GREAT
ARCHITECTURE
OF THE
WORLD

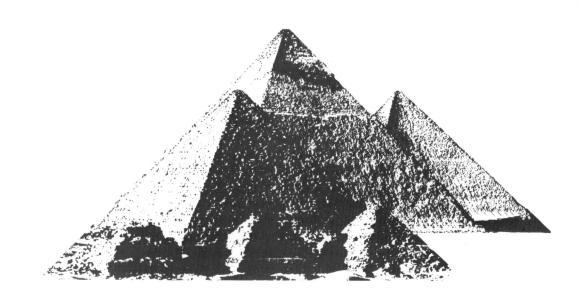

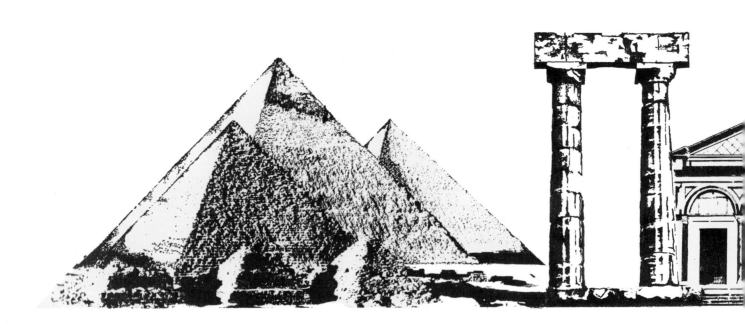

GREAT ARCHITECTURE OF THE WORLD

General Editor: John Julius Norwich

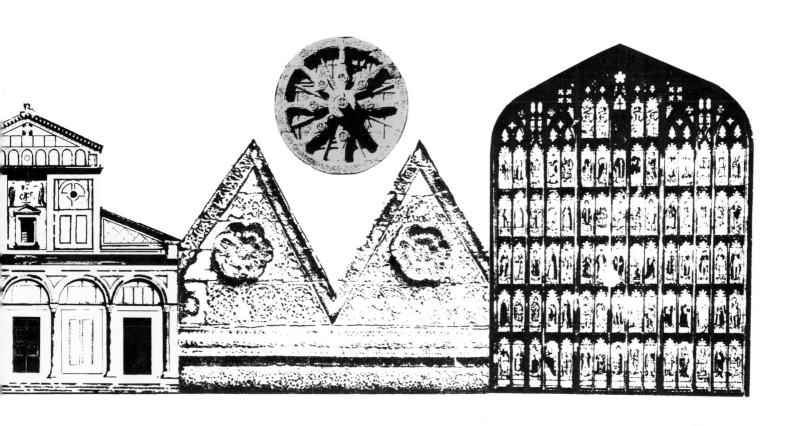

Da Capo Press

Contents

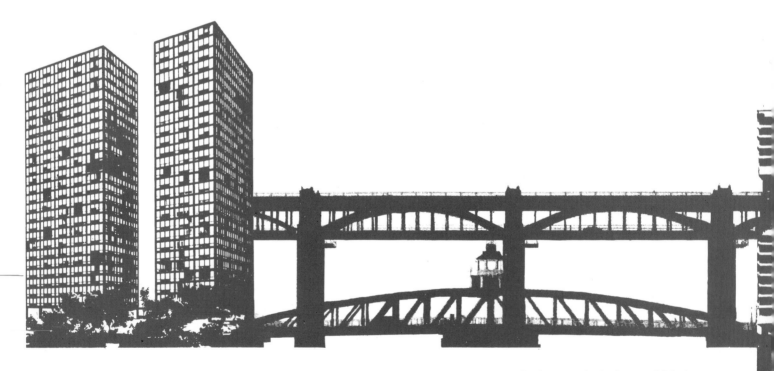

Great Architecture of the World
was edited and designed by
Mitchell Beazley Publishers Limited,
an imprint of Octopus Publishing
Group Limited
2-4 Heron Quays,
London, E14 4JB
© Mitchell Beazley Publishers Limited 1975
All rights reserved
Published by Da Capo Press
A Member of the Perseus Books Group
www.dacapopress.com

Great architecture of the world / general editor,
John Julius Norwich.
    p.   cm. — (A Da Capo paperback)
Reprint. Originally published: London:
Mitchell Beazley, 1975.
Includes index.
ISBN 0-306-81042-5
1. Architecture — History. I. Norwich, John
Julius, 1929-
NA200.G76   1990
720'.9—dc20
                        90-46098
                         CIP

This first paperback edition published
in the United States of America in 1991
by Da Capo Press, Inc.

Reprinted 2000

Printed and bound in China

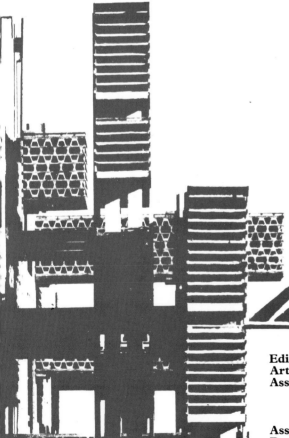

Editor	Elisabeth Brayne	**Picture Researchers**	Janice Jones
Art Editor	Linda Francis		Jackie Webber
Assistant Editors	Vivianne Croot	**Production**	Barry Baker
	Jinny Johnson	**Executive Editor**	Glorya Hale
	Jean McNamee	**Special Consultant**	Peter Blake, USA
	Helen Varley		
Assistant Art Editor	Mel Petersen		
Designers	Marianne Ingham		
	Kevin Maddison		
	John Ridgeway		
Editorial Assistant	Janet Wilson		

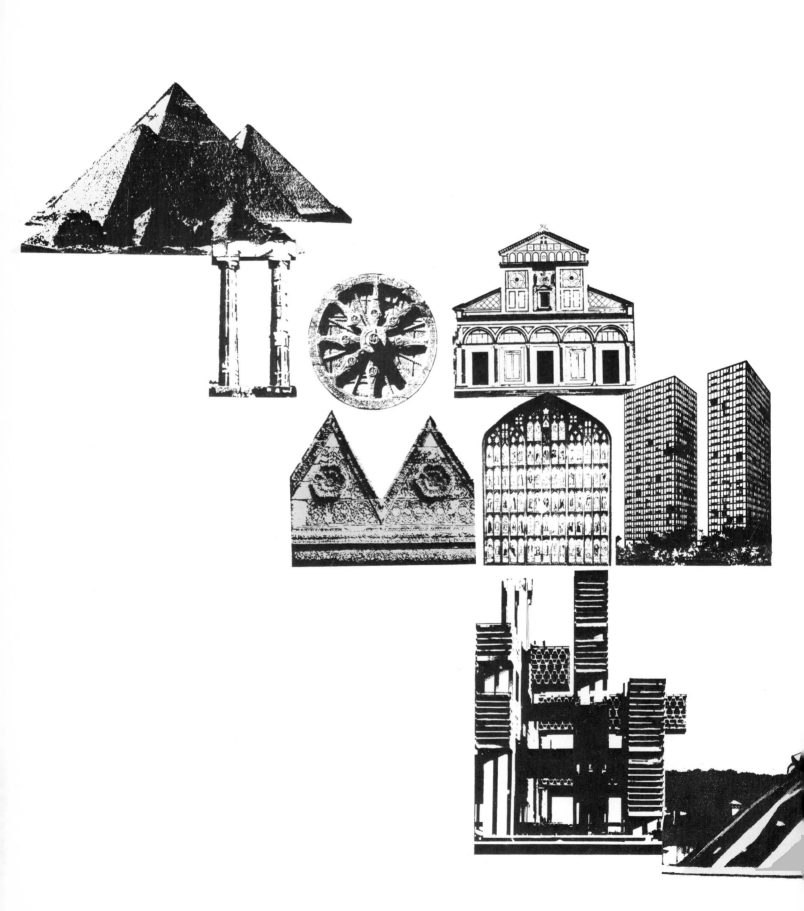

Foreword

by Sir Nikolaus Pevsner

The first world history of architecture was published 254 years ago. It is Fischer von Erlach's *Entwurff einer Historischen Architectur*. Fischer von Erlach was Architect to the Emperor Charles VI. His book consists of large etchings, each with two or three lines of caption. The pictures include the Temple of Solomon, Egyptian Pyramids, the Mausoleum of Halicarnassus, the Temple of Artemis at Ephesus, the Lighthouse of Alexandria, the Parthenon in Athens, the Golden House of Nero, several Roman triumphal arches, the Castel Sant'Angelo, the Palace of Diocletian at Split, the Ruins of Palmyra, Stonehenge, three of the main mosques of Istanbul, the Imperial Palace of Peking and Fischer's own buildings: Schoenbrunn, the Palace of Prince Eugene, the church of St Charles in Vienna, and the Collegiate Church at Salzburg. The assortment is amazing, even though most of the distant buildings are free restorations (very free indeed), and even though all Romanesque, all Gothic and all Renaissance are missing.

The present book is *Fischer Redivivus* with the gaps filled in, with serious texts instead of mere captions and with about 800 illustrations accurately presenting the buildings and accompanying photographic reproduction by drawings. In the latter feature in particular this book is not at all something usual in terms of today. Let me put before you the 20th-century possibilities of acquainting the layman with buildings. The best would of course be orally and in front of and inside the buildings themselves. Failing that, filming would do. But that also can be done only very rarely. So the accepted method is by printed word and printed illustrations. But in what proportion should they be to one another? There is no fixed answer to that question.

If I was asked by the editors of the present volume to provide an answer, the reason was no doubt that I have written a history of architecture myself. On the strength of that I would first of all say that text without pictures or pictures without text cannot be successful, nor can a short text or a few pictures. When in the war, in 1942, I published my own *Outline of European Architecture* it had a total of about 100 pages of text and 60 pictures on miserable wartime paper, and even when the book grew considerably, it yet remained short for what it wanted to be, that is a reading book, and not quite amply enough illustrated to be a picture book. The editors of this new book, when they apportioned texts and pictures, placed these questions to themselves completely afresh. For the text they assembled a team of authors, and for the illustrations they settled, as I have already said, for about 800. And what a team they succeeded in getting for the text, and what a variety of illustrations!

The use of colour is a great asset. For much architecture can come fully to life only in colour, whether a building operates with only two or three natural colours of stone, like St Michael at Hildesheim or Vézelay or Castel del Monte or Inigo Jones's Banqueting House before the 19th-century restoration, or whether it operates with a mixture of stone and varied bricks like Butterfield's churches, or whether it has the stained glass of medieval windows or the mosaic of Early Christian and Early Medieval buildings.

The other great asset is the many drawings—reconstructions, sections, plans, isometric and perspective cutaways. For only such drawings can convey the spatial character of buildings, and architecture of all ages—I cannot say it often enough—is space first and foremost, and so everything in a book on architecture which leads to richer spatial experiences is to be warmly welcomed.

Nikolaus Pevsner

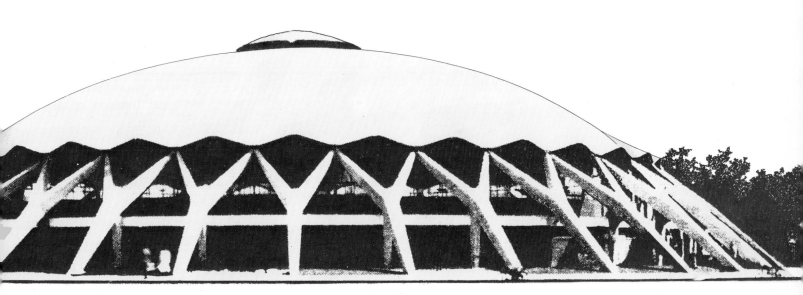

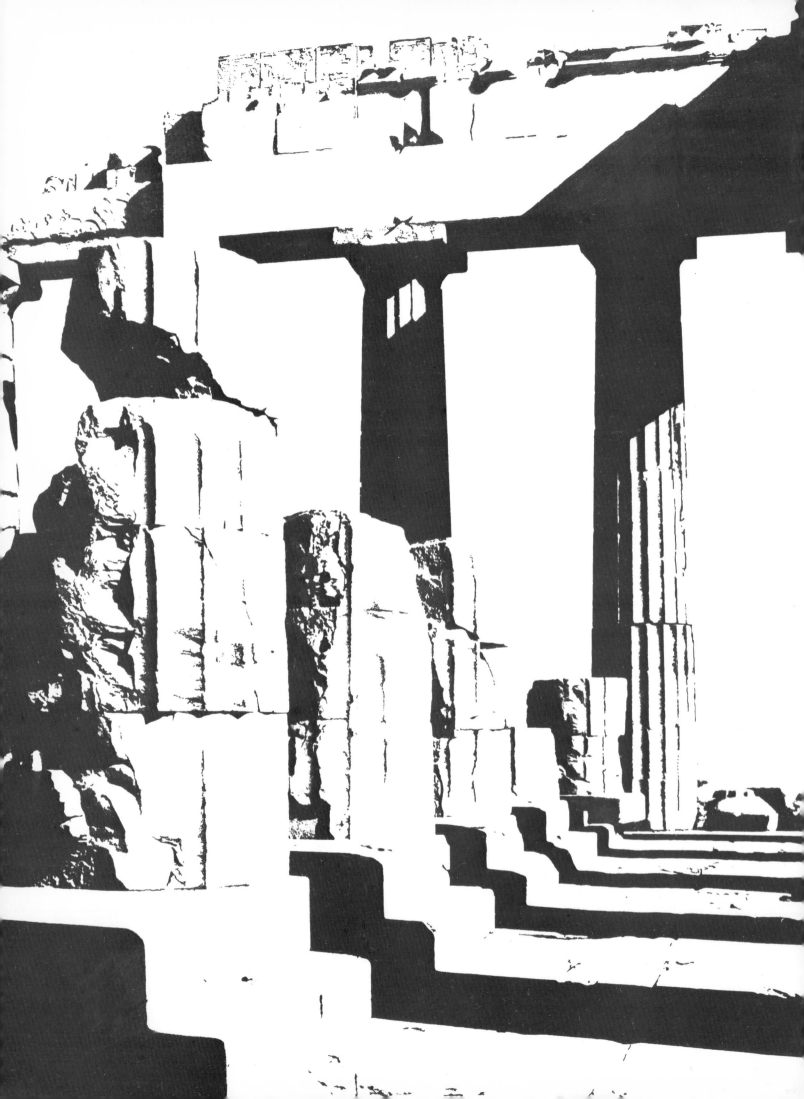

Introduction

by John Julius Norwich

Man has not always been a builder. When he depended on hunting for his survival, he was essentially a nomad, content with caves or makeshift shelters in the forest. But then, some nine or ten thousand years ago, he discovered the secrets of agriculture. For the first time he could indulge in the luxury of a settled habitation; and, from that moment, architecture was born.

Its early progress was slow. The fundamental principles of construction had to be learnt by trial and error; then there were tools to be invented and manufactured, materials to be found and transported, manual skills to be acquired and developed. Some civilizations managed to forge steadily ahead nevertheless, solving their problems as they arose. Others were held up, sometimes for centuries, because some vital secret remained undiscovered: the wheel perhaps, or the smelting of iron, or—much later—the arch. Gradually, however, the pace quickened. Man found that he had a natural talent for building. That same instinct that prompts a child, almost before it can walk, to pile one toy brick on top of another led him to ever more daring experiments. New challenges evoked new responses, and all the time his knowledge grew.

So too did his ambitions. It was no longer enough to have a house to live in—now he began to turn his mind towards a tomb in which to be buried, a monument by which to be remembered, a palace from which to be governed, a shrine where he and his fellows could worship their gods. Such buildings, by their very nature, must be built to last, and to impress. And so mud gave way to wood, wood to brick, brick to stone, and stone to marble. The invention of the arch led to that of the vault, the buttress and the dome.

Meanwhile, the architect had become an artist. He had learned that however brilliantly the painters and sculptors, the plasterers and mosaicists might embellish his work after its completion, the beauty that they created was essentially decorative and superficial. He realized that the artists were using his basic structure merely as a canvas, or at best as a frame, for their own virtuosity. True architectural beauty was something quite different and a good deal more abstract. If it were to exist at all, it must be inherent in the lines and proportions and perspectives of the building itself; it must reveal, to the responsive eye, an inner logic in which every individual feature had its own specific relationship with every other one, and with the whole.

This inner logic was obviously to some extent mathematical; but not entirely so. The Greeks of the 5th century BC, who understood the laws of architectural harmony better than any other people before or since, knew that the human eye was not only fallible but gullible as well; for best results, an architect must learn to take this into account and turn it to his advantage. Hence the invention of *entasis*; by which, in order to counteract the optical illusion which makes a strictly rectilinear column look concave, the Greeks deliberately swelled out their columns towards the middle—a trick which proved so successful that it was soon extended to horizontals. Examine their greatest monument, the Parthenon, and you will find that there is hardly a single straight line anywhere in the building.

But if architecture is an art, it is also by its very definition functional. Unlike music or painting or lyric poetry which—although they can occasionally be put to practical uses "to point a moral or adorn a tale"—are their own sole and sufficient justification for existing, architecture has a serious job to do. It is not enough for an architect to produce a beautiful building, as a painter might produce a picture or a composer a symphony; his work must also be suited to the purpose for which it was designed. If it is not, if he momentarily allows aesthetic considerations to outweigh practical ones to the point where his building fails in any degree to fulfil that purpose, then it fails also as a work of architecture. There is no great architecture that is not successful architecture too.

It is, I think, this functional aspect which has been responsible for making architecture the least appreciated of all the arts. That, and the fact that there is much too much of it. Because we need it to live, we see it all around us, all the time; and because we see it all around us we tend not to see it at all. We take it for granted, and our sensibilities no longer react to it in the same way that they would if we were confronted with a painting or a piece of sculpture. Often, alas, this is just as well. Few people are lucky enough to live in really beautiful cities like Rome or Venice or Bath; for those of us who are obliged to spend our lives surrounded by buildings ranging from the mediocre to the atrocious, some blunting of the aesthetic sense is, in such circumstances, as beneficial as it is inevitable. But this does not mean that we should not be able to resharpen it at will. The very fact that there is so much bad architecture around makes it all the more exciting when one comes upon a really distinguished building where it is least expected.

Naturally, few of us can hope to develop an eye like that of Sir Nikolaus Pevsner, who has honoured this book with a foreword and who, in his magnificent and compendious survey, *The Buildings of England*, has pointed out more unsuspected beauties to more devotees than any other architectural historian alive or dead. But we could, nearly all of us, become a good deal more receptive than we are at present, simply by looking, consciously, at the buildings we pass every day and asking ourselves, equally consciously, what we think of them.

The great buildings of the world, of course—those with which we shall be concerned in the pages that follow—fall into a rather different category. There is little risk of our not noticing *them*, particularly if we have travelled hundreds—perhaps thousands—of miles to see them. But all too often they too fail to be appreciated as they should be, for one simple if paradoxical reason: the camera. How easy it is to see a building merely as a composition in a viewfinder! From there it is only a short, slippery step to conceiving of architecture in terms of meter-readings, apertures and shutter speeds. Before a photograph is taken, there is one sovereign rule to be obeyed: look at the building for at least five minutes. Only then is there any chance of understanding it—and enjoying it—as it deserves.

For with architecture even more than with other arts, the secret of enjoyment is understanding; and it is in an attempt to increase that understanding that this book has been designed. It presupposes no advance knowledge of the subject or its history; it is intended, quite simply, for the layman who is anxious to learn.

Clearly it is impossible to encapsulate the whole of architectural history throughout the world in a single volume of manageable size. But we have cast our net wide—literally, from China to Peru—and if the lion's share of space has nevertheless been given to the architecture of Europe and the Western World, it is only because it is there that the most important and influential developments have occurred. This western mainstream has been treated chronologically; the more exotic sections, which cover a wider time span and do not therefore fit comfortably within this chronological framework, have been slotted in wherever the context seems most appropriate.

When I was invited to be General Editor of this book I little expected to collect a series of names half as distinguished as that which appears on pages 4–5. They are all acknowledged experts, often *the* acknowledged experts, in their fields. For all the contributors, it goes without saying that the opinions expressed are their own. This book has no editorial axe to grind. It makes no effort to preach, still less to pontificate. If it has a message, that message is simply this: that for every building mentioned in the following pages there are countless others, more modest perhaps, but every bit as worthy of preservation. And whereas the very greatest are probably safe for posterity—or at least one hopes so—most of these others are continuously at risk. If they are to be preserved, they must be fought for; and because buildings belong not just to those who live and work in them but are our common architectural heritage their preservation is the responsibility of every one of us. Too much of this heritage has been lost, irrevocably, in the past half-century. We must all fight to save what is left, while there is still something left to save.

John Julius Norwich.

THE
EXOTIC
WORLDS

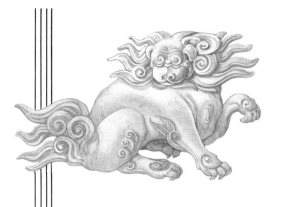

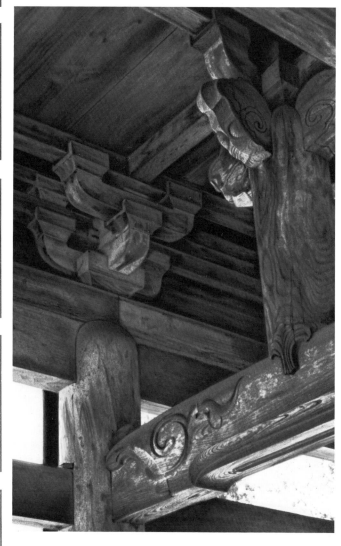

The use of the traditional wooden post and lintel construction and ingenious bracketing system of ancient China is exemplified in this bracketing detail from a 13th-century Japanese temple at Kamakura.

In China, whence sprang a tradition of wooden building which was adopted throughout eastern Asia, architecture cannot claim to be the mother of the arts. It is not prominent in painting or in the invention of ornament. But its principles of order and balance, as seen from the outside and as less obviously embodied in internal structures, echo the qualities of other branches of Chinese art. A system of pillar and beam architecture can be traced back to the neolithic period, in the late third and second millennia BC. It was confined to the region of the middle of the Yellow River Valley. Farther north, along the Amur, the first dwellings were virtually subterranean, while in southern China, and in Southeast Asia and the islands beyond, a tradition of wooden buildings raised on piles has persisted to the present time.

No brick was used in early times. Instead, walls and foundations were constructed of rammed earth. Since large timber was comparatively rare in central China, the architect had to be economical in his methods, using widely spaced pillars on a rectangular plan. Between the pillars were light walls of plaster, matting or lattice, allowing doorways and other openings to be altered freely. From the Han period onwards, interest centred on the elaboration of the roof and its supports above the pillar heads.

Stone barrel vaulting is first found in tombs of the 1st century AD, in which wooden architectural forms are imitated. Above ground, brick was used for the poorer dwellings and buildings associated with the rectangular city walls—command-posts, gate-houses, watch-towers and arsenals. It is in the large, solemn building—the palace, magistrate's hall or temple—that the growth of an artistic architecture can be followed. These edifices were ideally built wholly of wood, apart from roof tiles and plaster partitioning. When

China and Japan

buildings in brick and stone are of real merit, as notably in Kublai Khan's palace and its Ming successor, they are found to be governed in their proportions and ornamental features by the standards of wooden pillars placed within, if not actually on, the façade.

The regular dimensions of the pillared wooden buildings raise the question of the adoption of a pervasive module. It was natural to the carpenter's craft, so essential to the production of intricate bracket systems, that such proportions as width to length and length to vertical step should be simple multiples of an initial unit. In some early instances this can be shown to be the vertical breadth of the bracket arm. In AD 1103, Li Chieh's *Ying tsao fa shih*, or "Methods and Designs of Architecture", was officially promulgated. This book established the modular system, and thus uniform proportions of the size and spacing of pillars and beams were prescribed for the whole empire. At first the unit was the *ts'ai*, or vertical breadth of the bracket arm, or the *tsu ts'ai*, the ts'ai measurement taken together with the space between superimposed brackets. The *Ying tsao fa shih* also deals exhaustively with all manner of carved ornament, animal and floral, with panelled ceilings, and the great variety of lattice which was at the architects' disposal for windows and the surrounds of balconies. It is a repertory of Sung decorative art. In the 17th century, the Palace Office of Works of the newly established Ch'ing dynasty promulgated the horizontal width of the bracket arm as the new module. Finesse was observed in the profile of the larger pillars, which swell slightly towards a point somewhat below the middle of their height, while the corner pillars of a large building will often lean slightly inwards, as a corrective to the optical illusion which suggests an inclination outwards.

The designs of palaces built in the later Han period and in the following few centuries were adopted by the Chinese Buddhists for their temples. A typical temple layout was enclosed in a south-facing rectangular perimeter, with peripheral gallery, gate-houses and a succession of buildings following one behind the other along the north–south axis. But religious needs clashed with the ceremonial symmetry demanded of the palace. The main image-hall of a temple ranked about equal with the pagoda, and the earliest plans show them side by side, spaced suitably in regard to their very different elevations.

It was in this religious form that the wooden architecture of China was exported, in the wake of the Buddhist missions. First it reached Korea, and from there Japan. It is in Japan that examples of existing early buildings in this style can be seen, for, more carefully than the Chinese Buddhists, the Japanese abbots preserved much of their architectural heritage through troubled times. They adhered closely to tradition as they replaced or expanded, and innovated only in response to particular changes of fashion reported from China.

In addition to their early temples, the Japanese have preserved some noble secular residences of medieval date in which the Chinese styles blend pleasantly with the native tradition of the country house. It was in Japan, too, at the beginning of the 20th century, that the first experiments were made in adapting decorative features of the trabeate style to the roofs of stone buildings erected in more or less close imitation of French architecture. The success of this venture was always disputed in Japan. More recently the architects of the People's Republic of China tried to reconcile the new with the old on similar lines, notably in buildings of the Peking University, and were eventually decried by the officialdom.

The origins of the trabeate style

FROM THE EXCAVATIONS at the Shang dynasty capital near Anyang in north Honan it can be deduced that both palaces and temples were raised entirely on wooden pillars in alignment with the thatch roof. Assuming that there was a continuous roof, the arrangement of the roof timbers must have been considerably more sophisticated than in the smaller houses of the neolithic period. Already some features of the trabeate style were present: the buildings were raised on a podium of rammed earth about three feet high; the entrance was in the eaves façade, not in a gable-end, and it is likely that the spaces between the pillars were filled with only the lightest materials.

The capitals and eaves brackets, essential to the historical style, cannot be traced archaeologically before the 5th century BC, when some miniature representations of elevations show simple pillar capitals supporting eaves-beams. These pictures give a misleading impression of double storeys, with an upper row of pillars not vertically aligned with those below. The stepped rectangular earthen mounds which survive on some 5th- and 4th-century sites provide an explanation. The recessed terraces of these mounds carried galleries with a lean-to roof, so that the succession of eaves lines, seen in elevation, did not imply any superimposed living floors. This method of constructing an imposing ceremonial building, with a central earth mound rising to the level of the topmost floor, is thought to have persisted at least until the middle Han period (1st century BC to 1st century AD). Later, the bays of large pillared buildings had to be roofed over.

From the 3rd century BC, or possibly a little earlier, roofs were covered by ceramic tiles of semicircular section, the eaves tiles terminating in rondels, which bore a great variety of decorative devices. Pottery models of the later Han period show ornate buildings with single lines of brackets springing from pillar capitals, or sometimes from corbels, and gable-ridges ending in elaborate acroteria. The system of beams used here to raise the roof can only be guessed at, but it is probable that the classical systems of the T'ang and Sung periods were already anticipated.

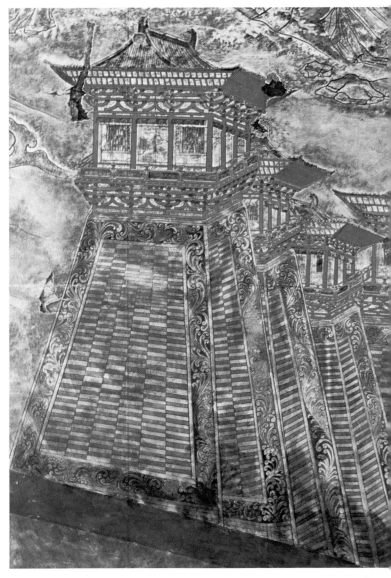

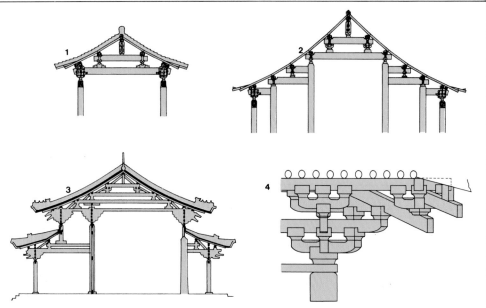

CHINESE ROOF CONSTRUCTION
The most striking feature of the roof is the absence of triangular tied frames. This made it necessary to ensure a vertical thrust upon the pillars by multiplying the points of support under the rafters. The archaic design (1), with narrow eaves and span, could be enlarged (2), but the increased number of pillars cluttered the interior, thus reducing the transverse spacing of the outer pillars. A solution was found by increasing the area of support afforded by each pillar (3). To achieve this the brackets, tou-kung, supporting the eaves rafters and purlins were increased to two or more tiers, the arms of a lower bracket carrying in turn similar brackets. The bracket cluster expanded upwards like an inverted pyramid, jutting both longitudinally and transversally (4). From the 8th century, cantilevers, pinned at the inner end against a purlin, were made to penetrate the bracket clusters and support a further bracket or series of brackets at a point still farther from the eaves pillar.

Soochow Lake Pagoda is one of the brick towers scattered in the northern and eastern parts of China. The pagodas belonged to Buddhist temples built from the 11th to 13th centuries.

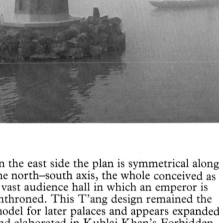

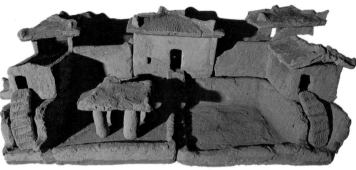

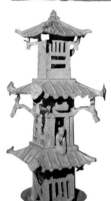

The Han pottery models placed in tombs of the later Han period (1st and 2nd centuries AD) are of buildings with plastered brick walls, in which only the roof details resemble the wooden architecture of the time. The farmstead (above) consists of several buildings surrounded by windowless walls, making it like a defensive keep. The tower (left) was the type on which the wooden pagodas of Buddhist temples were modelled.

Ta Ming Palace (below). Details of this reconstruction of the 8th-century palace are taken from contemporary paintings, but the plan has been established from excavations. Corner-towers and gate pavilions punctuate the pillared gallery built along the inner side of the walls. Except for a detached tower on the east side the plan is symmetrical along the north–south axis, the whole conceived as a vast audience hall in which an emperor is enthroned. This T'ang design remained the model for later palaces and appears expanded and elaborated in Kublai Khan's Forbidden City in Peking.

T'ang Watch Tower. This detail of a mural of the T'ang period shows typical 8th-century buildings crowning massive fortified walls. Gateways and corner-towers were the most striking parts of Chinese city walls.

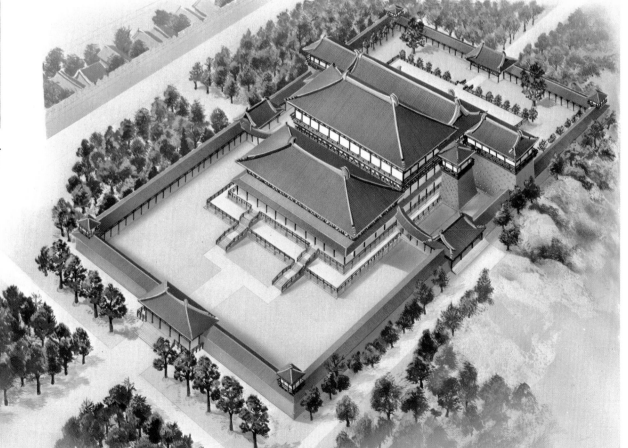

Early traditions adapted and preserved

UNTIL ABOUT 200 BC all Japan was occupied by the Jōmon culture. Their small houses had rough gabled or conical roofs, simply framed and probably thatched, raised over sunken floors, and were on much the same principle as the huts of neolithic China. During the period 200 BC to AD 200 this essentially northern tradition was replaced by another, of uncertain origin, associated with the Yayoi culture. The Yayoi houses, known only from models, were probably constructed entirely of timber, with floors at ground level.

In contrast to these traditions is the trabeate architecture, which reached Japan from China, by way of Korea, under the auspices of Buddhism in the 6th and 7th centuries. Structures surviving from this early phase are the earliest Chinese-style buildings in existence today. Most notable among them are the main buildings of the Hōryūji temple, Nara. Chinese practice was adopted to the last detail, and after the 670s, when Korea ceased to be the intermediary, Chinese architects, tile-makers and sculptors flocked to the Japanese capital to take advantage of the imperial patronage. Nevertheless, some features of the Japanese handling of the pillar, beam and bracket system were peculiar to the islanders, and the woodworking tradition was probably superior to that of China. The need to dismantle and re-erect the buildings, following the peregrinations of the imperial seat—it was fixed at Nara in AD 710—led to carpentry of surpassing neatness and great modular accuracy.

The interaction of palace design incorporating Japanese features with the designs derived from China created original plans and elevations even in some temple schemes, and introduced a freedom of invention in the wooden idiom which distinguishes the Japanese evolution from the more conservative heritage of China.

NATIVE JAPANESE ARCHITECTURE
One of the most primitive and holy of the Shintō designs, the Izumo shrine (right) shares with the Yayoi house model (below) the beetling gables, gable-end entrance (contrasting with the Chinese main-façade entry) and the peculiar round timbers balanced on the ridge. The crossing and projection of the gable rafters is a feature no less primitive, consecrated in the design. The shrines as they exist today are poems of carpentry. The subsequent evolution of Shintō temple design combined these initial forms with styles adopted from the Chinese.

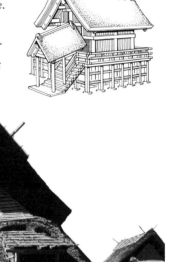

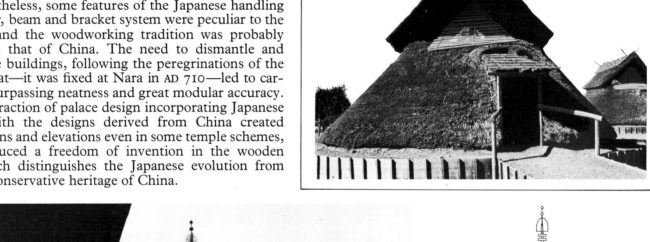

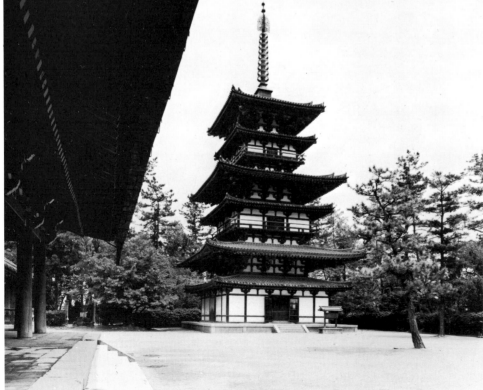

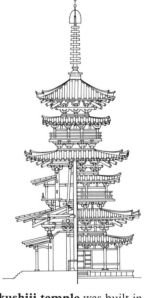

The Yakushiji temple was built in AD 680, but of its many buildings only the East Pagoda (left and above) survives. It differs from other towers of the period in having three roofs instead of five—compare the Hōryūji Pagoda—and compensates with three intermediate lean-to roofs. From the ground to the *hōshō*, or crowning sacred gem, the pagoda measures 103 ft.

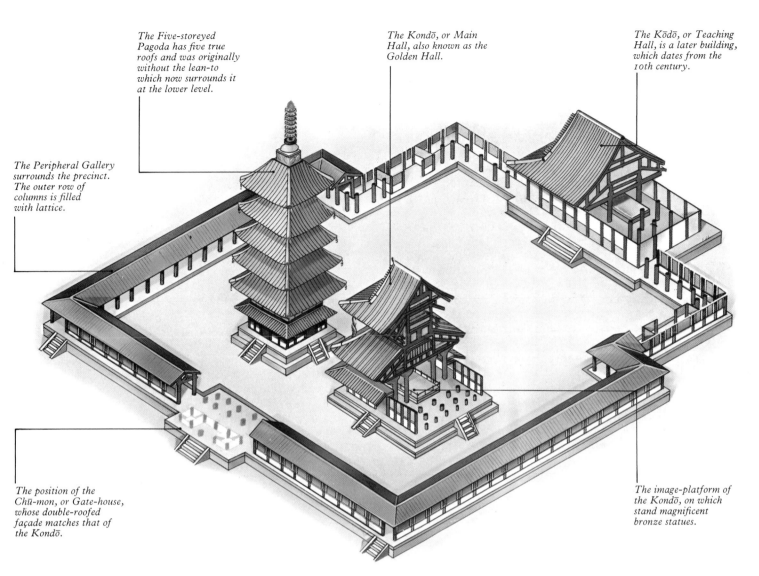

The Five-storeyed Pagoda has five true roofs and was originally without the lean-to which now surrounds it at the lower level.

The Kondō, or Main Hall, also known as the Golden Hall.

The Kōdō, or Teaching Hall, is a later building, which dates from the 10th century.

The Peripheral Gallery surrounds the precinct. The outer row of columns is filled with lattice.

The position of the Chū-mon, or Gate-house, whose double-roofed façade matches that of the Kondō.

The image-platform of the Kondō, on which stand magnificent bronze statues.

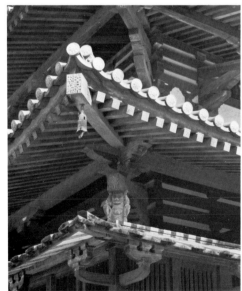

In this comparatively simple 7th-century bracket system of the Kondō, the arm-bracket and the cantilever rafter are combined in the eaves support without elaborate joinery. Later, when the cantilever plunges through the centre of a three- or four-tiered bracket system, the design can be baffling to the eye, and the purpose becomes decorative as much as structural.

Hōryūji temple at Nara (above and below). The surviving 7th-century structures of this temple—Main Hall, Five-storeyed Pagoda, Gate-house and Peripheral Gallery—are the earliest extant representatives of east Asian wooden architecture. The Kondō, or Main Hall, adopts the design of ceremonial buildings known in China from the Han dynasty onwards. The suggestion of an upper storey is illusory, for inside only a latticed ceiling separates the image-platform from the roof. The pagoda stands to the west and the Kondō to the east of the main north–south axis—a position unique to this complex.

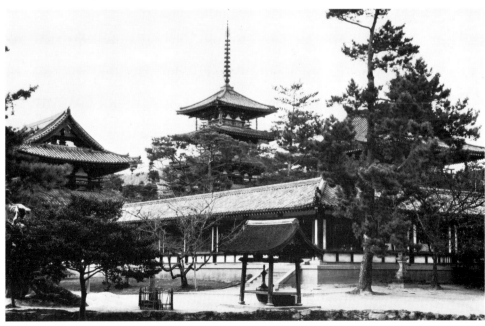

The Forbidden City, Peking

WHEN MARCO POLO arrived in China in 1272, Kublai had completed his conquest of the Sung Empire of southern China and was engaged in building two capitals. The northern one, beyond the Great Wall, was Shang-tu (Coleridge's Xanadu). The southern one was Khan-balik, the Lord's City, or Peking, Northern Capital, which remains the most impressive embodiment of the Chinese ideal of a ruler's fortified city.

Peking's rectangular plan, with south-facing entrance, north–south axis and central palace and command post, was inherited from the pre-Han period. In theory, Kublai's Peking was intended to hold the whole population of the city within its walls. The walls themselves were to house soldiers and ammunition. The Palace, or Forbidden City, walled and moated, was contained within the similar perimeter of the Imperial City, and all was surrounded by the outermost wall and moat defining the Inner City. The outermost wall, of which a gateway was recently excavated, is now to be seen as only a few traces. The Imperial City wall no longer exists. The Outer City, now merged into the modern town, was a rectangular enclosure adjacent to the south. What chiefly remains is the mighty Forbidden City, its vast gates, squares and halls extending for about a mile on a strict axial and symmetrical plan.

From the modern entrance at the T'ien-an Gate the visitor passes northwards through the Tuan Gate and so reaches the Wu Men, or Meridian Gate, which admits to the Forbidden City. Five marble bridges—one of which is seen below—span the branch of the moat which crosses the next great court. Ahead is the T'ai-ho Men, or Gate of Great Peace, the imposing entrance pavilion of the main precinct. Next comes the T'ai-ho Tien, or Palace of Great Peace, the most impressive of all, in which the emperor gave audience to officials massed and kowtowing in the court below. This palace is raised on a three-tiered marble podium, which skirts it to the sides and continues around two rear halls used for the emperor's robing and retirement. Beyond lie the inner courts of the imperial residence.

Apart from the grandiose logic of the plan, with its exhilarating development of roof line seen across wide uninterrupted spaces, the Forbidden City epitomizes two trends of the Ming architectural pomp. One is the combination of brick and marble with wooden pillars, and the bayed design which these impose; the other is the loading of stairs, balustrades and eaves with many-coloured and intricately carved ornament. Beneath the eaves, continuous clusters of polychrome brackets fill the recess without clarifying or even symbolizing the structural function from which they take their origin. Cloud scrolls on column capitals echo the ornament of the marble balustrades. The present decoration of the residential parts owes much to the 18th-century Emperor Ch'ien Lung.

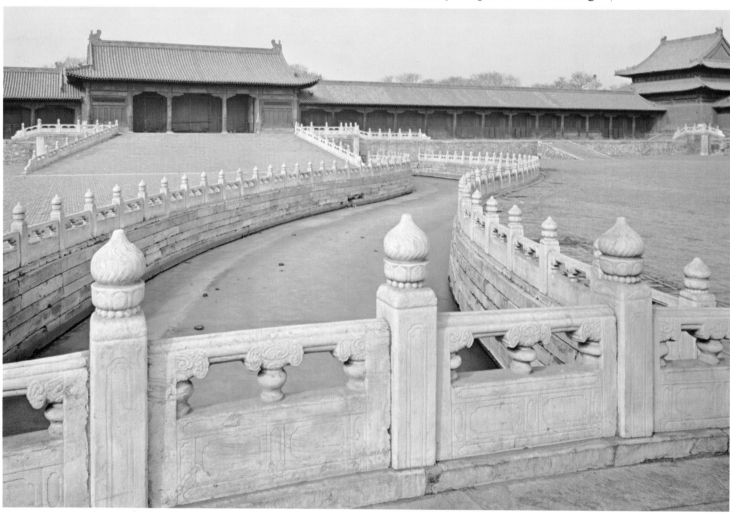

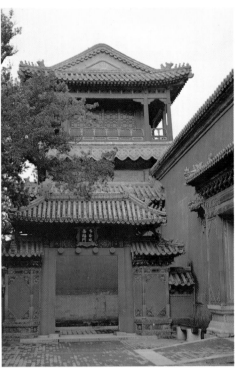

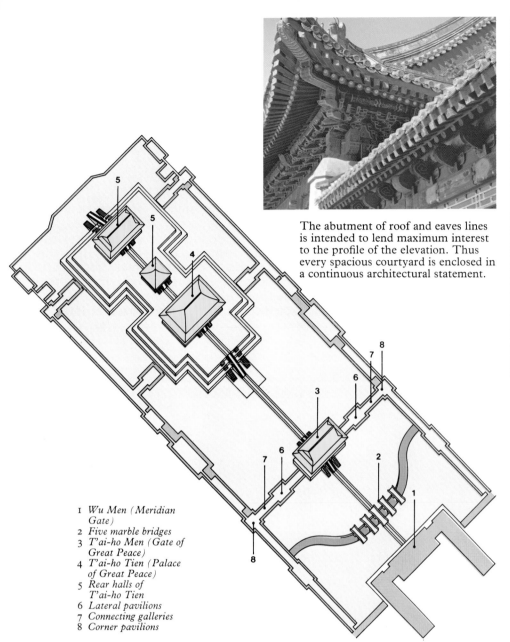

The abutment of roof and eaves lines is intended to lend maximum interest to the profile of the elevation. Thus every spacious courtyard is enclosed in a continuous architectural statement.

In the residential courts of the palace the reduced scale of pavilions and their narrower spacing give something of domestic intimacy. Here are shady nooks which might once have sheltered flowering bushes grown in the porcelain garden bowls of the Ming and Ch'ing potters.

1 Wu Men (Meridian Gate)
2 Five marble bridges
3 T'ai-ho Men (Gate of Great Peace)
4 T'ai-ho Tien (Palace of Great Peace)
5 Rear halls of T'ai-ho Tien
6 Lateral pavilions
7 Connecting galleries
8 Corner pavilions

The first highly ornate feature of the Forbidden City (above) is the T'ai-ho Men (below), approached from the five marble bridges in the forecourt. The western end of the gateway's main hall, in the foreground, links with the gallery, lateral pavilion, further connecting gallery and the corner pavilion, from which starts the lines of rooms enclosing the courtyard on east and west. The marble balustrades belong to the early Ming refurbishing; the gilded bronze guardian lions were placed by the Emperor Ch'ien Lvng.

CHINESE DECORATION
The lead-glazed pottery of architecture represents a distinct branch of Chinese ceramics, whose history can be traced before the T'ang period. The famous Dragon Wall is the greatest of the ceramic ornaments. Formal scrolls of flowers and leaves fill the lower corners of walls or appear in medallions on walls dividing the courts. On the gable edges of the roofs are rows of figurines representing fabulous creatures.

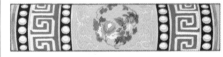

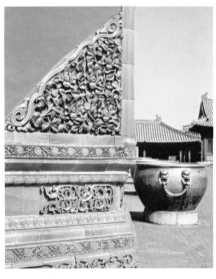

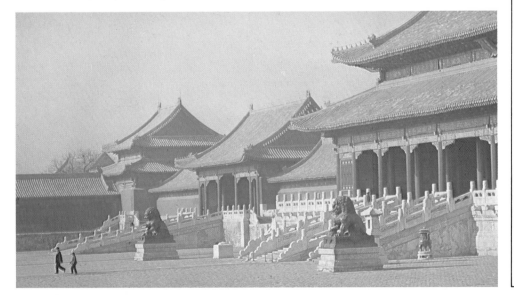

Katsura Palace, Kyōto

SET IN WOODED surroundings within the ancient perimeter of the imperial capital, Kyōto, the *rikyū*, or separated residence, of the Katsura Palace is the finest product of a secular and unofficial tradition. It was built in the opening decades of the 17th century by Kobori Enshū, tea ceremony master and architect, who sought to express his ideals of rustic simplicity and picturesque nature on a larger scale than had been attempted before.

Of the three main component buildings, Ko-shoin, Chū-shoin and Shin-goten, the first is in the more ceremonial *shoin* style and the latter two in the more intimate *sukiya* style. From the 14th century the cultivated nobility increasingly rejected the ornate grandeur of the town palace for an architecture designed above all to harmonize with a natural setting. Sukiya traces its origin to the farmer's cottage and the mountain hut, whose aesthetic was already distilled in the ceremonial tea-hut.

The buildings of the Katsura were framed in light timbers, using the triangular truss in the roof, and closed by plain walls, lacking the pillars, brackets, foundation podium and lean-to ambulatory of the Chinese style. Intimacy, almost too carefully contrived, is the keynote. From the start, the rooms and bays were laid out in multiples of the *tatami*, or rice-straw mats, used on floors in all classes of domicile for sitting and lying. Wood was left plain, sometimes even retaining its bark. Beauty of proportion and the comfort of plain material must speak for themselves.

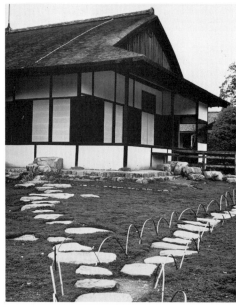

Verandahs, constructed at gable-ends—the most natural and inviting place for access—are an unemphatic link between house and garden. The solid partitions of earlier buildings are replaced by sliding panels covered with translucent paper. Sliding doors take the place of swinging half-doors at the entrance.

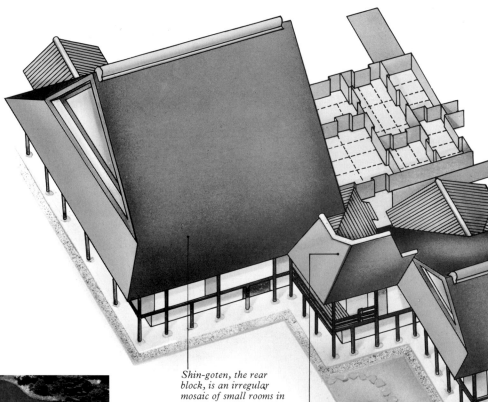

Shin-goten, the rear block, is an irregular mosaic of small rooms in rectangular plan, used as bedrooms, washing-rooms and the like. The service quarters are annexed to it on the north side.

This transitional block illustrates the structural principle of sukiya : one building depending on another, in a rambling, domestic way. It contains a store for musical instruments and a small tea-room for use by female guests.

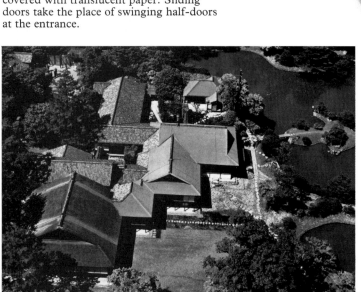

Katsura rikyū realizes most poetically the sukiya ideal of the marriage of house and garden. The garden is cited as the most beautiful of its kind.

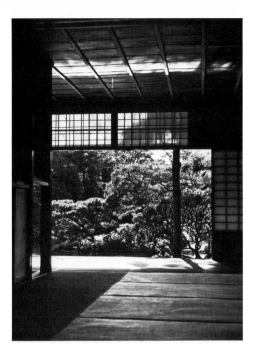

The front entrance of the Shōkintei pavilion, like those of the other buildings, frames a view of the garden, the natural scene replacing the landscape murals of the ornate palace.

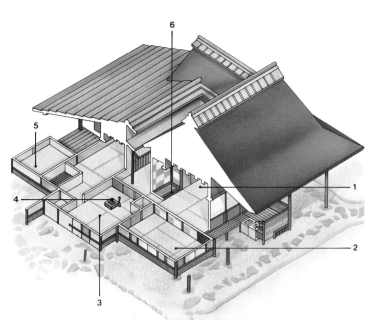

1 First guest-room
2 Second guest-room
3 Tea ceremony room
4 Hearth for brazier
5 Room for keeping tea ceremony water
6 Toko-no-ma

The Shōkintei, "Pavilion of the pine-tree harps", is divided inside in terms of the tea ceremony, the *cha-no-yu* rite, which has flourished since the 13th century. The rooms give only the austerest comfort. Their beauty lies in the structure, ornaments appearing only in the *toko-no-ma*, alcoves where flowers or works of art are displayed for contemplation. The tea ceremony demands above all tranquillity, in which the artificialities of social life are to be discarded.

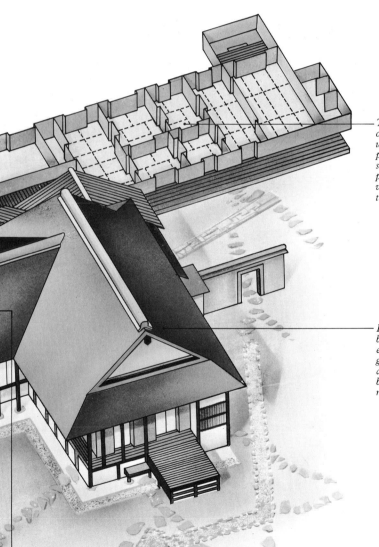

The back of this sector of ceremonially unallotted rooms was probably meant for servants. The east side provided shelter from which to contemplate the garden.

Ko-shoin, the entrance block, opening to the east, contains two large guest-rooms at the front, a warming-room with brazier and a refreshment-room.

Chū-shoin, the middle block, assumes more of the tea-hut character. The rooms are smaller than in other blocks, and one room has the toko-no-ma alcove, where the only ornament is displayed.

Stone paths laid out in traditional manner cross the moss garden to the Ko-shoin. Each stone is part of the meticulous overall design of the garden.

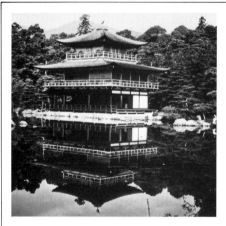

THE KINKAKU, OR GOLDEN PAVILION, *one of the most famous sites of Kyōto, is built at the edge of a pond, in a setting of shrubs and trees. It was built by the Ashikaga Shōgun Yoshimitsu in 1397 as the centre of a fabulous garden joined to his Kitayama Palace. After Yoshimitsu's death the building became a Zen temple, taking as its name the Buddhist posthumous title of its author Roku-en-ji, the "Temple of the sacred deer's cry". The pavilion consists of three storeys, all with windows opening under wide eaves. The gay lightness of structure, the perfect setting and invincible intimacy of the Kinkaku have made it, of all historic buildings, the dearest to Japanese hearts. (Unhappily burnt down in 1951, the Kinkaku has been rebuilt in perfect facsimile.)*

Temple, castle and farmhouse

DURING THE HEIAN AND FUJIWARA periods, AD 784 to 1185, Japanese architecture developed in isolation from China. The close adherence of the ruling nobility to the Buddhist faith, with which Shintō observances in no way conflicted, is reflected both in the secular grand house, based on a traditional native lay-out, and in the design of the Buddhist temples themselves. The Buddhist temples prolonged the T'ang style, delaying the decorative elaboration which was taking place at this time in China.

Capital cities were laid out in rectangular blocks, with the broad avenues and central palace area of Chinese convention, and in-town buildings accordingly favoured rectangular plans. But the clan structure of the Japanese nobility kept alive a love of country residence in the ruling class, and the rambling design of the *bessō*, or country residence, was a solvent of Chinese rigidity. The Katsura Palace is the secular climax of this trend, and the Byōdōin shows similar inventiveness with a religious building.

The only large stone buildings of old Japan were the creation of the civil war period, which led to the establishment of the Tokugawa shogunate, 1616 to 1868. They are many storeyed, built massively of stone, with high battered pedestals of uninterrupted masonry, and thick white-painted walls. The sudden resort to such robust methods was in response to the introduction of artillery during the civil wars, and defensibility rather than architectural nicety governed the complexities of approach and plan. Behind these characteristic Japanese developments, in temple and castle alike, stood the farmer's house, with its plain timber walls, steep gables and high thatched roof.

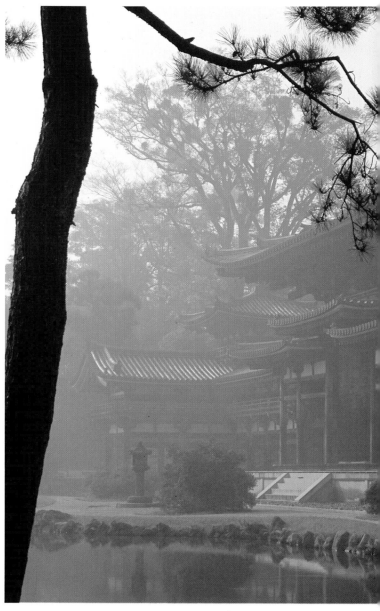

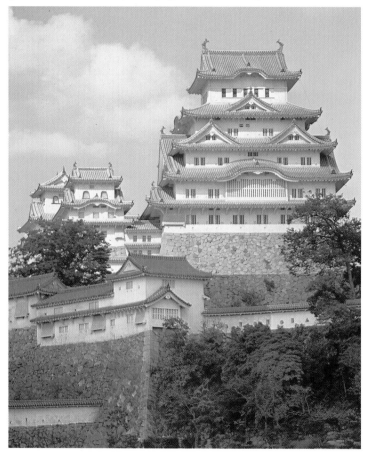

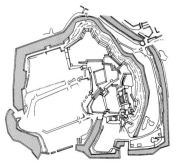

A moat and a labyrinth of earthen ramparts surround the central keep with its high battered walls. The whole construction was designed to make the castle impregnable.

The keep of Himeji Castle (left and shown on plan above) is the most impressive of the fortified residences built in the late 16th and early 17th centuries by the protagonists of the civil wars. These tall, stone-built structures attempted something without parallel in China—the superposition of many storeys each retaining the curving eaves and hipped gable of the Chinese style.

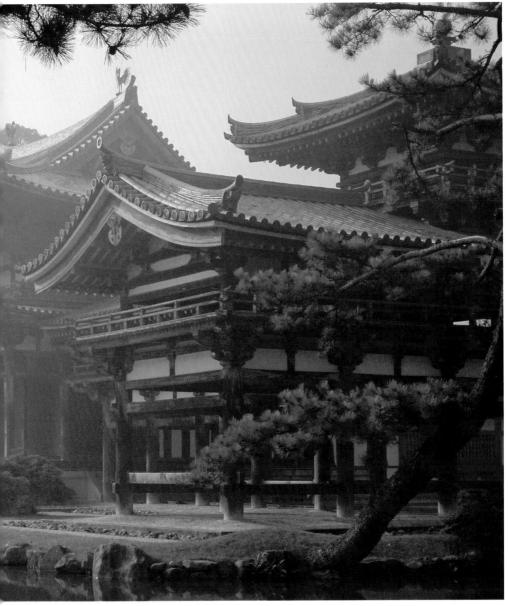

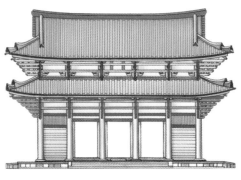

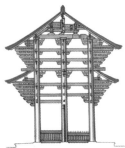

The Great South Gate, or Nandaimon, of the Tōdaiji temple was erected in AD 1199, and was intended to be in keeping with the archaic, 8th-century, character of the rest of the temple. The façade in general resembles that of the Hōryūji gate, but the system of brackets reflects the arrival in Japan of a later method of bracing the eaves.

The farmer's house (below) stood apart from Chinese tradition and its Japanese adaptations. Its design can have changed little in the last fifteen centuries beyond the systematizing of its proportions. The entrance and service areas are on ground level, traditionally floored with trodden earth, and the rest is raised a foot or two. Between the rooms are sliding doors—a feature used more extensively in palaces, such as the Katsura, which imitate the farmhouse style and idealize its beauties of proportion.

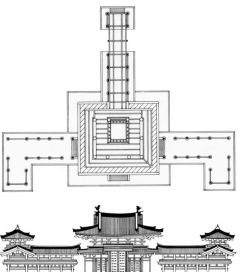

The Phoenix Hall of the Byōdōin (above). This most striking of Japanese Buddhist buildings owes its design to the nobleman Fujiwara Yorimichi, who built it as an ornament of his bessō, or country residence, situated in the rural Uji-machi of the Kyōto prefecture. It was consecrated in AD 1053 as the Amida Hall of the Byōdōin temple, but from its suggestion of a bird fronting pond and garden it is universally known as the Hōōdō, or Phoenix Hall. It houses the image carved by the great Jōchō. The front elevation (left) reproduces in miniature the features of a Chinese palace of the T'ang period, with its central pavilion, lateral connecting galleries and corner pavilions. The ambulatory lean-to roof of the hall echoes the curves of the main eaves above. The double line of brackets in the lateral galleries—elaborate below and simple above—repeats this division, while the rear gallery displays triple bracket lines, closely spaced. All of this retains the clarity of T'ang design.

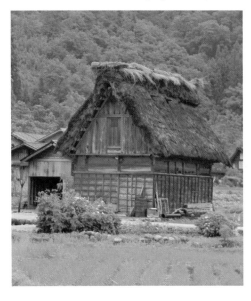

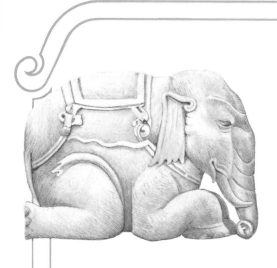

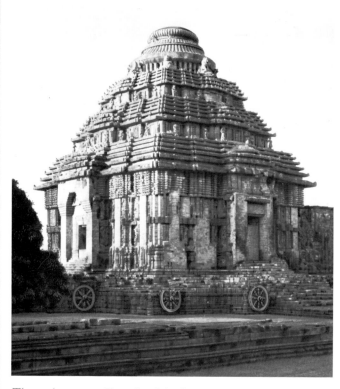

The 13th-century Temple of the Sun at Konarak in Orissa, of which only the entrance hall remains, is one of the best examples of Indo-Aryan architecture.

The history of architecture in India is not a continuous story. In India, as in other countries, all material expression of culture, and especially architecture, is connected with political power. Although religion was the main inspiration behind the greatest architectural achievements of the past, in every country the religion itself was that of its dominant political order. No cathedrals were built by the caliphs, no mosques by Christian rulers. The correlation is clearly seen in India, where the political history of the country is divisible into three separate cycles and where three distinct motivations and styles of building were created in three successive ages.

In the earliest of these cycles, whose beginnings cannot be precisely dated, but which lasted until the end of the 12th century of the Christian era, the country was ruled and dominated by a people who came later to be known as Hindus. Their own name for themselves was, however, *Arya*, or Aryan, and they were undoubtedly colonizers from outside. It was these people who brought into existence the ancient Indian civilization in which there were two religious elements—Brahmanism, popularly called Hinduism, and Buddhism. In the next cycle, which lasted from the beginning of the 13th century until the middle of the 18th century, northern India was ruled by Muslims, who came from Central Asia and from Persia and Afghanistan. Later, parts of South India were also ruled by them. These Muslims created an independent colonial order for themselves in India. The third cycle was the period of British rule from 1858 to 1947.

Naturally, these three political cycles, with their ethnic and religious diversities, also created three distinctive cultures. The first of these might be called Indo-Aryan, the second Indo-Islamic and the third Indo-British. The Indo-Aryan culture, irrespective of the foreign origins of the people who

India

brought it into existence, became and remained self-contained and wholly Indian, in spite of borrowings from outside. The affiliation of the Indo-Islamic culture was with the Middle East; it was, in fact, only a regional form of the culture of the entire Islamic world. The third political cycle saw the emergence of a culture through the impact of Western civilization.

In each of these cycles Indian architecture remained with equal naturalness within the framework of the culture of the dominant political régime. Thus its history can be divided into three periods: the first, that of the Hindu and Buddhist monuments; the second, that of Islamic monuments; and the third, that of Western-style building. It is curious that during the two centuries of British rule, which was the most stable period of political, economic and social life of the Indian people, few buildings of any individual architectural merit were erected, except towards the end of that rule. In contrast, the Muslim period with all its dynastic changes, wars and intermittent anarchy witnessed the building of innumerable monuments of the greatest beauty.

The political bearing of Indian architecture is also illustrated by its expansion overseas. Hinduism, Buddhism, and the general culture connected with both the religions and, with these, Hindu commerce and colonization, spread from various parts of India, especially from the south, to Burma, Indonesia and Indo-China. These elements created not only a colonial form of Indian civilization in these regions, but also found an architectural embodiment which was no less impressive than in India. Indian sculpture, too, was an accompaniment of this extension of art.

India's political history made yet another, destructive, impact on her architecture. It is responsible for a completely one-sided view of ancient Indian architecture, in which the importance of the south is emphasized at the expense of the north. The impression which exists is that South India is the land of temples and is different from the Gangetic basin in material culture. This is due to the historical fact that the temples of the Gangetic basin were destroyed by the Muslims, who, in their iconoclastic fury, razed to the ground all Hindu temples wherever they found them. With the exception of a short respite during the reign of Akbar, 1556–1605, this vandalism went on for five centuries. Even before the establishment of Muslim power in India, in the 10th century Sultan Mahmud of Ghazni had sacked most of the great religious centres in northern India in the course of his repeated invasions.

As a result of this widespread destruction, Hindu and Buddhist monuments survived in northern India only in those regions into which the Muslims did not penetrate—Bundelkhand, Orissa, Rajputana, Nepal and the Himalayan foothills. In the northern plain, temples began to be rebuilt only in the 18th century, when the Marathas became dominant. Thus the older examples of Hindu architecture which are to be found in the north were the creations of minor provincial rulers. Hindu architecture as created by the great North Indian imperial dynasties goes by default.

All the surviving examples of ancient Indian architecture are religious monuments. No residential buildings or any other form of secular architecture have survived. In the south, the elaborate palace complex of the Hindu Kingdom of Vijayanagara was sacked by the Muslims after their conquest of the city in 1565. But Sanskrit literature contains numerous references to splendid mansions and palaces which rose to the sky and there can be no doubt that the domestic architecture of ancient India was elaborate.

The earliest temples and shrines

NOTHING DEFINITE can be said about the origins of architecture in India. Early building was certainly in wood, but nothing of it has survived, with the exception of parts of a railing from Pataliputra, the capital of the Maurya Empire. It is, however, a reasonable assumption that architecture in stone was derived from ancient Persia. The earliest surviving stone monuments—the cave temples and the columns of Asoka—indicate a Persian origin. The cave temples were imitations of the Achaemenid tombs, which were built in Persia in the 6th and 5th centuries BC, and the columns, Persian in technique, style and feeling, were in fact probably built by Persians. Nothing like them was ever made again in India. Instead, a strange transformation took place in the handling of stone, which was treated as though it were wood. The previously developed craft of wood-carving was now applied to stone in order to create linear decoration rather than the effect of masses.

The Hindus did not learn to enclose large areas of space internally until very late, and even then only the audience-halls and passages were spacious. Not only did they scoop out caves to convert them into halls, they even carved whole temples from solid rock. None of the temples built by traditional architectural methods are earlier than the 7th and 8th centuries AD and most of them are much later. However, image worship, which must have been taken over from the Greeks who were in northwestern India for about three hundred years after Alexander the Great, was not part of the original Brahmanic worship, which may account for the late appearance of the temples. The earliest ruin of a Hindu temple is in Afghanistan and probably dates from the 2nd century AD. It has not only a peristyle plan, but also inscriptions in Greek letters.

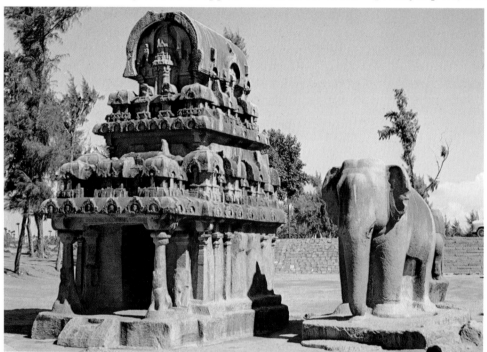

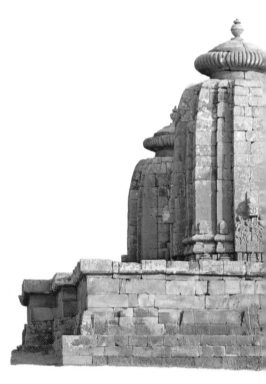

The Temple of Brahmeswara (below), at Bhubaneswar in Orissa, erected at the end of the 9th century AD, is richly carved inside and out. At Bhubaneswar, 7,000 Hindu shrines, dating from the 8th to the 12th centuries, once encircled Bindu Sarovar, the sacred artificial lake. Today, 500 remain. The basic structure of the Orissan temple has two connecting buildings. The smaller is the *jagamohan*, or assembly hall. Behind it is the *sikhara*, the towering sanctuary. Later temples have two additional halls in front—one for dancing, the other for banquets.

A rock-cut chariot, or *rath*, and an elephant, also carved from a single block of stone (above), at Mahabalipuram, near Madras in South India, are part of a unique group of monoliths. They, together with the temples at Mahabalipuram, were created by the kings of the Pallava dynasty, which flourished from the 7th to the 8th centuries AD.

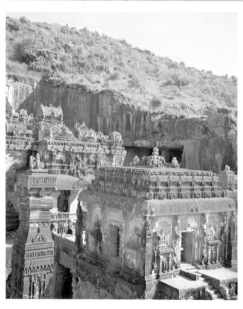

The Kailasa Temple (left), at Ellora in Maharashtra, is the largest and most splendid rock-cut temple in India. Attributed to a king of the Rashtrakuta dynasty in the 8th century AD, the Kailasa was carved out of the black volcanic rock of the hillside. It measures 164 ft deep, 109 ft wide and is 98 ft high, and to create it some 200,000 tons of rock are estimated to have been excavated. One of the finest of all Indian temples, the Kailasa strikingly illustrates how Hindu architecture was, basically, extended and magnified stone-carving.

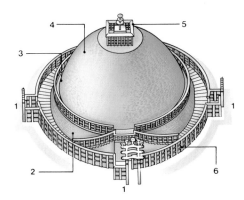

1 Toranas, or gateways
2 Medhi, or base
3 Pradakshina, or processional path
4 Anda, or dome
5 Harmika, or railed balcony
6 Vedika, or railings

The Great Stupa at Sanchi, in central India (left), is the largest of a group of stupas dating from the 2nd century BC to the 3rd century AD, which are among the first and most impressive Buddhist monuments in India. They display the earliest manner of transferring techniques of wood-carving to stone. The sculptures in the round and in relief on the stone railings and gateways (below) are remarkable, more like the work of skilled carpenters than of stone-masons.

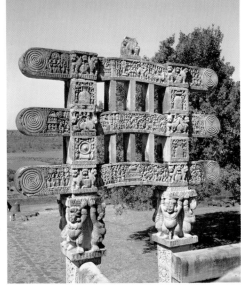

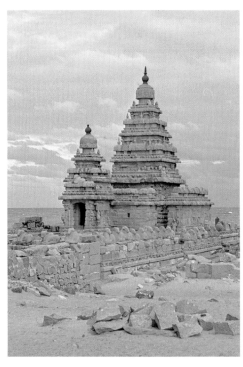

The Shore Temple of the Seven Pagodas at Mahabalipuram (above) dates from the 8th century AD. This five-storeyed Hindu monument is a pyramidal structure 60 ft high and 50 ft square at the base. In front is a small temple, which was the original porch.

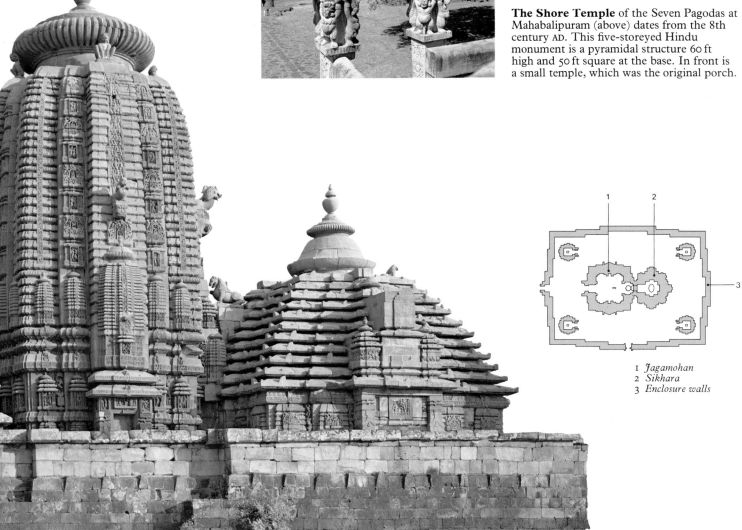

1 Jagamohan
2 Sikhara
3 Enclosure walls

Indian architecture in Southeast Asia

THE ANCIENT INDIAN architecture which flourished in regions outside India is equal, in both artistic conception and technical execution, to anything in India itself. This spread of Indian architecture was the result of a colonialism which took and acclimatized the culture of India, based on Hinduism and Buddhism, to the entire region of Southeast Asia, comprising Burma, Thailand and Indo-China on the mainland, and Sumatra, Java, Bali and other islands on the Indian Archipelago. It was, however, a peculiar colonization because there was no settlement of large numbers of Indians, and, therefore, the ethnic character of the indigenous populations was not altered. It created a dominant minority of rulers and, perhaps, an aristocracy, who were fully Indianized in culture. The masses, however, remained attached to their old life and culture. None the less, the ruling order gave the regions their most magnificent architectural monuments.

The expansion of Indians and their culture came from the coasts of the Bay of Bengal. It began in the early centuries of the Christian era, but reached its full strength only about four centuries later. At first the motive for this expansion was commercial, perhaps a quest for gold. The commercial adventure was accompanied by Buddhist missionary activity, which converted the whole region to that religion. It is also certain that at some later period Indians who were of the higher Hindu castes went to those same areas, particularly to Cambodia, for there, even when the ruling dynasties were indigenous, the names of the rulers were Sanskrit names and the religion was the highest form of Hinduism.

The two greatest monuments, which are due to the adoption of Indian culture abroad, are Borobudur in Java and Angkor Wat in Cambodia. Borobudur, built in the 8th and 9th centuries, is an immensely magnified Buddhist stupa which is carved out of a hill. It rises in terraces, which are decorated with small stupas and friezes, to the relatively small central stupa at the summit. It commands a wonderful view of the plains below and architecturally it is unlike any other monument of its kind.

The temple complex at Angkor Wat, begun in the 12th century, is Hindu and it is, in extent and grandeur, comparable to the largest temple complexes in South India. It is so large that the pilgrims who wished to go around the temple, in accordance with Hindu custom, had to walk almost thirteen miles.

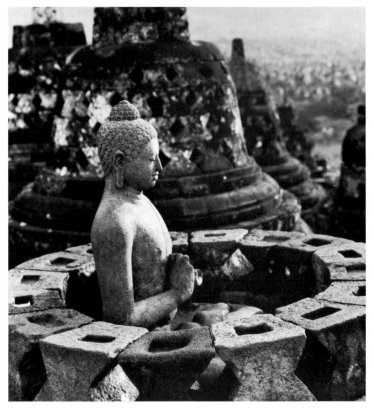

Borobudur, a monumental Buddhist temple-mountain (plan below), was built in Java *c.* AD 800. The pilgrim ascended along the corridors (1) of the square lower terraces (2), and then around three terraces (3) rising in concentric rings of 72 stupas (4). The great sealed stupa (5) is the symbol of Eternal Truth and the goal of the pilgrimage.

Huge stone Buddha figures were enclosed in each of the 72 bell-shaped, stone, open lattice-work stupas on the top three circular terraces.

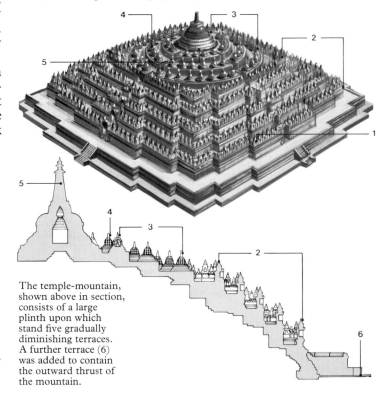

The temple-mountain, shown above in section, consists of a large plinth upon which stand five gradually diminishing terraces. A further terrace (6) was added to contain the outward thrust of the mountain.

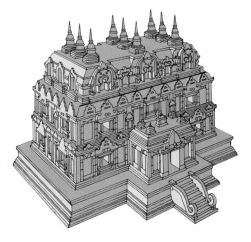

Chandi Sari (left), crowned by stupas and covered with sculpture of fine quality, is a unique 9th-century Buddhist shrine in Java. It appears from the outside to be a large, rectangular, three-storeyed house. Inside, however, it is hollowed out, with only a processional corridor around three shrines.

The main entrance to Angkor Wat (below), a monumental ceremonial gateway about 220 yds long, has three pavilions, each crowned with a tower. It is on the west side of the enclosure, the walls of which form a rectangle 1,425 by 1,640 yds. The approach road, with a magnificent serpent balustrade, is built on a wide stone causeway and crosses a moat 625 ft wide.

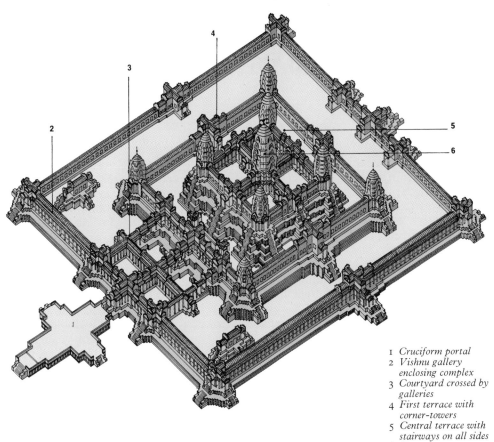

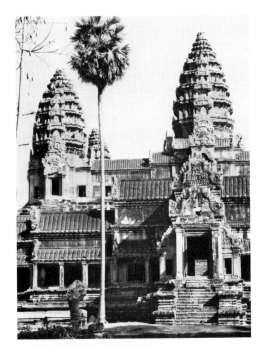

1 *Cruciform portal*
2 *Vishnu gallery enclosing complex*
3 *Courtyard crossed by galleries*
4 *First terrace with corner-towers*
5 *Central terrace with stairways on all sides*
6 *Central tower*

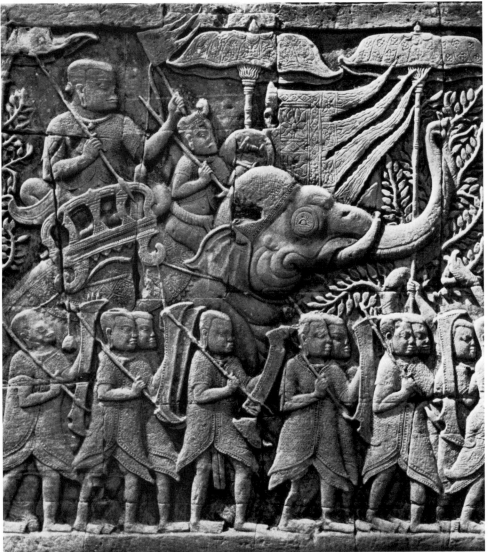

Angkor Wat, the great temple complex in Cambodia (plan above), is the crowning work of Khmer architecture and is probably the world's largest religious structure. A vast sculpture in stone, it was originally dedicated to the royal cult of Vishnu, a god of the Hindu pantheon, but was later used as a Buddhist shrine. It was begun early in the 12th century by Suryavarman (AD 1113–50), King of the Khmer Empire, as his dynastic temple and his mortuary shrine. Built in sandstone and richly sculpted throughout, the temple reflects Khmer cosmology—mounting terraces of diminishing size are topped with five towers symbolizing Mount Mehru, the home of the gods. From the triple gate of the outer enclosure, the stone causeway runs between what were two libraries and ceremonial tanks, or artificial lakes. A cruciform platform leads to the majestic triple-pavilion western gateway. Inside there is a courtyard with cross-shaped shrine galleries, which give on to the first corner-towered terrace. The shrine galleries of the central terrace are broken by entrance pavilions and are linked by triple aisles, in a cruciform shape, to the inmost shrine. This central tower, which soars 215 ft, is reached by exceedingly steep stone steps. The Wat was constructed by erecting the plain stone masses and then setting the sculptors to work. Even the stone roofs are carved. Convex-curved, they are slightly re-curved at the eaves. Most of the pillars are square, with huge square-cut capitals stepped out to carry the weight of the great architraves.

Great narrative bas-reliefs fill the galleried cloisters and are part of the wonder of Angkor Wat. Delicately and shallowly carved, the sculpture, which illustrates scenes from Hindu epics (left), complements without dominating the architecture.

The Indo-Islamic style

THE EXOTIC architecture of the Islamic world came to India with the Muslim conquest. It was derived from Romano-Byzantine architecture, but from the 7th century the Islamic style became a fully developed artistic expression in itself. In India, Islamic architecture remained traditionally Islamic. At the same time, it also adopted certain features of the pre-existing Hindu architecture, including brackets and corbelled construction. This assimilation of the indigenous elements was interrupted from time to time by the introduction of new and purely Islamic styles, which appeared in Persia and Central Asia from the 13th to the 17th centuries. As a result the architecture of the Muslim period in India alternated between purism and eclecticism.

The first mosques in India, which were built in Delhi and Ajmer in the last decade of the 12th century to celebrate the Muslim conquest, incorporated whole colonnades taken from Hindu and Jain temples, which gave them a very un-Islamic look. Very soon, however, Muslim builders were brought in, and in the course of the 13th century a recognizable Indo-Islamic style was created. But in the 14th century it was superseded by a severe and puritanical style which was introduced by the Tughluqs. This again was followed by a period of assimilation of indigenous Indian styles.

With the establishment of the Mogul Empire in the mid-16th century, Indian architecture found another splendid expression. The first Mogul buildings were in the eclectic style, but in the 17th century a purely Persian style dominated. During the whole Mogul period (c. 16th–18th centuries), even the independent Hindu princes built in the Indo-Islamic style and the palaces and forts of the Rajput princes cannot be distinguished from Muslim buildings of the same period. The most notable examples of such buildings are to be found at Jaipur in Rajasthan. The Marathas who followed also built in the Indo-Islamic style. Even Hindu temples in northern India have many Islamic features, including the dome and the arch.

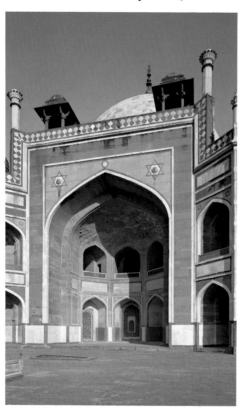

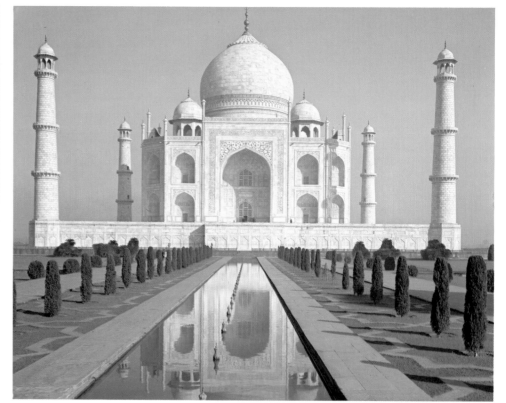

The central gateway of Humayun's tomb in Delhi takes the form of a deep, octagonally recessed bay—a treatment repeated in the central bay of the mausoleum. The tomb is 156 ft square and the height to the top of the dome is 125 ft. The red sandstone exterior is picked out in relief with white marble. The lower openings of the recessed windows are filled in with lovely lattices of stone and marble. Built in 1564 by the Emperor Humayun's widow, the mausoleum is a splendid example of Indo-Islamic architecture. It marked the introduction in India of the new and purely Islamic building styles of Persia and Central Asia.

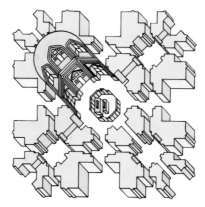

The Taj Mahal (1632–53) in Agra, the most famous example of Indo-Islamic architecture, is the mausoleum which the Emperor Shah Jahan erected for his favourite wife, Mumtaz Mahal, and in which he, too, is buried. Built of marble and decorated with exquisite *pietra dura*, a form of inlay work, the Taj stands on a platform 22 ft high and 313 ft square. The minarets at each corner rise to 137 ft. The tomb itself is 186 ft on each side and the great central dome soars to 187 ft. In the centre of the mausoleum, in an octagonal chamber (plan left), enclosed by a white marble trellis-work screen, are the two tombs. From each corner room spiral stairs lead to the roof.

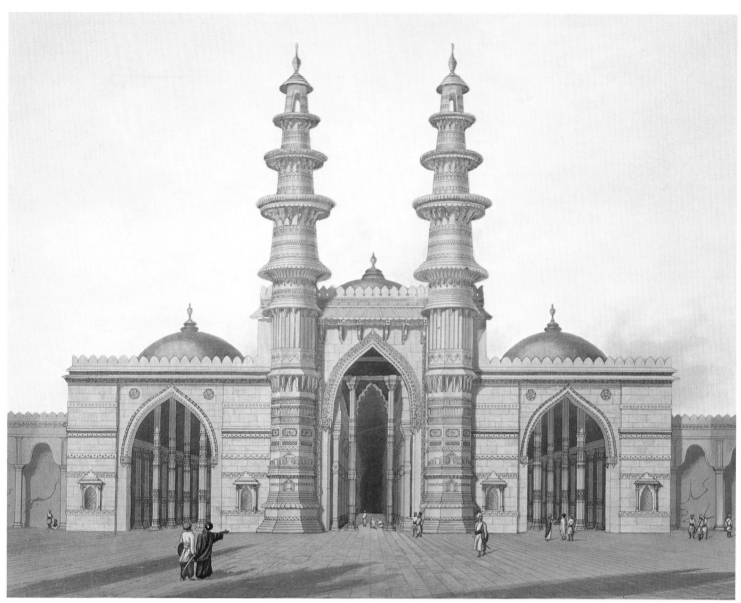

The Jami Masjid, at Ahmadabad in
Gujarat (above), was built in 1424. The roof
of the mosque, supported by 260 columns,
has 14 cupolas. This illustration is from a
water-colour done by an English officer in
1809. The minarets, known as the "shaking
minarets" because they shook in the wind,
lost half their height in an earthquake in 1819.

Gol Gumbaz, or Round Dome, at Bijapur
in the Deccan (below), is the mausoleum of
Sultan Muhammad Adil Shah (1626–56).
The tomb is square with 196-ft exterior sides.
The great dome in the centre is 124 ft in
diameter—16 ft larger than St Paul's in
London. The great hall beneath, the largest
domed space in the world, is 18,225 sq ft.

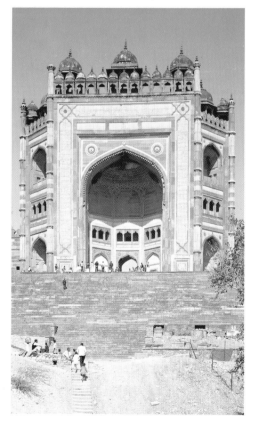

Fatehpur Sikri, the sandstone city founded
by Akbar in 1568 and abandoned 17 years
later is built in the Mogul eclectic style.
Almost seven miles in circumference, it
is surrounded on three sides by a wall
pierced with eight gateways. In the south
wall the Buland Darwaza, the Gate of
Victory (left), towers to a height of 176 ft,
its grandeur increased by the great flight of
stairs leading up to it. It was built by Akbar
to celebrate his conquest of Gujarat. The
Diwan-i-Khas, the hall of private audience
(below), gives the impression from the outside of having two storeys, but inside it is a
single room with a beautifully carved
octagonal pillar which supported the
Emperor's throne.

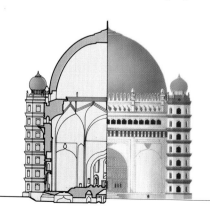

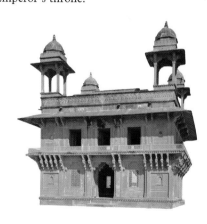

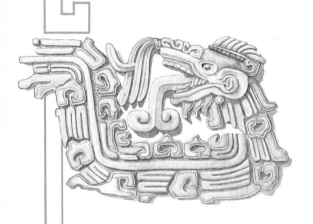

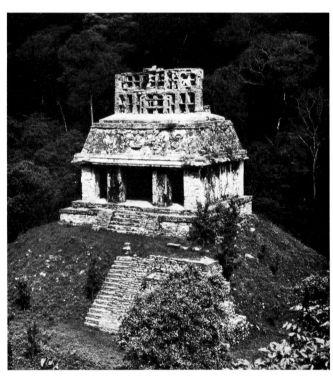

The Temple of the Foliated Cross is one of the distinctive and diverse buildings at Palenque, a hilltop city built by the Maya. Here, the Maya talent for stucco sculpture and low-relief ornament reached its finest expression. The range and elegance of these monuments are among the high points of pre-Hispanic architecture.

Once only in the long history of mankind have explorers or conquerors come upon a highly developed civilization that possessed not only no obvious links but no possible ones, however indirect, with their own. Anthropologists may—and doubtless will—argue for ever about whether the Indians of the Western Hemisphere are genuine aboriginals, or whether their forefathers came from Siberia to Alaska across the frozen Bering Strait, or even drifted over the Pacific on rafts; the question is intriguing but irrelevant. What matters is that their civilizations developed *in situ* and, until the arrival of the Spaniards in the early 16th century, owed nothing to influences from outside the continent.

In such fields as astronomy and the measurement of time they excelled, but in other respects they were woefully defective. They had no wheel, no beasts of burden—except when, latterly in Peru, the occasional half-domesticated llama could be persuaded to carry a light load over a short distance—no scales or weights, no implements of iron; nor did they ever discover the principle of the true arch. And yet somehow, despite these handicaps, they were able to build on a colossal scale: pyramids and temples and cyclopean walls that can still evoke astonishment and awe.

Of all the multifarious races of pre-Hispanic America, three stand out above the rest: the Aztec, the Maya and the Inca. Of these the Aztecs, denizens of the high central plateau of Mexico, can quickly be dismissed from any architectural history, since scarcely any of their monuments survive. This is not simply because they were warriors rather than builders; it is due principally to the fact that their watery capital, Tenochtitlán, which stood in the middle of a huge lake on the site of the present-day Mexico City, was destroyed in 1521 by the Spanish Conquistadors under Hernán

Pre-Hispanic

Cortés. They had hoped to preserve it: but the determination and courage of its defenders obliged them to continue the fighting until not one stone was left on another. Only thirty miles away, the tremendous ruins of Teotihuacán, now mercilessly restored, mark the site of the greatest metropolis in the ancient Americas; but Teotihuacán, which flourished at the same time as Imperial Rome, was already long abandoned and overgrown by the time the invading Aztecs first saw it, in about AD 1170.

It is difficult to feel fond of the Aztecs, whose constant warfare was directed towards a single object—that of taking enough prisoners to keep their sacrificial altars supplied with a constant stream of human hearts, torn still beating from the victims' bodies before being offered up to their insatiable gods. The Mayas, although they, too, practised human sacrifice on occasion, were far less bloodthirsty and infinitely more gifted. Hundreds of their monuments still dominate the steamy rain-forests of the Yucatán peninsula, Guatemala and Honduras; thousands more remain unexplored.

But for all their extraordinary feeling for design and proportion, the Mayas remained hamstrung by their ignorance of the arch. This meant that, although they could build long, they could never build high. In other circumstances, among other races, such a disability might not have mattered very much; but the peoples of ancient Mexico, in almost all their ceremonial building, set out to overawe if not actually to terrify. Height and mass consequently assumed vital importance, and most of their architects solved the problem in the only way they could—by means of huge mounds and pyramids crowned, as often as not, with tiny temples of just one or two rooms.

Anyone who has seen the eight temple pyramids at Tikal in Guatemala, the jungle-haunted ruins of Palenque or the Pyramid of the Soothsayer at Uxmal will know how thrillingly this apparently simple technique could work out in practice. Also at Uxmal, however, and at certain other sites such as Kabah, Labná and Sayil—all these are in Yucatán, where the vegetation, dense as it is, tends to be more stunted than in the rainier south—an alternative solution was produced, with long, low structures raised on terraces and making their impact by their proportions alone.

High in the Peruvian Andes, the Incas could not match the Maya talent for decoration, proportion or design. Their strength lay in the craft of architecture rather than in its art; for they were, arguably, the best stone-masons the world has ever known. Whether they were working with basically rectangular blocks of ashlar, as at Cuzco, or with irregular, polygonal ones, as at nearby Sacsahuamán, these blocks were quarried without explosives, shaped and chamfered without iron chisels, transported without wheels or draught animals for anything up to twenty miles of mountain terrain and finally fitted into position, using only the crudest forms of leverage, until it was impossible to slip a knife blade between them. Of carved decoration there is scarcely a trace. Either a surface was thought to be not worth decorating or, if it was, there were other, more satisfactory methods of doing so. The first Spaniard ever to see Cuzco reported "a quadrangular building . . . measuring three hundred and fifty paces from corner to corner, entirely plated with gold; of these gold plates they took down seven hundred, which together weighed five hundred *pesos* of gold. . . ."

And so, just a dozen years after Cortés had been forced to destroy Montezuma's Tenochtitlán, Pizarro massacred Atahualpa and his six thousand unarmed followers under a flag of truce and ravaged Cuzco. The city was too rich; the temptation too great; the loss incomparable.

Cities of the Mayas, Toltecs and Aztecs

ANY APPRECIATION of ancient Meso-America's architectural splendour must begin with Teotihuacán, the City of the Gods. Its two gigantic pyramid temples, dating from about the time of Christ, are the largest and oldest in the Americas and were models for all the rest. There, too, stand the remains of the Pyramid of the powerful god Quetzalcoatl, the Plumed Serpent. Teotihuacán was destroyed by fire in the 7th century, but the worship of Quetzalcoatl was subsequently adopted by the Toltecs, who settled in central Mexico in the 10th century and established their capital at Tula. Their Aztec conquerors were, in turn, heirs to the cult of the Plumed Serpent.

Remarkable though the temple ruins are at Tula, Toltec architecture is best seen at Chichén Itzá, the Maya city in Yucatán, which they occupied in the 10th and again in the 12th centuries. Nearly all the principal monuments, including the *Castillo*, or main temple, the Observatory and the Temple of the Jaguars, display strong Toltec influence, notably in the plumed-serpent columns and in the use of repeating jaguar and eagle motifs.

Pure Maya work is found elsewhere in Yucatán, in Guatemala and in Honduras. Although Maya civilization became recognizable by about the 2nd century BC and flourished until the 15th, its important architecture dates from about AD 624, with the building of Palenque, to 987, when Uxmal, the most sophisticated of all Maya sites, was founded. Here an architect of genius produced a "Governor's Palace", which has been described as "the single most magnificent building ever constructed in the Americas".

Another important Mexican site is Monte Albán, near Oaxaca, where from *c.* AD 300 the Zapotec people developed a culture which reached its apogee in the 9th century. An immense complex of tombs and temples, which they built on an artificially flattened hilltop, it still retains a strange and numinous beauty.

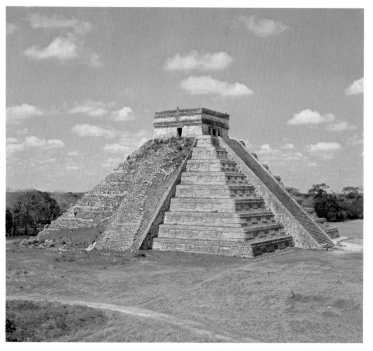

El Castillo (above) is the most impressive monument of the Toltec-Maya city of Chichén Itzá, in Yucatán. The temple pyramid was built at the end of the 12th century AD by Toltecs who had migrated there from their capital Tula, near Mexico City, in the 10th century. Breathtaking stairways rise on all four sides to the richly carved temple, dedicated to the god Kukulcán (or Quetzalcoatl, the plumed serpent-god). The serpent motif is used everywhere—on the balustrades of the stairways and on the temple columns. The façade is carved with figures of Tula warriors.

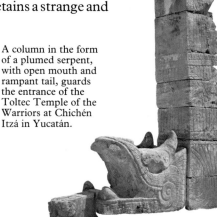

A column in the form of a plumed serpent, with open mouth and rampant tail, guards the entrance of the Toltec Temple of the Warriors at Chichén Itzá in Yucatán.

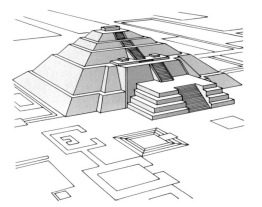

The Pyramid of the Moon is one of the oldest buildings at Teotihuacán, the city of eight square miles which flourished from 200 BC to AD 750 as a major centre for religious ceremony and ritual. This immense pyramid, companion to the even larger Pyramid of the Sun, dominates the northern part of the site, and although its original splendour has disappeared its vast size can still be appreciated. The structure was flat on top to provide space for a temple. The stairs, broken by terraces, appear continuous from below.

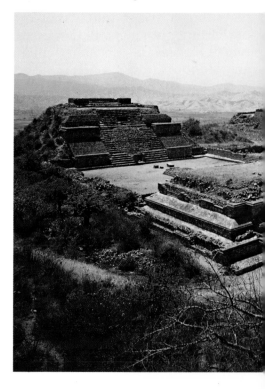

Monte Albán (right), the great temple city of the Zapotecs, is ideally situated on a mountain-top in Oaxaca. To the people in the valley it must have seemed the city of the gods. Although the stuccoed and painted decoration has now disappeared from the stone-work, the perfect proportions and symmetry of the complex, set on its terraces and platforms, establish it as an architectural masterpiece. The origins of Monte Albán are still shrouded in mystery. Certainly occupied from 500 BC to AD 1469, it presents a record of ever-changing cultures.

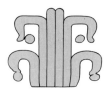

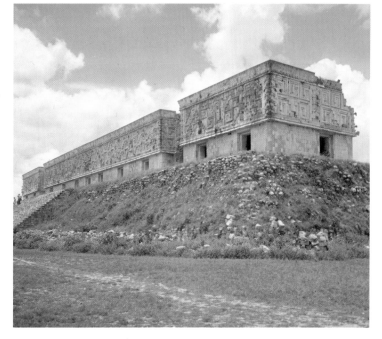

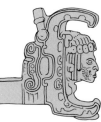

Maya artists excelled in low-relief carvings and achieved a sophisticated ornamental style full of grotesque elements, as seen in the head emerging from a serpent's jaw (above).

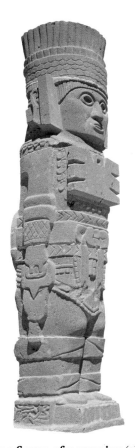

The Toltec figure of a warrior (above), over 15 ft tall, is one of many that supported the roof of a major temple at Tula. Each colossal figure carried a bag of incense and the *atl-atl*, a deadly throwing device. Gigantic sculptures of figures and serpents are the most distinctive and awesome features of Toltec work.

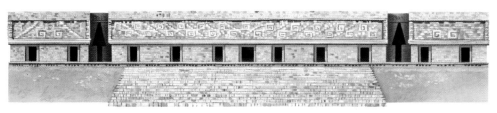

The "Governor's Palace" (above and top) is one of eight groups of buildings at Uxmal, perhaps the most beautiful of all Maya cities. Built towards the end of the 10th century AD, at the height of the Maya artistic renaissance, Uxmal was the principal ceremonial centre of the Puuc. This region of low-lying hills in northwest Yucatán is dotted with the remains of smaller cities in a similar elegant style. The so-called Governor's Palace is a magnificent example of Puuc building. Its characteristic exterior, the lower half plain, is incrusted above with a stone-mosaic frieze (320 ft long, 40 ft wide and 26 ft high), exuberantly and skilfully carved with about 20,000 geometric and symbolic motifs. The palace is remarkable not only for its carved decoration but also for its superb proportions. It consists of a large central building and two identical wings, which were originally connected by hallways whose vaults were the tallest of the Maya world. The doorways with their corbelled arches (the true arch was unknown in ancient Mexico) enhance its beauty with contrasts of light and shadow. The palace is set on an artificially constructed platform, which is reached by stone steps on all sides.

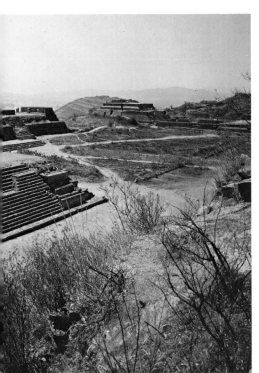

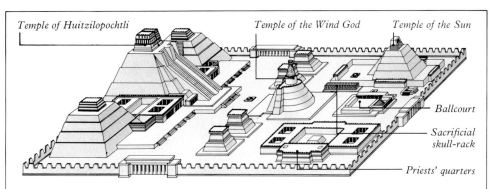

Temple of Huitzilopochtli · Temple of the Wind God · Temple of the Sun · Ballcourt · Sacrificial skull-rack · Priests' quarters

TENOCHTITLÁN

The ancient capital of the Aztecs, Tenochtitlán stood 8,000 ft above sea level in a landscape of bare volcanic mountains and forested valleys. The city, begun in AD 1325, was built on an island in Lake Texcoco. It was divided by a network of canals and connected to the mainland by three great causeways raised on dykes. Its magnificence and excellent planning amazed the Conquistadors who, in 1521, captured Tenochtitlán and burned it to the ground.

The sacred centre, the Great Plaza of Tenochtitlán, now lies buried under Mexico City. It is reconstructed here from archaeological evidence and is shown enclosed in a crenellated wall. Highly organized religions existed among the Pre-Hispanic peoples of Central America. The plaza probably contained temples to the gods of the Rain, the Winds and the Sun, as well as to Huitzilopochtli, the tribal god of the Aztecs. His temple is at the summit of the largest pyramid.

The Incas' unparalleled achievement

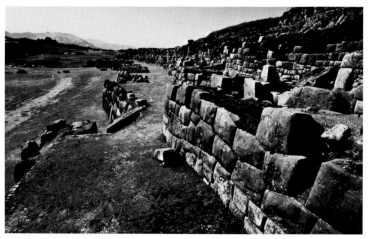

THE INCAS HAD no wheel, few draught-animals, no weights or scales, no iron implements. Architecturally there was a yawning gap in their knowledge, for they never discovered the principle of the true arch. Yet their building achievement is unparalleled in history. Inca architecture was a triumph not only in their houses, palaces and temples, but also in the roads and bridges with which they assured communications throughout their immense and straggling Empire. This Empire, which began as a small kingdom established at Cuzco *c.* AD 1200, had by 1530 expanded to include much of Ecuador and stretched southwards, through Peru and Bolivia, into parts of the Argentine and northern Chile.

The Inca Royal Road of the Andes, 3,250 miles long and passing through terrain as challenging as any in the world, was, until the 19th century, the longest arterial road ever constructed, and their coastal road was only slightly shorter. Rivers were spanned by cantilever or pontoon bridges, deep valleys by rope suspension bridges, one of which, the San Luis Rey, has passed into legend.

The cities of the Incas, strung along the entire length of the Empire, were unfortified, putting their trust in separate fortresses on nearby hills, to which the people retired to defend themselves when it was felt necessary. Most of these cities were designed around a central plaza, with a sun temple flanked by the palaces of the notables; their very uniformity showed the firmness of central control. Ironically, it was this brilliantly maintained centralization which was the cause of their ultimate destruction; for when the great Inca Atahualpa fell to the army of Pizarro in 1532, his Empire perished with him.

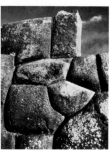

The great walls of Sacsahuamán (above) are built with huge polygonal stones, some of them up to 27 ft high.

Sacsahuamán (above), a mountain fortress defending the Inca capital Cuzco, is a spectacular example of the engineering skill of the Incas. From AD 1438 to 1500, 30,000 Indians, using only the most primitive of tools, helped to erect this gigantic structure, whose unbroken north wall is 1,500 ft long.

Machu Picchu (below), a fortress city dramatically situated above the Urubamba gorge, consists of an elaborate cluster of sacred plazas, temples and houses clinging to the terraced mountain-side. Although it now lies in ruins, the surviving walls, all of solid granite, remain as impressive testimony to its former austerity and grandeur.

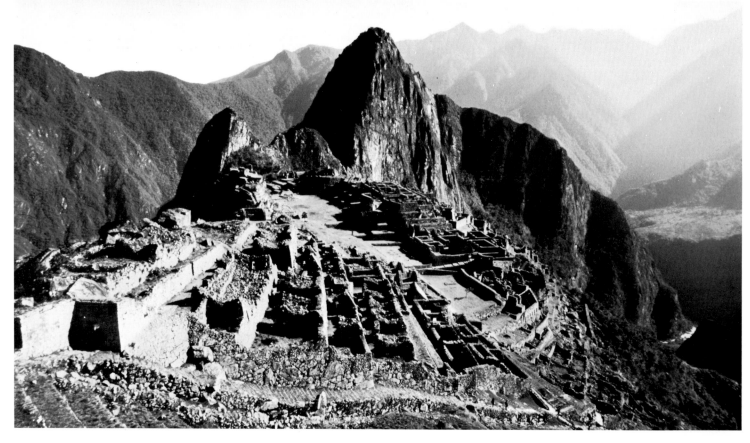

THE
ANCIENT
WORLD

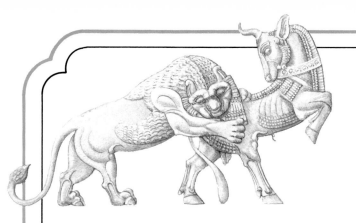

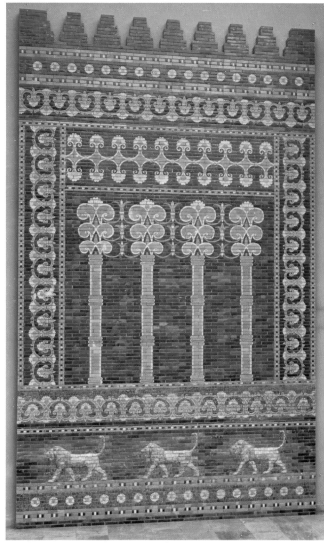

Mesopotamia lacked stone for carving, and so the Babylonians decorated their buildings with brilliant glazed ornament, as seen in this throne-room panel from Nebuchadnezzar's palace.

In the Near East, examples of man's first experiments in the craft of building have been found at many prehistoric sites. Circular huts or rectangular buildings of clay and stone have replaced the cave dwellings of earlier times and the camp sites of nomadic peoples. Their functional shape was dictated by the materials available and they cluster together for mutual protection. The first buildings consciously contrived to create an aesthetic effect are found during the 4th millennium BC and are confined to territory occupied by the antecedents of the Sumerians in southern Mesopotamia. The concept of architectural design was, therefore, a regional invention. Characteristic of the Sumerians were well-defined religious beliefs of a sort to which monumental architecture could give material expression. Their earliest public buildings accordingly took the form of temples.

In a treeless country with no stone available, sun-dried bricks soon became the standard building material, although the design long retained some memory of the reed architecture favoured by earlier marsh-dwellers. Parapets and internal walls were often decorated with mosaics consisting of terracotta cones. Alternatively, rooms were enlivened by painted murals depicting religious scenes. During the centuries preceding 3000 BC, the planning of these temples became remarkably sophisticated with a central sanctuary, sometimes cruciform like a Christian basilica, rising above its lateral chambers to allow clerestory lighting. Because mud-brick buildings were short-lived, the practice of building a new temple upon the ruins of its predecessors led to a convention by which such shrines were raised above the surrounding buildings on a high artificial platform. In later days, such platforms increased in scale and complexity, to create the great staged towers, or ziggurats, of which the summit temple was a culminating feature.

Mesopotamia and the Near East

During the period of the Sumero–Akkadian dynasties, c. 3000 to 2000 BC, art and architecture kept pace with developments in technology and political organization. Temples were surrounded by new forms of public buildings, including pretentious royal palaces. The 2nd millennium BC saw the adornment of great cities in central and northern Mesopotamia, including Babylon under its great king Hammurabi, the prosperous city-state of Mari on the middle Euphrates and the first Assyrian capital at Ashur on the Tigris. All of these required new forms of accommodation for the seat of government, and the planning of palaces acquired a new complexity. From representations in Mesopotamian art something is known about the external appearance of buildings and fortifications at this time. Gateways were flanked by high towers, their parapets decorated with crenellations. Façades were ornamented with a complex system of vertical pilasters and three-quarter columns, their brickwork sometimes carved to represent palm trunks. Whole towns, or their inner citadels, were surrounded by fortress walls, modelled on contemporary Egyptian defence systems.

During this same period, the understanding of architectural design had extended westwards to the cities of the Levant, northwards to Anatolia and in the east to Elam, with its capital at Susa. In all these centres, the middle centuries of the 2nd millennium BC saw great accomplishments in the realm of architecture. Differences of style could once more be attributed to the building materials locally available. In Anatolia, from the earliest times, timber-framed buildings with brick filling were the rule. The Hittites, however, in their capital at Hattusas, built great temples of dressed stone, and a double fortification with a substructure of "cyclopean" masonry enclosed a city of three hundred acres. Its gates were ornamented with portal sculptures centuries before this device was adopted in Mesopotamia. In Elam, kings of this period built, partly in stone, a religious complex centred around a colossal ziggurat, today better preserved than any in Mesopotamia.

In Assyria, during the 9th to 7th centuries, its great imperial rulers made their capitals successively at Nimrud, Khorsabad and Nineveh. From the hills above Nineveh a royal canal brought clean water to the city over stone aqueducts. It was from their palaces that excavators of the 19th century brought such a wealth of architectural sculptures to the European museums.

After the fall of Assyria in 612 BC, Mesopotamia saw a final revival of monumental building in Babylon. Nebuchadnezzar's vast city had a nucleus of formal planning, with temples and palaces connected by a raised Procession Street. All of these were lavishly decorated with glazed tiles showing heraldic animals and other motifs in relief. By contrast, when the contemporary rulers of Persia built a new capital at Persepolis, their palaces were grouped closely together on a huge terrace of natural rock and showed a strongly individual style. The employment of captive Greek craftsmen lent a new delicacy to the Assyrian style of carving, but the columnar ornament of opposing façades reflected the creative genius of indigenous peoples.

Some traces of this aptitude for architectural design are still to be seen in the few surviving buildings of the Sassanian kings, the third Persian dynasty to dominate the Near East in the 3rd century AD. A primary feature of Sassanian palaces was the huge *iwan*, or vaulted hall, open on one side, like that which distinguishes the ruins of Ctesiphon in central Iraq. For the rest, its flanking façades suggest a decadent form of the blind arcading used in Roman buildings, while the plan of the palace anticipates those of Muslim times.

The Sumerians, Elamites and Hittites

THE FIRST CONSCIOUS attempts at the design of public buildings must be attributed to the inhabitants of southern Mesopotamia in the final centuries of the 4th millennium BC. In a land without stone or wood, temples were built of sun-dried brick and ornamented with mural paintings or coloured mosaics. Alternating buttresses and recesses relieved the monotony of their plastered façades, and gateways were flanked by high towers. Kings of the Sumerian dynasties lived in formally planned palaces. The brick platforms supporting their primary religious shrines were later heightened and elaborated to create complicated staged towers, or ziggurats. Other temples, at ground level, were enclosed in a sacred precinct with protective walls.

Far to the north in central Anatolia, during the 2nd millennium, Hittite rulers soon emulated the architectural achievements of Mesopotamia. Temples and fortress walls were now built on a substructure of heavy stonework, and portal sculptures were a new feature of their monumental gateways. In the Zagros Mountains to the east, a dynasty of Elamite kings enriched their capital at Susa and founded a provincial religious centre at Dur-Antash.

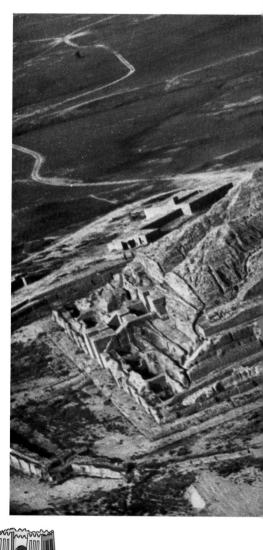

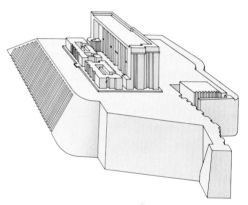

The White Temple (left), at the Sumerian city of Uruk, or Warka, was built *c.* 3000 BC. It stood upon a platform with sloping façades of panelled brickwork 40 ft above ground level. Externally it was white-plastered, but showed traces of wooden ornament between the projecting buttresses. The long sanctuary and lateral chambers are characteristic. The entrance for worshippers was through a side-room, but there were also imposing doorways at either end, one of them displacing the altar from its axial position. Scholars have explained this by attributing to such temples the function of a "portal", through which a deity might pass on his visits to earth.

A Sumerian platform-temple (below), at Khafaje, east of modern Baghdad. Built *c.* 2600 BC, it was enclosed in an oval-shaped precinct, with subsidiary chambers at ground level. An outer enclosure wall was extended to protect a priestly residence, with its own private chapel. The inner courtyard was provided with offering-tables and showed evidence of animal sacrifices. The temple itself and its platform were much denuded and are here tentatively reconstructed. A similar, better-preserved example at Al'Ubaid, near Ur-of-the-Chaldees, had façades decorated with pictorial friezes of coloured stone inlay, and copper animal figures in high relief.

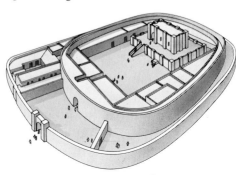

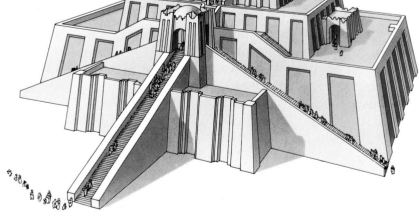

The great ziggurat tower at Ur-of-the-Chaldees, reconstructed after Sir Leonard Woolley, was built by Ur-Nammu and Shulgi, two Sumerian kings of the 3rd Dynasty, 2113–2048 BC. Incorporating the remains of an earlier structure, it was constructed of mud-brick, reinforced with thick layers of matting and cables of twisted reeds. A triple stairway with heavy bastions leads to the summit of the first stage, where one passed through a portal, perhaps covered by a dome. A fourth stairway gave access to the second and third stages. Nothing remained of the summit shrine itself, save a few fragments of glazed ornament, and the form suggested here is, therefore, hypothetical.

The temple of Ishtar-Kititum (right), at Ishchali, east of modern Baghdad, is dedicated to a form of the Mother-Goddess. This is the largest and most important of the three temples which make up the ingeniously planned assembly of religious buildings at Ishchali. It was built *c.* 1800 BC, by a ruler of the independent state called Eshnunna.

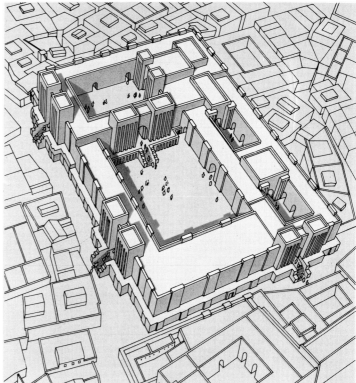

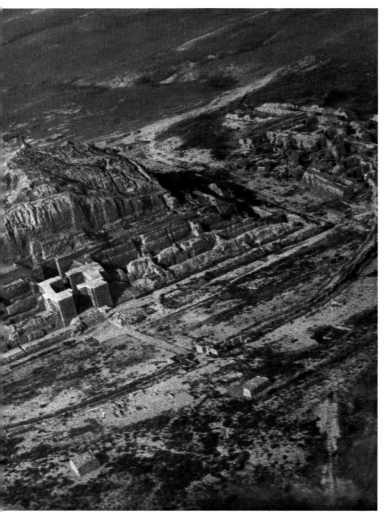

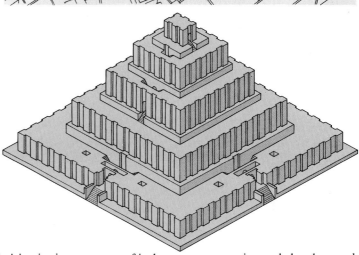

The Choga Zanbil ziggurat complex, twenty-five miles east of Susa, was constructed in the mid-13th century BC by King Untash-Gal of Elam. It is seen here after excavation (above), and reconstructed (above right). The city had three concentric fortification walls. The innermost wall enclosed the tower itself, rising in six stages from a base 110 yds square to a vertical height of almost 54 yds. Unlike those of Mesopotamia, this Elamite ziggurat had stairways leading to the summit which passed through vaulted passages within its structure. Also incorporated in the periphery of its lowest stage were internal chambers and chapels, dedicated to Inshushinak and other gods of the Elamite pantheon. Adjacent to the tower at its foot were formally built altars and shrines, while temples dedicated to minor deities occupied sites within the second enceinte.

THE KING'S GATE, BOGHAZKÖY
At the time of the Hittite Empire in the 14th century BC, the fortifications of its capital city, Hattusas (modern Boghazköy), were extended to enclose an area of almost three hundred acres. Its powerful walls were built on a substructure of "cyclopean" masonry, with rubble-filled casemates and projecting towers. Of the five main gateways, with their elliptical arches of corbelled stone, two are flanked by sculptured figures of lions or sphinxes, but a third—the so-called King's Gate (right)—has one lateral jamb of the inner archway ornamented with a larger-than-lifesize figure, carved in high relief. It represents a Hittite warrior of the Empire period wearing the characteristic "kilt" and conical helmet with ear-flaps. Other fine Hittite reliefs are to be seen in the rock-cut shrine at Yazilikaya, outside the city.

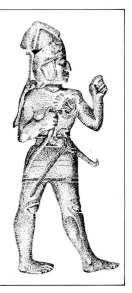

The Assyrians and Neo-Babylonians

UNDER THE ASSYRIAN king-emperors of the 9th to 7th centuries BC, Mesopotamian architecture acquired a new vitality. Ashurnasirpal II made his capital at Nimrud, or Calah, twenty miles south of Nineveh. Sargon II built a new capital at Khorsabad, or Dur Sharrukin, in the hills to the northeast. Sennacherib and his successors preferred Nineveh itself, which they rebuilt on a magnificent scale. In these walled cities, palaces took precedence over religious buildings, and it was their remains—first discovered and excavated during the 19th century—which so astonished the world. Raised on brick platforms, level with their surrounding fortifications, their principal gateways were flanked by "guardian" figures of human-headed bulls or lions sculptured in stone. Inside, their halls and corridors were lined with pictures and inscriptions carved in relief on stone slabs up to nine feet high. Some idea of the richness and luxury with which these buildings were decorated has been obtained from fragments of painted murals and the plentiful remnants of ivory furniture. City walls, often more than twenty feet thick, were further strengthened by innumerable towers with crenellated battlements.

After the fall of Nineveh in 612 BC, the focus of Mesopotamian civilization returned to the south, where a new dynasty of kings, including Nebuchadnezzar, revived the glories of Hammurabi's Babylon. Much rebuilding took place in the old Sumerian cities, while the capital itself was enormously enlarged, heavily fortified and adorned with magnificent new buildings. Here the traditional style of architecture reached its zenith and was enhanced by a new form of façade ornament consisting of figured designs in coloured glazed brickwork. The inner city alone, on the east bank of the Euphrates, had a five-mile circuit of walls. Public buildings were concentrated around a raised Procession Street, leading from the famous Ishtar Gate to the splendid ziggurat Etemenanki in its own walled precinct. The vast throne-room in the palace of Nabonidus, rebuilt and enlarged by Nebuchadnezzar, may have been the scene of the biblical "writing on the wall", and raised above the vaulted buildings which surrounded it were the Hanging Gardens of classical tradition.

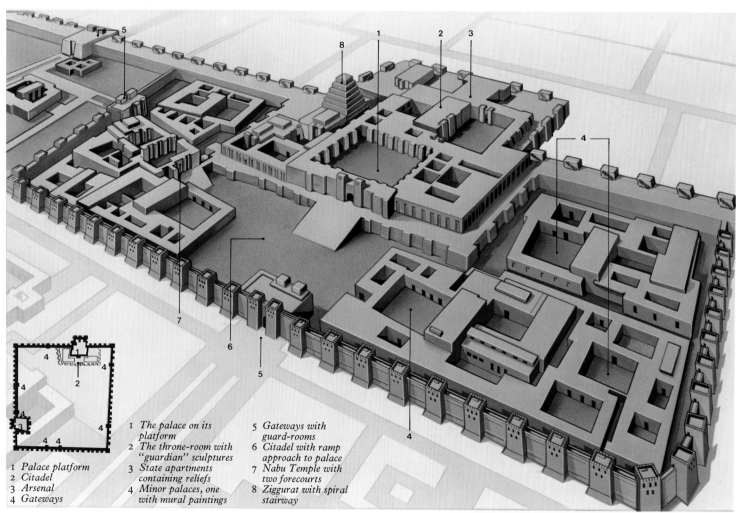

1   *The palace on its platform*
2   *The throne-room with "guardian" sculptures*
3   *State apartments containing reliefs*
4   *Minor palaces, one with mural paintings*
5   *Gateways with guard-rooms*
6   *Citadel with ramp approach to palace*
7   *Nabu Temple with two forecourts*
8   *Ziggurat with spiral stairway*

1 *Palace platform*
2 *Citadel*
3 *Arsenal*
4 *Gateways*

Khorsabad, the ephemeral capital of Sargon II of Assyria, 721–705 BC, was built, occupied and abandoned all within a score of years. The double fortification wall encloses an area of one square mile and has seven city gates. The royal palace, with its three private temples and small ziggurat, stands astride the wall at parapet height on the northwest side of the city. It is approached at ground level through a walled citadel, containing other groups of public buildings, and a great temple, dedicated to the god Nabu, is linked to it by a stone bridge. A second raised building near the southwest corner of the town has the function of an imperial arsenal, or *ekal mashati*, used for the assemblage of military equipment and the storage of spoils of war.

1 *Procession Street*
2 *Ishtar Gate*
3 *Palace of Nebuchadnezzar*
4 *Temple of Ninmakh*
5 *Ziggurat precinct of Etemenanki*
6 *Temple of Marduk*
7 *Stone bridge to the "New City"*

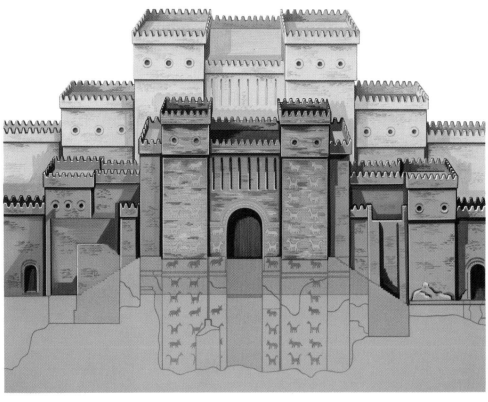

The old city at Babylon took the form of an irregular quadrangle on the east bank of the Euphrates. To this Nebuchadnezzar added a smaller "New City" on the west bank. He joined the two by a bridge and surrounded them by a huge double fortification wall, with projecting towers and a navigable moat,

making a total circuit of five and a quarter miles. Later he added an extended outer rampart, forming a triangle eight miles in circumference, around the eastern part of the town. There was a Summer Palace at the northern apex of the outer enclosure, and from here the great Procession Street

approached its entrance to the inner city through the famous Ishtar Gate (above), built astride the double fortification, with two pairs of towers and roomy internal chambers. At this point the street, paved with marble slabs, was raised high above the surrounding buildings, but its foundations penetrated

ASSYRIAN AND NEO-BABYLONIAN MOTIFS
The scene of King Ashurnasirpal hunting lions (1) is one of the innumerable subjects depicted in Assyrian palace reliefs. As documents of contemporary life, they have proved an invaluable supplement to the written texts. Characteristic motifs of Assyrian ornament are palmettes, chevroned feathers and buds, with a running "guilloche" pattern (2) adopted from North Syria. Pendant fronds (3), arcaded palmettes (4) and pillared panels alternating with rosettes (5) all suggest the familiarity of Neo-Babylonian artists with classical design.

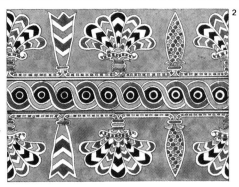

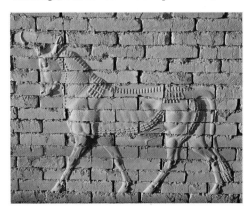

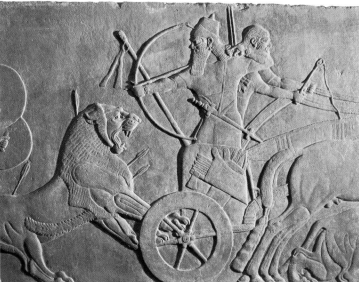

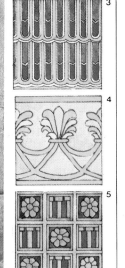

some 30 ft beneath. All façades of the gateway and those of the adjoining street were faced with blue-glazed bricks and ornamented with figures of heraldic animals—lions, bulls and *sirrush* dragons—modelled in relief and glazed in other colours. These figures were repeated, without glazing, on the façades of the hidden foundations (above). Nebuchadnezzar's palace was planned around five successive courtyards. Facing the third of these was the entrance to his colossal throne-room, in a façade once more decorated with brilliant glazed ornament. Farther south, the Procession Street skirted two sides of a broad open *temenos*, or dedicated precinct, surrounding the multicoloured ziggurat, so carefully described by Herodotus after his visit to Babylon in about 460 BC. As a result of quarrying activities in the past, not a vestige of this building remains. Of the Ishtar Gate, too, the ruins which survived above ground level were removed by German excavators in 1913 and the building re-constructed in the Berlin Museum.

The Persians and Sassanians

CYRUS THE GREAT, founder of the first Persian Empire in the mid-6th century BC, made his headquarters in the city of Pasargadae, three hundred miles southeast of Susa. Darius I (522–486 BC) and his successors built a new ceremonial capital at Persepolis, thirty miles to the south. By this time a new Persian style of building was already well developed; but whereas the monumental buildings of Pasargadae were widely spaced among gardens and plantations, those at Persepolis were concentrated closely upon a terrace of natural rock measuring approximately 550 by 330 yards.

Today the ruins of Persepolis give a faulty impression of the city's original appearance. The roofs of its great halls were supported by multiple columns, and some of these, made of stone, have survived. But the mud-brick fabric of its palaces and the high wall enclosing the whole terrace have perished completely, leaving only the sculptures, which adorned doorway or window openings, and the reliefs ornamenting its monumental stairways. Carving in stone is the leitmotiv of Persian design. It differs considerably from that of Assyria, where reliefs were used as interior ornament and their narrative content could be studied at leisure by visitors. At Persepolis they formed an integral part of the exterior design, which explains the occasional monotony of their processional subjects. The receding planes and engraved detail of the Assyrian sculptors gave way at Persepolis to delicate modelling, almost resembling the work of metal-smiths. In the Greek manner, drapery suggested the form of the human body. Portal figures imitated Assyrian formulae; but a striking innovation is to be seen in the sculptured capitals of columns on which Greek and Egyptian enrichment was added to the new animal forms.

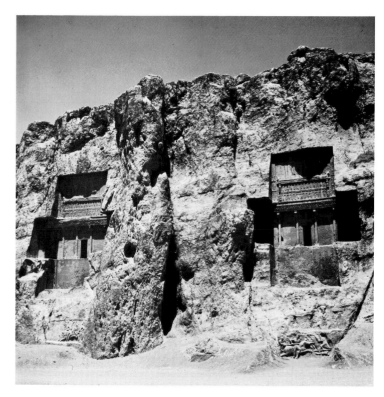

Cliff sculptures surrounding the burial chamber of Darius I at Naqsh-i-Rustam (above). In the upper panel the king sits facing the sacred fire, beneath the winged figure of the god Ahuramazda. Beneath him is a dais supported by thirty figures, representing the countries of his empire.

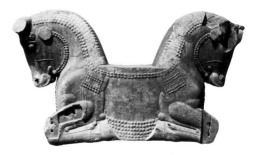

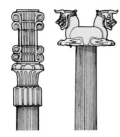

Stone columns at Persepolis are fluted, and often stand on inverted bell-shaped bases. Their capitals—combining Greek motifs such as drooping sepals and double-scroll volutes with the Egyptian palm-leaf—are surmounted by imposts of paired beasts.

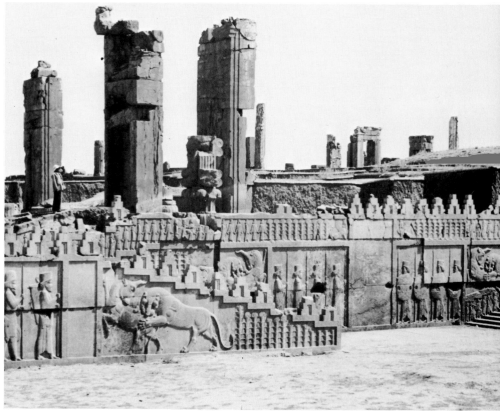

Sculptured reliefs ornamenting the stairways of Persepolis (right) show delegates from the many countries of the Persian Empire, bringing precious gifts and rare animals to the king, perhaps during the New Year Festival. Also appearing are the soldiers of the royal guard, both Persians and Medes, and the nobles of the imperial court. Elsewhere the king is seen in conflict with animals or seated beneath a ceremonial umbrella.

Persepolis. The terrace is approached by a double stairway at the northwest corner. A gate-house, built by Xerxes, leads southwards to the Apadana and eastwards to a second, unfinished, gateway facing the Throne Room. Centrally, a complex portal separates these ceremonial buildings from the royal apartments, with harem quarters surrounding an open courtyard. In the southeast, a treasury building is securely isolated.

1 *Main gate-house*
2 *The Apadana, or Great Audience Hall*
3 *Gate-house*
4 *The Throne Room, or Hall of One Hundred Columns*
5 *The Tripylon, or complex portal*
6 *Palace of Darius*
7 *Palace of Artaxerxes*
8 *Palace of Xerxes*
9 *The harem*
10 *The treasury*

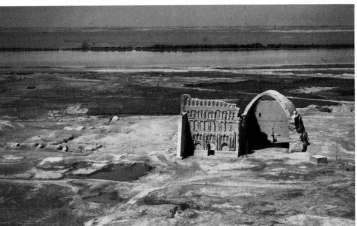

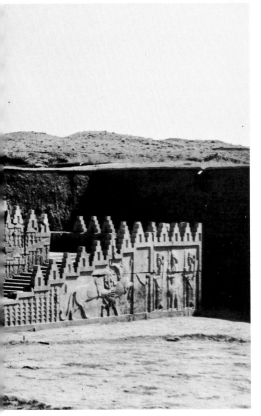

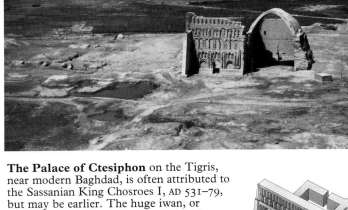

The open-fronted iwan later became a common-place of Muslim architecture. The lateral halls with their corridors are also characteristic; but the arrangement of chambers behind them is not fully understood.

The Palace of Ctesiphon on the Tigris, near modern Baghdad, is often attributed to the Sassanian King Chosroes I, AD 531–79, but may be earlier. The huge iwan, or audience-chamber, open on one side, has a vault of kiln-baked brick 120 ft high, with a span of 83 ft. The arch-rings of which it is composed are set obliquely, each one supporting its neighbour, in order to obviate the necessity for temporary support while under construction. The façades on either side (right), of which one survives, are also of brick, and decorated with blind arcading in the manner of some Roman buildings.

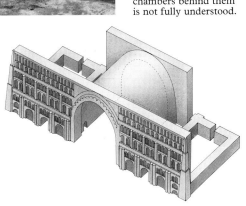

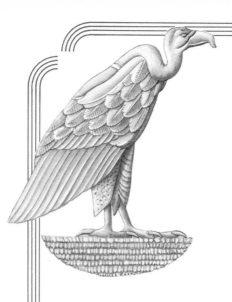

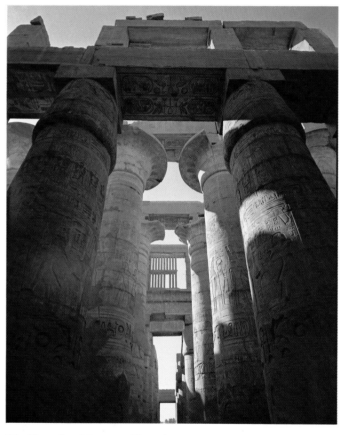

The Temple of Amon at Karnak, which has this monumental hypostyle hall at its centre, was Ancient Egypt's greatest temple, the cumulative creation of a succession of Pharaohs from 1530 to 323 BC.

The pyramids, rock tombs and temples of Ancient Egypt, solemnly set between the great river and the desert, span nearly three thousand years (roughly from 2800 BC to the first centuries AD). This architecture gave the world the earliest buildings in dressed stone, invented the column, capital and cornice, and throughout its long history reflected the fine craftsmanship which seems to have come naturally to the Nile people.

In Egyptian architecture great importance was attached to elaborate low-relief carving, making it an integral part of an architectonic whole. These bas-reliefs have both an aesthetic appeal (not always found in the monuments themselves) and an unparalleled human interest. No other architecture is as explicit about the thought and custom of a vanished civilization. In dark tombs and on sun-drenched walls, the stylized figures and the hieroglyphs betray secrets, the minutiae of beliefs and lives, lost to the world until the 19th century, when these stone pages were finally deciphered by Champollion.

In a sense Egyptian architecture was an infant prodigy. Born mature at Sakkara in the ambitious funerary complex of Zoser, some 2,800 years before Christ, it was to have neither youth nor age. Although developments might occur—the substitution of the rock-tomb for the pyramid, or the introduction of the pylon and the obelisk—the conceptions which underlay this architecture were as unchanging as the Nile Valley.

Such conservatism implies a certain mental apathy. For all their virtues, the buildings of Egypt are not distinguished for those intellectual qualities which find expression in proportion, balance and the harmonious subordination of parts to the whole. It is significant that the Egyptians were never prompted to explore the possibilities of enclosed interior space, and their weighty hypostyles,

Egypt

like the vast hall at Karnak, remain crowded halls of passage. In the architecture of the Nile, although the hand never falters and the craftsmanship never fails, the stimulus of intellectual curiosity, the tension that springs from avid enquiry, is often absent.

Little domestic architecture, built in perishable sun-dried brick, has survived, but there is ample evidence to show that it was of high quality, sensibly designed and comfortable. The palaces of the great were enriched with faience and gold inlay, cedarwood doors and painted stucco decoration. Even the workmen had seemly accommodation, and probably the *fellah*, the peasant, was more comfortably housed in 1500 BC than he is today.

The religious and funerary works of Ancient Egypt were by contrast built in stone for eternity, and it is these which have come to symbolize the architecture of the Nile. The pyramids of the Old Kingdom, 2700–2300 BC, majestically planted on the desert edge, are the most spectacular of all funerary works. Built to contain the burial chamber and the mummy of the pharaoh, they were habitually associated with a temple on the river, a causeway leading inland and a second temple for offerings adjacent to the pyramid. In the Middle Kingdom, 2134–1786 BC, the gigantic pyramid gave place to smaller-scale pyramid tombs. But, coincidentally, the sarcophagus in the tomb chamber assumed vast dimensions and might weigh as much as a hundred and fifty tons.

From early times such technical devices as the portcullis and the false chamber were employed to foil robbers. It was partly their signal failure to do so that prompted the pharaohs of the New Kingdom, 1570–1085 BC, to abandon the pyramid for the hidden rock-cut tomb, of which the most famous are those situated in the Valley of the Kings at Thebes. Decorated almost exclusively with scenes of a religious nature, the royal rock-hewn tomb usually incorporated an inclined corridor leading to an antichamber and from there to the sarcophagus chamber. These tombs, although furnished with every protection that ingenuity could devise, unfortunately proved hardly more burglar-proof than the pyramids.

From the time of the Old Kingdom onwards the funerary arrangements of the pharaohs were echoed in the tombs of the nobility. Although they were naturally more modest in scale, they often reveal in their reliefs and paintings work that is more sensitive and more human, with a finer feeling for nature. Tombs such as those of Ti and Mereruka at Sakkara, or those of Nakt and Ramose at Thebes, represent all that is most appealing in Egyptian art.

Religion in Ancient Egypt centred on the cult temple, which was the dwelling of the god or gods. Most of the earlier examples of such temples have disappeared, and it is the type established in the New Kingdom, of which the temple of Amon at Luxor is an early and elegant example, that has primarily survived. It is a type that remained virtually unaltered from the middle of the second millennium to the age of Cleopatra. Vast in scale, axial in plan and commonly entered through a pylon gateway, its basic elements consisted of a colonnaded forecourt and hypostyle hall set before a dark, narrow sanctuary in which stood the statue of the deity. The walls were lavishly, and often beautifully, decorated with stylized carvings in either low or sunken relief, representing the exploits of the pharaoh or the rites of the cult, and effective use was made of architectural statuary of vast dimensions. Closely related to the cult temple, but including a funerary chapel, was the mortuary temple, of which Hatshepsut's unique terraced design and the Ramesseum, both at Thebes, are notable examples.

Memphis and the pyramids

DUST AND PALM groves cover the scanty remains of Memphis, the ancient capital of the early pharaohs, but their pyramids, the most indestructible of man's creations, are still strung out southwest of Cairo, for fifty miles along the fringe of the western desert. Precisely oriented to the points of the compass, these vast objects, about two dozen in number, are designed with the precision of a Swiss timepiece. Although built nearly five thousand years ago as tombs, mostly for the rulers of the Old Kingdom, 2780–2300 BC, these sepulchres, set in the limitless space of the desert, are truly the first great works of abstract art.

The oldest of these monuments is the Step Pyramid of Sakkara. Its successive "steps" indicate how the pyramidal form evolved as a brilliant inspiration from the simple *mastabas*, or rectangular tombs, of the earliest Egyptian dynasties. The Step Pyramid was the focal point of the vast funerary complex of King Zoser, who reigned in the 28th century BC. The complex is a work without precedent, for at Sakkara are found, for the first time, brick and wood techniques translated into stone. Here in the desert rise the first ashlar walls known to man; here the earliest engaged columns, some of them with beautiful proto-Doric mouldings, support the earliest known capitals (of papyrus form). Here, a hundred years before the pyramids of Giza, formal architecture begins.

Near by, in the extensive necropolis, the painted bas-reliefs—probably the supreme artistic achievement of Ancient Egypt—found full expression two hundred years later in the tombs of the great court dignitaries. The paintings, usually during this period in delicate raised relief, as opposed to the sunken relief that became more common in the New Kingdom, are astonishingly eloquent and sophisticated. Working to a convention now familiar in the paintings of Picasso and Braque, these Ancient Egyptian artists were not concerned with perspective, but were intent to convey in diagrammatic shorthand the essence of their story. They did so with unfailing success and the subtlest craftsmanship.

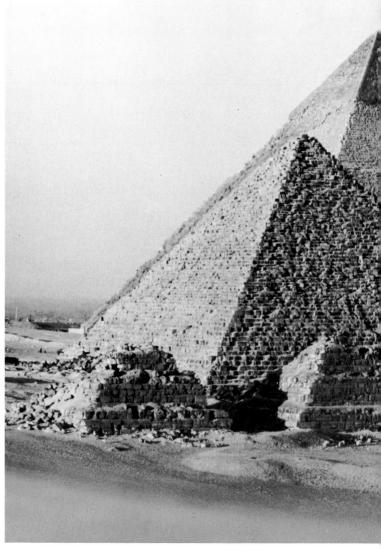

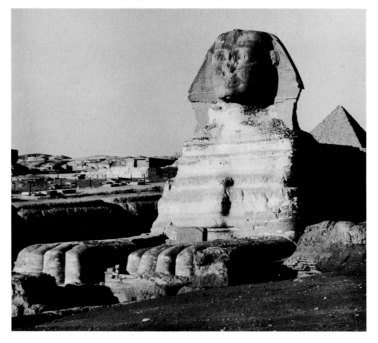

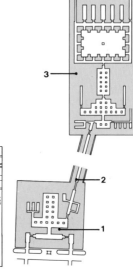

The Great Pyramids of Giza, most famous of Egyptian antiquities, defy time and mortality; built more than a century after Zoser's pioneer pyramid, they entomb the great Pharaohs of the Fourth Dynasty. Each perfectly proportioned pyramid was once encased in a smooth limestone skin. On the plan (below), the Pyramid of Cheops is seen on the right, Chephren's in the middle and Mycerinus' on the left. Of the valley temples associated with the pyramids, only Chephren's (right) survives. The T-shaped hall within (1), which housed statues of the dead king, was probably used for purification and embalming rites. A causeway (2) led to the mortuary temple (3).

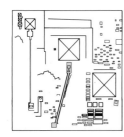

The colossal sculptured mountain of the Sphinx (left) guards the pyramids at Giza. The human-headed lion, once painted and gilded, represents Chephren as both king and sun god. A small temple nestles between the gigantic paws.

Zoser's funerary precinct (right) provides only one entrance for the living, a narrow passage, just one yard wide, in the southeast corner. To allow the departed king's spirit royal freedom of movement, 13 false doors were carved in the 30-ft-high surrounding wall. The panelled wall was unbonded and composed of small limestone blocks.

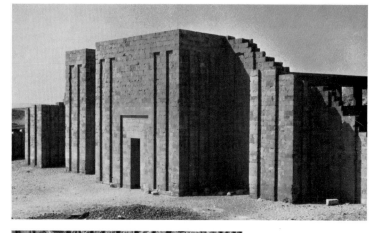

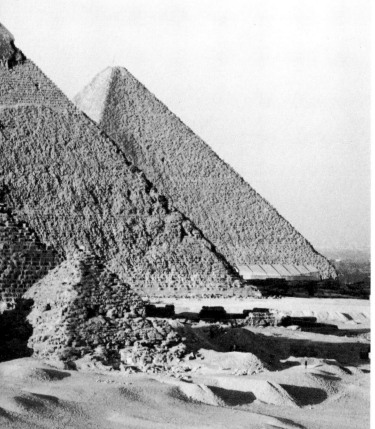

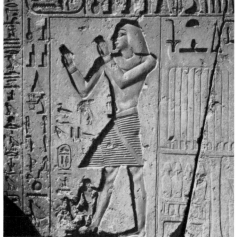

The supreme Egyptian art form is the painted relief, which covered the walls of tombs and temples. Many of the nobles' tombs contain delightful representations of everyday life in Ancient Egypt. This relief from Sakkara shows the son of King Unis.

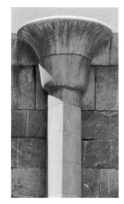

The first stone capital in the world (left), shaped like a papyrus flower, crowns a column in Zoser's mortuary complex. As the Greeks did after them, the Egyptians interpreted the physical details of their earlier building materials—the papyrus and mud-bonded palm leaves—in stone. These "translations" often retained all the vitality of their vegetable prototypes. Column capitals (below) were carved and painted to look like tied bundles of lotus flowers (1), papyrus buds (2), papyrus flowers (3) and palm leaves (4). These capitals had a symbolic as well as a functional purpose: the lotus was the emblem of Upper Egypt and the papyrus represented Lower Egypt.

The Step Pyramid (below), nucleus of Zoser's necropolis at Sakkara, revolutionized tomb-building and heralded the age of the pyramid. Built *c.* 2760 BC by Imhotep, the earliest named architect, it was the first structure to use dressed stone throughout. Rising in six great steps, it towers 200 ft above the desert.

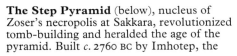

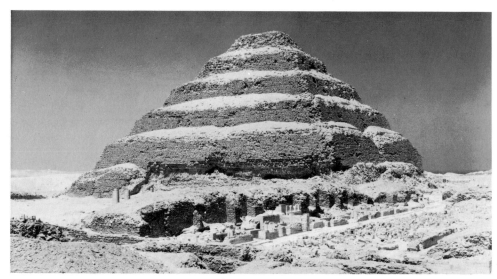

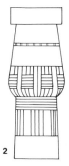

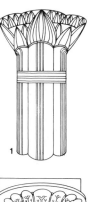

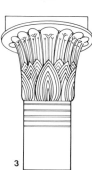

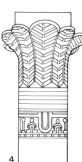

Thebes and the great temples

THE GROWTH OF the New Kingdom from 1570 to 1085 BC coincided with the imperial phase of Egyptian history. The wealth of the empire financed unparalleled architectural activity. For centuries Thebes, the capital of Upper Egypt, resounded to the hammers of innumerable masons, while the Nile flood annually floated down thousands of tons of Aswan granite. At Karnak alone, on the outskirts of the capital, there were once twenty temples.

Time has partially spared many of the tombs and temples of these frenetic builders. Although the pharaohs of the New Kingdom abandoned the pyramid, their hidden rock-hewn tombs in the Valley of the Kings, prudently disassociated from their funerary temples, were imperially conceived. Tutankhamun's hugger-mugger burial in a restricted sepulchre is exceptional in its relative simplicity.

Even more ambitious than the tombs are the temples of the New Kingdom. Although the basic plan of the temple remained unchanged, these pharaohs worked on a grandiose scale, often duplicating their immense forecourts and ponderous hypostyle halls. At the same time, they gave currency to new architectural features—to processional avenues of sphinxes, to massive pylon gateways, to colossi of the pharaohs and to towering obelisks of red granite; while on temple walls they never wearied of portraying their imperial victories. Although the temples of the New Kingdom impose primarily by their sheer mass, many of them, and above all the Temple of Queen Hatshepsut at Deir el-Bahri, are deeply impressive for their purely architectural qualities.

The temple as developed in the New Kingdom persisted substantially unchanged into the Christian era. Thus, oddly, it is in the splendidly preserved Ptolemaic temple at Edfu that the plan and intention of the great Theban temples is today most explicit.

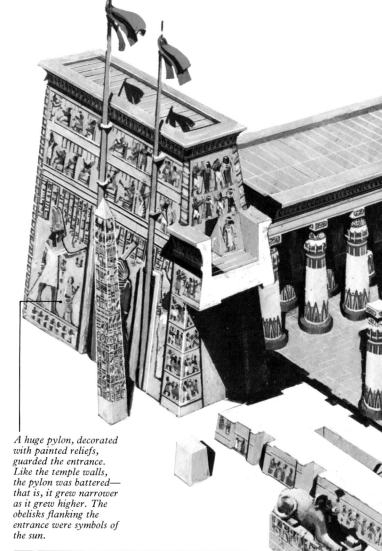

A huge pylon, decorated with painted reliefs, guarded the entrance. Like the temple walls, the pylon was battered—that is, it grew narrower as it grew higher. The obelisks flanking the entrance were symbols of the sun.

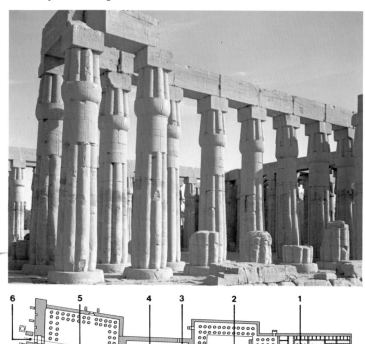

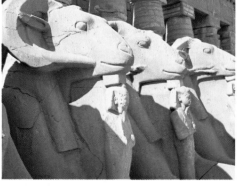

Sphinx avenues, or Ways of God, were associated with some New Kingdom temples. Ram-headed sphinxes with lion bodies linked the Temple of Amon at Luxor with that of Khons at Karnak. Symbol of generative power, the ram was sacred to Amon.

The Temple of Amon at Luxor was begun by Amenophis III in the 14th century BC. He planned the customary sanctuary (left) with its preceding hypostyle (1). The grand open court (2), enclosed by a double colonnade of papyrus-bud columns (above, left), was originally entered through a pylon gateway (3). A narrow, pillared hall (4), with papyrus-flower capitals, was added later, perhaps to connect with the avenue of sphinxes leading to Karnak. Ramesses II contributed a second colonnaded court (5) and another pylon (6). The axis of this court creates a disturbing optical effect and a sense of false perspective.

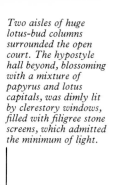

The small, dark sanctuary, forbidden to all but the initiated priests, contained the image of the god and his sacred barque. The boat originally symbolized the one in which the Sun God was believed to travel daily across the heavens.

The Temple of Khons (reconstructed above) stood in the precinct dedicated to the god Amon, at Karnak. Khons was the son of Amon, and his filially modest temple was built in the 12th century BC by Ramesses III. The heart of such temples was the sanctuary, ringed with subsidiary chambers, in which the image of the god was seated sometimes in a sacred barque. It has been suggested that

the Egyptian concept of ever-continuing life was symbolized in the plan of the temple. Congregational worship was not a feature of religion in Ancient Egypt and the public was usually restricted to the forecourt. Seclusion was imposed by the towering pylon gateway framing the narrow entrance and by the high mud-brick wall which enshrouded the temple.

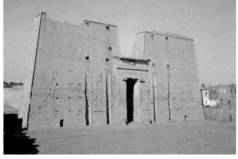

At Edfu, a massive pylon gateway, over 100 ft high, guards the 3rd-century BC Temple of Horus, son of Osiris.

Queen Hatshepsut's Temple at Deir el-Bahri (right) combined the conventions of the Egyptian funerary precinct—valley temple, causeway, mortuary temple—in an elegant, almost Greek, construction unprecedented in Egyptian architecture. Built in the 15th century BC, its colonnaded limestone terraces, linked by gently sloping ramps, are set against the mountain precipice. This break with architectural tradition characterized Hatshepsut's forceful personality. The only woman pharaoh, she usurped the rights of her son, Tuthmosis III, who later defaced the statues in her temple.

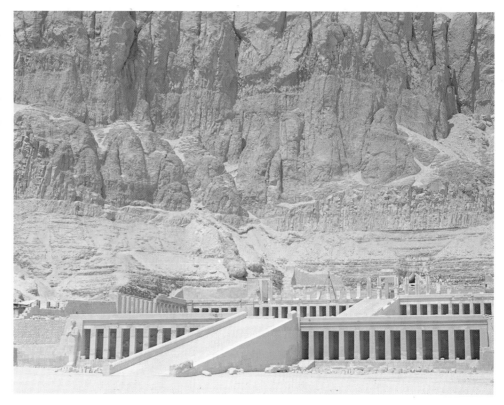

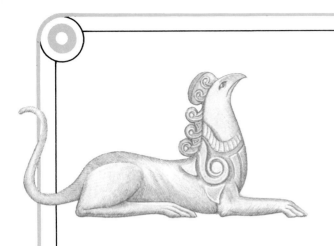

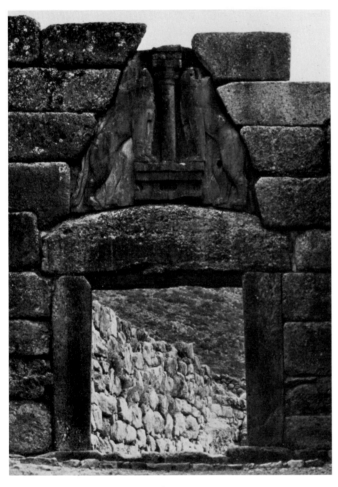

Two carved lions, the earliest known relief sculpture of Western civilization, face each other above the monumental Lion Gate, entrance to the hilltop citadel at Mycenae.

Aegean archaeology got off to a sensational start with Heinrich Schliemann's discoveries at Troy in 1873 and Mycenae in 1876. Schliemann was looking for material evidence that Homer's narrative was grounded in history. It is ironical that, although his intuition proved to be correct, what he uncovered in the two excavations that made him famous had nothing whatever to do with Homer's epics, but belonged to a much earlier world. Excavations at Knossos and Phaistos on the island of Crete, both started in 1899, finally put an end to any doubts as to the splendour and the antiquity of this Aegean civilization. The sheer scale and complexity of the Cretan palaces, and the quality of the works of art they contained, created a strong presumption that Crete was the home of this civilization. It seemed to follow that anything pre-Hellenic in Greece was derived from Crete, and for a long time Mycenae was regarded as a kind of Cretan outpost on the mainland.

It is now clear, however, that the civilizations of Crete and Mycenae, although obviously related in certain details, were not strictly contemporary. The fortunes of Mycenae rose while those of Crete declined. The great days of Mycenae came after the destruction of the Cretan palaces, when Knossos itself seems to have been a Mycenaean colony.

The people who built the palaces came to Crete, almost certainly from Asia Minor, towards the middle of the 3rd millennium. The three great palaces, at Knossos, Phaistos and Mallia, date from only c. 1900 BC. Their history was curiously uniform. Not only were they built at roughly the same time, but all three were destroyed together c. 1700 BC, and then rebuilt and destroyed again c. 1400 BC. Both catastrophies were precipitous and comprehensive, more likely to have been acts of God than the work of human hands. The second, for which the evidence is better, has given rise

The Aegean

to the theory of a gigantic tidal wave, launched by a volcanic explosion on the nearby island of Santorini (Thera), of which a folk-memory has been preserved in the legend of Atlantis.

The palaces are the best-known Cretan buildings, but there were many small country-houses scattered over the countryside, and several towns, of which the one attached to the palace at Knossos achieved considerable size. What the excavations have uncovered are essentially plans. Everything else is a matter of inference. The most striking feature of the palaces is the extraordinary number of chambers they contained. This also struck the Greeks of later times, who called them labyrinthine. The term seems to have been derived from the symbol of the *labrys*, or double axe, which was prominent at Knossos in what appears to have been a religious context. However, this proliferation of rooms at ground-floor level, most of them utterly unsuited for domestic purposes, suggests storage, somewhat reminiscent of the temples and palaces uncovered at Hattusas, in Turkey, or in Mesopotamia.

Crete has been thought of in terms of near-divine kings presiding over intricate bureaucracies largely concerned with commerce. Yet the paintings show ceremonies or games involving bulls, which have no counterpart elsewhere. These have been construed as indicating a taste for sport, which may have been true. The absence of fortification has also evoked impressions of a relaxed and easy-going society, unlike anything known in the Ancient World. The Cretan world is an almost total enigma and as long as this remains the case its architecture will also defy our attempts to understand it.

By comparison, the Mycenaean palaces of mainland Greece present fewer difficulties. The documents in Linear B script which were recently deciphered, make it clear that these palaces were the centre of meticulous administrations.

Mycenaean bureaucracies, however, enjoyed far less in the way of architectural amenities than those of Crete. They practised on the scale of estate management rather than of empire. The palaces were essentially fortified residences. The principal apartments, which were situated at ground level, were simple halls, where the rulers lived in a style not much different from that of feudal barons. By race they were Greek. Many Greeks remained in the mountains, but those who came down to the coast soon made contact with the more civilized peoples who inhabited the coasts and islands of the eastern Mediterranean. All they had to offer to this world was their prowess as fighting men.

Mycenaean society was military through and through. Their domestic apartments were protected by fortifications, which at Mycenae and Tiryns achieved a high degree of sophistication. These defences were derived from Hattusas, and there can be little doubt that eventually the parvenus of Mycenae were grudgingly acknowledged by the Hittite emperors. The seriousness with which Mycenaean rulers aspired to the status of oriental monarchies is reflected in the grandeur of their tombs. Mycenaean *tholos*, or beehive, tombs seem to have been unprecedented in putting a dome over a funeral monument. Some of the rituals associated with them persisted long after the end of the Mycenaean world, and the tholos tombs may have formed one of the links between the heroic age and Classical Greece. There was no obvious counterpart in Crete, and although both groups of palaces seem to have accommodated cults, only in the case of the Mycenaean buildings is it possible to detect a direct line of descent between the *megaron*, or great hall, which was their focal point, and the *naos*, or sanctuary, of the Classical Greek temple of later times. As Homer wrote, "Athena took up her abode in the house of Erechtheus."

Crete's island palaces

THE PEOPLE WHO built the Cretan palaces had lived on the island for half a millennium before they felt an urge to provide themselves with large buildings. What happened to cause this revolution is totally obscure. There are abundant signs that they were seafarers and familiar with the coastlands of the eastern Mediterranean. Their prosperity may have come by trade; and their architectural ideas certainly owed much to Egypt and Anatolia.

Before Sir Arthur Evans uncovered Knossos between 1899 and 1932, the term labyrinth was associated primarily with a monument built by the Pharaoh Ammenemes III in the Fayum, seen and described by the historian Herodotus. As far as can be judged, however, the Cretan obsession with labyrinthine storage cellars must have had some connection, if only in terms of function, with the temple storerooms of Mesopotamia and the Hittite lands. The palaces at Knossos, Mallia and Phaistos were contemporary, their histories remarkably similar, and none of them was ever fortified. These factors strongly suggest that the palace communities were not autonomous. If this were so, why three of them should be so close together is a mystery. In design, they resemble each other in having a central courtyard from which rooms spread out in all directions, with no evidence of conscious planning. There was no defensive outer wall; the Cretans evidently considered their supremacy at sea protection enough. The central courtyards seem to have been arenas where the so-called bull games, shown in one of the frescoes at Knossos, took place. Whatever these ceremonies meant, they were clearly an important part of palace life.

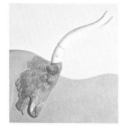

A charging bull, part of a painted relief near the main gate of the palace at Knossos. The bull, a recurrent motif in all forms of Cretan art, presumably had great religious significance.

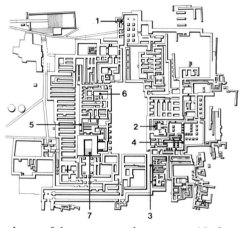

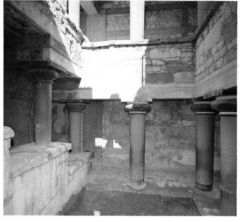

The grand staircase at Knossos led to the upper rooms of the west wing. Sadly, restoration indicates that it has been aesthetically overrated. It was lit, like the other palace stairs, by a light-well—a hole made in the roof to cast light over a specific area below.

The palace at Knossos, home of the legendary King Minos, was the largest and most elaborate of the Cretan palaces. Its plan (above) appears to have evolved organically around a large central court. The main entrance was defended by a guard-house (1), one of the few fortified structures in Crete. Archaeological evidence suggests that the main apartments were on the upper levels. A staircase (2) and a ramp (3) led to the upper chambers in the east wing. The queen's suite (4) boasted a bathroom which had a sophisticated drainage system of earthenware pots fitted together. The ground floor was given over to jewellery-making, pottery and other light industries. On the lower level of the west wing, a series of narrow storerooms opened from a long passage (5). Facing the central court was a throne-room (6), frescoed with heraldic griffins and containing an alabaster throne. The magnificent main staircase (7) led to the state apartments above. Staircases, light-wells and folding double doors allowing a whole wall to be opened up, were characteristic of the Island palaces, and, together with the wealth of decoration, suggest a marked fondness for gracious living. Few Cretan architects, however, were blessed with architectonic imagination; although they built big, they had little sense of the monumental. Their cypress wood columns tapered downwards, and the bases and capitals were rudimentary or featureless. The Cretans' talent lay elsewhere. They loved colour; most of the walls were sheathed in alabaster, and the frescoes and painted reliefs which adorn them are exquisite.

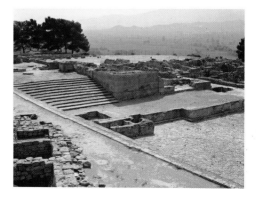

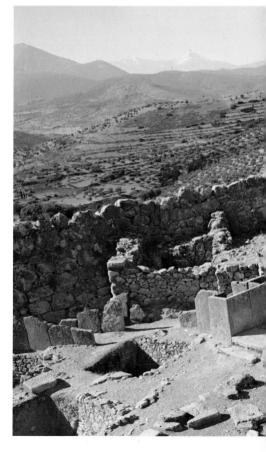

The palace at Phaistos (left), begun c. 1900 BC, is the most architecturally interesting of the Cretan palaces. Excavated at the same time as Knossos, it was overshadowed by the more sensational discoveries there. The elements of the design were similar; a great courtyard was surrounded on different levels by many rooms, their proliferation unhindered by a boundary wall. An unusual feature was the monumental flight of steps which swept up to what must have been an impressive formal gateway. Unlike the other palaces, Phaistos faces south. Egyptian influence was perhaps stronger here than elsewhere in Crete.

Mycenaean citadels and tombs

MYCENAE, INACCESSIBLE and easily defended, stands midway between Corinth and Argos on the eastern shoulder of the Peloponnese. Tiryns, on the coast, was in effect a castle, guarding the beachhead that served as the port of Mycenae. Other citadels and palaces at Athens, Sparta, Thebes, Pylos and elsewhere developed along similar lines. Perhaps at the outset they were autonomous, but the later archives of the Hittite Empire knew only one king of Achaea, the name by which the north Peloponnese is still known, and it is hard to resist the view that he was the Lord of Mycenae, of the House of Pelops.

Unlike Cretan palaces, the architecture of Mycenae was always in some sense known. What was required was interpretation and, more precisely, an accurate chronology. When, in 1876, Heinrich Schliemann found gold masks in the shaft graves at Mycenae, they were at once identified with the infamous House of Atreus, as were the later tholos, or beehive tombs. Atreus was the son of Pelops, and the father of Agamemnon and Menelaus. The association survives, although it is now clear that the masks at least belong to a much earlier period. How did gold come to Mycenae? One possibility is that it was payment for military service in Egypt, when the occupying Hyksos rulers were expelled and the New Kingdom established.

Greek legend names Perseus as the founder of Mycenae, his dynasty being later displaced by the House of Pelops. The historical value of this story is dubious, but it is consistent with the most plausible explanation of the beginnings of Mycenaean civilization in the 16th century BC and its later development.

1 Lower bailey
2 Upper bailey
3 Main gateway
4 Inner gateway
5 Grand entrance
6 Casemates
7 Great court
8 Main hall

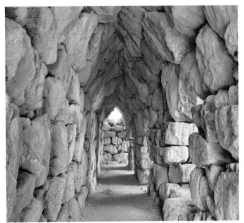

The royal residence at Tiryns (far left), one of the best-preserved Mycenaean fortifications, was guarded by immensely thick walls and a series of gates. Casemates, or covered galleries (left), protected and concealed the troops within.

The Treasury of Atreus (below) exhibited some of the best masonry and the most careful and ambitious construction to be found at Mycenae. If the Lion Gate proclaims the military pride of the Mycenaean tribal chiefs, such tombs reflect their divine aspiration.

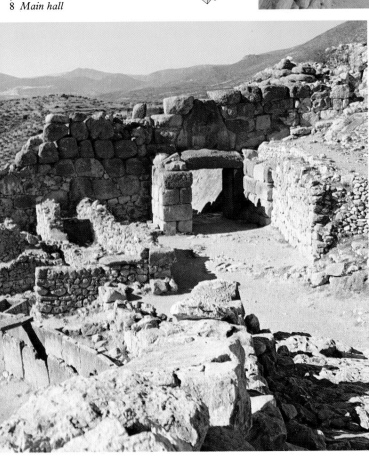

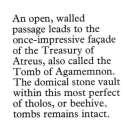

An open, walled passage leads to the once-impressive façade of the Treasury of Atreus, also called the Tomb of Agamemnon. The domical stone vault within this most perfect of tholos, or beehive, tombs remains intact.

At Mycenae, the mighty citadel (left) stood in an incomparable strategic position, commanding both the Argive Plain and the passes from the Peloponnese to Corinth. Huge limestone boulders made up its massive walls. Direct approach was difficult, and surprise impossible.

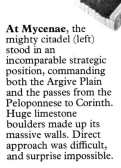

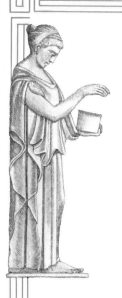

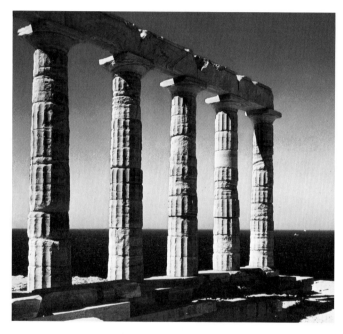

The care with which the Ancient Greeks chose the perfect setting for their temples can be seen at the Temple of Poseidon at Sounion. Set on a cape at the most southwesterly point of Attica, its Doric columns overlook the Aegean.

For the Greeks, as for their predecessors in Egypt, Mesopotamia and Anatolia, architecture began in the service of religion. The first and most persistent question that Greek architects were called upon to answer concerned the right form for temples. Their first efforts are totally lost; their earliest surviving works date from the 7th century BC, when there was already a measure of agreement as to what were the proper shapes, sizes and materials. Then they can be observed altering, refining and perfecting, until they finally arrived at a series of well-defined norms, which were generally accepted as the essence of good temple design.

Greek temples were purely formal objects. They were the abode of gods; and the task of architecture was to make them beautiful. The Greeks regarded beauty as an attribute of the gods, and the conscious pursuit of beauty as a religious exercise. They convinced themselves that the secrets of beauty lay in ratios or proportions; so their temples were conceived in mathematical terms. And they constantly sought to improve the materials out of which temples were made. As their experience accumulated, they seem to have reached decisions as to what would go with what, and the result was a codification of the Orders.

Their attitudes to architecture were modified when they went overseas. Some went east, to the coasts of Asia Minor, including Ionia, others went west, to Sicily and southern Italy. In both regions they showed a tendency towards megalomania in the scale of their temples, which Greeks who stayed at home avoided. The Asiatic Greeks soon made contact with the older civilizations. The column capital, which became the distinguishing feature of the Ionic Order, was ultimately derived from regions farther east; and for a time, in the 6th century BC, Egypt exercised considerable influence on the development of Ionian temples. During this

Greece

period the Ionic Order emerged as an alternative to the Doric, which was favoured in Greece proper and the West. There was, however, no exact geographical distinction. Ionic temples were built in the West, and, in later times, a species of Doric was used for civic buildings in Ionian cities.

The most important religious sanctuaries of Greece, including those at Delphi, Olympia and Delos, grew up outside, and partially independent of, the major cities. But it was from the cities that the impetus came which led to the great developments in Greek temple-building. The Greeks were convinced that what distinguished them from other peoples was the particular quality of their civic institutions and the vitality of the political life which these defined. To be cultivated was to be political, to participate to the full in city affairs, and these included religion.

The circumstances under which certain cults came to be absorbed into political life are obscure. But with the appearance of the tyrants of the 6th century, it is possible to discern signs of conscious manipulation in the conduct of festivals. Patriotism was given a religious slant, and many of the first great temples were built to provide obsessive focal points of admiration for citizens otherwise temporarily deprived of scope for political initiative.

In this way, temples became the principal ornaments of cities, and every city, even Sparta, had at least one. Gradually, there emerged the second great achievement of Greek architecture: its conception of the city itself as a work of art, and with it the extension of forms and features originally devised for temples, to a wide range of secular, civic buildings. The oldest Greek cities, such as Athens, had the irregular street-plan, which always implies uncontrolled growth. But when the Greeks went overseas they adopted the gridiron street-plan. In Classical times, the demands made

by Greeks on the ingenuity of their architects were not great. Apart from temples, they needed walls to protect them and covered halls in which to meet, do business and store merchandise. Houses were extremely simple. Markets, political assemblies and courts of justice were conducted in the open air. But, gradually, a wide variety of architectural amenities made their appearance. This process was encouraged by the Macedonians who, by putting an end to the autonomous city states, initiated a new kind of city life which was much closer to that of today. Thus, Hellenistic cities contained public fountains and theatres; specially devised council chambers; gymnasia, schools and libraries; even public baths and lavatories.

Many new cities were founded by Alexander and his successors; others were virtually rebuilt. In these cases it is often possible to recognize conscious, overall planning. Buildings were zoned into appropriate quarters. The market-place became a focal point, around which were grouped commercial and administrative buildings. Cities like Alexandria and Corinth are known to have enjoyed a limited form of street lighting.

When the Greeks could no longer indulge their passion for politics, something akin to modern private life took its place. Instead of meeting in the assembly, influential Greek citizens took to clubs, often attached to athletic or bathing institutions. Purely domestic life was also taken seriously. Houses became more elaborate; rooms acquired specific functions, and the planning and decoration of houses offered new scope for architectural talent. For the first time in Greek experience, interiors began to matter. This must have been most apparent in the palaces of rulers; none of these survives, but it is reasonable to presume that imposing halls for audiences were not unknown at Alexandria, Antioch, or Pergamon.

The Doric temple, a quest for perfection

THE EARLIEST known form of Greek temple resembled and almost certainly derived from the Mycenaean megaron, or house of a chief. It was simply a hall with a high-pitched roof and a front porch. None survive, but pottery votive models remain. Presumably these first temples were timber-framed, this being the only plausible explanation for certain features in the extant stone buildings which replaced them. The triglyph and metope sequence of the Doric frieze is a petrified, much enlarged and structurally meaningless version in stone of a series of timber trusses.

The development of Greek temple design shows a conservative attachment to this early type, combined with a restless quest for perfection, leading to endless changes in materials, proportions and ornament. The megaron was raised on a platform, its shape was varied in plan and elevation and a surrounding colonnade was added. Terracotta tiles, invented in the mid-7th century BC, allowed the pitch of the roof to be lowered. The most important innovation was the replacement of wood by stone, probably during the 6th century BC. The change was monumental in every sense of the word, and with it Greek architecture as we know it came into being. It was agreed that everything could no longer go with anything; some forms were mutually compatible, others not. Thus distinct styles or "Orders" of columns, each with its own form of entablature, began to emerge—Doric, Ionic and, lastly, Corinthian.

The development of the temple
1 Mycenaean megaron at Tiryns, c. 1300 BC.
2 The earliest temple (probably Ionic) at Samos, 9th century BC; a timber colonnade surrounded an unusually long chamber; inside, the roof was supported by a single row of columns.
3 Temple C at Selinus, Sicily, mid-6th century BC: a chamber placed asymmetrically on a platform allowed a more imposing façade.
4 Temple of Zeus at Olympia, c. 470 BC: its mature plan of 6 × 13 columns was popular in the early 5th century BC.

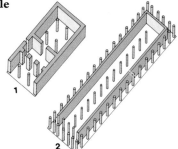

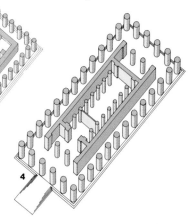

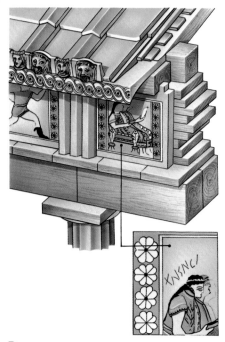

PROTOTYPES IN TERRACOTTA AND WOOD
Painted terracotta slabs found at Thermon have been identified as ancestors of the carved stone metopes of monumental Doric temples. Such slabs, thought to have formed part of the entablature of timber temples, were of a scale far removed from those of the earliest wooden temples. Seemingly, even during the timber period, the Greeks felt impelled to build monumental temples; the transition to stone was a response to the new sense of how a temple should look.

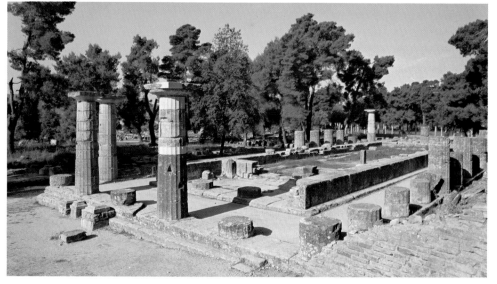

The earliest stone temple of which there are any considerable remains is the Temple of Hera at Olympia. Built at the end of the 7th century BC, its stylobate, or platform base, some of the columns and the upright bottom courses of the walls of the naos, or sanctuary, survive.

It was a long, low, unpretentious building, evidently devoid of the qualities that made mature Doric temples so impressive. But thanks to Pausanias, who wrote a guide-book for tourists c. AD 170, it is known that in his day a wooden column was still standing in the porch. It is almost certain that all the columns were originally wood. By the 5th century BC, however, those of the colonnade had been entirely replaced by stone columns. The surviving echinus blocks, or mouldings

on top of the columns, seem to belong to more than one period. Most point to the 5th century BC, but one at least of those surviving is a 6th-century BC form. The profile of the echinus changed in the course of time, the broad flat curve of the Doric form later becoming almost straight. This suggests that the construction of the temple was a piecemeal process. Perhaps it began with repairs, and ended with a wholesale smartening-up of the exterior so as not to disgrace the great Temple of Zeus, which was built close by c. 470 BC.

The inner building seems to have been left untouched. Only the footings of the naos wall were made of stone; as all trace of the superstructure has disappeared, it must have been made of some less-durable material.

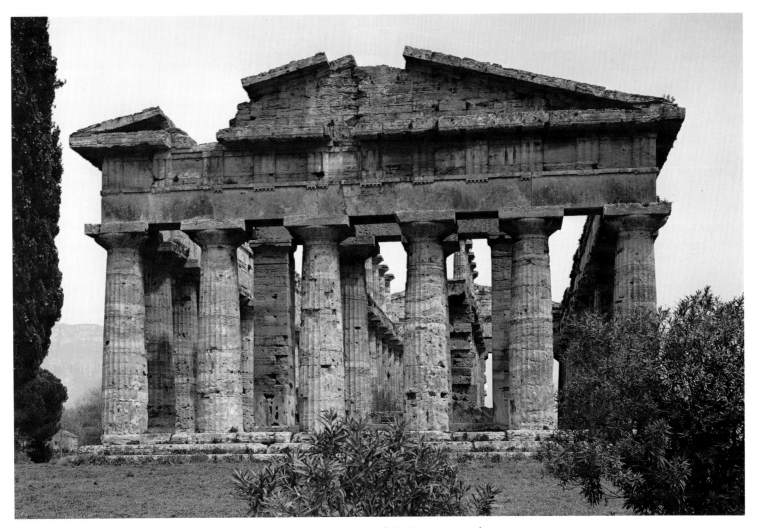

The Doric temple reached its maturity at the end of the 6th century BC, when a set of almost universally approved proportions seems to have been adopted. The formula was repeated many times on various scales. The Temple of Aphaia at Aegina (below), *c.* 490 BC, is perhaps the earliest example. The largest of its group, its pediments were lavishly sculpted, although this did not become a standard feature—the façade of the Temple of Hera Argiva at Paestum in Italy

(above), *c.* 460 BC, one of the best preserved, is imposing enough without it. Both temples had internal colonnades, composed of two orders of columns, one above the other, supporting the roof timbers. Most of the visual refinement for which Greek architecture is famous was present in these buildings. How much such subtleties were appreciated against the strident colours which seem to have been part of the traditional decoration of Greek temples remains arguable.

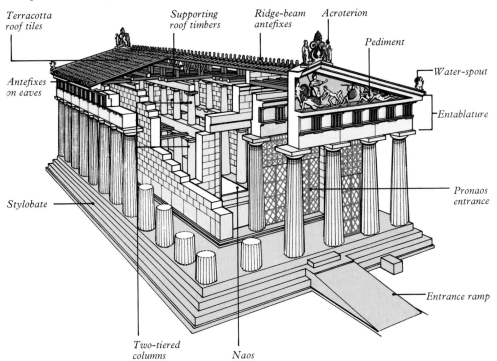

Terracotta roof tiles

Antefixes on eaves

Stylobate

Supporting roof timbers

Ridge-beam antefixes

Acroterion

Pediment

Water-spout

Entablature

Pronaos entrance

Two-tiered columns

Naos

Entrance ramp

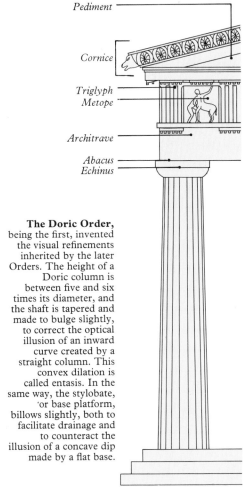

Pediment

Cornice

Triglyph
Metope

Architrave

Abacus
Echinus

The Doric Order, being the first, invented the visual refinements inherited by the later Orders. The height of a Doric column is between five and six times its diameter, and the shaft is tapered and made to bulge slightly, to correct the optical illusion of an inward curve created by a straight column. This convex dilation is called entasis. In the same way, the stylobate, ·or base platform, billows slightly, both to facilitate drainage and to counteract the illusion of a concave dip made by a flat base.

The Ionic and Corinthian Orders

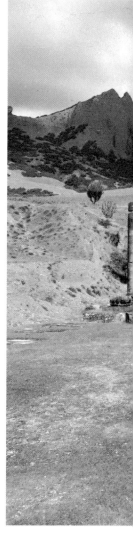

THE GREEKS WHO settled on the Aegean coast of Asia were better placed to make contact with the older civilizations of the Middle East than those who remained at home, and from the 7th century BC onwards, their art and architecture began to reflect such encounters. The Ionians had a treaty port in the Nile Delta, and from the middle of the 6th century BC a succession of colossal temples reflecting their lively appreciation of the scale of Egyptian monuments appeared at Ephesus, Samos and Didyma. From their Asiatic neighbours, they seem to have adopted the idea that columns ought to have bases and capitals. In characteristic Greek fashion, they took over the simple volute, or scroll capital, which had been ubiquitous from Palestine to Persia, and developed it into the satisfying decorative object which has proved one of their most enduring bequests to posterity. By the 5th century BC, the Ionic Order could be used at Athens in conscious antithesis with Doric—its forms being more suitable for smaller temples.

The idea of combining the Orders came into its own during the Hellenistic period of the 4th century BC, when two-storeyed buildings became more common. This was also the great age of Ionic architecture. The ancient cities of the Asiatic coast revived and were largely rebuilt, and most of the cities founded farther east by Alexander the Great and his successors were modelled on them. Pytheos, Hermogenes and other architects who used the Ionic Order, acquired reputations for academic correctness which endured into the period of the Roman Empire.

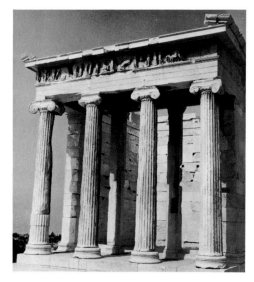

The Temple of Athena Nike (above), at the gateway of the Acropolis, is one of the earliest surviving Ionic buildings in Athens and a little gem of the Ionic Order. It was commissioned in 448 BC, after the peace with Persia, and built *c.* 427 BC by Callicrates. Dismantled by the Turks in the 17th century, it was reassembled in 1836 and again in 1935. The corner columns show one of the limitations of the Ionic capital—it was designed to be seen from the front only.

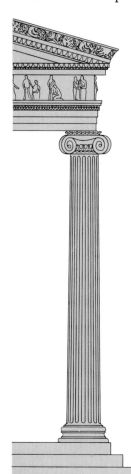

The Ionic Order in its mature form had a height of eight or nine times its diameter, compared with the bulkier Doric proportion. There were usually 24 flutes—more than on a Doric column, even though the circumference was less. Adjacent flutes were separated by a fillet and were rounded off at top and bottom.

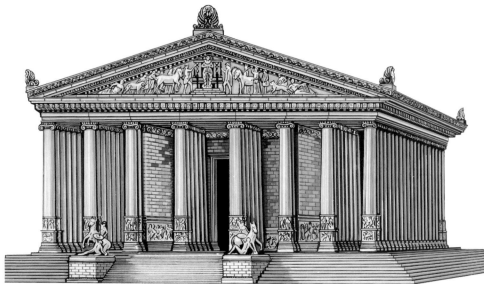

The Temple of Artemis at Ephesus (above). When the Greeks went to Asia, they seem to have taken over established cults. Only the names were changed—the Artemis worshipped at Ephesus was very much an Asiatic goddess. This may have been reflected in the size of the temple. Although some of the 6th-century BC temples of Ionia were among the largest the Greeks ever built, they have almost entirely disappeared, leaving only a few traces, from which archaeologists have reconstructed their former appearance. For the temple at Ephesus there is more than usual in the way of literary records. The original 6th-century BC temple—itself a marvel in its own day—was reputedly destroyed by fire on the night Alexander the Great was born in 356 BC. It seems he believed the story, because he helped to pay for its successor, shown reconstructed here, which took its place among the Seven Wonders of the World. Surviving fragments of carved ornament from its entablatures suggest that it fully deserved its reputation. One of its peculiarities was the relief carving on the lower parts of the columns, an idea copied from its predecessor. Pliny noted that 36 columns were decorated in this way, and presumably these were all at the front of the building.

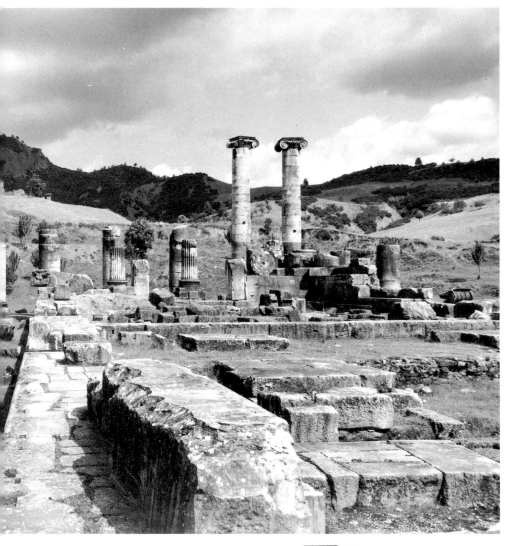

The Temple of Artemis at Sardis in Asia Minor dates from after 334 BC, when Alexander the Great took the city. It had once been the capital of Lydia. The Lydian temples had been destroyed by the Athenians in 498 BC. The ruined temple now visible (left) clearly took a long time to build, and some of it is Roman. Although not as large as those at Ephesus and Didyma, it approaches their colossal scale, and this may explain the slow construction and certain peculiarities in design. The columns of the façade were unevenly arranged, and unfluted. It was perhaps the first Ionic "pseudodipteral" temple—intended for double colonnades, but with the inner one omitted.

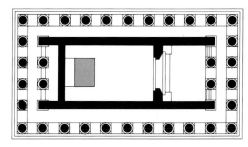

The Temple of Athena Polias at Priene (above) was dedicated by Alexander the Great in 334 BC. Although small, this Ionic temple enjoyed a high reputation in antiquity for the perfection of its proportions.

The Corinthian Order

The Corinthian capital was supposedly invented, at Corinth, by Callimachus, towards the end of the 5th century BC, but Vitruvius' tale of the goblets surrounded by acanthus leaves catching the Athenian sculptor's eye need not be taken too seriously. Essentially, the Corinthian Order is the Ionic Order with another kind of capital. Unlike the Ionic capital, which was designed to be seen only from the front, the symmetry of this new capital avoided problems at the corners of colonnaded buildings. Its attraction, however, seems to have been based not so much on this structural convenience, but on its very rich decorative effect. The earliest known example stood on an isolated column inside the 5th-century BC Temple of Apollo at Bassae.

Perhaps because it was regarded as ostentatious, or possibly because Greek capital carvers were intensely conservative, the Corinthian Order seems to have made little impact in Greece. It was, however, enormously popular in Rome, where it fitted well with the vulgar opulence of imperial taste. In Roman hands, the column became taller than was usual in Greek building, and this entailed a chain reaction which affected every part of the Order. Taller columns meant taller capitals. The Corinthian was in this respect more versatile than the Ionic, for it was easy to add to it another row of acanthus leaves. The Ionic Order was not entirely displaced: a peculiar hybrid form of capital was sometimes used, in which Ionic volutes were intermingled with Corinthian acanthus leaves in a combination known as the Composite Order.

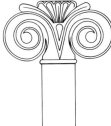

This archaic capital (left) probably dates from the 7th century BC. At first the volute element stood high and free between the column and the entablature. The spirals on the volutes were rudimentary. So were any leaves around the column neck.

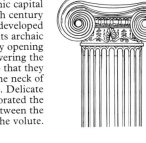

The Ionic capital (right), late 5th century BC, was developed from its archaic predecessor by opening out or lowering the volutes so that they embraced the neck of the column. Delicate ornament decorated the echinus between the column and the volute.

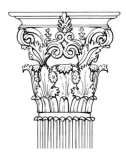

The Corinthian capital (left) makes a virtue of symmetry. The core is shaped like an inverted bell. The volutes, borrowed from the Ionic Order, are reduced to diagonally placed features at the corners. The main decorative effect is achieved by rows of carved acanthus leaves.

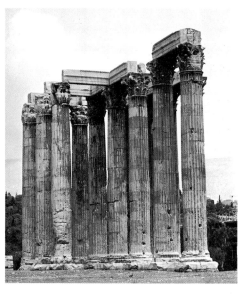

The Temple of Olympian Zeus at Athens was begun in the 6th century BC by the Pisistratids—the tyrants of Athens—seeking to emulate their Ionian counterparts in the construction of gigantic temples. The project was abandoned when the tyrants were expelled, and was not revived until the 2nd century BC. Antiochus Epiphanes, King of Syria, wishing to be represented at Athens by a prestige monument, put it in the hands of Cossutius, a Roman architect, who changed the Order from Ionic to Corinthian. The temple was only completed through the generosity of the Roman Emperor Hadrian, more than 600 years after it was started.

The Acropolis

THE ACROPOLIS today is a monument to the 19th century's vision of Periclean Athens. During the last hundred and fifty years, all traces of its medieval and Turkish buildings have been erased, just as all the previous history of the Acropolis was effaced by the Persians in 480 BC. What is left are the ruins of what was itself a vision—a group of buildings, mostly temples, which collectively embodied the more exalted aspects of the Athenian dedication to the pursuit and enjoyment of imperial power. The prime mover was Pericles himself; but the successful fulfilment of his ideal was entirely due to the genius of the men who executed it—Ictinus, Mnesicles and, above all, the sculptor Phidias. The calculated contrast which they evoked—between the Acropolis and the city below, and between pure masonry and sculpture—makes it perhaps the only seriously successful example of architecture in the service of politics.

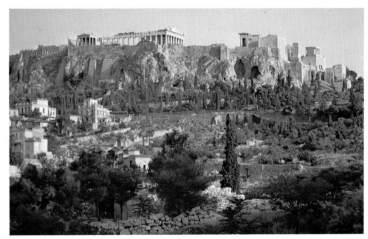

Seen from the Agora, the commercial centre of Athens, the Acropolis (above) was a reminder to Athenian businessmen of the higher purposes to which their city was dedicated.

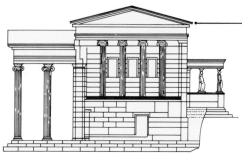

The Erechtheion was the antithesis of the Parthenon. Ionic, small in scale and built on two levels, which excluded any continuous colonnade, it was devoted to traditional rather than martial cults, which were grouped around and inside. Though temporarily overshadowed by the imperial associations of the Parthenon, they came into their own again when the Athenian Empire collapsed.

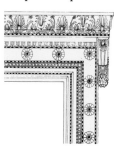

The caryatids (left) of the Erechtheion represent maidens who assisted in cleansing rituals.

An example (right) of the carved detail in the Erechtheion, which is unsurpassed in Classical architecture.

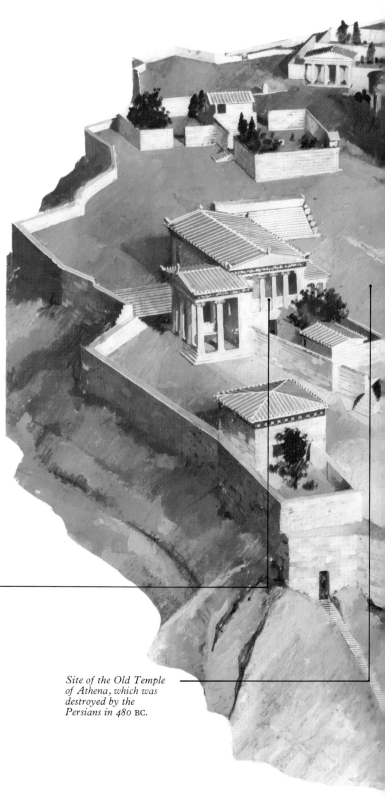

Site of the Old Temple of Athena, which was destroyed by the Persians in 480 BC.

The Acropolis, reconstructed here as it was at the end of the Classical era. Doric and Ionic Orders were combined to perfection in a composition of three magnificent structures: the Propylaea, the Parthenon and the Erechtheion. In the centre of the group lay the site of the old Temple of Athena, perhaps left as a memorial of the Persian Wars. Subsidiary temples and sanctuaries lined the walls of this citadel, sacred to the spirit of Athens.

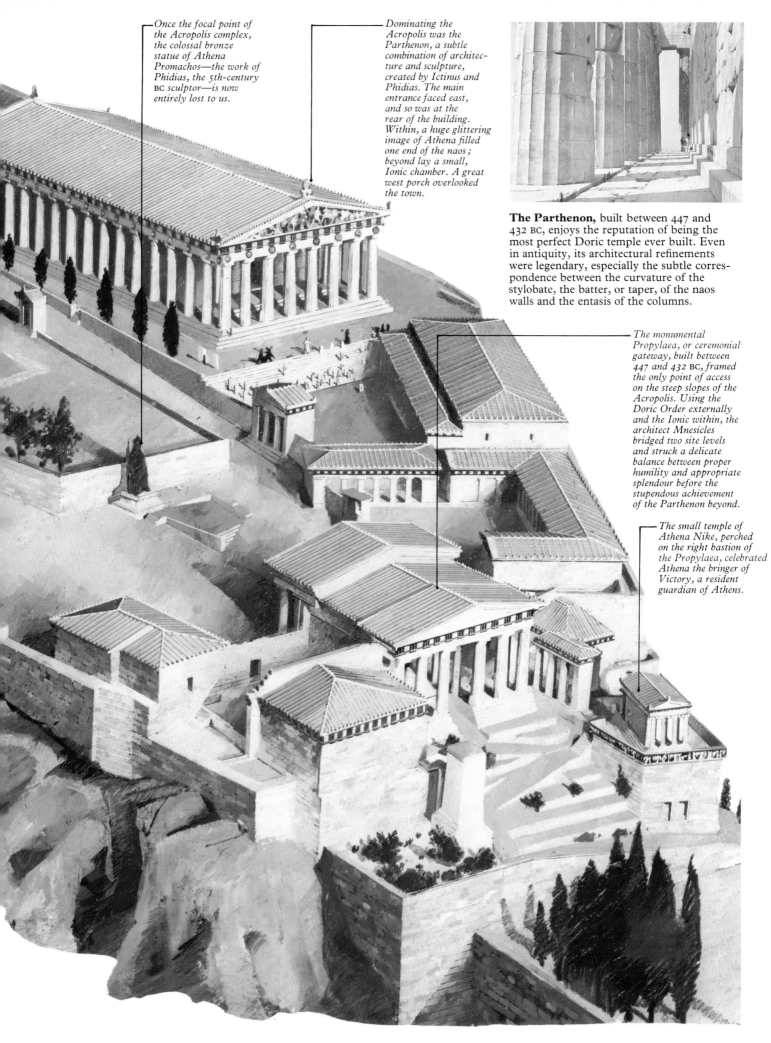

Once the focal point of the Acropolis complex, the colossal bronze statue of Athena Promachos—the work of Phidias, the 5th-century BC sculptor—is now entirely lost to us.

Dominating the Acropolis was the Parthenon, a subtle combination of architecture and sculpture, created by Ictinus and Phidias. The main entrance faced east, and so was at the rear of the building. Within, a huge glittering image of Athena filled one end of the naos; beyond lay a small, Ionic chamber. A great west porch overlooked the town.

The Parthenon, built between 447 and 432 BC, enjoys the reputation of being the most perfect Doric temple ever built. Even in antiquity, its architectural refinements were legendary, especially the subtle correspondence between the curvature of the stylobate, the batter, or taper, of the naos walls and the entasis of the columns.

The monumental Propylaea, or ceremonial gateway, built between 447 and 432 BC, framed the only point of access on the steep slopes of the Acropolis. Using the Doric Order externally and the Ionic within, the architect Mnesicles bridged two site levels and struck a delicate balance between proper humility and appropriate splendour before the stupendous achievement of the Parthenon beyond.

The small temple of Athena Nike, perched on the right bastion of the Propylaea, celebrated Athena the bringer of Victory, a resident guardian of Athens.

The later civic splendour

TEMPLES APART, the most consistent and urgent demand the Greeks made on architects was to provide fortifications. Callicrates, who imported the Ionic Order into Athens, is first mentioned as the designer of one of the long walls, built *c*. 460 BC, which linked Athens and its port, Piraeus. But city life, which enjoyed a special prestige, carried with it an implicit demand that the city itself should be an object of beauty. Gradually, government buildings and the *agora*, or market-place—the centre of city life—qualified for the embellishments which had once been reserved for the temples of the gods. Then, by a strange paradox, as Greek cities declined in status, their pride found consolation in splendid public amenities. Athens was probably never more beautiful than when it subsided into the role of a Roman provincial university town.

Town-planning became a matter of prime importance when Alexander the Great and his successors founded strings of colonies across the length and breadth of Asia. Tradition accords the invention of the gridiron street plan to Hippodamus of Miletus, who laid out Piraeus and Thurii for the Athenians in the days of their ascendancy. Miletus itself, as rebuilt *c*. 466 BC, after the Persian Wars, shared this plan; but the idea was as old as the colonies themselves, and Hippodamus probably earned his reputation because he gave thought to the way that cities were actually used. He grouped together their commercial, political and religious elements, arranging them on different levels to make some more imposing than others. The cities of the Hellenistic world were remarkably consistent in plan. An agora, partly surrounded by porticoes, a council house, a theatre, a public fountain, gymnasia and temples—these were the basic ingredients. Exceptional cities—capitals like Pergamon, or international trading places like Ephesus—acquired buildings suitable to their status. Pergamon had a veritable upper city, including a palace, barracks and civil service quarters; while Ephesus had markets and warehouses at both ends of the town.

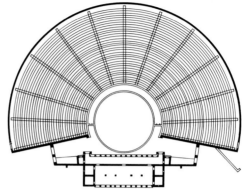

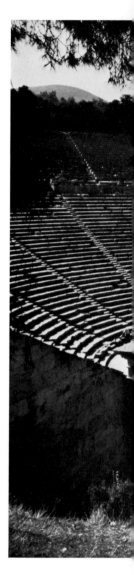

The Greek theatre plan, perfectly preserved in the sophisticated 4th-century BC theatre at Epidaurus (above and right), was devised to accommodate a drama which had evolved out of the performance of choral odes during the festivals of Dionysus. These ceremonies demanded separate assembly areas for the chorus and spectators. The chorus, who both chanted and danced, performed on an orchestra—a circular dance-floor with an altar at its centre—an arrangement which determined much of the subsequent development of Greek theatre.

Initially, the spectators sat on temporary wooden banks of seats, but an accident at Athens in 499 BC led to safer and more permanent seating—wedge-shaped blocks of stone banks, approximately concentric with the orchestra, cut into a convenient hillside. At Epidaurus, the banks of seats extend more than halfway round the orchestra, and are not built to a standard radius; a broad passage divides them horizontally, and the upper banks are steeper than the lower; these arrangements improved acoustics. Later theatre design emphasized the raised stage at the expense of the orchestra, reflecting the decline of the chorus and the rise of the individual actor.

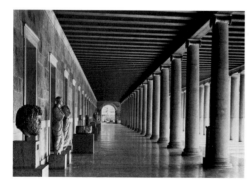

The Agora, or market-place, in Athens, here reconstructed (right), was moved or extended to its present position in the early 6th century BC. Originally an open space, it was gradually filled with buildings—mostly for religious or political purposes—beginning with the west and south sides. The great two-storeyed *stoa*, or colonnaded portico (above), filling the east side was built by Attalus II of Pergamon during the Hellenistic period. Later, the Romans further reduced the central space by adding a concert hall and transferring thither a temple to Ares.

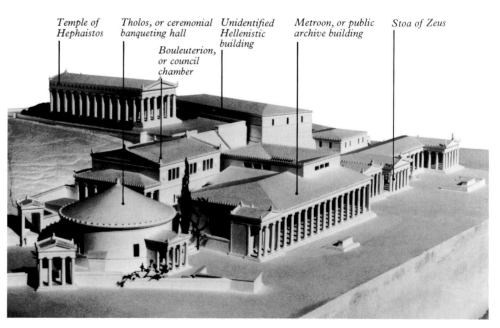

Temple of Hephaistos

Tholos, or ceremonial banqueting hall

Unidentified Hellenistic building

Bouleuterion, or council chamber

Metroon, or public archive building

Stoa of Zeus

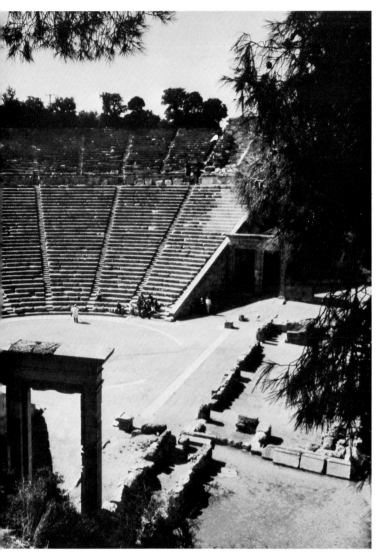

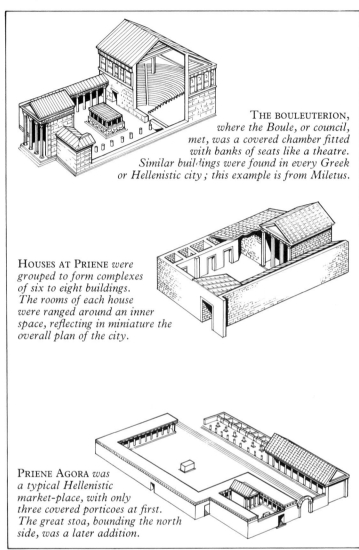

THE BOULEUTERION, *where the Boule, or council, met, was a covered chamber fitted with banks of seats like a theatre. Similar buildings were found in every Greek or Hellenistic city; this example is from Miletus.*

HOUSES AT PRIENE *were grouped to form complexes of six to eight buildings. The rooms of each house were ranged around an inner space, reflecting in miniature the overall plan of the city.*

PRIENE AGORA *was a typical Hellenistic market-place, with only three covered porticoes at first. The great stoa, bounding the north side, was a later addition.*

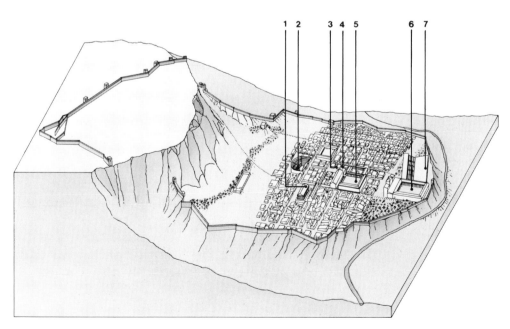

Priene, although a small and politically unimportant city, was a model of Hellenistic town-planning. In the 4th century BC, it was moved from its original, unknown site to its present position on Mt Mycale in Asia Minor. The upper slope made a formidable acropolis, 1,000 ft high, and the city's grid plan was carefully adjusted to the site. Six main thoroughfares running east–west were intersected by 15 secondary roads running north–south up the hill. Within the city were built a temple (1), a theatre (2), town hall (3), council chamber (4), agora (5), gymnasia (6) and stadium (7). The focal point of the town must have been the Temple of Athena Polias, a perfectly proportioned building, much admired by contemporaries.

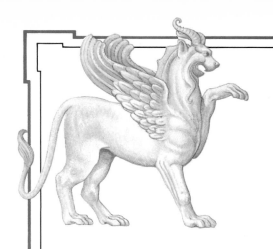

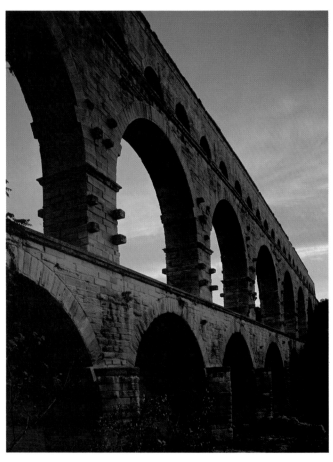

Some of the most beautiful Roman constructions were purely functional. The Pont du Gard at Nimes, a three-tiered aqueduct in southern France, is a lasting reminder of the genius of Roman engineering.

In a history which extended over a thousand years, Roman architecture not only underwent a series of drastic transformations, but came to mean several different things. In its narrowest sense, it was the architecture of the city of Rome. But the Romans did not stay at home and, in so far as their style of architecture travelled with them, it was the architecture of the Roman people. Beyond that, the Roman Empire included many provinces, especially in the eastern Mediterranean, which possessed highly developed architectural styles before the Romans arrived, and to which the Romans contributed little apart from patronage. Although materials, designs and functions varied prodigiously, the unity of the Empire in its prime made it impossible for differences to group themselves on a regional basis.

Given these ambiguities, it is not easy to summarize the architectural achievements of the Romans. During the first half of their history, that is, roughly, the Republican period, their expectations of architecture seem to have been modest and practical. Not a great deal of this architecture has survived, but enough to show that they were impressed by their Etruscan and Latin neighbours, who were themselves in some degree influenced by the Greeks. The highly conservative character of the Romans, however, and their contempt for art tended to inhibit experiments. The turning point came at the end of the Republican era, when the great generals of the civil wars, notably Sulla, Pompey and Julius Caesar, began to provide the city of Rome with monuments worthy of a world capital. Caesar started to remodel the entire centre of Rome. Augustus, Caesar's heir, boasted that he had found Rome a city of brick and left it a city of marble. Augustus' own successors turned much of it into a city of concrete.

The intense building operations of the early

Rome

Empire brought Rome into line with the Hellenistic cities of the eastern Mediterranean. Vitruvius, who dedicated his "Treatise on Architecture" to Augustus, seems to imply that many of the architects were Greeks. Indeed, the surviving fragments are Hellenistic with idiosyncracies. But the idiosyncracies are important. They occur in the entablatures of temples, making these both richer and deeper. The increase in scale implies a radical change in the proportions of the entire design. Roman temples were loftier and grander than their known Hellenistic equivalents. But our almost total ignorance of the public buildings of Ptolomeic Alexandria makes it difficult to evaluate this trend at Rome.

Whatever the initial purpose may have been, the desire to make Rome the most splendid city in the world produced a whole range of buildings that had never been seen before. The Forum Romanum, no longer a centre of active political life, was given up to the celebration of the city's greatness, past and present. Its commercial and social functions were taken over by a series of new Imperial Fora. Basilicas replaced stoas; baths and gymnasia coalesced into huge, people's palaces. The state policy of bread and circuses produced theatres, amphitheatres and stadia of immense size and ingenuity of design. The emperors, when in Rome, withdrew to the Palatine, which acquired the character of a kremlin, and built palaces that matched their megalomania. Very little is known about the architects who designed these colossal works. Many of them were Greek or Greek-trained; there are a few clues as to ways in which they prepared their designs. Their attitude towards the Classical tradition which they inherited, and never formally repudiated, was ambiguous. Their technical methods owed almost nothing to the past. Building with concrete was something they developed themselves. So, also, was the art of vaulting, which made possible the vast interiors which were their most distinctive achievements.

The Orders survived simply as veneers of ornament, applied to great masses of concrete on a scale hardly ever contemplated in Greece. The variation known as the Giant Order came into its own—without it, it is hard to see how Greek architectural ornament could have survived. The frank recognition that the Orders were nothing but ornament encouraged architects, especially in the eastern provinces of the Empire, to take liberties that would have been unthinkable to the more fastidious Greeks of the Classical period. Architraves could be interrupted, broken forward, or curved forward, or bent upwards into arches. The Giant Order was accompanied by the Miniature Order, applied to windows or tabernacles. These could be repeated or alternated with different pediments; and pediments could be used to link adjacent tabernacles instead of surmounting each one separately. Paradoxically, once the Orders ceased to be taken seriously, they became a fruitful theme for invention, none of it acknowledged in the academic rules preserved for posterity by Vitruvius. The term Roman Baroque has been applied to it; but the fantasy element could equally be called theatrical, for it may have derived from the permanent stage structure of Roman theatres.

The Imperial and Baroque themes in Roman architecture are perhaps the most conspicuous. But alongside them must be placed a third, a purely utilitarian one, which produced quantities of houses, apartment buildings, factories, roads, bridges—all those amenities which have returned to the world of architecture only in recent times, and which give the Romans a claim to be the only true precursors of the modern architect.

The Forum, city centre of an Empire

IN ITS FINAL form, the Roman Forum must have presented the most splendid collection of temples, public buildings and commemorative statues ever assembled in the Ancient World. Arranged almost without order, the different angles, shapes and styles combined to produce an effect which was at once picturesque and overwhelmingly monumental.

At first a swamp and then a burial ground, the Forum only became an effective city centre when it was drained by the Etruscans. The apparatus of politics—the rostra, the curia, or senate house, and the voting pens—grouped themselves at the west end, while the religious activities gravitated towards the east. This was where the sacred hearth was tended by the Vestal Virgins, and where the chief priest, the Pontifex Maximus, had his official residence. On either side, shops developed indiscriminately.

As at Athens, architectural embellishment came as a kind of compensation for the decline of political vitality. The process began in 78 BC with Sulla's Tabularium, or Record Office, overlooking the west of the Forum, and was continued spasmodically for over one hundred and fifty years by Caesar, Augustus, Tiberius and Vespasian. Temples were rebuilt, shops absorbed into basilicas and new buildings added. The proliferation of triumphal arches, columns and statues continued for centuries, the Column of Phocas being erected as late as AD 608.

Although the Forum was always in use, from Caesar's time onwards it became imperial policy to transfer many of its functions elsewhere. During the later Empire, the entire Forum must have seemed an increasingly comprehensive memorial to the glorious past of the city. Fourth-century senators probably felt much as Gibbon did when they contemplated its redundant magnificence.

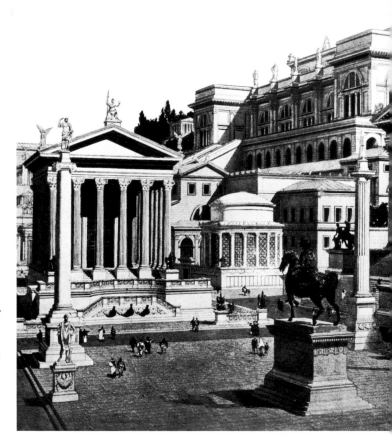

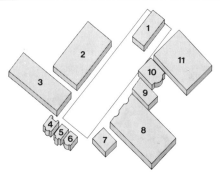

1 Temple of Jupiter
2 Temple of Apollo
3 Basilica
4 Magistrates' offices
5 Senate house
6 Administration block
7 Election hall
8 Eumachia building
9 Temple of Vespasian
10 Temple of the
   city deities
11 Covered market

PROVINCIAL VARIATIONS
Although the Forum Romanum had no counterpart elsewhere, the formula which underlies the Imperial Fora was familiar throughout the Roman Empire. At Pompeii, the Forum was an elongated rectangle with a temple of Jupiter at one end, and temples and sanctuaries on either side. The rest of its perimeter was taken up by a council chamber, magistrates' offices, a basilica, a covered market and warehouse.

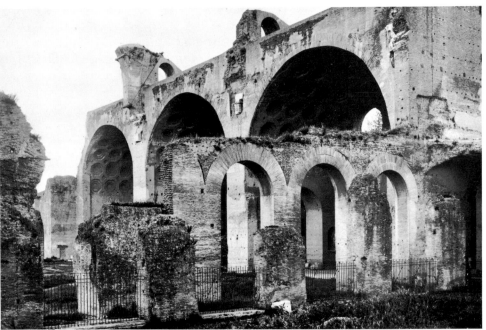

The Basilica of Maxentius was the most imposing of its kind in Rome. The term basilica in Roman architecture usually indicates a large, unvaulted hall; this example is different. Begun by Maxentius and finished early in the 4th century AD by Constantine, it was, in effect, the great concourse usually associated with the imperial baths, extracted from its usual context and set up as an independent building. The vast interior, 280 ft long, 85 ft wide and 120 ft high, required only three groined vaults to cover it.

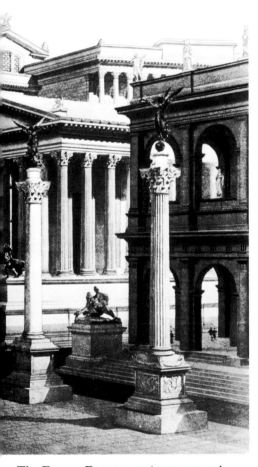

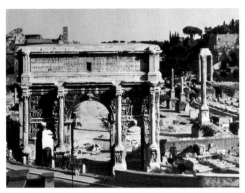

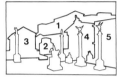

Forum Romanum
1 *House of the Vestal Virgins*
2 *Temple of Vesta*
3 *Temple of Divus Julius*
4 *Temple of Castor and Pollux*
5 *Basilica Julia*

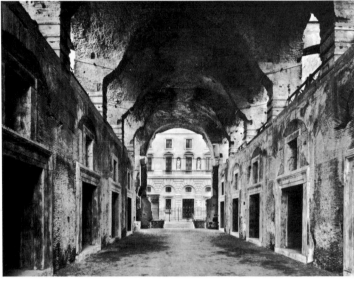

The Forum Romanum (reconstructed
above) was the oldest and most important
in the city. Caesar added a second forum in
46 BC, and his precedent was followed by
Augustus, Vespasian, Nerva, and by Trajan,
who rounded off the whole Imperial Fora
development (right) by taking it up the
slopes of the Quirinal hill. Caesar, Augustus
and Vespasian associated their fora with
votive temples; Trajan went further and
included a basilica, two libraries—one
Greek and one Latin—on either side of his
column, and a temple. Although the Ancient
Romans deserved their reputation for
unimaginative practicality, the city centre
discloses quite another side of their character:
even in ruins (below) it is difficult not to see
it as the work of men indulging in an orgy of
histrionic self-congratulation.

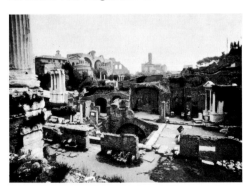

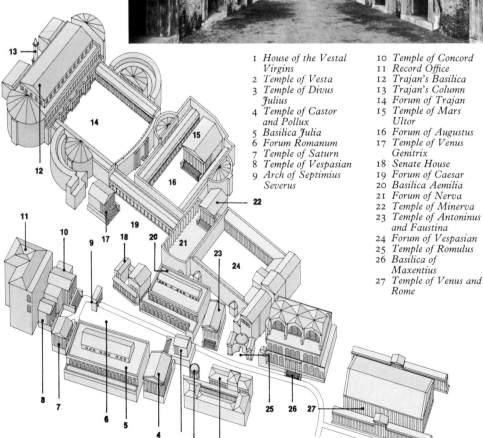

1 *House of the Vestal Virgins*
2 *Temple of Vesta*
3 *Temple of Divus Julius*
4 *Temple of Castor and Pollux*
5 *Basilica Julia*
6 *Forum Romanum*
7 *Temple of Saturn*
8 *Temple of Vespasian*
9 *Arch of Septimius Severus*
10 *Temple of Concord*
11 *Record Office*
12 *Trajan's Basilica*
13 *Trajan's Column*
14 *Forum of Trajan*
15 *Temple of Mars Ultor*
16 *Forum of Augustus*
17 *Temple of Venus Genitrix*
18 *Senate House*
19 *Forum of Caesar*
20 *Basilica Aemilia*
21 *Forum of Nerva*
22 *Temple of Minerva*
23 *Temple of Antoninus and Faustina*
24 *Forum of Vespasian*
25 *Temple of Romulus*
26 *Basilica of Maxentius*
27 *Temple of Venus and Rome*

Amphitheatres and theatres

AMPHITHEATRES WERE amenities for which the Greeks had little use. The entertainment value of killing—whether the victims were wild beasts, criminals or gladiators—was first recognized by the Campanians of southern Italy, and later keenly appreciated in Rome. Such exotic spectacles occurred infrequently at first, and were usually staged to celebrate military triumphs; for these, it was enough to close off the forum or put up temporary wooden structures. With the imperial policy of bread and circuses, initiated to keep the idle populace of Rome in good humour, spectacles in the arena became a popular and frequent pastime, and soon permanent buildings were being designed to house these disgusting festivities.

While similar in some ways to theatres, amphitheatres presented particular problems of safety and access. The needs of performer and spectator differed considerably. Natural amphitheatres do not occur frequently, least of all in towns, and early examples, raised on a natural depression, like that at Pompeii, set the pattern for later buildings. The essence of the exercise was the provision of artificial ramps, or slopes, for the seats. In the 1st century AD, the transition was made from wood to stone, but only the stone buildings remain as evidence.

At the Colosseum in Rome, and Arles and Nîmes, in France, the seating ramps were converging wedges of masonry, with vaulted passageways between. These passages were grouped in threes, the central one sloping downwards, flanked by two sloping upwards; the vaulted ceilings all sloped downwards. The passages opened on to circulation corridors, from which further slopes or stairs led to other levels. This ingenious interconnection of concentric corridors and inclines must have facilitated the handling of large audiences.

Amphitheatres presented every conceivable vaulting problem, except that of covering a wide span. The passageways not only tapered and sloped, but were also placed at varying angles, because the arena had more than one geometric centre. Concentric corridors also required a complex vaulting system. It has been justly claimed that the architect who could build an amphitheatre could build anything.

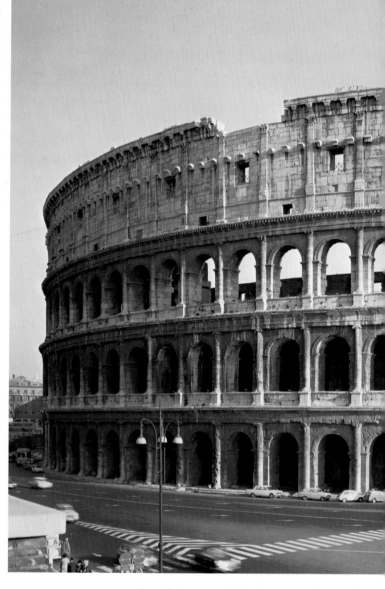

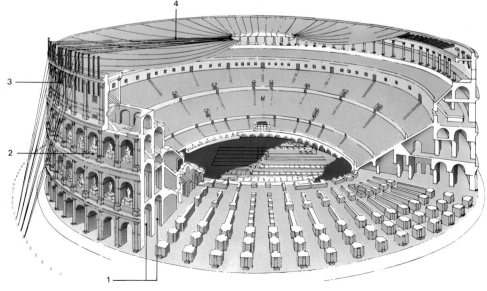

The Colosseum (above) was the largest of the Roman amphitheatres, but its name— now synonymous with its size—in fact, derives from a colossal statue of Nero near by. Vespasian began it *c.* AD 70, siting it on the lake intended for Nero's Golden House, which was never completed; occasionally, the lake was used to flood the arena for aquatic events. The design of the Colosseum, shown reconstructed (left), is similar to surviving Provençal amphitheatres, but it was unique in having two complete passageways (1) encircling the converging ramps of seats. Extra banks of seats could thus be added above, making a third order of arches necessary in the outer wall (2). A fourth storey (3) was soon added. All trace of the upper seats has disappeared, suggesting that they were made of wood. Canvas awnings (4), maintained by a squad of sailors, could be stretched across the arena, shielding the audience from the sun. The Colosseum could easily hold 48,000 people, and was still being used for animal games as late as AD 523.

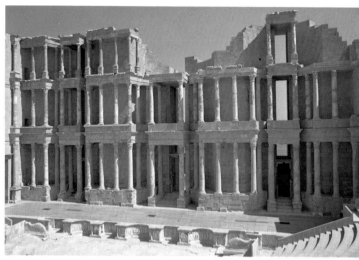

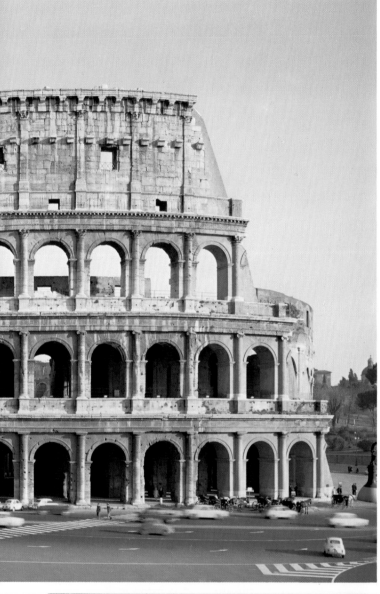

The scaena frons, or stone backdrop, of the theatre at Sabratha in north Africa (above), built *c*. AD 200, has been splendidly restored. Its position in the theatre is marked (below).

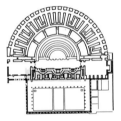

Theatre design was revolutionized by the Romans. Although the Greeks invented the drama, their theatres were little more than prepared landscapes, designed to seat large audiences and ensure good acoustics. The Romans transformed them into works of architecture, often raising an artificial *cavea*, or seating area, on vaulted ramps when no convenient hillside was available. This arrangement was much like an amphitheatre, but archaeological evidence suggests that the innovation was first made for theatres. Romans also worried about access to seats, and passages and stairs were installed behind the cavea to enable people to reach the top back seats easily from behind.

The other great Roman innovation was the *scaena frons*. In contrast with the Greek open theatres, which relied on the splendid distant landscapes provided by nature, this was essentially a wall behind the stage, which set the background scene for the action of the play. This feature was first used in the 4th century BC, but reached its apotheosis in the 2nd century AD, when it became an excuse for architectural conceits, which often assumed an almost Baroque exuberance.

Both Arles (left) and Nîmes in Provence, France, boast well-preserved amphitheatres; both are still used for bullfights. Built entirely of stone, they are marvels of convenience from the point of view of crowd control.

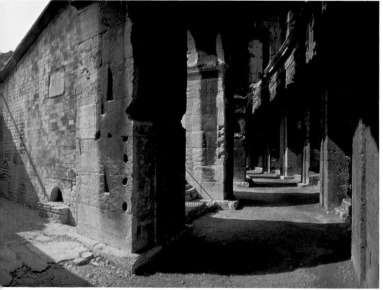

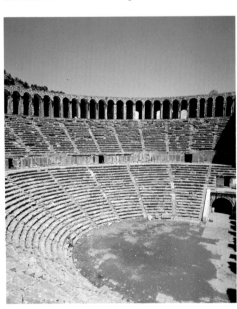

The theatre at Aspendos in southern Turkey rivals that of Orange in France in size and preservation, indicating that theatre design was fairly standard throughout the Roman Empire.

The temple

TEMPLE-BUILDING on a serious scale began in Rome in the 6th century BC. Roman temples differed from Greek both internally and in their relationship to their surroundings. Often, three gods were housed together, and although their *cellas*, or individual chambers, were narrow, the temples as a whole tended to be very broad. Instead of being placed symmetrically on a stylobate, or platform base, the divine accommodation was usually pushed to the back of a high podium approached by a flight of stairs. This produced an imposing façade which invited inspection from only one viewpoint. The ideal position for a Roman temple was, therefore, at one end of an open space, which is where they are found at Pompeii and in the ruins of the Roman Fora. Most of the temples in Rome were rebuilt by Augustus and Tiberius in the 1st century AD, and while the distinctive ground plans were retained, the exteriors were radically transformed to accord with either the current Hellenistic fashion or the Roman variant of it.

Roman temples, even more than those of Greece, were designed as imposing backdrops to open-air rituals. During the 2nd century AD, however, the religious life of the Ancient World changed profoundly. New religions made a powerful appeal and even the ancient cults, which had merged with the official worship of the state in the person of the emperor, felt the effect. The last great pagan temples, such as those at Baalbek, or the Pantheon at Rome, broke with tradition: their interiors were conceived in terms of unwonted magnificence. What went on inside was clearly of great importance; and the gulf between these temples and the first Christian churches was perhaps not as wide as is sometimes imagined.

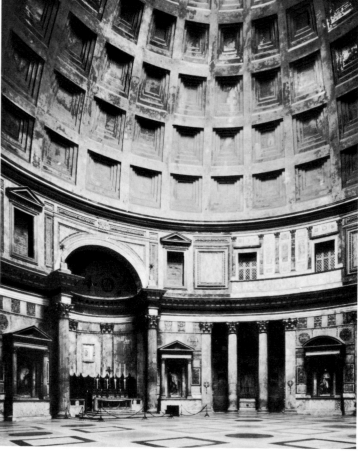

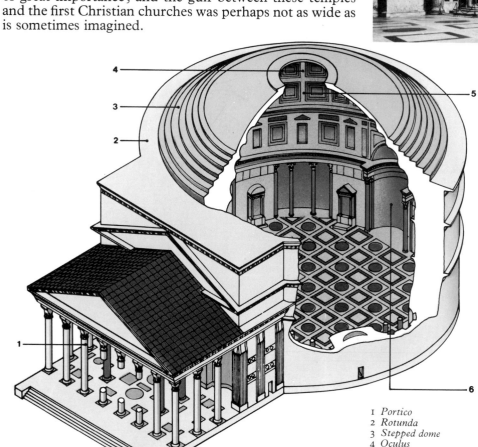

1 Portico
2 Rotunda
3 Stepped dome
4 Oculus
5 Coffered interior
6 Recess

The Pantheon (above and left) is unique among the buildings of Imperial Rome in having survived intact. Converted into a church in the 7th century AD, it has been relatively well cared for since. It is known today as S. Maria Rotonda. Its portico, of granite columns surmounted by Corinthian capitals, was originally part of a temple built in 25 BC by Agrippa, son-in-law to Augustus, whose name can still be seen on the frieze. The rotunda itself was built by Hadrian between AD 120 and AD 124.

The idea of a round temple was not new, but the scale of Hadrian's temple was unprecedented. It was planned with eight great recesses; one formed the entrance, while the remainder sheltered statues of the seven major Roman gods. The diameter of the drum and the height of the stepped dome are both 147 Roman feet (a Roman foot was one-third of an inch shorter than the English foot). A 30-ft-wide *oculus*, or round opening, in the top of the dome, illuminates the interior. The dome had an outer covering of gilt bronze until 655, when this was replaced with lead. Inside, the coffering, once embellished with stucco ornament, was a means of reducing the massive weight of the dome. The 21-ft-thick walls of the Pantheon were built of concrete, sandwiched between layers of brick facings and sheathed in marble veneer. They were not solid, but honeycombed with arches—yet another feature to relieve the dome's thrust—some of which spanned niches housing statues.

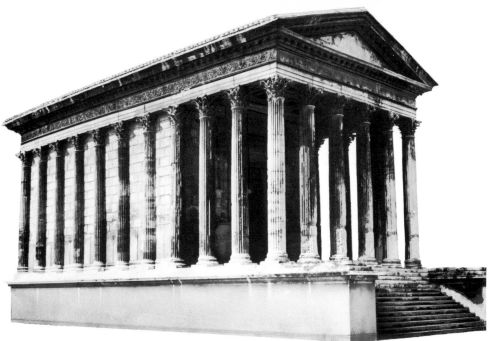

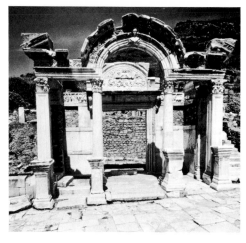

The Temple of Hadrian at Ephesus (above) was built in honour of the Emperor. Although small, it had several unusual features, including an architrave broken upwards in the form of an arch over the entrance to the porch; over the entrance to the inner cella is a carved tympanum, the semicircular arch between the top of the doorway and an arch above. Hadrian travelled widely in the provinces of the Empire, where many other buildings owed their inception or completion to his generosity.

The Maison Carrée (above) at Nîmes, in Provence, France, which must originally have stood in the Forum, is one of the best-preserved early Roman temples. Inscriptions associate it with the imperial family, and it was probably designed by one of the imperial architects. The cella, or chamber housing the cult image, was set well back on the podium and was reached by a flight of steps. The exterior is virtually intact and displays Corinthian columns in their enriched Roman form, supporting an opulently carved entablature. Provence, where colonies were founded by Caesar and settled by Italian veterans, was in many ways more Roman than Rome. Much imperial wealth was lavished on these new colonial cities, and their temples were as sumptuous as any in Rome.

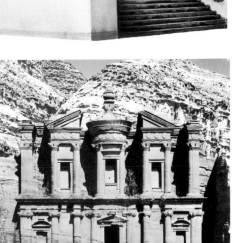

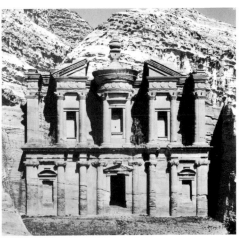

The rock-cut tombs of the desert city of Petra (left) display the most extraordinary use of architectural features. The tombs, which resemble temples, have façades divided horizontally into contrasting halves, with porches below and a turret-like device bisecting a pediment above. Tentatively placed in the 2nd century AD, the date of these eccentric buildings has not been fixed.

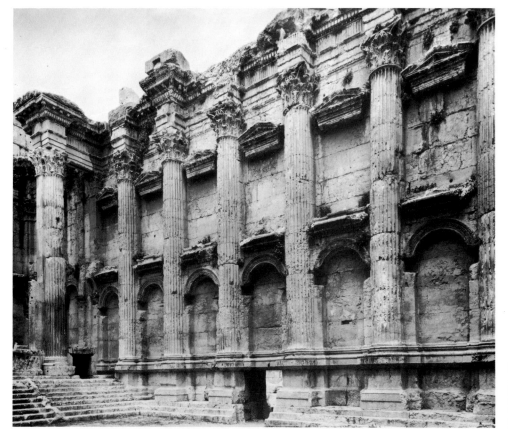

The Temple of Bacchus (left) at Baalbek in the Lebanon, dating from the 2nd century AD, is one of a group of temples. The history of this great temple complex goes back to pre-Classical times, and the pattern of their rituals remained essentially oriental, even though the Romans reconstructed the buildings in the Classical manner. Baalbek features the Giant Order—huge Corinthian columns or pilasters superimposed on a two-storeyed elevation. This order was used to even greater effect inside, where the naos became an assembly hall, and the *adyton*, or sacred chamber, was raised at one end and emphasized by a shallow vault. This plan (below) must have developed from something akin to Solomon's Temple at Jerusalem, and its essential lay-out survived in some medieval churches.

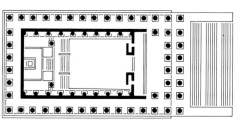

Palaces, villas and tenements

ROMAN DOMESTIC architecture, of which much survives, encompassed a variety of social levels. At the top were the imperial palaces, above all the Palatine itself, in Rome. Below this were the less elaborate country villas, typified by Piazza Armerina in Sicily, and Emperor Diocletian's residence at Spalato, modern Split, in Yugoslavia. Still farther down the social scale were the smart town houses at Ostia, Pompeii and Herculaneum. Finally, there were the tenement buildings, which must have been a feature of every well-populated town, although little trace of them remains. Sociologically they are perhaps the most interesting; nothing comparable has been found in earlier cities.

The smarter residences of Pompeii and Herculaneum were occupied by the well-to-do Romans. Their life-style cannot have differed much from that of their Greek counterparts, and their houses were designed on much the same lines as those at Priene. Men of property lived most of their lives in public and the affairs of the family were conducted from their houses, which were divided into two parts, one relatively accessible and the other strictly private.

In archaeological terms, most is known about the imperial palaces. The Palatine, built by a succession of emperors from AD 3 to AD 212, is a total ruin, but its plan has been preserved and the stages of its development worked out. Augustus evidently lived modestly; megalomania set in with Caligula and Nero; but it was Domitian who gave the public apartments of the palace their monumental form. The *aula regia*, or great audience chamber, must have been one of the most stupendous buildings in Rome—nearly 150 feet high, if it was vaulted, as seems likely. In a sense, this was the ultimate version of the ancient megaron, although as far as is known no continuous tradition linked Imperial Rome with the remote past of the Mediterranean world. What inspired Domitian's Palatine is a mystery. It had no equivalent in Greek cities; only at Antioch or Alexandria did palace life achieve the degree of ceremonial that would interest men like Domitian; and in neither city has anything comparable yet come to light.

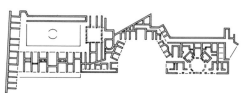

In the manner of a typical Roman army camp, two broad intersecting streets, running north–south and east–west, divided the palace into four rectangles. The northern rectangles probably contained the barracks of the imperial guard, stables, shops, bakeries and warehouses.

High walls, each with a fortified central gateway and huge defensive towers, guarded the three landward sides.

The imperial apartments lay within the corner of the southwest rectangle. To the north of the emperor's private chambers stood a temple, and to the east a splendid library, beyond which stretched a two-storey reception suite.

The palace built by Diocletian for his retirement at Spalato, modern Split, in Yugoslavia, was unlike any other known imperial residence. Built in AD 300, it was modelled on a legionary fortress, and while retaining many of the features of an army camp, none the less combined them with the kind of accommodation that an emperor, even a retired emperor, might expect. The reconstruction (right) indicates the extreme formality of the contemporary imperial style.

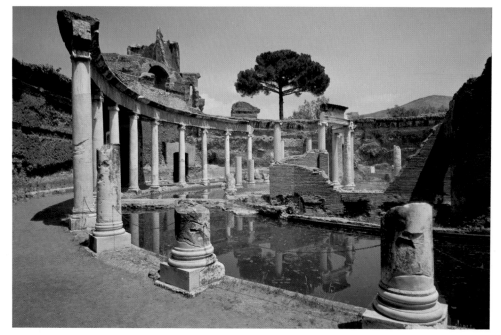

Hadrian's villa at Tivoli (left), built in AD 124, was a delightful blend of sculpture, architecture and waterworks, which produced that special kind of illusion later associated with 18th-century English taste.

The Golden House (above) was an extravagance planned by Nero—a seaside villa in the heart of Rome. Begun after the fire of AD 64, it was never finished, and has now mostly disappeared. It covered a huge area east of the Forum, parts of which were later occupied by the Colosseum, the Temple of Venus and Rome and the baths of Titus and Trajan. Its painted corridors inspired Raphael, and its principal apartment, a domed octagonal room lit from above, evidently foreshadowed a succession of imperial monuments, including the Pantheon.

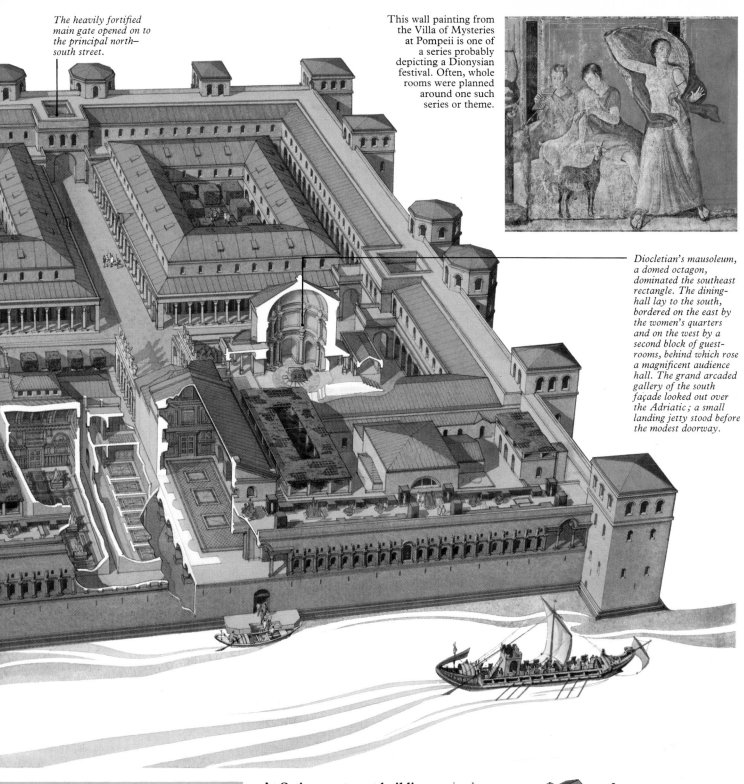

The heavily fortified main gate opened on to the principal north–south street.

This wall painting from the Villa of Mysteries at Pompeii is one of a series probably depicting a Dionysian festival. Often, whole rooms were planned around one such series or theme.

Diocletian's mausoleum, a domed octagon, dominated the southeast rectangle. The dining-hall lay to the south, bordered on the east by the women's quarters and on the west by a second block of guest-rooms, behind which rose a magnificent audience hall. The grand arcaded gallery of the south façade looked out over the Adriatic; a small landing jetty stood before the modest doorway.

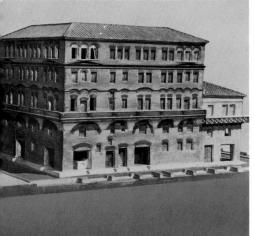

At Ostia, apartment buildings or *insulae*, shown reconstructed (left), rose to perhaps five storeys and represented the accommodation available to the common people. The population density in these tenements was probably not far off that of modern Naples.

The House of the Mosaic Atrium (right) at Herculaneum, preserved by the volcanic mud which covered the city in AD 79, indicates the standard of living enjoyed by the Roman upper classes in the 1st century AD. Like Greek houses at Priene, the plan includes a large garden: an entrance hall (1) leads to the mosaic-floored atrium (2), behind which is a reception room (3) for friends and clients; bedrooms extend along the west wall (4), and at the south end is the private family living area (5).

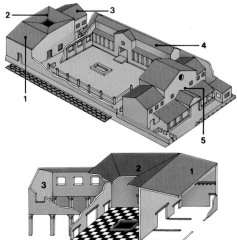

Engineering genius

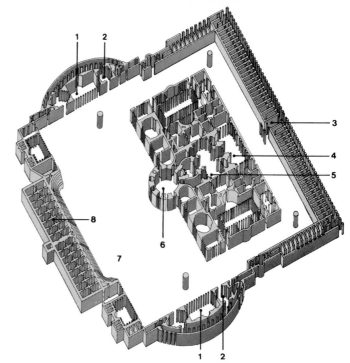

ALTHOUGH THE Romans did not discover that lime has the curious faculty of transforming itself into a rigid substance when mixed with water, they exploited it as no one else did before them. Plaster, cement and concrete are all variations on this theme. It is sometimes argued that the invention of concrete made possible the huge vaulted halls of the imperial palaces, baths and other buildings, but it seems more likely that it was simply the most convenient material in which to execute these grandiose visions.

The really important innovations which the Romans made in the design and construction of large buildings stemmed from their realization of the potential of the arch and its derivative, the vault. The arch was certainly known to and used by the Greeks, but as it played no part in their sacred architecture, it would seem that for them it had no spiritual overtones. The imperial architects of Rome used the arch in both a purely practical way—for bridges, sewers and aqueducts—and in a symbolic way for the triumphal arches which immortalized a succession of emperors. The same was true of vaults: cellars and passages were vaulted for convenience; great halls were vaulted for effect. The Romans used all forms of vault, and even anticipated the medieval ribbed vault in the baths of Diocletian.

The Baths of Caracalla were planned to combine bathing installations, gymnasia and libraries in one vast palace of recreation and culture. Begun by the Emperor Caracalla in AD 211, the construction used barrel vaults, groin vaults and domes. Rome boasted several such establishments, affording the ordinary citizen a taste of imperial splendour.

1 Library
2 Octagonal hall
3 Entrance
4 Frigidarium
5 Tepidarium
6 Caldarium
7 Garden
8 Stadium

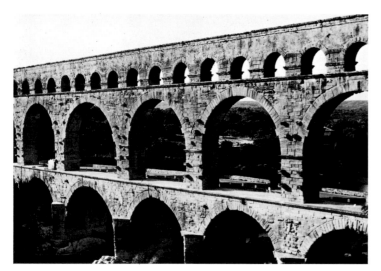

The prestigious Pont du Gard was built c. AD 14, as much perhaps to impress the natives as to supply Nîmes with water.

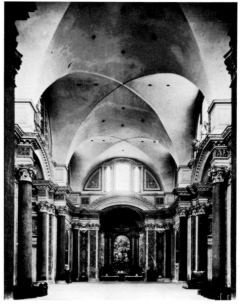

The great groin-vaulted concourse of the Baths of Diocletian, built AD 302, survived the Middle Ages and was incorporated into the Renaissance church of S. Maria degli Angeli. Something of the sumptuous effect of the original Roman design can still be felt.

ARCHES, VAULTS AND WALLS
The Romans made great use of the arch, built up from wedge-shaped blocks, or voussoirs. Prolonging the arch, they achieved the tunnel, or barrel, vault, a row of brick ribs infilled with concrete, the ubiquitous Roman building material. Intersecting vaults formed cross, or groin, vaults. Another form of vaulting, the semidome was also developed from the arch. Concrete was used for walls, but needed a framework to hold it until it set: opus incertum was the first rough stone frame; opus reticulatum, a cross pattern of diagonally set bricks, came next, followed by the triangular blocks, laid with points inwards, of opus testaceum.

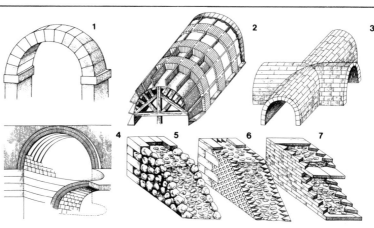

1 Round arch
2 Tunnel, or barrel, vault
3 Cross, or groin, vault
4 Semidome
5 Opus incertum
6 Opus reticulatum
7 Opus testaceum

THE
MIDDLE
AGES

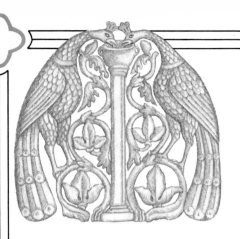

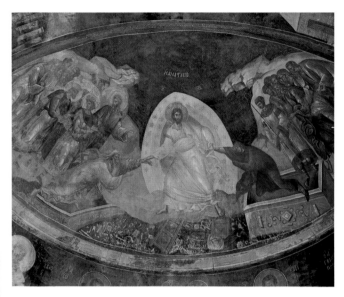

Glowing frescoes with Christ as the central figure adorned the walls of even the simplest Byzantine churches. This detail is part of a 14th-century series in the church of St Saviour in Chora, in Constantinople, now a mosque. The Gospel stories depicted here were executed with a skill rivalling that of the Ancient Romans.

It was not until the Emperor Constantine adopted Christianity as the state religion in 313 and in 330 moved the imperial capital to Byzantium (which was renamed Constantinople) that church-building began on a wide scale. From the start, these early churches were of two types. The first, the basilica, was rectangular, with twin colonnades separating the nave from the side aisles, which were built lower to allow for ranges of clerestory windows above them. There was no vertical division into bays; the axis was horizontal, with the eye travelling down the vista of columns, along the entablature, to the altar and the apse. The second type consisted of a circular or octagonal space surrounded by an ambulatory; it, too, had clerestory lighting.

In the early years, both types were popular in East and West alike. There were round churches, like San Vitale, Santa Costanza or Santo Stefano Rotondo, in Italy, just as there were basilicas, like St John of Studium, in Constantinople. Gradually, however, polarization set in. The West, with its increasing emphasis on congregational worship, preferred the basilican model—from which transepts soon began to sprout to give the long-naved, cruciform plan we know today. The East inclined towards the more mystical properties of the circle; to give this most perfect of forms still greater emphasis it developed the dome; and, barely two centuries after Constantine had inaugurated his new capital on the Bosphorus, it produced, in the church of Santa Sophia, an architectural miracle.

But if Santa Sophia was one of the earliest examples of the style now known as Byzantine, it was also its ultimate masterpiece. To the question of why the style showed so little development over the next fourteen centuries the short answer is, therefore, that it had nowhere particular to go.

Early Christian, Byzantine and Carolingian

There were other reasons, too: unlike its sisters in the West, the Orthodox Church during those later centuries never sought to impress. It had no desire to build ever larger and higher. Its liturgy, designed solely for the glorification of God, was performed for the most part behind a screen, from which the clergy appeared only briefly and at rare intervals. Instrumental music, statuary and even seating for the faithful were banned. It mistrusted the huge congregations, pealing organs and massed choirs beloved of the West, preferring intimacy, mystery, silence, and a semi-darkness relieved only by the flicker of a lamp on an icon or the glint of a mosaic in the candle-light. And it could not forget the mother church at Constantinople, and that great, magical, floating dome.

Now, domes in themselves present no particular structural difficulties; the Romans had already used them to stunning effect—notably with the Pantheon in the 2nd century—and for a less sophisticated example one has only to think of the igloo. But the igloo and the Pantheon are both in themselves circular; the problem arose when the dome had to be set upon a square base. No one is sure who hit upon the final solution, but that solution—the pendentive—must rank with the arch and the vault as a key invention in architectural history. Its soundness had been triumphantly proved at Santa Sophia, where each giant pendentive is over sixty feet high, and thereafter the dome-pendentive arrangement became the dominant feature in Byzantine churches. The result was to change the axis of the whole church, which in the early basilicas had been horizontal; now, the horizontals disappeared and the eyes were drawn, instead, upwards to the dome—where, in all probability, they were met by those of Christ.

The Eastern Church has always held very strict views about the representation of the Godhead. Above all, the hierarchy of Heaven must be respected: Christ at the top, then the Virgin, then the Archangels, and so in descending order through the Evangelists, Apostles, Old Testament prophets, saints and fathers of the early Church. To such a scheme Byzantine architecture, with its gradation of dome, drum, pendentive and apse, and its flat wall spaces, provided the ideal response. Where necessary, of course, it made its own adaptations. The desirability of having Christ centrally placed led to the general adoption of the cross-in-square plan—fundamentally cruciform, but with the angles of the cross filled in at a lower level so as to produce a square plan on the ground and a cross above. This innovation ended the practice by which the western arm was elongated, a tradition which in Latin lands produced the nave as we know it today.

As the centuries passed, there were other developments, but none of these was of real significance. Such important variations as occur within the Byzantine canon are not chronological but geographical. Thus, the pages of this book relating to Constantinople, though principally concerned with Santa Sophia, also include the frescoes in the church of St Saviour in Chora, which date from eight centuries later; and the pages that follow deal first with the mainstream in Greece and the Balkans and then with the two principal regional offshoots, the Russian and the Armenian. (It is a debatable question whether the Armenian should be described as Byzantine at all, but it would be unthinkable to leave it out.) Finally, we come to the last great stronghold of the Byzantine tradition in the West and its supreme example, St Mark's in Venice.

Early Christian and Byzantine architecture cover an immense but inexhaustibly rich field. They are styles of architecture that set out to portray, in plastic terms, the very Spirit of God.

Rome builds for a new faith

FROM AS EARLY as the middle of the 1st century Christianity was gaining converts in Italy. Even before 313, when the Emperor Constantine granted the new faith equal status with other religions, there were at least forty small churches in Rome. These early churches were of both the basilican and the centralized type. The prototype of the basilican church was probably the private basilica, or great hall, found in the mansions of the Roman plutocracy. The clerestory, or upper storey pierced with windows, a common feature of such halls, was adopted in churches of this kind. Basilican churches were the more popular, but centralized churches were also built, although, at first, not as places of congregational worship, but to mark some specially sacred spot or to house a tomb or baptistry.

Rome preserves more than a dozen early churches, dating from the 7th century or before. Despite alterations and restorations, many retain their Early Christian character. The least spoiled are the smaller, more remote churches, erected near or outside the walls of the ancient city, often over the tombs of apostles or early martyrs. The basilican church of Sant'Agnese fuori le Mura, although not the earliest, is one of the best preserved. Its design shares much, on a smaller scale, with that of Old St Peter's, Rome, which was pulled down to make way for the present cathedral. Columns for these old churches were almost invariably appropriated from ancient buildings. The churches were often, as at Sant'Agnese, enriched with mosaics. The two surviving centralized churches in Rome are Santa Costanza and Santo Stefano Rotondo.

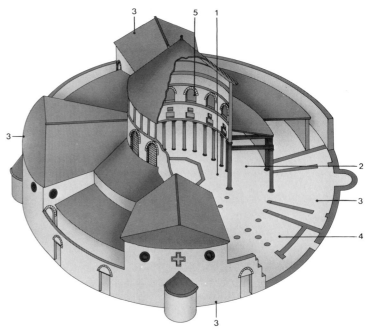

Santo Stefano Rotondo, built *c.* 468, with a diameter of 210 ft, is the largest circular church in existence. Its unusual plan blends a cross with concentric circles. The huge central nave is encircled by Ionic columns and lit by 22 clerestory windows. An ambulatory surrounds this colonnade and opens on to four deep chapels set crosswise.

1 *Nave*
2 *Ambulatory*
3 *Chapels*
4 *Aisles*
5 *Clerestory*

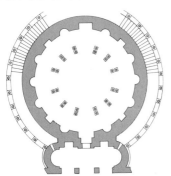

Sant'Agnese fuori le Mura was rebuilt *c.* 630 to replace the original basilican church established by Constantine in 324. The new church was a galleried basilica with antique columns supporting the arches along the aisles. The apse is at the west end of the church, an unusual position, also adopted in Old St Peter's.

Santa Costanza, one of Rome's two surviving circular churches, is symmetrical in plan, with a central space beneath the domed brick roof and an encircling aisle. Built *c.* 330 as a tomb for Constantine's daughter, it was converted into a church in 1256.

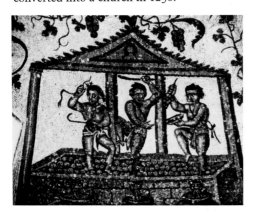

Mosaics dating from the 4th century decorate the barrel-vaulted ambulatory of S. Costanza. Still remarkably well preserved, they depict scenes from the grape harvest.

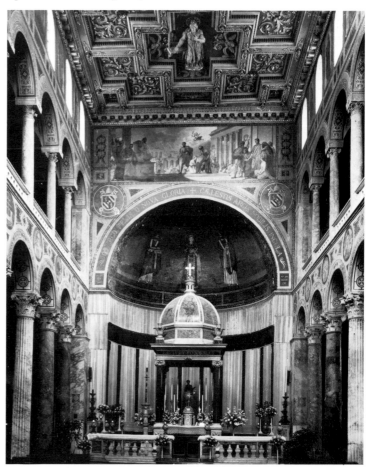

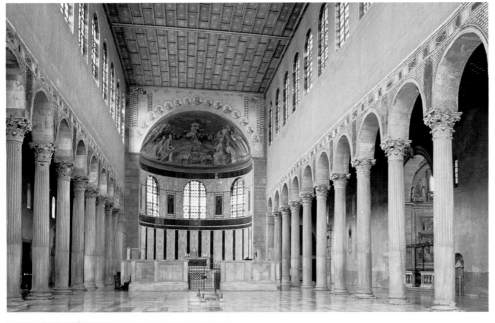

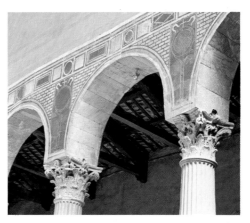

Santa Sabina. The tall, narrow nave of this elegant and well-preserved basilica (left) has arcades carried on antique marble columns with Corinthian capitals and bases. The spandrels of the arches (above) have decorative marble revetments, or facings, depicting chalices and pattens, symbols of the Eucharist.

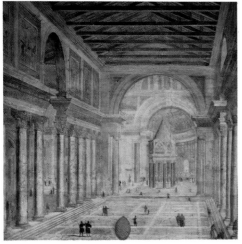

This unsigned painting hangs in the Church of S. Martino ai Monti in Rome. It shows the nave of Old St Peter's as it must have appeared before the building was pulled down in 1505 to make way for the present basilica.

Old St Peter's, the most renowned of Early Christian basilicas, was built *c.* 326 by Constantine near the site of St Peter's martyrdom. Although enormous—the nave was about 200 ft long—the church was structurally simple, with a plain timber roof. Rows of closely spaced columns divided the building into a nave with double aisles. Nave and aisles terminated at the west in five arches, of which the central was a triumphal arch. Behind this was the *bema*, a space which may have been the origin of the transept in later cruciform churches, and beyond this lay the apse. An atrium, or forecourt, to the east led through the narthex to the main body of the church.

The bema, or transept, contained St Peter's shrine, within a baldacchino.

The transept opened centrally in a western apse, from which the bishop and high clerics emerged to officiate at services.

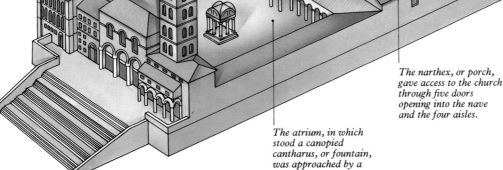

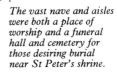

The vast nave and aisles were both a place of worship and a funeral hall and cemetery for those desiring burial near St Peter's shrine.

The narthex, or porch, gave access to the church through five doors opening into the nave and the four aisles.

The atrium, in which stood a canopied cantharus, or fountain, was approached by a flight of 35 steps.

Ravenna, city of mosaics

ON THE DEATH of the Emperor Theodosius I in 395, the Roman Empire was divided between his two sons, the eastern part being ruled by Arcadius from Constantinople and the western part by Honorius from Rome. Rome at this time was being attacked by the Goths from the north and was plagued by malaria from the surrounding marshes. In 402, Honorius moved his capital to Ravenna, whose port, Classe, had been the Roman naval base in the Adriatic since the time of Augustus Caesar. Ravenna fell to the Ostrogoths in 476 but was recovered by Justinian in 540, when the Empire was reunited, and remained under Byzantine rule until 751. By this time Ravenna's great period was over. Indeed, all the art for which the city is so famous was concentrated into the 5th and 6th centuries.

Ravenna faded out of history more than twelve hundred years ago. For centuries it was left to brood over its splendid past, a forgotten backwater. Its rediscovery in recent times was artistically of great importance, for Ravenna exemplifies the Early Christian and early Byzantine city *par excellence*. It is renowned for its architecture, but above all for its mosaics, which are the finest in the world. Roman mosaics are of stone, laid on floors; the Ravenna mosaics are mainly of glass and adorn walls and vaults. The preparation of the gold *tesserae*, as the little cubes are called, was a delicate task. The usual method was to cover each piece of glass in gold leaf and then fire another very thin film of glass on top. But many other colours of varying density were used, some reflecting the light much more than others. Light and colour, the chief delights in the art of mosaic, are seen to perfection at Ravenna.

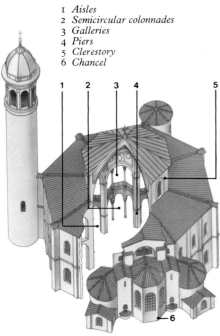

1 *Aisles*
2 *Semicircular colonnades*
3 *Galleries*
4 *Piers*
5 *Clerestory*
6 *Chancel*

San Vitale, founded by Justinian in 526 and completed in 547, is one of the finest Byzantine centralized churches in the West. It is composed of two concentric octagons, which form a central space surrounded by an aisle with vaults and galleries. A chancel opens from one side of the inner octagon, and the piers on the other sides act as anchor points for the semicircular colonnades supporting the galleries. The dome—ingeniously made of clay pots, fitted into each other, then covered with a timber roof and tiled—is so light that it needed no buttressing and is supported on arches alone. Round-headed arches in the clerestory and the outer aisle light the church, which, despite the later addition of Baroque decoration, retains its subtlety and elegance.

The mosaics of San Vitale depict sacred and secular themes, including the story of Isaac (below) and contemporary mosaic portraits of the Emperor Justinian and his queen, Theodora.

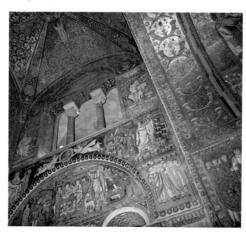

The Arian Baptistry. The mosaic (below) in the dome of the baptistry, built *c.* 500 by Theodoric the Ostrogoth, who ruled Ravenna from 493 to 526, shows Christ being baptized by John the Baptist.

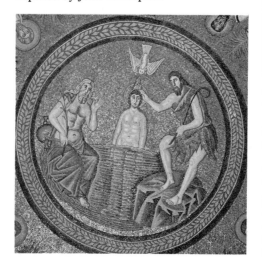

Sant'Apollinare Nuovo (below), a standard basilica except for an unusually high and wide nave, is noted for its fine mosaics. These include scenes from the Life of Christ, a view of the palace of Theodoric, who established the church in 493, and pageant panels from the time of Justinian, who completed the church in 525.

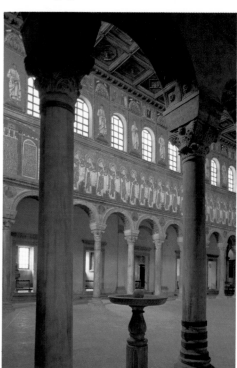

The Mausoleum of Galla Placidia (right), built *c.* 420, is a tiny building, measuring only 33 ft by 39 ft. Yet the interior, a dazzling display of mosaics, gives the illogical impression of being bigger than the outside. The interior walls are faced with marble slabs, and the mosaics, which include figures of the Apostles, St Lawrence suffering on the gridiron and the Good Shepherd with his flock, cover the dome, recesses and barrel vaulting. Still in their original positions are the sarcophagi of Galla Placidia, who ruled in Ravenna from 425 until 450, her husband and her brother, the Emperor Honorius.

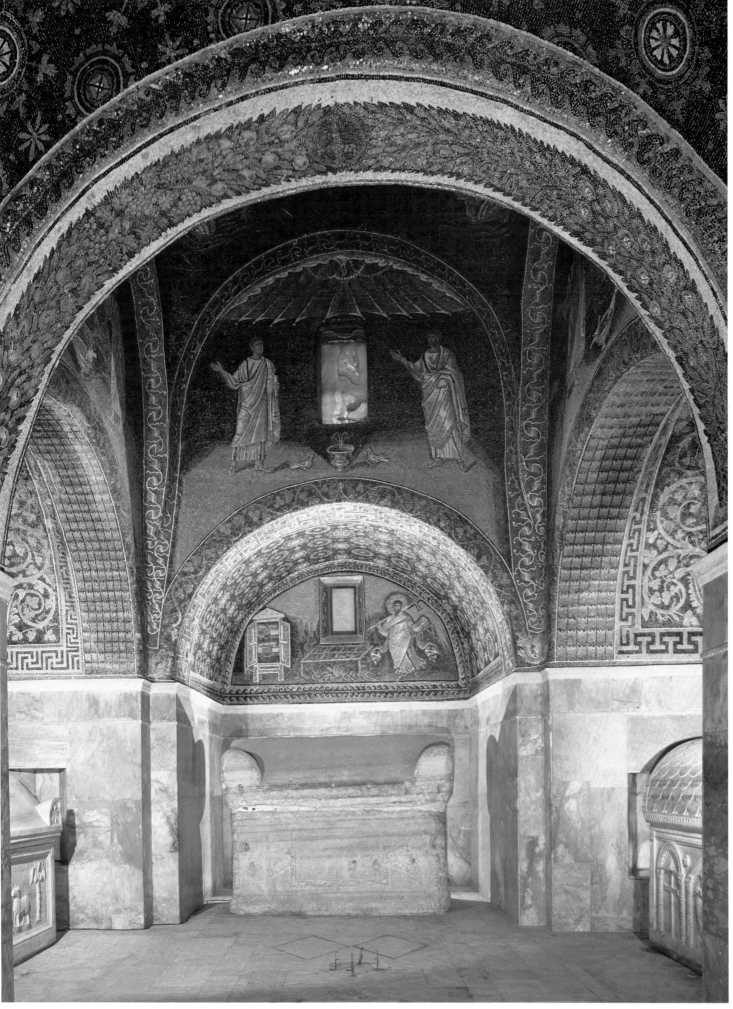

Santa Sophia, masterpiece of an age

IN TERMS OF sheer architectural daring, Santa Sophia, the Great Church of the Holy Wisdom, in Istanbul ranks as one of the most ambitious constructions known to man. No one, not even the Romans at their most vainglorious, had attempted such an enclosure of space; and the two engineers, Isidore of Miletus and Anthemius of Tralles, who in AD 532 were commissioned by the Emperor Justinian to create what was to be in effect the religious focus of his empire, had no practical experience of the problem that confronted them. Yet, on the day after Christmas in 537, Justinian dedicated his new church and, as he did so, murmured the words, "Solomon, I have surpassed thee."

Even ignoring the splendour of the polychrome marble and mosaic decoration—a splendour of which all too little, alas, remains today—the beauty of the building itself still has breathtaking power. The ground plan is almost square, the walls broken by aisles, colonnades and galleries, rising through half-cupolas and four gigantic pendentives to that incredible dome, shallowest of saucers, its diameter only eight feet less than that of St Paul's Cathedral in London. It is a dome, pierced by forty windows, which, in the words of a contemporary, "seemed not to rest upon a

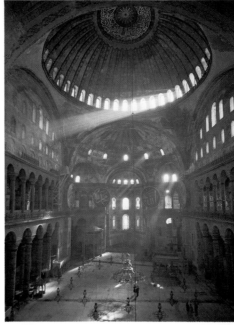

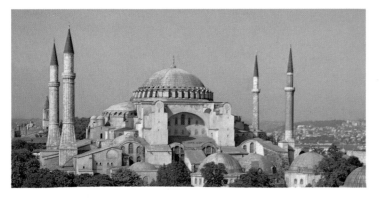

solid foundation, but to cover the place beneath as though it was suspended from heaven by a golden chain".

With the fall of Constantinople to the Turks in 1453, Santa Sophia, like most other churches in the city, became a mosque. Now, sadly secularized, it is a lifeless museum, its point and purpose gone. Many of its perspectives are still bedevilled by the trappings of Islam, many of its mosaics still hidden under layers of Turkish whitewash. No matter. In any age, under any condition, this tremendous building would proclaim its greatness. When it is remembered that it was built in less than six years fourteen centuries ago, the masterpiece becomes a miracle.

Vaulted aisles, 50 ft wide with upper galleries, surround all but the east side of the nave, from which they are separated by a beautiful screen of marble columns.

The interior of S. Sophia (above) is a marvel of space, engineering and the play of light. Nave, aisles and exedrae all open upwards and outwards into vaults and the great dome above.

Sombre and unadorned, the exterior of S. Sophia (left) creates its impact through massiveness and symmetry. The minarets were added after the church was made into a mosque in 1453.

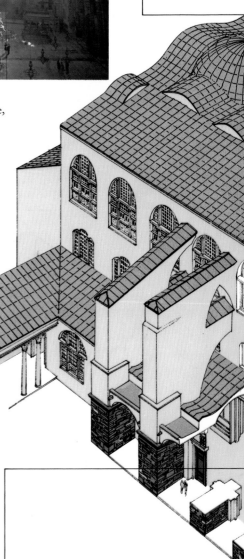

SS. SERGIUS AND BACCHUS, *Constantinople. Built in 527, this church, which slightly predates S. Sophia, is related to it in design. It exploited the beautiful Byzantine concept of the surrounding aisle. The central, domed octagon, just 52 ft across, has small but true pendentives. The dome is built not over a square— that great structural step remained to be taken—but over an octagon.*

S. Sophia is approached by an outer and a main narthex, or porch. The lower storey of the main narthex was used by catechumens and other penitents.

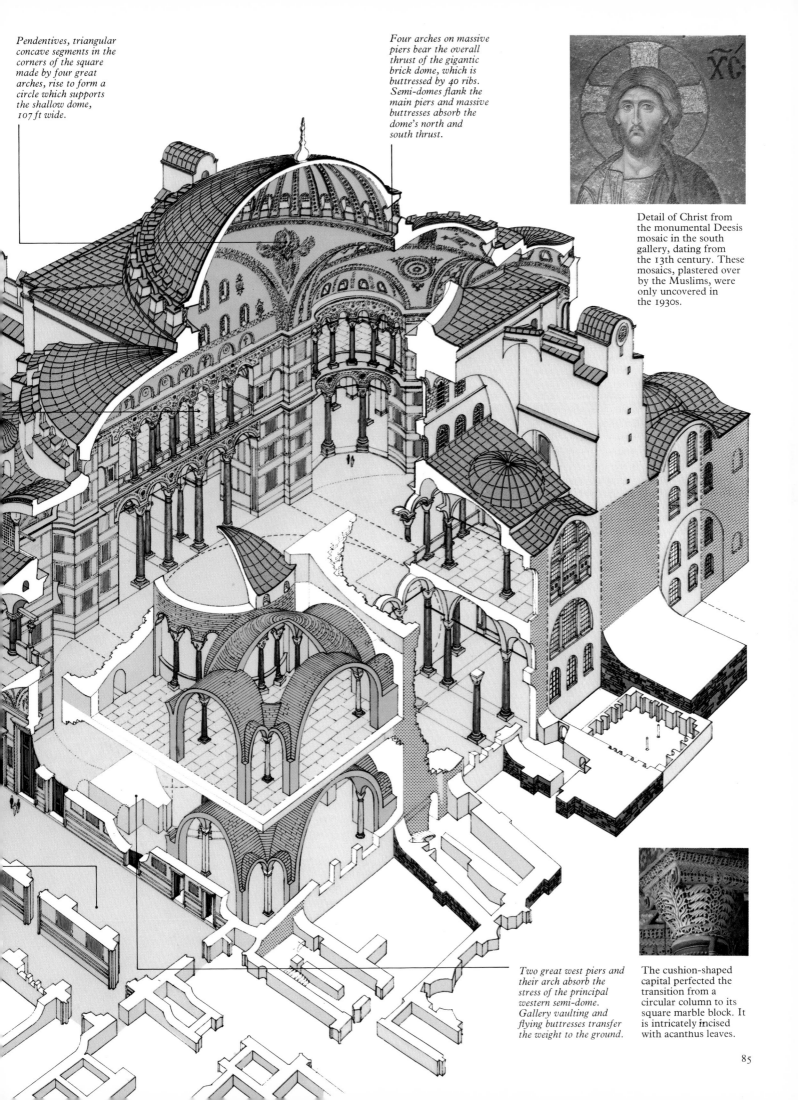

Pendentives, triangular concave segments in the corners of the square made by four great arches, rise to form a circle which supports the shallow dome, 107 ft wide.

Four arches on massive piers bear the overall thrust of the gigantic brick dome, which is buttressed by 40 ribs. Semi-domes flank the main piers and massive buttresses absorb the dome's north and south thrust.

Detail of Christ from the monumental Deesis mosaic in the south gallery, dating from the 13th century. These mosaics, plastered over by the Muslims, were only uncovered in the 1930s.

Two great west piers and their arch absorb the stress of the principal western semi-dome. Gallery vaulting and flying buttresses transfer the weight to the ground.

The cushion-shaped capital perfected the transition from a circular column to its square marble block. It is intricately incised with acanthus leaves.

Greece and the Balkans, the regional styles

FOR FIFTEEN OF the sixteen centuries that Constantinople was capital of a great empire—first the Greek Empire of Byzantium and then, after its fall in 1453, the Ottoman Empire of the Turks—Greece and the Balkans were merely outlying provinces. During the Ottoman days the Greeks, Serbs and Bulgars were also subject peoples, professing a minority religion which, although never persecuted, was obliged to maintain a fairly low profile. It is, therefore, hardly surprising that these lands never produced great architectural *tours de force* on the scale of Santa Sophia, Istanbul, or St Mark's, Venice.

One Greek city, however, preserved its importance throughout the Middle Ages because of its position on the Via Egnatia, the Roman road that crossed the whole peninsula from the Adriatic coast to Constantinople. This city was Salonica, which still boasts some half-dozen churches of great beauty, at least three of them dating from the 5th century. There are fine things at Kastoria, to say nothing of the wonderfully frescoed churches around Lake Ohrid, in South Serbia, and in northern Macedonia

—particularly those at Gračanica, Peć, Dečani and Nerezi. Most remarkable of all—for those of the male sex, since no female has been admitted for over a thousand years—is the peninsula of Mount Athos, whose twenty monasteries and innumerable dependencies still exhale, miraculously, the spirit of Byzantium.

Farther south, at the church of Hosios Loukas near Delphi and, just outside Athens, at the monastery church at Daphni, are the two supreme mosaic cycles, dating respectively from the beginning and the end of the 11th century. Near Athens, too, on the slopes of Hymettus, is another monastery, frescoed this time—the Monastery of Kaisariani, now beautifully replanted and restored. Latest in date, but among the loveliest, are the churches of Mistra, climbing up a remote Peloponnesian hillside, where the 14th-century paintings testify, as eloquently as those of the Chora in Constantinople, to that wonderful late flowering of Byzantine art before the Sultan's janissaries battered down the walls of the capital and the Byzantine Empire perished.

The Church of the Holy Apostles,
Salonica, most magnificent of all the late Greek churches, dates from the early 14th century. Its height is emphasized by the raising of its five domes on drums, with the simultaneous lowering of the roof line of the narthex and side aisles. The mosaics and frescoes in the church are of excellent quality, while the Byzantine decorative brickwork on the exterior of the east end is the finest of its kind anywhere.

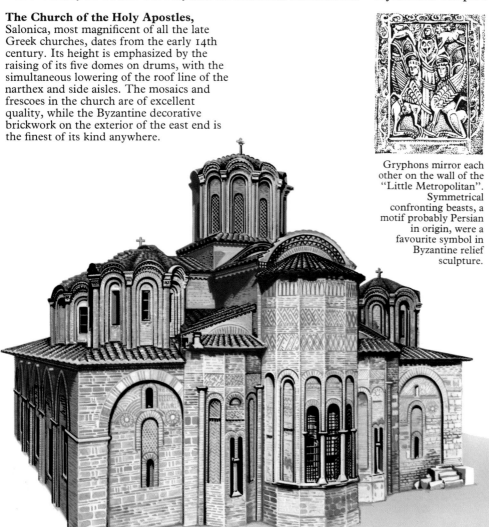

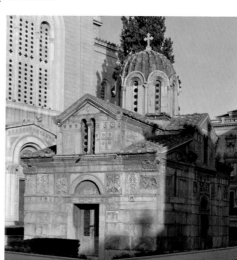

Gryphons mirror each other on the wall of the "Little Metropolitan". Symmetrical confronting beasts, a motif probably Persian in origin, were a favourite symbol in Byzantine relief sculpture.

The "Little Metropolitan" in Athens is perhaps the smallest cathedral in the world. Measuring only 38 ft by about 25 ft, it testifies by its minuteness to the humble state of the city in later Imperial times. Yet it remains a jewel of 13th-century Byzantine architecture, its walls studded with antique marble reliefs, which include a 4th-century BC recital of the zodiac along the west front, Corinthian capitals, Byzantine crosses and even the coat of arms of the Villehardouin family, who held the city of Athens after the Fourth Crusade.

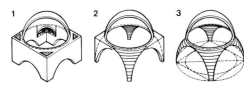

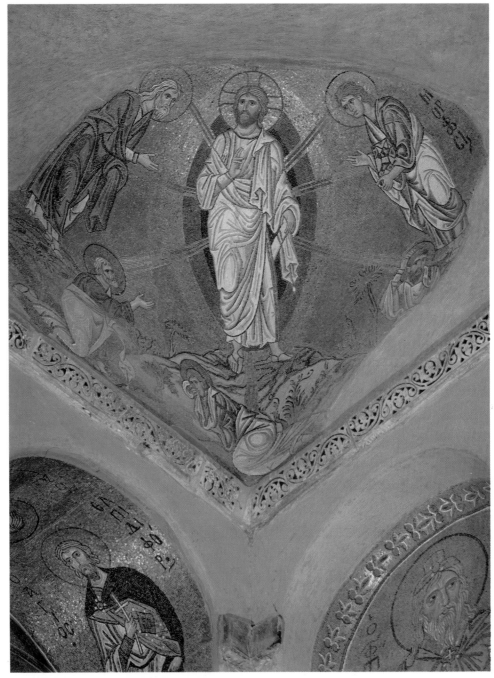

Pendentives solved the problem of placing a dome over a square base (above). A squinch arch built across each corner of the square (1) produces an octagonal base for the dome, but this makes an awkward transition from square to circle. The pendentive, an inverted concave triangle, springs from the corner of the square, curving up and out to meet with the other pendentives (2). The bottom points of these triangles form a square and the tops form a circle (3), allowing a dome to be placed on a circle from a square base. The pendentive arrangement can be seen beneath the dome in the Monastery of Daphni (below). Dome and pendentives (right) are decorated with superlative examples of late 11th-century mosaics.

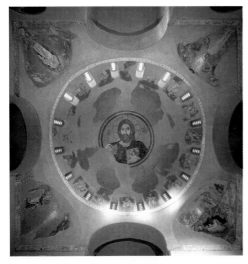

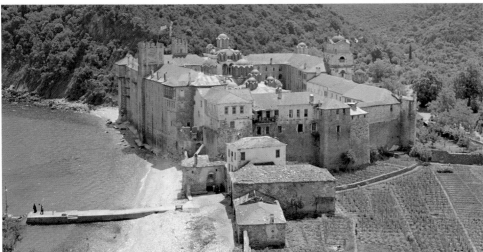

Lake Ohrid, in the southwest corner of modern Yugoslavia, was the principal religious centre of the medieval Serbian Empire before the Turkish conquest. This little church, with its patterned brick exterior, is one of several built here between the 11th and 13th centuries.

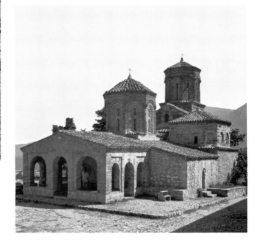

Mount Athos, the Holy Mountain, a 40-mile peninsula in the northeast of Greece, has been an independent monastic community for well over 1,000 years. During this time, access to the Holy Mountain by females, whether human or animal, has been strictly forbidden. Esphigmenou, seen here, is one of the 20 monasteries, each with its own hermitages and dependencies, which govern this mountain settlement.

Armenia, an independent approach

THE KINGDOM of Armenia, remote on the high plateau east of the Euphrates, under the shadow of Mount Ararat, was the first ever to adopt Christianity as a state religion—which it did in 301, nearly seven hundred years before the Christian faith was officially embraced in the emergent Russian Empire. The Armenians were architects of genius. The foremost of them, Trdat, was celebrated enough to be invited to restore the dome of Santa Sophia in Constantinople after its destruction by earthquake. His cathedral at Ani, although Byzantine in its cross-in-rectangle plan and its domed crossing, also possesses clustered piers, pointed arches and a profusion of blind arcading, as do the dozen other churches still standing in ruins on the rolling meadow that is Ani today. But it is no use looking for European influences. Trdat completed his cathedral in 1001, almost a century before such features were generally adopted in the West.

Armenian architects used two other devices that make their churches immediately identifiable. They covered their domes with conical caps and their walls with reliefs—crude perhaps, but lively and curiously endearing. Few nations in the early Middle Ages showed such artistic promise. It is one of the tragedies of history that this promise remained unfulfilled.

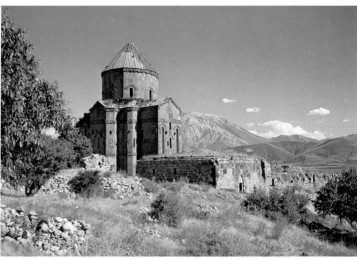

King Gagik's Church. The Armenian Church of the Holy Cross (above) was built by King Gagik of Vaspurakan between 914 and 921, on the island of Aght'amar in Lake Van, now in Turkey. David and Goliath (right) is one of many reliefs, unsophisticated yet full of life and humour, which cover the walls.

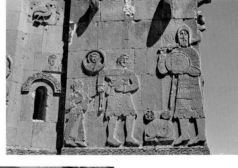

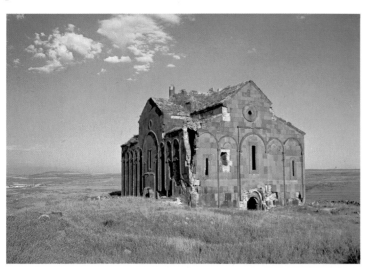

The Cathedral of Ani, once domed, was created by Armenia's greatest architect, Trdat, in 989–1001, almost a century before pointed arches, clustered piers and blind arcading appeared in the West.

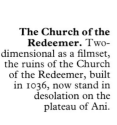

The Church of the Redeemer. Two-dimensional as a filmset, the ruins of the Church of the Redeemer, built in 1036, now stand in desolation on the plateau of Ani.

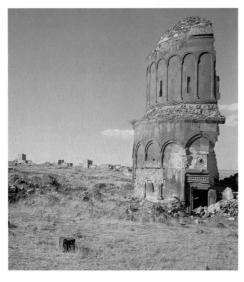

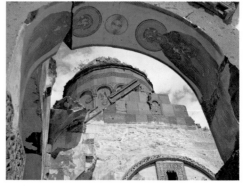

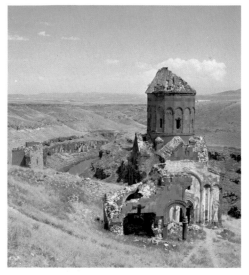

Church of St Gregory. In 961, the Armenian capital was established at Ani, "the city of a thousand churches". Today only a dozen churches remain, all in ruins. One of these, the Church of St Gregory the Illuminator, is poised above the ravine formed by the River Arpa Tchai, which now marks the frontier between Turkey and the Soviet Union. It is the only one to preserve traces of its original frescoes (above left).

Russia's late response

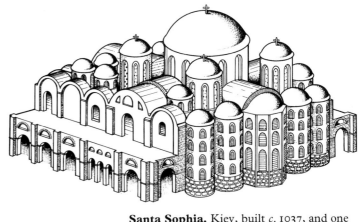

WHEN, IN AD 988, Prince Vladimir of Kiev adopted Christianity for himself and his embryonic empire, he borrowed not only his faith but also his architecture from Constantinople. There was only one drawback: the shallow, saucer-shaped Byzantine domes collapsed under the weight of the snow. The farther north the churches were built, the graver grew the problem; and it was in Novgorod, or possibly Pskov, in the 12th century, that the characteristically Russian onion dome finally took shape. In the 13th century the Mongol invasions cut the country off from Byzantium. From the 14th century the Italian craftsmen called in to work on the Kremlin introduced a flavour of the Renaissance style, an uneasy bedfellow of the Russian Orthodox tradition, that has never been entirely lost.

Santa Sophia, Kiev, built *c.* 1037, and one of the first great Byzantine-inspired churches in Russia, has suffered from both neglect and restoration. This reconstruction shows the original 11th-century building, a brick-domed basilica on the Byzantine pattern. There were five aisles, terminating at the east end in semicircular apses, with open arcading around the other three sides. A striking Russian feature was the construction and arrangement of the 13 domes, representing Christ and the Apostles. During the 17th and 18th centuries, four more aisles and eight extra domes were added in the local Baroque style so that the church today bears little resemblance to the medieval structure.

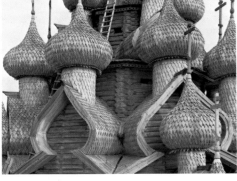

The perfection of wooden architecture in Old Russia is seen in the beautiful church of the Transfiguration, on Kizhi Island, built in 1714. Its magnificent roof, a pyramid of 22 onion-shaped domes, rises over 100 ft high. Each dome and its drum rests on a *bochka*, a roof shaped like a pointed horseshoe, and is covered with intricately carved aspen shingles.

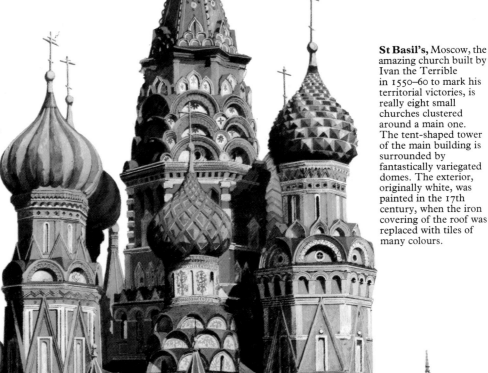

St Basil's, Moscow, the amazing church built by Ivan the Terrible in 1550–60 to mark his territorial victories, is really eight small churches clustered around a main one. The tent-shaped tower of the main building is surrounded by fantastically variegated domes. The exterior, originally white, was painted in the 17th century, when the iron covering of the roof was replaced with tiles of many colours.

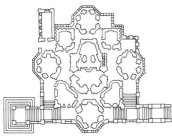

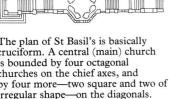

The plan of St Basil's is basically cruciform. A central (main) church is bounded by four octagonal churches on the chief axes, and by four more—two square and two of irregular shape—on the diagonals.

St Mark's, a gilded link with the East

NO ONE COULD ever forget their first sight of St Mark's. Seen from afar, across the length of the Piazza, it seems to smack of some magic palace out of an oriental fairy tale, a pleasure-dome in Xanadu. Even at closer range, when the eye has had time to pick out those Gothic pinnacles, those innumerable statues of saints and angels, those four great horses of bronze and those hideous late-Italian mosaics in the lunettes, it looks anything but Byzantine. The cupolas themselves are somehow wrong. It comes as quite a shock to learn that this incredible building was created in the 11th century by a Greek architect, who drew his inspiration from Justinian's Church of the Holy Apostles in Constantinople.

St Mark's is unlike any other church in the world simply because Venice is unlike any other city. Founded among the lagoon islands in the 5th century AD as a refuge from the barbarians, and thus deliberately cut off from mainland Italy, Venice remained technically part of the Byzantine Empire for five hundred years. Even after she had become an independent republic, she continued to look East rather than West. Later, as her own commercial empire grew, she became Europe's principal crossroads and clearing-house. St Mark's reflects both her double heritage of culture and—dazzlingly—her wealth.

The first church on the site was completed in 832 as a gigantic reliquary for the body of the Evangelist himself, stolen from Alexandria by a couple of enterprising Venetian merchants four years before. The church is embellished with mosaics, mostly Byzantine, many superb. It also shamelessly flaunts much of the loot—including the four horses—deriving from the abominable sack of Constantinople by Venetians and Franks in the so-called Fourth Crusade of 1204–5. Beneath all this exuberant incrustation, however, the 11th-century building has been preserved virtually intact and, once inside the great bronze doors, reveals itself in all its splendour—a painted harlot with a heart of gold.

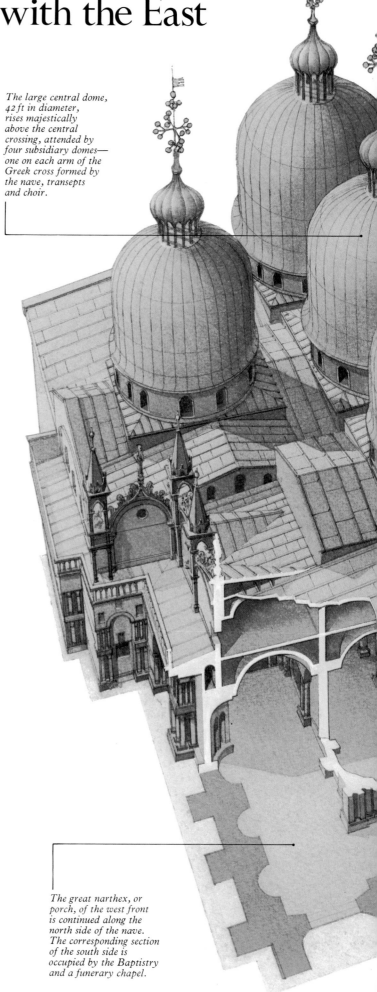

The large central dome, 42 ft in diameter, rises majestically above the central crossing, attended by four subsidiary domes— one on each arm of the Greek cross formed by the nave, transepts and choir.

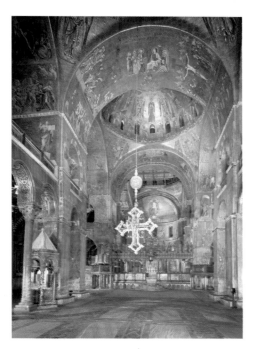

The cavernous interior of St Mark's, rising to almost 100 ft under the central dome, shimmers and glows with an unbroken expanse of mosaic, spreading over the walls, arches, piers and domes. The mosaics date from many different periods. Those of the 12th to 14th centuries— almost certainly executed by craftsmen brought from Constantinople—are among the finest in the Byzantine world.

The great narthex, or porch, of the west front is continued along the north side of the nave. The corresponding section of the south side is occupied by the Baptistry and a funerary chapel.

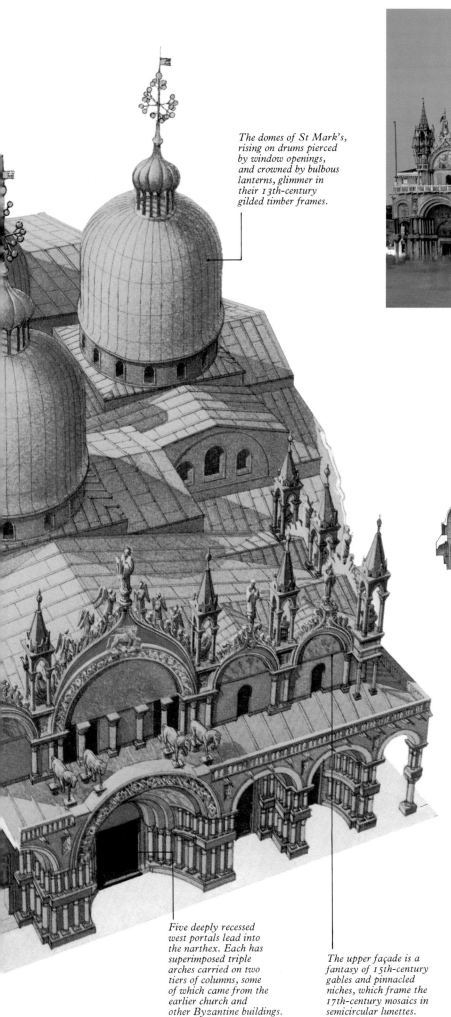

The domes of St Mark's, rising on drums pierced by window openings, and crowned by bulbous lanterns, glimmer in their 13th-century gilded timber frames.

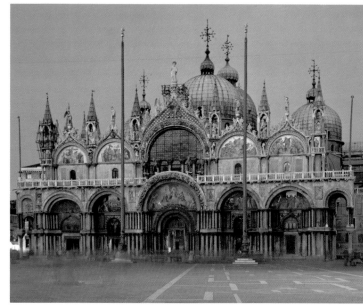

St Mark's Square, essentially an open-air atrium to the church, was described by Napoleon as "the greatest *salon* of Europe".

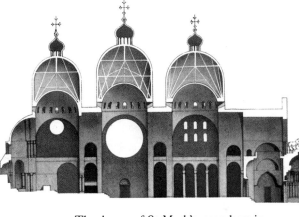

The domes of St Mark's, seen here in section, rise above a typical late Byzantine, Greek cross structure. Remodelled in the 11th century, on the pattern of Justinian's Church of the Holy Apostles in Constantinople, the present church stands on the site of a 9th-century basilica.

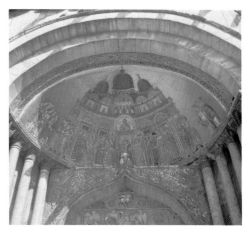

This 13th-century mosaic above the Porta di Sant'Alipio shows St Mark's body being transported to its new shrine. The church as it was *c.* 1210 can be seen in the background, unencumbered by Gothic pinnacles and Renaissance enrichments, but already flaunting the four bronze horses looted from Constantinople in 1205.

Five deeply recessed west portals lead into the narthex. Each has superimposed triple arches carried on two tiers of columns, some of which came from the earlier church and other Byzantine buildings.

The upper façade is a fantasy of 15th-century gables and pinnacled niches, which frame the 17th-century mosaics in semicircular lunettes.

A light in Europe's Dark Ages

THE FIVE HUNDRED years that followed the building of San Vitale at Ravenna in the mid-6th century were the doldrums of western architecture. In Italy, despite successive waves of barbarian invasion and the resultant political chaos, churches continued to be built, but they kept closely to the old basilican model. Throughout the period, only one ruler of incontestable greatness appeared on the European scene: Charlemagne, King from 768 and Emperor from 800 to 814. Just as Charlemagne overshadowed his fellow princes, so Carolingian architecture, the style named after him, which extended into the 10th century, produced almost the only noteworthy buildings of these years. Although these buildings were derivative, the sources of their inspiration are not always clear. At Santa Maria de Naranco, near Orviedo in Spain, the fluted buttresses murmur of Rome, but the airy lightness within hints unmistakably that Islam was not far away. Similarly, the beauty of the little church of Germigny-des-Prés near Orléans has been variously ascribed to Spanish, Byzantine and even Armenian influences.

Of the principal monument still extant, however, Charlemagne's own palace chapel at Aachen, there can be no doubt. It is unblushingly based on San Vitale itself, but is plainer and sturdier—more suited, in fact, to the tastes of this semi-literate Frankish soldier–administrator, whose energy and genius left him little time for excesses of Greek refinement. Only one secular Carolingian work survives—the gatehouse at Lorsch, in the Rhineland, one of Charlemagne's favourite monasteries. With its arches evoking Ancient Rome and its zigzag arcading, it shows that Carolingian architecture, however transitional and eclectic, could still boast a grace of its own.

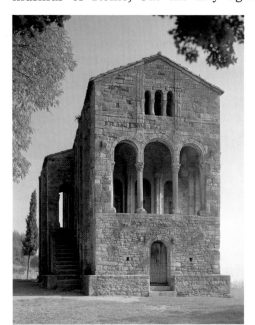

The Church of Santa Maria de Naranco (left), built *c.*848, was once a royal chapel. A tiny, oblong hall set over a crypt, it had a short, projecting arm on each side. The south arm, now gone, probably housed the altar and the north arm contains the entrance. This odd lay-out, like that of a Germanic palace hall, turned the body of the church into a wide, east–west transept for king and court. The populace outside followed the liturgy through open arcades at each end.

The gatehouse at Lorsch (below) in West Germany, built *c.*800, and all that remains of the monastery here, is a small essay in that curious mixture of local styles and Roman classical revivalism which typifies Carolingian architecture. Its masonry technique is derived from antique Roman methods, and the three round arches, separated by engaged columns topped with carved, composite capitals, recall the triumphal arches of the Roman Forum. The pattern-work, especially that of the pointed-arch blind arcading, suggests adaptation from wooden prototypes.

The Church of San Riquier at Abbeville in France, begun *c.*790 but later destroyed, was the earliest known Carolingian double-sanctuaried church. The forerunner of many future churches, its most influential feature was the tower-like "westwork"—an outer porch, flanked by stair-turrets leading to a chapel over the vaulted inner porch.

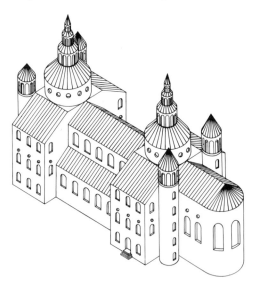

The monastic Church of St Michael at Hildesheim (below), begun *c.*1001, was planned by its bishop, Bernward. Its twin transepts, double aisles and double apses greatly influenced later, Romanesque churches in Germany. Another much-copied feature was the entrance in the south aisle. The church was severely damaged in World War II, but has since been restored to its original design.

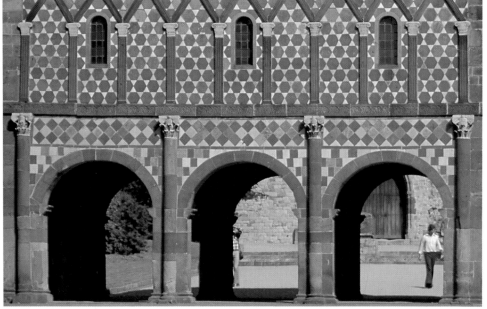

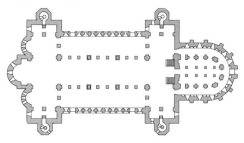

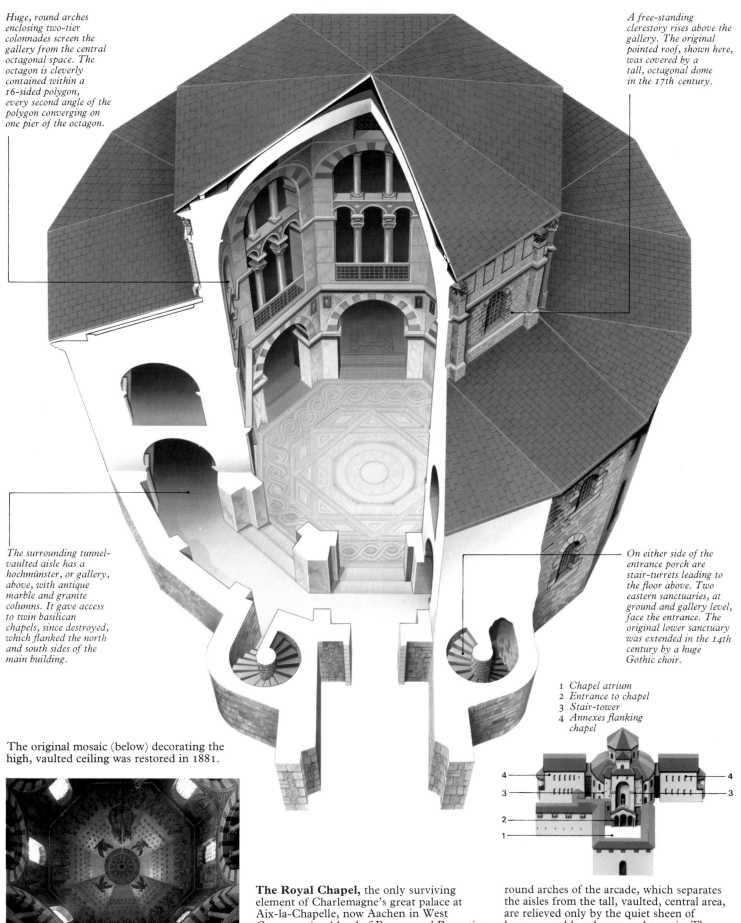

Huge, round arches enclosing two-tier colonnades screen the gallery from the central octagonal space. The octagon is cleverly contained within a 16-sided polygon, every second angle of the polygon converging on one pier of the octagon.

A free-standing clerestory rises above the gallery. The original pointed roof, shown here, was covered by a tall, octagonal dome in the 17th century.

The surrounding tunnel-vaulted aisle has a hochmünster, or gallery, above, with antique marble and granite columns. It gave access to twin basilican chapels, since destroyed, which flanked the north and south sides of the main building.

On either side of the entrance porch are stair-turrets leading to the floor above. Two eastern sanctuaries, at ground and gallery level, face the entrance. The original lower sanctuary was extended in the 14th century by a huge Gothic choir.

1 *Chapel atrium*
2 *Entrance to chapel*
3 *Stair-tower*
4 *Annexes flanking chapel*

The original mosaic (below) decorating the high, vaulted ceiling was restored in 1881.

The Royal Chapel, the only surviving element of Charlemagne's great palace at Aix-la-Chapelle, now Aachen in West Germany, is a blend of Roman and Byzantine influences. Its excellent construction techniques are Roman, as is much of the stone fabric, for which Ancient Roman ruins were looted. The design was derived from San Vitale in Ravenna, but the lightness and elegance of the Italian church is missing in this sombre, solid building. The heavy square piers and round arches of the arcade, which separates the aisles from the tall, vaulted, central area, are relieved only by the quiet sheen of bronze, marble columns and mosaic. The chapel is intact, despite subsequent restorations. Dedicated in 805, it was designed by Odo of Metz as both palace chapel and a mausoleum for Charlemagne. It has always had cathedral status and was used between 936 and 1531 for the coronations of 30 German kings.

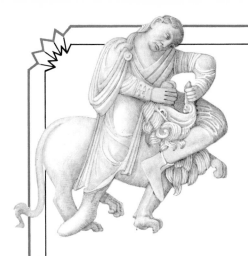

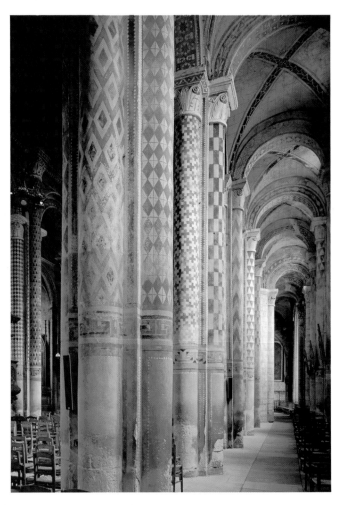

The interior of the 12th-century
Church of Notre Dame La Grande, at
Poitiers, is a dazzling reminder that
many great Romanesque churches were
once radiant with colour and light.

The term Romanesque is used here to describe
the style of architecture which arose in western
Europe towards the end of the 9th century and
which lasted until the rise of Gothic in the 12th.
Any appreciation of the Romanesque style is hardly
found before our own century. In the 18th, it was
fashionable to dismiss all the medieval arts with a
patronizing smile, while even in the 19th century,
Romanesque architecture was widely regarded
as a mere prologue to the study of Gothic. The
truth is that the age of Romanesque, like any era of
struggle towards an ideal, was one of vigour and
sincerity. As a definition, the word Romanesque,
which originated in the 19th century, is somewhat
misleading, for it suggests a style derived solely
from Ancient Rome. Although there are important
affinities linking it with Rome, Romanesque was
a compound of many influences—Roman, Byzantine,
Carolingian and Ottonian, Viking, Celtic, Saracenic.

The principal countries in which Romanesque
architecture flourished were France, England,
Italy, Germany and Spain. In all these countries
political conditions were in a state of turbulence;
the southern half of Spain was still in the hands
of the Moors. Such absence of political unity,
combined with other factors—widespread
illiteracy, small and scattered populations and poor
communications—favoured the evolution of local
styles so divergent, even within a single country,
that it is sometimes a problem to determine whether
or not all of them may be accurately described as
Romanesque. These variations, heightened by
differences in climate and building materials, all
help to make the Romanesque style such a
fascinating field of study. Yet the architecture and
art of this period is unified by certain characteristics
of a distinctly international flavour. This is
because its greatest patron was the Christian
Church. Most of the peoples of western and

Romanesque

central Europe by now professed the same faith, and Latin, the language of the Church, was freely understood by most Europeans of any education.

Within the Church itself, the monastic orders were the dominant force until the middle of the 12th century. It was they, almost alone, who championed intellectual and artistic life. Not that the great founders of the various monastic orders, men like St Benedict and St Bernard, were devotees of the arts; on the contrary, they tended to preserve an ascetic aloofness from such sensuous delights. Only as their coffers filled and their outlook broadened did many of the monks begin to realize that there could be no better way of honouring their Creator than by building fine churches and adorning them with sculptures and paintings.

The Romanesque style probably appeared first in Italy, in Lombardy, late in the 9th century. The Abbey of Cluny, the cradle of Benedictine monasticism in France, was originally founded in 910, but it was only in the first half of the 11th century that church-building in western Europe really gained momentum. There was a widely held belief that either the year 1000, the thousandth anniversary of the birth of Christ, or 1033, that of His Crucifixion, would mark the Second Coming of Christ and the end of the world. When both these anniversaries passed without mishap, there was general relief. Before long, in the words of Ralph Glaber, the Cluniac chronicler, "it was as though the very world had shaken itself, and, casting off her old age, was clothing herself everywhere in a white robe of churches". (White, because much of the limestone used was pale, while dark stone was usually given a coat of limewash.)

Who undertook the task of building these churches? Certainly not the monks, who, when they were artists, generally devoted themselves to gentler, more sedentary activities, like book-illumination, ivory carving and embroidery—the arts of the cloister. The monasteries were erected by stone-masons, unlettered men, most of whom were no more than ordinary workmen, hired by the monks to do the job. Architecture was classified as one of the mechanical arts. Not one of the seven liberal arts, it ranked with sculpture, painting, harness-making, carpentry, cobbling, pot-making and navigation. Its practitioners were men of decidedly inferior social status, which is why there is such scant biographical material about them; their achievements, however astonishing, were not considered to be worth recording. Nothing could have been wider than the gulf separating abbots, the most learned men of their time, from artists, who were completely under monastic control.

Christian influence was omnipresent. In Romanesque architecture, this is seen, so obviously, in the cruciform plan, the bell-tower and the cloister. In sculpture and in painting the subject matter of every artist's work was preordained by religious requirements. It was Christianity that imbued the arts with that element of mysticism so foreign to the work of the Romans, which preceded it. Christianity inspired all the symbolism in Romanesque art, as well as its elaborate iconography.

The architecture makes a brave story, one of faith and courage to build anew in the face of continual disasters from fire and faulty building technique, to say nothing of the havoc wrought by pillage and by acts of war. Architecturally, it was an age of unceasing experiment, so that, despite affinities of detail, few buildings of this period resemble one another very closely as a whole. It stands to reason, too, that few, if any, of the great Romanesque buildings have survived unaltered. Yet in all the principal countries there are some which preserve their Romanesque qualities to a remarkable degree.

France, cradle of great abbey churches

THE GREAT PERIOD of French Romanesque architecture was the hundred years between 1050 and 1150. Because at this time France was still split into a number of quite independent domains, it may seem surprising to find even a comparatively unified architectural character. The explanation lies in the cult of relics, which distinguishes this intensely credulous age. It induced people to move about the country, and indeed well beyond it, on pilgrimages. The pedigrees of these relics were usually dubious, but people were willing to believe in them. This blind faith made possible the erection of huge buildings, generally abbeys, the scale of which far exceeded local needs.

Great churches like Vézelay and Conques were constructed to accommodate the continuous influx of pilgrims, whose offerings provided the principal source of finance. The earlier of these churches tend to be plain and austere, while the later ones often exhibit an abundance of sculptural enrichment, the original function of which was didactic rather than decorative.

Among the various regions Burgundy, the cradle of the great monastic foundations of the Cluniacs and the Cistercians, is of particular interest. Of equal importance is the southwest, where the churches at Conques, Moissac and Souillac are among the highlights. The churches of Aquitaine are especially notable for the exuberance of their surface sculpture. Other regions with individual styles of Romanesque architecture are the Massif Central, Provence and Normandy.

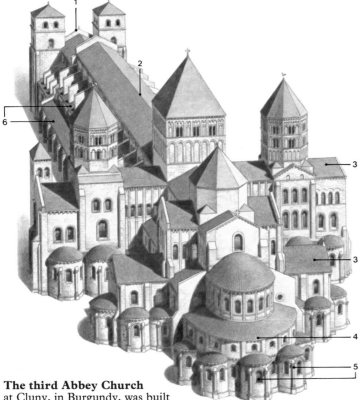

The third Abbey Church
at Cluny, in Burgundy, was built 1088–1130 and wantonly demolished in 1810. The longest church in France, it had massive walls, an immense nave, double aisles, twin transepts and many chapels and towers. Part of the greatest abbey in Christendom, it inspired many subsequent churches.

1 *West porch*
2 *Nave*
3 *Transepts*
4 *Ambulatory*
5 *Radiating chapels*
6 *Double aisles*

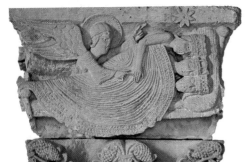

This carved capital in Autun Cathedral in Burgundy is one of many that crown the columns of the nave and great west porch. The sleeping Magi are gently awakened by an angel, who indicates the rising Star of Bethlehem. The sculptures here, executed c. 1125, are similar in treatment and theme to those which once existed at Cluny.

Sainte Madeleine (below) at Vezelay, in Burgundy, a beautiful Cluniac pilgrimage church, was built between c. 1089 and 1206. Its great and disciplined nave, nearly 200 ft long, has unusually high vaulting. Such proportions, and the elegance of the Gothic choir beyond, give the interior a lightness and gaiety which is heightened by the pink and grey bands of the massive nave arches. These mark the bays of the nave and divide each groin vault above. The nave is entered through a magnificently carved portal, leading from a wide west porch, where pilgrims were marshalled for processions.

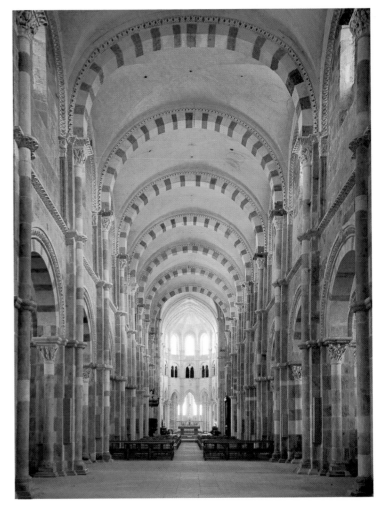

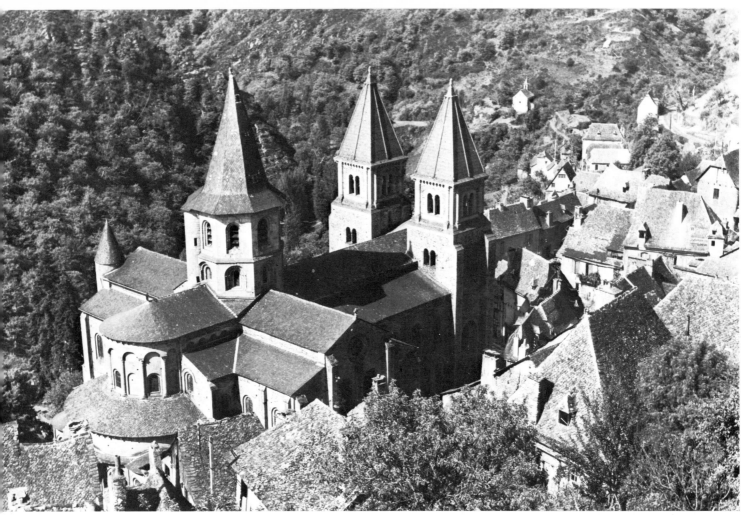

The Church of Sainte Foy (above) nestles in rural seclusion in a valley at Conques, in southern France. Built between *c.* 1050 and 1130, S. Foy was one of the great abbey churches along the pilgrimage route which led to the renowned medieval shrine of St James at Santiago de Compostela in Spain. Although the smallest of the group, it contains all the essential features of a pilgrimage church. Large windows and a tall, spacious nave and sanctuary accommodated the volume of air needed by throngs of pilgrims and provided perfect acoustics for the accompanying Roman chant. The church was constructed throughout in stone to lessen the fire hazard from the flaming torches which lit the interior.

To enable pilgrims to circulate with ease, the plan of S. Foy (below) was designed with a beautiful system of continuous aisles. These bound the nave and extend into the transepts, which are thus greatly widened. An aisle, encircling the apse at the east end of the church, opens outwards into small chapels, in the typically French Romanesque development known as the chevet.

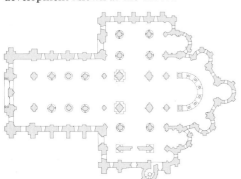

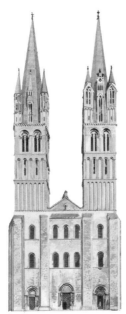

Saint Etienne (above), the celebrated church of William the Conqueror's Abbaye-aux-Hommes, stands grandly, but bereft of its abbey buildings, on the outskirts of Caen, in Normandy. Founded by William *c.* 1068, it typifies the great early Norman churches, which influenced Norman architecture in England, southern Italy and Sicily. The simple west façade has two Norman towers, which were unusually high even before they acquired their delicate, 14th-century Gothic spires. Shallow buttresses dividing the façade echo the interior division of nave and aisles, each of which has its own fine portal.

The fine nave of S. Etienne (right), long and lofty, is divided along its length by a rich and typically Norman three-tier system of arches. The arcades separating nave and aisles are topped by an arcaded triforium, or gallery, above which are the arches of the clerestory.

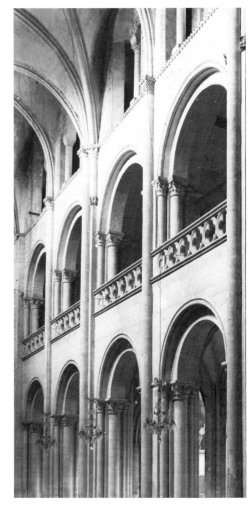

England, the Saxon and Norman phases

AT THE TIME of the Norman Conquest in 1066, England had been Christian for a little more than four hundred years. Among the survivals of those few centuries are some remarkable works of art—the Northumbrian stone crosses and book illuminations, Anglo–Saxon embroidery, sculpture and more manuscripts. Less is known about the best Anglo–Saxon architecture because, with the exception of Brixworth Church in Northamptonshire, the larger churches have all perished.

The Normans initiated the second phase of English Romanesque architecture, generally called "Norman" after the dynasty established by William the Conqueror. They soon launched an ambitious building programme. This predominantly monastic enterprise, which produced some of the largest, and longest, churches in Europe, received the active encouragement of the early Norman kings. The extremely long naves at such cathedrals as Winchester, Ely and Norwich were built because these cathedral churches were also Benedictine abbeys. The entire eastern part of the churches was the preserve of the monks. The laity, with their own altar before the rood screen, were restricted to the nave, which inevitably grew larger. The east end was usually apsidal, as in France, but not many Anglo–Norman apses survive. Stone vaults—highly desirable as a precaution against fire and by the 12th century used throughout major churches in Normandy—were still the exception in England. The arcade piers in these churches are sometimes composite, but are more often just huge cylinders, which, although often imposing, create aesthetic problems at the point of transition with the arches.

Except at Exeter, where the Norman towers crown the transepts, almost all these big churches had central towers, and some had, at the west, an additional pair—a glorious extravagance, as the purpose of a tower was to house the bells, for which only one tower was necessary. Many Norman towers later collapsed.

Norwich Cathedral was begun at the east end in 1096. The nave, not started until c. 1121, accommodated both the Benedictine monks and the laity. Norwich boasts at its crossing one of England's few intact Norman towers.

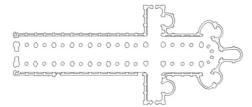

Peterborough Cathedral (below), once a great Benedictine abbey church, was begun by the monks in 1117. Unlike most other Romanesque cathedrals, its nave, begun about 28 years later, was never subsequently vaulted. It is among the finest in Romanesque architecture. Long and stately, its superb arcading of creamy-white Barnack stone is offset by a high, elaborately painted wooden ceiling, now carefully restored.

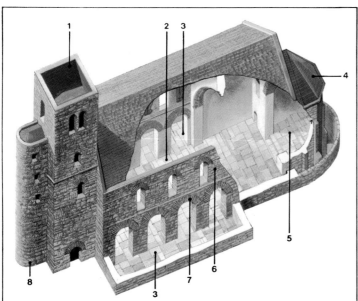

ALL SAINTS' CHURCH AT BRIXWORTH
Founded c. 670, it is the most ambitious surviving Anglo–Saxon church. An apsed basilica, it was built with powerful nave arcades—now walled up but still visible—and arched clerestory windows above. This evidence of the systematic use of arches by Saxon masons is perhaps the most significant and revealing aspect of the church. The aisles and the triple arcade separating nave and chancel have gone, and there are many later modifications. These include a 10th-century turret staircase beyond the west tower and a 14th-century spire.

1 *West tower*
2 *Nave*
3 *Aisles*
4 *Apse*
5 *Chancel*
6 *Clerestory*
7 *Nave arcading*
8 *Stair-turret*

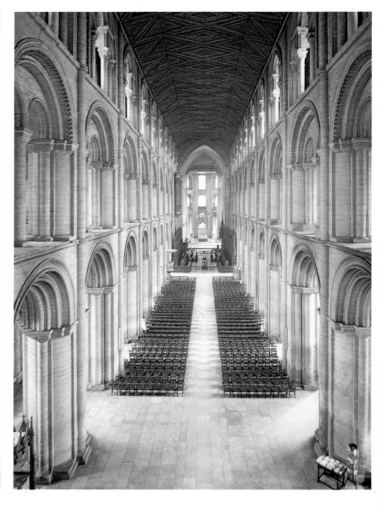

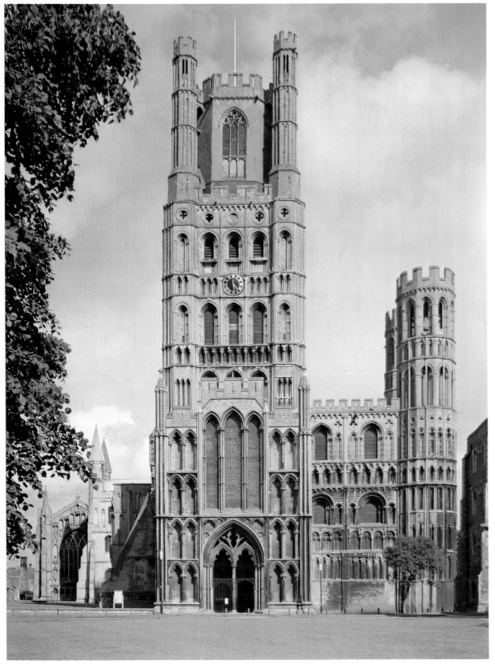

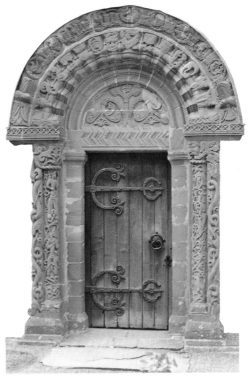

The richly carved south door of the Church of SS. Mary and David at Kilpeck in Herefordshire is its most interesting feature: flowers, fruit, serpents, soldiers and dragons intertwine in a strange fusion of motifs, not traceable to any Norman source. Small and almost perfectly preserved, the church was built *c.* 1145. Inside, the carving on the chancel arch recalls that in the Church of St James at Santiago in Spain.

Ely Cathedral (left), begun *c.* 1090, boasts a splendid and unusual west front formed by a second, western transept with a lofty central tower which spans the entire width of the nave. The north arm of the transept collapsed in the 15th century and was, sadly, never replaced. In the 13th century a porch was added in front of the tower, which was crowned with an octagon and turrets in the next century. Among the delights of the west front are its carved decoration and the imaginative use of blind arcades.

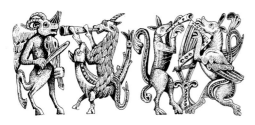

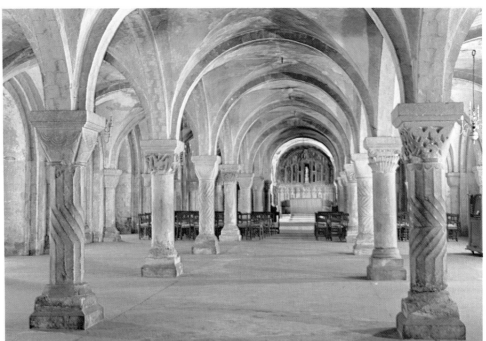

The crypt of Canterbury Cathedral (right) survived the fire of 1174 which destroyed most of the Norman church, begun *c.* 1070. The largest crypt in England, its powerful groin-vaulting is carried on sturdy columns, some of their capitals carved with the liveliest of Romanesque sculpture. One of the best (above) shows fantastic musical beasts: a hybrid ram-woman plays a primitive violin, accompanied on the recorder by a goat who struggles with a dragon. These carvings are inspired in their splendidly decorative interpretation of textures and their skilful adaptation to the shape of the capitals.

Durham, a pioneer of vaulted grandeur

ENGLAND IS fortunate to possess, in the Anglo–Norman Cathedral of Durham, one of the world's supreme masterpieces of Romanesque architecture. Even in the beauty and drama of its situation it is almost unrivalled, for it straddles a lofty sandstone bluff around which the River Wear, flowing through a wooded gorge, describes an elongated horseshoe. The neck of this peninsula faces towards Scotland, once the source of potential danger, from which it was protected by the powerful Norman castle of the prince–bishops. From several directions, views of the cathedral are magnificent. The best are from the Prebends' Bridge to the southwest and from the hill opposite.

Begun in 1093, the cathedral was built mainly in the 12th century and its west towers were completed by 1220. After this, the most significant changes were the replacement of the Norman apsidal east end by the Chapel of the Nine Altars, started in 1242 and completed in 1280, and the rebuilding, between 1465 and 1490, of the central tower, which had been struck by lightning in 1429.

The impression on entering the cathedral is one of overwhelming grandeur. The lofty nave arcading is borne on alternating composite and circular piers. The circular piers have boldly incised patterns: the chevron, the diaper and the vertical flute. Above the aisles is a deep tribune or gallery that harbours flying buttresses, which date from 1133—the earliest in England. And then the eye lights upon the vaults. Durham Cathedral was the first building in Europe to have ribbed vaults throughout, and one of the earliest to have pointed transverse arches in the nave. Although such features are more usually associated with Gothic building, the spirit at Durham is not in the smallest degree Gothic. The cathedral was also a great Benedictine abbey and most of its former monastic buildings survive.

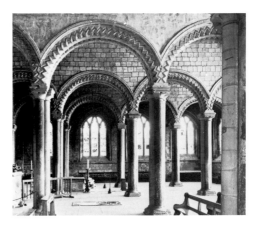

The unusual situation of the Lady Chapel, also known as the Galilee, is traditionally attributed to the misogyny of St Cuthbert, the 8th-century saint who lies enshrined in the crypt beneath the altar. Each time building began at the east end, his ghostly intervention caused the foundations to collapse. In 1170, the chapel was placed far away, beyond the west porch.

The lower stages of the western towers preserve much of their Romanesque character, as do parts of the nave, choir and the east and west walls of the large transept. The rest of the exterior incorporates many Gothic features.

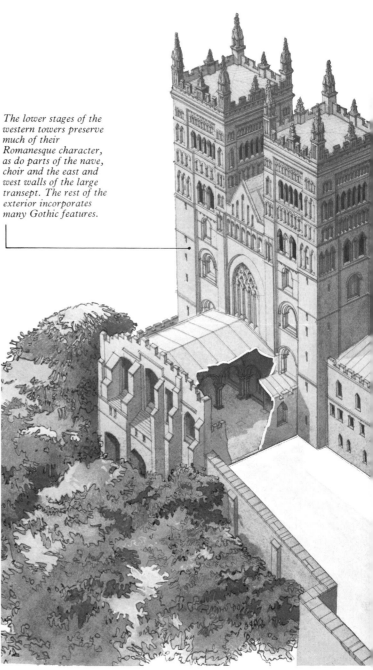

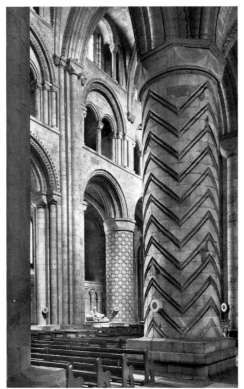

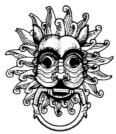

The bronze sanctuary knocker on the door of the north transept is a superlative and highly stylized piece of Romanesque sculpture. The eye sockets were originally decorated with coloured enamel, long since worn away.

Massive circular piers, alternating in the nave with clustered piers, are boldly incised with splendidly barbaric decorative motifs. These include the chequered diaper and the chevron, popular in England throughout the 12th century.

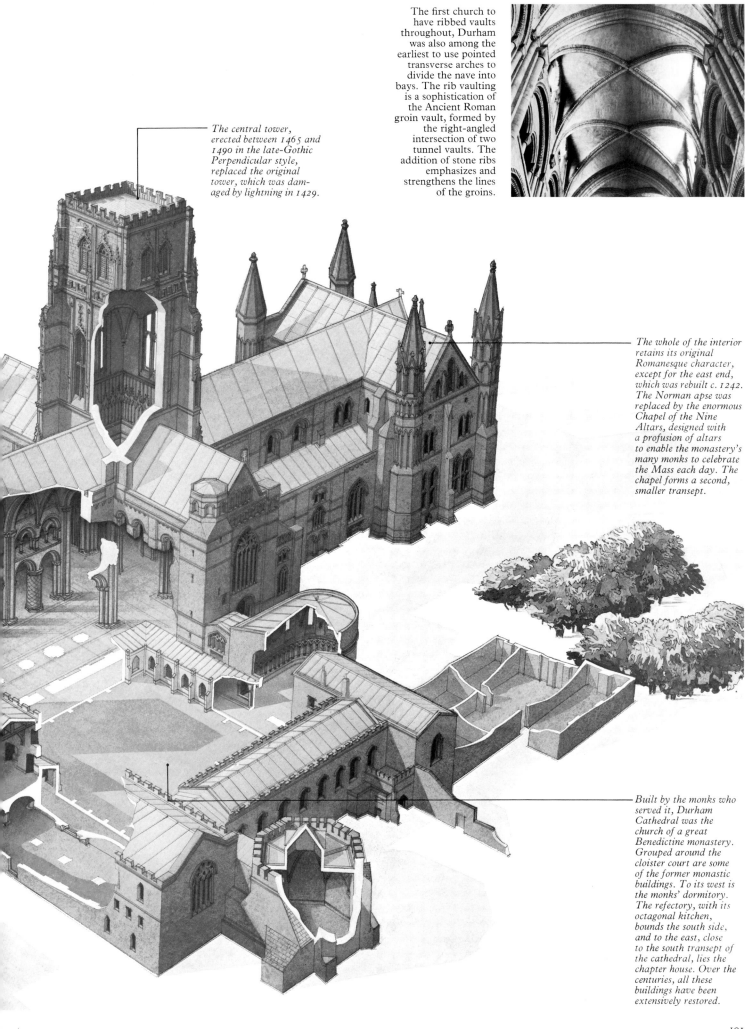

The central tower, erected between 1465 and 1490 in the late-Gothic Perpendicular style, replaced the original tower, which was damaged by lightning in 1429.

The first church to have ribbed vaults throughout, Durham was also among the earliest to use pointed transverse arches to divide the nave into bays. The rib vaulting is a sophistication of the Ancient Roman groin vault, formed by the right-angled intersection of two tunnel vaults. The addition of stone ribs emphasizes and strengthens the lines of the groins.

The whole of the interior retains its original Romanesque character, except for the east end, which was rebuilt c. 1242. The Norman apse was replaced by the enormous Chapel of the Nine Altars, designed with a profusion of altars to enable the monastery's many monks to celebrate the Mass each day. The chapel forms a second, smaller transept.

Built by the monks who served it, Durham Cathedral was the church of a great Benedictine monastery. Grouped around the cloister court are some of the former monastic buildings. To its west is the monks' dormitory. The refectory, with its octagonal kitchen, bounds the south side, and to the east, close to the south transept of the cathedral, lies the chapter house. Over the centuries, all these buildings have been extensively restored.

Italy, synthesis of sunlight and marble

ROMANESQUE architecture can be seen throughout Italy, although the style never won general acceptance: it scarcely penetrated into Rome; Venice adhered to the Byzantine mode and Sicily admitted several other important influences. Yet there are many Italian Romanesque churches with great appeal. A special feature is the external adornment of the walls. Their bare surfaces are articulated by means of shallow pilasters, known as "Lombard bands", that are linked at the top by a succession of small corbelled arches. This is already evident in the earliest Italian Romanesque churches, which date from the closing years of the 9th century.

Several important churches date from the 11th century, but it was in the following century that the Romanesque style enjoyed a magnificent flowering. The bright light, in combination with a profusion of the finest marbles, made possible effects of astonishing brilliance, as can be seen at Pisa, Lucca and Pavia. Even where, as was often the case, the basic material was brick, as at Milan and Murano, the external enrichment of the walls is still striking. At Florence, the church of San Miniato al Monte established a fashion for patterned wall surfaces in contrasting colours —here white marble and the dark green stone known as *verde antico*. In Apulia, the age-old Byzantine domination of the south of Italy ended in 1071 with the capture of Bari by the Normans. The oldest and most important church here is the fine white limestone basilica of San Nicola at Bari, which was begun in 1087.

In Italy, as in England, Romanesque churches with high vaults are unusual—most have trussed rafter roofs. The canopies of porches frequently rest on the backs of lions or other beasts, whose origin and significance remain, to this day, a mystery.

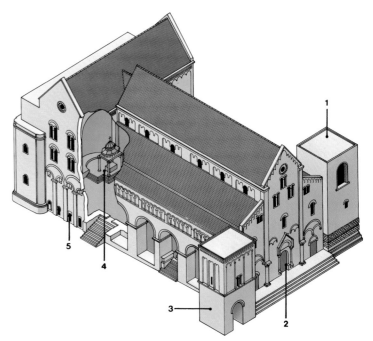

The Church of San Nicola at Bari is dedicated to St Nicholas, Bishop of Myra, more familiar as Santa Claus. To house his relics, a large vaulted crypt was built beneath the raised chancel. A wooden-roofed basilica, built between 1087 and 1197, the church has a west façade bounded by two towers, one Lombardic, the other semi-oriental in appearance. The columns of the porch rest on the backs of beasts, reputedly oxen, a popular Italian feature.

1 *Semi-oriental tower*
2 *Porch*
3 *Lombard tower*
4 *Raised chancel*
5 *Position of crypt*

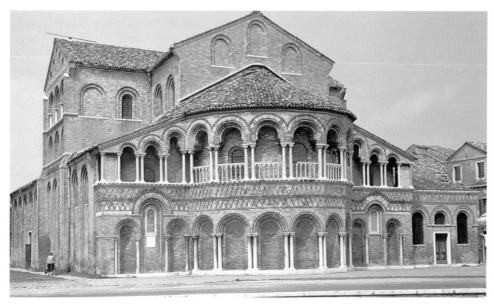

The Cathedral of SS. Maria and Donato, on the island of Murano in the Lagoon of Venice, was completed *c.* 1140. Although it is the most Romanesque of Venetian buildings, this cruciform church, built of brick, retains a distinctly Byzantine flavour. The east end, shown here, has a beautiful arcaded and galleried apse.

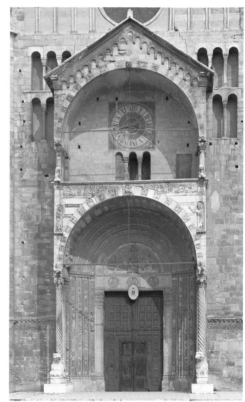

The 12th-century Cathedral of Verona (right) was almost entirely remodelled in the 15th century, except for the Lombardic Romanesque west front. The canopy above its porch is supported by free-standing columns, which rest on the backs of carved stone lions. The origin of these beasts remains uncertain.

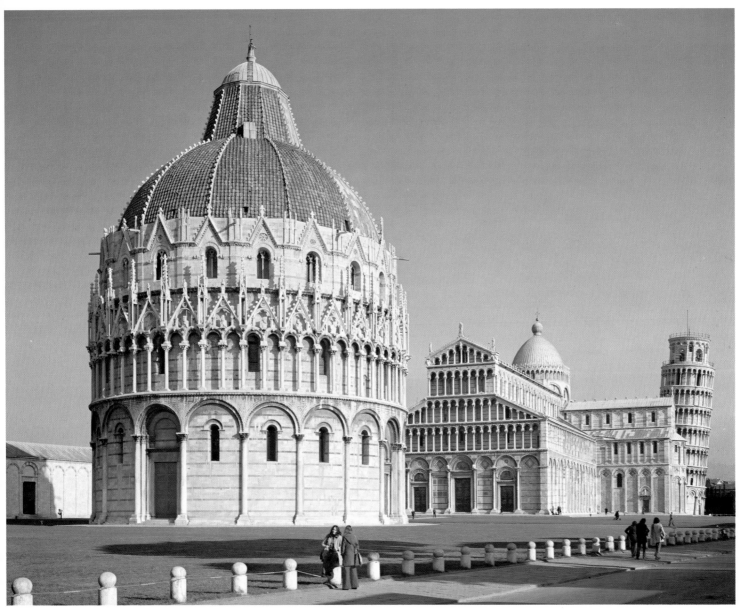

The Cathedral, Baptistry and Tower
of Pisa have a happy unity of style,
even though their construction lasted
from 1063 to 1350. Set in a grassy piazza,
which enhances the brilliance of their marble
exteriors, these widely differing buildings
are stylistically linked by the recurrent use of
open arcades and inlaid marble decoration.
The cathedral, with its fine west front
(below) rising in arcaded tiers, displays a
harmony rarely seen since the Greek temples.
The perilous angle of the celebrated campanile
adds to the character of this marvellous group.

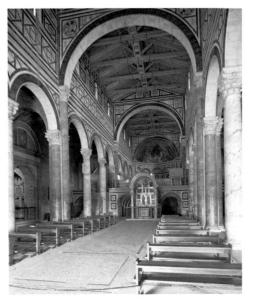

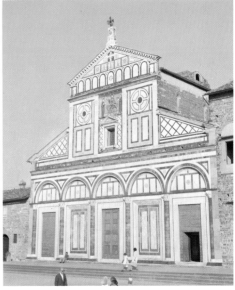

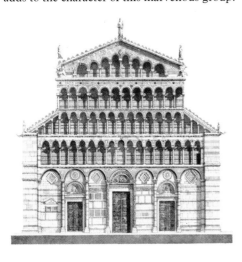

San Miniato al Monte, Florence, built
c. 1013–90, is a simple, beautifully
proportioned basilica. The arcading between
the nave and aisles is carried on columns
with antique capitals, and an open wooden
roof with patterned timbers covers the
building, the whole arrangement recalling an
Early Christian church. Transverse arches,
which span the nave, dividing it into bays,
were an important prologue to the vaulted
bays of later buildings. The decorative
arcading in the apse and rich, inlaid marble
ornament inside the church are repeated on
the entrance façade, which has five arches at
its lower level, beneath a gable with windows
and a central mosaic.

Spain, local and imported styles

THE SOUTHERN half of the Iberian Peninsula has no Romanesque architecture, because during the Romanesque period the area was still in the hands of the Moors. Over the years Christian Spain drove the Moors southeastwards and Córdoba, the Moorish capital, fell to Ferdinand III of Castile in 1236. In the northern half of Spain there was a variety of local architectural developments, often based on influences from abroad. Catalonia looked towards Italy; elsewhere, Spanish Romanesque art derived mainly from France. The seminal influence was the pilgrimage to the reputed relics of St James at Santiago de Compostela in Galicia. Enthusiastically supported by the Cluniac order in the 11th and 12th centuries, this pilgrimage was second only in importance to the pilgrimage to Rome.

Away from the pilgrims' road there were a few more specifically Spanish characteristics. There are beautiful central lantern towers, flanked by corner-turrets, at the cathedrals of Salamanca and Zamora, while a special feature of Castilian Romanesque churches, well seen at Segovia, is the open arcade carried around three sides of the church to form a kind of cloister. Often, as at Segovia and Soria, the arches are borne upon coupled columns, which have capitals of a distinctly Moorish type. The remote Benedictine monastery of Santo Domingo de Silos, south of Burgos, contains what is perhaps the most remarkable survival of early Spanish Romanesque. Here, in the double cloisters, is some of the most moving sculpture of the age. In Catalonia, only the celebrated west portal of the Abbey of Ripoll, the leading Romanesque church, escaped destruction in the Carlist wars of the 1830s. But both at Ripoll and in a number of remote village churches in the foothills of the Pyrenees the builders followed North Italian prototypes. A remarkable collection of Catalan Romanesque wall paintings, formerly in these Pyrenean churches, can now be seen in the Museum of Ancient Art in Barcelona.

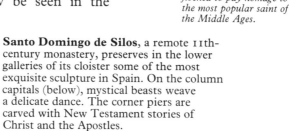

St James's is the archetypal pilgrimage church. Galleried aisles flank the huge barrel-vaulted nave and surround the wide transepts. This arrangement linked with the ambulatory around the apse to provide a continuous passage for the many pilgrims who flocked to pay homage to the most popular saint of the Middle Ages.

Santo Domingo de Silos, a remote 11th-century monastery, preserves in the lower galleries of its cloister some of the most exquisite sculpture in Spain. On the column capitals (below), mystical beasts weave a delicate dance. The corner piers are carved with New Testament stories of Christ and the Apostles.

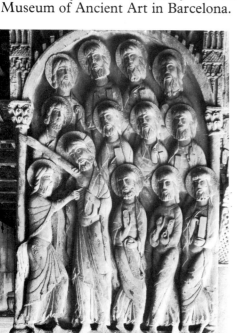

Doubting Thomas is movingly depicted on a corner pier of the Cloister at Silos.

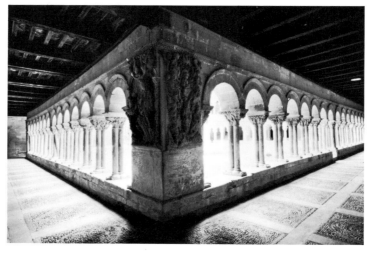

The 12th-century south transept doorway, the Puerta de las Platerías, was named after the silversmiths who, even today, work near the cathedral. Its sculpture is earlier than that of the Pórtico de la Gloria, just west of the nave. The casual arrangement of figures suggests that carvings from other parts of the church were used to fill the gaps caused by fire damage in 1117.

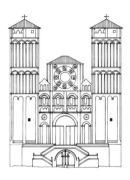

The original Romanesque west front boasted a monumental staircase. It led to a vestibule above the unusually high crypt, which contained the supposed relics of St James. Between the vestibule and the nave, the 12th-century Pórtico de la Gloria remains, superbly sculpted in the French Romanesque style.

A heavy octagonal lantern tower above the central crossing filters light into the transepts below.

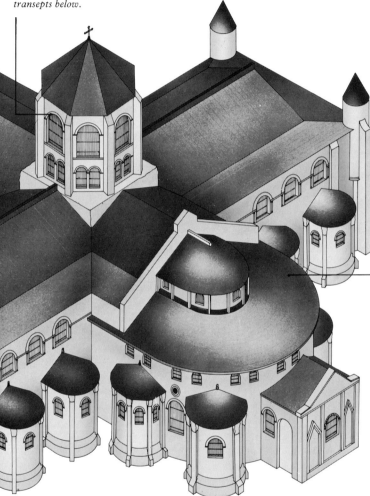

A Baroque screen masks the east end of St James's, which is seen here with its beautiful French Romanesque chevet—its aisle encircling the apse and opening out into five chapels. The east aisles of the transepts, with chapels of their own, continue this harmonious scheme, designed to furnish the pilgrims with stopping points on their tour of the church.

The Cathedral of St James at Santiago de Compostela (above), was journey's end for the myriad pilgrims who trod the great European pilgrimage routes to the shrine of St James in remote Galicia. The undisputed masterpiece of Spanish Romanesque architecture, the cathedral was influenced by the design of French pilgrimage churches and, in turn, inspired many others. It was built between 1078 and *c.* 1211, on the site of the modest 9th-century church which formerly enshrined the reputed tomb of St James, and was modified by successive generations until the 18th century. The Romanesque exterior is now disguised in a cloak of 17th- and 18th-century Baroque extravagance. The illustration, a reconstruction, shows the cathedral in its original form. The interior, hardly altered, is a fine example of Romanesque austerity.

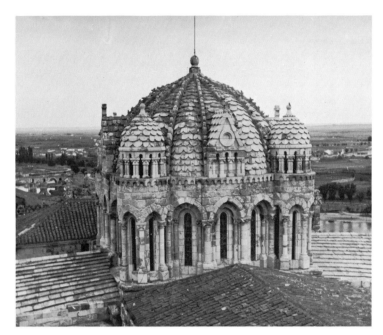

The lantern tower of Zamora Cathedral (above), a 12th-century Romanesque church, is crowned with an intriguing ribbed dome, which has been described as Byzantine, French and Islamic. It is a distinctive and characteristic feature of the Douro region of western Spain, near Portugal. The ribbing, emphasized on the outside by stone mouldings and within by paintwork, separates 16 concave segments, which taper to a central point. Four corner-turrets alternating with four gables complete the construction. The cupola and the small turret-domes are covered with tiny stone "fish scales".

The Abbey Church of Santa Maria at Ripoll, dedicated *c.* 1032, was virtually demolished in 1835, during the Carlist Wars. Only the 12th-century west portal screen (below) survives, battered but still retaining its graceful vitality. Its almost free-standing sculptured beasts are cousins of the animal column supports in the west porches of Italian Romanesque churches. Parallel bands of carving, depicting Old Testament scenes, frame the doorway, while an upper band, known as the attic, displays the hierarchies of Heaven. The rest of the church is a 19th-century approximation of the original design.

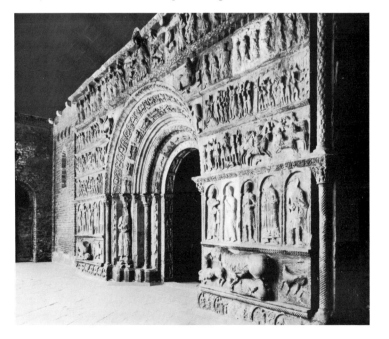

Sicily, a magical fusion of cultures

THE GEOGRAPHICAL location of Sicily, which looks towards Europe, Africa and the East, has made it a natural outpost of several great empires. The perfection of the climate, the charms of the scenery and, in places, the luxury of the vegetation have prompted many princes and peoples to covet the island. The Carthaginians, Greeks, Romans and Byzantines and, from the 9th century until 1072, the Saracens, or Arabs, all made Sicily their colony. Then came the Normans, who conquered the island *c.* 1091 and ruled until 1194. It was they who introduced the Romanesque style.

At Palermo, their capital, the Normans achieved a miraculous fusion with two artistic traditions totally unlike each other and unlike their own—the Byzantine and the Saracenic. At Monreale, on a hill above Palermo, the plan of the cathedral is predominantly Romanesque, but the nave, which resembles an Early Christian basilica, has imposing antique columns beneath arches that are both pointed and stilted, as in Saracenic architecture. The mainly Romanesque cathedral at Cefalù, inspired by the Benedictine churches of Normandy, has splendid Byzantine mosaics in the apse.

The explanation for much of this assimilation of local styles is simple. The men who carried out the work had been trained in a Saracenic tradition of building; and it was certainly Byzantine Greek craftsmen, working for Norman masters, who were responsible for the remarkable mosaics in which Sicily is so rich.

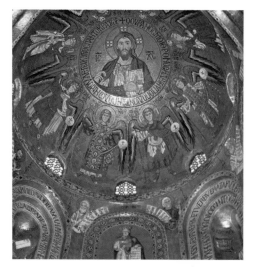

The Palatine Chapel at Palermo (left), begun *c.* 1132, contains this Byzantine mosaic in its tiny, 18-ft-wide dome. The chapel, a remnant of the Norman Royal Palace, is the most perfect example of the Sicilian Romanesque fusion of several architectural traditions. A miniature basilica, it has Islamic pointed arches in the nave, is overhung with an Islamic "stalactite" ceiling, and has opulent Byzantine wall mosaics.

The Benedictine cloisters at Monreale (right), completed *c.* 1200, are among the finest in late Romanesque architecture. Famous for their sumptuous decoration, they have Arabic pointed arches, which spring from capitals carved with a lively variety of sacred and secular subjects. The paired columns supporting them are alternately plain or incrusted with chevrons, spirals and fluting in coloured mosaic.

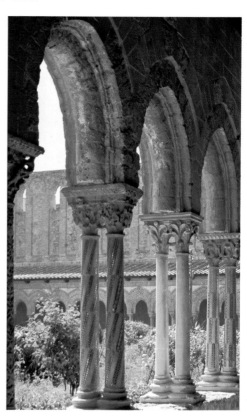

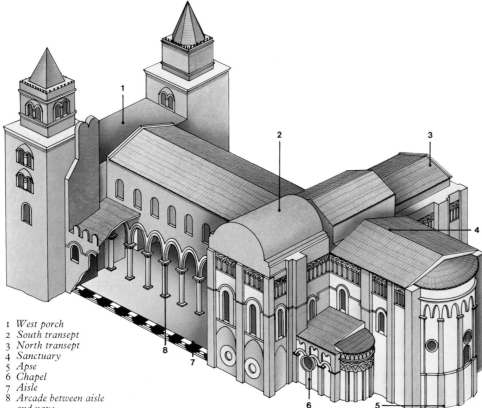

1 *West porch*
2 *South transept*
3 *North transept*
4 *Sanctuary*
5 *Apse*
6 *Chapel*
7 *Aisle*
8 *Arcade between aisle and nave*

Cefalù Cathedral (left) is the grandest expression of northern Romanesque architecture achieved by the Normans in Sicily. Built *c.* 1131–1240, this basilica was inspired by the Benedictine churches of Normandy. The unusually modest nave is eclipsed to the west by an imposing narthex, or porch, and to the east by the powerful transepts and the sanctuary. The sober massiveness of the exterior, emphasized by thick masonry walls, is relieved only by small windows and interlaced blind arcades. A tiled wooden-trussed roof covers the church, except for the south transept, which is roofed with a stone barrel vault. The sanctuary is flanked by twin barrel-vaulted chapels and ends in an apse with a pointed semi-dome. Two square towers, reminiscent of minarets, bracket the columned west porch.

Germany's distinctive outlines

WELL-PRESERVED Romanesque architecture is less commonly found in Germany than in any of the countries where it flourished. Due in part to an unfortunate scarcity of limestone, the use of sandstone, lava and other less durable building materials has necessitated drastic restoration. Even before the destruction of the Cologne churches in World War II, it was usual to look in vain for the patina of age. Despite such disadvantages, German Romanesque churches are novel in planning, striking in scale and often quite rich in external ornament.

The distinctive feature of the planning is the placing of the apse at each end, a feature retained from the Carolingian style of architecture, which evolved late in the 8th century and extended into the 10th century. Its origin has not been

Circular towers containing spiral staircases, almost a trademark of German Romanesque, are placed symmetrically at each end of the church. An octagonal tower, occupying the focal position over the central crossing, is echoed by a smaller octagon between the west turrets.

Italian open arcades encircle the towers and pilaster strips punctuate the walls.

The polygonal apse at the west end, begun in 1234, is a semi-Gothic addition. It contrasts with the earlier apse at the east end of the church, which is concealed in a straight wall. Here, as is usual where apses appear at both ends, the entrances are at the side of the church.

Sturdy piers support the arcading in the nave, which is divided into square bays. Rib vaulting covers both nave and aisles, and there are clerestory windows high in the nave walls.

Worms Cathedral, symmetrical in plan and restrained in decoration, is a typical 12th-century Rhineland church, built c. 1110–81, with apses at both ends and many towers.

fully explained, but may have been monastic, the monks assembling for worship in the east apse and the nuns in the west. Consequently, as can be seen at Worms Cathedral, these churches had no great west entrance. Doors were placed laterally in the aisles. The close political association between Germany and northern Italy during this period would seem to account for the Italianate character of the external wall surfaces, with the open gallery below the roof, the open arcading encircling the towers and the succession of shallow wall-projections linked at the top by corbelled arches. All these features are evident at Worms. The interiors of these churches, although often large, are somewhat bare. The piers are frequently square, the arches are unmoulded and there is a marked economy in the use of ornament.

Romanesque architecture in Germany developed early and lasted a long time; much dates from well into the 13th century, in a style little altered from a century earlier.

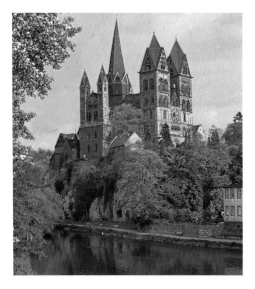

Limburg Cathedral is an elegant late-Romanesque church, completed in 1242. Rising on a hill above the River Lahn, it has six square towers, dominated by a spired, central, octagonal tower. This compact and masterly piling up of many towers suggests a questing towards the next architectural style— the Gothic.

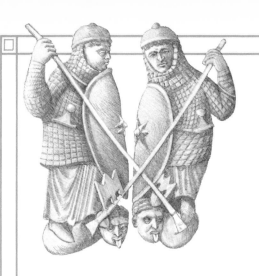

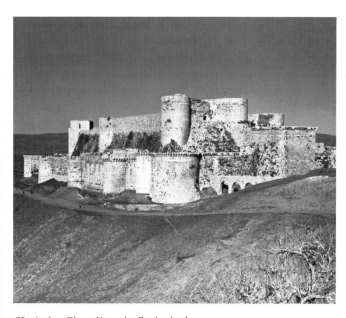

Krak des Chevaliers, in Syria, is the most complete and splendid surviving castle. During the 12th and 13th centuries, the Hospitaller Knights transformed a small fort captured by the first Crusaders into this massive concentric castle, which remained impregnable until 1271.

Fortifications come in all sizes and shapes. Some are a straggling line like Hadrian's Wall or the Great Wall of China, others are more or less circular, such as an earthwork crowning a hilltop; some are rectangular like a Norman keep, others are irregular and multisided as, for example, town walls, while still others are like a Russian doll, castle within castle. All were designed for strength, not beauty. Yet their massiveness and skilful masonry convey a sense of grandeur and of style. There is no mistaking the character of a Norman keep or a 14th-century gate-house. Their style was a function of their military purpose. It is only with modern technology that weapons can be custom-built to meet specific military problems. Castles were designed to deal with weapons and tactics which changed only slowly; and the availability of materials, manpower and skills was also influential. The shortage of timber in Palestine, for example, encouraged more stone vaulting than in Europe.

Some fortifications had a purely defensive purpose; they were intended as dykes to hold back the Barbarians, or as places of refuge in time of trouble. Others had a more aggressive purpose; they were intended to push forward and secure the occupation of new territories or to overawe a town. At the simplest level, fortifications, whether defensive or aggressive, protected the lord's family and immediate retainers from surprise attack and, equally likely, from treachery. At a more sophisticated level, castles could resist sieges for upwards of a year. When the tide of the invading army had receded, the defenders could reassert their authority over the surrounding land.

For some centuries, the security of life in towns depended upon their fortifications, and the constricting girdle of walls and towers did much to shape the architecture of cities. As with the island of Manhattan, they encouraged high rather than

Castles

wide building. Castles were fortified villages, sheltering people of every level of society and providing a store for grain against famine as well as imminent siege. Often, they were also administrative centres.

Hundreds of castles still exist in Europe and the Levant as evidence of the fact that building fortifications and guarding them was an important part of medieval life. The cost of these activities also formed an important charge on royal and baronial budgets. But there is no doubt that for several hundred years they were cost effective. Quite small numbers, measured in terms of trained men, could hold a fair-sized castle for weeks against a besieging army; there are cases of garrisons as small as thirty holding off 3,000. Famine was their worst enemy and sickness among the besiegers their best ally. The Crusaders captured Jerusalem in 1099 by wheeling tall towers up against the walls and taking them by storm. But a more certain and effective method of assault was to drive a mine under a tower and then set light to the mine props, so that the weight of the tower caused it to fall in. The only sure defence against mining was to build on rock or to cut a water-filled moat round the castle. In the end, cannon was the great leveller; but it was only slowly after their introduction in the early 14th century that cannon affected castle design. Many castles in northern Italy of the 16th century bear witness to this; the basic design is little changed, but the towers are more squat and the thicker walls are pierced with gun embrasures.

The purpose of a castle determined its site and to some extent its shape, but its detail and character depended upon the state of military art. Where commanders could deploy large forces, they designed armed camps which allowed their men to line the walls and launch their weapons against the enemy. Hence, the Roman *castrum*, or camp, and the Byzantine field castle with its long, thin walls and meagre towers. But where men were lacking, as with the Crusaders, towers and walls had to take their place; massive masonry had to deter attack and withstand battery, twisting walls and projecting towers threatened the attackers in their rear or on their flanks, and elaborate entrances were designed to trick the unwary. All castle designers had to provide water and living quarters for the garrison. Hence, deep wells and cavernous cisterns, now the haunt of bats. Hence also, great halls for the men-at-arms and airy apartments for the ladies.

The design of castles has always been a subject worthy of princes. Château Gaillard in France, one of the most original designs, was the personal achievement of Richard I of England. The great Military Orders, the Hospitallers and the Templars, had their own distinctive "house style". The owners of most castles played a large part in their design, more, in all likelihood, than in the design of their civil and ecclesiastical buildings; in doing so they were exercising the profession of arms to which they had been bred.

The evidence is scanty, but we can reasonably surmise that there was a close working relationship between the princes and peers who designed the castles and their usually anonymous master masons, who nevertheless signed their work with their individual marks. The masons were a well-paid fraternity, who ranked high in the hierarchy of medieval craftsmen; and their military work has endured as well as their ecclesiastical. The turbulence of the times provided reason for building castles more speedily than churches, but often they were not less carefully constructed. Their masonry, now largely unroofed and uncared for, was intended to resist not merely time and weather but also to withstand the mine, the battering-ram and the catapult.

The evolution of stone fortifications

THE DATING OF fortifications is often conjectural. It is not merely that the archives are imprecise; it is also that many sites retained, through succeeding ages, a particular military significance. Thus frequent repairs and adaptations to existing fortifications often employed the masonry to hand, which may have been shaped centuries earlier. Nevertheless, there was a reasoned evolution in the design of fortifications and there were several distinctive architectural features which can be broadly dated with confidence.

The Byzantines built two types of castle; each intended to protect, and to be defended by, large numbers of people, not all of whom would necessarily be professional soldiers. One type of castle consisted of elaborate town defences with massive walls and boldly projecting towers, sometimes in the shape of horseshoes, as at Nicaea, in Turkey, or pentagonal, as at Ankara, also in Turkey. It is likely that more fortifications were captured through storming the gates than through scaling the walls. In their town fortifications the Byzantines occasionally incorporated "bent entrances", whose design forced an attacker to turn one or more times, thus exposing his back or his flank, preferably the right flank, which would normally be unprotected by a shield. The other type of Byzantine fortification was an altogether flimsier affair. The walls were thin, but were broadened at the top by the addition of a wooden wall-walk supported on corbels; the towers were usually square or irregular, following the configuration of the ground, and were of slight projection; the entrances were simple and straight; only concealed postern gates introduced any element of surprise. Saône in Syria, built mainly in the 11th century, is the exemplar of such a field castle.

Both types of Byzantine fortification were derived from Roman models. There were similar defences in western Europe, and these were copied by the successors of the Romans. Such, for example, were the great city fortifications at Carcassonne in France, built by the Visigoths in the 6th century. But whereas in the East the central authority of the state persisted, in the West it disintegrated. The result was that for some centuries virtually no stone fortifications were built in western Europe.

When, in the 11th century, after a lapse of about four hundred years, the building of stone castles was resumed, it was frequently a case of stone simply replacing wooden palisades. Thus the Normans began with motte and bailey castles. The motte was a tall mound surrounded by a moat, while the bailey was an irregular area of much greater

The city walls of Constantinople, though built in the 5th century, were frequently repaired. This early Byzantine work matches the sophistication achieved by the Crusaders, other western Europeans and the Saracens in the 13th century. A moat, a breastwork and two lines of walls provided defence in depth. The bold projection of the towers, the provision of loopholes and the dominating height of the inner walls allowed an aggressive defence.

At Carcassonne, in France, the 13th-century city walls (below) stand on 6th-century foundations built by the Visigoths. Their work, in the same Roman tradition as Constantinople, is the last pre-Norman sophisticated stone defence in the West.

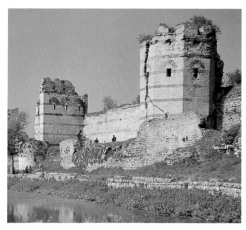

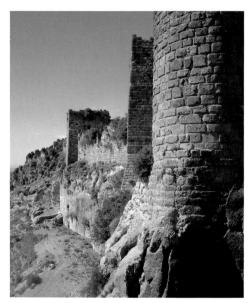

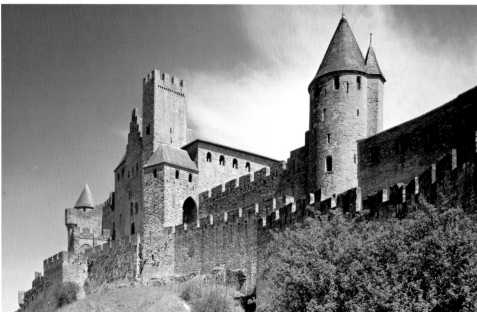

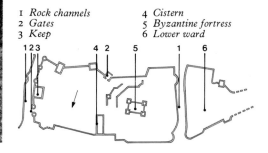

At Saône (above and below), in Syria, the south wall has a round tower and three huge square ones. The bossed masonry, c. 1120, is Crusader work, as is the squat keep at the east face. Below it, a vast rock-cut channel isolates the castle at the end of a mountain ridge. The original castle and some of the existing curtain wall are Byzantine.

1 *Rock channels* 4 *Cistern*
2 *Gates* 5 *Byzantine fortress*
3 *Keep* 6 *Lower ward*

extent, defended by a mound crowned with wooden stakes. Basically, the motte was for the lord and his immediate retainers, while the bailey was for his villagers and cattle. By the 12th century it was common to replace the palisade at the top of the motte and the mound around the bailey with stone walls. The stone palisade on the top of the motte, as seen at Carisbrooke, on the Isle of Wight, is called a shell keep. But another kind of keep, the great foursquare Norman keep, was in vogue simultaneously. The first and greatest of these is the White Tower at the heart of the Tower of London, begun in the 11th century by William the Conqueror.

The Norman keep, which flourished in the 12th and 13th centuries, was the epitome of passive defence. It was difficult to harm those inside but, equally, they could do little damage to their attackers. The Normans' sway depended partly upon winning pitched battles, mainly through the weight of their armoured cavalry and partly upon the stone armour of the keep, which protected the knight in his off-duty moments. The comparatively small Norman stone castle (impervious to fire, unlike its wooden predecessors) was well suited to conditions of feudal fragmentation and did much to perpetuate them.

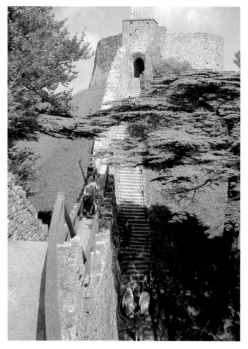

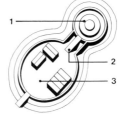

A motte and bailey castle of the 10th to 12th centuries usually consisted of a stockaded mound with a tower (1), and an inclined bridge (2) leading to a lower stockaded bailey (3) with stables and domestic buildings. It was ringed by a ditch and counterscarp. The stockade on top of the motte was sometimes later replaced by a curtain wall called a shell keep. Carisbrooke shell keep (left) dates from the middle of the 12th century.

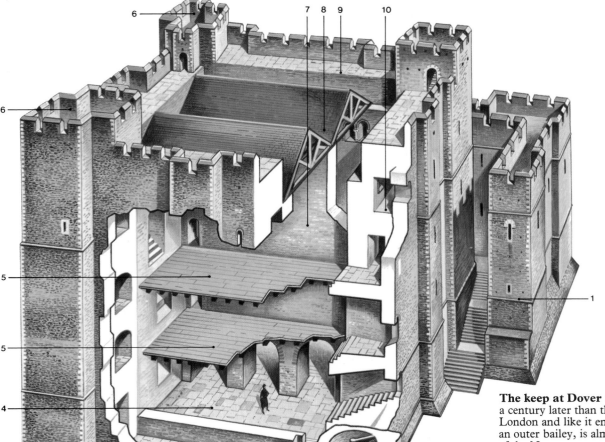

1 Forebuilding and entrance stairs
2 Spiral staircase in corner tower
3 Pilaster buttresses
4 Basement for storage
5 Main floors
6 Tower turrets, 12 ft above level of keep walls
7 Cross-wall subdividing the keep
8 Double-pitch roof below wall-walk level
9 Wall-walk
10 Wall chambers

The keep at Dover Castle, built c. 1180, a century later than the White Tower in London and like it enclosed in an inner and an outer bailey, is almost the largest and last of the Norman rectangular donjons. Its three storeys rise to 83 ft, with walls from 17 to 21 ft thick. The entrance is at the third storey, via stairs in the forebuilding and an internal drawbridge. The keep contains living apartments, chapels and a well. As usual, the spiral stairs twist to the right to give a right-handed defender sword room.

The Golden Age

WHEN KINGS AND military orders, with their great resources and greater numbers, came to predominate over the individual knight they built larger and more complicated castles. The finest examples of these are the English castles in, or on the borders of, Wales, constructed between about 1220 and 1320, and the Hospitaller castles built in the Crusading principalities between 1150 and 1250.

The inspiration of these castles has been disputed. No doubt the Crusaders learned a good deal from the weakness of the Byzantine field castles and from the strength of their town fortifications. But it is a matter of record that the earlier Crusader castles did not follow Byzantine models. Their addition of massive square towers to the Byzantine castle at Saône was in the spirit of the contemporary 12th-century castles being built in western Europe. The Hospitaller style, which came to its full flowering with the castle of Krak des Chevaliers in Syria in the 13th century, was characterized by boldly projecting round or horseshoe towers, concentric lines of fortification, bent entrances,

well-sited loopholes and by massiveness of construction.

The Crusading principalities and the Armenian kingdom to the north were forcing-houses for military architecture. Their shortage of manpower meant that castles were the condition of their continued existence and as a result of the skill of their opponents in siegecraft the castles had continually to be strengthened. The same was thought to apply to the English castles in Wales (although in fact they were never fully tested) and also in turn to both the English and the French castles during the Hundred Years' War. These sophisticated castles were designed to take a heavy toll of the attackers through their arrangements which exploited the improved power of the crossbow and longbow.

While the complicated new castles of the 13th and early 14th century were being built, some of their more notable features, for example the better provision of loopholes, were being incorporated in older castles. By this date, keeps in the old style were no longer built. Instead, the chief defences of the castle were found to give better value—both

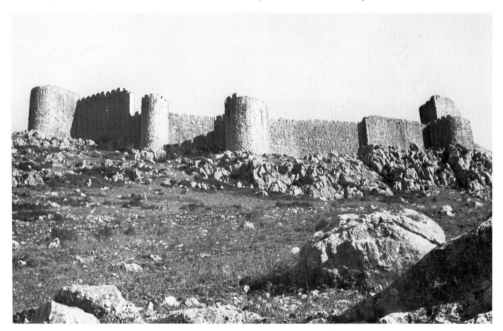

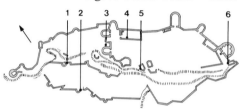

1 Gate, middle ward   4 Cistern
2 Gate, lower ward   5 Chapel
3 Gate, upper ward   6 Postern

Ilan (left and above), *c.* 1200, in the Armenian kingdom of Cilicia, occupied a naturally strong site. The main purpose of the southern and western walls was to push attackers out to the steepest slopes. The boldly projecting rounded towers, placed where the gradient is easier, are early examples of the revival of the Roman–Byzantine tradition. Loopholes at different levels have splayed feet to cover the ground near the walls. The linked entrance towers of the upper ward flank a bent entrance, forming a unit unconnected with the curtain wall.

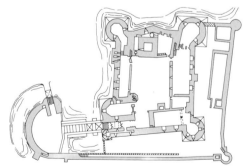

At Goodrich, a late 12th-century English castle was pulled down, but its three-storey keep was incorporated within a much-strengthened castle of *c.* 1300, with a rock-cut moat and with huge masonry spurs. To force entry, attackers had to cross a drawbridge, carry the barbican, make a right-angle turn and cross a bridge with two more draw-bridges, while under fire from the walls.

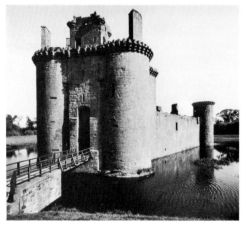

Caerlaverock gate-house in Scotland, dating from the 14th and 15th centuries, shows remnants of machicolation—a gallery commanding the base of the walls.

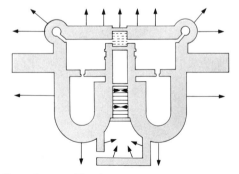

Gate-houses like that at Beaumaris, in Wales, *c.* 1300, superseded keeps. Loopholes (represented by arrows) covered every approach, for the gate-house, like the keep, was often designed to repulse attack from within as well as without. The extensive use of mercenaries made treachery ever possible. The barbican confined an attack on the gate to a restricted space, covered from every angle.

militarily and psychologically—at the most, instead of the least, vulnerable point. Hence, the great gate-houses of the 14th and 15th centuries. The towers in the outer defences became squatter and thicker to resist the batter of siege engines and artillery; at every point the inner fortifications dominated the outer fortifications.

Soon the power of attack outran the means of defence. On the one hand cannon, and on the other central governments, with the resources to carry out prolonged sieges and to sap the defences by extensive undermining, put an end to castles. Throughout Europe castles declined in importance as the 15th century progressed.

The last sieges of medieval castles took place during the English Civil War, in the mid-17th century. As the cannon battered them to bits, Sébastian Vauban (1633–1707) the most celebrated of military engineers, was receiving his apprenticeship in France and the Low Countries in a new form of fortification, whose strength once again lay more in earthworks than in masonry.

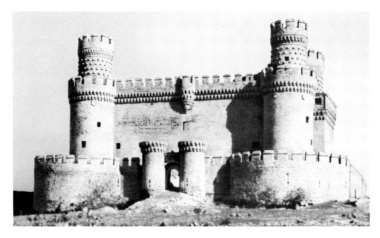

Manzanàres el Real, in Spain, *c.* late 15th century. Its inner fortifications so dominated the outer that attackers could be under fire from both simultaneously.

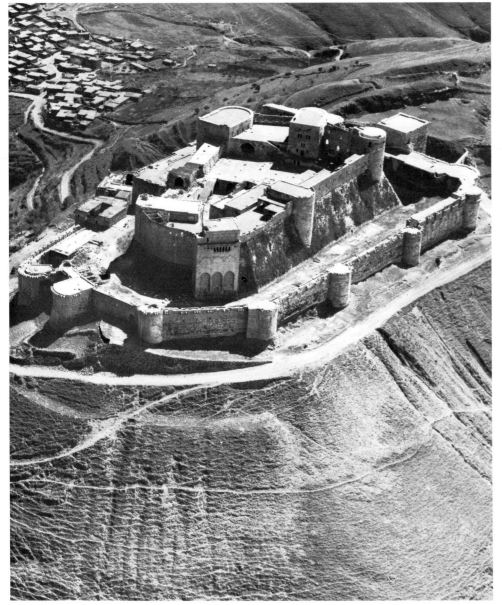

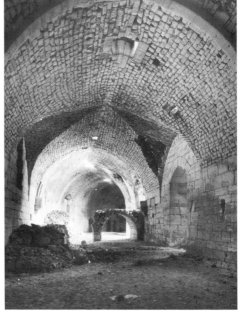

Krak (left) was a fully concentric castle, the outer ward completely surrounding the inner. The square tower of the outer ward, at the top of the picture, is later Arab work. Beyond it is a triangular outwork covering the only feasible approach for heavy siege engines. In the inner ward there are early Crusader square towers, but others were later transformed by the Hospitallers into rounded bastions. In the last phase of Crusader building, represented by the two towers at the bottom left of the picture, the projection of the rounded bastions became increasingly pronounced. These towers flank one of the three postern gates. The main entrance is through the square tower just beyond them. It gives on to a vaulted ramp which, in a series of sharp bends, winds past four gates, one portcullis and several machicoulis. In its heyday, Krak maintained a garrison of 2,000. Meticulous restoration has preserved the delicate stonework of the storage undercrofts (above), the great hall and the chapel.

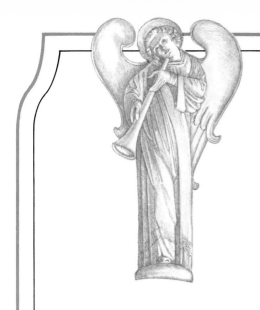

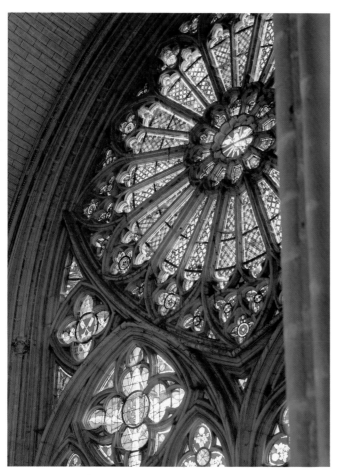

In many great Gothic cathedrals, such as Bourges, walls are pierced by large expanses of stone tracery filled with stained glass. In some cathedrals, walls almost give place to windows, thus reversing the normal proportions of void and solid.

In the Gothic age, even more than in the Romanesque, the dominant art was architecture. And happy are the times when this is so, for architecture is the great harmonizer. The Gothic epoch, which north of the Alps spanned nearly four centuries, produced many splendid secular buildings, but the highest expression of the style —literally no less than metaphorically—was in the cathedrals. They depended for their enrichment chiefly upon sculpture and stained glass. The bulk of Gothic sculpture is architectural, while stained glass, at best the most thrilling of the medieval crafts, is completely the servant of architecture. But in an age when few people could read or write and when art therefore had also to serve a didactic purpose, the level of these two arts was sometimes —not by any means always—unashamedly popular. In architecture, Gothic art was at its most intellectual. But whatever its character, it was church- and cathedral-building which provided the great outlet for the creative activity of the age.

Why did the Gothic church take the form that it did? Formerly it was customary to explain its evolution in terms of engineering: the pointed arch, it was held, was adopted as a matter of necessity, in the development of the ribbed vault. The whole weight of the Gothic vault, it was believed, rested upon a skeleton of ribs: hence the development of the big buttress and, as the churches grew loftier, of the flying buttress, to counteract the outward thrust. As regards abutment, this is perfectly sound; what is not true is the supposition that the whole vault does rest upon a skeleton of ribs. It is now recognized that the old structural distinction between a groined vault and a ribbed vault is largely fictitious; in World War II this was clearly demonstrated, for at a number of places the ribs were smashed without bringing about the total collapse of the vault. It was thus proved that the

Gothic

reason for the ribs of a Gothic vault is not functional, as used to be believed, but aesthetic. The ribs provide a pleasing finish to the angles of intersection of the cross-vault, and so delight the eye. The reasons why the vaults of, say, Rheims or Amiens, although very high, have stood for more than seven hundred years without giving the slightest indication of instability, even through the ordeal of World War I—while many Romanesque vaults have sagged so badly, or even collapsed, as at Vézelay—are that Gothic vaults were constructed much more lightly, of carefully dressed stone, and were properly buttressed.

As for pointed arches, it is true that they were structurally convenient; they introduced an element of flexibility which was lacking in Romanesque churches. A cross-vault could now be erected over a bay of any shape, simply by varying the sharpness of the angles of the arches. But, so long as it was properly buttressed, a high vault could have been erected which made use of nothing but round arches. Furthermore, pointed arches and ribbed vaults can be found, although infrequently, in Romanesque churches, most notably at Durham. For an explanation of the almost universal adoption of the pointed arch in Gothic architecture one must look into the realm of aesthetics. The Gothic age used the pointed arch because it loved this form, which was felt to be the right vehicle for the expression of certain moods, even of spiritual states, which were outside the emotional range of the round arch—still more of the post and lintel form.

The markedly vertical emphasis of Gothic buildings can be accounted for in much the same way. The structural miracle of the Gothic cathedral was achieved as the result of man's ceaseless striving to build vertically. It is the high vault, functionally so splendidly unnecessary, which was mainly responsible for the cathedrals taking the particular form that they do. People with a strong preference for classical architecture often dislike what they regard as the excessive verticality of Gothic and are also likely to have a special distaste for flying buttresses, which they may feel to be restless and ugly, looking as if the scaffolding had still been left in position. But the builders themselves were certainly not ashamed of them, and others have regarded them as being like great sentinels on duty around the cathedral.

Gothic architecture, which first developed in France c. 1140, covered a somewhat wider area of Europe than Romanesque, but the principal countries were the same. There was, however, one new factor of great importance: the growth of the towns, particularly in France, which, as they became more prosperous, wanted their own churches—churches of quite a different kind from the abbeys; churches which could also be symbols of civic pride. The clergy, because they almost alone had any education, still took the initiative and directed operations, but usually in cordial collaboration with the laity. An entirely different spirit could now be detected: less cloistered, less introspective, more confident, more optimistic. There appeared for the first time since the very beginning of Christian art an appreciation of nature, typified—and sanctified—by the teaching of St Francis of Assisi. All this is reflected in the art of the time, which became much more outward-looking, revealing a new freshness of observation.

Structurally, prodigious strides were made; the Gothic architects ended by performing feats of extraordinary virtuosity, almost to the point of occasionally overreaching themselves. Compared with Romanesque architecture there was a quicker rhythm, a heightened tension, a new subtlety, a greater warmth of feeling, and often a finer, more delicate sensibility.

France, birthplace of the new style

HISTORY OFFERS no parallel to the outburst of cathedral-building which occurred in France between about 1150 and 1300. So audacious are these buildings in conception, so prodigious in scale, that even today they dominate their surroundings and thrill the senses. Religious zeal was no longer exclusive to the monks in their monasteries, but was shared by the people as a whole. Agnosticism was unknown. The building of churches and cathedrals was, therefore, truly popular and everyone who had anything to contribute had a share in it. There is the well-known story of how, in the 12th century, the people of Chartres harnessed themselves to the carts and dragged from the quarry the enormous limestone blocks for their new cathedral. Donations flowed from both rich and poor and the Church drew additional revenue from the rental of its properties. Above all, it was the much-increased power and authority of the French kings, and the resultant peace and prosperity, which made such grand-scale cathedral-building possible.

Laon and Notre Dame de Paris are the two great cathedrals in the earliest Gothic style, while Chartres, Bourges, Rheims, Amiens, Le Mans and Beauvais are the most famous cathedrals of the early maturity. But France has many other glorious Gothic cathedrals, among them Sens, Troyes, Auxerre, Tours, Metz, Strasbourg, Narbonne and the great brick fortress–cathedral of Albi. Rouen and Coutances are the leading cathedrals of Normandy. The world's finest stained glass is found in some of these cathedrals, and in a few others architecturally less distinguished, such as Angers and Poitiers. For sculpture, Rheims is surpassed only by Chartres. The late Gothic Flamboyant style appeared about 1400. Although its ornamentation is often excessive, some of this late work is masterly. There are, for example, superb towers at Saint Ouen at Rouen, and many lovely rose windows.

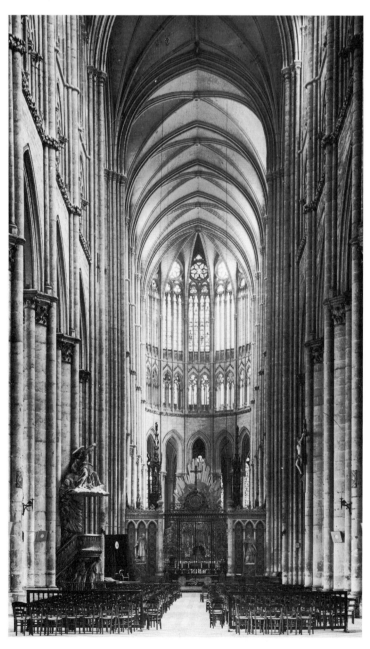

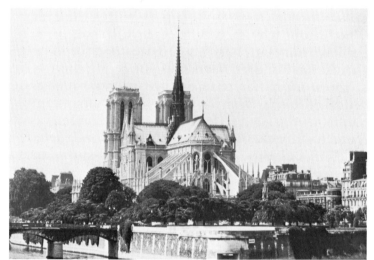

Notre Dame Cathedral in Paris (above), begun in 1163, was seminal in the evolution of the French Gothic style. It is 110 ft high—the first cathedral built on a truly monumental scale. With its compact, cruciform plan, its sexpartite vaulting, flying buttresses and vastly enlarged windows, it became a prototype for future French cathedrals.

The nave at Amiens (left). The incredible height—139 ft—and dramatic verticality of the nave, so designed that the eye is drawn ever upwards, is the supreme fulfilment of the Gothic ideal. Begun in 1220, the nave was completed within 16 years. The classic three-stage interior, established at Chartres, was perfected here.

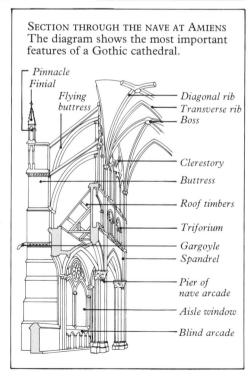

SECTION THROUGH THE NAVE AT AMIENS
The diagram shows the most important features of a Gothic cathedral.

- Pinnacle
- Finial
- Flying buttress
- Diagonal rib
- Transverse rib
- Boss
- Clerestory
- Buttress
- Roof timbers
- Triforium
- Gargoyle
- Spandrel
- Pier of nave arcade
- Aisle window
- Blind arcade

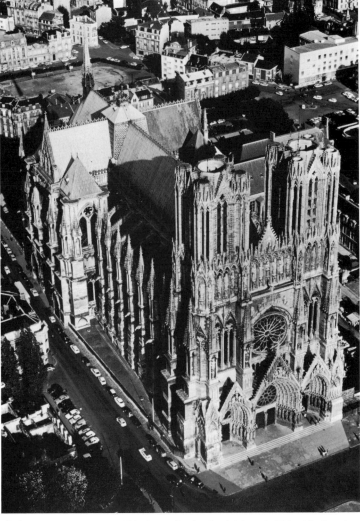

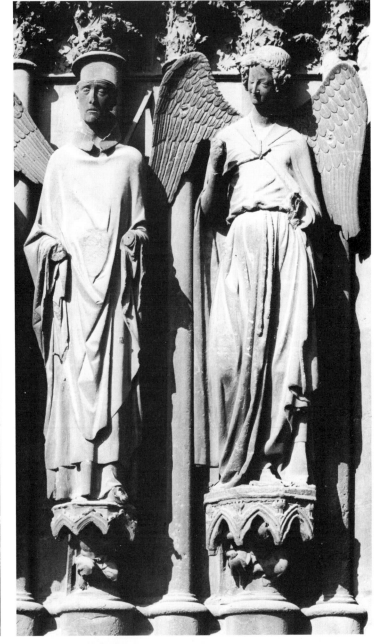

Amiens

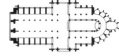

Notre Dame, Paris

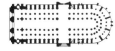

Rheims

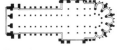

French cathedrals tend to be short, wide, symmetrical and compact. Transepts project only slightly and naves often have double aisles. At the east end, an ambulatory and radiating chapels form the typically French rounded chevet.

Rheims Cathedral (above). Dignified and stately, the coronation cathedral of the kings of France rises regally above modern Rheims. It was begun in 1211 and, though not completed until 1481, it has a splendid unity of style. The church is cruciform in plan, and to provide the space necessary for the coronation ceremonies, held on this spot since the year 496, the nave, aisles and east end were broadened to embrace the transepts.

Solemn and restrained in decoration, the interior suggests limitless height and spaciousness. The avenue of clustered piers lining the 460-ft-long nave leads the eye to the intersecting vaulting 125 ft above. The architects of Rheims used the classic interior arrangement of arcades, triforium and clerestory, but instead of using single lancet windows, as at Chartres, they employed paired lancets at both aisle and clerestory levels.

Stained glass windows over the doors of the west façade replace the traditional tympana. Rheims is renowned for its complex system of elegant flying buttresses, which support and ornament the sculptured exterior. The spires were never added to the 268-ft-high western towers. The sound construction of this cathedral proclaims the skill of High Gothic master-masons.

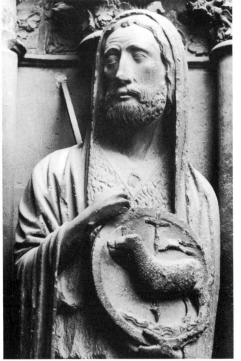

On the west portals of Rheims Cathedral there are nearly 500 carved figures, some larger than life-size. One of the earliest is John the Baptist (left) in the right-hand portal, carved in traditional style. The statues of St Niçaise and the famous Angel of Rheims (above), in the left-hand portal, are later figures in the style most typical of Rheims sculpture. These ecstatic figures were widely imitated all over medieval Europe.

Chartres Cathedral

As a work of architecture, Chartres is surpassed by the Cathedrals of Rheims, Bourges and Amiens, which were all being built at the same time. But Chartres preserves better than any of these its sculpture and much better its glass. As a synthesis of Gothic art Chartres is supreme. Some would even say that, despite deplorable alterations to the choir in 1763, it is one of the loveliest works of man.

The present cathedral, begun in 1194 and roofed by 1220, replaces a succession of churches built on the site and razed by fire. Rising high above the town, it has an interior height of one hundred and twenty-one feet six inches. There is, as is so often the case in France, no central tower, for such a tower would have had to be very large and therefore expensive to be in scale with the rest of the building. Instead, there are two towers at the west end, while six more, intended to flank the transeptal façades and the apse, were never carried up. The crypt and the west front alone antedate the disastrous fire of 1194. The spire rising over the south tower, completed *c.* 1160, is one of the earliest and finest true spires in Europe. The west, north and south fronts all have triple portals, which are profusely enriched with sculpture, arranged according to carefully worked-out iconographical schemes. Among these carved limestone figures are several of the greatest masterpieces of French art.

The cathedral has one hundred and seventy-six windows, most of which date from the 13th century and still preserve their medieval glass. Some of the windows are very large, yet replacements amount to less than six per cent of a total area of about twenty-six thousand square feet of glass. Here, indeed, is what John Ruskin, the Victorian art critic, called "flaming jewellery", one of the most moving visual experiences to be had anywhere.

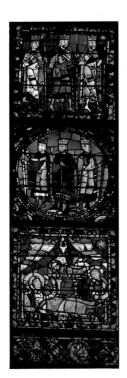

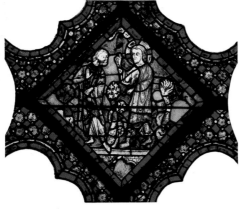

The stained glass windows at Chartres are unique in loveliness and quantity. The impact of sunlight on intense reds, blues and violets creates a magical effect of light and colour, made more remarkable because the medieval artists designed these windows "on the bench" and did not see the finished effect until the glass was in position. A 13th-century panel (above) shows God with Noah. Three panels (left), depicting the Nativity and the Magi, are from a lancet window, one of three under the west rose window. They rank among the finest examples of 12th-century stained glass.

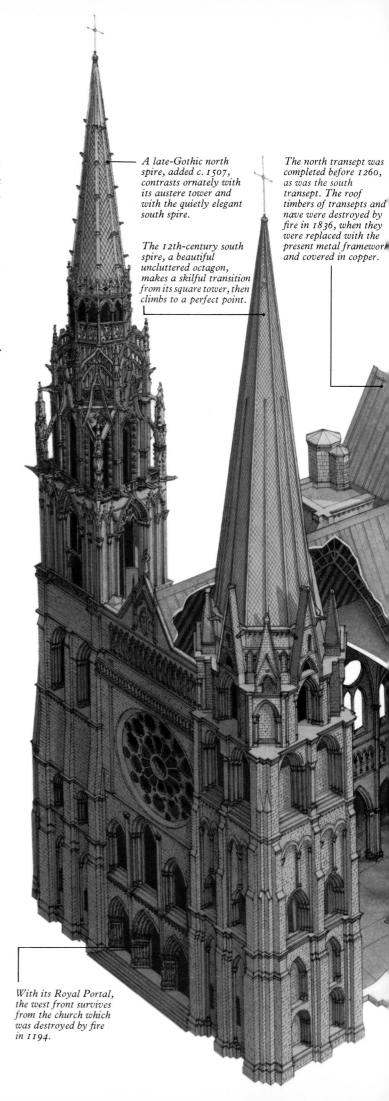

A late-Gothic north spire, added *c.* 1507, contrasts ornately with its austere tower and with the quietly elegant south spire.

The 12th-century south spire, a beautiful uncluttered octagon, makes a skilful transition from its square tower, then climbs to a perfect point.

The north transept was completed before 1260, as was the south transept. The roof timbers of transepts and nave were destroyed by fire in 1836, when they were replaced with the present metal framework and covered in copper.

With its Royal Portal, the west front survives from the church which was destroyed by fire in 1194.

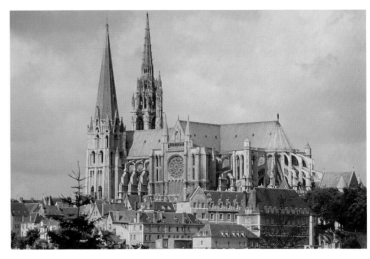

An inspired architect rebuilt the nave after 1194. Forced to work on earlier foundations, he built audaciously high. Over the nave arcades he made a triforium, a gallery hiding the aisle roofs, above which he heightened the nave walls dramatically. Windows gained new importance; each bay in the upper nave has twin lancets and a rose window. From this experiment came the style of Gothic building in which windows eclipse walls.

The outward thrust of the huge vault is counteracted by flying buttresses, here of a somewhat archaic form.

The lofty apse is surrounded by a double ambulatory encircled by chapels; a good example of the French chevet.

The cathedral rises above Chartres, its spires and weathered copper roof visible for miles around.

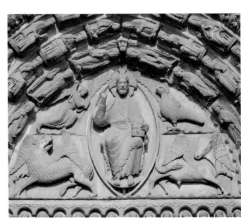

Christ in Majesty, surrounded by the symbols of the four Evangelists, dominates the tympanum above the central door of the magnificently carved Royal Portal. Romanesque in its highly stylized treatment, yet Gothic in the serenity and humanity of the figures, this sculpture, which dates from *c.* 1150, is the finest in this transitional style.

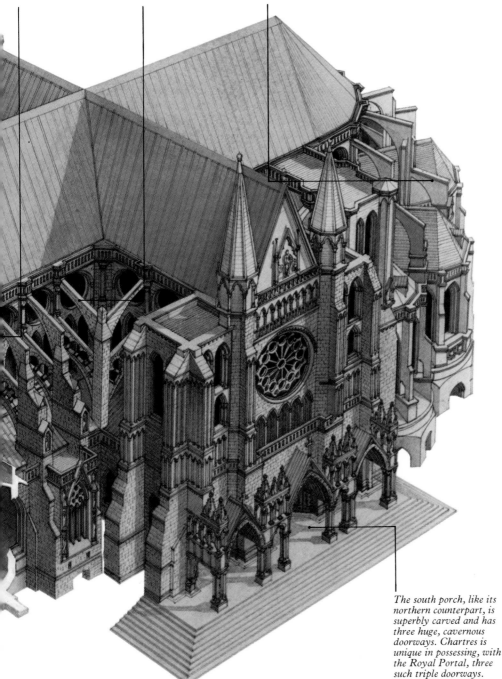

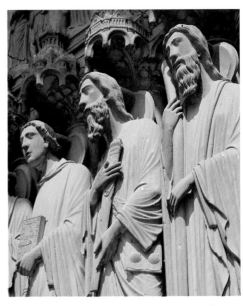

The south porch, like its northern counterpart, is superbly carved and has three huge, cavernous doorways. Chartres is unique in possessing, with the Royal Portal, three such triple doorways.

The Apostles stand against the splays of the central doorway in the south transept. The sculpture of the transepts was executed nearly a century after that of the Royal Portal. The figures, although now Gothic in their realism, are still perfectly integrated with their architectural setting.

119

Early English, the springtime of a style

THE GOTHIC STYLE in England was introduced through the spread of the French monastic orders, especially the Cistercians, and by the French designer William of Sens, who was invited to rebuild the east part of Canterbury Cathedral after its destruction by fire in 1174. Before long a new English style developed. In the cathedrals, it appeared first in the transepts and nave of Wells. There is a striking contrast between the dry, somewhat charmless style of the choir of Canterbury and the rich linear elaboration of the piers and arcades at Wells, as well as the liveliness of the sculptured capitals and corbels.

Spatially, however, English cathedrals are far less compact than those of the Continent, particularly those of France. The emphasis is on length rather than on width or height. The transepts project considerably and sometimes there is a second pair. Massive stone screens at the crossing further emphasize the separateness of the parts. Except at Westminster Abbey, where Henry III deliberately followed French models, there was, in place of the French chevet, a reversion to the flat east end of Anglo–Saxon times, probably because more light was felt to be necessary at the high altar. In England, small chapels for the accommodation of secondary altars were therefore usually confined to the eastern sides of the transepts, or were placed within the body of the church itself. Here, too, more than in any other country, west fronts tended to be designed as screens. The west front at Wells, far broader than the nave, is the outstanding example, while that at Peterborough Cathedral, still wider, is the most original.

Early English, the first phase of English Gothic, is often called the springtime of the style. It was fresh and almost severe in its classical simplicity, comparable to that of the Cathedral of Bourges in France. The purest expression of the style is Salisbury Cathedral, begun in 1220. The richest example of 13th-century architecture, and probably the finest of all English cathedrals, is Lincoln.

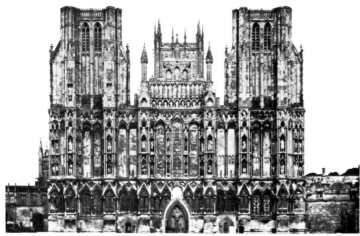

The façade of Wells Cathedral
(above), 150 ft wide, is a gigantic screen displaying nearly 400 13th-century figures, which were once gilded and painted.

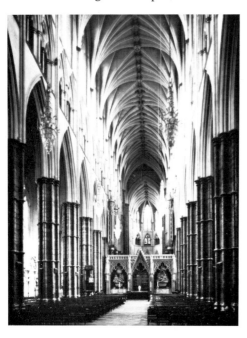

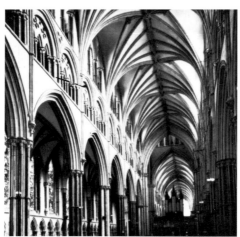

The nave of Lincoln Cathedral (above) is long, somewhat low and typically Early English. It contrasts sharply with the height and verticality of the nave at Westminster, which is nearer in style to French Gothic cathedrals than any other English church.

The nave of Westminster Abbey (left), 102 ft high, is England's tallest medieval vault. It follows the style of the choir and transepts, begun 150 years earlier, in 1245.

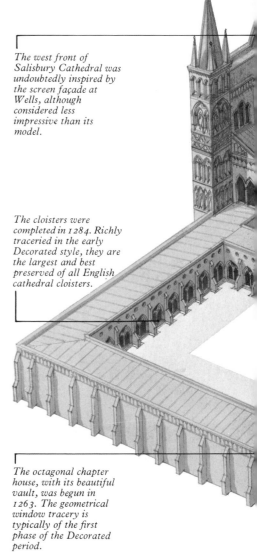

The west front of Salisbury Cathedral was undoubtedly inspired by the screen façade at Wells, although considered less impressive than its model.

The cloisters were completed in 1284. Richly traceried in the early Decorated style, they are the largest and best preserved of all English cathedral cloisters.

The octagonal chapter house, with its beautiful vault, was begun in 1263. The geometrical window tracery is typically of the first phase of the Decorated period.

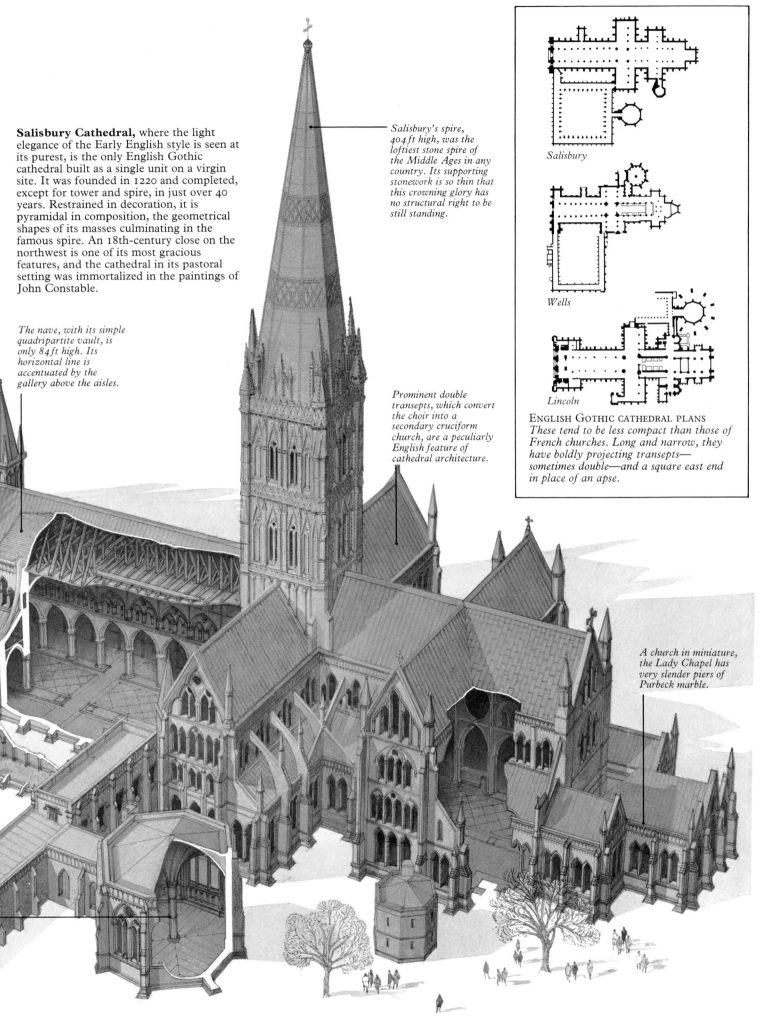

Salisbury Cathedral, where the light elegance of the Early English style is seen at its purest, is the only English Gothic cathedral built as a single unit on a virgin site. It was founded in 1220 and completed, except for tower and spire, in just over 40 years. Restrained in decoration, it is pyramidal in composition, the geometrical shapes of its masses culminating in the famous spire. An 18th-century close on the northwest is one of its most gracious features, and the cathedral in its pastoral setting was immortalized in the paintings of John Constable.

The nave, with its simple quadripartite vault, is only 84ft high. Its horizontal line is accentuated by the gallery above the aisles.

Salisbury's spire, 404ft high, was the loftiest stone spire of the Middle Ages in any country. Its supporting stonework is so thin that this crowning glory has no structural right to be still standing.

Prominent double transepts, which convert the choir into a secondary cruciform church, are a peculiarly English feature of cathedral architecture.

A church in miniature, the Lady Chapel has very slender piers of Purbeck marble.

Salisbury

Wells

Lincoln

ENGLISH GOTHIC CATHEDRAL PLANS
These tend to be less compact than those of French churches. Long and narrow, they have boldly projecting transepts— sometimes double—and a square east end in place of an apse.

England's glorious later phase

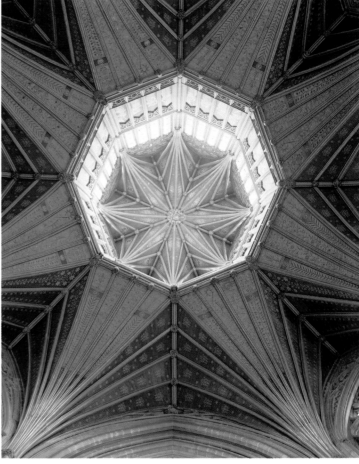

THE FIFTY YEARS preceding the Black Death of 1348–9 was a brilliant period for Gothic architecture in England. The country was prosperous and money poured into the coffers of the Church. Architects were bold, resourceful and endlessly inventive. This period saw the creation of, among much else, Exeter Cathedral, with its wonderful tierceron vaulting; the chapter house and the whole of the eastern part of Wells Cathedral, the most poetic Gothic interior in England; the brilliantly original octagon of Ely Cathedral; the commencement of the tower and spire at Salisbury, the highest and also the loveliest stone spire of the Middle Ages, and, at Lincoln, England's loftiest medieval cathedral tower.

Ornament was now often highly luxuriant, yet it always remained subordinate to structure. The Decorated Period, c. 1250–1370, was succeeded by the Perpendicular, c. 1330–1540. Although compared with its French counterpart, the Flamboyant, this long last phase of English Gothic was an age of architectural sobriety, many gloriously extravagant towers, of which the finest of all is at Canterbury, and some of the most beautiful vaults in existence, date from this period. Tiercerons were succeeded by lierne and fan vaults which, in the very boldest examples, as in the choir of Oxford Cathedral and in Henry VII's Chapel in Westminster Abbey, were constructed with large pendants.

In all this architecture the abundance of excellent limestones was a great boon. At this time England also had a vast supply of oak. The interiors of some parish churches, which before the end of the medieval period numbered over nine thousand, still preserve remarkable displays of woodwork, and the angel roofs of East Anglia have no parallel.

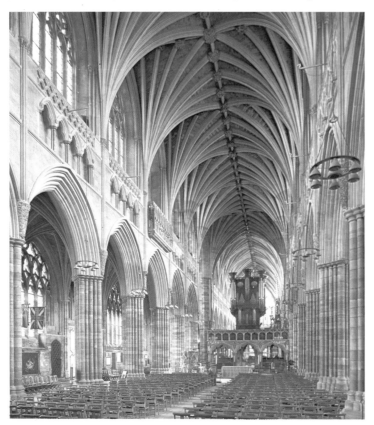

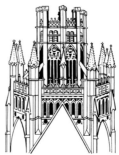

Exeter Cathedral. At Exeter the architectural style of the eastern parts, begun c. 1275, was continued in the nave (left), which was not completed until nearly 100 years later. The glorious "palm" vault, with multiple tiercerons, extends unbroken along the entire 300 ft of nave and choir. This vault, together with the exuberant wood and stone carving, and the elaborate window tracery, combine at Exeter to present English Decorated Gothic at its best.

The octagon of Ely Cathedral is the only Gothic dome, a daring and ingenious solution to the problem created by the collapse of the heavy Norman tower in 1322. The exterior stone octagon (left) carries a lead-clad wooden lantern and belfry. Wood was also used for the beautiful 70-ft-wide interior vault (above).

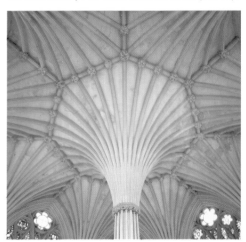

The chapter house at Wells Cathedral is perhaps the most beautiful of the polygonal chapter houses, unique to English cathedral architecture. The vault (above) is supported by a central pier from which no fewer than 32 ribs radiate.

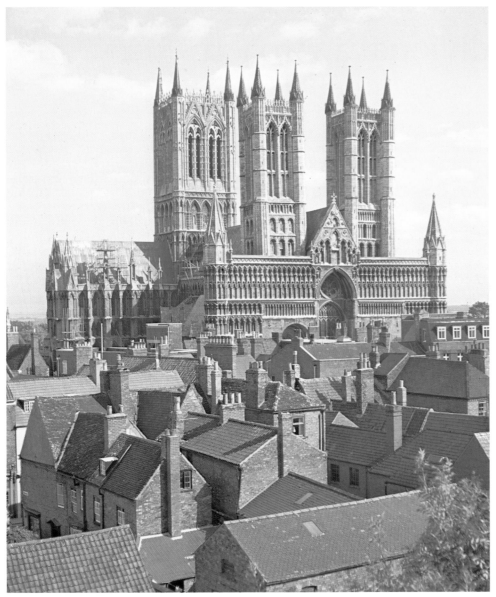

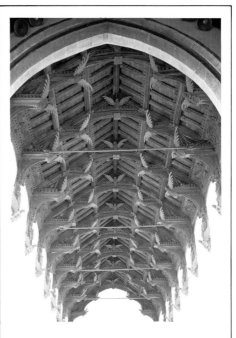

Lincoln Cathedral (above), standing high above the city, is widely regarded as the finest of England's cathedrals. The west façade with its imposing sculptured Gothic screen, and the lower parts of the two huge western towers are all that survive of the Norman cathedral, destroyed by earth tremors in 1185. The present church, completed by 1400, is mainly Early English and has the earliest and largest decagonal chapter house. With their original spires, Lincoln's towers must have been even more impressive, for, at 271 ft, the central tower is still England's tallest cathedral tower.

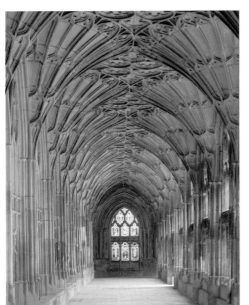

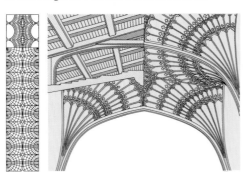

King's College Chapel, Cambridge (above), is roofed with an early 16th-century fan vault, the finest of its kind. A gilded boss is the focal point for each bay. The 14 identical ribbed panels which emanate from each springer are adorned with decorative ribs and tracery.

The cloister of Gloucester Cathedral (left). This cloister owes much of its grace to its fan vaulting, which is among the earliest in England.

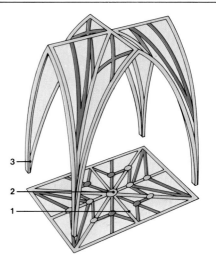

▭ *Rib vault*	1	*Ridge rib*
▭ *Tiercerons*	2	*Central boss*
▭ *Liernes*	3	*Main springer*

RIB VAULTING
This bay is divided into four cells with tiercerons (secondary ribs) leading from springer to ridge rib. Liernes (tertiary ribs) touch neither springers nor central boss. From below, these appear as the star-shaped pattern of the stellar vault.

Germany, an individual approach

GERMANY IS rich in Gothic buildings. Some of them are works of marked individuality, but many are marred by over-extensive restoration. Because the style arrived here very late, there is little Gothic architecture before the second quarter of the 13th century. Bamberg Cathedral, for example, built for the most part in 1237, is still predominantly Romanesque.

Germany's special contribution to Gothic architecture was the *hallenkirchen* or hall-churches. These were built with aisles as high as the nave and the choir. The fine ordonnance of arcade, triforium and clerestory was thus sacrificed, but some daringly tall aisle windows were possible. The 13th-century Sankt Elisabeth-Kirche at Marburg is a typical hall-church.

The citizens of prosperous towns, particularly in northern Germany, built almost all the principal Gothic churches, some on a bold scale and often with tall towers. Choirs tended to be short, because there were not many priests. In the north, where there was a scarcity of building stone, brick was generally used, sometimes with admirable resourcefulness. The intricacy of lierne vaulting was much favoured by German builders in the late Gothic period.

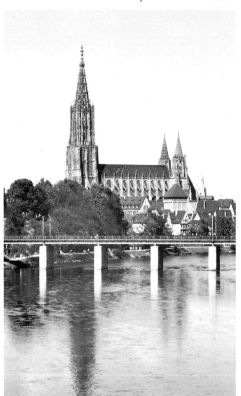

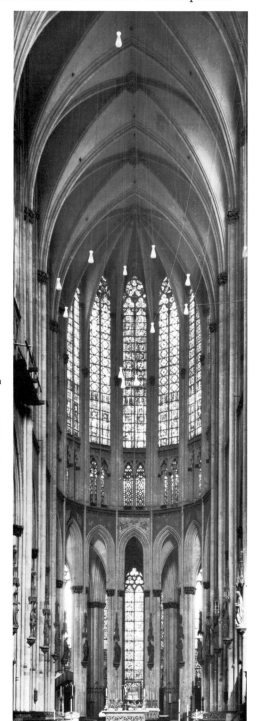

Ulm Minster (left), with its sharp, unmistakable profile and the loftiest spire in Christendom, built in 1890, is typical of High Gothic burghers' churches. A hall-church built in brick and stone, its aisles were extended, in the 14th century, to the same width as the nave, and daringly but successfully covered with star-shaped lierne vaulting. After 1502 the aisles were subdivided with slender pillars. The overall width of nave and aisles is an immense 147 ft.

The interior of Cologne Cathedral (right), looking into the choir, is the oldest part of the church, begun in 1248 and modelled on that at Amiens. The 150-ft-high nave, completed only in the 19th century, closely followed the style of the choir.

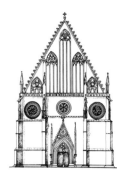

The Church of the Holy Cross (left) at Schwäbisch-Gmünd was the work of Heinrich Harler, an influential stone-mason. Begun *c.* 1350, it heralded the golden age of the German hall-church. The lines of its façade are echoed in the symmetrical placing of the decoration and of the tall, German lancet windows.

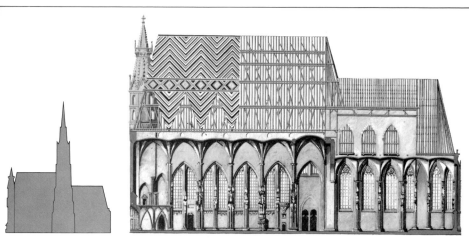

ST STEPHEN'S, VIENNA
This modified Romanesque church, rebuilt from 1300 to 1450, retains its original west front, capped by two small towers. A fine 448-ft-high steepled tower, decorated with filigree sculpture, was raised above the south portal between 1368 and 1433. The enormous roof, steeply pitched against heavy winter snowfalls, has polychrome tiles arranged in chevron and diamond patterns.

Spain's richly varied churches

SPAIN, WHICH remained in a state of political disunity throughout the Middle Ages, until 1479, has a Gothic style as lacking in uniformity as its Romanesque. The most traditional Gothic architecture is found in the north, in the old kingdom of Castile and León. It began not as a gentle evolution from Spanish Romanesque but as a mature import from southern and western France, introduced in the 13th century by the French monastic orders. The finest French-inspired cathedrals are Toledo, Burgos and León, which has the best display of stained glass in the country.

In Catalonia, Gothic churches also show a debt to France. Hence the extraordinary cathedrals of Barcelona, Gerona and Palma de Majorca, with their powerful external walling enclosing huge internal buttresses interspaced with chapels, and their broad naves, often aisleless, with the widest Gothic vaulted spans in Europe—at Gerona 73 feet.

In the south, another group of cathedrals reflects Spain's Moorish heritage. The late Gothic Cathedral of Seville, begun c. 1402, is the earliest of these. Europe's largest medieval church, its size and rectangular plan were dictated by the site of the mosque on which it stands; its bell-tower was the minaret of the mosque.

The last phase of Spanish Gothic has splendidly exuberant vaults, towers and cloisters and rich Plateresque ornament—stone carving deriving its name from *platería*, the Spanish for the silverwork which it resembles. This popular form of surface decoration, of which the west façade of Salamanca Cathedral is a prime example, continued from Gothic into Spanish Renaissance architecture.

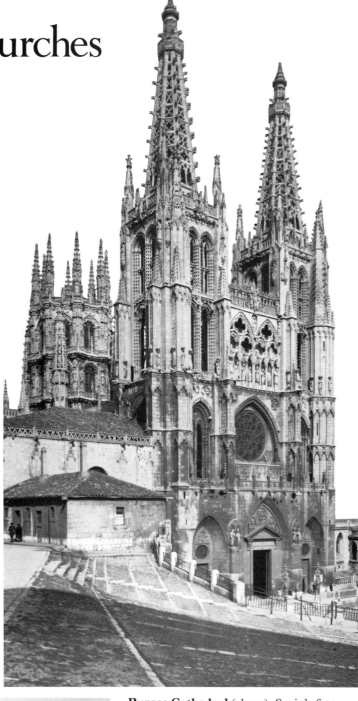

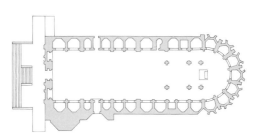

Gerona Cathedral plan (left); the aisleless, 72-ft-wide nave is Europe's widest vaulted room. Vast buttresses with chapels between them surround most of the church. The choir, in typically Spanish fashion, occupies two bays of the nave.

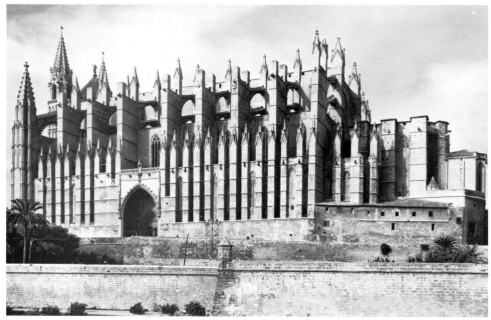

Burgos Cathedral (above), Spain's first great Gothic cathedral, was begun in 1221 as a defiant symbol of Christianity and an inspiration for the Reconquest. It was started on a French cruciform plan, but its symmetry was charmingly disturbed by the multiplicity of levels on which it was laid out, and by the addition of cloisters, the archbishop's palace and beautiful late Gothic side chapels. The interior carving is essentially Spanish and the *cimborio*, the central tower, is encrusted with 16th-century Plateresque detail; but the openwork western spires were the work of Hans of Cologne. The T-shaped "Golden Staircase" in the north transept was created by Diego de Siloe, the Renaissance sculptor.

Palma Cathedral (left), palisaded with buttresses and spiked with pinnacles, was begun in 1229, just after the recapture of the Balearic Islands from the Moors. The vast, cavernous interior glows with colour from stained glass windows, placed to catch the morning light. The nave, 141 ft high, is separated from the aisles by slender piers, below 60,000 sq ft of vaulting.

Italy, a classically tempered style

CONSIDERING ALL that was achieved north of the Alps, it is sometimes said that, apart from Milan Cathedral, the only Italian building with a transalpine flavour, there are no truly Gothic churches in Italy. This, surely, is an oversimplification which discounts differences in climatic conditions, building materials, architectural inheritance and popular requirements.

In church architecture, differences of climate are reflected mainly in the size of the windows and the pitch of the roofs. Where, as in Italy, the light is strong and the summers very warm, big windows were not favoured; and because of the Italians' long-standing devotion to fresco painting, there was little interest in stained glass. The fabric of many Italian churches is brick, sometimes with a cladding of coloured marbles, in which, unlike the northern countries, Italy abounds. Thus the emphasis was not on broken surfaces, so suitable to limestone, but on flat, polychromatic patterns. And while the northern Roman-

esque and Gothic churches had been erected on what was, artistically, virgin soil, in Italy at least three civilizations—Etruscan, Roman and Byzantine—had come and gone. So, in Italian Gothic, there was an admixture of styles.

Italian church builders, unlike those farther north, were usually not monks, but were either mendicant friars or the people of the towns, some of which gained their independence earlier than their northern counterparts. The Italians, who were not greatly preoccupied with ritual in worship, went to church primarily for the preaching. Thus what was required, and achieved, was an abundance of unencumbered floor space. The Gothic style was, in general, tempered and modified by classical proportions and a Mediterranean respect for human scale—for breadth rather than height. Because, like Germany, Italy abandoned the Romanesque style with reluctance and turned to the Renaissance soon after 1400, nearly all Italian Gothic churches belong to the 13th or 14th centuries.

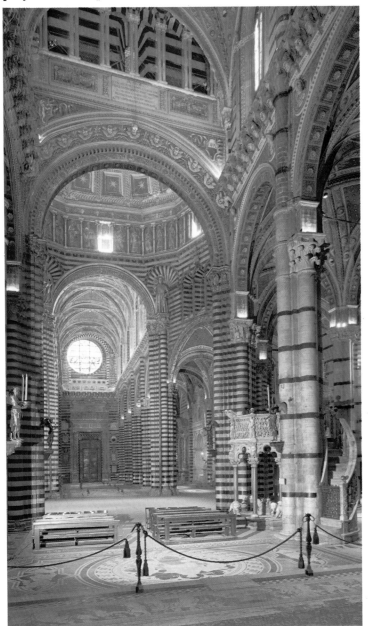

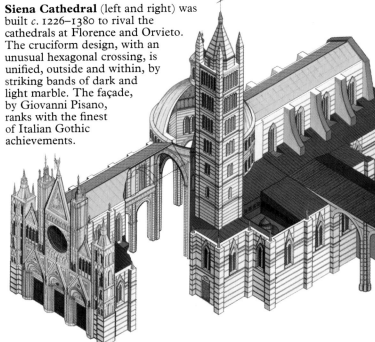

Siena Cathedral (left and right) was built *c.* 1226–1380 to rival the cathedrals at Florence and Orvieto. The cruciform design, with an unusual hexagonal crossing, is unified, outside and within, by striking bands of dark and light marble. The façade, by Giovanni Pisano, ranks with the finest of Italian Gothic achievements.

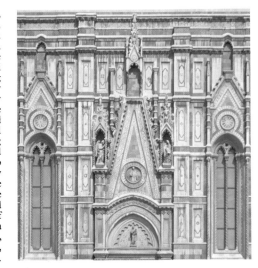

Florence Cathedral, or S. Maria del Fiore, took so long to build that it embraces both Gothic and Renaissance forms. Arnolfo di Cambio began building in 1296. Many architects subsequently enlarged and altered the design. These included Giotto, who created the free-standing campanile in 1334, and Brunelleschi, who added the essentially Renaissance dome *c.* 1420–34. The beautiful green and white marble shell of the church, set on a Gothic apsidal plan, encloses a cool, spacious interior.

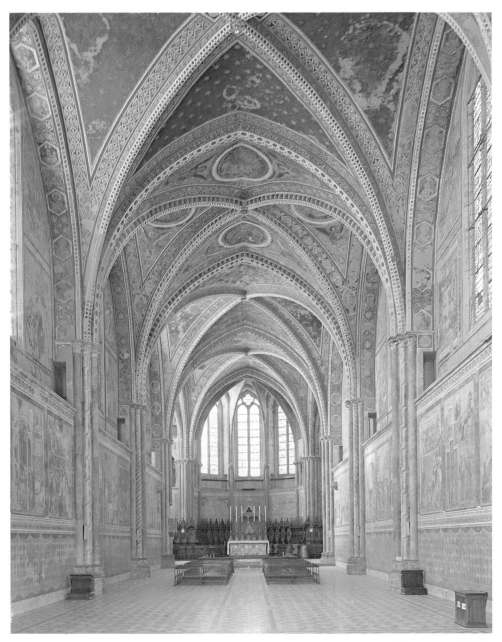

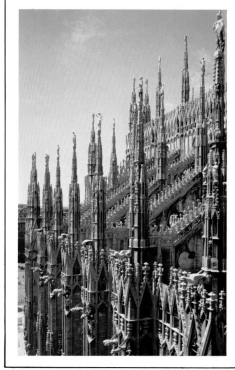

The Church of San Francesco at Assisi (right), which stands over the tomb of St Francis, was begun two years after the saint's death in 1226. Poised, in its monastic setting, on a hillside above the Umbrian plain, this most original of early Italian Gothic churches set a pattern for the spacious, hall-like churches demanded by the rapidly expanding Franciscan and Dominican orders.

A two-level basilica, its square campanile, massive buttressing and austere Umbrian façade—with triangular gable and a rose window—give the church an almost Romanesque flavour. However, both the upper church (above) and the crypt-like lower church are vaulted and end in polygonal apses. The aisleless interiors are a perfect foil for the frescoes of Cimabue and Giotto; recreating scenes from the life of St Francis, they adorn every available wall surface.

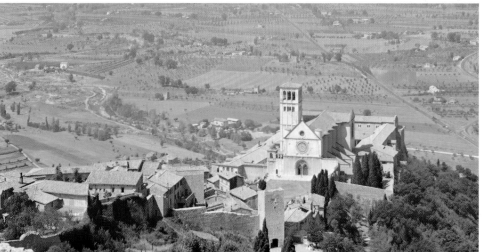

The secular splendour of the age

DURING THE latter part of the Gothic period a wealth of fine secular buildings sprang up all over western Europe. Italy led the way with a group of superb civic buildings—in Perugia the Palazzo del Municipio, 1281, in Siena the Palazzo Pubblico, 1289, and in Florence the Palazzo Vecchio, 1298, are three of many striking examples. The Doge's Palace in Venice has been described as "the most successful non-ecclesiastical building ever achieved in the Gothic style". Unsurpassed among the many once-private palaces in Italian cities is a group of palaces on the Grand Canal in Venice. Of these the Cà d'Oro, c. 1430, is the best known.

In the Low Countries, where the prosperous towns of Belgium and Holland vied with each other in the sumptuousness of their town halls, secular buildings outshone churches. The most imposing of all commercial buildings was the Cloth Hall at Ypres, a war casualty in 1915, which has been carefully rebuilt. Germany and Spain have some picturesque civic and domestic buildings of the late-Gothic period. In France the Palais de Justice at Rouen epitomizes the rich and well-preserved Gothic secular architecture of that country. Badly damaged in 1944, it is now immaculately restored.

England, fortunate in having never been much fought over, is unrivalled in the number and variety of its secular buildings of the period—manor-houses, alms-houses, hospitals, schools and colleges, guild and market halls, hostelries, huge tithe barns—the list is endless. The most remarkable single building is Westminster Hall, the only surviving part of the former Royal Palace of Westminster in London, with its enormous hammer-beam roof, erected in 1399. The most extensive building was the Palace of Hampton Court, before parts of it were rebuilt during the Renaissance by Sir Christopher Wren. Gothic castles were built in all these western European countries, but most of them are now in ruins or drastically restored.

The Palazzo Pubblico at Siena, with its 334-ft-high Torre del Mangia, Italy's highest bell-tower, symbolized the civic pride of wealthy Sienese merchants in their seat of government. Begun in 1288, it is light and palatial—one of Italy's most beautiful municipal buildings. The stone-built lower storey is pierced by characteristic Sienese arches, in which a depressed round arch is enclosed in a tall pointed one; the upper storeys are built of brick. With its mock crenellations and curved façade, the palazzo forms part of a graceful city centre around a shell-shaped piazza.

The Palais de Justice at Rouen is a fine example of a French municipal building in the Gothic style. The elaborately carved façade, the steeply pitched roof and the fine octagonal tower with turreted roof offset the horizontal emphasis of this magnificent Flamboyant building.

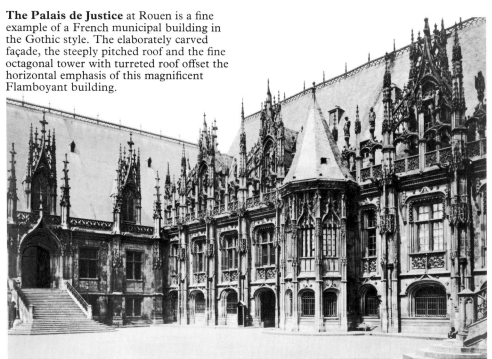

The Cloth Hall at Ypres (below) was Europe's outstanding secular medieval building. Begun in 1201 as an exchange for the prosperous Flemish woollen textile industry, this supremely dignified building took 100 years to complete. Its unbroken, 440-ft-long façade is relieved by an immense central square tower, corner spires and carved detail.

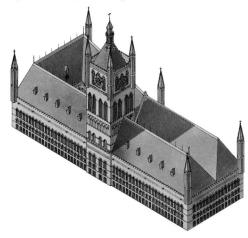

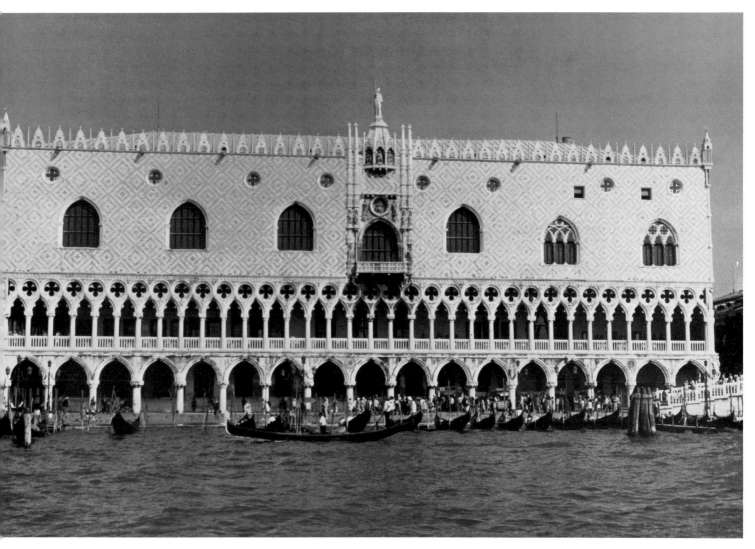

Palazzo Ducale, Venice (above). A lacy network of arcades and open stonework supports the colourful marble façade of the 14th-century Doge's Palace. Exuberant yet refined, it represents the climax of Italian Gothic. The oriental delicacy of the ornament is the fruit of Byzantine influence upon a city situated midway between East and West.

Westminster Hall, London (below left). An invention unique to English medieval builders was the hammer-beam roof. That of Westminster Hall, the only surviving part of the Palace of Westminster in London, is the most famous example. Built in 1397–9 and half an acre in area, it has one of the world's largest unsupported roofs.

The Guildhall at Lavenham in Suffolk (below) is one of several well-preserved late-Gothic buildings in the centre of this prosperous little town. An elegant timber-framed building with lath and plaster infilling, its excellent proportions disguise its true height—only 30 feet. The hall was built in 1529 during a boom in the wool trade.

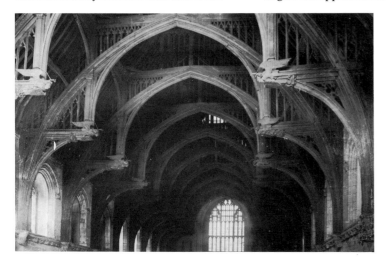

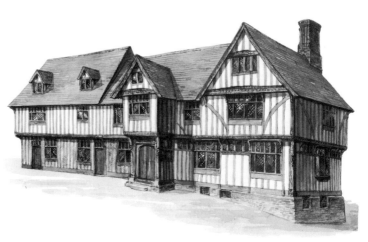

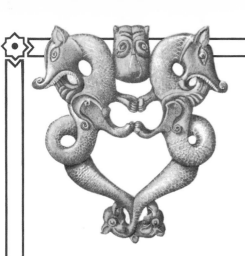

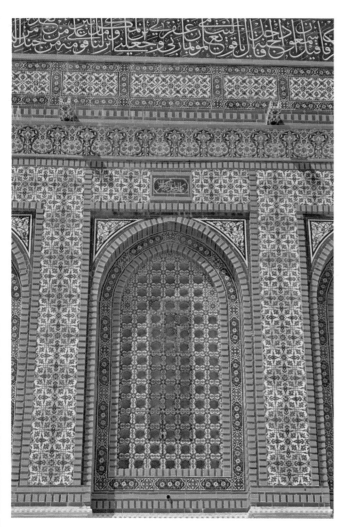

The Dome of the Rock, built by craftsmen from all over the Muslim world, expresses the eclecticism of Islamic architecture. The decorative glazed tiling used here originated among the ancient civilizations of the Middle East.

When the Arabs emerged from the deserts, impelled by the vital energy that, in less than a century, carried Islam westwards to Spain and eastwards to the confines of India, they had no architecture. The Faith, however, had ritual requirements, and these expressed in terms of the two major building traditions of the Near East—the brick and stucco tradition of Mesopotamia and the ashlar tradition of North Syria—created the first architecture of Islam.

Within eighty years of Muhammed's death in 632, the simple ritual requirements of the Faith were given formal architectural expression in a number of great congregational mosques. These buildings incorporated most of the features attributable to ritual, which have characterized Islamic architecture throughout succeeding centuries. They included an arcaded portico, derived from the shelter of palm leaves erected in Muhammed's courtyard after the Companions had complained of the heat; the *mihrab*, or decorated niche in the *qibla* (the wall oriented to Mecca), perhaps commemorating the spot where Muhammed had led his followers in prayer; the *minbar*, or pulpit, situated to the right of the mihrab, recalling no doubt the three steps from which Muhammed preached; the *maksura*, or railed enclosure, to protect the caliph or his representative when leading prayers; the basin for ritual ablutions; and lastly the minaret, an obvious convenience for the call to prayer five times a day.

As Muhammed's house had been simply the meeting place of the Faithful, so were the early mosques. Thus, the mosque was not the dwelling of the deity, incorporated no sanctuary in the Christian sense, and was served by no formal priesthood. On the other hand, the personnel of the mosque was formalized as early as its ritual features. It consisted of the *imam*, originally the

Islam

caliph or his representative, but later a paid official, the *khatib*, who preached from the minbar, and the *muezzin*, deriving his office from Muhammed's herald.

Although the ritual features of the mosque were constant, its form was to change dramatically as time passed. The 7th to the 11th centuries saw the building of *ulu Jami*, the great congregational, or Friday, mosques. These mosques, often of astonishing beauty, were essentially walled rectangular courtyards (spacious enough in theory to accommodate the whole Muslim community) surrounded by flat-roofed porticoes carrying rows of arches on columns or piers. Beneath the ample portico on the qibla, or Mecca side, usually four or more bays deep, were situated the mihrab, minbar and maksura. The porticoes on the other sides were narrower, often of two or three bays. The ablution fountain was situated in the centre of the open courtyard and the minaret at the end of the building farthest from the qibla.

With the 12th century came the development of the *medresa*, or teaching mosque, at first particularly associated with the Seljuks in Anatolia and Persia, and with the Ayyubids in Egypt. In these mosques, which were smaller but of great sophistication, porticoes were replaced by vaulted halls, or *iwans*, with imposing arched openings giving on the central courtyard. At the same time the entrance front, with an elaborate portal and sometimes flanked by twin minarets, became a prominent feature. (By the 15th century what remained of the courtyard was often enclosed and the central area surmounted by a dome or wooden lantern.) The introduction of the medresa coincided in many areas with the abandonment of brick and the rise of superb ashlar buildings, often with alternating courses of lighter and darker stone. Under the Bahri Mamelukes, who ruled in Egypt from 1250 to 1382, the medresa

achieved perhaps its finest expression.

The erection of mausolea, often with a splendid stone dome over the tomb, was another development that roughly coincided with the introduction of the medresa. These mausolea were often associated with medresas in a single and imposing architectural complex. From the 14th century another distinctive unit, the *sebil* and *kuttab*, a fountain with a charity school above, often found a place in the mausoleum–medresa complex.

Following the fall of Constantinople to the Ottomans in 1453, Islamic architecture suffered a profound change, for the works of the Ottomans came to reflect the overwhelming influence of the church of Santa Sophia and the Byzantine tradition. In the masterpieces of Sinan, the Ottoman architect, and in the other imposing Turkish mosques of the 16th and early 17th centuries, everything is subordinated to the central dome. In order that nothing may compete with it, the minaret, which in the 15th century had become a feature of immense elaboration, is reduced to a slender pencil. Although architects have rarely organized interior volumes with greater elegance and clarity than they did in Turkey in the 16th century, later Ottoman mosques tend to be a repetitive variation on a single theme.

Most of the important decorative features that we associate with the buildings of Islam were introduced at an early date. The pointed arch, free stucco work, the decorative use of calligraphy, and conventional floral patterns set in a geometrical framework were all established by the end of the 9th century. Two hundred years later, stalactite ornament and the joggled voussoir were coming into general use. Particularly in Persia, glazed tiles played an important role from early times, although both there and in Turkey the lavish use of ceramics is associated with the 16th and 17th centuries.

Syria and Egypt

THE UMMAYAD CALIPHS, who ruled the fast-expanding new Islamic Empire from 661 until 750, made Damascus their capital. Muslim culture was now in close contact with Byzantine civilization and with the ashlar building tradition of northern Syria. From the Syrians, the Ummayad builders perhaps derived the mihrab, which echoed the apse of Syrian Christian churches, and also the square-based minaret. In addition to such imposing desert palaces as the 8th-century Kasr al-Hayr, which shows little distinctive Islamic influence, the two surviving Ummayad buildings of outstanding importance are the Mosque of Walid I at Damascus (715) and the Dome of the Rock at Jerusalem (619) which is the earliest great Muslim building in existence. Yet neither of these is typical of Islamic architecture. Both show a strong Syro-Byzantine influence; furthermore, the Mosque of Walid I was built within the precinct of a Roman temple, and the Dome of the Rock was adapted to a site sacred since antiquity to Jews and Christians.

In 750, the Ummayad caliphate was replaced by the Abbasids, who ruled until 1258 from Baghdad, in Iraq, where the brick and stucco building tradition of the Persians was predominant. When the Mongols razed Baghdad in the 13th century, the major Abbasid buildings were destroyed.

It is, therefore, in Egypt that Islamic architecture of the 9th to the 14th centuries can be seen at its most vigorous. Cairo was not only immensely rich, but was spared destruction. Its medieval buildings are unequalled in their variety and number. The Tulunids, Fatimids, Ayyubids and Mamelukes contributed to a wealth of monuments, which reflect not only exquisite craftsmanship but also a profound feeling for structure. The 9th-century Mosque of Ibn Tulun, at Cairo, is the finest of surviving congregational mosques, while the 14th-century Medresa of Sultan Hassan, also at Cairo, is the finest of its kind. Until 1516, when Egypt was reduced to a province of the Ottoman Empire, such works as the Mosque Medresa of Qait Bey, completed in 1496, continued to exhibit an elegance and refinement hard to parallel in the architecture of Islam.

The Dome of the Rock at Jerusalem, begun c. 684 on the site of the old Jewish Temple, is Islam's earliest monument. Influenced by the Graeco–Byzantine rotunda, the building has a harmonious geometrical plan; the dome and clerestory beneath it are supported upon a circular colonnade of piers, while the outer lower storey is a double octagon. Multipatterned ceramic facings sheath the exterior. The sumptuous interior is decorated with marble panelling and mosaic.

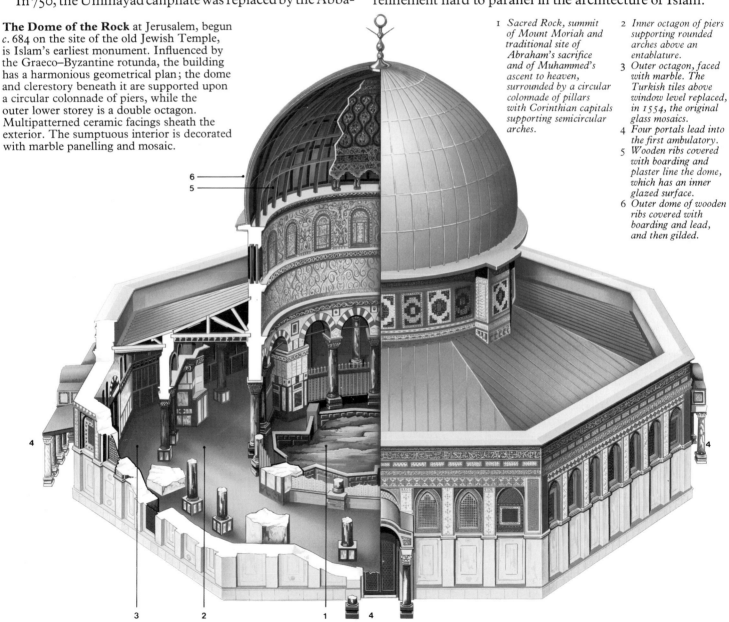

1 *Sacred Rock, summit of Mount Moriah and traditional site of Abraham's sacrifice and of Muhammed's ascent to heaven, surrounded by a circular colonnade of pillars with Corinthian capitals supporting semicircular arches.*

2 *Inner octagon of piers supporting rounded arches above an entablature.*

3 *Outer octagon, faced with marble. The Turkish tiles above window level replaced, in 1554, the original glass mosaics.*

4 *Four portals lead into the first ambulatory.*

5 *Wooden ribs covered with boarding and plaster line the dome, which has an inner glazed surface.*

6 *Outer dome of wooden ribs covered with boarding and lead, and then gilded.*

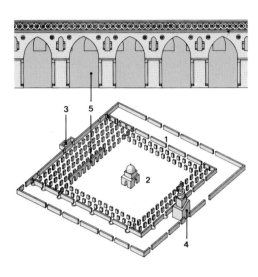

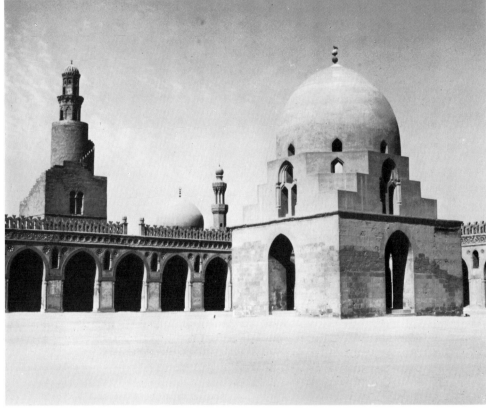

The Ibn Tulun Mosque at Cairo (above right), built in 876–9, is one of the most imposing early Islamic monuments. Its plan (above) is strongly influenced by the Great Mosque at Samarra. The perimeter wall, with a unique ornamental parapet, encloses on three sides a *ziyada*, or outer court (1). The Friday congregation gathered in the *sahn*, or central court (2), with its fountain, for the ablutions which are a feature of the Muslim rite. The devout prayed facing the mihrab (3), an ornate niche in the qibla (the wall indicating the direction of Mecca). Although the mosque is of brick faced with decorated stucco motifs, the later minaret (4), which echoes the spiral form of its Samarran predecessor, is built of limestone. Portals lead from the eastern ziyada into the arcading. The elegant pointed arches (5) are carried on piers with engaged colonettes. Facing the qibla, four rows of arcades form a beautiful aisled sanctuary.

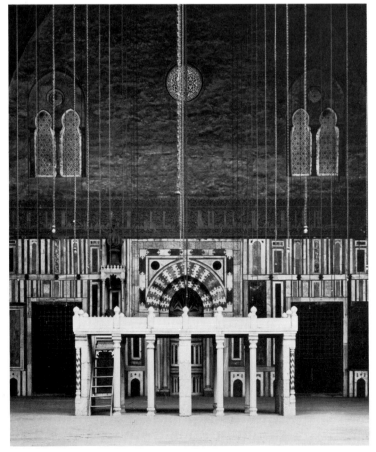

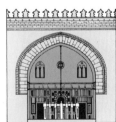

The Medresa of Sultan Hassan at Cairo, built in 1356–62, is a collegiate mosque, cruciform in plan. Four iwans, or recessed porches, with immense pointed arches (above), constitute the arms of the cross. There is a minimum of decoration, and the walls of the 100-ft sahn rise skywards with splendid architectural effect. The founder's domed mausoleum, situated behind the qibla (left), is enriched with stalactite decoration.

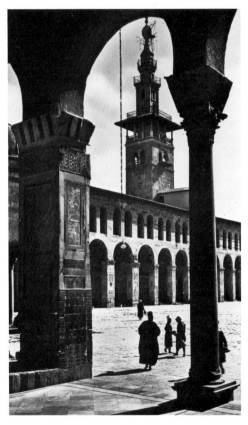

The Great Mosque at Damascus (above), Islam's oldest extant congregational mosque, was begun in 707 within a vast Roman sacred precinct. Existing Hellenistic buildings were incorporated in the plan, the corner-towers becoming Islam's first minarets. The sanctuary has a transept and features that recall the earlier Christian church on the site. The court, flanked by arcades, incorporates pierced-stone window-grilles, with the type of geometrical design that was to become characteristic of Islam. There are superb mosaics of Byzantine inspiration, particularly in the western arcade.

ISLAM
Persia

ON REACHING THE Euphrates in the 7th century, the Arabs came in contact with a vigorous Sassanian building tradition that soon imprinted itself on the emergent architecture of Islam. It was a tradition of brick and stucco, and these materials, with the addition of enamelled tilework, dictated the character of Muslim building in Persia, from the earliest surviving mosque of Tarik-Khana, built in the 8th century at Damghan, to the sumptuous Safavid works of the 17th century, such as the Masjid-i-Shah at Isfahan.

From the outset, brick and stucco were vehicles for lavish ornamentation. Nowhere else in Islam was brickwork so decorative, patterned and elaborate; nowhere else did stucco artists achieve such virtuosity, or combine floral motifs more effectively with geometric patterns and elegant calligraphy. Blue lustre tiles—found in Mesopotamia in the 9th century and developing later into multicoloured mosaic faience—were employed with such prodigality that by the 16th century they covered entire buildings.

In terms of architecture rather than decoration, Islamic building in Persia is distinguished by its unique tomb-towers, often with vertical flanged ribs, the most splendid examples dating from the 11th to the 14th centuries, and by the early emergence of the medresa plan, with four great arched iwans opening on a central courtyard.

From beyond the Euphrates, three important features of Islamic architecture were derived: the squinch, familiar to the Sassanians, which played so decisive a role in the erection of the beautiful stone domes of Egypt and Anatolia; stalactite decoration, which first appeared early in the 11th century in Persia and was destined to become a hallmark of Islamic building; and, lastly, the glazed tile, which was to contribute so greatly to the mosques of the West.

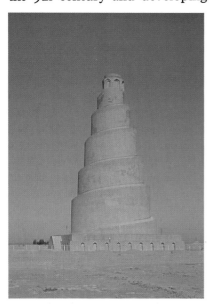

The Great Mosque at Samarra, begun in 847, is the largest mosque ever built. A burnt brick construction, it is famous for its curious cone-shaped minaret (above), the Malwiya, which is encircled by a spiral outer ramp like the ancient Assyrian ziggurats. The diminishing circuits of the tower are equidistant, so the ramp rises more sharply as it ascends. The plan (below) shows a mosque of the congregational type, with high, bastioned walls and a spacious inner court. The flat-roofed porticoes surrounding the court are supported on brick piers, nine rows deep on the qibla, or sanctuary, side. The entire mosque, 784 ft by 512 ft, is enclosed by an outer ziyada which is more than one-fifth of a mile square.

The Masjid-i-Shah, the Imperial Mosque at Isfahan, was skilfully built at a half right angle to the entrance, thus achieving the correct orientation with Mecca and at the same time aligning with the *maidan*, the city's great central square. Begun in 1612, it is a classic iwan mosque; dressed inside and out with predominantly blue and turquoise faience tiles, it is the city's largest and most brilliant building.

Main court overlooked by four iwans, containing symmetrical arcades and a wide ablution pool.

Portal minaret, 110 ft high.

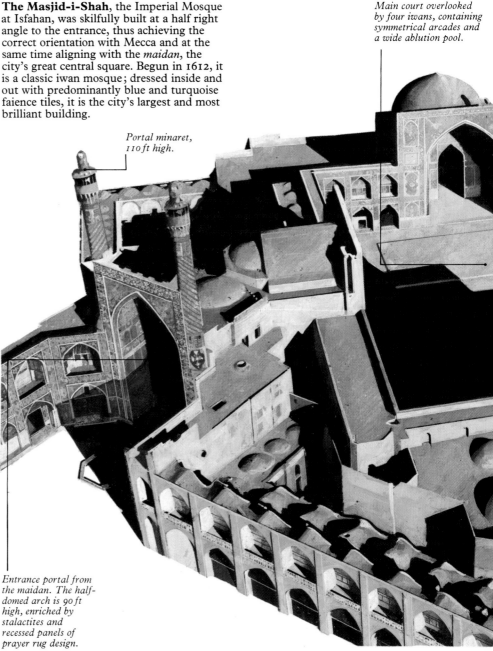

Entrance portal from the maidan. The half-domed arch is 90 ft high, enriched by stalactites and recessed panels of prayer rug design.

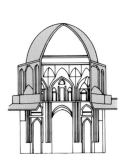

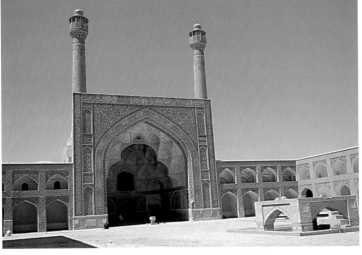

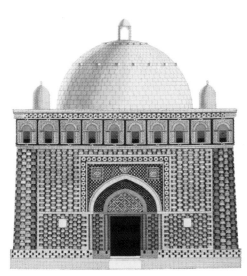

The Masjid-i-Jami is Isfahan's Friday, or congregational, mosque. Founded in 760 and subsequently enlarged, it displays over 800 years of Persian architecture. Its chief glories are the two domed chambers dating from the late 11th century. The Gunbad-i-Kharka or the Brown Dome (above), contains some

of Persia's finest Seljuk brickwork. Perfectly preserved, it is 33 ft square and 65½ ft high; four corner squinches bridge the transition between the octagonal ground plan and the circular dome. The four-iwan court (above), 196 ft by 230 ft, is lined with elaborate mosaic tiling.

The Tomb of Ishmail Samanid at Bokhara (above), built in 907, is remarkable for its decorative brickwork. The deeply etched pattern and texture of its exterior walls recall wickerwork and would seem to be derived from the carved wood techniques of the region's earlier mosques.

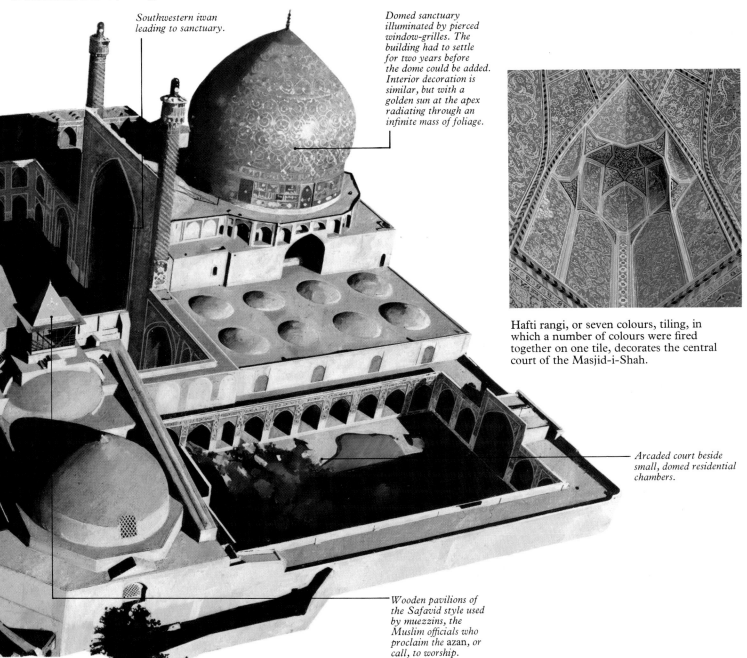

Southwestern iwan leading to sanctuary.

Domed sanctuary illuminated by pierced window-grilles. The building had to settle for two years before the dome could be added. Interior decoration is similar, but with a golden sun at the apex radiating through an infinite mass of foliage.

Hafti rangi, or seven colours, tiling, in which a number of colours were fired together on one tile, decorates the central court of the Masjid-i-Shah.

Arcaded court beside small, domed residential chambers.

Wooden pavilions of the Safavid style used by muezzins, the Muslim officials who proclaim the azan, *or call, to worship.*

The Seljuks

THE SELJUK TURKS who defeated the Byzantines in 1071 and overran central Anatolia, where they established their sultanate of Rum, were nomadic tribesmen, who had emerged from the steppes of central Asia only a generation earlier. Yet they proved prolific and splendid builders, who, in the course of the next two hundred years, left their bold architectural imprint on Asia Minor.

The distinctive characteristic of Seljuk work is the calculated counterpoint between plain surfaces of superb ashlar masonry and areas of rigidly controlled decoration. The confidence of their carved geometric patterns, conventional floral designs and decorative calligraphy was outstanding. Equally confident were their elegant patterned domes, raised on the squinches which are almost a sign-manual of Seljuk building. Although boldly eclectic—for they derived from Syria their stone-carving technique and the square-based minaret, and from Persia the use of glazed tiles, decorative brickwork and the round brick minaret—the Seljuks evolved an architecture that was distinctly their own. Nowhere is the originality of the Seljuks more apparent than in their beautiful *türbes*. Inspired by the shape of the nomad tent, or possibly by the churches of Armenia, these little mausolea, with their conical roofs and their bands of exquisite stone carving, are among the choice delights of Islamic architecture.

In the harsh climate of Anatolia, the open, congregational mosque was soon abandoned. Here, Seljuk building is associated with medresas, their recessed and highly decorated portals often flanked by twin minarets. The medresa, or teaching mosque, recommended itself to the Seljuks, who were devout propagandists of Muslim orthodoxy. Coincidentally with the usual cruciform medresa, they evolved a basilican type, probably owing something to Christian prototypes in Syria. The Çifte Minare at Erzurum, 1253, is a characteristic basilican medresa.

The distinguished architectural legacy of the Seljuks is not limited to the fine mosques in such towns as Sivas, Erzurum, Diyarbekir and Konya. In a country where fords are impassable when the snows melt, they threw across the rivers of Asia Minor those shapely yet sturdy bridges, so many of which survive. To further a revived traffic along the old Byzantine caravan routes, they also built the splendid four-square *hans*, or caravanserais, which are still the wonder of the Anatolian steppe.

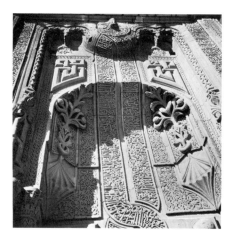

Although the unusual portal of the Ince Minare at Konya is overelaborate, the crisp carving of the conventionalized floral decoration and the Naskhi script is typical of Seljuk work of the 13th century.

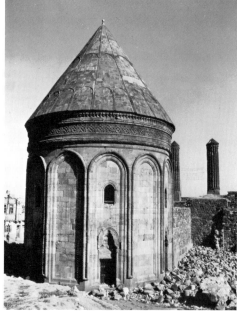

The türbe, or tomb-tower, was a mausoleum, with a small prayer chamber situated above a tomb-vault. The türbe at Erzurum (above) is circular in plan; others were square or octagonal. The overhanging stone roof was usually conical, like a tent roof, and vaulted with a stone dome within. The exteriors were often decorated with blind arcading and geometrically patterned bands of fine carved stonework.

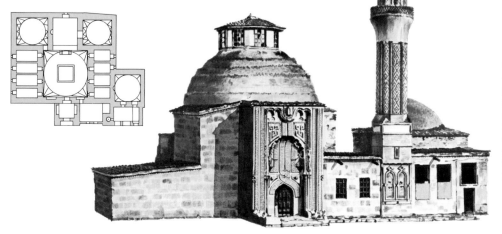

The Ince Minare, or Slender Minaret, at Konya, built between 1258 and 1262, and shown here in plan and in its original form, is one of the finest of the Seljuk dome-chambered medresas. An iwan hall opens on to the sahn, which is roofed with a brick dome that was originally surmounted by a lantern. The minaret is now half its original height.

This little twin-lobed plant motif was a favourite with the Seljuks. Superb carvers, they used a bewildering variety of patterns, even reproducing Persian stucco designs in stone.

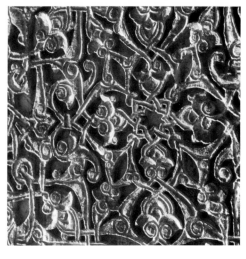

The Çifte Minare (right), the Double-Minaret Medresa, at Erzurum was built in 1253. The entrance front of this noble medresa shows the skill with which the Seljuks combined plain surfaces and rich decoration. The contrast between the carved bands framing the stalactite portals and the undecorated wall surfaces is characteristic of the best Seljuk work. Set on stone bases, the fluted cylindrical minarets are of brick and reflect Persian influence. The plan (below) is a compromise between an iwaned and an arcaded structure.

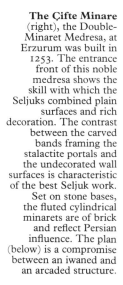

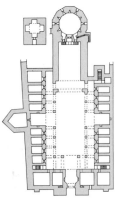

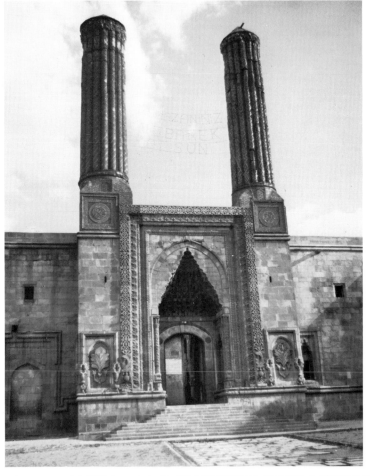

The Sultan Han (below), between Konya and Kaysari, begun in 1229, is a typical Seljuk fortified caravanserai, a rest house for caravans, built upon a main trade route. The finest date from the 13th century, and much thought was lavished on them. A decorated portal led into a severely functional courtyard, flanked by lodgings and storerooms. For the comfort of the merchants there was a *hammam*, or bath, coffee house, cobbler, and sometimes even an orchestra. A mosque normally stood in the centre of the courtyard. The camel stable, a great aisled hall, was architecturally the most impressive part of the complex.

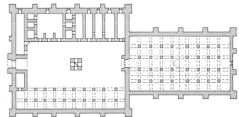

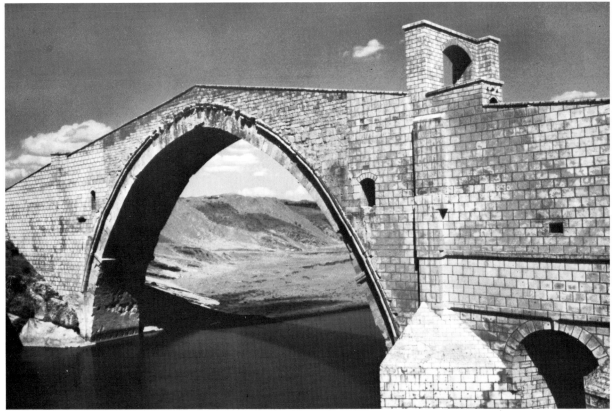

Seljuk bridges. Where the rivers of Turkey drop from the high central plateau of Anatolia, they are rarely fordable in spring and winter. To carry caravan traffic the Seljuks built imposing bridges. Many are still in use, such as this 12th-century bridge over the Batman, a tributary of the Tigris.

Spain and Morocco

ARCHITECTURE IN Spain and Morocco tended to develop somewhat independently of the rest of Islam. From the outset the horseshoe arch and the lobed or multifoil arch, which are rare in Cairo and Anatolia, characterized local building. Minarets were usually of the bold, square tower-form, often with arcaded windows, and relate to the Christian church towers of northern Syria. Rightly, the most famous examples are the Giralda at Seville and the tower of the Koutoubia Mosque at Marrakesh, both of the 12th century. The brick and stucco tradition of Mesopotamia is well exemplified in the 12th-century congregational Mosque of Tinmal, the first Almohad capital, which rises ruined but imposing in the High Atlas. The medresa plan arrived late in Morocco with the Merinid dynasty, *c.* 1250–1350, and a striking example is to be found at Fez in the Bou Inaniya Medresa, *c.* 1350.

The two most notable buildings on this fringe of Islam are the Great Mosque at Córdoba and the Alhambra Palace at Granada. Although its architectural forms have a certain restlessness characteristic of Muslim building in the West, the Mosque of Córdoba, begun by Abder-Rahman in 785, is a majestic building. A mosque of the congregational type, and utilizing—as the Arabs so often did—earlier classical columns and capitals, its eighteen *riwaqs*, or arcades, that precede the qibla create the impression of some extensive stone forest. Arches are stilted or even superposed to give additional height; complex multifoil arches are often employed; and there are vaults with interlaced arching of unusual complexity.

The Alhambra, substantially of the 14th century, is the sole Islamic palace of the Middle Ages that remains virtually intact. Evoking in its decoration all that is meant by the term "arabesque", it is an elegant affair of lath, plaster and stucco, an airy complex of pervasive charm.

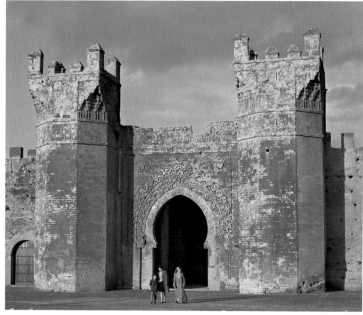

The walls of Rabat (above), with their splendid gates, date from the 12th century, when Saladin was fortifying Cairo. By then defences had become sophisticated; gates were furnished with bent entrances and portcullises; and the machicoulis was coming into use. Ceremonial gates, like the example from Marrakesh (right), were richly decorated.

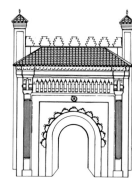

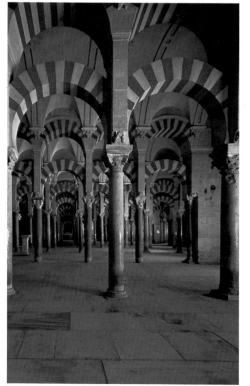

The Great Mosque at Córdoba, capital of the Ummayad Caliphate of Spain, was begun in 785. Its great hall (left) is a forest of arcades, 19 bays wide. The horseshoe arches, with alternating voussoirs of white stone and red brick, are carried for the most part on antique classical columns. To give added height to the hall, the arches were either stilted or an extraordinary double-tiered arch was employed. In the sanctuary before the mihrab ornately scalloped arches and half-arches are displayed in a unique combination. This chamber is roofed with two vaults of astonishing complexity, the domes deriving support from intersecting ribbed arches.

The Giralda Tower, Seville (right), was once a minaret, part of Seville's 12th-century congregational Mosque, erected for the Almohad caliphs. It is built entirely of brick, and following the Syrian Christian tower style adopted for minarets throughout North Africa and Spain, it is slender, square and lofty, with arcaded windows. In the 15th century the mosque was replaced, but for the Giralda and part of the sahn, by Seville's great cathedral. An ornate belfry, added in 1568, converted the minaret into a bell-tower, but the elegant panels of Islamic interlaced arches on the façade betray the oriental origin of this famous tower.

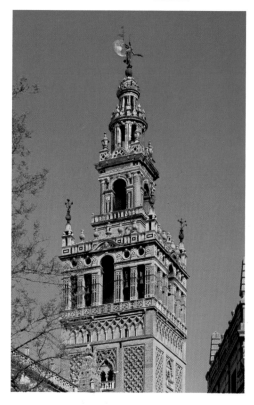

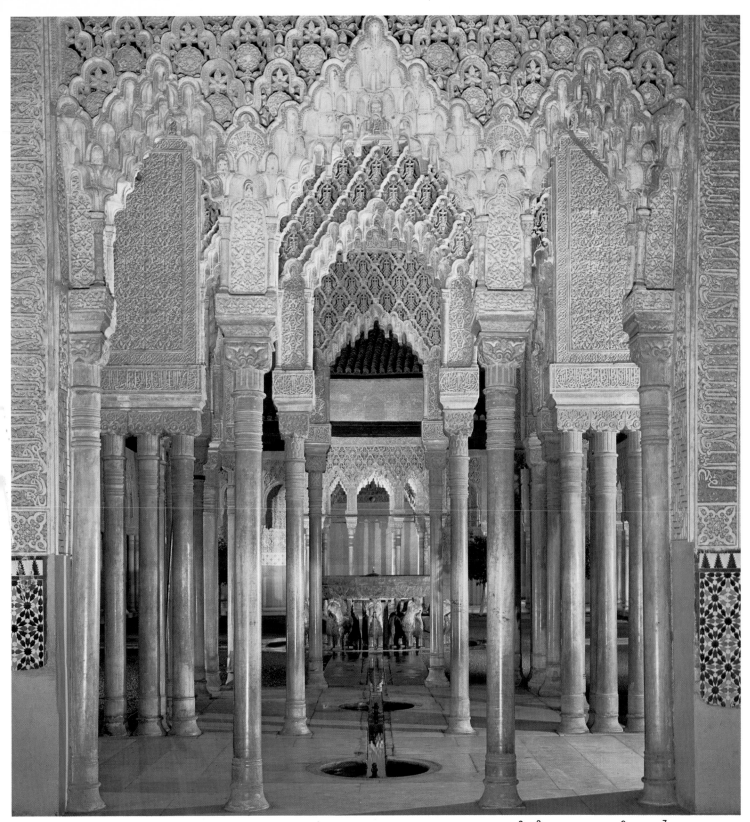

The Alhambra, Granada, built mainly in the 13th and 14th centuries, was the palace of the last Muslim rulers of Spain. From outside it looks like a vast fortress, with bright red burnt-brick walls. Inside, it is a sumptuous palace of effusively decorated rooms, courts and formal gardens, laid out in the curiously irregular style of Muslim palaces. The Hall of Judgement (above) has complex stalactite decoration—a gay profusion of brick stucco pendants. It is preceded by the arcaded Court of the Lions, which, it has been suggested, reflects the Muslim idea of paradise. A marble fountain surrounded by stone-carved lions splashes in the courtyard, coloured enamelled tiles line the walls of the shady loggias and delicate columns support fretted stalactite arches. Vividly coloured and gilded, the decoration of the palace—variegated marbles, lustre tiles, flowing stucco ornament—impart to each pavilion and court an air of light, impermanent fantasy. The ground plan (right) shows: The Court of the Myrtles (1); The Mosque (2); The Court of the Mosque (3); The Hall of the Barque (4); The Hall of the Ambassadors (5); The Baths (6); The Queen's Boudoir (7); The Lindarajas Garden (8); The Hall of the Two Sisters (9); The Hall of Judgement (10); The Court of the Lions (11); The Hall of the Abencerrajes (12).

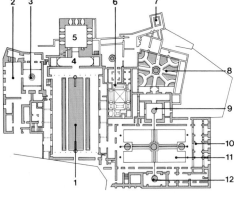

The Ottomans

WHEN, IN THE 14th century, the Ottoman Turks inherited the fragmented territories of the Seljuks, the buildings of the Ottoman capital at Bursa continued to reflect the Seljuk architectural tradition. Such was the vitality of this tradition that, fifty years after Byzantium fell to the Ottomans in 1453, the Seljuk style persisted in the new Ottoman capital at Istanbul. Only with the completion of the Mosque of Beyazit II, in 1505, did the great Byzantine Church of Santa Sophia begin to show its influence. During the next century and a half, it inspired the finest Ottoman architecture, which developed the concept of a unified, domed space even further than it had been taken by the Byzantines.

The Ottoman architect Sinan and his followers, who were concerned with the imposition of the perfect circle on the perfect square, designed austere geometrical masterpieces, in which decoration plays a secondary role. Everything is subordinated to the great domed interiors and to the sense of ordered space which they convey. Uncompromising and monumental, these Ottoman mosques echo and develop the theme of Santa Sophia. Unlike Justinian's cathedral, they are preceded by an open, pillared court and are commonly the focus of a group of buildings which include a founder's tomb, a hospital, kitchens, baths and teaching medresas. The scale of these architectural complexes was new to Islam and their harmonious planning is a striking feature of Turkish building.

Classic Ottoman architecture declined, as did the empire, from the middle of the 17th century, and an increasing European influence led to the development of a Turkish version of Rococo. This hybrid style, well suited to certain features of Islamic decoration, found its happiest expression in domestic building and flourished far into the 19th century. Although often technically shoddy, the style of these houses was eminently picturesque, and in the Romantic period its exotic charm came to symbolize Ottoman architecture for the West.

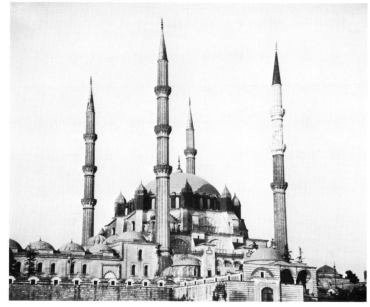

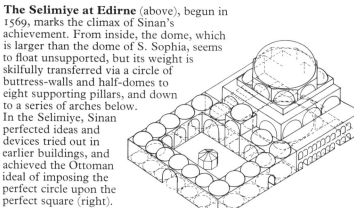

The Selimiye at Edirne (above), begun in 1569, marks the climax of Sinan's achievement. From inside, the dome, which is larger than the dome of S. Sophia, seems to float unsupported, but its weight is skilfully transferred via a circle of buttress-walls and half-domes to eight supporting pillars, and down to a series of arches below. In the Selimiye, Sinan perfected ideas and devices tried out in earlier buildings, and achieved the Ottoman ideal of imposing the perfect circle upon the perfect square (right).

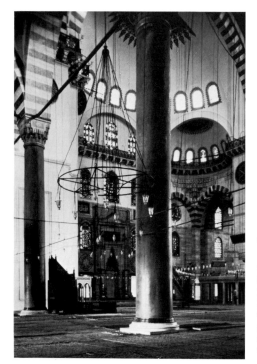

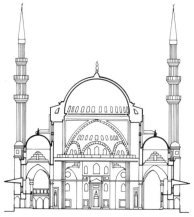

The Suleimaniye, Istanbul (above), is the largest of Sinan's mosques. Begun in 1550, its ground plan was based on S. Sophia, but it was intended to surpass Justinian's church in splendour. A cluster of cupolas and arches lead to the main dome, 181 ft high and 84 ft wide. Inside (left), four gigantic pillars support the central dome and the half-dome above the qibla, and 138 stained-glass windows admit a suffused light.

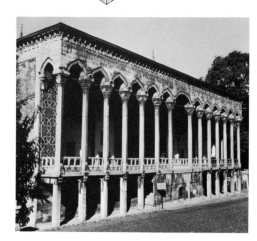

The Çinili Kiosk, or Tiled Pavilion, in the Topkapi Palace, at Istanbul, is decorated with glazed faience. Built as early as 1473, and possibly designed by a Persian architect, it exerted a powerful influence upon succeeding Ottoman architecture. Square in plan, it is preceded by an arcaded entrance portico (above). The interior is roofed with an elaborate arrangement of ribbed vaults and a lofty central dome.

THE
RENAISSANCE

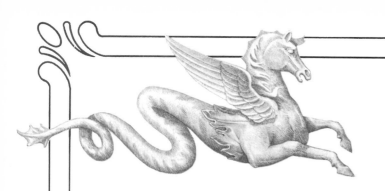

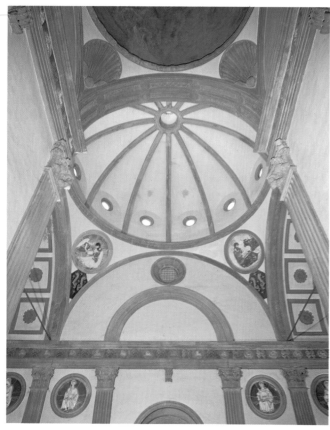

A language of architectural forms
derived from Ancient Rome was used
by Renaissance architects for new
purposes. The Pazzi Chapel, Florence,
designed like a Roman temple in
miniature, has classical decorative
detail and a Gothic ribbed dome.

What separates the architecture of the
Renaissance from that of the Middle Ages
is the Cult of Personality. The names of many of
the masons who worked on the great medieval
cathedrals are known to us, and it is clear that there
was no intentional anonymity: the real difference
lies in the fact that architects like Brunelleschi or
Alberti were consciously artists, not just leading
craftsmen in a team. They were deliberately
creating a personal style, founded on what they
knew of the buildings of Ancient Rome.

We know about Brunelleschi, Alberti and most
of the others, because their contemporaries thought
it worth while to record their doings: a long,
anonymous *Life* of Brunelleschi, written about forty
years after his death, is a polemic against everyone
who did not wholeheartedly support him in his
efforts to recover and restore the "good ancient
manner of building". The author tells us that
Brunelleschi, on a visit to Rome, "perceived the
method and the symmetry of the building
techniques of the Ancients, and he thought he could
discern a certain order, as it were of bones and
members, and it was made clear to him, almost as
if God had illumined him. He sketched almost
every building in Rome and the surrounding
countryside, with measurements . . . as closely as
he could estimate them. . . ."

Alberti took the muddled and obscure Latin text
of Vitruvius—the only ancient writer on architecture whose treatise has survived—and, in deliberate
emulation, wrote a Latin treatise of his own,
expounding the doctrine of mathematical harmony
and proportion in architecture. A few years later,
in a document of 1468 concerning the Palace at
Urbino, we have a statement by Duke Federigo
da Montefeltro, one of the most enlightened patrons
of the Renaissance, in which he says, "We judge
those men to be most worthy of praise and honour

Italian Renaissance

who are manifestly endowed with genius and talents, and most especially with such talents, honoured by the ancients and moderns alike, as that of Architecture; based, as it is, on Arithmetic and Geometry, which are among the Seven Liberal Arts. . . ."

This document is the strongest evidence for attributing the Ducal Palace at Urbino to Luciano Laurana, but there are several cases of major buildings created by unknown masters, or designed by a major architect but executed and modified by others. Thus, the churches of San Bernardino at Urbino or the Consolazione at Todi, the Palazzo Pitti in Florence in its original, smaller, form, and the vast Palazzo della Cancelleria in Rome still present unsolved puzzles.

By the end of the 15th century, the main structural and aesthetic principles of Ancient Roman architecture had been recovered and more or less assimilated. Most of the story of this recovery is told by Giorgio Vasari in his monumental *Lives of the Painters, Sculptors and Architects*, 1550 and 1568. Vasari was a painter and an architect who began serious collection of material for his great work in the 1540s. He therefore tells us about the history of the early Renaissance from the point of view of a professional architect rather more than a hundred years after Brunelleschi's first works in Florence had begun the whole movement. In the general introductory passages to the technical *Introductions*, and in the *Lives* of individual artists, Vasari makes it clear that the original impetus came from the same sources as those which had inspired the Humanists to revive the writing of Ciceronian Latin. All these men regarded Ancient Rome as a golden age of the arts which could be revived by the efforts of men like themselves.

This explains why contemporaries (and later generations) agreed that the apogee of classical architecture came with the work of Bramante in Rome in the first years of the 16th century. He inherited from his 15th-century predecessors a fully developed instrument, which enabled him, for the first time, to concentrate upon expression rather than on the recovery of a lost language. His works in Rome, and especially the designs for New St Peter's, came to be regarded as norms of a perfect classicism; but in the nature of things this was bound to produce a reaction, which was profoundly reinforced by the Sack of Rome in 1527 and the turmoils consequent upon the Reformation and the foreign invasions of Italy. Even before the Sack of Rome, Bramante's own pupil and successor, Raphael, in a celebrated letter, expressed the view that Bramante's art was more austere than that of antiquity, and that a greater richness of form and decoration could be justified from ancient precedents. Raphael's own pupil, Giulio Romano, and Michelangelo himself, are the two great exponents of a more intensely personal form of expression. Michelangelo made it clear that he did not intend to be bound by the rules of ancient architecture as, for example, his contemporary Sangallo was, and that he regarded it as the prerogative of a great artist to create new forms of his own. Much of the 16th century passed in a rather frantic search for a balance between an unrestrictedly personal style and the claims of a harmoniously classical style based on Bramante. Palladio, who died in 1580, was perhaps the last great architect to continue the austere style of Bramante. In his own treatise, published in 1570, he succeeded in formulating the abiding principles of classicism. His *Quattro Libri* remained the bible of all classically minded architects for at least three centuries, but, by 1600, a new balance between the claims of antiquity and the freedom of the individual artist had been attained, and the Baroque style arrived with Bernini at a new interpretation of the heritage of Ancient Rome.

Florence and the Renaissance

THE RENAISSANCE of classical architecture began in Florence just before 1420. Its symbol is the dome of the cathedral, begun by Filippo Brunelleschi in 1420 and completed after his death in 1446. The huge dome, 138½ feet across, could not have been built with the means available to the architects of the Gothic cathedrals, but Brunelleschi had made an intensive study of the vaulting methods of the Imperial Roman architects, as exemplified by the Pantheon in Rome, which is 140 feet across and made of cast concrete. It was this unique combination of "modern" —that is Gothic—constructional methods with those of Ancient Rome which made Brunelleschi's reputation and at the same time introduced the idea of a deliberate revival of ancient forms for modern purposes.

The conscious use of ancient forms, as a parallel to the revival of Ciceronian Latin in literature, can be seen in the loggia of the Foundling Hospital, in Florence, also by Brunelleschi and built between 1419 and 1424. It came to be accepted that a new language of architectural forms, derived from those of Ancient Rome, could be used for new purposes; the norms invented by Brunelleschi became definitive for Christian churches—the Latin cross plan derived from Roman basilicas in San Lorenzo and Santo Spirito, and the central plan in the Old Sacristy of San Lorenzo, the unfinished Santa Maria degli Angeli, and, above all, in the Pazzi Chapel at Santa Croce. These type-forms set by Brunelleschi (and, later, by Alberti) remained valid in Florence for the rest of the 15th century, but the development outside, in Mantua, Urbino and Milan, owed more, on the whole, to Alberti than to Brunelleschi.

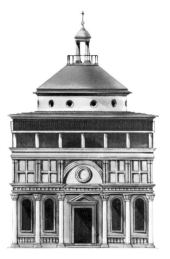

1 *Corinthian columns*
2 *Loggia*
3 *Nave, with position of overhead dome marked*
4 *Altar*

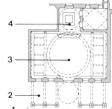

The Pazzi Chapel (above), an exquisite architectural jewel set in the cloister of S. Croce, was built by Brunelleschi for Andrea de' Pazzi, a member of the family which later became notorious for plotting to murder Lorenzo de' Medici. Begun in 1429 at the height of Brunelleschi's career and completed long after his death, it illustrates his free and highly inventive use of the different styles of the past. The chapel has a centralized plan, Byzantine in concept, covered by a rib-vaulted dome of Gothic construction, and barrel vaults with classical coffering. Smaller domes are set in the altar recess and in the vault of the colonnaded entrance loggia. Delicate carving and graceful detail lighten the geometric austerity of this tiny church. Of particular note are the charming roundels designed by Della Robbia in the dome of the loggia and the glazed terracotta frieze inside the chapel. The building has always been greatly admired as a superb expression of order and serenity.

San Lorenzo (right) was rebuilt by Brunelleschi for the Medici family. Here their children were baptized, their dead buried, and their marriages splendidly celebrated. The earliest part of the building is the Old Sacristy (1), begun in 1421. The mathematical purity and harmony of this centrally planned cubic chapel covered by a dome resting on pendentives, is in keeping with the spirit of the Renaissance and had a far-reaching influence. The main body of the church, a basilica with a light arcade of Corinthian columns (2) was completed much later. A row of side chapels (3) extends beyond the domed aisles (4), enhancing the space of the interior. The nave was completed by Antonio Manetti, with a dome above the crossing (5). The New Sacristy (6 and below), commissioned in 1520 to house the tombs of the Medici, was designed and embellished with sculpture by Michelangelo, who acknowledged Brunelleschi's sober and refined style.

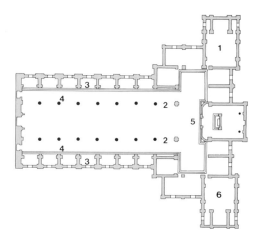

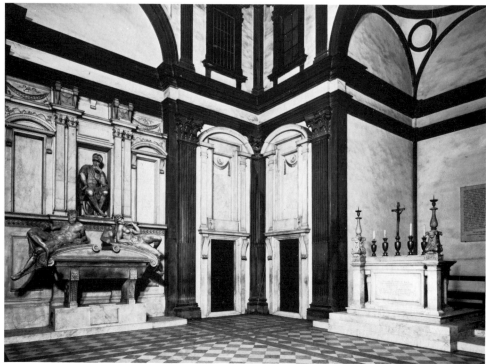

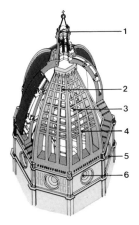

1 *Lantern*
2 *Main ribs*
3 *Minor ribs*
4 *Horizontal ties*
5 *Octagonal drum*
6 *Circular windows*

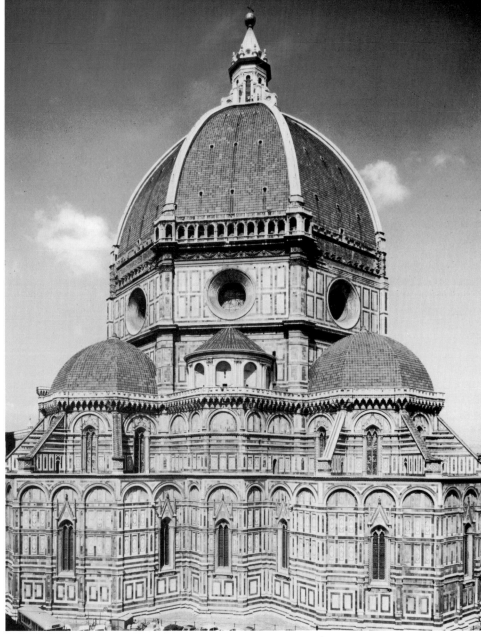

The dome of Florence Cathedral, rising like a crown of glory to the Renaissance, is a miracle of design and engineering. The pointed dome was begun by Brunelleschi in 1420 and built in the Gothic manner, with slender ribs and a light double vault. Brunelleschi was also inspired by Roman vaulting systems and used herring-bone brickwork for greater strength and ease of construction. The outer casing of red tiles contrasts with the green and white marble façades of the church.

Santo Spirito (below), Brunelleschi's last work, was designed in 1434 and completed in 1482. The church has a Latin cross plan and the proportions are based on a single module, giving the interior a sense of harmony, clarity and space, which is enhanced by the grey stone of the columns, arches and cornices.

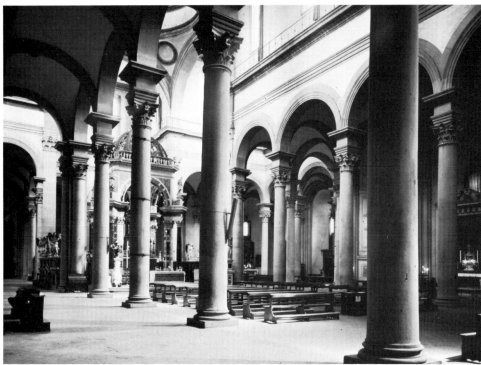

Santa Maria Novella (below), a Gothic building with a beautifully proportioned Renaissance façade of coloured marble, was the first of the great and influential Florentine churches. Scroll forms link the upper and lower storeys of the façade, which was designed by Alberti, and begun in 1458.

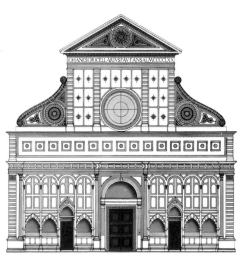

145

The spread of the new ideas

IT WAS NOT UNTIL after the death of Brunelleschi in 1446 that the new ideas began to make headway outside Florence itself. They began to spread, first to Rimini and then to Mantua, because Leon Battista Alberti, although he regarded himself as a Florentine, spent nearly all his life outside the city and much of it in Rome, where he was a passionate student of the remains of Antiquity. About the middle of the 15th century he was employed by Sigismondo Malatesta, the tyrant of Rimini, to convert the church of San Francesco into a Malatesta monument. The rebuilding was never completed, but Alberti took the decisive step towards a classical interpretation of the traditional church façade by an ingenious adaptation of the ancient Triumphal Arch, such as Constantine's in Rome. In a letter to his assistant at Rimini, Alberti used a phrase which sums up all the aspirations towards perfection of proportion which typified the Renaissance architect: "The measures and proportions of the pilasters," he said, ". . . if you alter anything, all that music will fall into discord."

In 1460 and 1470, Alberti designed two churches in Mantua—San Sebastiano and Sant'Andrea—which were to be his versions of the central plan and the Latin cross type, as distinct from Brunelleschi's. Almost nothing is known of Alberti's work in Rome, which remained an unimportant centre until much later, when Bramante arrived at the very end of the century. He came from Milan, where he had worked, along with Leonardo da Vinci, for the Sforzas. The church of Santa Maria delle Grazie was built partly by Bramante; and its convent contains Leonardo's *Last Supper*, both works dating from the 1490s. The Milanese cloister of Sant'Ambrogio and the Roman one at Santa Maria della Pace, both by Bramante, mark the transition of his style from the tentative "Early" Renaissance to that of the assured "High" Renaissance.

1 Dome
2 Coffered barrel vault
3 Pedimented entrance façade
4 Side chapels
5 Transepts
6 Apsidal sanctuary

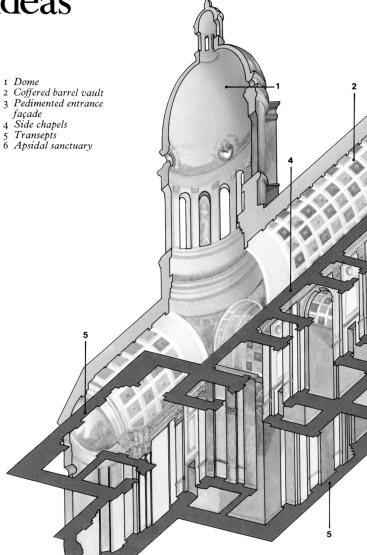

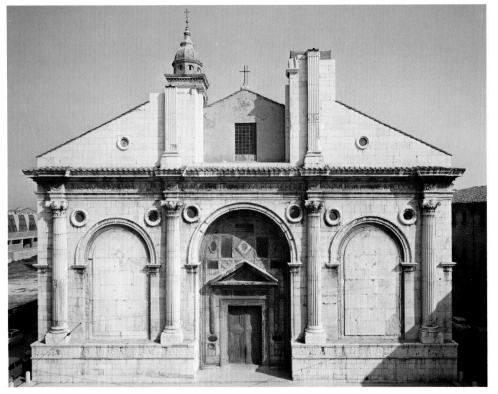

Sant'Andrea in Mantua (above) was begun by Alberti in 1472, the year of his death, and was finally completed with a dome in the 18th century. His design established the Latin cross type of plan with an aisleless nave and side chapels, adopted for many later churches. Alberti's debt to Ancient Rome is clearly seen in the splendid coffered barrel vault, which gives a sense of space to the interior. The most impressive external feature is the majestic façade, a combination of triumphal arch and temple front.

The Tempio Malatestiano at Rimini is a dignified memorial to Sigismondo Malatesta and his court of humanist scholars. About 1450 he commissioned Alberti to reclothe that existing Gothic church with an appropriate façade and interior. The work was never completed, but it is a clear manifestation of Alberti's skill in handling Roman forms and details in a new way. He adapted the triumphal arch form for the monumental entrance façade and added to the side walls arcaded recesses for the sarcophagi of the scholars and poets.

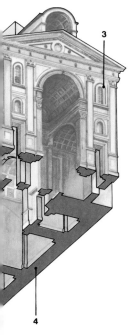

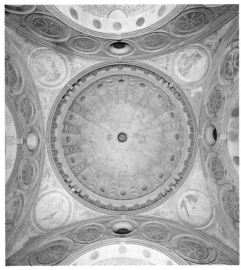

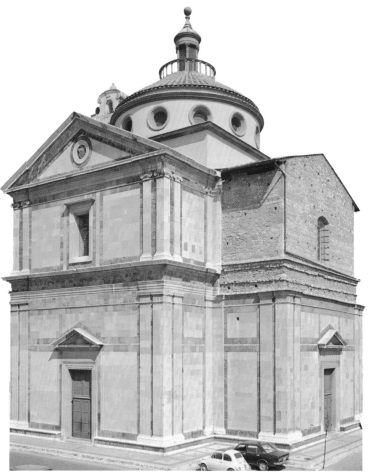

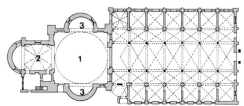

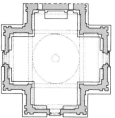

Santa Maria delle Grazie in Milan (above) is a Gothic church with an east end added by Bramante in the 1490s. He completely transformed the building with his spacious crossing (1) covered by a vast dome (top), while circular windows flood the interior with light. Graceful curves are repeated in the apsed choir (2) and transepts (3), enhancing the effect of space and unity.

Santa Maria delle Carceri at Prato (above and left) is an early work of Giuliano da Sangallo. It was built between 1485 and 1506 and was inspired by Brunelleschi's Pazzi Chapel in Florence, and, equally, by the Greek cross plan of Alberti's S. Sebastiano, at Mantua. The exterior is inlaid with coloured marbles, which give it a vitality but reveal its lack of classical proportions.

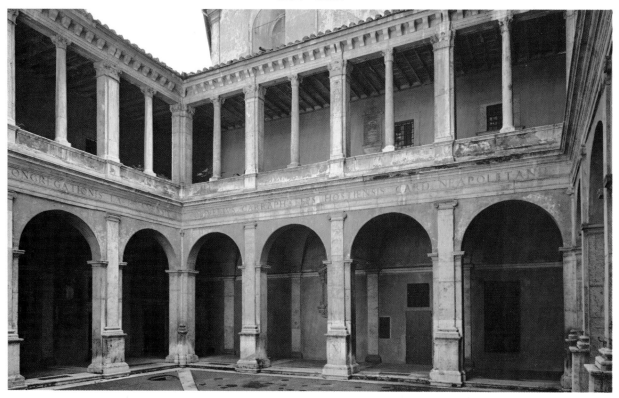

Bramante's cloister for the church of S. Maria della Pace, built between 1500 and 1504, was his first work in Rome. The beautiful two-tiered loggia is perfectly proportioned with sturdy piers, Ionic pilasters and arches on the ground floor, inspired by the Roman Colosseum. The upper storey is lighter, with twice as many openings.

Villas, princely and Palladian

PROBABLY BECAUSE town life began so early in Italy there was a feeling for the delights of country life from ancient times, as documented in the *Letters* of Pliny (*c.* AD 100) describing the two beautiful villas he owned; while the imperial villas, like that of Hadrian near Tivoli, although lost, were known from descriptions to be surrounded by an aura of luxury. In Roman times there were two types of villa; the *rustica*, or farm house, and the suburban villa, which was originally a small but splendid villa within easy reach of Rome or any other great city, to which the owner could retire at weekends or in the great heat of the summer.

By the 15th century, many noble families owned farm-like villas, the Medici villa at Cafaggiolo, near Florence, being a good example. These gradually became more luxurious, until they ceased to be working farms—like, for example, the Villa Medici at Poggio a Caiano. In Rome, the Villa Farnesina was a *villa suburbana*, built for an immensely rich banker. His example was followed by others, including cardinals and popes, at Frascati and Tivoli, which were near enough to Rome to be convenient, and much cooler in the summer. The Palazzo del Tè, at Mantua, and the Villa Farnese at Caprarola, near Viterbo, provide examples of magnificent villas for princely families, both of them designed and decorated by the leading architects and artists of the day.

It was in the region around Venice, however, that the finest villas were produced. These were designed by Andrea Palladio, mostly as practical working farms for the great Venetian families who were reclaiming derelict land in the Veneto and providing themselves, at the same time, with cool retreats for the summer. The Villa Rotonda, just outside Vicenza, is an example of the suburban type, comparable with those in Tivoli or Frascati, but rarer in the Veneto. It was these Palladian villas which provided models for the English and American country-houses of the 18th century.

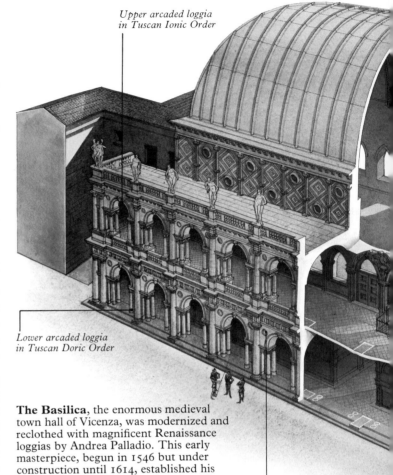

Upper arcaded loggia in Tuscan Ionic Order

Lower arcaded loggia in Tuscan Doric Order

The Basilica, the enormous medieval town hall of Vicenza, was modernized and reclothed with magnificent Renaissance loggias by Andrea Palladio. This early masterpiece, begun in 1546 but under construction until 1614, established his reputation as an architect of genius. The loggias consist of superimposed Doric and Ionic Orders, arches supported on smaller twin columns, balustrades and oculi, grouped to give an exciting effect of light and shade.

Oculi and the arches they pierce together create exciting patterns of light and shadow

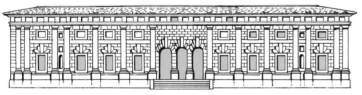

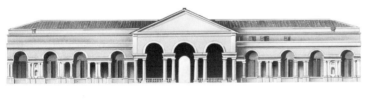

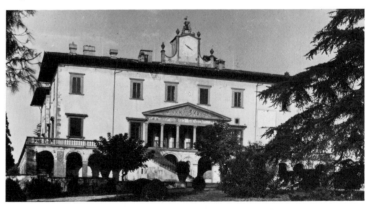

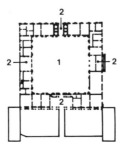

The Palazzo del Tè at Mantua was built by Giulio Romano for Federigo Gonzaga. This extraordinary single-storeyed summer pleasure-house was begun in 1526 and completed *c.* 1534. Its plan shows the typical lay-out of a Roman villa with a central court (1) surrounded by four low wings (2). Each façade is unexpectedly different. Novel and extravagant combinations of classical forms and details, often gigantic in scale, reveal Giulio's ruthless disregard for logic in his pursuit of drama.

The Villa Medici at Poggio a Caiano was an old fortified citadel, already altered as a residence when Lorenzo the Magnificent commissioned Giuliano da Sangallo to remodel it as a sumptuous villa for the reception of important guests from Florence. In the 1480s Sangallo created a loggia along classical Roman lines, which provided a continuous balcony for the piano nobile. It is one of the earliest strictly classical villas of the Renaissance, anticipating by several decades the designs and buildings of Palladio.

The Villa Madama in Rome had a typical Renaissance formal garden in the grand manner. It was begun by Raphael and Antonio da Sangallo the Younger *c.* 1516 and was continued, although never completed, by Giulio Romano. Raphael's loggia (right) with its vast open bays, rich stuccoed decoration and painted vaults, inspired by Nero's Golden House, was the model for many that came after.

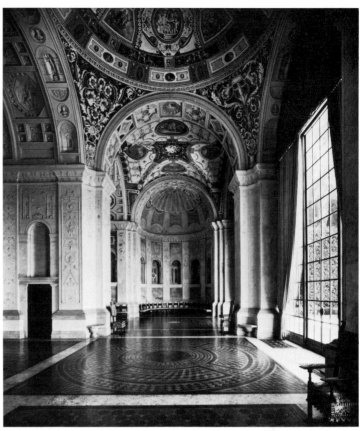

Medieval hall above ground-floor vaulting

Statues mounted on upper balustrade above each pier

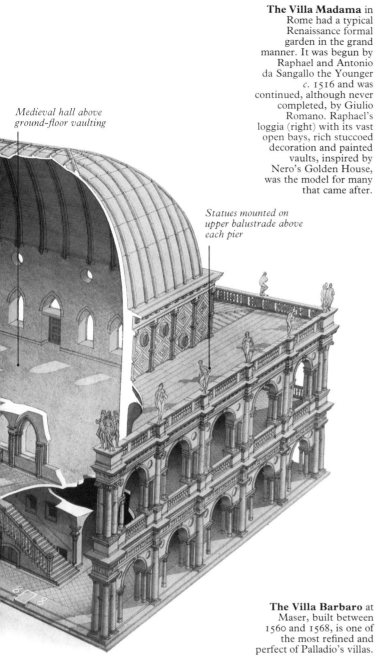

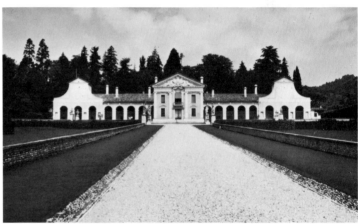

The Villa Barbaro at Maser, built between 1560 and 1568, is one of the most refined and perfect of Palladio's villas.

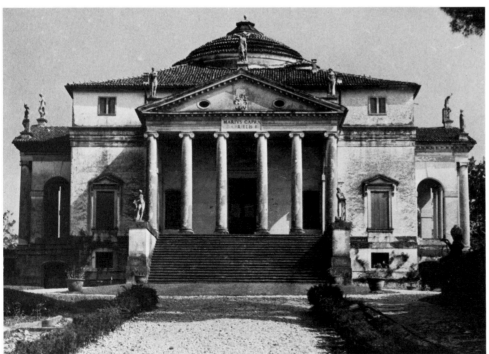

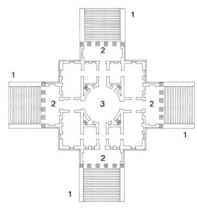

The Villa Rotonda (above and left), begun between 1567 and 1569, is set on a hill just outside Vicenza. It was designed by Palladio to command views of the countryside from all sides and has, on each façade, a flight of steps (1) ascending to an identical Roman temple portico (2). The remarkably symmetrical plan has a circular hall (3) covered by a low central dome. Although Palladio's inspiration was Ancient Rome, his beautiful villa with its fine proportions and harmonies was entirely original.

Palaces

THE RENAISSANCE palace derives directly from Ancient Roman forms, especially the *insula*, or block of flats, which was basically a series of ground-floor shops, with fine rooms on the first floor, or *piano nobile*, for the owner and his family, and upper floors for servants or for letting.

Brunelleschi built no private palaces, but the huge Medici Palace in Florence, designed by his follower Michelozzo, probably reflects his ideas on the subject, with the three main floors distinguished by varying textures and the whole crowned by a huge overhanging cornice.

Alberti, in his Palazzo Rucellai, also in Florence, introduced the idea of using the Classical Orders to decorate the façade. He adapted the Colosseum in Rome, but the difficulty of adjusting the proportions of the pilasters to the arrangement of the floors deterred many architects from following his example, the most notable adaptation being the huge Palazzo della Cancelleria in Rome, built by an unknown follower of his.

All these palaces are built around a central court, similar in arrangement to monastic cloisters, but mainly adapted from Brunelleschi's forms in the loggia of the Foundling Hospital. The most beautiful of them all, distinguished by the harmony of its proportions, is that in the Ducal Palace at Urbino, a unique masterpiece by Luciano Laurana, the Dalmatian architect, combining Florentine and Roman ideas.

By the 16th century some important developments had taken place. The so-called House of Raphael by Bramante is known to us only from drawings and an engraving, but it was the manifesto of a severer classicism, more closely based on the ancient insula type, and with only two components, the rusticated ground floor for the shops and the splendid paired half-columns to give dignity to the piano nobile. It must have lacked small rooms for service purposes, and, probably for that reason, although it was widely imitated, most versions had additional rooms or floors.

The enormous Palazzo Farnese, in Rome, about a hundred feet high, started a new trend towards sheer massiveness as a means of securing monumentality. In Venice the typical palace took a different form, partly because the waters of the Grand Canal meant that palaces were seen as façades, not blocks, and partly because of local tradition in the arrangement of the rooms.

The "Secret Garden" was laid out by Laurana as a geometric pattern of flower-beds and paths around a fountain. The Duke's and Duchess's suites were connected by a passage along the outer wall.

The Duchess's suite is approached through the great salon, where the court gathered for conversation and music.

The Duke's suite, lying behind Laurana's twin-towered west façade, included chapels, an antique bath, and a windowless study with trompe l'oeil inlaid panelling.

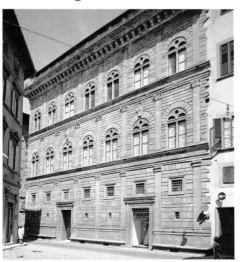

The Palazzo Rucellai (left), in Florence, is a semi-fortified townhouse built between 1446 and 1451 to Alberti's design. Its splendid façade is severely Roman in form and detail. The rusticated masonry creates an impression of strength, especially on the ground floor, which contained storerooms. A more elegant note is introduced by Orders superimposed as pilasters and by beautiful double windows on the upper storeys.

The Palazzo Farnese, in Rome, is Antonio da Sangallo the Younger's masterpiece. This fine Renaissance palace was begun in 1534, and completed after 1546 by Michelangelo. The building is an isolated rectangular block of monumental grandeur. Its courtyard (right) is composed of arches and engaged columns, enriched on the top storey by superimposed pilasters and corbels in Michelangelo's unique style.

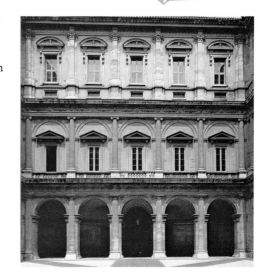

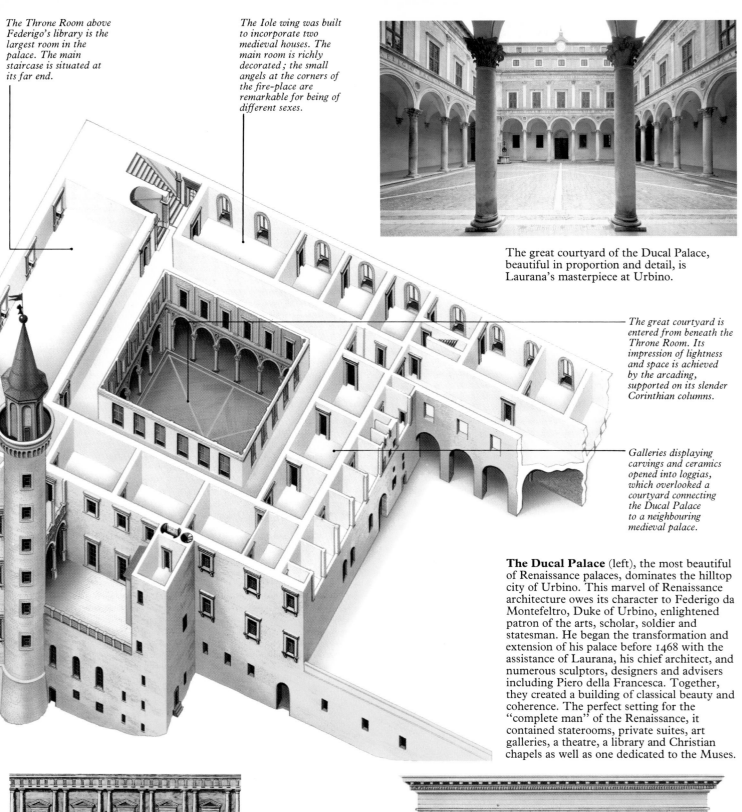

The Throne Room above Federigo's library is the largest room in the palace. The main staircase is situated at its far end.

The Iole wing was built to incorporate two medieval houses. The main room is richly decorated; the small angels at the corners of the fire-place are remarkable for being of different sexes.

The great courtyard of the Ducal Palace, beautiful in proportion and detail, is Laurana's masterpiece at Urbino.

The great courtyard is entered from beneath the Throne Room. Its impression of lightness and space is achieved by the arcading, supported on its slender Corinthian columns.

Galleries displaying carvings and ceramics opened into loggias, which overlooked a courtyard connecting the Ducal Palace to a neighbouring medieval palace.

The Ducal Palace (left), the most beautiful of Renaissance palaces, dominates the hilltop city of Urbino. This marvel of Renaissance architecture owes its character to Federigo da Montefeltro, Duke of Urbino, enlightened patron of the arts, scholar, soldier and statesman. He began the transformation and extension of his palace before 1468 with the assistance of Laurana, his chief architect, and numerous sculptors, designers and advisers including Piero della Francesca. Together, they created a building of classical beauty and coherence. The perfect setting for the "complete man" of the Renaissance, it contained staterooms, private suites, art galleries, a theatre, a library and Christian chapels as well as one dedicated to the Muses.

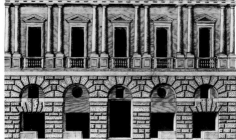

The House of Raphael in Rome was built by Bramante *c.* 1512. This engraving by Lafréry clearly shows the perfect contrast between the ground floor, with its heavy stone facing, and the main upper storey, gracefully articulated by Tuscan columns, pedimented windows and balustrades.

The Palazzo Strozzi, begun in 1489 by Benedetto da Maiano, is the finest palace of its kind in Florence. Rectangular in plan with loggias around a central court, the building has a simplicity and clarity typical of Florence. The outer walls are heavily rusticated and rise to a grand cornice inspired by an antique fragment. Cronaca completed the palace after 1504.

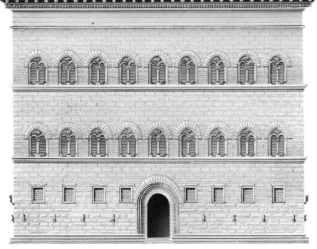

New St Peter's, Rome

OLD ST PETER'S, the greatest and most famous church in Christendom, was more than 1,100 years old in the 15th century and was showing signs of its age, but not until the Pontificate of Julius II (1503–13) was there any real attempt to restore or rebuild it. The fact that Bramante was available led Pope Julius to take the momentous decision to rebuild the ancient basilica in suitably Imperial Roman terms, as a modern rival, stylistically, to the Baths and the Pantheon. The basilica was, however, also the shrine of St Peter himself, and was, therefore, a martyrium or commemorative church. Similarly, the tiny Tempietto at San Pietro in Montorio was designed by Bramante at about the same time to commemorate the spot on the Janiculum Hill, which was thought, though mistakenly, to mark the place where the saint was martyred. Such martyria were usually centrally planned.

In practice, however, centrally planned churches are not convenient for great ceremonies involving thousands of people, and so a compromise was gradually evolved in the course of the 16th century. Caradosso's medal, dated 1506, and a half-plan drawn by Bramante must represent the earliest stages of the design, before any of the difficulties of so great an undertaking had forced modifications on Bramante (who died in 1514) and his successors. The large and ugly wooden model made for Antonio da Sangallo the Younger, who died in 1546, represents a compromise solution to several of the problems, especially in its awkward mixture of central and Latin cross plans.

Michelangelo, who took over in 1546, returned to the central plan and, like Bramante, was also able to think on a scale appropriate to the huge building. His ideas are known to us from some engravings, a few of his drawings and another large wooden model, which, however, has probably been altered. The great and justly famous dome was built from 1588 to 1593, long after his death, and is probably lighter and more pointed in shape than he would have desired. The major change from his design came with Maderno, who lengthened the nave to provide more space and thus modified the whole relationship between the dome and the façade. In the 17th century this was again drastically, but successfully, altered by the creation of Bernini's huge colonnade enclosing the Piazza.

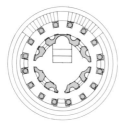

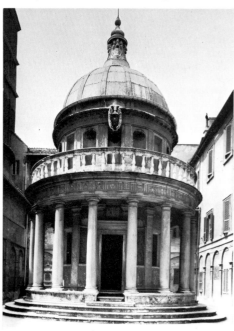

The Tempietto, Bramante's tiny chapel, was built after 1502 in the cloister of S. Pietro in Montorio, Rome. This perfect monument was designed entirely with reference to its outward appearance. A Doric colonnade encircles the two-storey building, enhancing its proportions and symmetry. Modelled on the antique temples of Rome, it is both a tribute to the classical past and a Christian memorial.

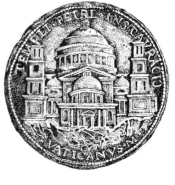

Caradosso's medal of 1506 illustrates Bramante's original intention for St Peter's. In emulation of the Pantheon, the vast central dome is raised from the base in steps. Four smaller domes are set over the arms of the Greek cross plan.

The wooden model of St Peter's, built from Sangallo's design in the 1530s, lacks Bramante's feeling for classical simplicity. Its most distinguishing feature is the curious bridge linking vestibule and nave.

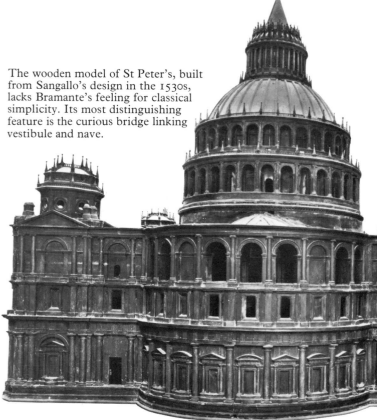

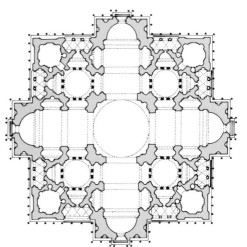

Bramante's plan for St Peter's was centralized and probably took the form of a Greek cross— symbol of the universal Christ—with four small Greek crosses in the arms. Although approved by Pope Julius in 1506, it was never executed.

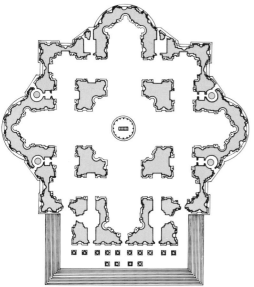

Michelangelo's plan of 1546 preserved the original centralized space of Bramante's design and surpassed it in clarity and economy. By opening the plan at its corners, he created a single integrated cross and square and a more unified interior.

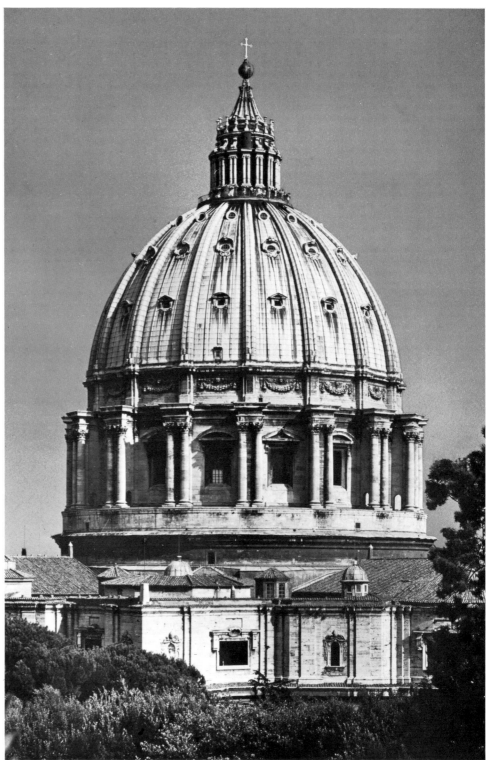

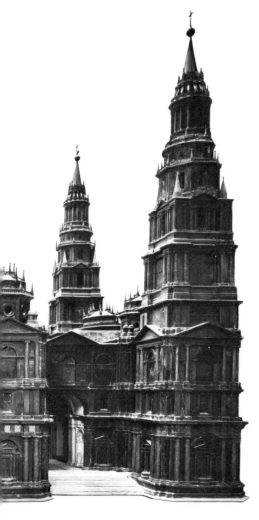

St Peter's, the most magnificent church in Christendom and the fruit of many talents, soars triumphantly above the Vatican Hill. For nearly 150 years, a succession of popes entertained the idea of glorifying the shrine of their patron saint. The scheme was finally completed in the 17th century by Bernini, who designed the monumental entrance Piazza. But, undoubtedly, most of the credit must go to Michelangelo and to Giacomo della Porta, whose dome towers 452 ft above the pavement and adorns the church with splendour. Della Porta took over the work in 1573, following Michelangelo's death in 1564, making certain changes to the design. It is buttressed by apsidal tribunes and supported internally by four massive piers, each 60 ft square. The stone ribs, rising steeply from a colonnaded drum to support the crowning lantern, enhance its dynamic outline.

153

Churches of the Counter-Reformation

THE CHURCH FORMS established by Brunelleschi and Alberti were continued and modified in the 16th century, particularly as a result of the new trend in church-building which arose from the Counter-Reformation. Centrally planned churches deriving from San Sebastiano, Santa Maria delle Carceri and the Tempietto can be found all over Italy and include some of the finest monuments of Renaissance design, often on sites of great natural beauty just outside towns. Bramante's influence, if not his actual presence, can be felt in the church of Santa Maria della Consolazione, at Todi, begun in 1508, and in the church of the Madonna di San Biagio, near Montepulciano, begun ten years later. He himself built two similar churches in Rome, but one is lost and the other profoundly altered.

Even more influential were the works of Giacomo Vignola. In the little church of Sant'Andrea in Via Flaminia, built in the 1550s just outside the gates of Rome, he introduced the oval form in the dome, and, just before his death, he used an oval ground plan in his chapel of the Papal Grooms. Oval plans were to be exploited by the great Baroque designers Borromini and Bernini, yet Vignola's church for the new Jesuit Order was the most influential of all. The Gesù in Rome, mother-church of the Society of Jesus, is a modernized version of Alberti's Sant'Andrea in Mantua of a hundred years earlier. The Gesù was designed for preaching, in accordance with the new ideals of the Counter-Reformation, and its design has been more widely copied than that of any other church. By contrast, Andrea Palladio, Vignola's great contemporary, designed two splendid Venetian churches—San Giorgio Maggiore and the Redentore—to meet specifically Venetian conditions.

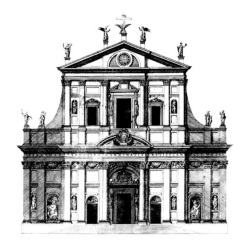

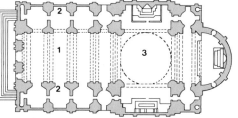

The Gesù was completed with a façade by Della Porta between 1573 and 1584. He gave it great richness by doubling the columns, and united the two storeys with large volutes. The design was soon copied throughout the Christian world

The Gesù, built for the Jesuits in Rome, inaugurated a new era in church design with its revolutionary plan and composition. Designed by Vignola in 1568 so that the congregation and clergy could be united more closely, it has a large nave (1) flanked by side chapels (2) instead of aisles. The sense of drama is heightened at the crossing (3), where light pours in from above.

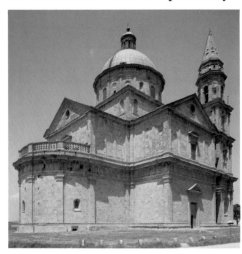

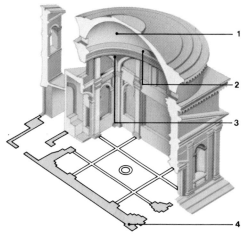

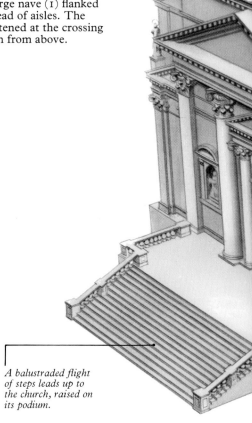

A balustraded flight of steps leads up to the church, raised on its podium.

The Madonna di San Biagio, standing by itself in a meadow on the outskirts of Montepulciano, is Antonio da Sangallo the Elder's greatest achievement. Begun in 1518 and completed in 1529, this quietly dignified church, inspired by Bramante's design for St Peter's, is set on a Greek cross plan and crowned by a lofty dome. Bell-towers were intended for two corners, although only one was completed. The arms are barrel vaulted, with the eastern one terminating externally in a huge apse, and the crossing is lit by a deep, fenestrated drum. The façades of golden travertine are not richly decorated and are of modest size, but the effect is monumental.

Sant'Andrea in Via Flaminia is one of the most forward-looking and experimental churches of the 16th century. It was built for Pope Julius III in 1554 by Vignola, the leading architect in Rome of the generation after Michelangelo. Although inspired by the Pantheon, this restrained and logical building has an elliptical dome (1) carried by a Corinthian cornice (2) and pendentives (3) above a rectangular plan (4). In this it heralded the oval plan, favoured by architects for small churches in the Baroque period. Its elegant entrance façade has a simulated temple front with a pediment and shallow Corinthian pilasters.

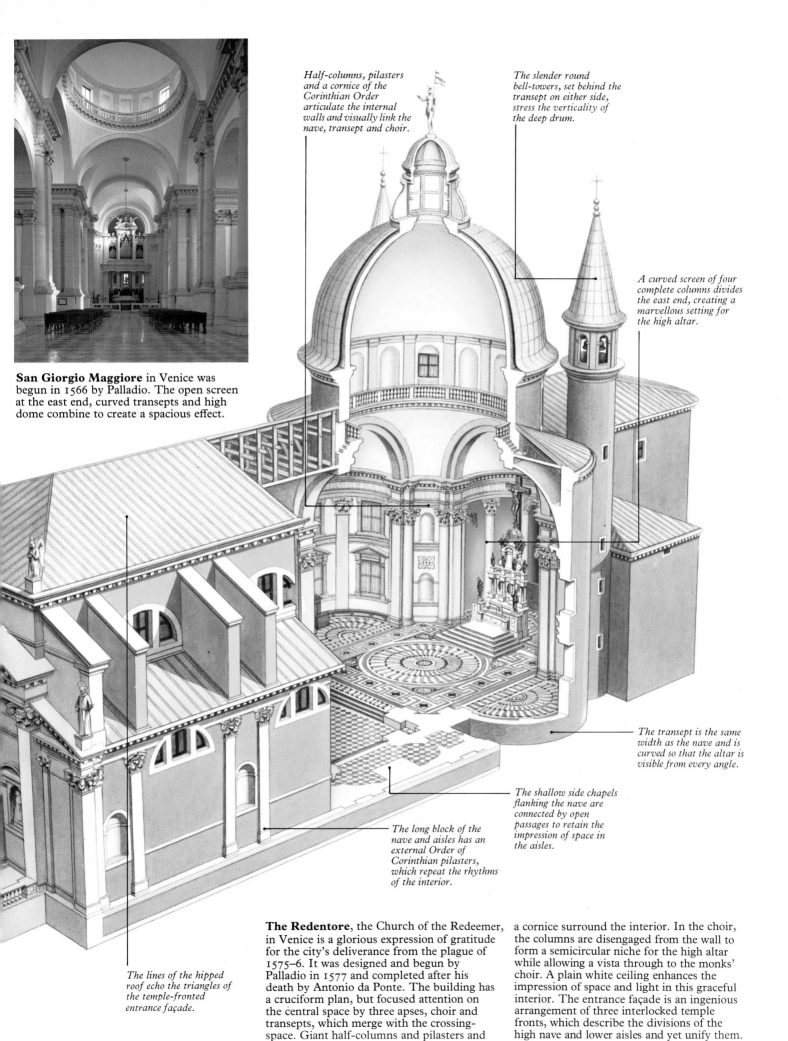

San Giorgio Maggiore in Venice was begun in 1566 by Palladio. The open screen at the east end, curved transepts and high dome combine to create a spacious effect.

Half-columns, pilasters and a cornice of the Corinthian Order articulate the internal walls and visually link the nave, transept and choir.

The slender round bell-towers, set behind the transept on either side, stress the verticality of the deep drum.

A curved screen of four complete columns divides the east end, creating a marvellous setting for the high altar.

The transept is the same width as the nave and is curved so that the altar is visible from every angle.

The shallow side chapels flanking the nave are connected by open passages to retain the impression of space in the aisles.

The long block of the nave and aisles has an external Order of Corinthian pilasters, which repeat the rhythms of the interior.

The lines of the hipped roof echo the triangles of the temple-fronted entrance façade.

The Redentore, the Church of the Redeemer, in Venice is a glorious expression of gratitude for the city's deliverance from the plague of 1575–6. It was designed and begun by Palladio in 1577 and completed after his death by Antonio da Ponte. The building has a cruciform plan, but focused attention on the central space by three apses, choir and transepts, which merge with the crossing-space. Giant half-columns and pilasters and a cornice surround the interior. In the choir, the columns are disengaged from the wall to form a semicircular niche for the high altar while allowing a vista through to the monks' choir. A plain white ceiling enhances the impression of space and light in this graceful interior. The entrance façade is an ingenious arrangement of three interlocked temple fronts, which describe the divisions of the high nave and lower aisles and yet unify them.

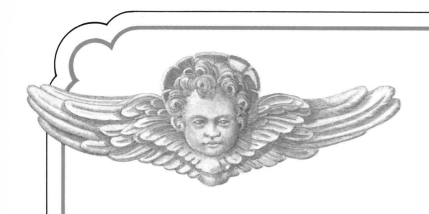

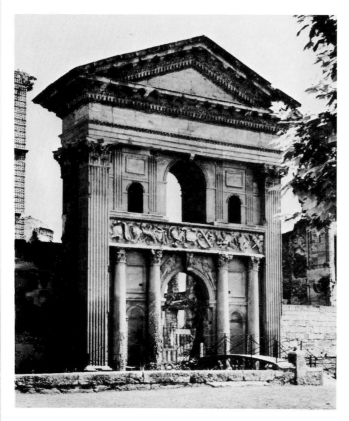

The Triumphal Arch of the Château of
La Tour d'Aigues in southern France,
which captures the character of a
Roman original, is a superb example of
the Renaissance quest for classical form.

In the last years of the 15th century knowledge of Italian Renaissance art began to spread across the Alps. Books being lighter than stones, and scholars generally more transplantable than architects, the new learning arrived first, and well before 1500 Greek was being taught in many centres outside Italy, and the philosophy and science evolved in Florence were studied with enthusiasm.

The arts followed soon afterwards. First movable objects, such as illustrated books, illuminated manuscripts and small paintings, but soon small architectural features, such as fountains and tombs, were exported to other parts of Europe. From these models artists in other countries learnt the decorative vocabulary of the Renaissance, which they began to apply to buildings being erected in the Gothic manner. The result was a hybrid style, still medieval in planning and structure, but up to date in its ornament, of which the most famous examples are the châteaux built in the Loire valley by François I and his courtiers. In Spain the same fusion took place, but Spanish Gothic was more fanciful than French and the result was an extraordinary and elaborate style called the Plateresque. In Portugal the same phenomenon occurred, but the style was called the Manueline after King Manuel I, who ruled Portugal at the time. The new manner penetrated to England under the aegis of Henry VIII, partly through the arrival of Italian artists such as Pietro Torrigiano, who came to design the tomb of his father, Henry VII, in Westminster Abbey, but more effectively through artists who had been trained in the Italianizing workshop set up by Cardinal Amboise, Archbishop of Rouen, at his country Château of Gaillon.

France was ahead of most other countries in the importation of the new style partly because, for a period of more than thirty years, the French kings, Charles VIII (1483–98), Louis XII (1498–1515),

Spread of the Renaissance

and François I (1515–47), were involved in campaigns in the north of Italy which brought them into close contact with the art of the country. François I invited many of the great Italian artists of the period, including Michelangelo and Titian, to come to his court. Only one—Leonardo da Vinci—settled there; but in the 1530s the king determined to make of his palace at Fontainebleau a real centre of the new art. The first two artists whom he attracted to Fontainebleau were the painters Giovanni Battista Rosso and Francesco Primaticcio, who created a completely new style of decoration, which found its first expression in the Galerie François I at Fontainebleau itself, but then spread over the whole of Europe, even to Italy, the country which had till then remained in the lead in architecture and decoration and had never accepted ideas from countries north of the Alps. The "Fontainebleau style" with its mixture of painting and high-relief stucco and its particular form of decoration called "strap-work"—which consisted of panels of stucco shaped like curled leather or parchment—became the common vocabulary of decorative art throughout the whole of Europe.

In the middle of the 16th century a new style of architecture emerged in France. Sebastiano Serlio, the Venetian architect, settled in France in 1540 and established there a much more maturely classical style than anything that had existed before. At about the same time certain French architects, notably Philibert de l'Orme, made the journey to Rome and came to know Ancient Roman architecture and the works of the great masters of the Renaissance at first hand. The result was a movement in French architecture which can really be seen as part of the Renaissance and not merely as an intersecting hybrid style.

Such mature variants of Renaissance style are rare in countries outside Italy—though individual examples can be found in Spain and Portugal—and in most parts of Europe the hybrid styles described above were succeeded by an equally complex manner, which is in a sense a derivation from the decorative style of the School of Fontainebleau. This style, which has certain features in common with Italian Mannerism, dominated northern and central Europe in the second half of the 16th century and in many places lasted till well into the 17th. In France its main protagonist was Jacques Androuet du Cerceau, who built little but whose engravings, often of architectural fantasies, were imitated all over Europe. In the Netherlands it produced the gabled houses of the great trading towns; in Germany it was carried to its most fantastic point in the engravings of Wendel Dietterlin and in the palaces of the German princes. In Denmark it was used for the royal palaces of Helsingør and Rosenborg. In England it flourished with special brilliance and produced the great houses of the Elizabethan and Jacobean eras.

In the 17th century this manner was gradually displaced by new styles. In Flanders, where the Catholic revival was particularly powerful, a variant of Baroque came into fashion; in Holland a more classical manner prevailed, as for instance in the Town Hall of Amsterdam. In Germany all artistic production was cut off by the Thirty Years' War (1618–48), but when the country was once again settled it plunged into a full and lively Baroque movement. In France and England a new classicism prevailed: in France, inspired by the study of Antiquity and the masters of the 16th century; in England, under the dominant influence of Palladio. Meanwhile, Italy had passed through the phase of Mannerism and was evolving the true Baroque style, and the stage was set for the full variety of 17th-century architecture in what we call the Age of the Baroque.

France, the School of Fontainebleau

THE INSPIRER OF what is called the first Renaissance in France was the king, François I, who in the early years of his reign added a wing to the old Château of Blois and built the vast Château of Chambord, which may have been partly designed by Leonardo da Vinci, who was then living in France under the king's protection. Chambord is famous for the magnificent chimneys and dormer windows which decorate its roof and for the ingenious double staircase. This consists of two ramps, which start at opposite sides of the circular well and intertwine without ever meeting. This plan may have been suggested by Leonardo.

The example set by the king was soon followed by the great nobles and also by a number of newly enriched bourgeois, who held offices connected with the royal administration. Chenonceaux, on the banks of the Cher, was begun in 1515 by the financier Thomas Bohier and Azay-le-Rideau a few years later by a relation of his called Gilles Berthelot, another eminent public servant. Azay was all built in a single campaign, but at Chenonceaux only the part on the north bank of the river was built by Bohier. Later, the château belonged to Henri II's mistress, Diane de Poitiers, a great protector of the arts, who commissioned Philibert de l'Orme to build the bridge across the river. The gallery was added by Henri's wife, Catherine de' Medici, who compelled Diane to cede the place to her after her husband's death.

The great creation of the king was the Château of Fontainebleau. Until his time it had been a small hunting lodge in the Forest of Fontainebleau, but he enlarged and transformed it into one of the great palaces of Europe. He built a wing running west from the old keep, which contained the famous Galerie François I, decorated by Rosso and Primaticcio. This led to the vestibule of the chapel and an elaborate staircase—replaced in the early 17th century by the existing one—leading to a large base court.

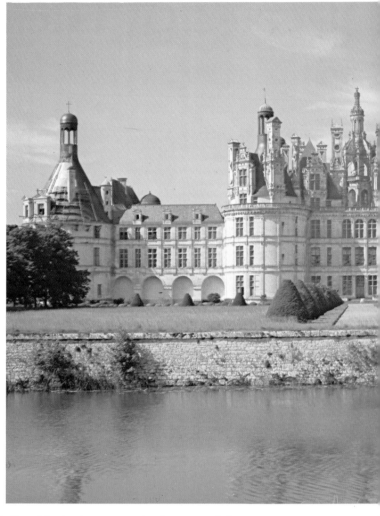

The Château of Chenonceaux was begun in 1515 for Thomas Bohier, who built the right-hand block. The architect's name is not known, but he was certainly French, although the decorative detail is Italian. The bridge to the left was built by Philibert de l'Orme in the years 1555–9, and the gallery over it was added by Jean Bullant after 1576.

The Château of Chambord (above), begun in 1519, was designed by the Italian architect Domenico da Cortona, but it is possible that Leonardo da Vinci modified it. The builders were French masons. The château is therefore a good example of the different elements which made up a French building in the early 16th century and which account for the hybrid character of the whole. The general conception of the château, with its huge round towers, is still medieval, but the regularity and symmetry of the plan (below) show the direct influence of Italian ideas. The double spiral staircase (right) is a great feat of design and engineering.

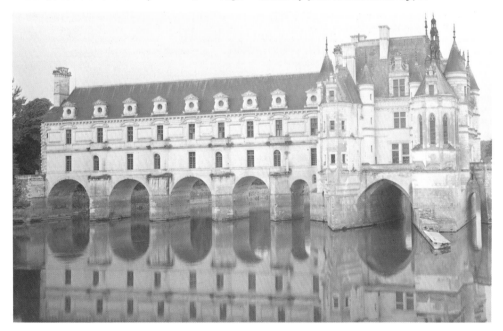

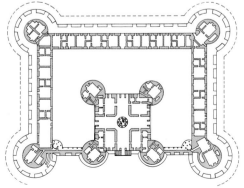

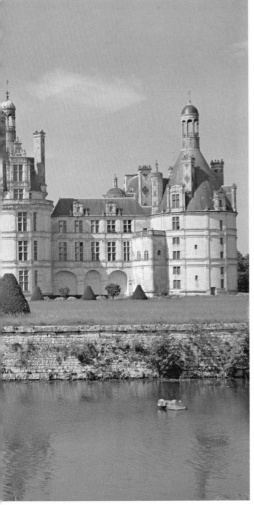

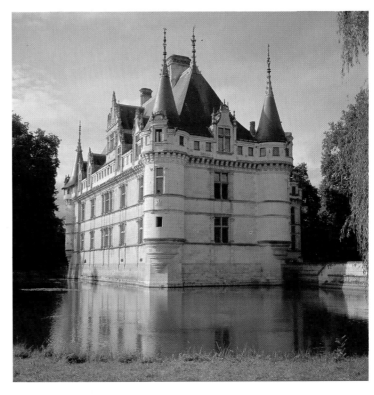

Azay-le-Rideau, the exquisite little château which stands in an artificial moat, was built between 1519 and 1527 for Gilles Berthelot. The unknown French architect incorporated Italian decorative detail in this most complete and most perfectly preserved of all the châteaux dating from the early part of François I's reign.

The Château of Fontainebleau (below) was built by François I round the keep of a small medieval castle, which imposed a certain irregularity on the plan. The Galerie François I (below left), recently restored to its original splendour, set a fashion in decoration which was imitated throughout the whole of Europe.

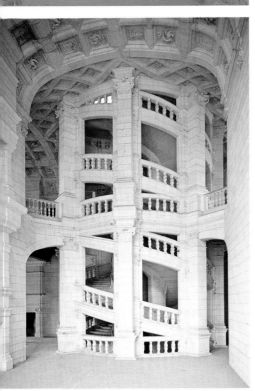

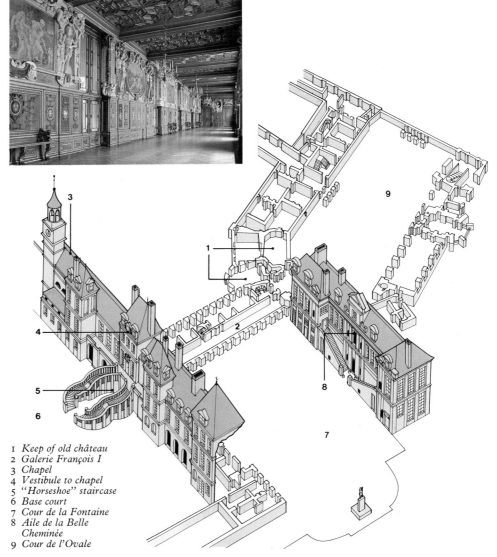

1 *Keep of old château*
2 *Galerie François I*
3 *Chapel*
4 *Vestibule to chapel*
5 *"Horseshoe" staircase*
6 *Base court*
7 *Cour de la Fontaine*
8 *Aile de la Belle Cheminée*
9 *Cour de l'Ovale*

France, the classical phase

APART FROM THE work of Inigo Jones in England in the early 17th century, the architecture of France in the mid-16th century is the most sophisticated version of the Renaissance style to be found outside Italy. The phase started in the last years of François I's reign, when Serlio built the Château of Ancy-le-Franc (though not for the king himself, who hardly employed him); but its full development took place through the patronage of his son Henri II (1547–59) and Henri's brilliantly intelligent mistress, Diane de Poitiers. François planned to rebuild the medieval Château of the Louvre, but the work was carried out by Henri.

At the same time Philibert de l'Orme was building for Diane the Château of Anet, in which he blended with unique success Italian and medieval French ideas. The plan of the chapel, with four equal arms rounded at the ends, enclosed in a circle, is based on northern Italian models, but the curved coffering of the dome could only have been invented by an architect familiar with late French Gothic vaulting. The gate, with its rounded "bastions", still has something of the character of the fortified entrance to a medieval castle, but in its detail and in the use of the Orders it is purely classical. Philibert de l'Orme's ideas were too advanced to take root and it was left to François Mansart, nearly a century later, to revive them and develop a new style from them.

In the last decades of the 16th century the dominant style in French architecture was that associated with the name of Jacques Androuet du Cerceau, who probably designed the Château of Verneuil, with its accumulation of complicated architectural forms and fantastic detail.

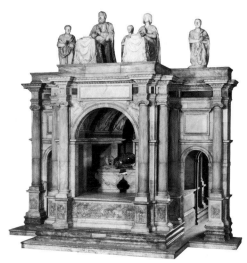

The tomb of François I, at S. Denis was commissioned by Henri II after his father's death in 1547. The architect was Philibert de l'Orme and the figure sculptures and bas-reliefs were by Pierre Bontemps. It was designed, like many late medieval tombs, to contain the figures of the king and queen, depicted as corpses under the arch but kneeling, surrounded by their children, on the top of the tomb. De l'Orme gave the structure the form of a Roman triumphal arch, executed with unusually rich and fine detail, the effect being heightened by panels of black marble.

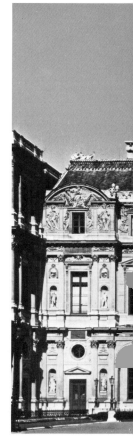

In the dome of the circular chapel of Anet with its curved coffering, the Renaissance principle of the circle as the perfect form worthy of the House of God was applied for the first time in France.

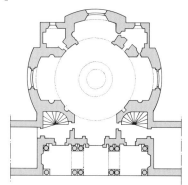

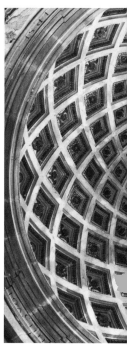

The Château of Anet was built by Philibert de l'Orme for Diane de Poitiers, the favourite of Henri II, immediately after Henri's accession as king in 1547. The general lay-out of the château follows earlier 16th-century models, with three wings round a courtyard, but the style is altogether novel. The entrance gate (right) is centred on Benvenuto Cellini's bronze relief of Diana, made for Fontainebleau but given to Diane by Henri and now in the Louvre (a modern cast now replaces it). The gate is surmounted by a clock with a bronze stag, which strikes the hours by tapping with its hoof. The chapel was the most advanced building of its day, elaborate but symmetrical in plan (above), inventive in the curved coffering of its dome and exquisite in its sculptures, probably by Jean Goujon. The rest of the château was pulled down during the Revolution.

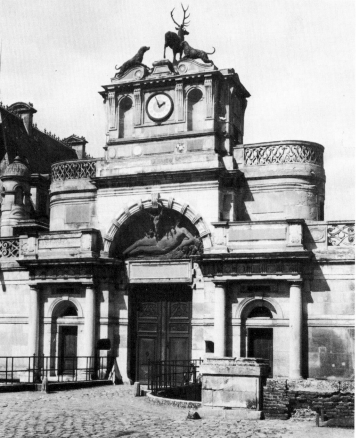

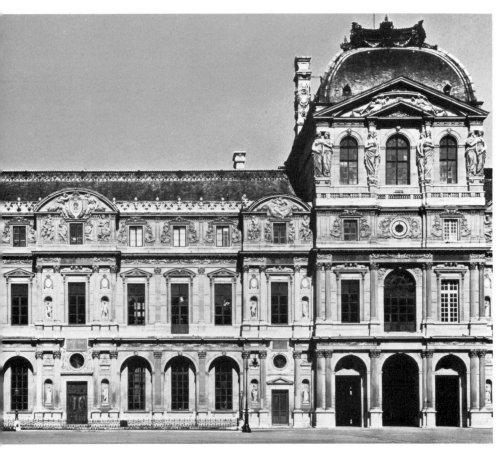

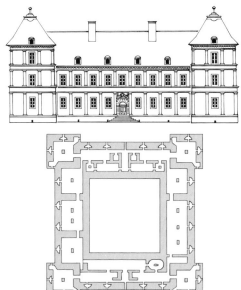

The Château of Ancy-le-Franc was designed by Serlio in 1546 for the Comte de Clermont-Tonnerre, an important member of the court of François I. This was the first French château to be laid out regularly, in this case with four identical wings round a square court. Serlio originally designed it with low roofs, but in the actual building he made them steeper, in accordance with a French tradition suited to the northern climate. Serlio exerted great influence through his treatise on architecture.

The Square Court of the Louvre (above). The decision to rebuild the old Château of the Louvre was taken by François I in 1527. In 1546, Pierre Lescot was commissioned to plan a building on the same scale as the old court—that is, with a façade of the length shown above. Soon, however, the scheme was enlarged with a façade double the original length, with a taller pavilion inserted in the middle. Work was interrupted by the death of Henri II in 1559 and the Wars of Religion, when only one wing had been built. The Pavillon de l'Horloge, on the right, was added by Jacques Lemercier from 1627 onwards, but the court was not finished until the mid-18th century.

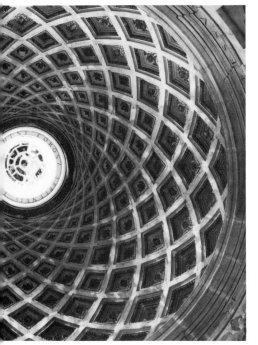

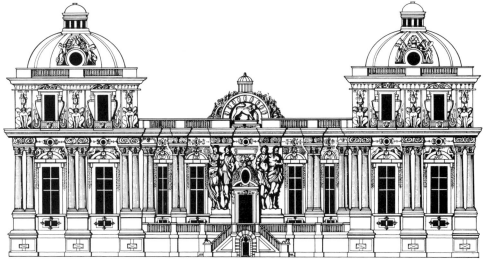

The Château of Verneuil was begun in 1568 for Philippe de Boulainvilliers, a rich landowner obsessed with the fact that he was descended from the early kings of France, whose images occur in the decoration of the château. It was pulled down after the Revolution, but its appearance is recorded in engravings by Jacques Androuet du Cerceau, who was probably the architect of the building. It is typical of the ornate and fanciful style of French architecture in the late 16th century.

Spain and Portugal

THE FLOW OF GOLD and silver from America into Spain and Portugal created an immediate if short-lived prosperity and caused a great outburst of building activity. In Spain there was an added political stimulus from the recent unification of the country and the need to build churches and palaces in the areas conquered from the Moors. Building was partly centred on the ports of Seville and Lisbon, but it also affected Toledo, still the capital of the new Spanish kingdom, and towns such as Tomar, Coimbra, Granada and Salamanca, which were great seats of religion and learning.

The first monuments of this revival, such as the royal chapels in Toledo and Granada, were in a late Gothic style, but gradually the Italian influence penetrated. In Spain this happened by direct contact, because for the greater part of the period under consideration Lombardy was under Spanish domination, and links between the two countries were close. Portugal was more cut off from Italy, and some of the most important artists working in the Italian manner were Frenchmen who had emigrated to Portugal to work for the king or the Church.

It is appropriate that Granada, as the capital of the newly conquered province of Andalucia, should contain some of the most important monuments of the new style. The cathedral is Gothic in its tall proportions, but the detail is mainly classical, except for the curling Gothic decoration on the vault. But the Palace of Charles V, begun in 1527 and built by Pedro Machuca in the Alhambra itself, is in a remarkably pure classical style, as if to assert the victory of the Christian king over the Moors. In Portugal the early phase is well represented by the cloisters of the Jeronymites at Belem near Lisbon, in which Renaissance decoration is applied to a traditional Gothic structure.

The mature classical style of the middle of the 16th century is represented in Portugal by buildings such as the cloister at Tomar and in Spain by the Escorial, a work of astonishing grandeur and severity, appropriate to the character of the king, Philip II, who built it and who, amid all the wealth of his kingdom, demanded a building which, though vast enough to include a palace and religious house, should also be completely simple.

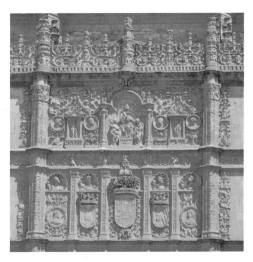

The University of Salamanca. The façade, begun in 1513, is one of the most complete examples of the mature Plateresque style, its combination of decorative panels and portrait medallions producing an effect of exceptional richness.

The college occupies the northwest quarter. Like the monastery, it is subdivided by four courts and is entered from the west façade.

The great court of the palace, in the northeast angle of the Escorial, is connected with the state apartments, which project behind the church.

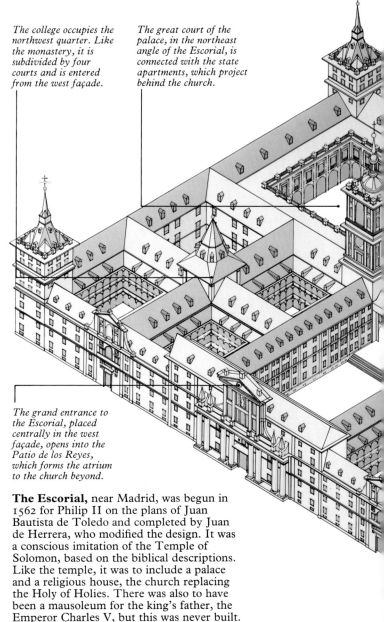

The grand entrance to the Escorial, placed centrally in the west façade, opens into the Patio de los Reyes, which forms the atrium to the church beyond.

The Escorial, near Madrid, was begun in 1562 for Philip II on the plans of Juan Bautista de Toledo and completed by Juan de Herrera, who modified the design. It was a conscious imitation of the Temple of Solomon, based on the biblical descriptions. Like the temple, it was to include a palace and a religious house, the church replacing the Holy of Holies. There was also to have been a mausoleum for the king's father, the Emperor Charles V, but this was never built.

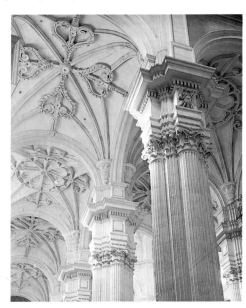

Granada Cathedral was built to the designs of Diego de Siloe from 1528 onwards. The cathedral is a traditional five-aisled building, with piers which are Gothic in their proportion, but classical in their detail, and Gothic decoration on the vaulting; but at the east end Siloe added a tall rotunda, in direct imitation of the church of the Holy Sepulchre in Jerusalem. To 16th-century architects "imitation" involved no obligation to copy the style of the model but merely its essential features, in this case its tall, circular form and the number of piers supporting the dome.

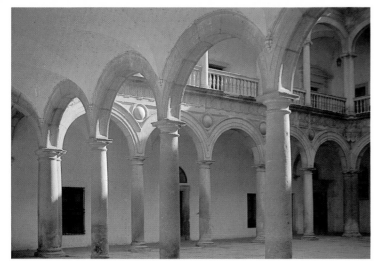

Afuera Hospital, Toledo, dates from about the middle of the 16th century. It was built for Cardinal Tavera, probably by Bartolomé de Bustamente. The most interesting feature is the double cloister, composed of superimposed round-headed arcades, the arcade between the two cloisters being open on both sides.

The fortified tower at Belem was built between 1515 and 1520 by Francisco Arruda on the coast near Lisbon as a defence against pirates. The little domes, divided into segments like an orange, show knowledge of Muslim architecture, and possibly even of buildings in the Portuguese settlements in India.

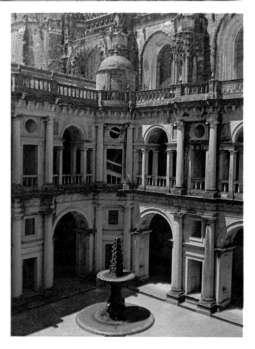

The church, which dominates this austere group of buildings, shows Italian influence, not least in its Doric-columned west façade and hemispherical dome of a type used by Bramante and others. The placing of the choir over the vaulted vestibule at the west end (thus shortening the long arm to give the church a Greek cross plan) is a Spanish feature.

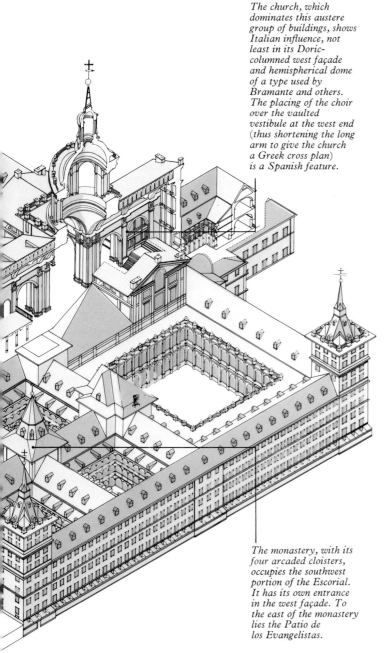

The monastery, with its four arcaded cloisters, occupies the southwest portion of the Escorial. It has its own entrance in the west façade. To the east of the monastery lies the Patio de los Evangelistas.

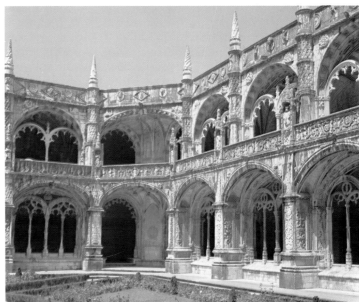

The Jeronymite Monastery at Belem (above) was begun in 1502, probably from the designs of the architect Diogo Boytac, who came from the south-west of France, and finished in 1519 by the Spaniard João de Castilho. In the cloister the most impressive feature is a series of deep recesses, behind which lie the aisles of the lower cloister.

The cloister of the Convent of Christ at Tomar, begun in 1555 by Diogo de Torralva, is the purest example of the full Renaissance style in Portugal. It is unusual in being composed of the "Serlian arch", a round-headed arch between two bays under a flat architrave.

The Low Countries

THE ARCHITECTS of the Low Countries took up the style invented by the school of Fontainebleau, elaborated it and applied it to their buildings, not only to the ornament but also to the forms of the gables, which become increasingly complicated. Houses of this type are to be seen in all parts of the Low Countries, a typical Dutch example being the Meat Hall at Haarlem. In Flanders, that is present-day Belgium, the style survived until a remarkably late date, and when the houses of the Grande Place in Brussels were destroyed in the siege of 1695, they were rebuilt in the traditional manner, though the figure sculpture was in higher relief and the architecture included a few features that could be called Baroque.

Flemish architects, working for a Catholic community deeply affected by the Counter-Reformation and the revival which followed it, naturally absorbed Baroque ideas, and the great churches of the 17th century in Brussels and other cities of the southern Netherlands are strongly marked by the style; but in Protestant Holland, architecture moved in the opposite direction towards greater classicism. The change can be seen from a comparison between two church towers in Amsterdam: the Oude Kerk of 1565 and the Westerkerk of 1620. The first has the broken curved forms of the early phase, with a half-onion dome in the middle of the tower and a flame-like crowning feature; the second is conceived in severe rectangular blocks, defined by clear, flat walls. This church, a typical example of the earlier classical work in Holland, was built by Hendrick de Keyser, but the movement reached its highest expression in Jacob van Campen's Town Hall of Amsterdam, now the Royal Palace. This is composed of large, clearly defined masses, with no ornament save two severe orders of pilasters. The same style could also be applied to buildings on a smaller scale, such as the Mauritshuis at The Hague, and was to have an influence on the building of country-houses in England.

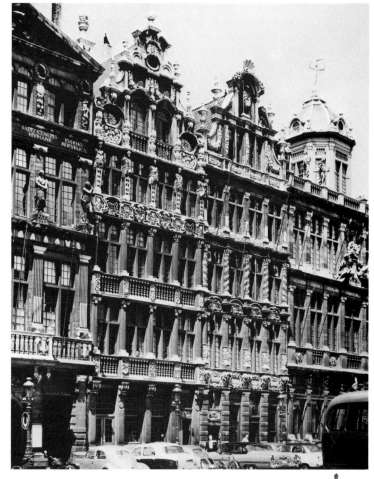

Houses on the Grande Place, Brussels. Built after the seige of 1695, this is the last of the public squares surrounded by guild houses, once found in all Flemish towns.

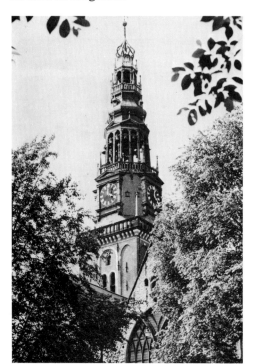

The Oude Kerk, Amsterdam (left). The tower of the Oude Kerk was built by Joost Bilhamer in 1565–6. The steeple is basically octagonal, but this fact is almost concealed by the variety given to the different stages: the lowest storey is decorated with four clocks; the next is surrounded by an open arcade of tall, thin arches supported on spindly wooden columns; then comes the half-onion dome; this is topped by another open stage and the whole steeple ends in the open wrought-iron "flame".

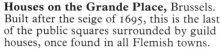

The Westerkerk, Amsterdam (right), was begun by Hendrick de Keyser in 1620. In plan it follows a medieval tradition in having double transepts (1), but it has a square east end (2) and no side chapels, in accordance with the practice of the Calvinist Church. The Calvinists had condemned the worship of saints and therefore did not need separate chapels dedicated to them; and they liked the altar to be placed near the congregation and not, as in a Roman Catholic church, set apart at the end of a chancel. The interior is a spacious three-aisled hall, suitable for preaching to large congregations.

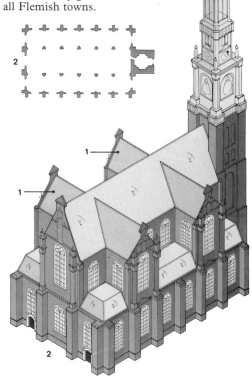

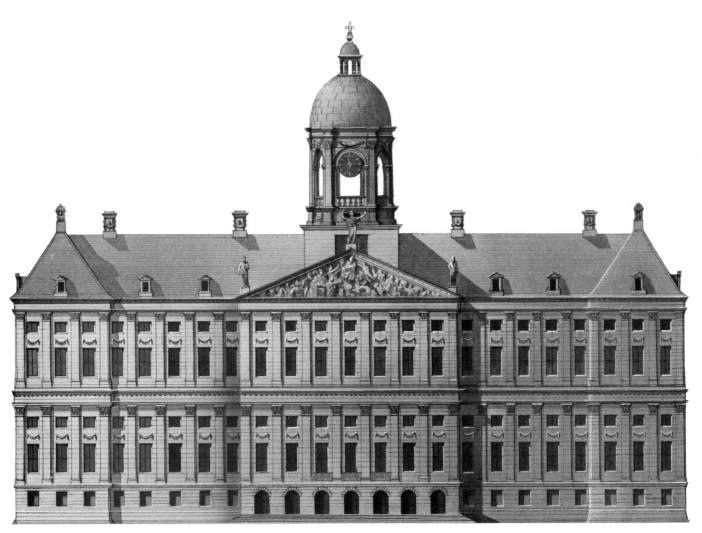

The Town Hall, Amsterdam, now the Royal Palace, was designed by Jacob van Campen. Begun in 1648, at the height of Amsterdam's power and wealth, it was to be a symbol of civic pride. Basically it is like the great 16th-century town halls, such as those found at Antwerp in Flanders and Augsburg in Germany, but the architect gave a splendidly classical form to the conception. The great central hall running right through the building, as at Augsburg, is placed between two courts and so can be lit by windows on both sides. This arrangement, combined with the fact that the room is painted white, makes it much more luminous than similar halls in earlier buildings. Rembrandt was among those commissioned to paint canvases for the Town Hall, but his composition was rejected.

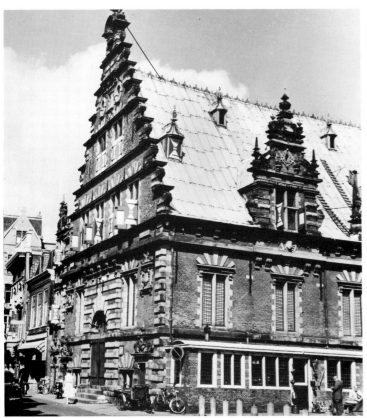

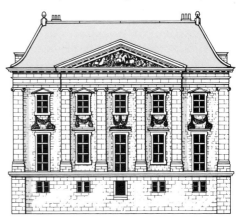

The Meat Hall, Haarlem, which was the hall of the Butchers' Guild, was built by Lieven de Key in 1602–3. De Key used the traditional stepped façade, decorated with finials, but gave subtle variety to the surface by intermingling stone and brick, on the ground floor, with bands of rustication around the door and at the corners, and above in the surrounds and balconies of the windows.

The Mauritshuis, at The Hague, was designed *c.* 1633 by Van Campen for Prince Maurice of Nassau. It stands on a small lake in the middle of The Hague, which it dominates in spite of its small size. This is due to the fact that the architect boldly used a Giant Order of pilasters, which give great grandeur to the façade. The restraint is superb, and the pilasters are the only decoration, apart from an allegorical bas-relief in the pediment. In its simplicity the building has some affinity with French classicism, although there is no trace of direct influence from France. The interior, is symmetrically designed about a central staircase.

Germany, Austria and Hungary

THE FIRST COUNTRY in central Europe to absorb the influence of the Italian Renaissance was, curiously enough, Hungary, where Italian craftsmen were introduced by the king, Matthias Corvinus, as early as the mid-15th century to decorate his palace in Buda. In the early years of the 16th century Bavaria began to be affected. In about 1540 Duke Ludwig of Bavaria imported a team of artists from Mantua to build his palace in Landshut, but unfortunately they had to rely on local and rather incompetent craftsmen to execute the work and the result is an unhappy hybrid. In 1560, Duke Albert V began to rebuild a large part of the Residenz in Munich with much more satisfactory results, and the Antiquarium is one of the finest Renaissance rooms in Germany. The ecclesiastical authorities were not slow to follow the Duke's lead and the church of St Michael presents a grand interior, Italianate in its feeling for space, but not directly imitating any specific Italian model or indeed style.

Curiously little architecture of this period survives in the former Hapsburg territories, mainly because the cities of Vienna and Prague were almost entirely rebuilt in the Baroque Age. A few examples survive, such as the Hofkirche in Innsbruck, a Gothic church with vaults carried by tall Ionic columns, and the Landhaus at Graz with three superimposed loggias, inspired by those built by Bramante in the Vatican.

The rich bankers and merchants of the great free towns such as Augsburg, Nuremberg and Frankfurt were aware of what was taking place south of the Alps through their commercial connections, and the Italianate style soon took root in these towns. The most spectacular manifestation of the new taste was the Town Hall of Augsburg, a vast cubical mass, which was gutted during World War II. It is typical of the mixture of ingenuity and naïvety which characterized the architects of the German Renaissance that the architect Elias Holl should have crowned the central section of the building with an element copied from the upper half of a Roman 16th-century church. The Italianate style was also taken up by individual bourgeois families, and the house and chapel built for themselves in Augsburg by the powerful banking family of Fugger, also destroyed in the war, were among the most accomplished imitations of the southern manner in Germany.

The Italianate style spread west and north through dynastic or commercial connections. The Electors Palatine, who belonged to the same family—the Wittelsbachs—as the dukes of Bavaria, introduced it with great éclat into their capital of Heidelberg. Their palace includes two wings in the new manner, one the Ottheinrichsbau, begun in 1556, in a relatively severe style, and the other, the Friedrichsbau, added in the first years of the 17th century, when a love of more contorted forms prevailed. This style is also to be found in the north of Germany in the town halls and the merchants' houses of the Hansa towns such as Lübeck and Bremen.

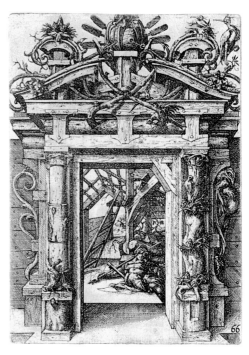

Wendel Dietterlin. This design for a door is from the series of engravings by Dietterlin published in 1593 under the title *Architectura*. The book was immensely influential and plates were copied by artists all over northern and central Europe.

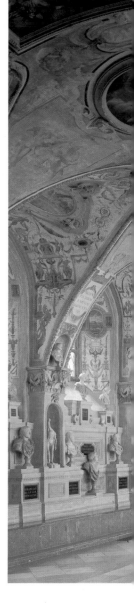

The Antiquarium in the Residenz, Munich (right), was built by Duke Albert V of Bavaria in 1569 to house his art collection, and decorated by the painter Friedrich Sustris in 1586. The room is of an unusual form, covered by a low barrel vault decorated with "grotesque" designs like those found in Ancient Roman palaces, such as the Golden House of Nero, and imitated by Raphael and his pupils.

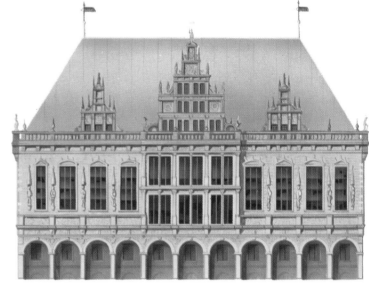

Bremen Town Hall was built between 1609 and 1614 under the influence of Flemish architects. The high-pitched roof and the stepped gables decorated with finials are typically northern, but the round-headed arcade and the decorative panels show Italian influence.

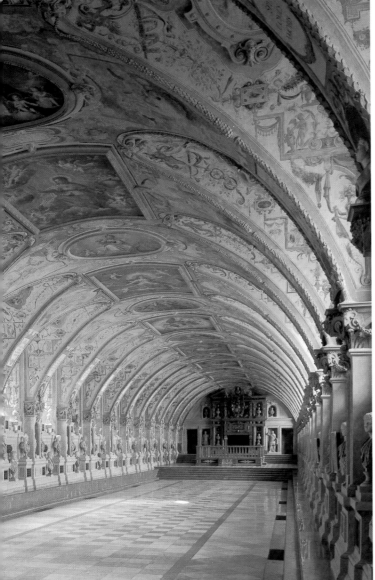

St Michael's Church, Munich, was built for the Jesuits, 1583–99. The original designer is unknown, but the choir was added by Sustris. It was badly damaged in World War II, but has been brilliantly restored.

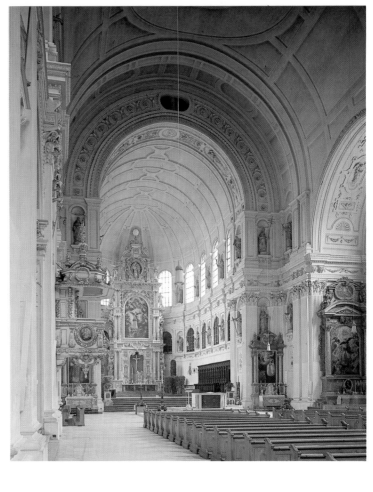

Augsburg Town Hall (below) was built in the years 1614–20 by Elias Holl, one of the most interesting German architects of the period. When the building was bombed during World War II the great hall, which ran across the middle of the building, was completely destroyed.

The Friedrichsbau wing at Heidelberg Castle was built 1601–7 from the designs of Johannes Schoch. Every inch of the surface of the building is covered with decoration and the gables are broken into forms as fantastic as those of the engraver Wendel Dietterlin.

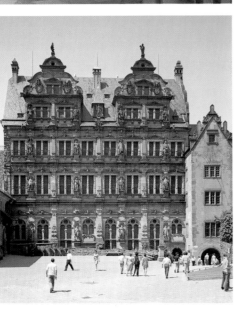

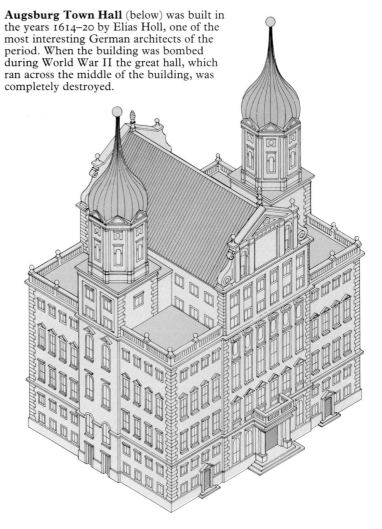

England, Tudor and Jacobean

WHEREAS THE Renaissance struck Italy in the 15th century, it barely touched England before the 17th. In this country the 15th century was one of civil turmoil. The stable and conservative Church alone provided education and social services, and dictated the rules of taste, which were traditionally Gothic. Henry VIII, encouraged by Cardinal Wolsey, prided himself on being a Renaissance prince. He welcomed to his court foreign scholars and artists. In his enlightened youth he commissioned the Italian Torrigiano to design his father Henry VII's wholly Renaissance tomb (1512) in Westminster Abbey. Yet beyond a few extraneous roundels of Roman emperors' busts by da Maiano, and carved dolphins and "putti" on window mullions and wainscot, architectural ventures in the Renaissance style were mere trimmings.

Henry VIII turned to France for inspiration. The splendid King's College, Cambridge, screen (1532–6) was a direct result of Gallic influence. Nevertheless the houses of the new nobility remained basically Gothic—Barrington Court, Somerset (c. 1530), and Sutton Place, Surrey (1523–5)—enlivened by a few Renaissance motifs on the surface. With Edward VI's reign came bolder emulation of French patterns. The Strand front of Protector Somerset's house (1547–52) was deliberately modelled on Constable Montmorency's palace at Ecouen. In Elizabeth I's reign influences came from the Low Countries, with whom England enjoyed close commercial and religious ties. Immigrant craftsmen brought over pattern books by de Vries and Dietterlin. Hence the popularity of grotesque second-hand Flemish strap-work designs, translated to the skylines of Burghley (1575) and Wollaton (1580).

With the prevailing peace after the Armada in 1588, Elizabethan and Jacobean architecture lost its fussiness and found a new confidence in simplicity. Domestic building—for after the Reformation church-building was minimal—assumed a character essentially English. Hardwick Hall (1590–7), Montacute House (1599), Audley End (1603–16), Bramshill House (1605–12) and Blickling Hall (1620), are among the glories of English architecture. They were not the work of trained architects, but of master masons and carpenters. Planning was conventional—entrance porch, axial screens passage, great hall, butteries, summer and winter parlour, with long gallery occupying an upstairs floor of one wing. Panelled walls and plaster ceilings were universal. In addition, manor-houses of the lesser gentry and merchants sprang up like mushrooms.

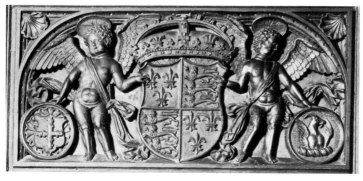

The Long Gallery, the Vyne, Hampshire. During the reign of Henry VIII, wainscoting, a cheap and attractive form of insulation, replaced wall hangings in large rooms. In this early 16th-century panel, above the door in the eastern wall, two angels support the Royal Arms of Henry VIII. The circles display the arms and crest of the Sandys family, who built the Vyne.

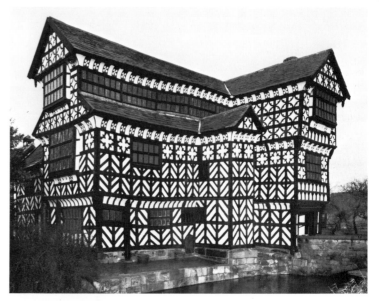

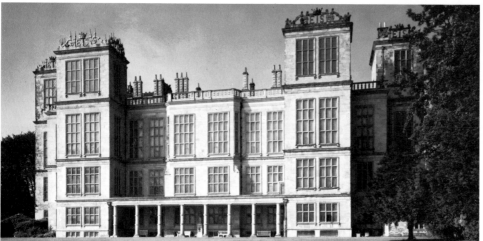

Little Moreton Hall, Cheshire (above), is a mid-16th-century house, a romantic half-timbered structure, surrounded by a moat. Its projecting long gallery, 75 ft by 12 ft 6 in, was superimposed in 1580. It has a ceiling of curved braces and plaster panels of emblematic devices. Its carved corner posts, gables and "magpie" surfaces are typical of the Tudor Midlands.

Hardwick Hall, Derbyshire, built 1590–7, is a later Elizabethan country-house, probably the work of the mason Robert Smythson. Designed on a squat H plan with projecting bays and a central hall, it is strictly symmetrical. The façade decoration is restrained, but inside is some of the richest Elizabethan decorative work. The predominance of windows gives rise to the idiom "Hardwick Hall, more glass than wall."

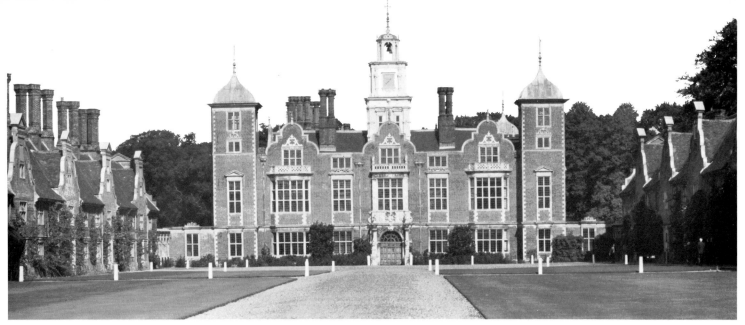

Blickling Hall, Norfolk (above), built
c. 1620, is a Jacobean brick house with stone
dressings. The rectangular plan contains
two internal courts, separated by a hallway.
There are traces of a medieval moat. The
house is dominated by a central clock turret,
and four corner-towers for staircases. The
plaster ceiling of the Long Gallery, one of the
most elaborate to survive from this period,
is decorated with pictorial panels taken from
a contemporary emblem book.

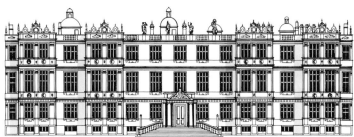

Longleat (left), begun
in 1553, was a
transitional country-
house, yet more strictly
Renaissance in concept
than any of its Tudor
predecessors. The three
Classical Orders are
conscientiously
displayed upon its
elegant façade.

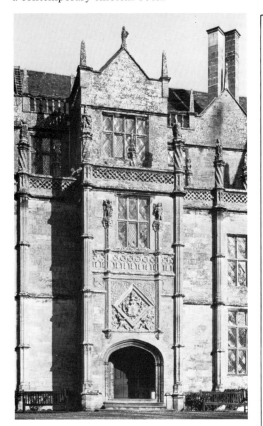

Montacute House, Somerset, built 1580–99,
is a late Tudor mansion. Its plan is E shaped,
with a central entrance and two end wings.
The elaborate west portal (above), flanked
by Gothic shafts, was imported from a
neighbouring house. Traditional English
decorative features are combined at
Montacute with Flemish conceits, which in
modified form gained ascendancy in England
during the Elizabethan period.

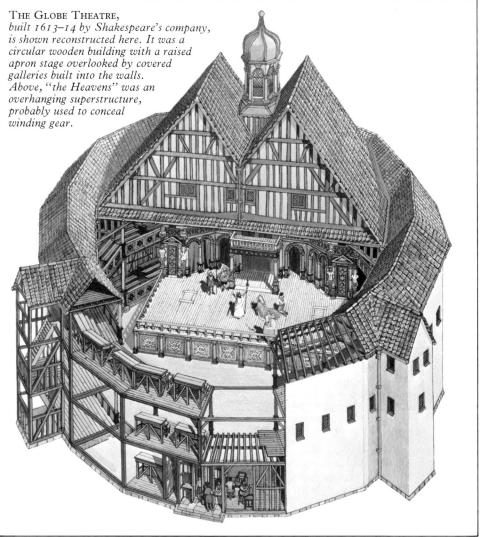

THE GLOBE THEATRE,
*built 1613–14 by Shakespeare's company,
is shown reconstructed here. It was a
circular wooden building with a raised
apron stage overlooked by covered
galleries built into the walls.
Above, "the Heavens" was an
overhanging superstructure,
probably used to conceal
winding gear.*

Inigo Jones and the new classicism

INIGO JONES (1573–1652) is to architecture what Shakespeare is to literature. Inigo is first heard of in 1603 as a skilled draughtsman and an imaginative producer of masques. In 1611 he was made Surveyor to Prince Henry of Wales, and in 1615 Surveyor of the King's Works (until 1642). In 1613–14 he travelled in the suite of Lord Arundel, the art connoisseur, to Heidelberg; thence to Venice and Rome. Italy, which he had visited once previously, became the mainspring of his culture. He was the first Englishman to make on-the-spot studies of Roman antiquities and to assimilate the Classical precepts of Vitruvius and Palladio.

Jones's surviving buildings are few indeed. His earliest significant works are the Queen's House, Greenwich, begun in 1616, and the Banqueting House, Whitehall, 1619–22. The Queen's Chapel at St James's followed in 1627. A cursory look at these three buildings reveals to the least trained eye a total departure from the vernacular style of architecture. Jones had produced for the first time on English soil a *quattrocento* villa, a Palladian palace and a *cinquecento* chapel. The three buildings were to determine the future Neo-Classical style of British architecture.

John Webb (1611–72) was articled to Inigo Jones at the age of seventeen and married his niece. He was a devoted disciple and the only contemporary to follow in the master's footsteps. But he was not an inspired creator. After Jones's death he received a number of private commissions—Lamport Hall, Northamptonshire (1654–7), and work at Belvoir, the Vyne and Amesbury. For the Crown he built the King Charles Block at Greenwich Palace (1665).

Such is Inigo Jones's reputation that numerous buildings of the mid-17th century with semi-classical pretensions have wrongly been ascribed to him. Several amateur gentlemen, like Sir Balthazar Gerbier, Sir Roger Pratt and John Evelyn, likewise went to study architecture abroad and practised it at home. The York Water Gate (1626), Coleshill House (*c.* 1650) and Clarendon House, Piccadilly (1664–7), are among their endeavours. Professional masons, bricklayers and carpenters, members of London companies, were vaguely affected by the Jonesian influence. Nicholas Stone, the monumental sculptor, built the Physick Garden gateway, Oxford (1632), and a wing at Cornbury Park (1632). Peter Mills, a City bricklayer, built Thorpe Hall, Northamptonshire (1653–6).

A lone figure of the immediate post-Jones epoch was Hugh May, 1622–84. He can claim to be a professional architect. The intimate friend of Lely, Pepys and Evelyn, he spent most of the Commonwealth in Holland. He remodelled some of the royal apartments in Windsor Castle, and built Eltham Lodge, Kent (1664), in a Dutch Palladian spirit.

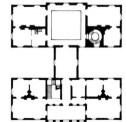

The Queen's House, Greenwich (left), was a conceptual departure from all foregoing English Renaissance architecture, the first English villa in truly Italian style. In plan (right) it was originally of two parts, connected by a bridge over a public road. Later the house was converted into a simple rectangle with a galleried hall, a 40-ft-wide cube, in the centre. The house is wholly symmetrical; the proportions are balanced with care. A restrained and dignified building, begun in 1616, it influenced later buildings in England.

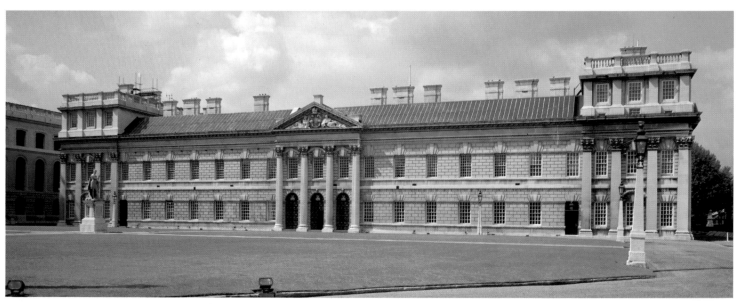

King Charles Block, Greenwich Palace, begun in 1665, was the major building of John Webb, who drew heavily for inspiration upon Inigo Jones's unrealized plans of 1647 for a palace at Whitehall. Webb anticipated the Baroque in this monumental façade, divided horizontally by two stone bands and unified by a central group of four columns and a pediment, with two groups of four giant pilasters at either end. The structure was the first stage of the projected Greenwich Palace, completed by Wren as a hospital.

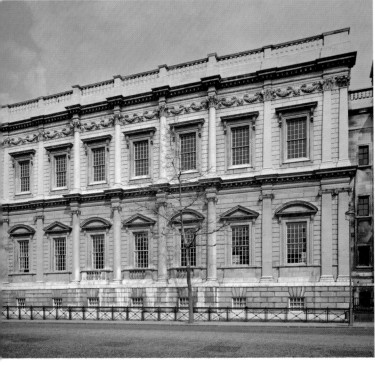

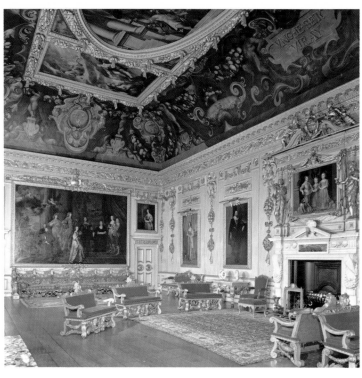

The Double Cube Room, Wilton House, Wiltshire (above), dates from *c.* 1649. Designed by Jones to display a number of Van Dyck portraits, it is decorated in white and gold. One of the best surviving examples of a 17th-century state room, its finest features are the great coved ceiling, the Corinthian pedimented chimney piece and the carved swags and drops of fruit and drapery.

The Banqueting House, Whitehall (above), completed in 1622, was Jones's masterpiece, strictly Palladian in concept. Like the Queen's House it is a double cube, and the central hall, with ceiling panels painted by Rubens, occupies the piano nobile and upper storey. The severely classical façade, incorporating the Ionic and Composite Orders, has three projecting centre bays of columns and entablatures, with festoons and masks below the upper of two horizontal friezes, symbolizing the revelry associated with a banqueting hall.

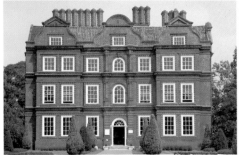

Brick houses became increasingly common during the 16th century and exploded into a vogue during the 17th, especially in areas short of wood and stone. Flemish influence is clearly discernible in façade decoration, where ornate gables are combined with classical features. Kew Palace (left), 1631, has splendid curvilinear gables, brick pilasters and moulded window and door surrounds. The brickwork of Swakeleys (below), 1629–38, is stone-dressed, a miscellany of gay curved and scrolled gables crowned with pediments.

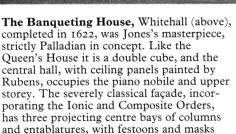

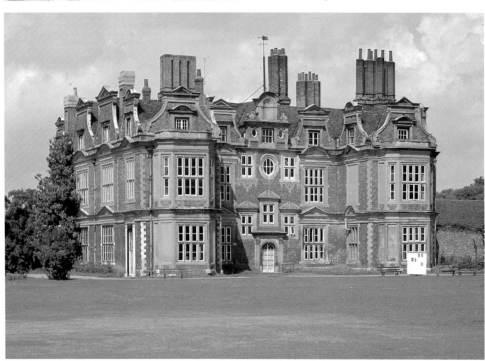

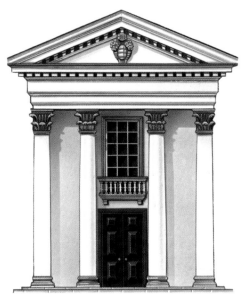

The portico of the Vyne, Hampshire, was designed in 1654 by John Webb. Brick columns and pilasters faced with moulded stucco are surmounted by a wooden pediment.

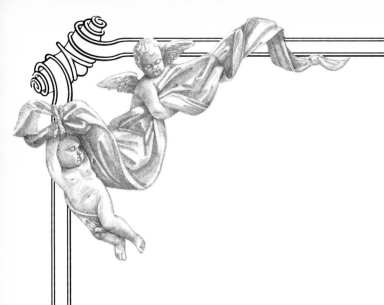

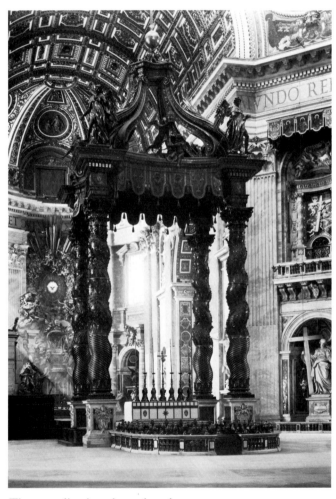

The ascending impulse and opulent forms so characteristic of High Baroque are seen in Bernini's bronze Baldacchino, rising on its spiralling columns more than 90 ft above the high altar of St Peter's in Rome.

The word "baroque" originally meant irregular or misshapen—particularly with reference to pearls—but it was applied by art historians in the 19th century to describe a type of architecture current in Europe during the 17th and 18th centuries which they condemned as being contrary to classical principles. It has stuck as a label for this period, but is no longer used as a term of abuse.

The Baroque is a style which was evolved in Rome in the years 1620–60, largely as the expression of the Catholic Revival which took place at this time, when the Roman Catholic Church, after its period of reform in the later 16th century, was recovering its temporal power and expanding actively through its missions in Asia and America. In its emotional tone and rhetorical power the Baroque expressed the spirit of the new Catholicism, while it also served the needs of the absolute rulers of the time, who found it admirably suited to the kind of propaganda which they needed to impress their subjects and their rivals. The architects who created the style in Rome were Gianlorenzo Bernini (1598–1680), Francesco Borromini (1599–1667) and Pietro da Cortona (1596–1669). These artists used new methods to convey their ideas and those of their patrons. Their buildings were generally on a vast scale and were based on curved forms, which produced an effect of movement and allowed the architects to use new types of ground plan and to experiment with new spatial inventions. They loved complexity and richness of materials rather than simplicity, and they indulged in dramatic effects of lighting. They exploited effects of illusionism and made one art imitate the methods of another. Sculptors introduced colour into their works in the spirit of a painter, architects used sculpture to support the members of a building and painters decorated the walls and vaults of churches with false architectural perspectives. The Baroque

Baroque

was invented in Rome, but by the end of the 17th century it had begun to spread to other parts of Italy and even beyond the Alps. In Turin, Guarino Guarini, a follower of Borromini, created a new kind of architecture in which openwork ribs—almost Gothic in feeling—replaced domes, and in Naples Cosimo Fanzago created fantastic effects with inlays of coloured marbles. In Venice the classical tradition of Palladio was so strong that the Baroque never took root, but Baldassare Longhena produced one great work in the style, the church of Santa Maria della Salute.

At the same time something of the Baroque spirit began to be felt outside Italy. In France, in the first half of the century, the spirit of classicism prevailed and inspired the exquisite buildings of François Mansart, such as the Château of Maisons, but Louis Le Vau, his contemporary, showed more feeling for the grand scale and dramatic effects of Italian Baroque architecture, which he applied to great effect, first in the Château of Vaux-le-Vicomte and later at Versailles, though here his successor, Jules Hardouin-Mansart, carried the methods of the Baroque much further in his additions to the château, above all in the Galerie des Glaces.

The most important and fruitful expansion of Baroque architecture was, however, towards Austria and South Germany. In Vienna, the capital of the Holy Roman Empire and a stronghold of Catholicism, it found a natural home, and the great palaces and churches built by Johann Bernhard Fischer von Erlach and Lukas von Hildebrandt are among the most splendid creations of the style. In the Danube Valley, Jakob Prandtauer built the great monasteries of Melk and Sankt Florian. In Germany the style was used by the ruling princes to build their palaces in imitation of Versailles, and in the south by the almost equally wealthy monasteries. A particular local form of

Baroque is to be found in the many pilgrimage churches, often built with the money of the pilgrims themselves, which have a slightly popular, even peasant, character.

From Germany and Austria the Baroque spread east to Hungary and Poland, and even to Russia, where the Italian architect Bartolomeo Rastrelli brilliantly adapted his Italian style to the needs of the Russian nobility and the Orthodox Church.

Naturally the Baroque did not take root easily in the Protestant countries of northern Europe. Although in England Wren, Vanbrugh, Hawksmoor and Gibbs represent a definite move towards the style, 18th-century England was dominated by the Palladianism revived by Lord Burlington and his friends.

Meanwhile in Europe a new style, which we call the Rococo, had grown up. It shared certain features with the Baroque—complexity of forms, fusion of the arts and illusionism—but it was invented to suit a different taste, that of Parisian society in the first decades of the 18th century which demanded elegance and convenience as opposed to grandeur. The style reached its first flowering in France, but it soon spread to other countries, particularly to South Germany, where it was brilliantly adapted to the decoration of churches.

The architecture of Spain and Portugal during this period presents special problems. The decorative forms of the Italian Baroque found an original interpretation in the palaces of northern Portugal, and Spanish architecture of the 18th century has a complexity which is in a sense Baroque. But no architect in either country showed any understanding of the basic principles of the Baroque. There is almost nothing in common between the churches of Borromini and, say, the Trasparente in Toledo Cathedral, except a love of ingenuity and fantasy.

Rome and the creators of the style

THE THREE ARCHITECTS who created the Baroque style in Rome—Bernini (1598–1680), Borromini (1599–1667) and Pietro da Cortona (1596–1669)—were remarkably different in their characters and in their approaches towards their art. Bernini startled Rome by his sculpture before he was twenty; he was also a skilful painter and he composed and produced plays and operas. He was the favourite of two popes, Urban VIII and Alexander VII. His art was splendid in conception and lavish in execution. He thought in terms of marble, gilding and dramatic lighting, and he loved a grand scale.

Borromini was the exact opposite. He was timid and neurotic, but wholly devoted to his art. He enjoyed little public success during his lifetime, and for more than two centuries after his death was regarded as a kind of madman who broke all the rules and debauched architecture. In fact, however, he was a passionate student of Antiquity and his designs are always based on a rigorous geometrical system. He normally worked on a small scale and had a preference for simple materials such as brick and stucco.

The third member of the group, Pietro da Cortona, made his reputation as a painter and only practised architecture on the side, so to speak. His church façades are designed almost like stage sets, planned to catch the dramatic contrasts of light and shade in the strong Roman sun.

The generation of architects after the three "founding fathers" was more timid, and Carlo Fontana (1634–1714) created a sort of compromise style in which the bold inventions of his predecessors were qualified by a taste partly influenced from France. The result was a style which may be called "Late International Baroque", which was palatable to foreigners and influenced the whole of Europe.

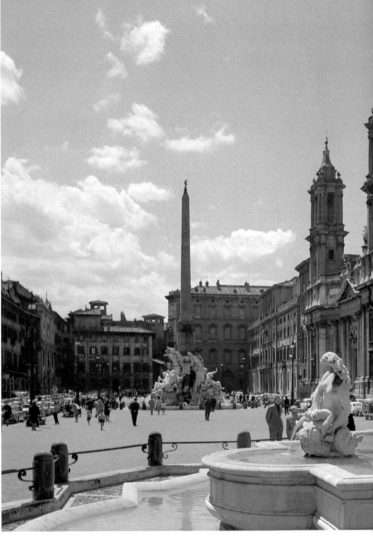

The Piazza Navona, most of which was built by the family of Innocent X (Pamphili), is a summary of Baroque Rome. The church of S. Agnese was designed by Borromini; two of the fountains are by Bernini; and Cortona painted the gallery in the Pamphili Palace.

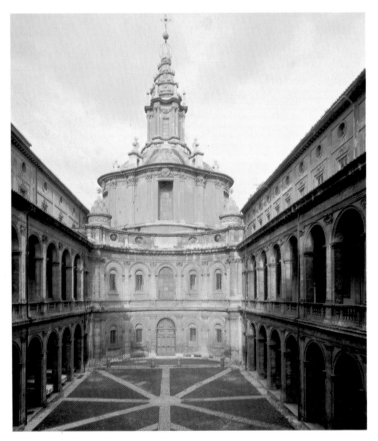

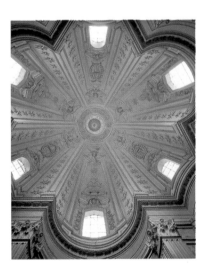

Sant'Ivo della Sapienza, the church of the University of Rome, is Borromini's masterpiece. The courtyard was already finished when, in 1642, he began the church, which had to be fitted between the two arcades. Borromini chose a centralized plan based on two interlocking equilateral triangles, forming a six-pointed star; out of this he evolved a form which compels the eye to move continuously round it. The church is full of symbolism, mostly alluding to the Temple of Solomon, the seat of Wisdom. The star of the plan is the Star of David; the decoration of the dome (right) includes the palms, cherubs' heads and pomegranates of the Holy of Holies; the ziggurat-lantern ends in the flame of Truth.

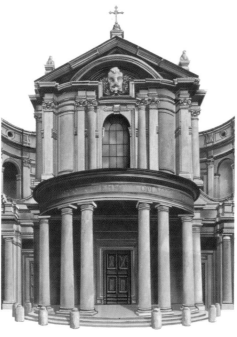

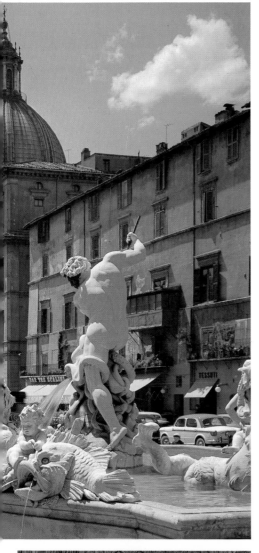

Santa Maria della Pace. The façade was added by Pietro da Cortona to an earlier building in 1656–7. Cortona contrived to give a symmetry to an irregular group of buildings and to solve the problem of providing enough room for aristocratic worshippers to turn their coaches (the street to the left of the church must be one of the first one-way streets ever established). At the same time he created a magnificently dramatic architectural effect by providing a semicircular back-cloth to the central section of the front, which closes the nave. In this part of the front Cortona has brilliantly exploited the rough veining of Roman travertine. The semi-circular porch influenced Wren at St Paul's.

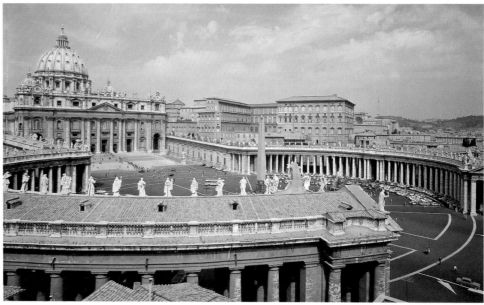

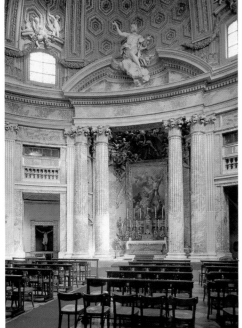

The Piazza of St Peter's was built by Bernini for Pope Alexander VII in 1656–67. It was conceived as a grand approach to the church, but had to be planned so that the greatest number of people could see the Pope give his blessing, either from the middle of the façade of the church or from a window in the Vatican Palace. Bernini made his design broad and low to minimize the squatness of the façade. Towers had been planned, but could not be put up for structural reasons, leaving an awkwardly long low façade.

Sant'Andrea al Quirinale (left and right). Bernini's son records that in his old age the architect often went to sit in this church, which he regarded as his most perfect creation. It was built for the Jesuits in 1658–65. The church has an unusual plan, an oval with the short axis leading to the altar. Externally, it is dominated by heavy scrolls, which support the dome, and by the elegant porch, which echoes the half-oval chapel to which it leads. In the interior, the walls are lined with delicate pinkish-red marble, hardly broken by relief, and the dome is richly coffered. Bernini here employed his idea of "extended action" to great effect. Over the high altar is a painting of the martyrdom of St Andrew; sculptures over the chancel arch show his soul being borne to Heaven, where the Holy Ghost and angels await him.

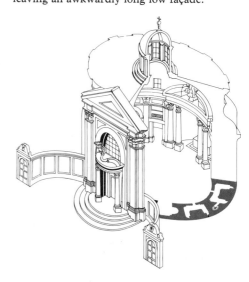

The Italian variations

OUTSIDE ROME THE Baroque took on a great variety of different forms owing to local conditions and building materials. In Naples the wealth of the Church and the desire of the nobles—often bearing newly created titles—to rival each other in display, led to a style of extreme richness, which was made possible by the fact that coloured marbles were readily available in southern Italy and lent themselves to the kind of rich effects which the Neapolitans love. To satisfy this taste architects such as Cosimo Fanzago (1591–1676) created some of the most sumptuous and richly coloured church interiors in the whole of Baroque architecture. In the first half of the 18th century Naples produced another major architect, Ferdinando Sanfelice (1675–1750), who was a master in the designing of dramatic staircases. In Sicily, too, coloured marbles were common and chapels, and sometimes whole churches, were decorated with patterned marble inlay, the effect of which is sometimes heightened by high-relief sculpture. Sicilian architects also evolved a special type of church design in which the tower is fused with a form of façade borrowed from Rome, as in San Giorgio, Ragusa.

In Apulia, the province which occupies the "heel" of Italy, there was also a great outburst of church-building in the 18th century, made possible by the prosperity of the country based on its agriculture; but it is doubtful whether the buildings put up in towns like Lecce can properly be called Baroque. They have almost nothing in common with the architecture of Borromini or Bernini and depend for their effect on a piling up of carved ornament, made possible by the soft golden stone found in the area, which allows deep and complicated cutting and then hardens in the atmosphere.

In the north of Italy the Baroque developed much more sophisticated forms. In Turin, Guarino Guarini (1624–83), who was an admirer of Gothic architecture and seems even to have been aware of Muslim structures, created web-like open domes, composed of ribs which stand out against the light from the lantern which they support. Guarini's successor as the dominant architect in Turin, Filippo Juvarra (1676–1736) was one of the most brilliant exponents of the international style. Whereas Guarini based his conception of architecture on his study of Borromini, Juvarra was a pupil of Carlo Fontana, but he added an almost theatrical sense to the rather staid manner of his master.

Much Italian Baroque is pedestrian, even poor, and this is one reason why the style fell into discredit. It must, however, be judged by its best works, those of the great architects of Rome, Turin, Naples and Sicily.

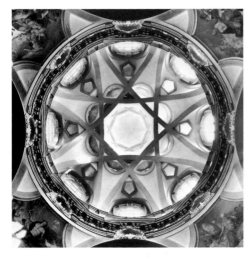

The Church of San Lorenzo, Turin, was begun by Guarino Guarini in 1668 for the Theatine Order, of which he was a member. The plan is remarkable for its curved bays pressing into the central domed space—an idea developed from Borromini—but the dome (above) is even more remarkable. It is a masterpiece of ingenious construction—the ribs actually carry the lantern above them—which is also used to produce dramatic contrasts of light and shade.

The Church of Santa Croce at Lecce is a striking example of the degree to which medieval features survive in the architecture of Apulia. The façade was begun in the 1570s and not finished until a century later, but the round windows and the grotesque beasts supporting the balcony might have come from a 12th-century church. The monastic buildings, of which one bay is visible here to the left of the church, are typical of the 18th-century architecture of Apulia.

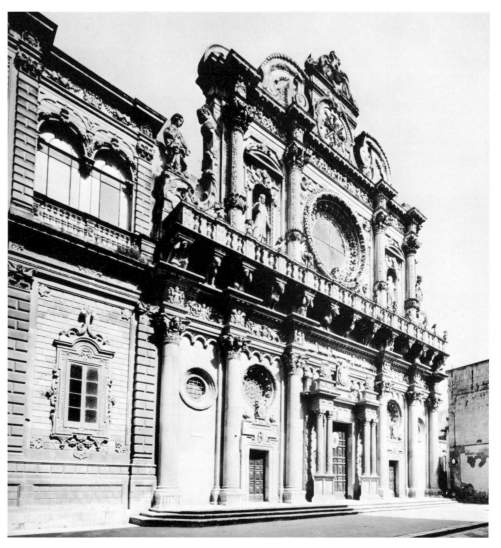

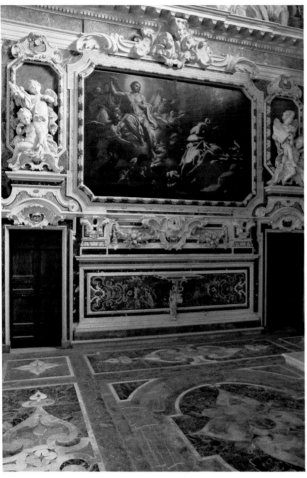

The Certosa di San Martino, Naples, was built 1623–31 by Cosimo Fanzago who worked for 30 years for the Carthusian Monastery of San Martino. He began the decoration of the church—which is perhaps the finest example of the Neapolitan love of colour, supplied by paintings and marble inlay—but it was not completed until the mid-18th century.

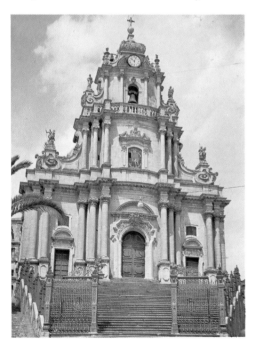

San Giorgio at Ragusa, Sicily, was built by Rosario Gagliardi in 1744–66 to replace a church destroyed by earthquake in 1693. Gagliardi, Sicily's finest architect of the period, understood the feeling for mass of the great Roman architects and produced some of the island's few genuine Baroque churches.

The Basilica di Superga, Turin, was built by Filippo Juvarra in 1716–27 as a thank-offering for the liberation of Turin after the siege by the French in 1706. Like most Baroque architects, Juvarra had an eye for a good position and the church stands on the top of a steep hill, 1,500 ft above the city. Juvarra designed it so that the simple masses of its dome and portico tell at a great distance. The dome, with its coupled columns and heavy ribs, is based on that of St Peter's; the porch is severely classical, but the crowning features of the towers are in the most mature Baroque style, deriving from Borromini, but with an extra complexity of curves rare in Italy and more generally associated with Austria and South Germany—a mixture typical of the Late International Style.

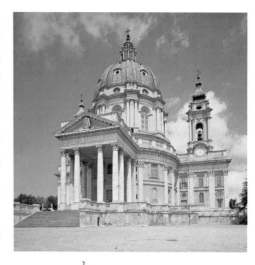

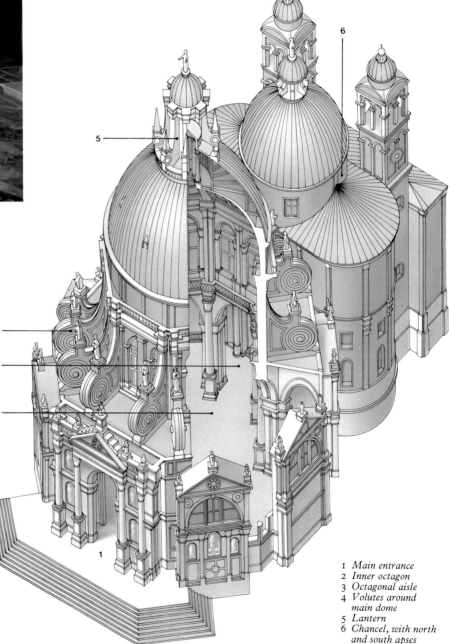

1 Main entrance
2 Inner octagon
3 Octagonal aisle
4 Volutes around main dome
5 Lantern
6 Chancel, with north and south apses

Santa Maria della Salute, Venice, the church which dominates the entrance to the Grand Canal, was begun by Longhena in 1631, but took more than half a century to complete. Its octagonal form, admirably suited to its situation, presents a coherent view from every side. In the lower storey, Longhena still shows a certain Palladian restraint, but the huge volutes, which carry the lateral thrust of the dome, create a fully Baroque movement. The exterior is built of white Istrian limestone, but the interior has columns of dark grey stone, which contrast with the white stucco of the main walls.

France, the spirit of classicism

AFTER HENRI IV (1589–1610) had freed his country from foreign invaders and internal factions he set about making Paris the true capital of his kingdom. His own contribution was a series of projects for public buildings, of which the Place Royale and the Place Dauphine on the Ile de la Cité still survive. The forty years after his death saw a great increase in the power of France owing to the political skill of Cardinal Richelieu, and at the same time a new class of rapidly enriched bourgeois came into power. Fortunately they showed great taste, and the development of the Paris *hôtel*, or townhouse, in this period is entirely due to them. They, rather than the Crown, were the patrons of François Mansart and Louis Le Vau, and they fostered the new classical style, which these architects introduced. These bourgeois also bought estates near Paris on which they built their châteaux, of which the most perfect is Maisons by Mansart and the most spectacular Vaux-le-Vicomte by Le Vau.

When in 1661, on the death of Richelieu's successor Cardinal Mazarin, Louis XIV decided to rule the kingdom himself, things changed and the most important building enterprises were once more undertaken by the king with the help of his able minister Colbert. The first objective was the completion of the Square Court of the Louvre, which had been begun in the mid-16th century but still lacked its east wing. After various abortive projects, including one by Bernini, it was finally decided to build the Colonnade, which stands today.

By the late 1660s, when the Colonnade was put up, Louis had decided to make Versailles the centre of his court and relatively little building was done in Paris in the last decade of the century. The two great exceptions were the church of the Invalides and the Place Vendôme. The former was probably designed to contain Louis XIV's tomb (paradoxically it now contains the remains of Napoleon), the latter, originally planned for various academies, was eventually let to private individuals.

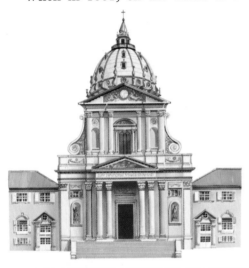

The Val-de-Grâce, Paris (left), was commissioned by Anne of Austria, wife of Louis XIII, to celebrate the birth of the dauphin, later Louis XIV, in 1637. Building was started by François Mansart in 1642, but he soon quarrelled with the queen and the church was finished by other architects not wholly in accordance with his design. The façade is however one of the purest examples of French classicism.

The Place des Vosges, Paris, originally called the Place Royale, was begun in 1605. It contained unit habitations (below), each house consisting of four bays over the open arcade, which was intended as a promenade for the inhabitants of the district. This particular house was later lived in by Victor Hugo and is now a museum.

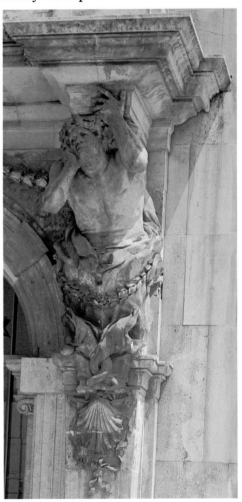

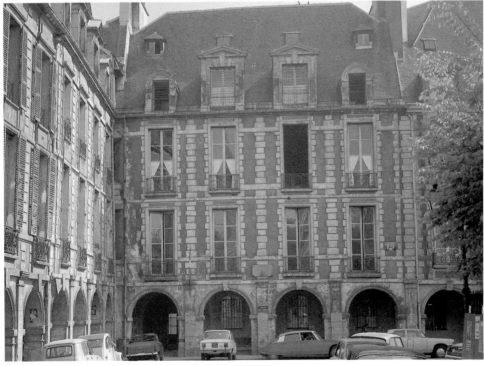

Pierre Puget, 1620–94, was primarily a sculptor and the tortured atlantes, or stone figures, which support the heavy balcony over the door to the Hôtel de Ville at Toulon (above), built in 1656, are the most spectacular features of the building. The shells are an allusion to the importance of Toulon as a port. The figures are inspired by Michelangelo, an artist generally neglected—even disapproved of—in France at this time.

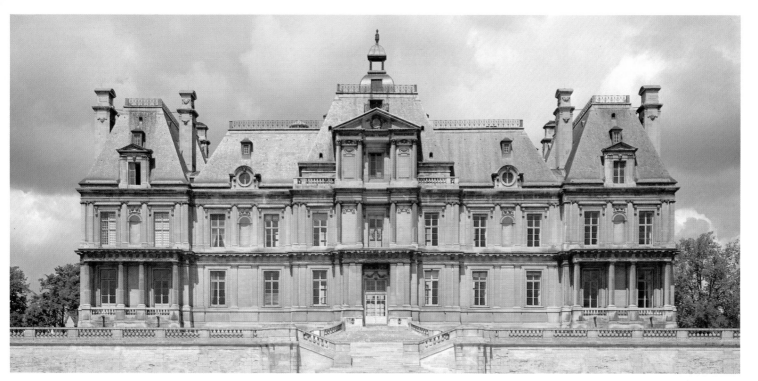

The Château of Maisons, now called Maisons-Lafitte, near Paris, was built by François Mansart between 1642 and 1648 for the wealthy René de Longueil, Marquis de Maisons. It was regarded by Voltaire and his contemporaries as the purest example of French classical architecture, and Louis XV contemplated buying it and adapting it to his needs, but decided that this would be vandalism. The building and the decoration of the interior have survived almost unaltered, but the magnificent gardens and park which surrounded it have been built over with modern suburban villas.

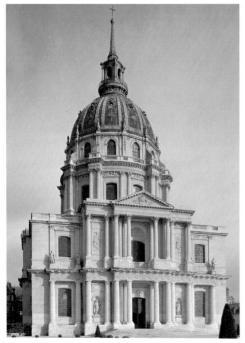

The Church of the Invalides was built by Jules Hardouin-Mansart, the great-nephew of François Mansart, between 1679 and 1691, but the decoration of the interior lasted into the 18th century. The lower part of the exterior is severe and classical, but in the dome the architect was much bolder. He raised the cupola itself by inserting a range of windows, which allowed him, in the interior, to light the outer shell of a double dome; and he decorated the exterior of the dome with gilt military trophies.

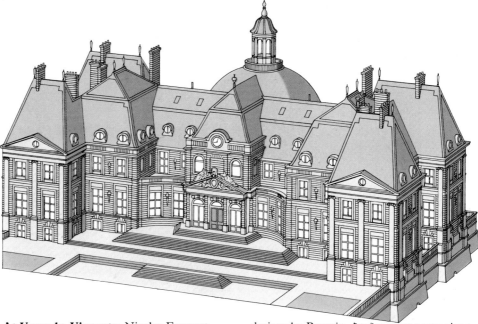

At Vaux-le-Vicomte, Nicolas Fouquet, Finance Minister to Louis XIV, brought together the team of artists who later created Versailles. The architect was Le Vau, the painter, Charles Lebrun; the gardens were laid out by Le Nôtre, with statues after designs by Poussin. At the great party given for the king in 1661 the play was by Molière, the prologue by La Fontaine, the music by Lully, and the dinner was cooked by Vatel. Within weeks Fouquet was charged with corruption and gaoled for life.

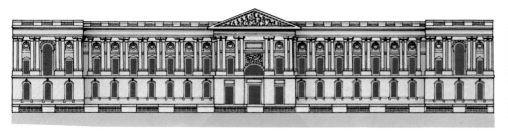

The East Front of the Louvre—often called the Colonnade—was begun in 1667 from designs by three artists: Le Vau, the first architect to the king, Lebrun, the first painter, and Claude Perrault, a doctor turned architect. Controversy has raged ever since as to which of these men was the real inventor of the scheme, but it is perhaps typical of the organization of the arts under Louis XIV that such complete collaboration was possible.

France's splendid later phase

ONCE LOUIS XIV had decided that Versailles was to be the centre of his court it became necessary to enlarge the existing château built by his father, which was little more than a hunting lodge. The first enlargement was undertaken in the late 1660s under the direction of Louis Le Vau, who added two flights of rooms round the earlier building, one for the king and the other for the queen. In the late 1670s, under Le Vau's successor, Jules Hardouin-Mansart, the great-nephew of François Mansart, the Galerie des Glaces was added to make one of the most resplendent suites of rooms in Europe. Both Le Vau and Hardouin-Mansart made use of certain Baroque features—scale, richness of materials and blending of painting and sculpture with architecture—but the *bon goût* of which the French were so proud inhibited them from indulging in the broken and curved architectural forms loved by Borromini and his followers.

In the last years of Louis XIV's reign and during the regency of his successor—and great-grandson—Louis XV, taste changed. Higher standards of comfort were demanded and the new style, the Rococo, was much more intimate than that of the Sun King as shown at Versailles. Many rooms in the royal palaces were redecorated in the new manner, but it also had a wide success in Paris, which once again became a centre of architectural activity.

During this period few public buildings were erected, but about the middle of the century, under the impulse of the Marquis de Marigny, brother of Madame de Pompadour, the Crown once again began to undertake great projects, of which the Place Louis XV, now the Place de la Concorde, was the most remarkable. Jacques-Ange Gabriel, the architect of the Place, was also employed on the royal palaces and was responsible for the Petit Trianon.

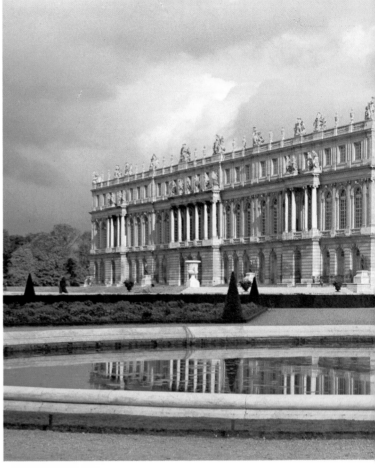

The Garden Front of Versailles (above) was built mainly by Louis Le Vau in 1669, but in his scheme the middle section of the main front, seen here on the left of the picture, was opened by a terrace. In 1678, this was filled in by Hardouin-Mansart to allow the construction of the Galerie des Glaces. At the same time the length of the palace was trebled by the addition of long wings, one bay of which is visible on the extreme right, to house the courtiers and the administrative staff of the State.

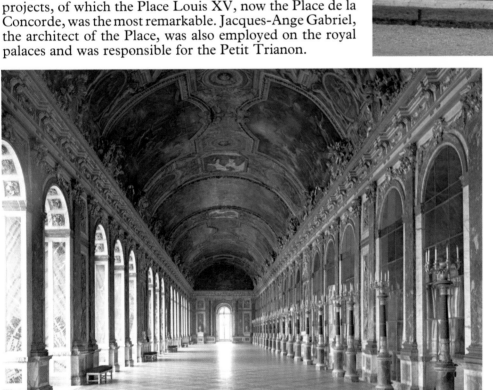

The Galerie des Glaces at Versailles is still the most splendid room in France. It was originally equipped with solid silver tables, chairs and furniture—benches against the walls, torchères to carry lights—and with the floor covered with Savonnerie carpets. The furniture lasted only ten years, as the king sent it to the Mint in 1689 to be melted for bullion needed to carry on the War of the League of Augsburg.

The Petit Trianon, Versailles (below), was built for Madame du Barry by Gabriel in 1763 and altered for Marie Antoinette, with whom it is mainly associated. Used by the queen as a private refuge from the formality of mid-18th century court life, the Petit Trianon is a real retreat, surrounded by an informal "English" garden.

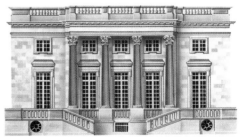

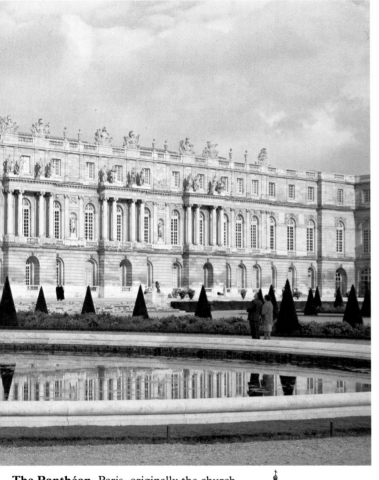

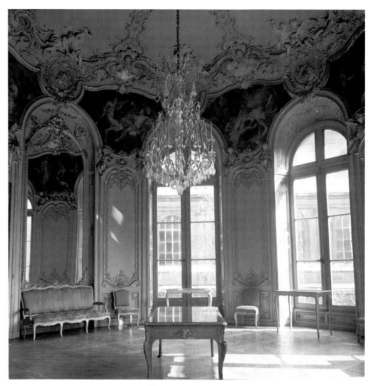

The Oval Salon of the Hôtel de Soubise,
Paris, was built by Germain Boffrand in
1738–40 and is one of the most elaborate
Rococo rooms in France. The light and gay
stucco work is typical of the period, but the
room is unusual in that paintings play a
considerable part in the decoration.

1 *Portico*
2 *Colonnaded drum
  supporting the dome*
3 *Dome with triple-
  shell construction*
4 *Towers, designed but
  never built*
5 *Crossing*

The Panthéon, Paris, originally the church
of S. Geneviève, was begun by Soufflot in
1757 but not finished until after his death in
1780. The structure of the building is very
bold: the columns supporting the dome are
unusually thin, giving an airy effect to the
interior, and the huge columns of the portico
are widely spaced, making the
construction of the pediment over it
difficult. The dome is a version of
Wren's at St Paul's, but with all
the bays of uniform pattern.

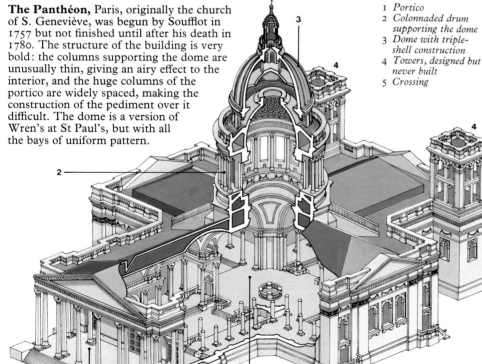

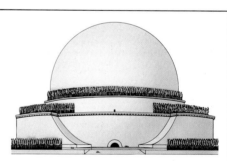

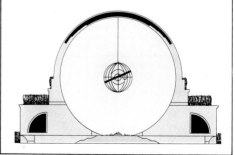

CENOTAPH FOR SIR ISAAC NEWTON
*Etienne-Louis Boullée's design (1784)
illustrates a most curious aspect of the
Neo-Classical movement, a sort of dream
architecture, too vast and strange ever to
have been realized. Boullée and his rival
Ledoux built houses in Paris; their great
inventions are recorded only in engravings.*

Austria, a natural home of the style

AUSTRIAN BAROQUE architecture falls into three main categories: public buildings, private palaces and monasteries, and the names of three architects are associated with the three categories: Johann Bernhard Fischer von Erlach was responsible for the public buildings (though he also built palaces), Lukas von Hildebrandt was primarily concerned with palaces and Jakob Prandtauer was solely a builder of monasteries.

The public buildings included not only the Imperial Palace, or Hofburg, in Vienna, to which Fischer added a court with the great library, but also the Karlskirche, commissioned by the emperor in 1716 to commemorate the cessation of a plague. Fischer was trained in Rome, probably in the studio of Fontana, and his adaptation of the Roman style was particularly suited to the demands of the Holy Roman Emperor, who saw himself as the successor not only of Charlemagne but also of the Roman emperors of Antiquity.

Hildebrandt was trained in Turin as a military engineer and took part in the Italian campaigns of Prince Eugene of Savoy—the companion in arms of Marlborough—for whom he built the splendid Belvedere Palace on the outskirts of Vienna, with vast gardens spreading down the hill to the stables and another smaller palace. Prandtauer never left his native country though he must have studied Italian models in engravings. His monasteries are almost all in the Danube valley.

The most important works of the Austrian Baroque are to be found in this area, but the style actually appeared first in the Tyrol, particularly in Innsbruck, and in Prague, which was then the second capital of the Empire. In Prague the Dientzenhofer family, who originally came from Franconia, built a number of palaces and churches before the end of the 17th century, at a period when activity in Vienna was hindered by the threat of attacks by the Turks. Another important centre was Salzburg, where the cathedral was rebuilt quite early in the 17th century in an Italian manner and where Fischer von Erlach started his career as an architect.

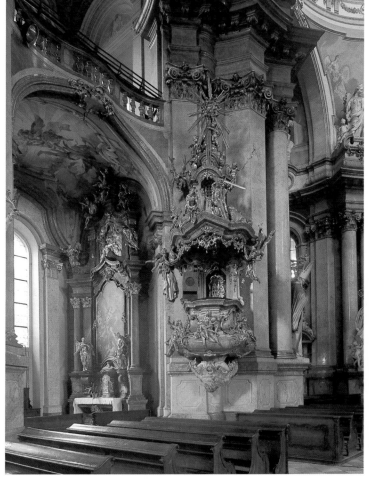

Sankt Nikolaus on the Kleinseite in Prague, was built 1703–11 by Christoph Dientzenhofer and his son Kilian Ignaz. The interior is a fine example of the complex interlocking vaulting and the curved balconies which give a strong sense of moment to much Austrian Baroque architecture.

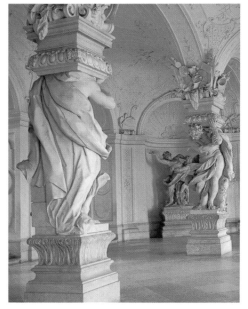

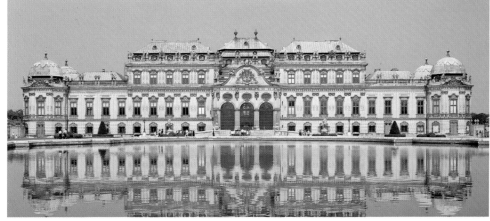

The Belvedere in Vienna was the summer palace of Prince Eugene of Savoy, built for him by Hildebrandt in 1720–4. The entrance front (above) shows Hildebrandt's love of curved forms, as in the pediment, and of a broken roof line which piles up towards the centre with Baroque vivacity. The vestibule (left) on the garden side is typical of Viennese architecture in that the vault is supported by stone figures instead of columns.

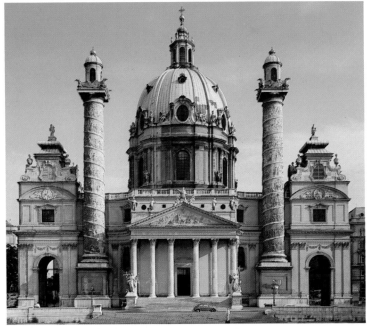

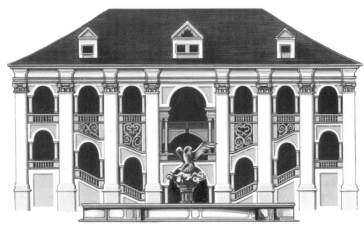

The Monastery of Sankt Florian (above), near Linz, was rebuilt, from 1711 onwards, by Prandtauer, who was responsible for the brilliantly designed staircase. It is unusual for Austria in being open and its design can only be paralleled in the staircases by Sanfelice in Naples, which at that time was under the rule of Austrian viceroys.

The Karlskirche in Vienna (above). The most remarkable feature of the church is the pair of columns in front of it. They allude to the columns outside the Temple of Solomon and to Roman triumphal columns of Trajan and Marcus Aurelius, thus identifying the emperor with the rulers of Israel and Rome.

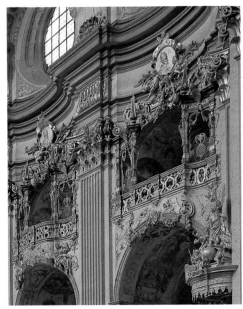

The Benedictine Monastery of Melk (above and right), the grandest and richest of all Austrian religious houses, was rebuilt in the first half of the 18th century by Jakob Prandtauer and his pupil Josef Munggenast. It stands on a bluff over the Danube and the whole design leads up to the climax of the domed church. The interior of the church combines something of the movement of the Dientzenhofers' churches with a greater richness: red stucco–marble pilasters and gilt ornament with an almost French elegance.

1 *Church*
2 *Kaisersaal, or hall for the reception of the emperor or other important visitors*
3 *Library*
4 *Monks' living quarters*
5 *Bastions for the defence of the monastery*

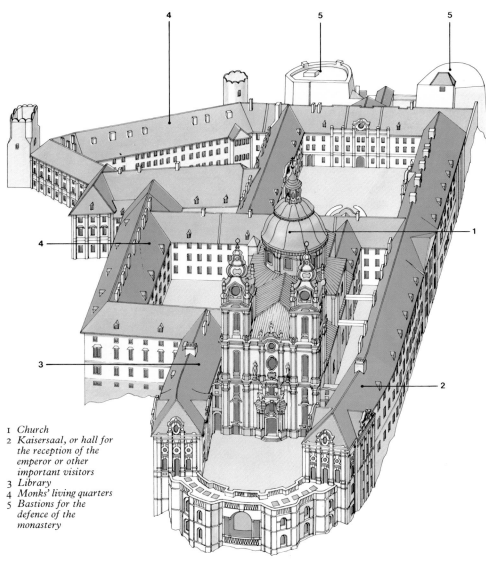

Germany, a magnificent flowering

IN THE FIRST HALF of the 18th century, when Germany had recovered from the effects of the Thirty Years' War, there was a great renewal of building activity. The princes, great and small, began to rebuild their palaces; in the Catholic south the monasteries, which acquired great wealth from the exploitation of their estates, began to restore and extend their buildings, which had hardly been touched since the early 16th century on account of the religious disturbances which followed the Reformation; and in the country districts, a great wave of religious fervour led to a demand for new pilgrimage churches to house the venerated images or relics.

The new styles of Baroque and Rococo first took root in Bavaria, where the Electors redecorated the Residenz in Munich and built the Palace of Nymphenburg just outside the town, famous for the little pavilion called the Amalienburg, one of the most perfect Rococo buildings in existence. In the 1730s the Asam brothers, who between them covered all three arts of architecture, painting and sculpture, produced maturely Baroque churches such as that of Weltenburg, near Regensburg; but the greatest masters were active about the middle of the century: Johann Michael Fischer (1691–1766), the creator of Ottobeuren and other vast monastic churches, and Dominikus Zimmermann (1685–1766), who specialized in pilgrimage churches such as Die Wies. At about the same time a little farther north, in Franconia, Balthasar Neumann (1687–1753) built the palace for the wealthy bishops of Würzburg with ceiling paintings by the Venetian Tiepolo, one of the most splendid palaces in Europe, and a series of churches, such as Vierzehnheiligen, which are remarkable for the brilliant new spatial forms which the architect introduced.

In Dresden the Electors of Saxony built the Zwinger, and in Prussia Frederick the Great produced, in Sanssouci, a palace which almost rivals the Amalienburg Pavilion for its Rococo decoration.

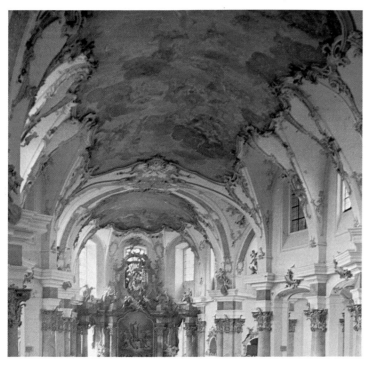

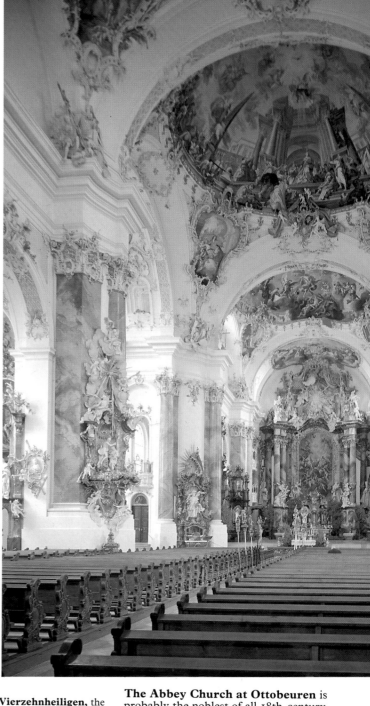

Vierzehnheiligen, the Pilgrimage Church of the Fourteen Helper Saints, was built in 1743–72 by Neumann. His complex system of ribs and domes created brilliant spatial effects, and enabled him to give equal importance to the high altar and the Fourteen Saints in the nave.

The Abbey Church at Ottobeuren is probably the noblest of all 18th-century German churches. This is the more surprising in that the foundations had already been laid when Johann Michael Fischer was called in to carry on the building in 1748. Its size is enormous and its decoration is a sumptuous combination of coloured stucco-marble, frescoes and white and gold stucco frames, but the whole is saved from fussiness by the simplicity of the main lines of the arches and the clarity of the planning.

Die Wies (right), built by Zimmermann in 1745–54, is the most famous and enchanting of all the pilgrimage churches in Bavaria. Its simple exterior, painted white, gives no hint of the splendour of the interior, which demonstrates how perfectly the Rococo, invented for sophisticated Parisians, could be adapted for use in a country church. To Protestant eyes this type of architecture for long seemed simply profane, but it expresses a genuine, if simple, piety which argues that the image of the Virgin—the centre of the pilgrimage—should be given as gay and luxurious a setting as possible.

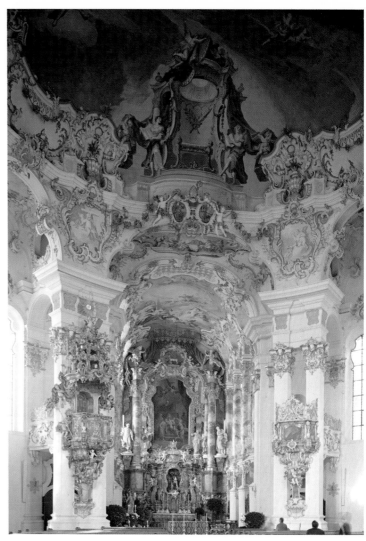

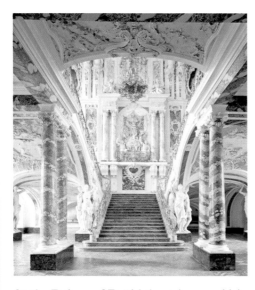

At the Palace of Brühl the staircase, which was constructed in 1740–1 by Neumann, combines Baroque grandeur with exquisite Rococo detail, for instance in the wrought-iron balustrade.

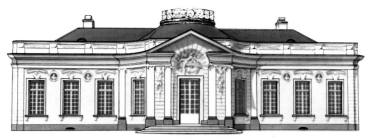

The Amalienburg Pavilion (left), in the park of Nymphenburg Palace near Munich, was built for the Electors of Bavaria in 1733. It was designed by François Cuvilliés, a Flemish-born architect who learned the latest Rococo style in Paris. To this he added certain personal features, which make the Amalienburg one of the most perfect Rococo buildings ever conceived.

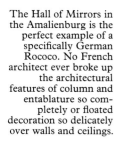

The Hall of Mirrors in the Amalienburg is the perfect example of a specifically German Rococo. No French architect ever broke up the architectural features of column and entablature so completely or floated decoration so delicately over walls and ceilings.

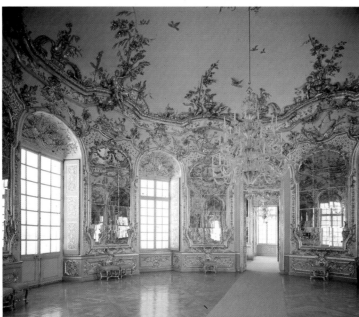

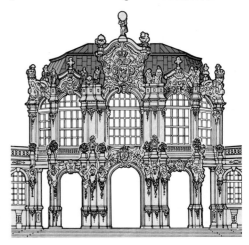

The Zwinger, Dresden (above), part of the Palace of the Elector, was built in 1718–28 by Daniel Pöppelmann. Dresden was, till World War II, the most perfect 18th-century German town, and the Zwinger was its most characteristic building.

Spain and Portugal, original approaches

As HAS ALREADY been said, it is doubtful whether the term Baroque can properly be applied to the 18th-century architecture of Spain. It is sometimes described by the term Churrigueresque, after the family of architects called Churriguera who built many of the most important buildings in the style, including the Plaza Mayor at Salamanca, and although the word is cumbersome there is much to be said for its use. The main centres of activity were Seville and Granada in the south, Valencia on the Mediterranean coast, Toledo, which though no longer the capital of the country was its principal religious centre, and the great pilgrimage town of Santiago de Compostela in the northwest. The work in Toledo is the most sophisticated, and that of Andalucia the wildest and furthest removed from true Baroque.

Portuguese architecture of the 18th century is quite different from Spanish. Some of the earlier churches in the north (Oporto, Aveiro) have altars formed of repeated round-headed arches—almost Romanesque in character—entirely covered by gold leaf; others are more Italianate in spirit. Many of the churches are approached by elaborate open staircases, of which the most dramatic example is that leading in six stages to the pilgrimage church of Bom Jesus, near Braga.

Secular architecture also flourished in Portugal during the period. Houses, such as the one at Guimarães in northern Portugal, have their parallels in a series of beautiful country-houses scattered all over the country. The Royal Family built on a larger scale. The huge palace-monastery of Mafra, in conception based on the Escorial, is impressive but cold, and the relatively small palace of Queluz has much greater charm. The interior decoration of the time is brilliantly represented by the library of the University of Coimbra, the greatest centre of learning in Portugal.

The sacristy of the Cartuja (right), the Carthusian monastery at Granada, is the supreme example of the way Spanish architects dissolved architectural forms into decorative features. The entablatures vanish into curves and the half-columns disappear behind jagged scrollwork. The agitated effect of the whole is difficult for northern eyes to assimilate.

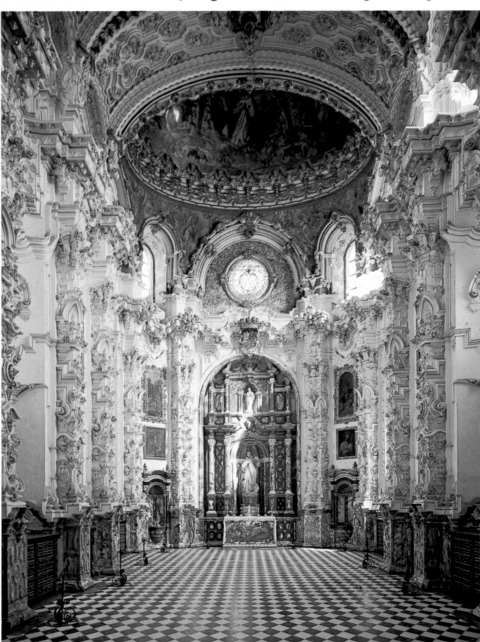

The Trasparente in the Cathedral of Toledo, designed by Narciso Tomé in 1721, fills the Gothic Lady Chapel behind the high altar. It is composed of sculpture and light. The Last Supper is represented in life-size stucco figures, on which the light floods down from an opening ingeniously inserted in the Gothic vaulting of the chapel.

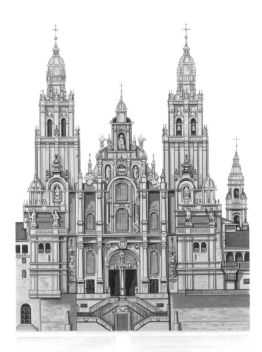

Santiago de Compostela Cathedral.
About 1667 it was decided to complete the
medieval cathedral by adding a façade and
towers to the main front. The height of the
Romanesque nave and the strong feeling for
the old traditions of the church led the
architects to construct what looks almost
like the façade of a French medieval
cathedral, but the decoration of the middle
section (1738) is typical of the Spanish
Churrigueresque style.

The door by Brocandel, the painter (right),
at the Palace of the Marqués de Dos
Aguas in Valencia, was built—or "modelled"
—from 1740 to 1744. It goes back to a type
used by Puget, in which athletic figures
support a balcony over the door, but here
figures and balcony have been merged in a
diaphragm of sculpture which almost fore-
shadows Art Nouveau.

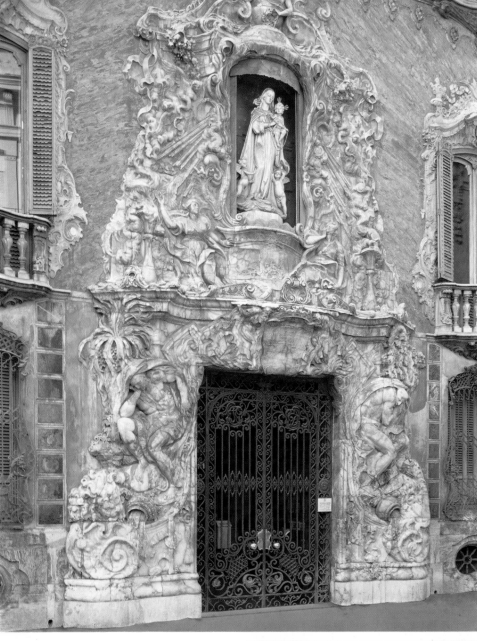

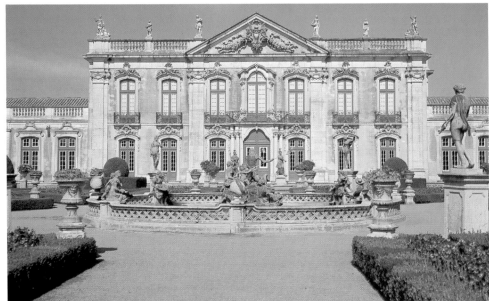

The Palace of Queluz, north of Lisbon,
was built in 1747–52 by Mateus Vicente de
Oliveira for one of the sons of King João V
and typifies the Portuguese version of the

International Baroque. Its general design is
like Gibbs's Senate House in Cambridge, but
the shape of the windows is French and the
pediments over them derive from Borromini.

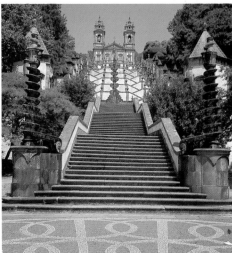

Bom Jesus, near Braga, in Portugal, was
laid out in 1723–44 as a pilgrimage way up
steps flanked with chapels, each containing a
carved representation of one of the Stations
of the Cross. Its effect is made more dramatic
by the zigzag plan of the steps, with their
angles pinpointed by fountains, statues and
obelisks in granite.

England, Wren and his contemporaries

IF INIGO JONES was something of a myth, Christopher Wren (1632–1723) was a miracle. Primarily an astronomer and physicist, he was incidentally an amateur architect. He was also a genius. His first tentative but competent buildings were at the universities, the Oxford Sheldonian (1662–3) being modelled upon Serlio's woodcut of the Roman Theatre of Marcellus. Ever afterwards Wren's architecture was notable for an academic restraint. Although his visit to Paris in 1665–6 opened wide his eyes to the sophistication of Mansart, Le Vau and even Bernini, his own work was never to indulge in continental Baroque flights: it was staid and masculine. Yet the catalogue of Wren's architectural library proves the eclecticism of his studies. This in turn is reflected in his buildings.

Wren's great opportunity arose after the Fire of London in 1666. He was made responsible for the rebuilding not only of St Paul's Cathedral—a stupendous enterprise—but fifty-one City churches, the designs of each to be approved when not devised by him. St Lawrence Jewry, St Mary-le-Bow, St Clement Danes and St Stephen, Walbrook, were among his masterpieces of planning and design. Perhaps his greatest contribution was the complex and inventive steeples, which gave unique beauty to the City of London skyline. In the course of these operations he trained an army of expert craftsmen—in the mason carvers Strong, E. Pearce, C. Kempster and C. Cibber. His secular work included Chelsea Royal Hospital, the south and east wings of Hampton Court, Kensington Palace and Greenwich Palace.

Wren no more established a school of architecture than Jones. His chief associates were Robert Hooke (1635–1703), builder of Montagu House, Bloomsbury, in the French manner with "cour d'honneur", and Willen Church, Buckinghamshire; William Talman (1650–1719), architect, under Roman influences, of Chatsworth and Dyrham; William Winde (d. 1722), of Dutch extraction, whose Buckingham House (1703) became in George I's and II's reigns the prototype of a Baroque country-house formula (giant pilasters, attic storey with flat parapet, spreading pavilions); William Samwell (1628–76), gentleman architect of Felbrigg Hall's red brick west wing of prosaic pattern; Sir William Wilson (1641–1710), a mason contractor from Leicester, who built houses in the Midlands; and Henry Bell (c. 1653–1717) of King's Lynn.

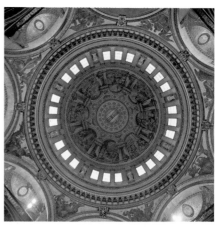

The saucer-shaped interior dome of St Paul's, its "eye" 214 ft 3 in above the floor, was painted with scenes from the life of St Paul by Sir James Thornhill, who also worked with Wren at Blenheim and Hampton Court palaces, and at Greenwich Palace.

The two Baroque steeples which flank the west façade and frame the great dome are 212 ft high. Added in 1708, the north steeple houses a belfry and the south a clock tower.

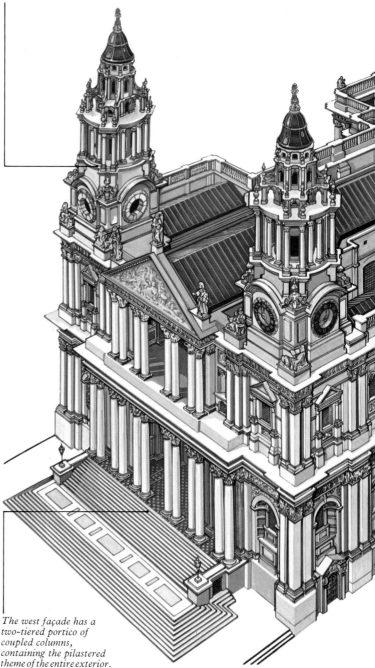

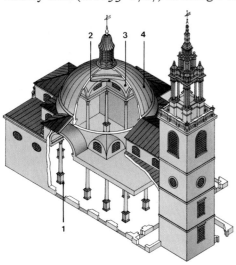

St Stephen, Walbrook, built in 1672–87, was one of Wren's important City churches, an experiment prior to St Paul's. The interior is divided into five aisles by 16 Corinthian columns (1), of which eight in a central circle support eight arches (2), thus converting the upper central area into an octagon. Pendentives (3) between them reconvert the octagon into a circle which carries the light wood and plaster dome (4), the earliest, perhaps, in England. Wren's steeples were an innovation of this period.

The west façade has a two-tiered portico of coupled columns, containing the pilastered theme of the entire exterior.

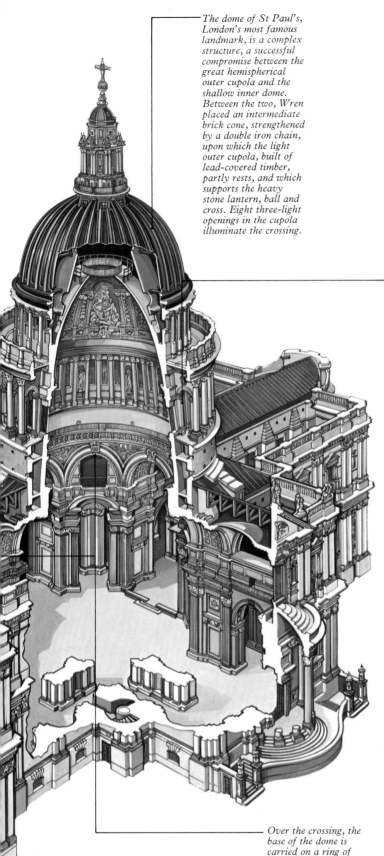

The dome of St Paul's, London's most famous landmark, is a complex structure, a successful compromise between the great hemispherical outer cupola and the shallow inner dome. Between the two, Wren placed an intermediate brick cone, strengthened by a double iron chain, upon which the light outer cupola, built of lead-covered timber, partly rests, and which supports the heavy stone lantern, ball and cross. Eight three-light openings in the cupola illuminate the crossing.

The 32 buttress walls radiating from the drum terminate in three-quarter columns, making a peristyle. Every fourth space is blocked, thus lending strength and solidity to the dome. The balustrade above, vilified by Wren as mere feminine frippery, was added against his will by the fashion-conscious Cathedral Commissioners.

Over the crossing, the base of the dome is carried on a ring of eight arches supported on piers. The arch and dome motif is continued into the nave, which is ingeniously vaulted with a succession of small domes, 91 ft above the ground, separated by transverse rib arches.

St Paul's Cathedral was built between 1675 and 1710 on the site of the medieval cathedral destroyed in the fire of 1666. It was designed in the shape of a Latin cross, 463 ft long and 101 ft wide, with a vast circular space at the crossing, where eight pillars support the great dome. England's only classical cathedral, St Paul's was the result of considerable modifications of Wren's original scheme for a church in the shape of a Greek cross.

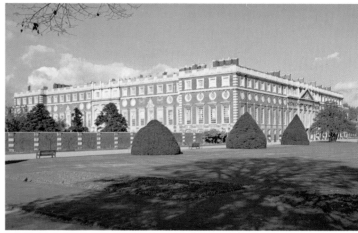

Hampton Court Palace (above), built *c.* 1520 for Cardinal Wolsey, was presented to Henry VIII in 1526. John Molton added the north and south wings, the Great Hall and the Chapel in 1531–6. The eastern section was rebuilt by Wren in 1689–1701 in Renaissance style, using brick and stone.

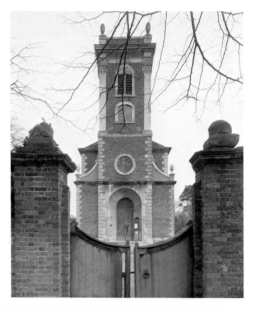

Willen Church, Buckinghamshire, built 1677–80, was designed by Robert Hooke, an experimental physicist who worked closely with Wren as a surveyor for the rebuilding of London after the Fire. One of the few churches in classical style built in the counties during the 17th century, it has a square tower, a parapet with finialled corners, and arched windows.

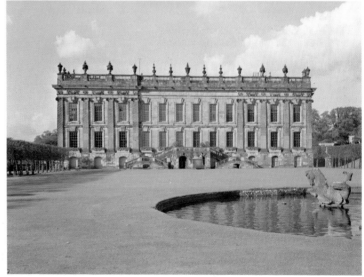

Chatsworth House, Derbyshire, rebuilt 1687–96, was designed by William Talman, a former pupil of Wren. A stately house of the English Late Renaissance, it comprises a block of superbly decorated apartments arranged around a central courtyard. The west façade is noted for its fine carving.

The first English exponents of the style

THE BAROQUE which originated in Rome of the Counter-Reformation underwent strange secular changes in its translation to England a hundred years later.

Its first recognizable exponent in England was Nicholas Hawksmoor (1661–1736). He began his career as "clerk" to Wren. A conscientious, scholarly man of humble origins, he attained no high offices. In 1699, he linked up with Sir John Vanbrugh (1664–1726). In their remarkable partnership Vanbrugh stole the limelight. He was gentleman-adventurer, dramatist and good fellow.

Hawksmoor's earliest essay in the Baroque style was Easton Neston House (1696–1702). The steeple of St George, Bloomsbury, is a striking example of Hawksmoor's learning and inventiveness. His Westminster Abbey towers reveal a romantic sympathy with the Gothic.

The first outcome of the Hawksmoor–Vanbrugh partnership was Castle Howard, an enormous Yorkshire palace, begun in 1701. Blenheim Palace, Kimbolton, Kings Weston, Seaton Delaval and Grimsthorpe followed in quick succession. Their architecture is massive Doric, defiant, uncompromising. The use of cyclopean elements against a rusticated background is invariable.

Thomas Archer (1668–1743) actually travelled to Rome in search of Baroque sources. Borromini seems to have been his paramount inspiration, as Heythrop House (1706) and St John's, Smith Square (1713–29), testify. He gleefully reproduced Borromini's capitals and weird vegetable-like window corbels.

James Gibbs (1682–1754) was likewise trained in Rome. His master was Carlo Fontana, a late Baroque, if not post Baroque, Roman architect. Consequently Gibbs's style was never as bizarre as Archer's. His St Mary-le-Strand (1714–17), with its two main storeys and tabernacle windows, is more Roman Mannerist than Baroque. His St Martin-in-the-Fields (1721–6) is almost a reversion to Wren's academic classicism. Gibbs's *Book of Architecture* (1728) was for many years the provincial builders' manual.

Gibbs had no followers. On the other hand, William Wakefield in Yorkshire, William Townesend of Oxford and Francis Smith of Warwick built numerous houses for the lesser gentry, in a sort of emasculated Hawksmoor–Vanbrugh style, well into the middle of the 18th century. And Nathaniel Ireson and the Bastards of Blandford continued to sprinkle the west country with eccentric Archerian details long after the Baroque style was forgotten in London.

St Mary Woolnoth, 1716–27, was the smallest of the so-called Fifty New Churches built in the City of London under the 1711 Act. It is Nicholas Hawksmoor's masterpiece, adapted to a narrow and awkward site. The style, however, is massive. The fortification motif is exemplified by the blind window (right), framed with heavy blocks and flanked with columns.

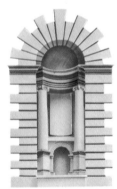

At Easton Neston in Northamptonshire Hawksmoor's task was to provide a centre-piece, in 1702, to conform to a pair of brick wings built in 1682. The rectangular block is distinguished by the rhythm of closely packed pilasters in the Giant Order. Subtle "breaks" relieve the monotony of a highly concentrated surface. The material is a beautiful silvery stone.

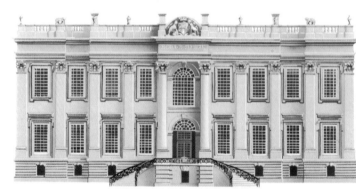

Blenheim Palace in Oxfordshire (right), built between 1705 and 1724 and presented to the first Duke of Marlborough by a grateful nation, is a monument rather than a house. The architect, Sir John Vanbrugh, sacrificed convenience and comfort for symmetry and pomposity. The wings of the palace (below) are spread around a great court, and themselves contain courtyards. The kitchen court on the left (1) is mirrored by the stable court (2) opposite; both are connected to the main wing (3) by colonnades. The projected grand northern entrance façade (4) was never built.

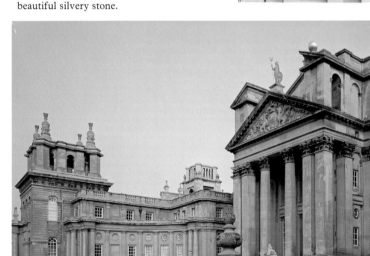

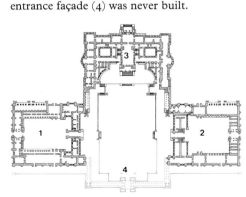

The Radcliffe Camera at Oxford (left)—Dr Radcliffe's "physic library"—was built between 1737 and 1749 to James Gibbs's design. An effect of monumental rotundity is achieved by its plan of two concentric cylinders, the inner of which is domed, and a rusticated base. This was originally an open vestibule, but the openings have now been glazed or filled in to provide a second reading-room.

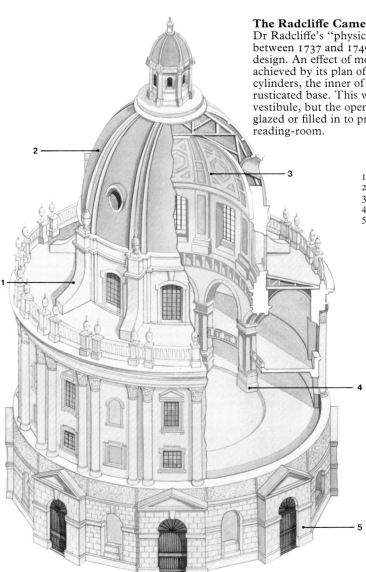

1 *Curved buttresses*
2 *Lead-covered dome*
3 *Interior coffering*
4 *Piers supporting dome*
5 *Rusticated base*

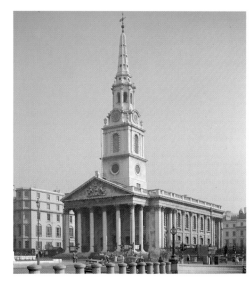

St Martin-in-the-Fields in London (above and below), built between 1721 and 1726, is James Gibbs's best-known and most influential church. It displays his innovatory combination of a classical portico with a Gothic steeple, which tapers from a square base to a concave-sided spire. The interior plasterwork was the work of Italian craftsmen.

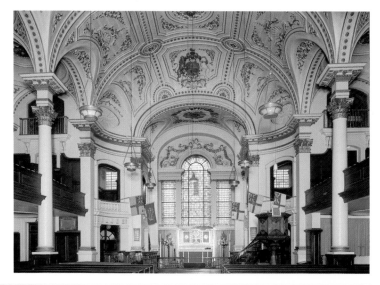

Ragley Hall in Warwickshire was renovated and repaired for the Earl of Hertford by James Gibbs between 1750 and 1755. The work evidently included the decoration of the main hall (below).

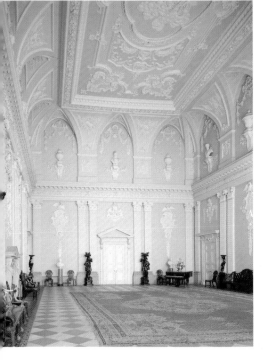

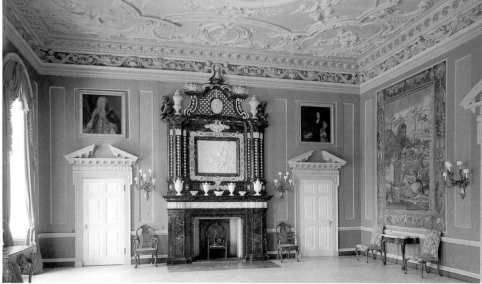

Clandon Park, near Guildford in Surrey, was built between 1717 and 1735 by Giacomo Leoni, a Venetian architect who came to England in 1715. The house is in essence Palladian. But whereas the façades are very severe, the state rooms, including the saloon (above), are decorated with Baroque verve.

BAROQUE
The Palladian revival

THE PALLADIAN VOGUE lasted from approximately 1715 to 1750. Ostensibly a protest by leading men of taste against the licentiousness of the Baroque style, it was in effect a political expostulation by the Whig oligarchy against Jacobite Toryism, which had received a knock-out blow with the death of Queen Anne. Its patrons, and indeed several of its practitioners were rich Whig landowners, notably the Earls of Burlington, Pembroke and Leicester.

Burlington was of course regarded as the high priest of the new cult. Vitruvius, Palladio and Inigo Jones were the three pre-eminent saints in the Burlingtonian calendar. The narrow canons of the revered trinity were set down in numerous treatises, notably Campbell's *Vitruvius Britannicus,* Leoni's *Architecture of Palladio* and Kent's *Designs of Inigo Jones,* all published within a few years of each other. They fairly launched the movement. It was practically restricted to country-houses, if we may include in that category Burlington House, Piccadilly, a large house in its own grounds, begun by Colen Campbell in 1715. On its

completion Lord Burlington, his head crammed with memories of what he had seen on his Italian grand tour, set about turning Chiswick House into a Vicentine villa. With the co-operation of his protégé William Kent, a garden was laid out on the lines of what they believed Pliny's in Tuscany to look like. Henceforth Palladian gardens became an extension, if not a part, of the houses. At Rousham Park, Oxfordshire, Kent introduced literary and painterly allusions. He remodelled the glades, wildernesses, serpentine paths, bedecked with grottoes, obelisks and urns, upon descriptive passages in Thomson's poetry and the pictures of Salvator Rosa and Claude.

Lord Pembroke soon built a Thames-side villa for his friend Mrs Howard at Marble Hill. Prime Minister Walpole followed suit with a far more ambitious project at Houghton, Norfolk (1721). Walpole's neighbour, Thomas Coke, not to be outdone, began Holkham Hall in 1734. This vast house was in truth a complex of villas, namely a central block and four pavilions at the end of colonnades. Through-

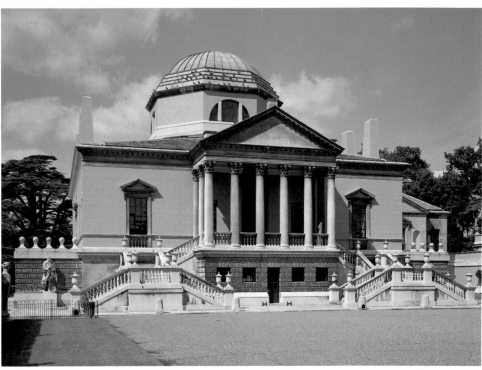

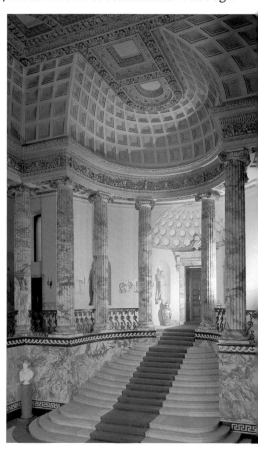

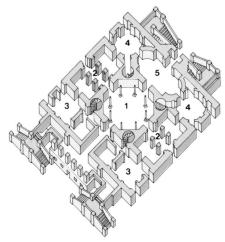

Chiswick House (above), a domed Italianate villa which Lord Burlington built for himself in 1726 with the assistance of William Kent, exemplifies his academic and doctrinaire approach to classical design. He sought to revive the pure classicism of Vitruvian Rome through a study of Palladio's writings and buildings and from his knowledge of Roman remains. Chiswick House, although modelled on the Villa Rotonda by Palladio, is fundamentally different in several ways. Its plan (right) is not symmetrical and only the two side façades are identical. The rooms are varied in shape and in spatial effect as were many of the baths of Ancient Rome. They radiate from the domed octagonal hall (1), and include lobbies (2), offices (3), libraries (4) and an apsidal room (5) opening on to the formal gardens.

Holkham Hall in Norfolk, a huge Palladian country-house begun in 1734 by Lord Burlington and William Kent for Thomas Coke, has a severe and rather forbidding brick exterior in marked contrast to its ornate interiors. The house was planned primarily as a show-case for the owner's collection of Classical antiquities. Its most impressive room is the entrance hall (above), a complex design on two levels connected by a grand flight of steps and an Ionic colonnade. The richly coffered ceiling, frieze and apse were derived appropriately from the Antique.

out the land the Whig aristocrats were raising giant villas, their severe façades pierced with rows of rather small, plain windows, relieved maybe by one central tripartite, or lunette, window. They filled the Royal Works with their placemen—Campbell, Kent, Flitcroft, Ware, Vardy, Roger Morris and Brettingham.

The second generation of Palladians included John Wood (1704–54), who, inspired by Burlington's development of his Mayfair property into streets of contiguous houses, made Bath a city of crescents, squares, a circus, straight and serpentine streets, set in a wooded valley. The twenty-two-year-old E. L. Pearce carried the Palladian theme across the Irish Sea. His Castletown (1722) inaugurated a spate of country-house building. In England Sir Robert Taylor (1714–88) with Asgill House and Heveningham Hall, James Paine (1716–89) with Nostell Priory and Wardour Castle, and John Carr (1723–1807) with Tabley House, Basildon Park and Buxton Crescent (as late as 1780) continued to tread the well-worn Palladian path.

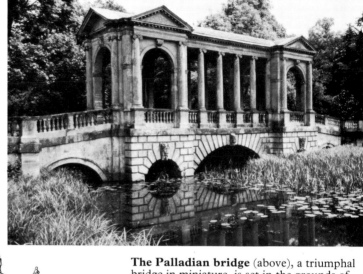

Stourhead in Wiltshire (right), begun by Henry Hoare, the banker, in the 1720s from the designs of Colen Campbell, was directly influenced by Palladio's Villa Emo at Fanzolo and became one of the models of English classicism. It has a perfectly proportioned temple-fronted façade. Away from the house is one of the most carefully planned and idyllic landscape gardens of the period.

The Palladian bridge (above), a triumphal bridge in miniature, is set in the grounds of Stowe House, Buckinghamshire, a vast and imposing Palladian country residence. The fine grounds were landscaped by Bridgeman, Kent and Brown successively. An informal garden was considered the ideal complement to the classical house and was usually embellished with small temples, arches and bridges of classical design. These charming garden structures were used to punctuate serene and harmonious vistas, like those in the paintings of Claude Lorraine, and were sometimes one-sided like stage scenery.

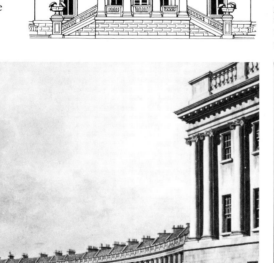

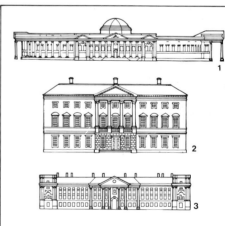

The Royal Crescent is part of the brilliant and ambitious town-planning scheme which transformed Bath into the most elegant resort of the 18th century. Much of the work was carried out by John Wood and his son, who, following the ideals of Palladio and the Ancient Romans, designed the fronts of their terraced houses to give the impression of one palatial façade. Building began in 1728 with Queen Square, designed by Wood the Elder. He was also responsible for the famous Circus of 1754–70, whose façades were suggested by the Colosseum. Wood the Younger gave the 30 houses of the Royal Crescent, begun in 1767, a continuous frontage of giant Ionic columns.

DUBLIN IN THE 18TH CENTURY
The city of Dublin underwent an amazing expansion during the 18th century, giving it the Palladian and Georgian character still much in evidence. Palladianism is best represented by the dignified public buildings in the eastern part of the city. Its leading exponent was Sir Edward Lovett Pearce, who began the old Parliament House (1) in 1728. It originally occupied three sides of a square with a grand Ionic colonnade. A classical façade was added to adjacent Trinity College (3) in 1759. Leinster House (2), built by Cassels in 1745, is based on English models.

The English Neo-Classicists

NEO-CLASSICISM in England was brought about by a reaction from the inflexible rules of the Palladians and by architectural students travelling abroad farther than Italy. The two dominant architects of the new movement were William Chambers (1723–96) and Robert Adam (1728–92). Adam's strong personality and teeming visions gave his name to a style which prevailed in the British Isles from 1760 until the end of the century.

Chambers's earliest buildings, like the exquisite little Casino at Marino outside Dublin, are still Palladian in plan but already Gallic in several details. As to interiors, he introduced Louis XV Rococo ceilings and fireplaces. His Somerset House (1776–80) is a monumental combination of separate entities, overlaid with French elements in doorways, windows and attic storeys.

Robert Adam was a creative genius of immense confidence. He derived inspiration from Etruscan, Pompeian, Raphaelesque, even Vanbrughian, Burlingtonian and Greek sources. The outcome of all this eclecticism was a distinctive style of his own which was essentially decorative and feminine.

The next generation of Neo-Classical architects was numerous. Robert Mylne (1734–1811) built bridges and town and country houses. John Yenn (1750–1821) was an undeviating follower of Chambers. Thomas Hardwick (1752–1829) built London churches and chapels. George Dance (1741–1825) was a designer of Piranesian power. The work of Henry Holland (1745–1806), a protégé of the Prince Regent, was pre-eminently Louis Seize. James Wyatt (1746–1813), extremely versatile and prolific, became the Adam brothers' serious rival. James Stuart (1713–88), a late starter, was the first British architect to design in the Greek style from first-hand researches. John Soane (1753–1837), an eccentric and edgy genius, was the youngest of the Neo-Classical group.

In the last decades of the 18th century a counter-movement was asserting itself. The Picturesque School, of which John Nash (1752–1835) was the leading exponent, resurrected the Gothic, introduced some exotic styles like the Moorish and sought variety in asymmetrical dispositions.

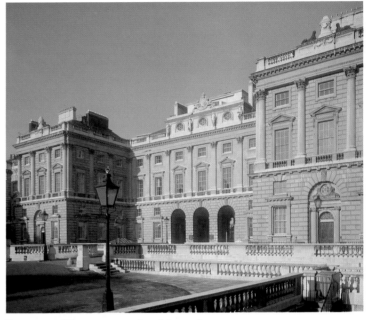

Somerset House, a grand and imposing government building in the Strand, was begun by Sir William Chambers in 1776. It consists of four main blocks surrounding a vast open court.

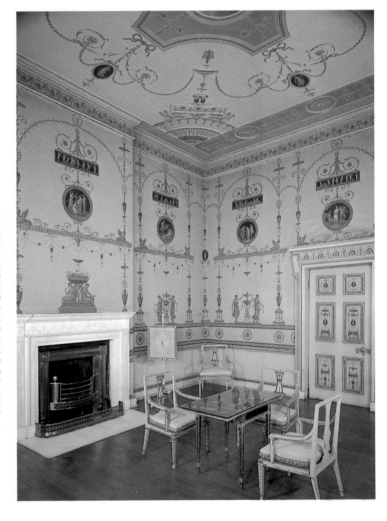

Osterley Park in Middlesex is a Tudor mansion reclothed in Neo-Classical dress by Robert Adam. Between 1761 and 1780 he joined two projecting wings with a portico and transformed the interiors. His light and graceful decorative style is clearly seen in the Etruscan Room (right), where the walls and ceiling are enhanced with shallow stucco work and painted motifs and medallions inspired by early Greek vases.

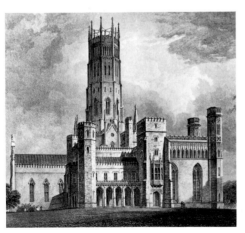

Fonthill Abbey, Wiltshire, by James Wyatt, was a country-house in the guise of a medieval religious establishment. This curious and sensational monument of the Gothic taste was begun in 1796. Its tower collapsed in 1825.

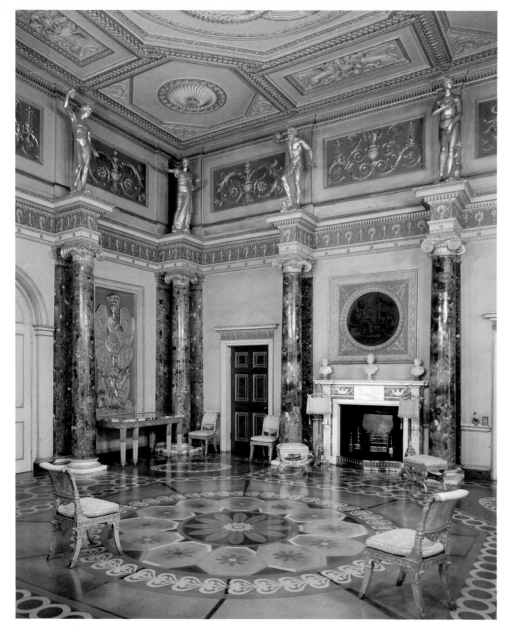

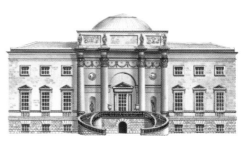

Kedleston Hall, Derbyshire, is the dignified creation of several architects. In 1761, work was taken over by James Paine, who planned the central block with a domed saloon and a great basilican entrance hall. Its most important architect was Adam, who took over the work in 1765, designing the south façade (above). The front of the saloon has free-standing columns boldly projecting from the main block, emphasized by curved stairs leading down to the garden. He also completed the interior decoration, giving the hall (below) a deeply coved ceiling with three oval skylights and cladding its columns and floor with Derbyshire marble.

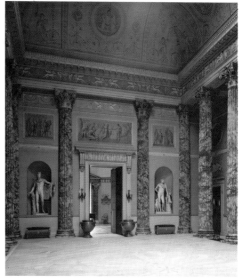

Syon House at Isleworth was a Tudor building almost square in plan. Adam completely remodelled its interiors in 1762–9. In the Roman ante-room (above), marble, gold and colour reign supreme.

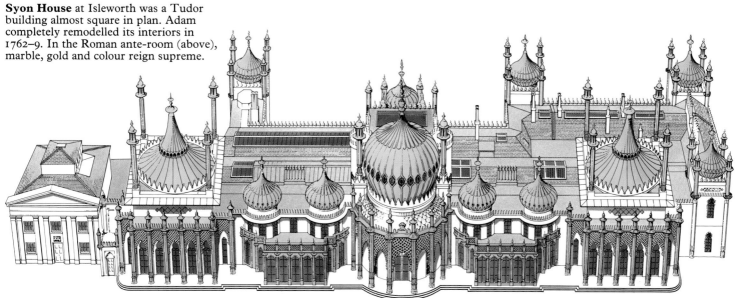

The Royal Pavilion at Brighton, extensively rebuilt for the Prince Regent by Nash, with an extravagant mixture of Hindu, Chinese and Gothic elements, is one of the most delightful examples of the Picturesque style. The house had been partially enlarged and redesigned in the Palladian manner when Nash took over in 1815. He preserved the classical symmetry of the main façade, but created an exotic skyline of domes, minarets and pinnacles. Much of the construction is of cast-iron, used here for the first time in a private domestic building. Banqueting and music rooms with pagoda roofs complete the façade at either end.

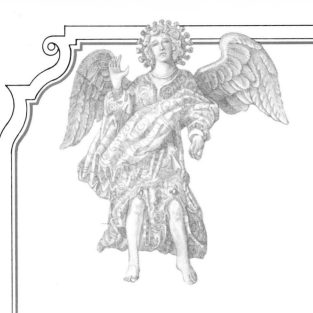

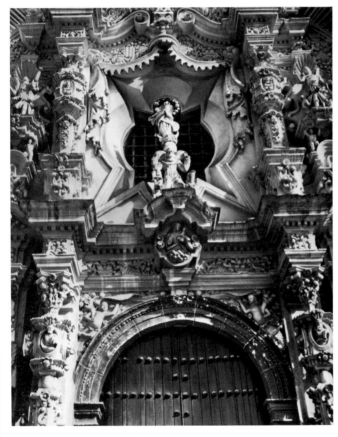

A fantastic ensemble of moulded white stucco and red unglazed bricks, the Sanctuary at Ocotlán is an interesting synthesis of 18th-century Spanish style and native craftsmanship. Designed by a Franciscan parish priest, its exuberant façade was carved by Francisco Miguel, an Indian sculptor from Tlaxcala.

Colonial architecture has its special problems. When one nation conquers another, or when a body of men move from one country to another and settle there, they are faced, when they come to build their towns, with a different climate, new kinds of building materials, probably the need for defence and—most complex of all—the problem of using local craftsmen, trained in a quite different artistic tradition.

These problems have been tackled in different ways by different colonizing groups. When the Greeks planted colonies in Asia Minor, Sicily and southern Italy, they brought with them an art so superior to anything they found that they made hardly any changes in their methods. They did, however, make two innovations which were to remain regular features of colonial architecture: they laid out their towns on a grid system, which they were able to do because they were building on new and clear sites; and they made their temples larger and more elaborately decorated than those in Greece proper, no doubt "to impress the natives".

Sometimes, if the civilization of the conquered country was very advanced, the process could be reversed, and so, for instance, when the Turks captured Constantinople in 1453, they took Justinian's church of Hagia Sophia as the model for their own mosques.

The first great colonial enterprises of modern times were those undertaken in South America by the Spaniards and the Portuguese. From the military, political and religious points of view the two nations faced similar problems, but when they came to build cities there were important differences. In Brazil, the Portuguese found a country with no stone architecture and only very primitive traditions in the other arts. They were therefore able to impose their own style, and the architecture of Rio de Janeiro or Ouro Preto is a

Colonial Styles

direct development from that of the home country.

The Spaniards were faced with a quite different situation. In Mexico and Peru they found civilizations of an extraordinarily high order, which had found brilliant expression in the field of the arts, and, since they were compelled to rely on local craftsmen, the buildings which they erected were immediately impressed with a local flavour. In Peru, the Incas had produced some of the finest masonry ever seen, and in Mexico sculptors trained in the workshops of the Aztecs had a skill greater even than that of Spanish craftsmen, and they made possible the creation of a fantastic style of decorative sculpture which incorporated many Aztec features.

In both the Spanish and the Portuguese colonies the presence of almost unlimited supplies of gold and silver enabled architects to add to the richness of the sculpture that of precious materials, and the effect of the churches erected in these areas depends to a great extent on the magnificence of their gold altars and panels. In making this display of richness the Spaniards must have been partly impelled by the desire to show that the Catholic Church was as rich as the gods of the Aztec or Inca religions.

The Dutch and French colonists were not such great builders as the Spaniards or the Portuguese— partly because they were not so intent on converting the natives and only needed simple churches for their own use; but they took with them their own styles and applied them with a certain rustic charm.

The last great colonial builders were the British. In countries such as India, which they conquered by force, the British simply exported their own style of buildings, and views of Calcutta or Madras in the early 19th century show a series of classical buildings, which remind one of the great public buildings of Bath, Edinburgh or Dublin.

The English settlers in North America produced a style of colonial architecture which has no parallel elsewhere. This is not surprising because the conditions in which it was created were different from all other cases. The first English colonists were not, like Cortés and Pizarro, brilliant and ruthless adventurers in search of immense wealth, and they were not, like the British in India, the representatives of a government supported by a regular army. They were simple, hard-working people who had either left their country to seek a place where they could worship as they wished, or who had emigrated with the knowledge that their new life would be hard and the rewards probably not enormous. Many of them were themselves craftsmen, who brought with them their own traditions of building. There was no question of either trying to impress the natives or of fusing their own culture with a local tradition.

The first buildings of these settlers were very simple frame houses, but by the first half of the 18th century American architects had evolved a style which, while wholly English in derivation, had an individual flavour. This was partly due to the fact that stone was rare and lime not available, so that brick building was impossible, with the result that almost all buildings, whether houses, churches or public offices, were of wood. Many houses were faced with wooden shingles, and, when classical porticoes came into fashion, the columns, being of wood, could be much slimmer than those in stone.

The simplicity of the architecture was not, however, entirely imposed by the materials; it also reflected the severe puritanical taste of many, at least, of the settlers. The result was the well-planned and practical kind of building of which many are still to be seen in the towns of the eastern states, and of which the cumulative effect is still preserved in Williamsburg, Virginia.

Iberian themes in the New World

ROMAN BAROQUE architecture shocked the "classical" taste of France and England for generations and the architecture of the Iberian Peninsula even more so. The ultimate outrage, however, was the architecture of the Spanish and Portuguese colonies in Central and South America which was considered to be the last word in barbarous irregularity. But now we recognize that it has a fiery, imaginative quality, which may not be in accordance with European standards, but which has a validity of its own.

The architecture of the Portuguese colony of Brazil is slightly more orthodox than that of the Spanish colonies, but only an architect with Indian blood could have created the churches of the gold-mining district of Minas Gerais, such as those at Ouro Preto.

In Mexico, the influence of native traditions was much stronger. Basically the style is that of southern Spain, particularly of Andalucia, from which the colonizing expeditions set out. The *estípite*, or broken pilaster, a decorative theme so skilfully used in the sacristy of the Cartuja at Granada in Spain, is the theme of much Mexican church decoration, both external and internal. But the luxuriance of the all-over high-relief carving shows clearly the influence of local traditions, most obviously of Aztec sculpture; and the overpowering use of gold is something which is not to be found even in the richest Spanish churches.

From the point of view of planning, the churches are conventional, usually based on the normal late Gothic scheme consisting of a long nave with two or four aisles. Hardly any architects in the Spanish or Portuguese colonies took cognizance of the new forms invented by the masters of the Italian Baroque. Their treatment of individual features owes much to European models, but they took liberties with the architectural members which they borrowed.

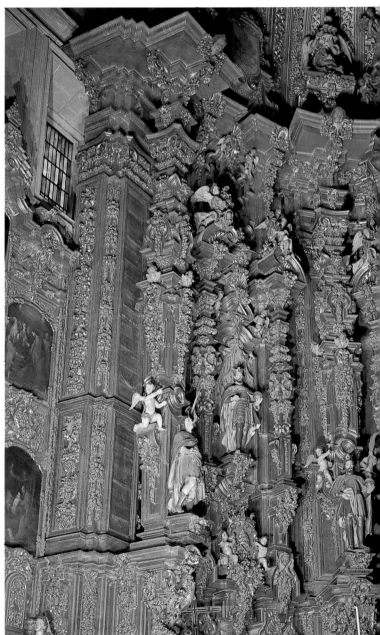

The Church of São Francisco at Ouro Preto (left), the centre of the gold-mining district of Minas Gerais, was built by Antonio Francisco Lisboa between 1766 and 1794. The façade of the church is unusual in having round towers, but its great feature is the door (below), which shows the artist's gifts as a decorative sculptor. Lisboa was the one really original architect of the period in South America. He was a mulatto and is always known by his nickname of Aleijadinho, or Little Cripple. He was born in Ouro Preto in 1738 and lived until 1814; most of his work was done when both the Baroque and the Rococo were outmoded in Europe.

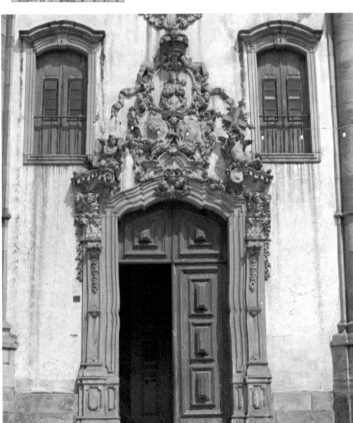

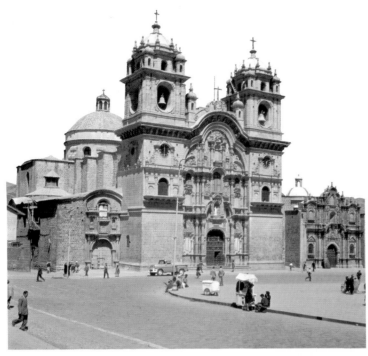

The Compañía, or Jesuit church at Cuzco, in Peru, is remarkable for its façade. The towers are of a design unknown in Europe, with four little turrets flanking the cupolas which top them. The central panel is also unusual, having very steep arches, interrupted by windows and ending in a triple cusped arch. Above this swings a heavy entablature, which breaks up over the central feature. The church was begun in 1651, but the façade and towers are almost certainly later.

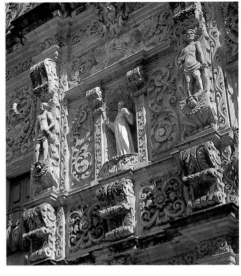

São Francisco (above) is the richest church in Bahía (or Salvador) on the coast of Brazil. The whole interior is covered with gilt wood and plaster decoration and the façade is fretted with sculpture. The figures on the latter are very crude, but the decoration of the interior is of finer quality.

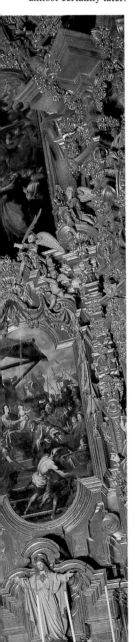

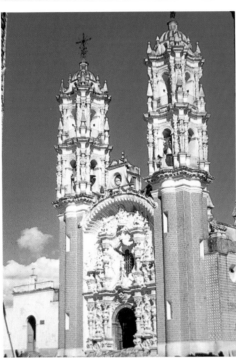

The Church of Ocotlán is unique among Mexican churches for its tall, elegant and richly decorated towers and for the material from which it is built. The lower parts of the towers are constructed of bright-red unglazed bricks, cut in unusual shapes and separated by white mortar, creating the impression of red fish-scales.

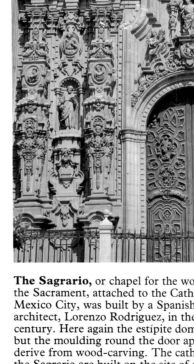

The Cathedral of Mexico City is the largest and most impressive church in the country, and the chapel dedicated to the Three Kings (left) is its richest feature. The chapel was built in the years 1718–37 by Jerónimo Balbas, an architect, who probably came from southern Spain. It is a riot of gilded wooden estípites and statues, centred on a painting of the Adoration of the Kings.

The Sagrario, or chapel for the worship of the Sacrament, attached to the Cathedral of Mexico City, was built by a Spanish architect, Lorenzo Rodriguez, in the 18th century. Here again the estípite dominates, but the moulding round the door appears to derive from wood-carving. The cathedral and the Sagrario are built on the site of one of the largest Aztec temples.

Colonial variations

THE THREE BUILDINGS here reproduced represent three distinct types of colonial building: an administrative office, a large private house on a country estate and a small farmhouse; the styles employed by the three architects are appropriate to their different characters. The Town Hall at Calcutta is grand, classical and slightly pompous; the South African farmhouse is rustic, simple and charming; Monticello, the private house in Virginia, is impressive and very carefully planned for convenience. None of the three would rank among the greatest buildings of the world, but all fulfil their functions admirably.

The Indian Town Hall is simply an up-to-date English building designed no doubt in London and transplanted without any concession to the problems of the hot climate in which it was to be built, not even with the addition of verandahs, which were accepted as essential in private buildings.

The Dutch house is in a style which in Holland itself would have been regarded as quite out-of-date at the time it was built, and is an example of the time-lag which is a common feature in colonial architecture.

Monticello is perhaps unique among colonial buildings in that it was designed and built by a great man, with a highly original mind, for his own use. Thomas Jefferson wanted a combination of French ideas of comfort with English simplicity, and he was a sufficiently skilful amateur architect to produce the result himself. Monticello makes the other two buildings look conventional and commonplace.

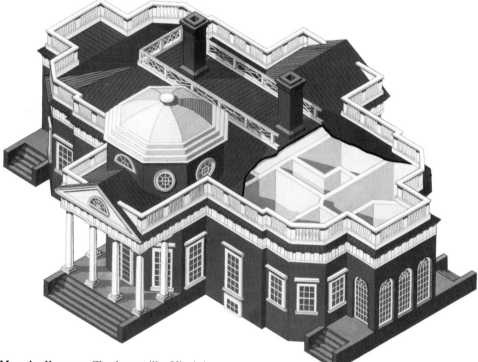

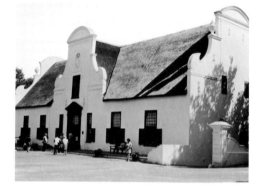

Groot Constantia near Cape Town, a small house at the centre of what is now a wine-growing estate, is typical of the few remaining Dutch houses of the 17th and 18th centuries in the colony. When the Dutch first came to build in South Africa they were faced with fewer problems than most colonists. The climate and the building materials available were not very different from those of their native country; there was no native tradition to fuse with their own, and like the English colonists in North America they were putting up buildings purely for their own use.

Monticello, near Charlottesville, Virginia, was designed by Thomas Jefferson as his own country-house. It was originally planned in 1772 as a small house in the English Palladian style, then current in the eastern states of America, but Jefferson's long stay in France led him to remodel it later—between 1796 and 1808—on the pattern of an 18th-century Parisian hôtel, with projecting bays containing rooms of unusual shapes. The internal arrangement is full of ingenious devices, such as a bed in the wall between bedroom and sitting-room, so that the occupant can get out of it into either room.

The Town Hall at Calcutta, built by John Garstin between 1807 and 1813, represents the phase of English architecture when Neo-Classical taste was just beginning to impose itself. The arcade and the windows are still Palladian, but the portico is in the severe Roman Doric Order. Twenty years later—as, for instance, in the Mint in the same city—full Greek Doric was introduced in accordance with current English taste.

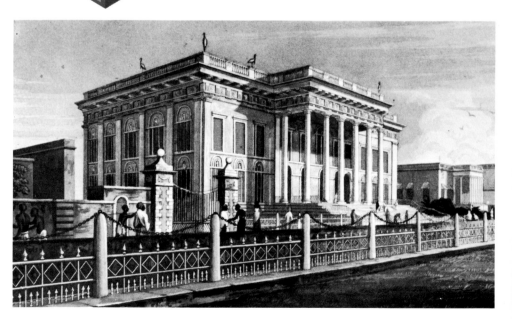

THE
MODERN
AGE

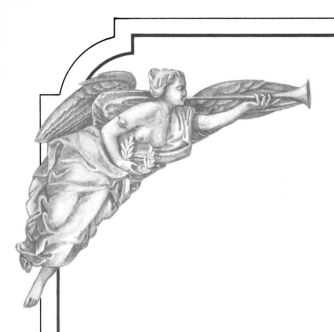

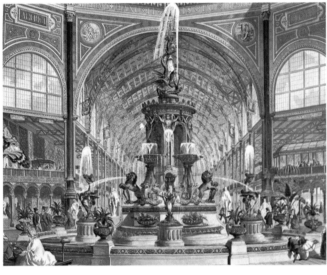

Much of the architecture of the 19th century revived the styles of the past, but some buildings used new constructional methods and materials, such as the Crystal Palace, Hyde Park. Its content, however, was at variance with the spirit of its architecture.

Around the beginning of the 19th century, architecture in the Western World underwent an abrupt change in its nature as well as in its style. There were three main interrelated causes: the introduction of new materials and techniques; the demand for new types of building to meet new social needs; and changes in the cultural climate and the sources of patronage, from both of which arose a new succession of styles and fashions.

The first two of these causes are closely associated with the Industrial Revolution, which had begun in Britain in the last quarter of the 18th century and spread during the 19th to Europe and America. It demanded new types of building for transport and industry and, at the same time, created the techniques that made these possible. The most progressive buildings of the time were therefore the work of engineers rather than architects, using iron, the principal new material, boldly and adventurously. It was engineers who created the impressive array of simple, dignified and refreshingly functional buildings, the viaducts, dockyards, textile mills and railway stations that still dominate British industrial areas and remote valleys where water-power was freely available—areas not otherwise endowed with much distinguished architecture. Some of these buildings possess a nobility of scale and presence that makes them comparable with the cathedrals, castles and great country-houses of the centuries before. Many buildings, nevertheless, were made to appear less unorthodox than they really were by façades and embellishments applied by architects in fashionable current styles: classical frontispieces to give railway terminals monumental significance; Georgian pediments designed to lend grace to an otherwise featureless mill building.

In other types of building the new techniques came into use only gradually, as they made, for example, the large covered spaces that the new

The Nineteenth Century

functions required easier to provide. Some of these new types such as hospitals, stores and offices, derived from social and commercial developments. Others, including town halls and big hotels, were the result of increasing urbanization, in which Britain led Europe with its rapid movement of population into the towns. They offered architects a challenge which was accepted with confidence, although with varying aesthetic success. Now, for the first time, buildings that dominated the expanding towns and cities were, in Britain and then all over Europe, the new civic and commercial buildings, rather than the churches and fortresses that had previously been the only structures of outstanding size.

Equally significant were the changes in patronage. Until the early 19th century, fashions had been set and trends in architecture had been influenced by the aristocratic classes and the buildings they commissioned. The middle classes that had increased in power and numbers as a result of the growth of commerce had neither the same scholarly background nor tradition of conformity. When they built in order to celebrate either their own wealth and substance or the civic dignity of the growing industrial cities, correctness of taste was seldom their objective. When taste did aim at correctness, the scholarship on which it was based had changed too, the world being opened up by new communications and the growth of commerce, as well as by a new interest in archaeology. This interest had already shown itself among architects late in the 18th century. In the 19th an increasingly wide-ranging antiquarianism developed into a fashion for basing whole buildings on Ancient models and especially for reviving the Greek and Gothic styles.

Gothic, which was favoured in Britain more than anywhere else, was thought particularly appropriate for churches, although later it was used, in Britain and throughout Europe, for buildings of many kinds, including hospitals, law-courts and hotels. In Britain, the Gothic Revival went through a number of phases: romantic, when architects were chiefly concerned with recapturing the spirit of the Middle Ages; antiquarian, when correctness of form and detail was the aim; and eclectic, when architects felt free to improvise, using material gleaned, with the help of the sketch-book, over the widest possible field.

Throughout Europe, too, nearly every past style was re-examined and reused, but as the century wore on styles of the past were no longer imitated exactly, but were looked on as a quarry from which architects could extract whatever elements struck their fancy. A succession of rival styles came, vied with each other and went: Neo-Roman and Venetian Gothic, Flemish, Byzantine, Neo-Baroque and many others, some conforming conscientiously to historical precedent, but many more mingling reminiscences of different periods and countries. Richness of form and picturesqueness of effect were the principal aim.

In the hands of architects of understanding and sensibility some notable buildings were produced, and much ingenuity was shown in adapting the styles of the past to the new and bulkier types of building now demanded. This was the age of some of the major architectural monuments—and particularly of major changes in the skyline—of nearly every town and city. What would London be without the Palace of Westminster and St Pancras Station, Paris without the Sacré-Coeur, Liverpool without St George's Hall and Berlin without the Gedächtnis Church? The total effect of all this on European towns and cities was, however, to replace the erstwhile unity of the street by a chaotic miscellany of buildings, each asserting its own individuality.

Britain and the new structural advances

THE INDUSTRIAL REVOLUTION is inseparable from the growth of communications which, indeed, made the revolution possible; and so most of the great buildings and feats of construction of this heroic age are connected with transport. First came canal-building, initiated on an industrial scale in the 18th century, but reaching a climax in the 19th century with Thomas Telford's waterways, bridges and aqueducts and the handsome warehouses that served them.

Then came road-building, of which the heroes were McAdam and Telford, whose Menai Suspension Bridge of 1826 was the first great example of its kind (although the first iron bridge, at Coalbrookdale, had been constructed as long before as 1779). Next was railway-building, of which the heroes were the Stephensons and the younger Brunel. Railways endowed Britain not only with such major works of engineering as bridges, tunnels and viaducts, but with the great terminal stations, the requirements of which produced the iron and glass arched roofs that are among the most spectacular achievements of 19th-century architecture. Station exteriors and other railway structures were sometimes as austerely functional as King's Cross, London,

by Lewis Cubitt (1857). At other times they were put into monumental dress; witness Brunel's "Tudor" train-shed at Temple Meads, Bristol, and Stephenson's "Egyptian-style" Britannia Bridge over the Menai Straits.

After the railway age came the age of ocean trade, on which the growth of Britain's manufacturing industry equally depended and which necessitated enlarged harbour basins (in London, Liverpool and elsewhere) surrounded by tall warehouses that were made more capacious by the use of iron columns and beams. Iron was used similarly in the great textile mills, whose masonry walls concealed the earliest experiments in iron-frame construction (the very first, a flax-mill at Shrewsbury, was built by Charles Bage in 1796), which led eventually to the steel-framed sky-scrapers of the United States.

The use of iron to cover vast spaces was also carried forward by Joseph Paxton, experimentally in his plant-houses at Chatsworth and then triumphantly at the Crystal Palace, built in 1851, which held additional significance for the future because of its comprehensive use of standardized and prefabricated parts.

The Clifton Suspension Bridge spans 702 ft across the Avon Gorge near Bristol. It was designed in 1836 by the great railway engineer I. K. Brunel and completed in 1864, five years after his death, as a memorial to him. Its chains were taken from Brunel's Hungerford footbridge in London which had been demolished.

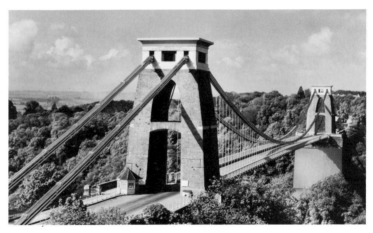

The Central Railway Station (below) at Newcastle upon Tyne is the first of the great surviving stations. It was built between 1846 and 1850 by John Dobson, who pioneered the form of the iron and glass arched roof leaping over railway tracks and platforms. This type of roof was soon used for similar structures. Dobson also gave the station its handsome Neo-Classical front.

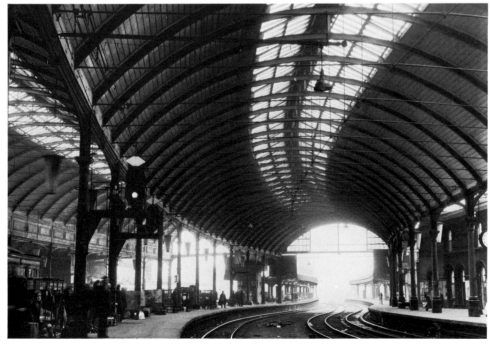

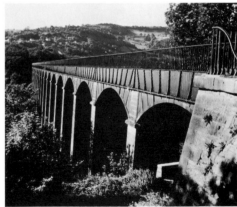

The Pont Cysyllte Aqueduct, carrying the Ellesmere Canal across the River Dee in Wales, is an engineering work of grandeur and historical importance. The 1,000-ft-long aqueduct, begun in 1795 by Thomas Telford, demonstrated the enormous architectural potential of cast-iron. Its 19 masonry piers, each 120 ft high, support a cast-iron canal trough with tow path and railings also of iron. It was completed in 1805.

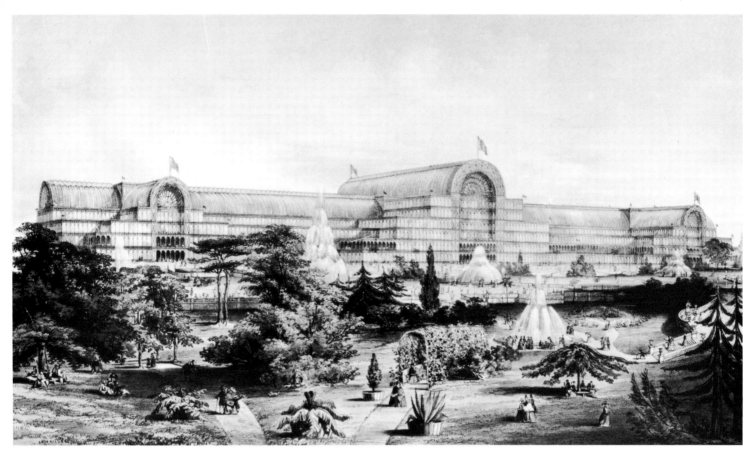

The Crystal Palace was designed by Joseph Paxton for the Great Exhibition of 1851, held in Hyde Park, London. It was afterwards re-erected on Sydenham Hill, where it stood until accidentally destroyed by fire in 1936.

Its iron frame was prefabricated in sections and its glass panels, set into wooden sash-bars, were of standard 4-ft lengths. In 1851, it was the largest building ever constructed, with an area of 770,000 sq ft.

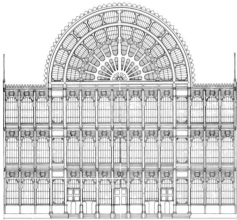

This detail of the entrance shows the standard units of metal and glass which made up the Crystal Palace.

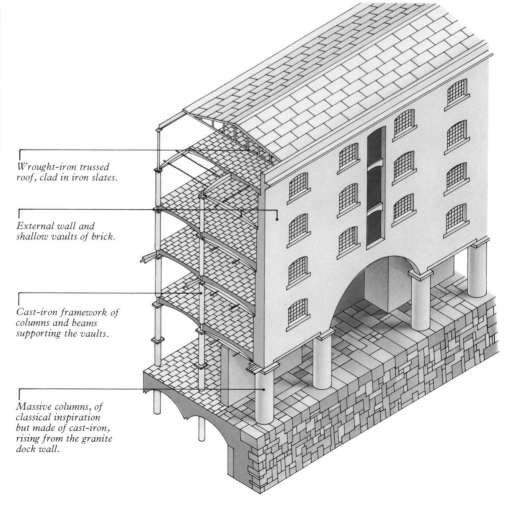

Wrought-iron trussed roof, clad in iron slates.

External wall and shallow vaults of brick.

Cast-iron framework of columns and beams supporting the vaults.

Massive columns, of classical inspiration but made of cast-iron, rising from the granite dock wall.

The Albert Dock is the culmination of a series of docks built at Liverpool from the end of the 18th century onwards. Its architect, Jesse Hartley, who was the city's dock surveyor from 1824 to 1860, endowed his docks and warehouses with a monumental simplicity and directness, which place them among Liverpool's finest buildings. The Albert Dock, which was opened in 1845 by the Prince Regent, may have been influenced by Philip Hardwick's earlier St Katherine's Dock in London. It is surrounded on all four sides by five-storeyed warehouses over a colonnade of cast-iron Doric columns rising from the dock wall. The warehouses are built mainly of red brick with iron supports.

The Paris Exhibition of 1889

GREAT EXHIBITIONS, since their birth in London's Hyde Park in 1851, have served repeatedly as testing grounds for new architectural ideas. Paxton's Crystal Palace soon became the model for other experiments in iron and glass. New York built its own Crystal Palace two years later, in 1853. Paris held exhibitions, at least partly housed in this still novel type of building, in 1855, 1867, 1878, 1889 and 1900, as did Vienna in 1873 and Philadelphia in 1876. The most notable of all was that held in Paris in 1889, on the centenary of the French Revolution, sited, like several of its predecessors, on the Champ de Mars.

Although many of its buildings were ornately conventional, the Paris Exhibition of 1889 included two great structures, which dominated the whole complex. One of these was the Machine Hall, which carried a stage further the British experiments with large-span glass roofs first made in plant-houses and railway stations. The other was a steel tower, the tallest structure in the world at that time, designed by Alexandre-Gustave Eiffel, whose glass-roofed station, built at Budapest in 1877, had already rivalled some of those constructed in Britain.

The Paris Machine Hall, by the engineer Contamin and the architect Ferdinand Dutert, spanned about 380 feet. Although it embodied structural experience accumulated during half a century, it was original in several ways. The supporting frame was steel instead of iron, so that it represented another step on the road towards the steel-framed buildings of the 20th century. The side walls of glass did not span between the arched girders, but stood outside them, being thus a precedent for 20th-century curtain walling.

Eiffel's tower, one thousand feet tall, unlike the Machine Hall, still stands. Its structure was based on Eiffel's experiences with earlier exhibition buildings and with such bridges as that over the Douro in Portugal, built in 1875, and the Garabit viaduct of 1884. The tower rests on four pylons anchored to separate foundations, and only falls short of fully expressing the nature of steel construction because of the curved arches that link the pylons. These were added for decorative reasons and have no structural function.

The Machine Hall, Paris (right), now demolished, was a masterpiece of engineering, created out of the need for a vast covered space to display industrial machinery. The building, designed by Contamin and Dutert, owed nothing to historical styles, and was constructed almost entirely from the new materials, steel and glass.

The Paris Exhibition of 1900 (below) was one of a remarkable series. The galleried machine hall is shown in a contemporary photograph with its industrial exhibits.

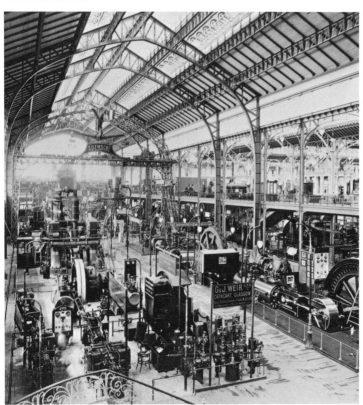

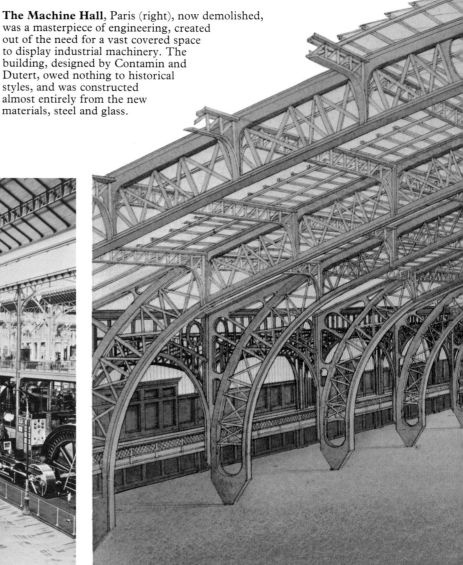

1 *Eiffel Tower*
2 *Hall of Fine Arts*
3 *Hall of Liberal Arts*
4 *Halls of various industries and nations*
5 *Grand vestibule of Machine Hall*
6 *Machine Hall*

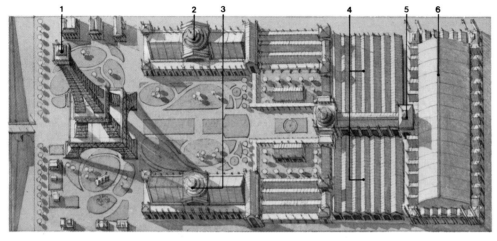

The Eiffel Tower, symbol of modern Paris, was commissioned in 1887 to commemorate the Exhibition of 1889. This important steel structure exceeded in height all the skyscrapers of its day.

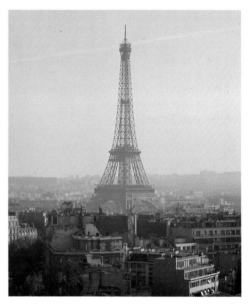

The Paris Exhibition of 1889, held in commemoration of the centenary of the French Revolution, surpassed all earlier exhibitions in novelty and scale. Built on the Champ de Mars, an established exhibition site near the heart of the city, the main part of the exhibition, which consisted of the Machine Hall and the immediately adjacent halls representing various industries and nations, occupied an area of 50 acres.

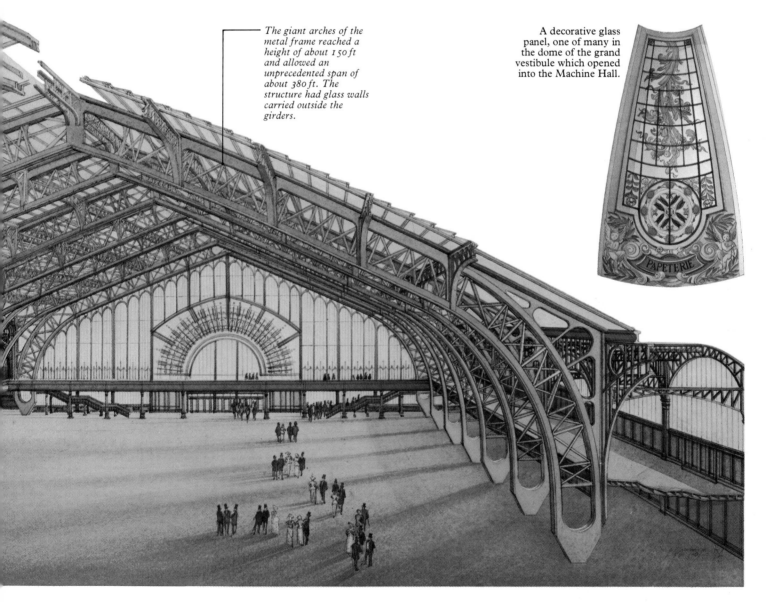

The giant arches of the metal frame reached a height of about 150 ft and allowed an unprecedented span of about 380 ft. The structure had glass walls carried outside the girders.

A decorative glass panel, one of many in the dome of the grand vestibule which opened into the Machine Hall.

Spread of the new techniques

THE NEW TECHNIQUES, especially those involving the use of iron, that had originated in Britain as a by-product of the Industrial Revolution, spread later in the 19th century to the other industrialized countries. In Britain, these techniques had at first been used to do things impossible without them—to cover great spaces or to support heavy loads such as goods in warehouses or machinery in textile mills—and were therefore specially identified with transport and engineering. Well before the end of the century, however, in Britain and in Europe, they were being adapted to nearly every kind of building. They showed themselves particularly well suited to solving the problems posed by the new types of building for which recent social developments and the movement of populations into towns and cities had created a demand.

Wholesale and retail trade, for example, was being concentrated into larger buildings, and the new forms of construction were used to provide market halls with the advantage of unobstructed floor space and department stores with the capacity to accommodate large crowds. Civic buildings, too, took advantage of the freedom of planning and easier manipulation of space that the new forms of structure encouraged. With a few bold exceptions, however, these new structural forms were generally regarded as a mere technical convenience and were clothed in some style that referred back to the pre-industrial age.

As land values increased, office buildings made use of the new framed structures to multiply the number of storeys, but these buildings, too, were normally clothed in masonry and were indistinguishable from the earlier types of stone-built structure. Style and technique had still to be reintegrated. Only in America did office buildings begin to evolve the expressive style that was soon to make American city architecture famous.

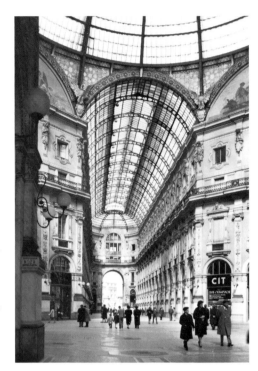

The Galleria Vittorio Emanuele, Milan, is a vast arcade sheltering shops and cafés. Designed in 1861 by Giuseppe Mengoni, it was built by an English firm between 1865 and 1877. The largest and loftiest of its kind, it is cruciform in plan with a large domed octagon at the intersection. Although shopping arcades had been popular in Britain for half a century, iron and glass construction now made it possible to cover what was, in effect, a street.

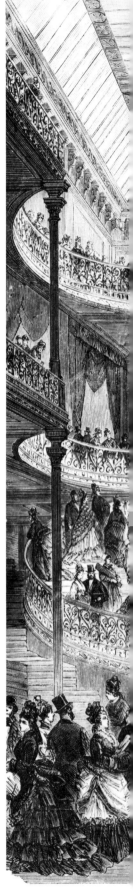

The Library of Sainte Geneviève in Paris (right and below), designed in 1843 and built between 1845 and 1850 by Henri Labrouste, is a handsome, classical building with lofty interior spaces created by the very early use of iron. Although the outer walls (1) are conventional masonry, the double vaulted roofs (2), and the columns (3) which support them independently of the walls, are all of wrought- or cast-iron. The long, rectangular building contained both an upper and lower reading-room, and served as the model for the Boston Public Library, completed in 1893 by McKim, Mead and White.

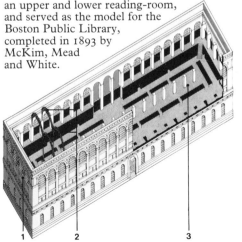
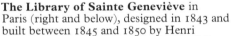

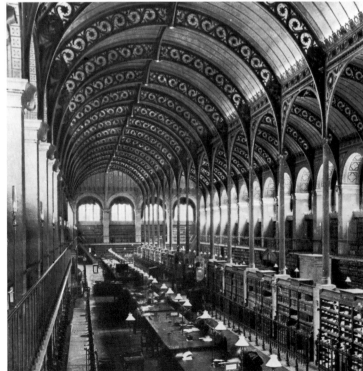

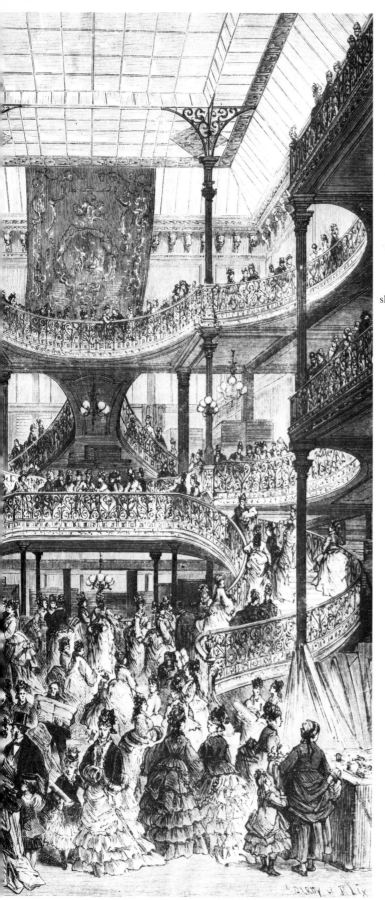

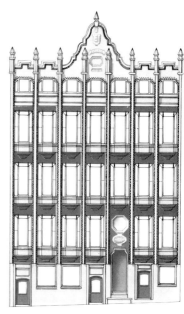

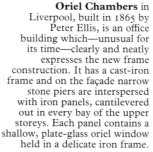

Oriel Chambers in Liverpool, built in 1865 by Peter Ellis, is an office building which—unusual for its time—clearly and neatly expresses the new frame construction. It has a cast-iron frame and on the façade narrow stone piers are interspersed with iron panels, cantilevered out in every bay of the upper storeys. Each panel contains a shallow, plate-glass oriel window held in a delicate iron frame.

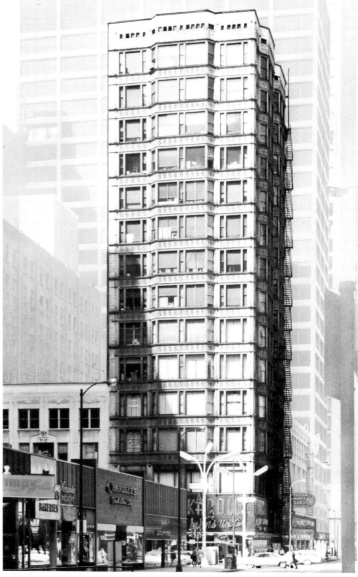

The Magasin au Bon Marché, Paris, built in 1876 by L. A. Boileau and Gustave Eiffel, was one of several Paris department stores that used the new iron construction to create spacious, well-lighted interiors. Although the ornamental detail belongs to the past, the bold use of iron, with its flying bridges, gives the interior an air of fantasy that is wholly of its period.

The Reliance Building, Chicago, one of the ancestors of the modern skyscraper, was designed by Daniel H. Burnham and John W. Root. Its vigorous design is based on the proportions, and its elegance on the structural economy, of its steel frame. The four-storeyed structure, completed in 1890, was extended in 1894 to 13 floors. The frame is faced with terracotta.

209

The Classical Revival

THROUGHOUT THE 18th century classical architecture as an expression of an intellectual idea was triumphant. By the beginning of the 19th century, stimulated by the publication, in 1762, of Stuart and Revett's *Antiquities of Athens*, by the activities of the Dilettanti Society, and by the sculptures of Flaxman and Chantrey, the more advanced thinkers were turning away from Rome and towards the noble simplicity of Greece. John Nash the theatrical space-master—so Victorian in his energy and enterprise if Georgian in his architecture—was still transforming the architectural landscape of London, and Sir John Soane continued to pursue his lonely and original way, but the "Young Greeks"—Wilkins, Smirke, Decimus Burton and Inwood—were taking over. The most brilliant of these was Harvey Elmes (1814–47), the pupil of Schinkel and designer of St George's Hall, Liverpool; the most scholarly,

Charles Cockerell (1788–1863), who combined a successful commercial practice with the Surveyorship of St Paul's.

In Germany, Schinkel was the fashionable master, in France, Hittorff. In the United States, nourished by the New World's admiration for the Greek War of Independence, the deep classical tradition of the American educational system, and also by the fact that at a time of fabulous economic expansion a system of democratic government was gradually crystallizing, it was to sweep the country from 1820 to 1850. By 1860, in England the movement had lost its impetus. Traces survived in the great mid-Victorian speculative developments of Belgravia and Pimlico, and in the less fashionable watering-places and spas, and in coarser forms it was still called upon occasionally—though not so often as Gothic—to express commercial stability or civic display.

The Doric Euston Arch in London (left), disgracefully demolished in 1962, was designed by Philip Hardwick for the London and Birmingham and Great Western Railways as a majestic gateway to the North. It was the earliest part to be built (1835–7), and together with two flanking pavilions designed in the classical manner, formed the centre-piece of the Euston Station approach. To the Victorians, railway travel was an adventure demanding appropriate drama from its architecture.

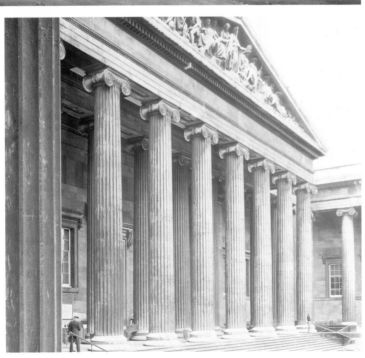

The British Museum in London, with its intimidating screen of marching columns, was built by Sir Robert Smirke between 1823 and 1847 to house the nation's important collections of Classical antiquities. Art and knowledge were treated seriously by the Victorians, and museums and galleries were thus expected to look like temples. The British Museum was built on the site of Montagu House, the old museum, and consists of four main wings around a central court, now the domed Reading-Room.

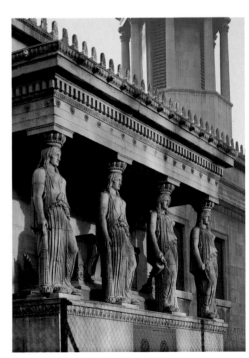

These sculptured ladies staring stonily into the traffic of the Euston Road, London, are replicas of the caryatids from the porch of the Erechtheion on the Acropolis. They form part of St Pancras Church, perhaps the finest church of the Greek Revival, built 1819–22 to the designs of William and Henry Inwood. The design of the tower was based on the Tower of the Winds in Athens.

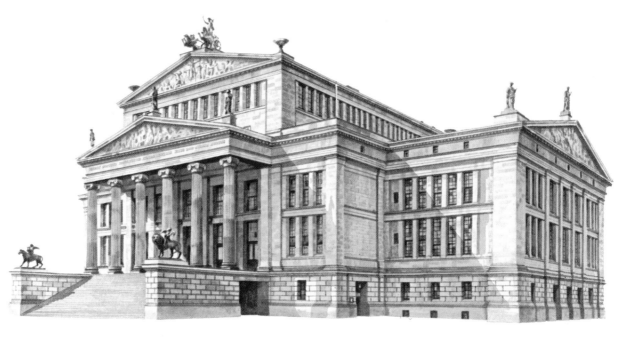

The Schauspielhaus, Berlin, completed in 1821, was the first internationally celebrated work of Karl von Schinkel (1781–1841). Designed, in the architect's words, "to emulate as far as possible Greek forms and construction", the theatre stood as the symmetrically planned and formal centre-piece of the Platz der Akademi, flanked on each side by two early 18th-century churches. Schinkel also designed the drop-curtain for the opening performance.

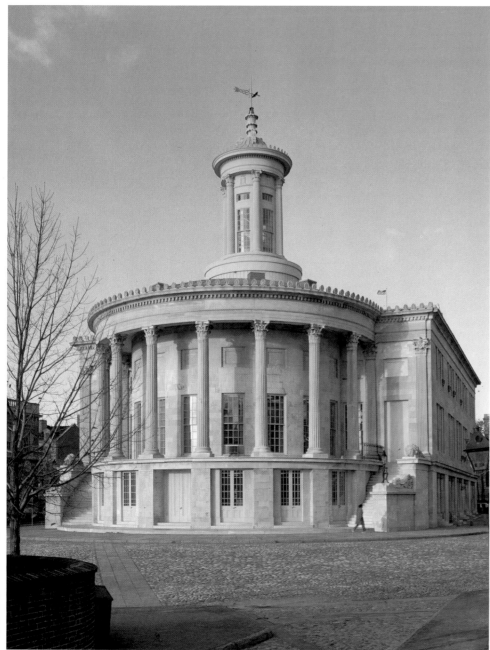

The Philadelphia Merchants' Exchange (left) of 1832–4, by William Strickland, is a brilliantly handled solution to a difficult corner site and one of the masterpieces of the period. In the early days of the new republic, Boston remained under the architectural influence of English Georgian, while Philadelphia, at that time the metropolis, became one of the main centres of the Greek Revival, launched in 1798 by Benjamin H. Latrobe, Strickland's mentor, with the building of the Bank of Philadelphia.

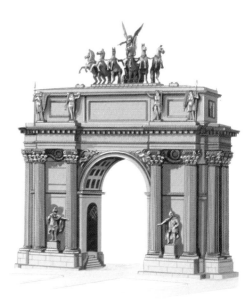

The Narva Arch. Leningrad, like Venice, is built on a swamp. This did not prevent Peter the Great and his successors from erecting the heaviest and most solid-looking buildings for their Imperial City. The Narva Arch, scene of bloody street riots in 1905, was one of many classical-style structures erected over 200 years by a series of European architects.

The Gothic Revival

THE GOTHIC REVIVAL means what it says. Beneath the stony weight of 18th-century classicism, Gothic—like a thin, delicate but tenacious weed—had managed to struggle on, nourished by the poetry of Pope and Gray and by the writings of Walter Scott and *The Gentleman's Magazine*, flowering bravely in the workshops of country builders, in gazebos and garden lay-outs, in the gimcrack charm of Horace Walpole's Strawberry Hill, in the fashionable scenery of Fonthill, Ashridge and Windsor, until by 1830 the Middle Ages had successfully superseded Classical times as the cultural ideal. This sophisticated opinion was given popular impetus by the publication in 1836 of *Contrasts*, an illustrated manifesto by A. W. N. Pugin (1812–52) that claimed Gothic to be both morally and aesthetically the only correct and universal style. By 1845 the style had entered an even sterner phase—"the organ", it was said, "after the harpsichord."

Gothic became more a matter of faith than of fashion. Its English prophet was John Ruskin, its priests the Oxford Movement and the Camden Society, founded in 1839, who for fifty years were the rigorous arbiters of ecclesiastical taste. Its busiest architect was Sir George Gilbert Scott (1811–78), with eight hundred buildings, including St Pancras Hotel and St Nicholas, Hamburg, to his credit; its most original William Butterfield (1814–1900), designer of Keble College and All Saints', Margaret Street, London; its most romantic, William Burges (1827–81), the restorer of Cardiff Castle. By 1860, to Ruskin's dismay, it had conquered the world of commerce and civic pomp. But its glories were over, and by 1880 it had flickered out into the embers of eclecticism, from which sprang the sparks of the Arts and Crafts movement. It had been perhaps the most influential art movement ever to spring from this country, changing the face of England, and leaving as its most splendid monument the "amiable and august" Houses of Parliament, of all English buildings perhaps the best loved.

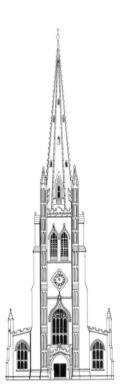

Trinity Church, New York, is one of the best-known Neo-Gothic churches in the United States. It was designed in the Decorated style by Richard Upjohn and completed in 1846.

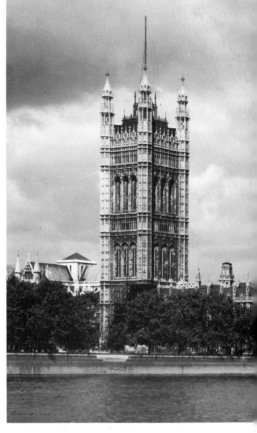

The Houses of Parliament, dominating the skyline at Westminster, established Gothic as a style befitting major public monuments. Built 1840–65, it owes its classical plan and general form to Sir Charles Barry and its marvellous Tudor-Gothic detail and fabulous interiors to A. W. N. Pugin.

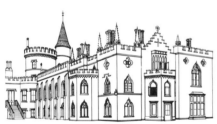

STRAWBERRY HILL
The earliest phase of the Gothic Revival, remarkable for its fanciful, picturesque romanticism, is exemplified at Strawberry Hill, Horace Walpole's "medieval" dream-house at Twickenham. Walpole, author of a highly successful Gothic horror story The Castle of Otranto, *bought the square Georgian building in 1747 and began to extend and "gothicize" it in the following year. The additions included the Long Gallery wing, the round west tower, the Beauchamp turret and "medieval" battlements. As the work progressed the house became increasingly asymmetrical in plan and grouping and more elaborately exact in its Gothic detail.*

The Law Courts in the Strand (1874–82) is the last notable building, and a *tour de force*, of the Gothic Revival. It was designed by G. E. Street, who, inspired by French Gothic of the 13th century, created an asymmetrical, dramatic main façade of stone towers and pinnacles. Behind the great vaulted entrance hall in the style of a 13th-century church nave, dark staircases and passages give access to the first floor, where the courts extend on three sides.

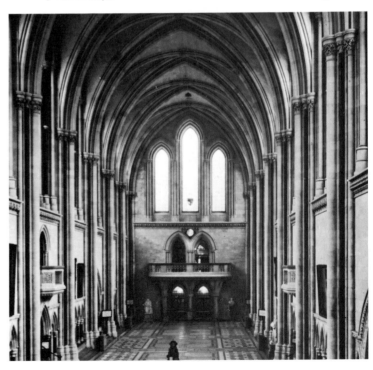

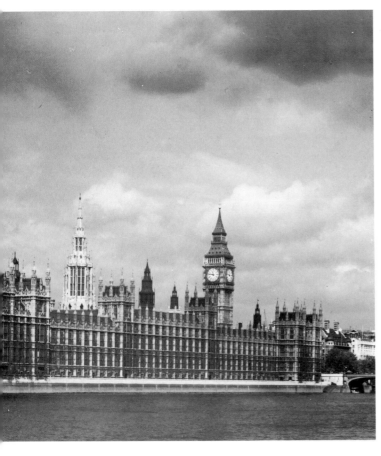

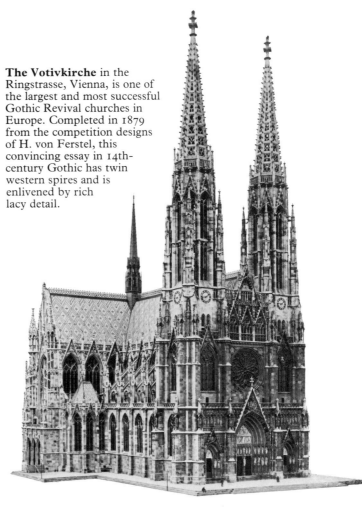

The Votivkirche in the Ringstrasse, Vienna, is one of the largest and most successful Gothic Revival churches in Europe. Completed in 1879 from the competition designs of H. von Ferstel, this convincing essay in 14th-century Gothic has twin western spires and is enlivened by rich lacy detail.

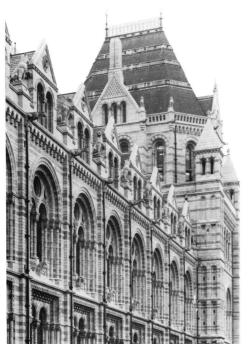

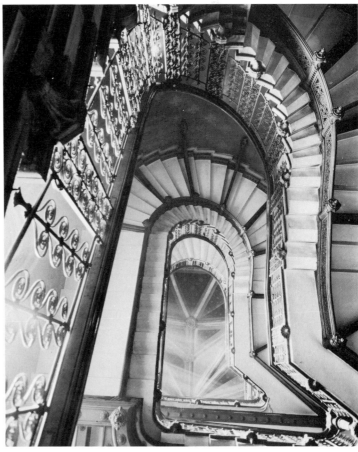

The Natural History Museum is part of Prince Albert's ambitious scheme of cultural institutions at South Kensington, London. Begun in 1873 from Alfred Waterhouse's design, this vast building is in the Romanesque style and is richly decorated with honey-coloured terracotta slabs, moulded in relief.

The grand staircase of the Midland Hotel, at St Pancras Station in London, is rich in metalwork and elaborate ornament, as is the entire interior. The exterior of the hotel, built in 1865–71 by Sir George Gilbert Scott, is a fairy-tale composition of pointed arches, gables, chimneys and spires, set on a ramped and terraced base. An incongruous frontage to W. H. Barlow's great iron train-shed, the hotel is the epitome of High Gothic Victorian taste and a symbol of the age.

The Opera House, Paris

BETWEEN 1850 AND 1870, Napoleon III, with the help of his Prefect, George Haussmann, transformed Paris from a congested, unhealthy and often squalid medieval city into a modern capital of wide, well-lit boulevards and generously planted parks, of squares, markets and spectacular public buildings. It was a task complicated by a fast-growing population, immense legal and financial difficulties and public resistance to change. Napoleon and Haussmann decided it could only be done by keeping the reins in their own hands. Napoleon, who fancied himself as an architect, drew up many of the preliminary sketch plans. Haussmann was his "creative collaborator".

In 1857, a new opera house—the need for which had been hastened by an assassination attempt on the emperor in the narrow street outside the old building—was proposed and a design competition announced. It was won on the second round by the young Charles Garnier, and the building was completed in 1874. Although described by a contemporary critic as "looking like an overloaded sideboard", it is now regarded as one of the masterpieces of the period. Here Garnier triumphed over a cramped and difficult site, handling the carriage-ramps and approach steps, the foyers and staircases, both in section and plan, with confidence and skill. The style is monumental, classically based and opulently expressed, as the times demanded, in an elaborate language of multicoloured marbles and lavish statuary. Throughout his life, Garnier was criticized for his excessive use of ornament, as Napoleon and Haussmann are still accused of being inspired by an out-of-date and imperialist showmanship expressed in a language already debased. Such critics forget that every city needs its occasional monuments and occasions of grandeur, and that thanks largely to these three men, Paris remains one of the most beautiful cities in the world.

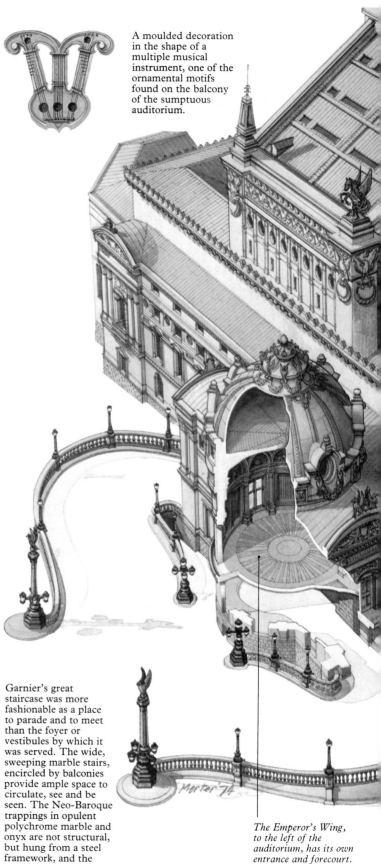

A moulded decoration in the shape of a multiple musical instrument, one of the ornamental motifs found on the balcony of the sumptuous auditorium.

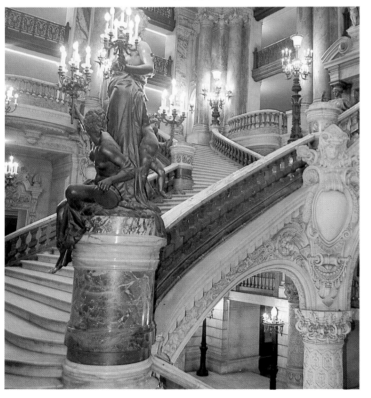

Garnier's great staircase was more fashionable as a place to parade and to meet than the foyer or vestibules by which it was served. The wide, sweeping marble stairs, encircled by balconies provide ample space to circulate, see and be seen. The Neo-Baroque trappings in opulent polychrome marble and onyx are not structural, but hung from a steel framework, and the whole concept has the boldness of the great Parisian department stores of the same time.

The Emperor's Wing, to the left of the auditorium, has its own entrance and forecourt. On the other side of the building, a similar wing is provided for season-ticket holders.

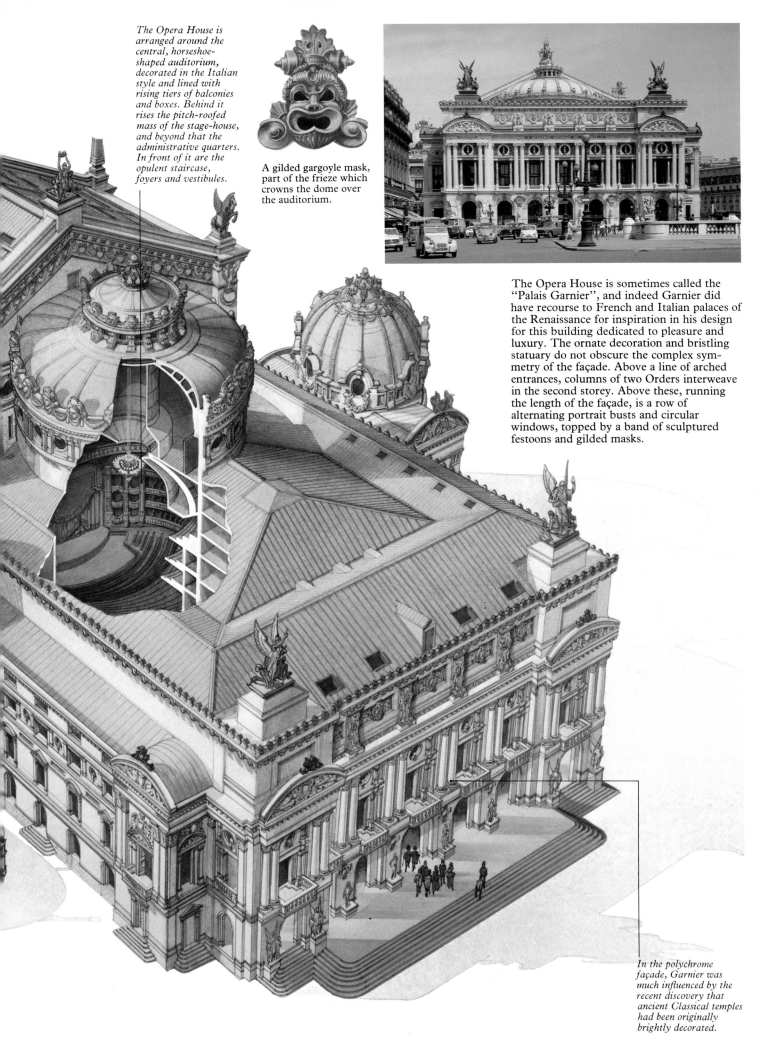

The Opera House is arranged around the central, horseshoe-shaped auditorium, decorated in the Italian style and lined with rising tiers of balconies and boxes. Behind it rises the pitch-roofed mass of the stage-house, and beyond that the administrative quarters. In front of it are the opulent staircase, foyers and vestibules.

A gilded gargoyle mask, part of the frieze which crowns the dome over the auditorium.

The Opera House is sometimes called the "Palais Garnier", and indeed Garnier did have recourse to French and Italian palaces of the Renaissance for inspiration in his design for this building dedicated to pleasure and luxury. The ornate decoration and bristling statuary do not obscure the complex symmetry of the façade. Above a line of arched entrances, columns of two Orders interweave in the second storey. Above these, running the length of the façade, is a row of alternating portrait busts and circular windows, topped by a band of sculptured festoons and gilded masks.

In the polychrome façade, Garnier was much influenced by the recent discovery that ancient Classical temples had been originally brightly decorated.

Eclecticism, an era of stylistic revivals

THE 19TH CENTURY was a time of enthusiastic and bewildering stylistic confusion. Picturesque Gothic, Graeco-Roman Classic, Ecclesiastical Pointed, Jacobethan Commercial had swept like invading armies across Europe, leaving the battlefields strewn with architectural debris of every size, shape, colour and style. Much of this was picked up and enthusiastically exported to the New World to enrich and inflate the American vernacular of skyscraper and shack. Improved communications, rocketing wealth and national confidence heaped the culture and produce of the industrial world at everybody's feet. Styles were chosen, not just for fashion but for their associative qualities. Historic styles were easily recognizable, understandable and spectacular. Roman for Justice, Gothic for Learning, Greek for Government, Venetian for Commerce, Oriental for Leisure, Hanseatic for Housing. Every building told a story and pointed a moral.

The master architect in England of this period was Norman Shaw (1831–1912), whose virtuosity and skill in handling the richer surfaces and livelier skylines demanded by the confident and rich was unrivalled. Behind this picturesque play-acting glittered the iron and glass architecture of the engineer-experimentalist—Bunning's Coal Exchange (1849), Paxton's Crystal Palace (1851), Labrouste's Paris Library (1843–50), the great railway arches and factories of the Industrial Age, the daring towers of the Chicago School (1880–1900). The "Japonism" of the Aesthetic Movement, the Arts and Crafts movement, the preachings of William Morris against opulence and the tyranny of the machine (to lead, ironically, to its 20th-century idealization), the stirrings of Art Nouveau and the folksy aspirations of the garden city movement can now be seen to have been the ancestors of modern architecture, but in 1900 there was little sign of any crisis of conscience to be seen in the flushed, confident, prosperous face that European architecture presented to the world.

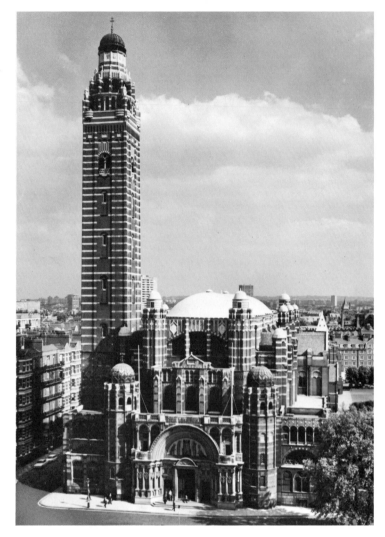

Westminster Cathedral in London (above), begun in 1895 by J. F. Bentley, was built in the Byzantine style, using a system of brick domes rising from pendentives covering the nave, choir and sanctuary. Outside, bands of brick and stone make a distinctive pattern, and from the northwest corner rises the dramatic campanile known as St Edward's tower.

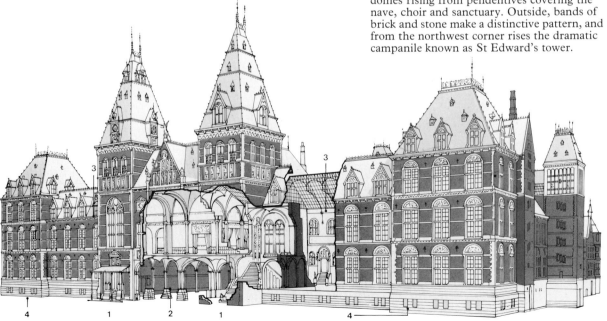

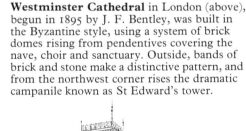

The Rijksmuseum (left), built between 1877 and 1885, is one of the most prominent 19th-century buildings in Amsterdam. It was built to the competition-winning design of P. J. H. Cuijpers, who until then was better known for his ecclesiastical architecture. The two main entrances (1) are in the bulky twin towers, which flank a central arcaded court (2). Iron and glass roofs cover the exhibition courts (3), which are bounded at each end of the building by side pavilions (4).

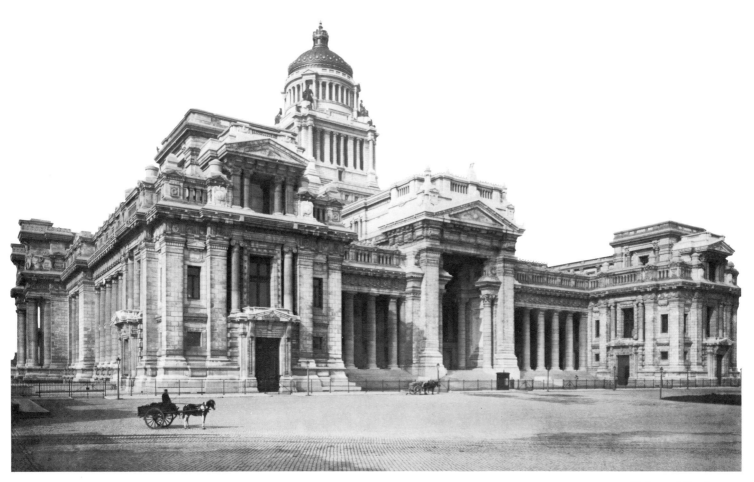

The Palais de Justice in Brussels (above) is a weighty and overpowering edifice, built between 1866 and 1883 by Joseph Poelaert. Its ponderous elements build up in a slow pyramid to the massive central tower; it is placed on such high ground and built on so huge a substructure that its bulky outlines are visible nearly all over the city.

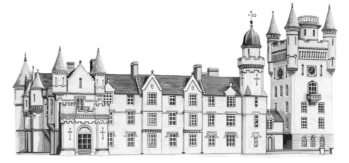

Balmoral Castle in Scotland (left) was originally a modest residence built by John Smith of Aberdeen in the 1830s. It was taken over in 1848 by Queen Victoria and remodelled in the "Scottish Baronial" style by William Smith, aided by Prince Albert, who incorporated a prefabricated iron ballroom.

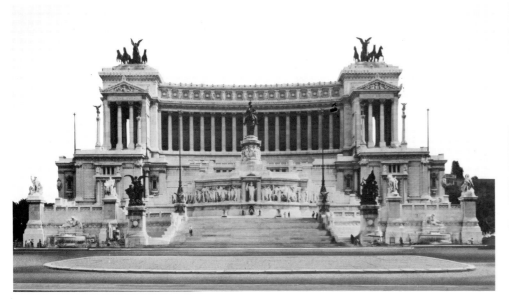

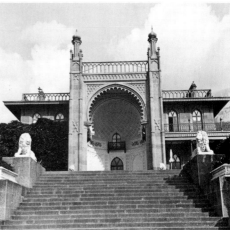

The Victor Emmanuel II Monument in Rome (above) stands gesticulating on the slopes of the Capitol, almost obscuring the remains of the Ancient Roman Forum. It comprises a vast platform with a terrace which supports an enormous equestrian statue of the king. It was designed in 1884 by Giuseppe Sacconi. After his death in 1905, it was continued by Manfredi and others, and was not completed until 1922.

The Palace at Alúpka, near the Crimean coastal resort of Yalta, was built in 1837 for the Prince Vorontzóv to the design of the English architect Edward Blore. The palace combines Gothic and Moorish styles and features a large Moorish gateway (above) in the middle of the south façade. A mosque and a minaret which stand in the extensive park surrounding the palace help to consolidate the Moorish atmosphere.

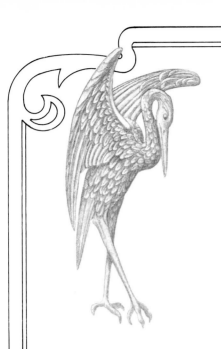

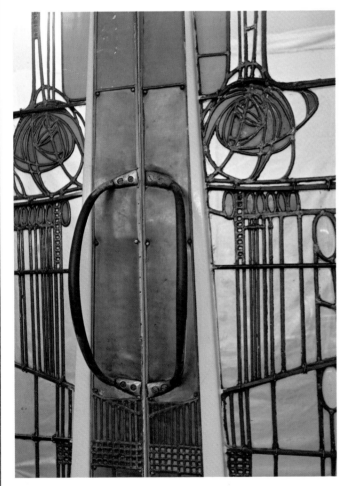

Art Nouveau, as represented by this door in the Willow Tea-rooms, Glasgow, by C. R. Mackintosh, highlighted the decorative value of the curved line, whether vegetable or geometric in origin.

The first signs of a revolt against the narrow historicism on the one hand and the wayward picturesqueness on the other, in which the architectural profession had been indulging since the early part of the 19th century, showed themselves in England in the 1850s. It was William Morris who led an attempt to re-establish in all the visual arts a more logical relationship between design and materials. He particularly opposed the Victorian practice of using new materials and methods merely to imitate the old more cheaply.

Although Morris's own designs, for furniture, stained glass, fabrics, wallpapers and much else, were medieval in inspiration and dependent on hand craftsmanship—he saw no aesthetic promise in designing for the machine—the Arts and Crafts movement he founded, and other movements, like the German *Werkbund*, that followed it, let in a breath of fresh air to disturb the somewhat stuffy atmosphere of academic professionalism. From these movements architecture was an early beneficiary. Although the new movement in Britain—which later spread to Europe—was almost wholly restricted to houses and their contents, it was the beginning of a new sense of architectural logic and aesthetic responsibility.

Another kind of reaction against 19th-century enslavement to historic precedent came nearer the end of the century, and on the Continent rather than in Britain. It, too, was concerned with decoration more than construction, and aimed to create a style—especially a style of ornament—that owed nothing to the past. It emerged in France and Belgium as *Art Nouveau* and in Germany, a little later, as *Jugendstil*. It spread to central Europe and Italy, and in a highly idiosyncratic form to Catalonia, where Antoni Gaudí created some astonishing buildings with a wide range of structural as well as decorative innovations.

New Beginnings

In other countries, too, Art Nouveau was associated with a move into a different future. In Finland it became closely linked with the National Romantic movement, which was using architecture and decoration, including a revival of the countryside vernacular such as the Arts and Crafts movement had fostered in Britain, as a vehicle for its declaration of independence from domination by Czarist Russia. This Europe-wide development attained special significance in Vienna, where the *Sezession* movement not only enriched the new decorative language but, in the work of architects like Josef Hoffmann, opened the door to a greater freedom of expression and a more experimental approach to architecture itself. It led on towards the more comprehensive revolution that was to preoccupy the 20th century.

As with the Arts and Crafts movement, all the arts were involved in these experiments. The characteristic idiom of Art Nouveau—its swirling lines and stylized plant forms—is to be found in the work of the painters and illustrators of the time. And, although its first aim was decoration, it did not fail to recognize the significance of the new structural materials that were playing an increasingly important role in architecture. Some of the pioneers of Art Nouveau, like Horta in Belgium and Guimard in France, used iron, for example, with unprecedented vigour and with regard for its inherent nature.

Meanwhile, other developments, concerned with a more wholehearted reappraisal of the relation of form to function and which may be considered the real beginnings of modern architecture, began in Austria, Germany and Holland. It was less a concerted movement than a series of independent steps forward by a number of individuals, each responding in his own way to the new spirit that was in the air and often inspired by advances in science, technology and social and philosophical thought: Otto Wagner in Austria, followed more ruthlessly by Adolf Loos, who declared war on all forms of ornament; Berlage and Van de Velde in Holland; Behrens and Olbrich in Germany. Britain, with her more emancipated architecture still limited to the domestic, was by now somewhat isolated from the main European stream. But the solitary figure of Charles Rennie Mackintosh provides a link with the ferment that was taking place on the Continent, just as he—and Beardsley in the graphic arts—represents the principal British claim to have contributed to Art Nouveau.

Before the end of the 19th century the United States, where the architects had been even more slavishly devoted to the pedantic classicism of the *Beaux Arts* school in Paris, dramatically came on the scene in two distinct but related developments: the work of one powerful individual, Frank Lloyd Wright, and that of a group of architects in Chicago, led by Louis Sullivan, whose pupil Wright had been.

Frank Lloyd Wright's departures from the orthodox were little appreciated at the time, but his flamboyant personality, backed by his prophetic utterances and the example of his "Prairie-style" houses, later became a powerful force in the world's gradual reappraisal of architectural conventions. It was a liberating process that had been tentatively begun by architects like Voysey and Norman Shaw in England, but which Wright carried further, so that indoors and outdoors often seemed to merge.

Sullivan and the other architects of the Chicago school continued the experiments with steel-framed structures that had been made earlier by such men as Jenney and Root, and produced a sequence of buildings out of which grew that American phenomenon the skyscraper. In one short generation America came to lead the world in the rapidity and confidence of its architectural progress.

Britain's new domestic architecture

IN TURNING AWAY from academic conventions, the English house architects of the later 19th century looked for inspiration chiefly to their own rural vernacular. Philip Webb (who built for William Morris), C. F. A. Voysey (probably the most widely admired of all those responsible for this new-style domestic architecture), Baillie Scott, Norman Shaw, Ernest Newton and others modelled their houses on the anonymous and timeless examples to be found in farms and villages all over Britain. Plans were opened up and the whole style was deceptively informal, a studied composition of roofs, chimneys and bay windows taking the place of period ornament. The result was a style that accorded with these architects' interest in the craftsmanlike use of traditional materials like brick and timber.

Although they opened the way for the far bigger changes that were to come, by discarding borrowed styles and insisting on the moral rightness of their attitude to design, many of them—like Morris himself—looked backwards as much as forwards and would certainly not have admired the modern buildings that historians now regard as their progeny. At the time, however, their work seemed revolu-tionary and it soon had an influence in many parts of Europe, especially in Germany. So interested were the Germans, in fact, that they went to the length of appointing to their embassy in London a special attaché, Hermann Muthesius, whose task was to report on the new English developments in architecture and design and who published, in 1904, a book, *Das Englische Haus*, which spread the new gospel even farther afield.

This new informality and rusticity affected planning as well as building. This was the era of the garden suburb, which was conceived also as a reaction against the insanitary and overcrowded Victorian slums. The first garden suburb, laid out and partly designed by Norman Shaw, was Bedford Park, in west London, begun in 1875; soon after came the garden city movement inspired by the social reformer Ebenezer Howard, and the housing estates laid out by altruistic industrialists on the fringes of manufacturing towns like Bournville and Port Sunlight. All were composed of winding roads lined with cottage-style houses set in gardens and among greenery. These, too, influenced housing and town-building in many parts of Europe.

The Orchard at Chorley Wood in Hertfordshire (below), built in 1899 by C. F. A. Voysey for himself, shows a return to local craftsmanship and skills. The house has a rectangular plan with the usual domestic rooms and a schoolroom around a central staircase. The pale decorative scheme of the interior gave a novel effect of lightness.

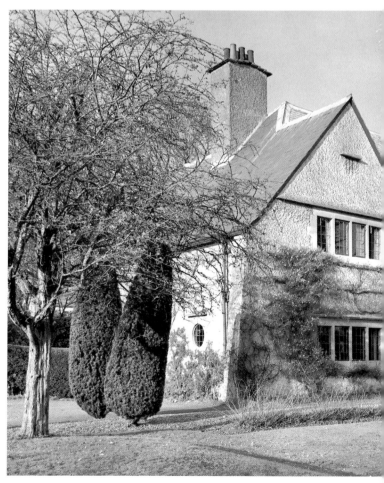

The Red House at Bexley Heath in Kent was designed for William Morris by Philip Webb in 1859. The house, which derives its name from the plain red brick of its exterior, was a startling contrast to the prevalent Italianate stucco villa. Although large and comfortable, it had no bathroom.

1 *Outhouses*
2 *Kitchen yard*
3 *Scullery*
4 *Kitchen*
5 *WC*
6 *Pantry*
7 *Dining-room*
8 *Stairs connecting the two wings*
9 *Hall*
10 *North porch*
11 *Waiting-room*
12 *Bedroom*
13 *Garden porch*

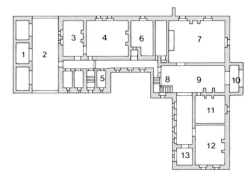

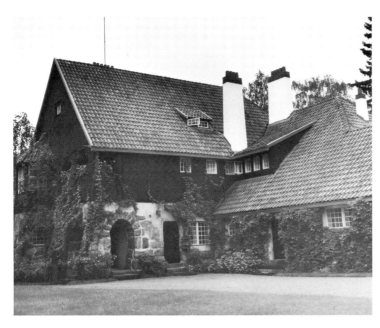

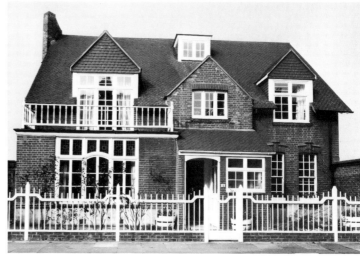

Bedford Park, London (above and below), was the first garden suburb. Laid out in 1875 it combined healthy surroundings with quick access to the city by way of the new Turnham Green station. The architects chiefly involved were Norman Shaw, E. W. Godwin, E. J. May and Maurice Adams. The houses were set along tree-lined streets and had informal gardens. The scheme was completed with a church, club, tavern and general store which gave the estate its community spirit.

Hvitträsk (above), a group of houses and studios built by E. Saarinen, A. Lindgren and H. Gesellius in 1902 for their own use, is situated in the Finnish countryside west of Helsinki. It shows a knowledge of the English Arts and Crafts movement transmitted to Finland principally through A. W. Finch, an English artist who lived and taught there.

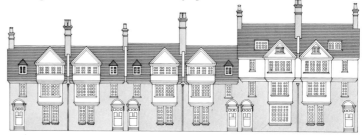

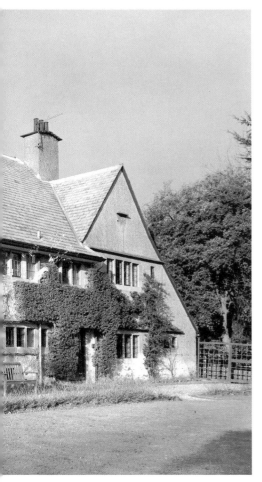

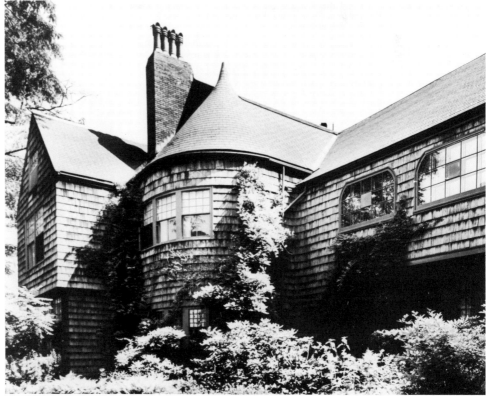

Stoughton House at Cambridge, Massachusetts, exemplifies the "Shingle Style", which influenced American house design in the late 19th century. Built in 1882–3 by H. H. Richardson, the house has outer walls clad entirely with wooden shingles. A more important and forward-looking feature is the informal plan, which gives spaciousness to the interiors and picturesque asymmetry to the exterior.

Art Nouveau, a break with the past

THE TERM ART NOUVEAU covers a wide range of stylistic approaches and individual design responses to what, around the turn of the century, was called "the new art". The lack of a cohesive Art Nouveau style is understandable in a period of experimentation. What common denominators there were in designers' work in France, Belgium, Austria, Germany and Scotland can probably be best understood with reference to nature and to the fascination to be found in the external appearance of natural—biomorphic and zoomorphic—forms. The tortuous twists and writhing curves, indentations and incrustations of the buildings of this period in Latin countries contrast with the ordered, and usually rectangular framed, approach of the Anglo-Saxon. The contrast of approaches is shown by comparing the work of Guimard in Paris and the Glasgow Four in Scotland. All of it was individualistic; the mass-produced version of the French type of Art Nouveau—principally concerned with domestic interiors—came much later, after the creative potency had been spent.

During its heyday, from 1890 to 1906, Art Nouveau in various countries was recognized largely by the name of the individual architects or designers; Van de Velde in Belgium (later Germany), Hoffmann and Olbrich in Austria, Guimard in France, Mackintosh in Scotland and Gaudí in Spain (although he was discovered much later). The outlet for the wide dissemination of the ideas of these and other, lesser, architects and designers was the contemporary art magazines, where innovations in graphic representation—from posters by Mucha and Lautrec to the title pages by Van de Velde and Behrens—were as much a part of the same genre as the studiously contrived photograph of an inventive piece of architectural design. Invention is indeed the keyword, as opposed to the slavish copying of past styles. Art Nouveau represented, above all, a break with the past in both arts and crafts, as well as providing a seedbed for those in search of what was called "an art appropriate to its time".

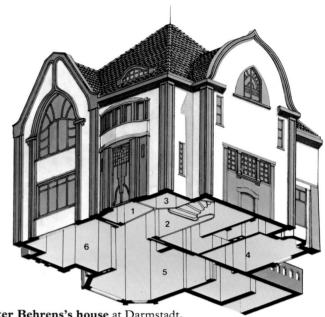

Peter Behrens's house at Darmstadt, Germany, his first building, was designed for his own occupation at the Artists' Colony, Darmstadt, in 1901. Its plan is similar in some respects to Frank Lloyd Wright's early work in Oak Park. Other, nearby, domestic buildings were designed by J. M. Olbrich.

1 *Entrance*
2 *Hall*
3 *Cloakroom*
4 *Mistress's sitting-room*
5 *Dining-room*
6 *Music-room*

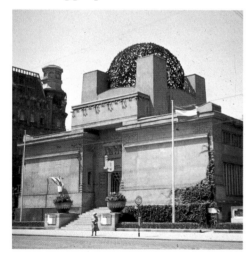

The Sezession House in Vienna, as its name implies, was a centre for those artists who broke away from the Academy. Designed by J. M. Olbrich in 1896, it poked fun at the notions of classicism. The dome itself, known locally as the Golden Cabbage, is symbolic of *Ver Sacrum*, the Sezessionist journal.

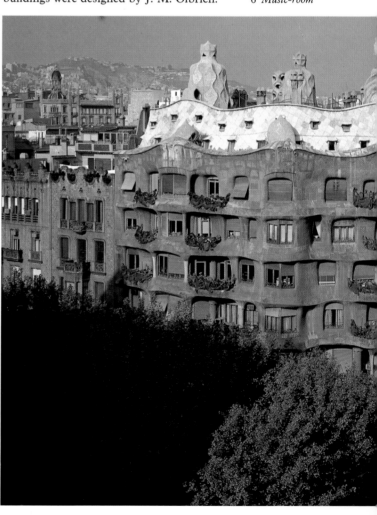

The Casa Milá in Barcelona, built between 1905 and 1910 by Antoni Gaudí, is often cited as the most "expressionistic" of his buildings, but still exhibits local, essentially Catalonian, motifs. Constructed in concrete and blockwork it is supported by elephantine columns. Internally a large open court provides light to the apartments. At roof level a weird idiosyncratic collection of chimneys and finials creates an exciting skyline.

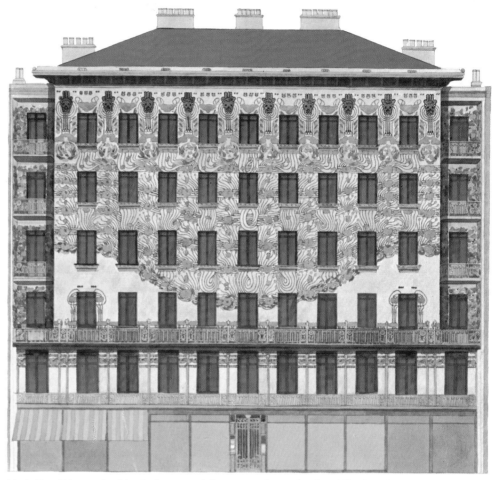

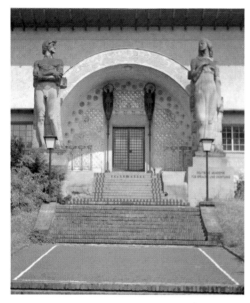

J. M. Olbrich's Artists' House at Darmstadt, 1899–1901, was the central building of the Darmstadt Artists' Colony. It brought a key Viennese Sezessionist to Germany, and also an unusual style of architecture combining simplicity with characteristic Sezession entrance detailing.

Majolica House, besides being one of the most highly decorated buildings in Vienna, also solved the difficult building problem of placing apartments over shops. The second-floor balcony indicates the point of change of construction. The façade above the balcony is faced in majolica tiles. At each side of the main symmetrical apartment buildings are flat-roofed recessed balconies. It was designed by Otto Wagner in 1898–9.

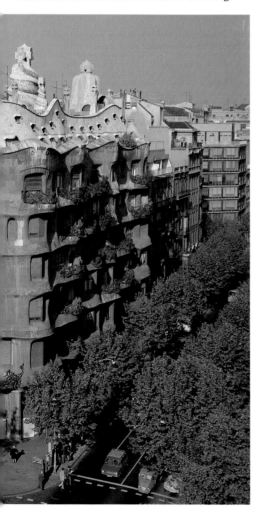

GUIMARD'S DECORATIVE ENTRANCES
Guimard was the chief exponent of the Art Nouveau style in Paris. The entrance to the Castel Béranger (1) indicates a much freer kind of decoration than his later wrought-iron Métro entrances, which are as famous as Lautrec's posters and characterize, to this day, the Belle Epoque. He developed a number of station types, including entrances with fan-shaped and enclosed pavilions (2) and others with balustrades (3) around them.

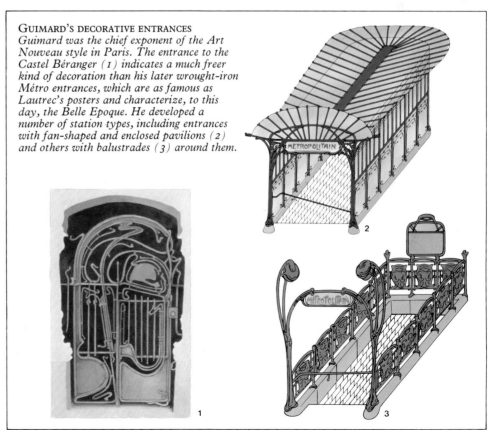

Art Nouveau, variations on a theme

THE ART NOUVEAU style involved the creation of an effervescent atmosphere in which the freely shaped, writhing forms of the designers seem to gesticulate in their own way at the current historicism of the more conventional work of the time. The aesthetic standards of Art Nouveau were both diverse and diffuse. It possessed no single stylistic purpose or intention, as far as one can see, other than that given to it by each individual designer. There were, however, many common characteristics. The Art Nouveau designer showed a delight in the dynamic forms found in nature, as well as in the deliberate simplification of structural elements in buildings and building interiors.

It was a romantic phase that took pride in the handmade object. This aspect of the style was mainly ". . . confined to ornamentation" and to interior design and furniture production. The naturalistic ornament was applied in a typically Mannerist way, accentuating the delicate but vigorous twists found in nature into exaggerated design effects.

The decorative aspects of the interior design movement were developing side by side with the use of new constructional techniques and methods. This can be seen in Victor Horta's Maison du Peuple, in Brussels (1896–9), and the work of the Viennese Sezessionists. In the Maison du Peuple, the ornamentation of the ironwork was a sharp contrast to the carefully articulated structural framing.

The two vital centres of Art Nouveau in France were at Nancy and Paris. Of the two, the Nancy school was established first and was quickly turned into the most comprehensive arts and crafts centre in the country. By 1900, the year of the Paris Exhibition—the year of triumph for the new style—Emile Gallé was employing as many as three hundred men in his Nancy workshops. With this emphasis on the simple idea that an article of "art production" should bring joy to the man who made it and satisfaction to the person who paid for it, Gallé showed his indebtedness to the English Arts and Crafts movement.

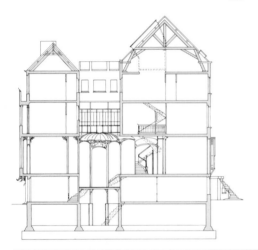

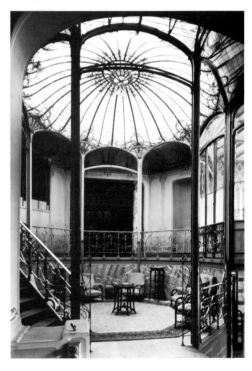

The Hôtel van Eetvelde in Brussels (left and right) was designed in 1898 by Victor Horta, undoubtedly the key European Art Nouveau architect. While most other architects flirted with the new style, Horta found it gave the best expression to his ideas. His skill is demonstrated in his ability to slip his domestic designs into narrow constricted sites. The interiors become of great importance as centres of light, which permeates through the filigree domes and skylights—usually in the centre of the building (left). The Hôtel van Eetvelde is a remarkable example of the way Horta handled the situation and used it to highlight the imposing staircase, which leads up to the first-floor reception rooms.

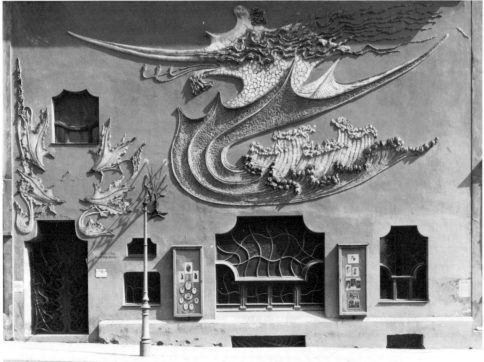

The Elvira Studios at Munich. Demolished long ago, the façade (left) has fascinated historians of Art Nouveau for many years. In reality little is known about its origins as a design, but as a symbol of the youthful exuberant German "new art" style it is unequalled. Designed in 1896 by August Endell, whose work owes a debt to Japan, it has a book illustrator's panache yet embodies very largely the theoretical framework which Endell, who trained as an aesthetician as well as an architect, established for his turn-of-the-century architecture. He spoke in his writings about forms having certain qualities of "lightness", "sharpness' and "speed".

The master bedroom in Hill House, near Glasgow (right), is shown with the original furnishings. The overall effect is one of simplicity, with white walls and woodwork relieved by subtle coloured decoration. Hill House, also known as the "Blackie" House, was designed in 1902–3 by Charles Rennie Mackintosh, who, at the turn of the century, was probably Britain's most inventive architect. It is now preserved as an historic building.

The Central Pavilion of the International Exposition of Decorative Arts held at Turin in 1902 was designed by Raimondo d'Aronco. Its key feature was the central rotunda (below), inspired by the dome of S. Sophia in Istanbul. With its undulating cornice and the general use of recesses and curved surfaces on the exterior, it is a rich and eccentrically modern version of the Baroque style, which inspired D'Aronco's version of Art Nouveau.

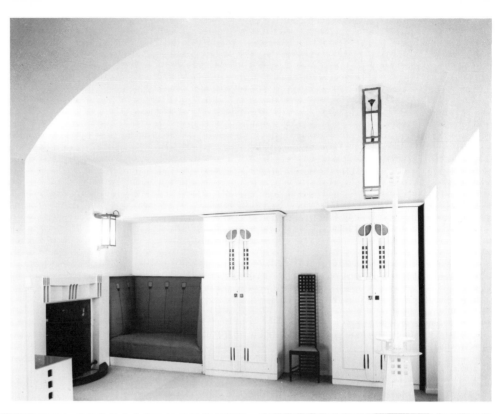

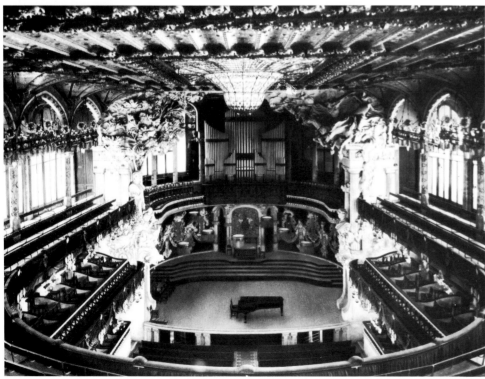

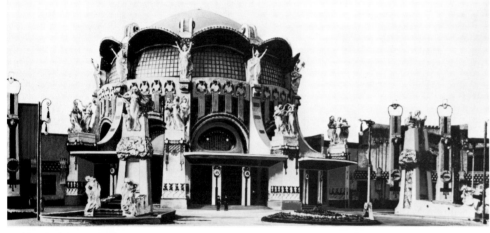

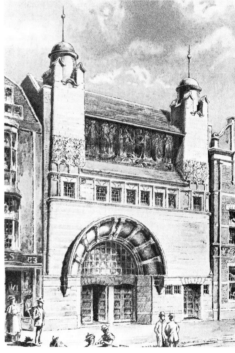

The Whitechapel Art Gallery in London (above) was designed by C. Harrison Townsend in 1901 and is one of his principal buildings. An active member of the Art Worker's Guild, Townsend shared their interest in decorative craftsmanship, but he was also influenced by the pioneer "modern" American architect H. H. Richardson.

The Palace of Catalonian Music at Barcelona (left), built 1905–8 by Luis Domènech, is similar in many ways to the work of his rival, Gaudí—at least as far as the visual pyrotechnics go. Paradoxically combined with this, however, is the controlled aestheticism associated with the rational development of modern architecture, which culminated with Gropius and the Bauhaus, and the arguments over functionalism.

The Chicago School and Frank Lloyd Wright

CHICAGO WAS the centre of architectural progress in the United States from the 1880s onwards, and Louis Sullivan and Frank Lloyd Wright were the two giants who gave it international significance. W. Jenney and other experimenters with steel-framed office buildings had laid the foundations, while H. H. Richardson, although not an innovator of structural technique, simplified the forms of large commercial buildings, giving them, notably with his Marshall Field warehouse of 1887, a new monumentality.

In Chicago, following the disastrous fire in 1871, importance was attached to fireproof construction, and this gave an impetus to the new styles then being evolved for the office buildings so much in demand in the expanding Middle West. A metal frame, sheathed in stone or brick, seemed to Louis Sullivan and to several others to require a form that kept frame and infill visibly separate and that owed nothing to period precedent. Although Sullivan was a prolific designer of free-flowing ornament, his early skyscrapers were a striking geometrical answer—on which other architects developed further after his early retirement.

When Frank Lloyd Wright broke with Sullivan, whom he always regarded as his master, to set up his own practice in 1893, he first devoted his efforts to houses. The horizontal emphasis and spatial flexibility of his many houses in the Chicago suburbs were brilliant innovations, but their quality was little recognized locally. In 1909, however, his series of Prairie-style houses culminated in the Robie House. Thereafter, their impact on European architects was dramatic. As early as 1901, Wright began to take an interest in the possibilities of concrete, and in such buildings as the Larkin office building at Buffalo and the Unity Church at Oak Park, he electrified Europe with his bold, expressive treatment of this hitherto despised material. He also experimented with concrete-block construction in a group of houses in California.

Wright's fame eventually spread throughout America, too. His own house at Taliesin, Wisconsin, 1911, a rambling romantic structure in a mixture of materials related to the landscape in which it stood, became a centre of pilgrimage. Here, he gathered disciples around him and became the patriarchal figure that the world recognized as a genuine, if sometimes outrageous and loquacious, genius.

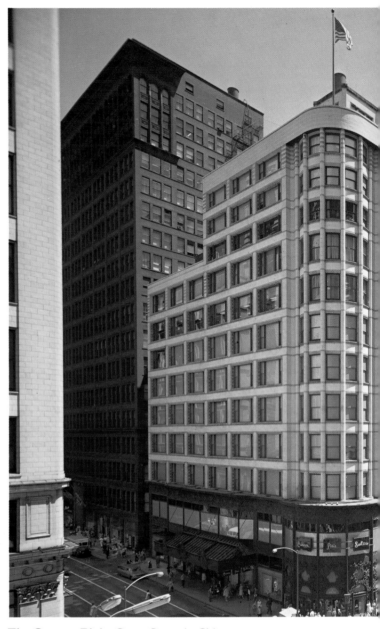

The Carson, Pirie, Scott Store in Chicago (above) was the climax of Louis Sullivan's career as an architect of big commercial buildings and a masterpiece of the Chicago school of steel-frame design. Many of the first multistorey buildings were put up in Chicago in the 1880s and 1890s to meet the great demand for new offices and stores after the fire of 1871. The technique of hanging the outer walls on a load-bearing metal frame enabled architects to erect structures of over ten storeys and allowed them to increase the window area significantly. These desirable features are clearly seen in the Carson, Pirie, Scott Store. The building, erected mainly in 1899 and in 1904, admirably met the need for extensive floor space and well-lit interiors. Around the entrance appears some of the elaborate surface ornament which Sullivan somewhat illogically combined with his functional conception of structure.

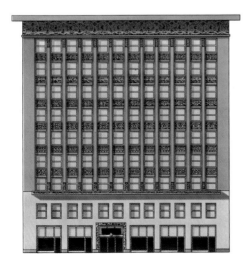

A breakthrough in the evolution of the skyscraper occurred in 1890, when Louis Sullivan used a framework entirely of steel in this St Louis office building known as the Wainwright Building. Its metal skeleton is clothed by brick piers, and the grid-like structure is suggested by the identical cellular window units on seven of the ten storeys.

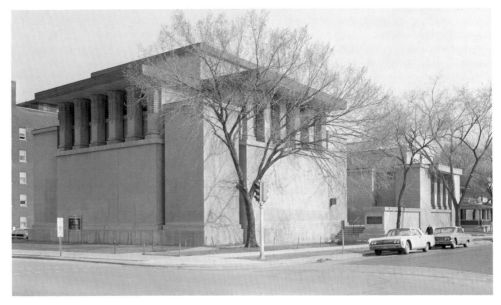

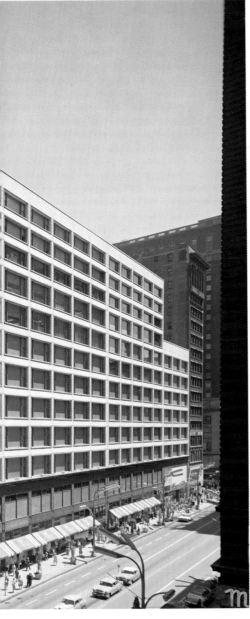

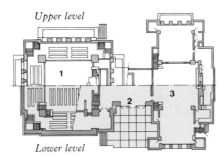

Upper level

1

2   3

Lower level

Unity Church at Oak Park, Chicago (above), was one of the most important buildings of Frank Lloyd Wright's career. Revolutionary when built in 1906, it owed its appearance to poured concrete, a material used here in a newly expressive way by Wright. On plan (left) the church consists of an auditorium (1) and parish house (3), linked by a common entrance (2) to make the letter H. This block-like form was a complete break with traditional church design. The interior is a spectacular display of complex spatial relationships and bold geometric ornament.

The Robie House, Chicago (below), 1909, most celebrated of Wright's early, Prairie-style houses, epitomizes his revolutionary contribution to a new, American, domestic architecture. In place of traditional, boxy shapes and self-contained rooms, low-slung, overhanging roofs shelter flowing internal spaces, which open outwards in terraces and continuous windows, to merge with the landscape beyond.

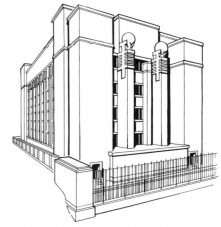

The Larkin Building, Buffalo (above), demolished in 1950, was built in 1904 for a large mail-order firm. It was designed by Wright who, boldly applying Sullivan's famous principle "form follows function", built an entirely new type of office building. His main aim was to liberate conventional office design from its box-like arrangement. He did this dramatically by building open galleries around a vast four-storey well topped by a skylight. Sealed off from the outside by massive brick walls and fixed windows, the building was also the first of its kind to be fully air-conditioned.

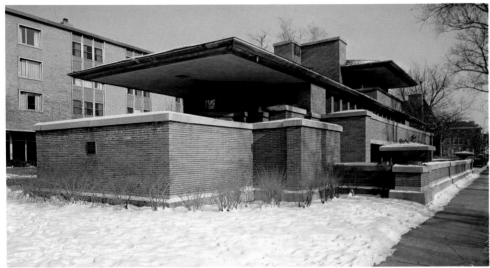

Europe, the spirit of change

THROUGHOUT EUROPE the period from 1890 to 1919 was an exceptionally creative one for the arts, and particularly for architecture. During these years drastic changes occurred both in the appearance of objects and in the artist's—including the architect's—approach to his subject. It was a period of expansion in almost every field of human endeavour. A succession of new movements, "isms" and tendencies developed; some overlapped, like the Dadaists and the early Expressionists and the Italian and Russian Futurists, while others were idiosyncratic to the extreme.

Almost all owed a common debt to the 19th-century innovations in French painting circles and Parisian public life, and also to the "psychological" artists and writers of Scandinavia. For architects, the work of the enterprising 19th-century engineers was of importance.

After a period of Romanticism, usually couched in nationalistic terms, the pressures of "modernity" (allied to notions of progressive evolution) for architects were applied in a number of ways: the need for an identifiable new architectural language; a theoretical framework of ideas that involved the consideration of new uses of old materials; the desire to move away from eclecticism; and a general disenchantment, among the *avant-garde*, with the Academies.

Notwithstanding the incentive to originality, provided by the revolutionary zeal of those artists and architects who were caught up in the atmosphere of the times, life itself was changing. New demands were placed upon architects to design for efficiency and for public use; pressures were also exerted by political power groups—from Grand Dukedoms to Leninists—to provide an architecture appropriate to their causes and aspirations. Much was left to the individual artist's vision: altogether it was an exciting period for the development of ideas. Architects sought to find a simpler expression for their design ideas; they also had to design many new types of buildings.

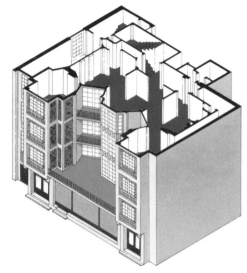

Auguste Perret's apartment house, 25bis Rue Franklin, Paris, built 1902–3, has been referred to as the first major 20th-century building. It is constructed with a reinforced concrete frame; the architect uses the trabeated form to provide a watered-down type of classicism. Between the columns the faience infilling panels and the windows indicate the period décor and fenestration. The novel features are the way the design is implemented with the part-courtyard on the face of the building and the effect this has in strengthening the vertical emphasis through recessed balconies.

The Post Office Savings Bank, Vienna (right), built 1904–12, is Otto Wagner's most forward-looking work. In 1903, Wagner's design won a competition of 37 entries. Externally the building is massive—the competition requirement had been for a building of "maximum solidity"—with a facing of marble slabs. Inside, the banking hall is a lightweight contrast with its elegant curved section and slender concrete supports. The hall is a good example of one of Wagner's architectural engineering structures. He was both architect and engineer to the king.

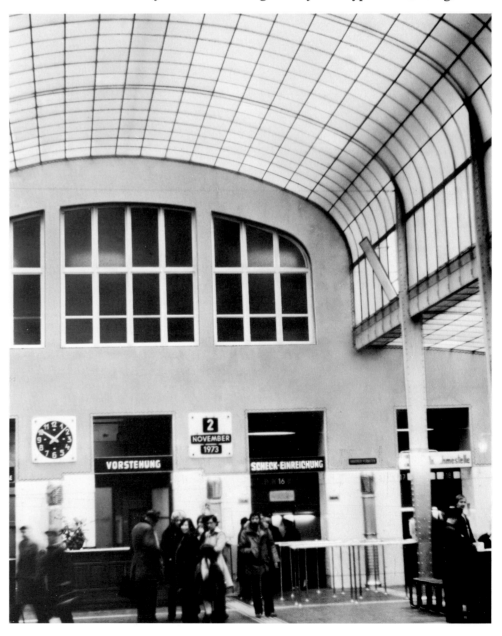

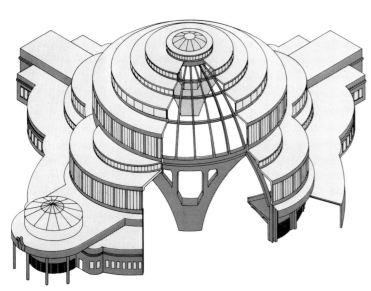

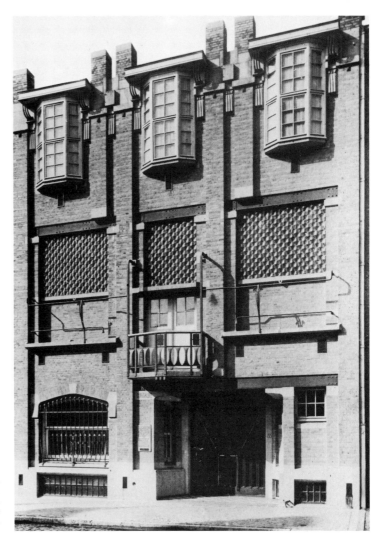

The Centennial Hall (above), in Breslau, now Wroclaw in Poland, is virtually the only building known to be designed by Max Berg. It was constructed in 1911–12 as the centre-piece of a whole series of exhibition structures. Berg's immense concrete-framed dome, with a diameter of 213 ft, height of 137 ft, and covering an area of 6,340 sq yds is one of the world's most impressive monuments to reinforced concrete.

The Clinic for Dr Van Neck, in Brussels, was designed by Antoine Pompe in 1910. A small infill building, it was built in brick and contained a number of innovations, including an internal ventilation system. The exterior still shows signs of Art Nouveau.

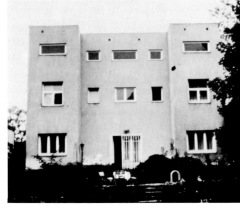

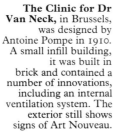

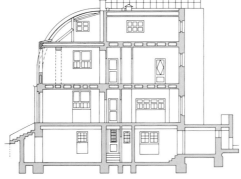

The Steiner House in Vienna, designed by Adolf Loos in 1910, has often been used by historians to demonstrate the typical appearance of the "new architecture", yet it predates most of the work of the modernists in Europe and the United States by some 15 years. However Loos himself had visited both the United States and Britain and had admired this kind of simplicity in Georgian and Colonial examples. Its plain garden façade (far left) was prophetic, but as the section (left) indicates it was a natural result of an ingenious design. The road elevation with its half-round roof is much less typical of the modern movement.

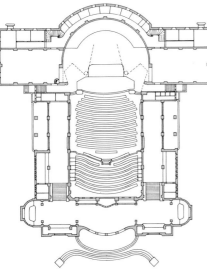

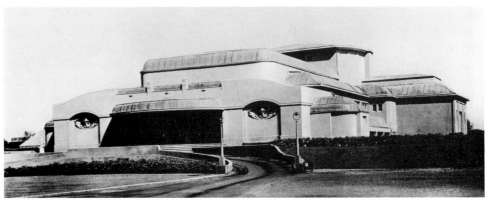

The Werkbund Theatre in Cologne was designed in 1914 by Henri van de Velde. Of all his buildings this was his most successful architectural solution. It went through many modifications as a cinema and a playhouse before maturing into a thoroughly modern, and immensely influential, theatre building (plan left). The curved exterior and the general massing of the building reflected Van de Velde's interest in Islamic architecture.

The architects of the new approach

THE PROTO-MODERN buildings that can be isolated from the general body of architectural work which was going on during the first years of the 20th century (ignoring the later manifestations of individualistic Art Nouveau) were those that embodied notions of simplicity and logic, structural ingenuity and plain façades. The work of Adolf Loos, the Viennese architect, is often cited as typical of this approach; clearly, too, it exhibits qualities to be found in the more decorative work of the Sezession architects. It was an architecture of transition, bridging the gap between the modishly inventive and the utilitarian. This period was to set the scene for what was later to be called "International Style" (a term introduced by Hitchcock and Johnson) or "Functionalism".

The Dutchman H. P. Berlage, foreshadowing a slightly different kind of modernity and initially drawing his inspiration from Viollet-le-Duc and a reapplication of Romanesque principles, propounded a theory based on what the Germans referred to as *Sachlichkeit*. This view was concerned with the appearance of such natural materials as brick, wood and iron, and the organization of spaces—qualities also to be seen in the early industrial design work of Peter Behrens in Berlin and suggested, at the turn of the century, in the work of the English Free School. Some of the structures, isolated as proto-typical of the later modern movement, involved the architect in experimentation with structure, with large areas of glass or with contemporary developments in specialist types of building. The vast interior of Berg's Centennial Hall at Breslau, powerfully vaulted in concrete and glass, was a structural *tour de force*. Wagner's Post Office Savings Bank Hall, Vienna, was a beautifully contrived enclosure in glass and metal, consistent down to the last glass floor tile.

After 1910, the architecture of Frank Lloyd Wright also found favour in Germany and the Netherlands. What has been called his "peaceful penetration of Europe"—via Wasmuth, Berlage and the more obscure Dutch architect Robert van't Hoff—can be seen as an early inspiration in the work of Gropius and other later important architects of the Bauhaus period.

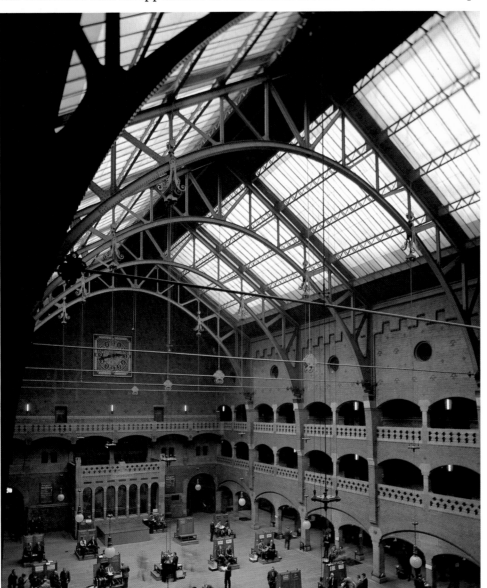

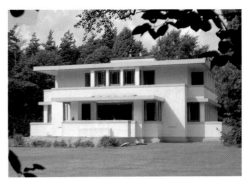

Villa at Huis ter Heide near Utrecht, designed by Robert van't Hoff, a Dutch architect, who, on a visit to the United States, had seen the work of Frank Lloyd Wright. This house, built in 1916, was an attempt to transfer the Wrightian "Prairie School" ideas to the Netherlands. Constructed in reinforced concrete and using an overhanging flat roof, it proved immensely influential in forwarding Wright's architecture in Europe. It was of significance to the De Stijl artists.

The Exchange in Amsterdam (left) was built between 1897 and 1909. Although considered to be one of the embryonic buildings of the modern movement, it was steeped in tradition. H. P. Berlage, the architect, envisaged an historically based modern architecture—one which exhibited qualities of form, structure and craftsmanship. Brick was one of his favoured materials. Stylistically he owed much to the French theorist Viollet-le-Duc and the great Romanesque masons. But the Exchange, still one of the most impressive civic buildings in Amsterdam, was not a hybrid; it was experimental and derived its influential importance from Berlage's attention to detail as much as his mastery of past forms.

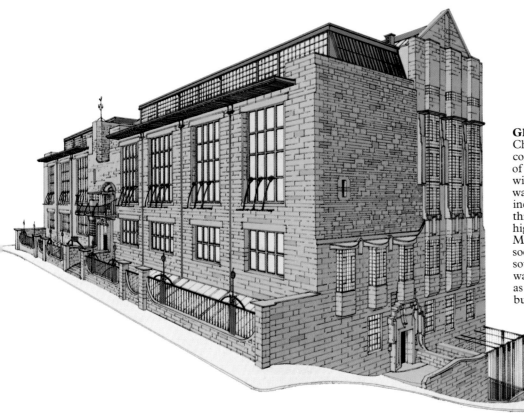

Glasgow School of Art was designed by Charles Rennie Mackintosh, who won a competition for the design of a new School of Art in Glasgow in 1896. By 1899 the east wing, designed in a somewhat baronial mode, was completed; the west wing (left), which included the remarkable library space, lit by three oriel windows each more than 26 ft high, was not finished until the end of 1909. Mackintosh virtually retired from practice soon afterwards and left his native city for the south of England. His greatest achievement was the Glasgow School of Art, justly famed as the most important proto-modern building in Britain.

The Stoclet Palace in Brussels (below), 1904–11, was designed by Josef Hoffmann. Amid the exciting but eccentric Art Nouveau-inspired domestic designs of central Brussels, this precise example of the sober geometrical Viennese version of the style comes as a surprise. Commissioned by the Belgian industrialist Stoclet, it is a carefully modulated building—the almost cubic geometry of the exterior builds up to a dominant staircase tower. The interior spaces are equally well controlled and the geometrical theme, possibly inspired by Mackintosh, runs right through.

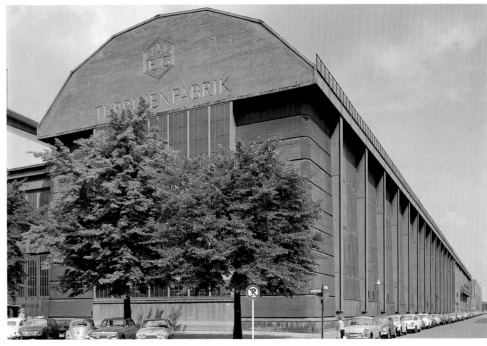

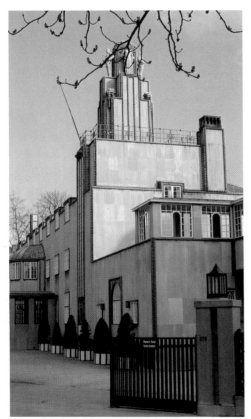

The AEG Turbine Factory in Berlin (above), another key monument of the early modern movement in architecture, was built by Peter Behrens in 1909, soon after his appointment as architect and industrial design consultant to AEG. Mies van der Rohe, Walter Gropius and Le Corbusier all worked briefly in his office. The Turbine Factory incorporates an iron three-pin frame on a massive scale.

The Theatre of the Champs Elysées in Paris (right), 1910–11, was originally designed as a competition scheme by Van de Velde. After a dispute it was modified and built by Auguste Perret with a complex concrete framework. Basically Neo-Classical in style, it also incorporated Van de Velde's ideas of a "three part" stage.

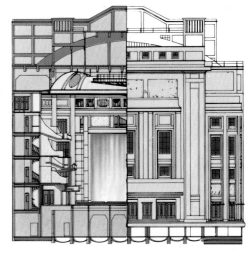

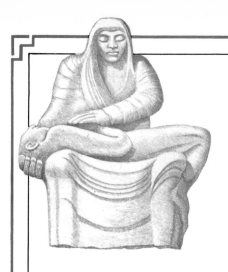

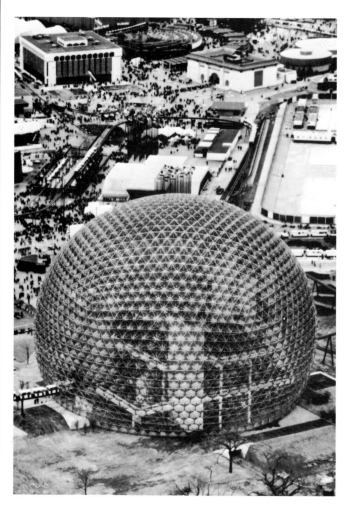

The United States Pavilion at Expo '67, Montreal, with an advanced and experimental building in the form of Buckminster Fuller's prefabricated geodesic dome.

Efforts to introduce a style of architecture which responded to new social needs and exploited new materials and techniques were tentative and fragmentary. The changed appearance of buildings was derived, in addition, from developments in the other arts, like cubism, and from an instinctive desire on the part of architects to break away from the confusions and contrivances of the 19th century.

These efforts were mostly individual; they were hardly yet part of a concerted movement. But the new buildings already had characteristics in common: simple rectangular outlines; avoidance of symmetry as a result of the insistence on a building's function determining its form rather than some picture in the architect's mind; absence of applied ornament; flat roofs and white walls, resulting from the use of reinforced concrete, now the favourite material; large windows, which new structural techniques permitted, but which were encouraged too by the spirit of the times, which believed in opening up the interiors of buildings to light and air. These characteristics, and the discipline imposed by post-1918 economic stringency, created what the historian Henry-Russell Hitchcock called, in an introduction to the first exhibition celebrating modern architecture's maturity (held at the Museum of Modern Art, New York, in 1932), the International Style. This development was reinforced by two events: a series of exhibitions at which architects from different countries saw and were influenced by each other's experiments, and the formation of an international architectural organization through which ideas could be exchanged and mutual support enjoyed.

The pioneer among these exhibitions was that at Stockholm in 1930. Its significance was that it provided the first opportunity to explore an environment created wholly by modern buildings; they had previously been experienced only as

Some Twentieth Century Architectural Developments

single structures against an alien background. The Stockholm buildings, designed by Gunnar Asplund, had a charm and elegance that contradicted the impression gained elsewhere that modern architecture was always heavy and inhuman. The next influential exhibition, held in Paris in 1937, was international like its great predecessors of 1867 and 1889, and, in fact, occupied the same site. Here the international style showed itself as a mature, Europe-wide movement. After World War II more such exhibitions followed—at Brussels in 1958, at Montreal in 1967 and at Osaka, Japan, in 1970—for by this time the movement was firmly established in the Americas and Japan as well as in Europe.

The international organization was the Congrés Internationaux d'Architecture Moderne, known as CIAM. At its meetings, the leading European architects formulated their beliefs and set them out in a series of manifestos. Founded in Switzerland in 1928, the organization lasted until 1959 and concerned itself especially with planning and the social role of architecture. During the period of CIAM's greatest influence, in the 1930s, among its members were most of the great architects of the day, including Walter Gropius, Le Corbusier and Alvar Aalto. The secretary was Sigfried Giedion, the Swiss art historian.

Until the 1930s, Germany was the main centre of the new architecture because of the presence there of another unifying institution, and one that produced designs as well as ideas. This was the Bauhaus, a college of design, first established at Weimar, where the old Arts and Crafts school had been refounded under Van de Velde, and again (in 1919) under Walter Gropius. It was Gropius who gave the Bauhaus its unique character, associating its work with the recently arrived machine age and with the needs of standardization and the mass-production of components. After the Bauhaus had moved to Dessau in 1925, where it inhabited a range of steel, glass and concrete buildings designed by its staff and students, Gropius recruited teachers from all over Europe and thus gave it an even wider international influence.

The Bauhaus was soon, however, persecuted by the Nazi régime, which disliked all forms of internationalism, and after being briefly in the charge of another leading German architect, Mies van der Rohe, closed in 1933. Paradoxically, this increased its influence, because many of its members fled, some to Britain and then on to America (like Gropius, Moholy Nagy and Marcel Breuer), or direct to America like Mies van der Rohe. Other German architects, like Erich Mendelsohn, did the same. The gospel the Nazis had tried to suppress now had prophets on both sides of the Atlantic, and the United States suddenly became a place of remarkable architectural energy.

In the years after 1945 the emphasis was on town-planning and housing, and in most countries also on legislation to control building in the public interest, in which activities Britain set the lead. This was the era of new towns, vast housing estates and attempts—too often abortive—to gear building programmes both to social needs and to industrialized systems and techniques. It was also the era of population explosions and the comprehensive redevelopment of town centres by property companies, for whom social priorities were irrelevant, resulting in the disruption, functionally and visually, of their age-old pattern.

In matters of architectural style, it became less a question of conflict between period revival and modern design than between buildings designed for effect and those that aimed at the creation of a modern vernacular and a humane and harmonious environment.

The modern movement in the Netherlands

THE MODERN MOVEMENT in Dutch architecture is usually considered as a dual development represented by the romantic school of Amsterdam and the rational approach of Rotterdam. Both owed a common debt to the architect–theorist H. P. Berlage, and to some extent both approaches involved an overlap of ideas and personalities. However, the distinction is a useful one when examining the work of the so-called Amsterdam School of designers, which pays lip-service to the 19th-century English Arts and Crafts movement, and the work of Rotterdam architects, which relates much more closely to the notions of the *De Stijl* group (1917–31). The Amsterdam School, through M. de Klerk, P. Kramer and F. Staal, was principally concerned with an ambitiously modelled and decorated architecture, often in brick. The success of this approach was enhanced by a vast house-building programme in the Amsterdam suburbs.

In Belgium, the modern movement is less easily defined. There was no cohesive development of ideas. Originality and invention in terms of architecture were shown in the work of those architects who saw their opportunities in following Horta's and Van de Velde's ideas, or in keeping in close touch with developments in neighbouring countries. Antoine Pompe, for example, was an important eclectic modernist, trained in Germany, having an admiration for English domestic design and pursuing an idiosyncratic but personally brilliant course. Victor Bourgeois, with his estate La Cité Moderne at Berchem-St-Agathe, built between 1922 and 1925, was the leading exponent of continental modernism.

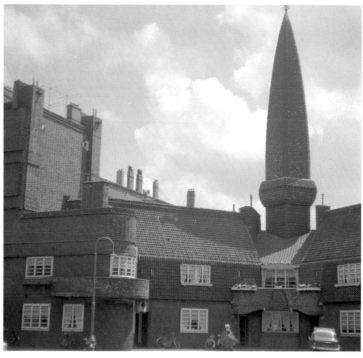

Michel de Klerk's Eigenhaard housing in Amsterdam is one of the most unusual estates in Europe. Built between 1913 and 1921, it is the prime example of the Amsterdam School of architects, with its mixture of undulating surfaces, decorative brickwork and sexual symbolism.

The Schröder-Schräder House in Utrecht (right) was designed by Gerrit Rietveld and Mrs Schröder-Schräder in 1924. Arguably the most modern house in Europe at the time it was erected, the Schröder house exhibits the principles of the De Stijl theory of art and architecture with its interpenetration of planes, recessions and colours. Clearly—apart from its logical planning—it was to be viewed as three-dimensional sculptural architecture. It has recently been restored.

1 *The Kiefhoek Estate*
2 *Outline of earlier houses surrounding Oud's estate*

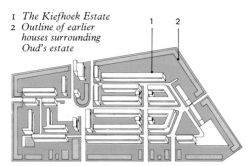

The Kiefhoek Housing Estate in Rotterdam was designed by J. J. P. Oud in 1925. As City Architect to Rotterdam in the early 1920s, Oud was a committed "modern" architect in a unique position. Not only was he able to commission work but he was also able to pursue his own ideas for a rationally based architecture.

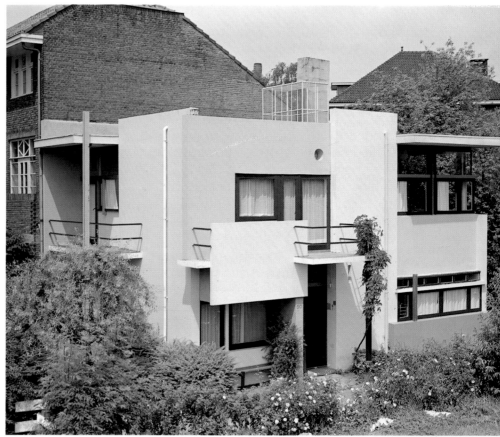

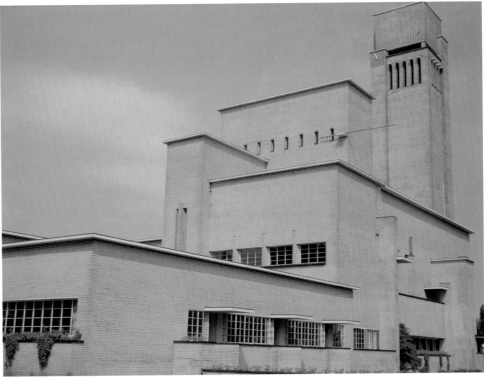

The Town Hall at Hilversum (above), built in 1930, is Willem Dudok's best-known building. Dudok was an individualist who pursued a middle-of-the-road line between the romantic ideas of Amsterdam and the rational notions of De Stijl. His aesthetic ideas were based on the use of plain surfaces of brickwork built up into cubic masses relieved by the occasional window opening. Admired by the British, plagiarizations of his work can be found in many English cities. Die-hard modernists on the Continent, however, felt his work compromised the "new architecture".

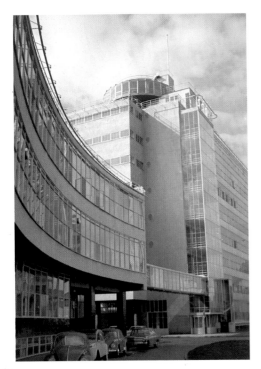

The Van Nelle Factory in Rotterdam (above) was a collaborative project by J. A. Brinckman, L. C. van der Vlugt and Mart Stam. It was built between 1927 and 1930 and became a major attraction for architects visiting the Netherlands in the 1930s, particularly the younger English modernists.

Aldo van Eyck's orphanage in Amsterdam (right) was built in 1960–1. Of the post-war architects working in the Netherlands, Aldo van Eyck, Bakema and Herzberger have produced the best work. Van Eyck's reputation as an original designer was enhanced by this low-profile brick-built orphanage on a site in the Amsterdam suburbs. It has had an influence on school buildings throughout the world.

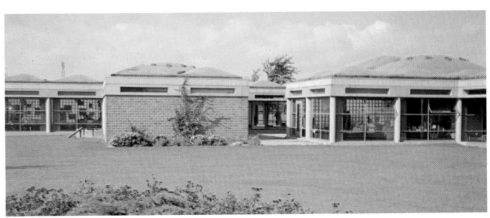

Bloemenwerf House at Uccle, near Brussels, built 1895–6, was the first house which Henri van de Velde designed; it was built for his own family use. This house, with its exaggerated gables and eaves and boldly striped gable ends heralded Art Nouveau. Apart from the gables, the most interesting feature is the spacious, central two-storey hall with window-like openings set between it and some of the rooms. The influence here is clearly that of the English Arts and Crafts movement.

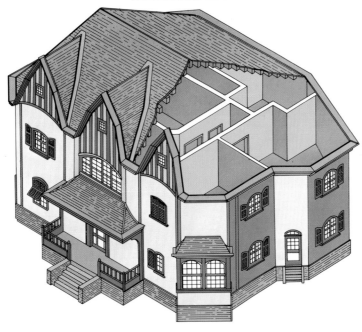

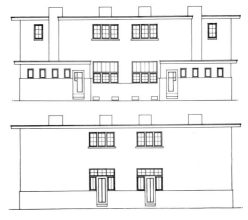

The Cité Moderne at Berchem-St-Agathe, Brussels (above), 1922–5, one of the first flat-roofed concrete housing estates in Europe, was designed by Belgian architect Victor Bourgeois. The layout was based to a large extent on the English garden city ideas, but the grouping and elevation treatment was original and exploratory.

Germany, centre of the new architecture

GERMANY'S IMPORTANCE in establishing the framework of what, in the 1920s, became known as the international functionalist "modern" architecture is well known. The continuity of ideas about architecture from the theoretical point of view, as well as the practical, is more clearly seen in Germany than in any other country. The search for a "new architecture" of the 20th century began with Jugendstil architects such as August Endell and the architect–historian Hermann Muthesius, and proceeded in the first decade of this century via Poelzig and such expatriates as Van de Velde and Olbrich. Through the activities first of the German Werkbund and then later the Bauhaus, the identity of a new architecture emerged; it was supported by the visionary ideas of the post-Great War Expressionists and the architect–planners who constructed a new, practical and efficient Germany after revaluation in 1923.

Le Corbusier's influence, however, should not be underestimated during the latter part of the 1920s; his was a two-way involvement. He had learned much from an early visit to Germany, when he had met Behrens, Gropius and Mies van der Rohe; he also built (with his cousin Pierre) two buildings at the 1927 Stuttgart Weissenhof-siedlung Exhibition. This exhibition was the testbed for the "new architecture"—after it, the success of the modern movement was assured in Germany. Many English critics who at the time disliked the "new architecture" pointedly dismissed it all as *Modernismus*, implying its Germanness. Hitler disliked it even more and by 1933 had stamped it out.

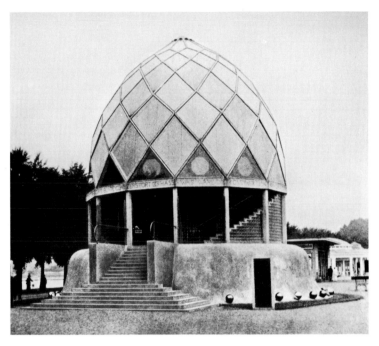

The Glass Pavilion of the 1914 Werkbund Exhibition in Cologne. This glass-faceted "crystal" structure designed by Bruno Taut was his prototype for a series of projects based on the Glass Architecture ideas of the Expressionist poet Paul Scheerbart.

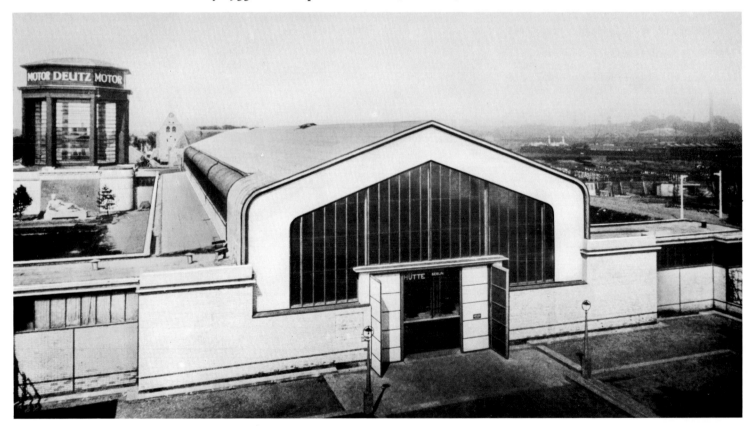

The Model Factory was designed by Walter Gropius and Adolf Meyer for the German Werkbund in 1914. It has been described as the first "functional" building of the 20th century; the plan was laid out with areas clearly defined for functional use, including an administrative block for the white-collar workers, separated by a courtyard from the blue-collar workers' machine hall. The alien Neo-Classical Deutz pavilion which is seen to the left of the picture, was merely an advertising symbol.

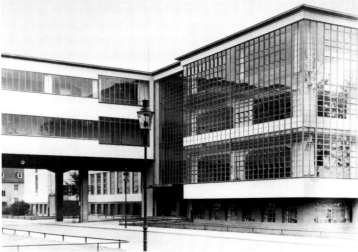

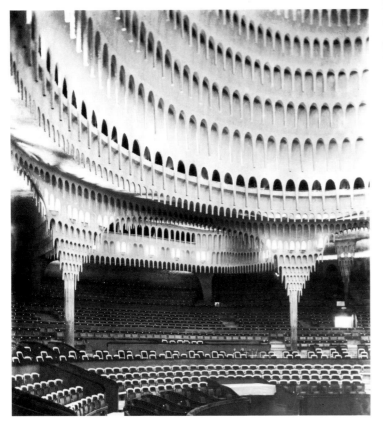

The **Bauhaus**—created in 1919 by Walter Gropius—moved from its first home in Weimar to these new premises in Dessau in 1925; the main entrance (above) has the glazed workshop block on its right. The diagram (below) shows the competent grouping of the irregular blocks.

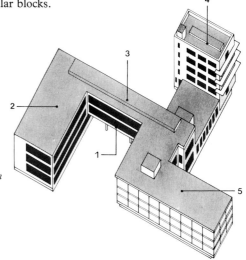

1 *Overhead bridge with entrance below*
2 *Teaching block*
3 *Administration offices*
4 *Student accommodation*
5 *Workshops*

The **Grosses Schauspielhaus** in Berlin (above) was designed by Hans Poelzig in 1919. The theatre held 5,000 people in a vast circular auditorium created from an existing circus building.

Walter Gropius's own house at Dessau (below), 1925–6, was one of a group of four houses designed for the teaching staff at the Bauhaus. It is L shaped and built in concrete blocks in a series of cubes, with cellular subdivisions within the house. It shows Gropius's interest in standardization.

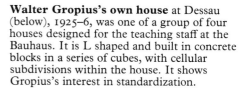

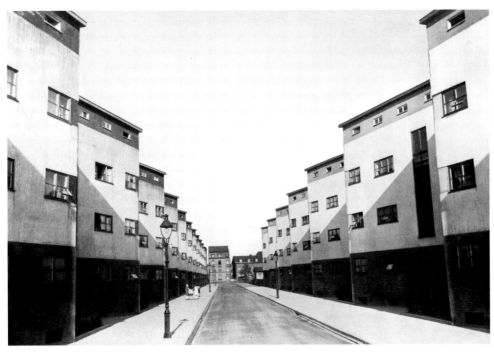

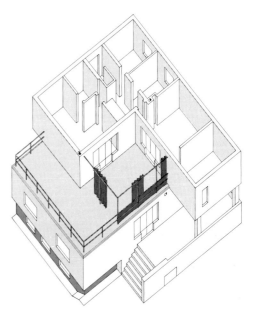

The **Bruchfeldstrasse Estate** at Frankfurt am Main was designed by Ernst May, who in 1925 was given unprecedented responsibilities by Frankfurt council to renew, and extend, the city as an expression of the "new architecture". Emphasis was placed on mass housing and the creation of modern utilitarian estates.

Germany, Expressionism and Rationalism

BEFORE THE REPRESSIVE régime of the Third Reich took hold in Germany, and creative work of the so-called "modern" architects and artists became unacceptable, the modern style that had emerged had two main components: the Expressionistic, or visionary, and the Rational bases of design. For many years they were inextricably mixed. Some architects, like Scharoun and Häring, developed their version of Rational architecture along Expressionist lines; others, such as Ludwig Mies van der Rohe and Walter Gropius, remained objective. This development prevailed after 1945, when German architects were able to pick up from where they left off in the pre-Hitler era. The post-war architects, including Eiermann, Kramer, Böhm and Gutbrod, together with those who had remained in Germany during the war years, re-established the tenets of the old modern movement. A few—notably Frei Otto and Oswald Ungers—pursued new avenues.

The post-war building programme was immense and many interesting school, theatre, recreation and civic buildings were erected by public authority architects. Most of these were ideologically based on the notions developed in the pioneer years in Germany from 1908 to 1933.

With the strength of modern architecture firmly established in the early 1930s, those German architects who had helped to create it escaped to other parts of the world. German architecture was transferred literally to other countries—via Gropius, Breuer, Mies van der Rohe and Erich Mendelsohn to England and then the United States; by Taut to Japan and Turkey. Today, probably the most Germanically inspired city in the world is Chicago, where Mies van der Rohe exerted his strongest influence.

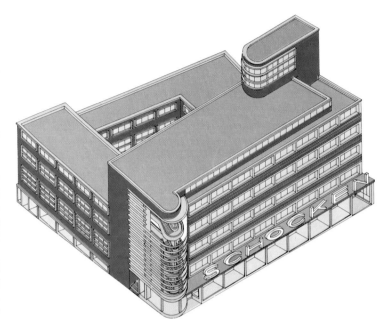

The Schocken Department Store in Stuttgart, 1926, was the best known of Erich Mendelsohn's numerous well-designed store buildings. The five-storey façade was banded horizontally with windows and panels, providing an emphatic contrast to the fully glazed curved vertical staircase tower. It has been a prototype for many, later, European store buildings.

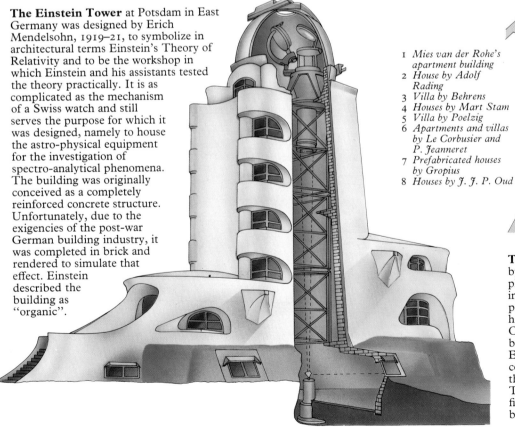

The Einstein Tower at Potsdam in East Germany was designed by Erich Mendelsohn, 1919–21, to symbolize in architectural terms Einstein's Theory of Relativity and to be the workshop in which Einstein and his assistants tested the theory practically. It is as complicated as the mechanism of a Swiss watch and still serves the purpose for which it was designed, namely to house the astro-physical equipment for the investigation of spectro-analytical phenomena. The building was originally conceived as a completely reinforced concrete structure. Unfortunately, due to the exigencies of the post-war German building industry, it was completed in brick and rendered to simulate that effect. Einstein described the building as "organic".

1 *Mies van der Rohe's apartment building*
2 *House by Adolf Rading*
3 *Villa by Behrens*
4 *Houses by Mart Stam*
5 *Villa by Poelzig*
6 *Apartments and villas by Le Corbusier and P. Jeanneret*
7 *Prefabricated houses by Gropius*
8 *Houses by J. J. P. Oud*

The Weissenhof Estate at Stuttgart (above) by Mies van der Rohe, architect and planner, and others, was part of a second influential exhibition of architecture promoted by the German Werkbund and held in Stuttgart in 1927; the first was held in Cologne in 1914. Under Mies's direction it brought together many of the leading European architects in order to present a consistent estate of model houses based on the principles of the "new architecture". The result was a predominantly white-finished cube form and flat-roofed group of buildings; the first such estate in the world.

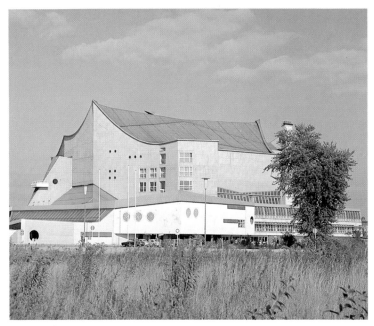

The Philharmonic Hall in Berlin, Hans Scharoun's best-known architectural work, was completed in 1963, towards the end of his career. It is a highly mature work, derived to a large extent from his earlier projects for theatres at Kassel and Mannheim. It also owes much to Scharoun's ideas on "organic functionalism". The Philharmonic Hall acts as the permanent home of the famous Berlin Philharmonic Orchestra.

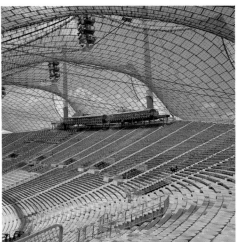

The Olympic Games Tent in Munich (left and below) was designed for the 1972 Olympics by Frei Otto. The various "tent" and "umbrella" roofs erected at Munich were the culmination of Otto's many years' experience. Earlier examples had indicated the potential of such temporary but economical large-span structures. But at Munich the scale was tremendous, involving the erection and linking of varied amoeba-shaped tents: the major areas covered included the main stadium, on one side only, linked to the arena and the swimming area, both wholly covered. The roof covering the main stadium consisted of a PVC-coated polyester fabric suspended on hangers independent of the cable net. The supporting masts held the main cables in tension, thus providing the necessary support for the hanging roof areas.

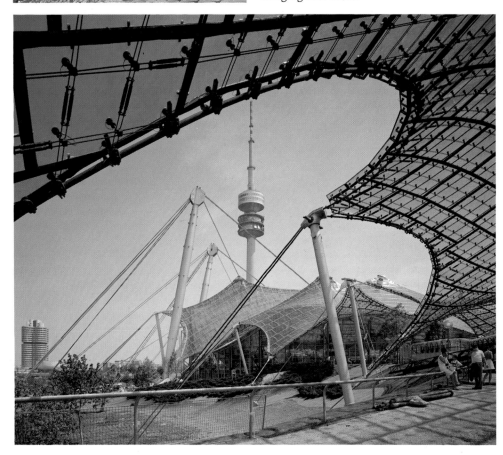

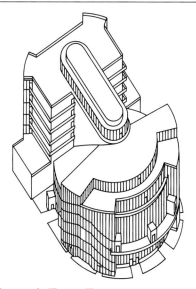

GROPIUS'S TOTAL THEATRE PROJECT
Gropius's "theatre of totality" was designed, in 1926, in response to the idea that Theatre itself was a political, and therefore participatory, act. Gropius attempted to meet this demand by technical means as well as aesthetic; the theatre had an inbuilt flexibility that allowed three acting areas as well as film projection on the ceiling and walls to give the audience the illusion of total involvement.

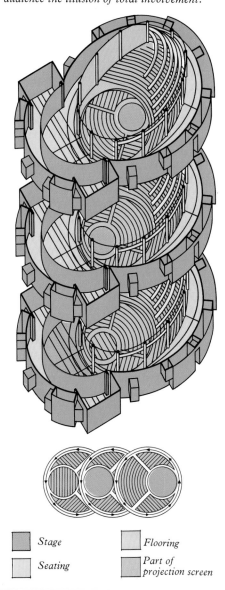

Stage	Flooring
Seating	Part of projection screen

France, Auguste Perret and Le Corbusier

FRANCE'S REPUTATION in the field of modern architecture rests almost wholly on two men—Auguste Perret and Le Corbusier. Perret approached architecture as a constructor. He used the classical elements like columns and beams and his achievement was to combine classical discipline with a vigorous use of reinforced concrete, a material he pioneered in several buildings in or near Paris and, after World War II, in the reconstruction of Le Havre.

Le Corbusier, born Charles Edouard Jeanneret, was Swiss by origin. Throughout his career he worked in France, where he was only belatedly honoured and little employed. He was a challenging polemicist and the author of controversial books on architecture and town-planning; an abstract artist as well as a constructor.

His early works, apart from the epoch-making Pavillon de l'Esprit Nouveau at the Paris Exhibition of Decorative Arts in 1925, were mostly houses. In them Le Corbusier fully exploited the qualities of reinforced concrete and incorporated the principles that were to be the basis of all his work, and of the new architecture itself, until his more monumental buildings transferred the emphasis to other, more sculptural, uses of concrete in the 1950s. These principles are summarized in his famous *Five Points of a New Architecture*, enunciated in 1925: columns to lift the building off the ground; the flat roof with a garden; the free plan; the long window; and the free façade with floors and walls extending beyond the supporting columns.

Le Corbusier's extension of these into principles of living in, and laying out, cities, was illustrated in his Unité d'Habitation built at Marseilles in 1952, as well as his other housing blocks in similar style. Later he surprised the world with less didactic and more poetic buildings including his chapel at Ronchamp (1955) and his majestic group comprising the capitol at Chandigarh, India, which was completed in 1957. His vigorous way of handling concrete reached a climax in his monastery of La Tourette (1959) in central France.

Le Corbusier, until the end of his life, was architect, prophet and teacher, and his visits to Brazil, North Africa and Japan, as well as to India, left their mark on the changing architecture of those countries.

Running the width of the block are 337 two-level apartments of 23 types, designed to accommodate tenants from one person to a family of ten. These domestic units fit into the main structure like drawers into a chest, allowing each apartment large windows and double balconies.

The wall of the south façade, like the east and west, is enlivened by the pattern of light and dark rectangles created by the alternating balconies. Their internal walls are brightly painted, contrasting with the raw concrete of the building fabric. The north wall is windowless against the erosive force of the mistral.

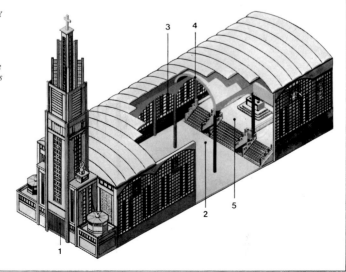

NOTRE DAME AT LE RAINCY
This church, near Paris, was built between 1922 and 1925 by Auguste Perret. Its columns, vaults and tracery are the equivalent in concrete of their medieval predecessors in stone. Reinforced concrete makes buttressing and load-bearing walls unnecessary. The walls comprising the north, the bowed east, and the south façades are of pre-cast concrete with variously shaped openings filled in with coloured glass and small painted panels.

1 *Main entrance*
2 *Nave*
3 *Transverse barrel vault*
4 *Longitudinal barrel vault*
5 *Chancel*

Concrete pilotis containing drainage pipes support the building, creating space for a car park beneath. Heating and power installations are placed above.

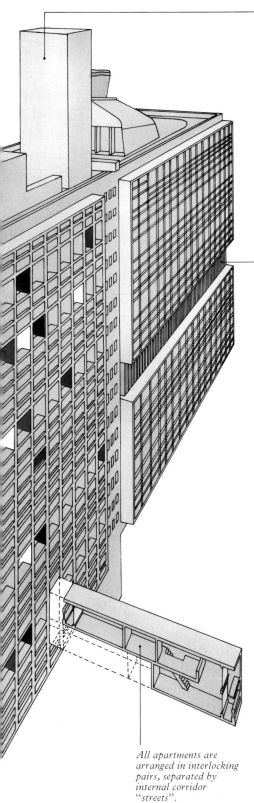

A central building containing the elevator shaft emerges on the roof; to the left is a ventilator shaft. A 300-metre running track loops around the edge of the roof with a swimming pool, gymnasium, theatre, nursery school and other facilities in the middle.

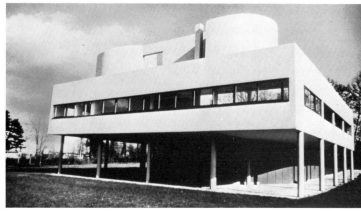

The seventh and eighth floors contain a communal centre, with shops, a post office, restaurants, studios, offices and workshops. Elsewhere in the building is a communal laundry. These are designed to make the building a self-contained social community.

The Villa Savoie at Poissy (above and right), built between 1929 and 1931, is one of Le Corbusier's most classic and influential buildings, embodying the principles set out in the architect's manifesto, *Five Points of a New Architecture*: raised on pilotis (1), it is designed on a free plan, with a free façade, almost continuous ribbon windows (2) and a roof garden with a solarium (3). On the first floor, the glass-walled living area (4) wraps in an L shape around a terrace (5). From ground to roof level winds an entrance ramp (6).

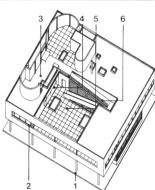

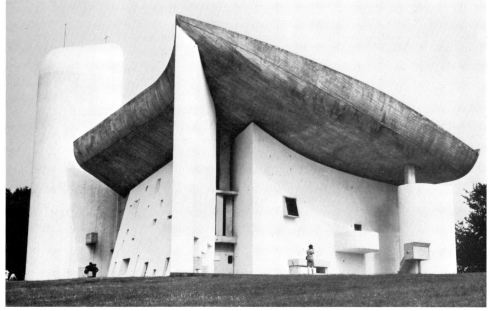

All apartments are arranged in interlocking pairs, separated by internal corridor "streets".

The Unité d'Habitation at Marseilles was built by Le Corbusier between 1947 and 1952. It was designed as one unit of a new-type city and contains a street of shops and social and service accommodation of various kinds, as well as two-level apartments to house 1,600 people. It is poised on thick columns, or pilotis. Use was made in the design of the building of the "modulor"—a system of fundamental dimensions, based on the measurements of the human body, designed by Le Corbusier to create harmonious proportions.

Notre Dame du Haut at Ronchamp (above and right). The pilgrimage chapel, finished in 1955, is the most personal of Le Corbusier's works; wholly original, but not wilfully so since every form and spatial effect is related to the architect's concentrated attempt to achieve a sense of religious dignity and purpose. The design solves the besetting problem of pilgrimage churches—the accommodation of a large but only occasional congregation—by grouping an altar and pulpit outside (1) and providing an outdoor nave for about 12,000 pilgrims. Within the main building, the small chapel (2) seats only 50. It is lit by irregular, wedge-shaped windows of varying size filled with coloured glass which allow diffused light to reflect on their sides. The roof is slightly raised on metal supports, creating a thin band of daylight between it and the top of the wall. Light filters through the rounded half-domed towers (3) and falls on the altars of the chapels below.

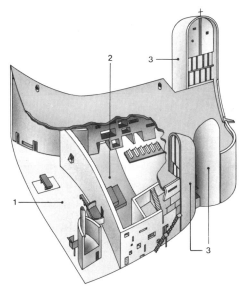

Italy's new generation of architects

ITALY WAS SHOWING every sign of making an interesting contribution to modern architecture when progress was interrupted by the Fascist régime, which demanded buildings that reflected its own pomposity and supported its claim to be a reincarnation of the Roman Empire. After 1945 a new generation of Italian architects, especially those working in Milan, gave Italy a fresh start and a reputation for buildings in which the age-old Italian tradition of fine craftsmanship was combined with the adventurous use of new materials. Then, as in recent times, however, Italian architecture suffered, when compared with that in other European countries, from Italy's failure to give building programmes much relationship to social priorities.

There was also a tendency towards wilful departures from orthodoxy. This was exemplified in the 1960s by the Neo-Liberty movement, an attempt to revive a fashion of half a century before, related to Art Nouveau and called in Italy the *Stile Liberty* after the London department store from which artistic fabrics and furnishing were then imported. An unorthodox approach is also evident in one of the most prominent buildings in Milan, the much-discussed Torre Velasca with its strange oversailing upper storeys. It was designed in 1957 by an influential group of architects known as BBPR, after its partners, Banfi, who had been killed in the war, Belgiojoso, Peressutti and Rogers, which exercised a degree of intellectual leadership through Ernesto Rogers's writings and his participation in CIAM, Congrès Internationaux d'Architecture Moderne.

Gio Ponti was another outstanding architect whose tall Pirelli building (1960) is one of the most elegant of its kind in Europe. But the most notable designer in Italy during the post-war years was Pier Luigi Nervi, an engineer. He did more than anyone in the world, except Le Corbusier and, perhaps, the Spanish–Mexican Felix Candela, to reveal the aesthetic potentialities, as distinct from the mere structural convenience, of reinforced concrete. Nervi's speciality was roofing-in great spaces with domes displaying their radiating concrete ribs. He built aircraft hangars, exhibition buildings and two spectacular sports halls for the Olympic Games held in Rome in 1960.

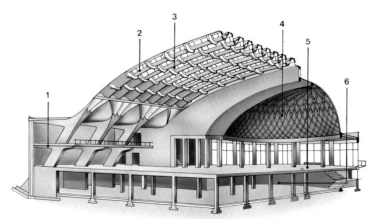

The Exhibition hall at Turin was designed by Pier Luigi Nervi in 1947 and covers an enormous area 312 ft by 250 ft. It is spanned by a large vault, made up from pre-cast, reinforced concrete sections incorporating glass panels as a light source.

1 Gallery
2 Pre-cast sections
3 Glass panels
4 Semicircular dome
5 Exhibition hall
6 Basement

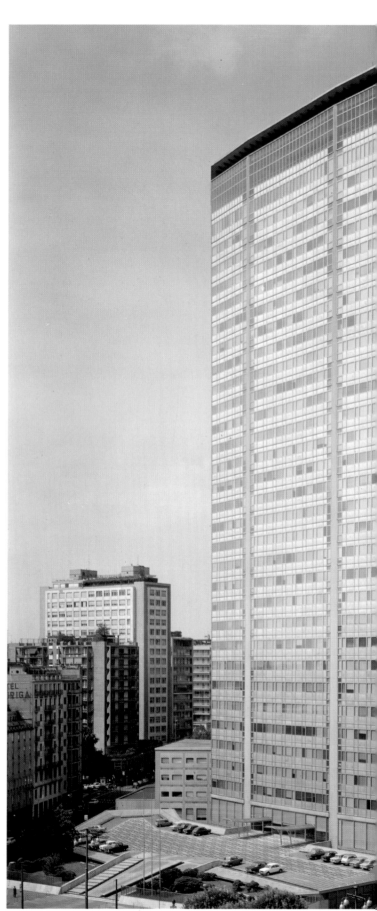

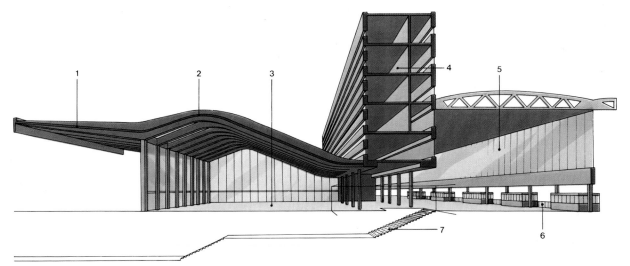

The Railway Terminus at Rome is a long, low structure of reinforced concrete and aluminium, built between 1947 and 1951 by Montuori and Associates. Behind the main concourse is a block of offices and shops and a gallery overlooking the platforms below

1 *Protective canopy*
2 *Concrete roof*
3 *Main concourse*
4 *Offices and shops*
5 *Gallery over platforms*
6 *Entrance to platforms*
7 *Stairs to subway*

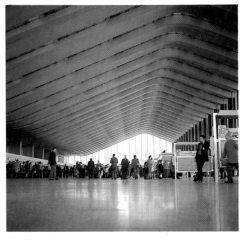

The main concourse of the Railway Terminus at Rome (above) is covered by a flowing concrete roof, which extends outside to form a canopy over the entrance. The roof is supported on multiple granite-faced pillars and decorated inside with white marble mosaic.

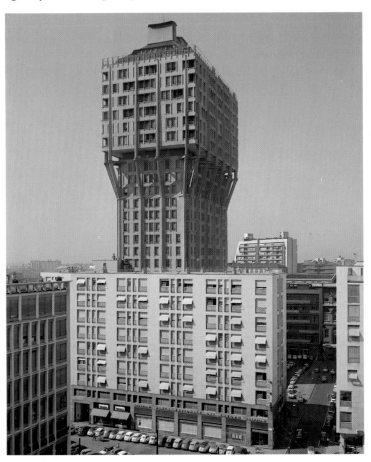

The Torre Velasca (left) thrusts up from the crowded streets of Milan's cathedral district. This much-discussed building with its strange oversailing upper storeys, has irregularly spaced windows and wide expanses of unglazed wall. Built in 1957 by BBPR, a leading Italian architectural group, it is related to the Neo-Liberty style, which echoed the Art Nouveau movement of the 19th century.

The Pirelli Building (left), 407 ft high, dominates the commercial centre of Milan. It was built by Gio Ponti between 1956 and 1960. Its slenderness is accentuated by the tapering of the side walls at either end of the building. Storey-high windows allow maximum light to penetrate into the open-plan offices within. Pier Luigi Nervi was the engineer.

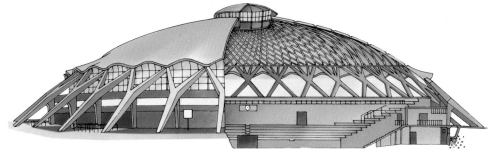

The Palazzetto dello Sport is the smaller of two sports halls built by Nervi and Vitellozzi for the 1960 Olympic Games held in Rome. Its dome rests on 36 Y-shaped concrete struts, which transmit the thrust to an underground concrete ring.

Switzerland, the respectable standard

SWITZERLAND, LIKE the Scandinavian countries, is more remarkable for the respectable standard of most of its new buildings than for its memorable or exciting monuments. The most progressive and interesting post-1918 buildings were schools and churches. In fact, Switzerland has more good modern churches than any other country except, perhaps, Germany. The earliest, and still one of the most impressive, was St Anthony's, Basel, designed by Karl Moser in 1927. It was followed by other churches by the same architect and by churches designed in a similar austere but dignified style by Hermann Baur, Ernst Gisel, Fritz Metzger and others.

Karl Moser was a professor of architecture at the University of Zürich, where he taught many of the best architects of the next generation. He was succeeded by O. R. Salvisberg. The presence in Zürich of Moser and Salvisberg and of many architects influenced by CIAM, and of a similar group in Basel, including Hannes Meyer (Gropius's successor as the head of the Bauhaus), was undoubtedly responsible for the architecture of German Switzerland being far more advanced than that of the French or Italian cantons. In 1955, Max Bill, a Swiss architect who was also associated with the Bauhaus and with CIAM, became the head of the influential and strictly puritanical school of design at Ulm, Germany.

Besides schools and churches, Switzerland was notable for hospitals and swimming pools—outstanding buildings were designed by Alfred Roth and the firm of Steiger, Moser and Haefeli—as well as, especially after 1945, for housing that also made a constructive contribution to town design. Typical of the Swiss talent for the soberly experimental is the Halen housing estate (1957), near Berne, designed by a group called Atelier 5.

Switzerland can claim one true pioneer in the person of Robert Maillart, the designer of bridges in reinforced concrete which astonished the world by their slenderness, tautness and grace long before such qualities had become associated with this new material. Among Maillart's many remarkable bridges, in which arch and roadway are one structural unit, a principle developed by him, are the Tavanasa Bridge over the Rhine at Grisons (which was built as early as 1905 and destroyed by a landslide in 1927), the more ambitious Salginatobel Bridge near Schiers (1930), with a span of 300 ft, and the Rossgraben, near Schwarzenberg (1932). Maillart also designed a dramatic barrel-vaulted exhibition pavilion at Zürich in 1939.

The Church of St Anthony at Basel (below), designed by Karl Moser in 1927, rekindled Swiss interest in church-building. Echoes of Auguste Perret's church at Le Raincy, finished two years earlier, are found in the exclusive use of reinforced concrete and the long stretches of glass walls. Here, however, the effect is altogether more massive and the scale more imposing. The square tower is over 180 ft tall.

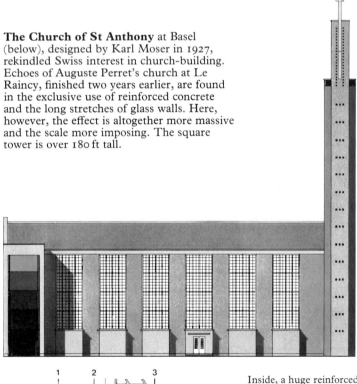

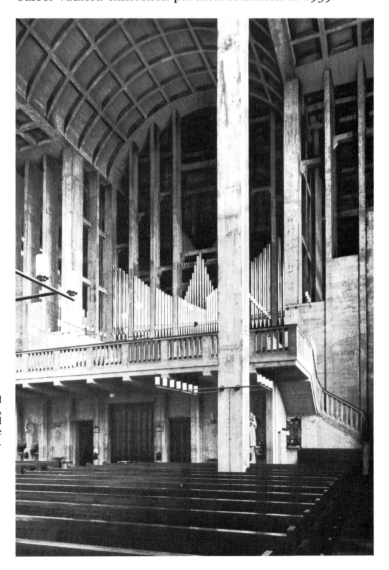

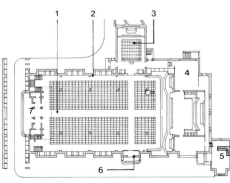

Inside, a huge reinforced concrete barrel-vault, flanked by flat-ceilinged aisles, rests on square concrete piers.

Planned around a wide, rectangular nave (1) with narrow side aisles (2) are a baptistry (3), vestry (4) and tower (5). There is a lateral porch (6) and a main entrance (7).

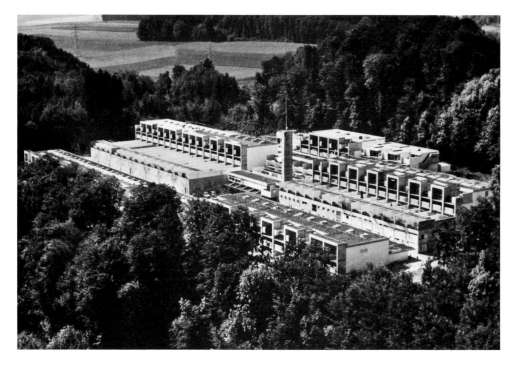

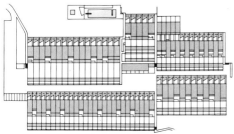

The Halen Estate (left), secluded in the beautiful countryside outside Berne, was built between 1957 and 1961 by a group of young architects called Atelier 5. It is constructed from standardized concrete units. Planned to spread over a gentle, southern-facing slope are 79 homes, sharing the communal facilities of swimming pool, restaurant, village square, heating plant and garage. The terraced houses are of two types: the one-and-a-half-roomed individual dwelling and the multiroomed family house. They fit together neatly without intruding on each other's privacy. Each house has its own private garden.

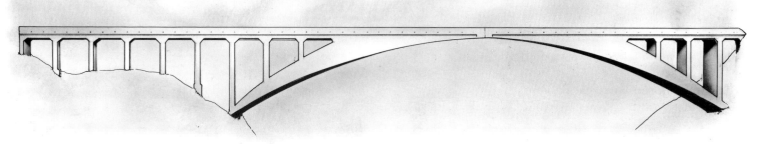

The Salginatobel Bridge (above) spans the Salgina gorge in one precise, elegant gesture. It was built in 1930 by the engineer Robert Maillart, who pioneered bridge-building in reinforced concrete. In Maillart's bridges, the traffic deck—usually a box girder—is an integral part of the structure instead of simply resting on it.

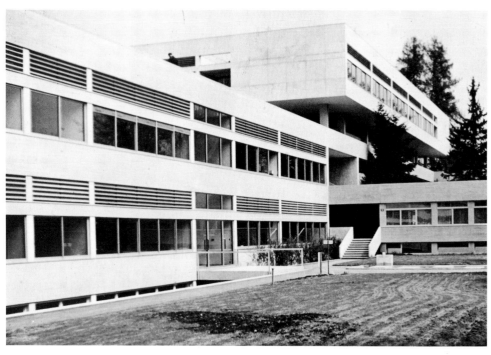

The Freudenberg School (right) at Zürich was built between 1958 and 1961 by Jacques Schader, who had to combine two different kinds of school on one limited, hilltop site. Five shallow rectangular or square buildings are massed together and interconnected with ramps and staircases. The buildings comprise a grammar school, commercial school, natural sciences building, gymnasium and assembly building with a theatre and dining-hall.

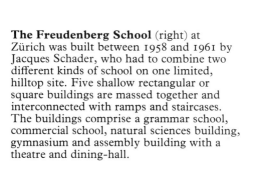

Scandinavia's particular achievement

THE CREATION OF A generally civilized standard of building, rather than sensational single monuments, and a concern for social priorities marked Scandinavia's particular architectural achievement after 1918. In those years, the northern countries set a lead to Europe in matters of housing —especially low-income housing—and in the planning of new communities within reach of the larger towns. While adapting their architecture to modern techniques, they continued to use traditional materials and to maintain traditional standards of craftsmanship, and there was therefore no abrupt change from old to new.

After the influential Stockholm Exhibition of 1930, Sweden produced a number of civic and public buildings that were admired throughout Europe for their freshness and sobriety and as prominent, but unpretentious, additions to the towns in which they stood. The architects of these buildings included Gunnar Asplund, the designer of Stockholm's city library (1928) and the Forest crematorium (1940), Sven Markelius, who designed Hälsingborg's concert hall (1932) and was also planner for the Stockholm region, and Sigurd Lewerentz and Peter Celsing, who specialized in the design of austere brick churches.

Housing in Sweden was notable, before and after World War II, for multistorey apartment buildings which yet preserved human qualities by good community planning and a sympathetic relationship to the landscape. Sweden built a number of successful satellite towns, of which the first was Vällingby, near Stockholm, begun in 1953 and planned by Markelius.

Denmark, too, acquired a reputation for housing and for educational and civic buildings of unassuming character, but with craftsmanlike attention to quality and detail. Leading architects included Kay Fisker and C. F. Møller, who were jointly responsible for Århus University, begun in 1931, the versatile Arne Jacobsen, who designed town halls at Århus (1937) and Søllerød (1942) and the SAS building at Copenhagen (1959)—which showed the direct influence, rare in Scandinavia, of modern American styles and techniques—and Jørn Utzon, who was responsible for much unusually sensitive housing until his career was distorted by his victory in the international competition for an opera house at Sydney in 1956.

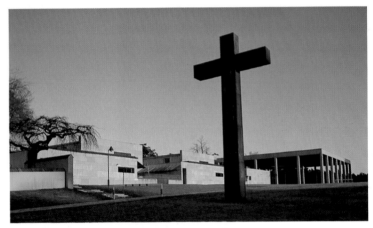

The Forest Crematorium at Stockholm, designed by Gunnar Asplund and built in 1940, is notable for its purity of form and sensitivity to the landscape. The existing site was improved by building up the hill on which the cross and chapels stand. A covered court in front of the main chapel can be used to provide extra congregational space when necessary, as the door between it and the chapel slides into the ground.

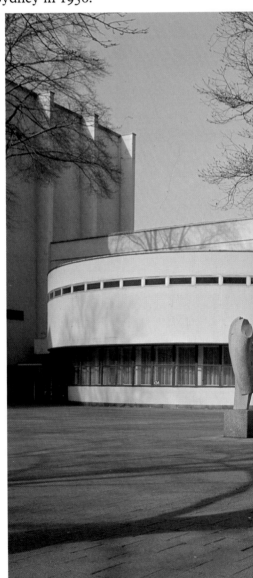

The Concert Hall at Hälsingborg was built by Sven Markelius in 1932. Sweden was commissioning civic buildings in the modern style at a time when, elsewhere in Europe, only private clients were so adventurous.

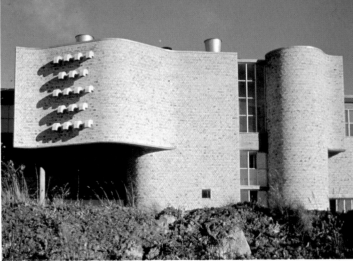

The cardboard factory at Fors in Sweden, a reinforced concrete and brick structure by Ralph Erskine, was built in 1953. The central, double-curving wall incorporates air-ducts, turned downwards against the snow, which remove excess condensation from within.

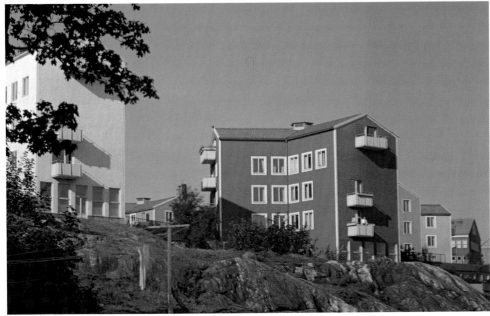

The Gröndal Estate outside Stockholm, built in 1947 to the design of Backström and Reinius, illustrates the careful study of form and landscaping typical of the best Scandinavian housing. The honeycomb lay-out (right) is built up from combinations of three-pointed "stars", each composed of three flats placed together.

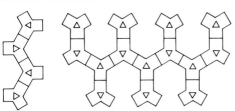

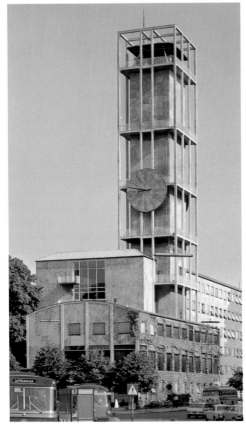

The Town Hall at Århus on the east coast of the Danish mainland, designed by Arne Jacobsen in 1937, draws some influence from the pioneering Swedish architect Gunnar Asplund.

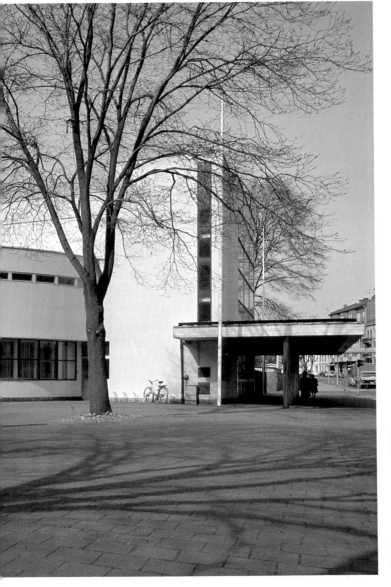

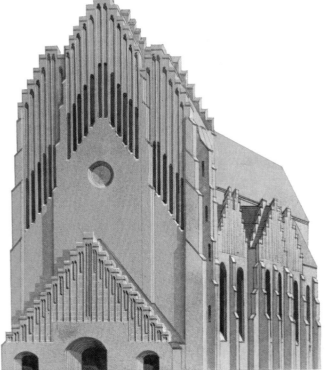

Grundtvig's Church in Copenhagen (above and right), with its organ-shaped façade, was designed by P. V. Jensen Klint in 1920. Built of brick, it is a modernized version of a style of church which was traditional in rural Denmark.

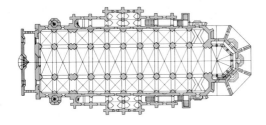

Finland, the inspiration of Alvar Aalto

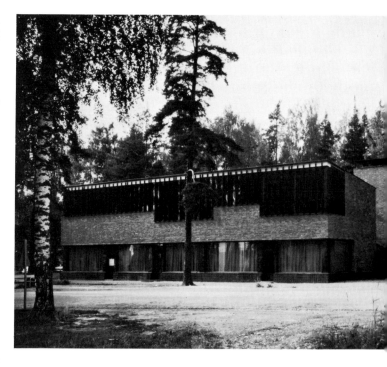

BETWEEN THE WARS, Finland was put on the architectural map of Europe by one man, Alvar Aalto, whose earliest buildings gave the first indication that something remarkable was happening in this remote northern country since, in 1904, Eliel Saarinen and his partners had won the competition for the Helsinki railway terminus with a design (not completed until 1914) that was far in advance of its time. For a generation after this, Finnish architecture was little more than an echo of the more conservative Swedish. A prominent example of this was J. S. Sirén's monumentally Neo-Classical parliament building at Helsinki, built in 1931.

But Aalto's first major buildings, his tuberculosis sanatorium at Paimio (1933) and his library at Viipuri (1935), offered a complete contrast: they were functional but humane; simplified to their bare bones, yet preserving a sensitive, even romantic, harmony with the landscape. They demonstrated, especially at Paimio, the spare elegance of which concrete construction was capable. These qualities were sustained in nearly all Aalto's later work, even when brick was preferred to concrete. Its affinity with the Finnish landscape, especially in such buildings as the civic centre at Säynätsalo (1952), was controlled by a

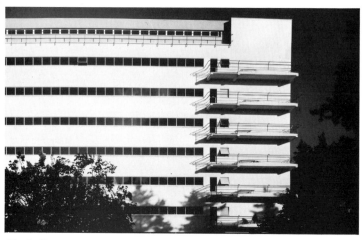

The Paimio Sanatorium (left), finished in 1933, is a reinforced concrete building by Alvar Aalto. Its wings radiating from the centre are angled according to the direction of the sunlight and view.

The Church at Vuoksenniska (below), in southeastern Finland, was built by Alvar Aalto in 1958, and is set among trees in an industrial area. The shape of the tower serves to identify the church in the distant view, which is crowded with factory chimneys. The interior of the church can be adapted, with the help of partitions, to congregations of different sizes.

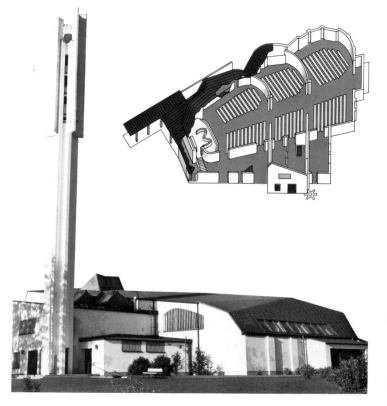

discipline not always possessed by his more romantic followers.

Aalto's furniture, based on new techniques of bending wood, also created world-wide interest when it was seen at the Finnish Pavilion at the 1937 Paris Exhibition—a building he himself designed and which revealed his talent for using timber freely and inventively. Although Aalto was the dominating figure, other architects who produced original work in Finland at this time were Erik Bryggman, who designed a chapel at Turku (1941), and P. E. Blomstedt, the designer of the Aulanko Hotel near Hämeenlinna, built in 1938.

After 1945, an alternative school of architecture arose, more rational and more closely related to contemporary work in post-war Europe and America. The initiators were Viljo Revell and Aulis Blomstedt. Leading architects since the 1950s have included Jorma Järvi, Kaija and Heikki Siren and Aarno Ruusuvuori. All are represented in one of the best-known Finnish post-war enterprises, the satellite town of Tapiola, west of Helsinki, which maintains the Scandinavian tradition of well-planned and sited housing.

The student restaurant of the Institute of Technology at Otaniemi, just outside Helsinki, was built by Kaija and Heikki Siren in 1952. Its interior (right) is typically expressive and vigorous in its use of wood.

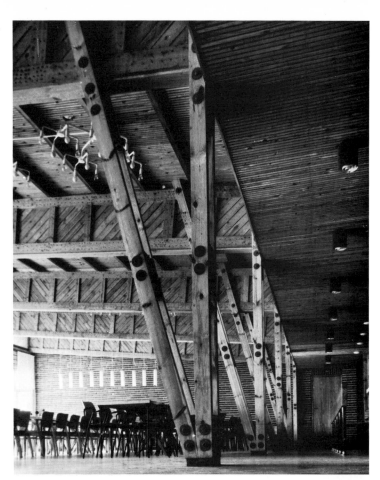

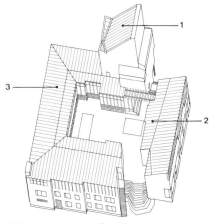

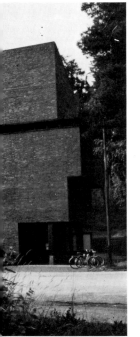

The Civic Centre at Säynätsalo (above and left), not far from Alvar Aalto's home town in central Finland, was designed by Aalto and built between 1950 and 1952. It serves a small, one-industry town and groups a council chamber (1), community library (2) and municipal offices (3) around a raised green courtyard. The buildings are of wood, copper and dark red brick.

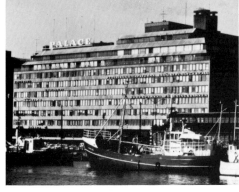

The Palace Hotel (above), which faces Helsinki's south harbour, was built by Viljo Revell in collaboration with Keijo Petäjä as the headquarters for the 1952 Olympic Games. Shops, offices and a restaurant are incorporated in this hotel building, which exemplifies the austerity of the post-war period and also the new emphasis on the rational initiated by Revell.

Housing at Tapiola. The satellite town of 17,000 inhabitants west of Helsinki was begun in 1952 and finished in 1969. Tapiola's original plan was by Aarne Ervi and most of the leading Finnish architects, except Alvar Aalto, contributed flats or houses. The town consists of three residential areas, made up of a mixture of terrace houses and blocks of flats (right) built to a fairly low overall density, in a wooded landscape. These neighbourhoods are grouped around an administrative and shopping centre, sited near a lake and a secondary school. One central power station supplies heat, water and electricity to the town.

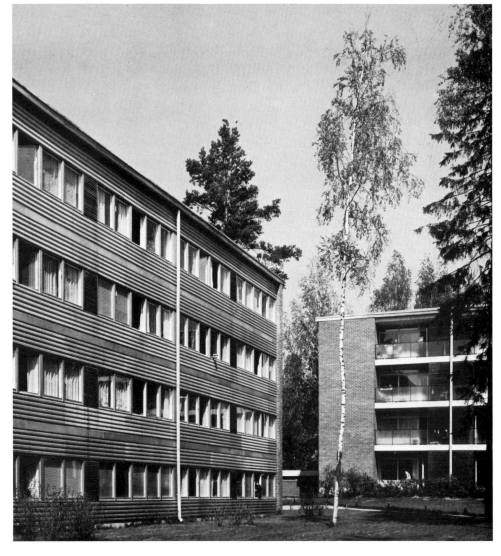

New building programmes in Britain

BRITAIN WAS SLOW to adopt the new architectural ideas current in Europe in spite of having been a pioneer of architectural change, and of new constructional techniques, in the previous century. In the 1920s and 1930s a few individuals became aware of what was happening overseas and began to experiment along similar lines, mostly with the support only of private clients. Notable among these architects were Wells Coates, Maxwell Fry, F. R. S. Yorke, Serge Chermayeff, the firm of Connell, Ward and Lucas and the engineer Sir Owen Williams. All but Williams were members of CIAM and the strongest European influence was that of Le Corbusier.

In 1930, Berthold Lubetkin, a Russian architect who had been working in Paris, came to England and formed a group with half a dozen newly qualified English architects. The group called itself Tecton and designed a number of distinguished buildings, notable for their strict geometrical discipline and their sophisticated use of reinforced concrete, in which they had the help of the engineer Ove Arup. Their work included several elegant zoo buildings, which did much to arouse public interest in modern architecture.

These rather tentative efforts were powerfully reinforced in the 1930s when a number of important German architects, including Gropius, Mendelsohn and Breuer, came to Britain as refugees from Nazi persecution. Although they were offered little chance to build in Britain and soon moved on to America, they brought an end to Britain's isolation, so that when civil building resumed after 1945 Britain was well equipped to answer the demands of post-war reconstruction with progressive architectural policies. British architects also had by then the benefit of relatively advanced town-planning legislation and controls.

Building programmes gave priority to housing and schools, the design of which was mostly in the hands of the large architectural offices built up by central or local government. The vast housing projects designed in official offices, like that of the London County Council, aroused world-wide interest; so did Britain's new towns, which were, however, although important as social experiments, conservative in their garden-city type of lay-out and their traditional architecture based on the two-storey brick and tile cottage. British school-building programmes led the world, especially in the use they made of mass-produced components and of prefabrication techniques.

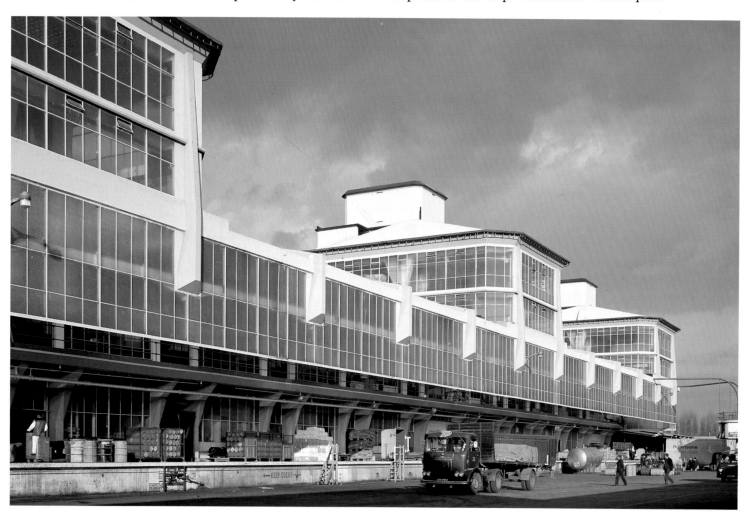

Boots Pharmaceutical Factory at Beeston, in Nottinghamshire, built between 1930 and 1932 by the engineer Sir Owen Williams, unites reinforced concrete and glass in a strictly functional structure. Concrete mushroom-pillars support concrete floors and glass curtain walls envelop the whole building; parts of the roof have thick glazed tiles. Loading bays with long ramps run the length of the north and south sides of the building. This engineer's buildings had an important influence on architects' work in Britain.

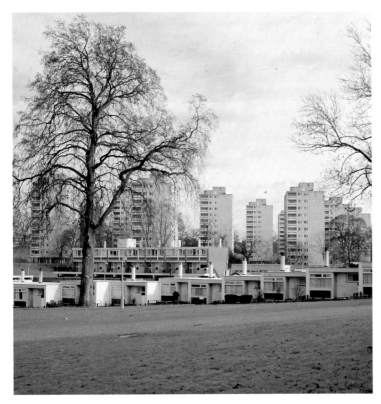

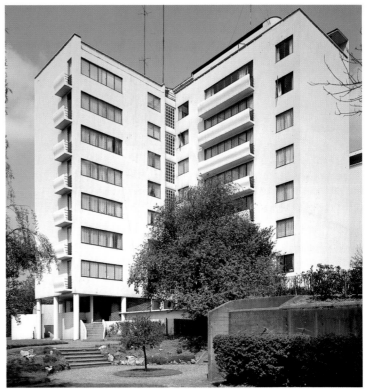

The Alton Estate at Roehampton, in London, houses some 9,500 people in an ambitious scheme by the architects of the London County Council, built between 1956 and 1960. Eleven-storey towers and slabs mingle with long four-storey buildings and terraced houses in 128 well-treed acres.

Highpoint I (above), a luxury apartment building at Highgate, London, built in 1933, typifies the early work of Tecton, the group of young English architects. The engineer was Ove Arup. An elegant eight-storey building raised on pilotis, it has a cruciform plan, designed so that each flat is separate and commands views through large windows with balconies. The ground floor (right) consists of a tea-room (1), maids' rooms (2), hall (3), small apartments (4), large apartment (5), stairs and lift (6) and porter's flat (7). Large and small apartments dovetail together on the upper floors. Highpoint II, added to the site in 1938, differs only slightly; its porch evoked surprise at this date by being supported by classical caryatids.

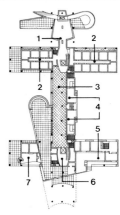

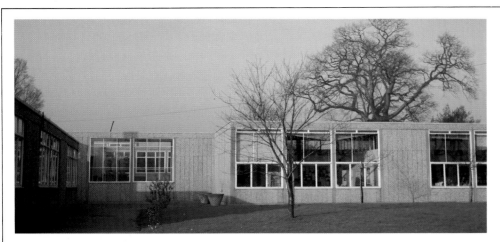

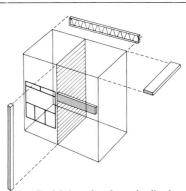

Prefabricated and standardized components are adaptable to the size and function of different schools.

THE HERTFORDSHIRE SCHOOLS

The British post-war school programmes were pioneered by Hertfordshire, a county where the need for new schools was urgent because London was growing fastest in this direction. The new schools were designed in the county architect's office, and the needs were met by devising, with the help of industry, a constructional system using light-weight steel columns and lattice-beams and wall-panels in various materials, all absolutely standardized. The components, however, were small enough to allow flexibility of design and adaptability to different sites. They were manufactured centrally, and sent to depots in various parts of the county from which they could be drawn according to the requirements of different schools. Speed of construction was as important as economy, and by this system, in spite of shortages of labour and materials, the county of Hertfordshire was able to build nearly 200 new schools during the first 15 years after the war. They were light and airy and provided flexible spaces designed to suit the changing teaching methods arising from the 1944 Education Act. Later their structural techniques were adapted for multistorey buildings, and other local authorities devised similar schemes, with several authorities in some cases pooling their resources and programmes in order to make such a highly industrialized method of building economically worth while. The illustration here shows part of the Junior School at Croxley Green in Hertfordshire.

Britain's special contribution

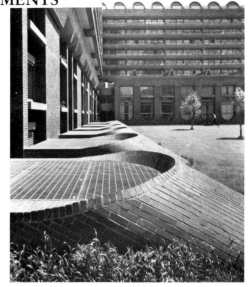

THAT BRITAIN, AFTER 1945, had no dominating architect figures indicates the nature of her special contribution to contemporary architecture: the recognition that architecture is as much a social service as it is a source of famous monuments, which led to the establishment of large public offices working in close collaboration with other departments of government. Although British architects created some original and individual buildings, it was the largely anonymous work of the public offices that gave British architecture—especially housing and schools—a high reputation in the 1950s and promised the emergence of a modern vernacular as ubiquitous as only the Scandinavian countries had hitherto achieved, with the added significance of being founded on industrialized building methods.

The merits of the British school-building programme have already been noted. Small house design in the hands of public authorities, especially those of the new towns, reached a consistent standard, although for the most part retaining traditional methods and materials for reasons

The horizontal apartment buildings in the Barbican are grouped around sunken grass quadrangles, planted with trees. The flat tops are relieved by the pattern made by a row of semicircular penthouse windows.

The Barbican housing project in the City of London was begun in 1955 by Chamberlin, Powell and Bon on a 35-acre site almost entirely cleared by war-time bombing. The medieval church of St Giles, Cripplegate, remained standing and is now the centre of a paved square flanked by a school and a lake. Across the lake is an arts centre, with a theatre, concert hall and art gallery. The project houses 6,500 people.

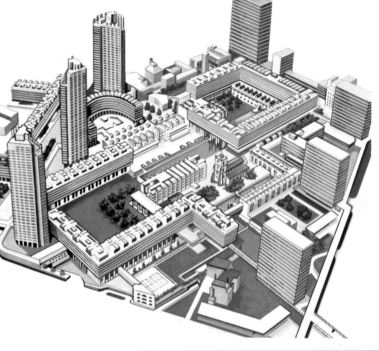

connected with the organization of the building industry. High-density city housing made more use of new methods, but generally failed to create a satisfactory living environment, especially when errors in planning and administration caused too much reliance to be placed on high-rise apartment buildings. But it was after economic restrictions had been lifted in the 1960s that it became evident that British architecture generally, and commercial architecture in particular, had not achieved the hoped-for vernacular restraint and orderliness. As in other European countries (with the notable exception of Germany and, to a lesser extent, the Netherlands and the Scandinavian countries), only a few distinguished buildings by the better architects emerged from a mass of commonplace and self-indulgent individualism. In Britain particularly, the latitude given to speculative property developers caused much environmental damage.

In 1960, the opportunities offered to more talented and responsible architects were increased by the Government programme of building new universities and expanding the existing ones. Some of the best British buildings of the 1960s and 1970s were for university purposes. This often involved fitting new buildings harmoniously into old settings, a process given much attention throughout Britain, publicly and professionally, as a result of a new interest in the quality of the environment and in the relation of a new building to its setting—which had been ignored by the pioneers of the 1930s. Methods of planning control continued, in spite of many failures, to be Britain's special contribution to architectural progress.

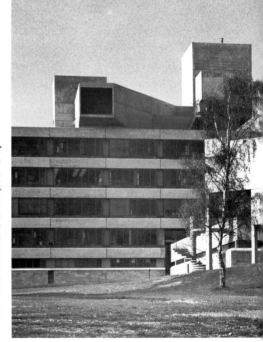

The University of East Anglia, near Norwich in Norfolk, was built in 1963 by Denys Lasdun. One of 11 new universities founded in the 1960s, it stands in a park-like landscape and, instead of being spread out campus-fashion like most of the others, is highly concentrated, being mostly contained in a linked pair of buildings. The teaching building lies behind the stepped-up residential quarter.

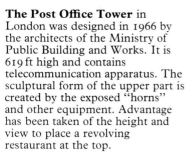

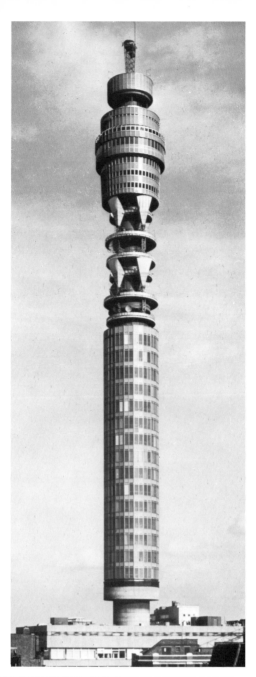

The Post Office Tower in London was designed in 1966 by the architects of the Ministry of Public Building and Works. It is 619 ft high and contains telecommunication apparatus. The sculptural form of the upper part is created by the exposed "horns" and other equipment. Advantage has been taken of the height and view to place a revolving restaurant at the top.

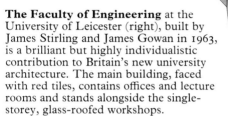

The Faculty of Engineering at the University of Leicester (right), built by James Stirling and James Gowan in 1963, is a brilliant but highly individualistic contribution to Britain's new university architecture. The main building, faced with red tiles, contains offices and lecture rooms and stands alongside the single-storey, glass-roofed workshops.

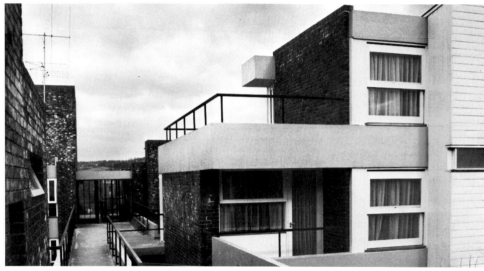

The hospital at High Wycombe (above) in Buckinghamshire was designed by the architectural partnership of Philip Powell and Hidalgo Moya. Using reinforced concrete floors and framework with brick walls, the project—begun in 1960 and scheduled to finish in 1980—will eventually hold about 370 beds. It is designed to serve an entire regional health area.

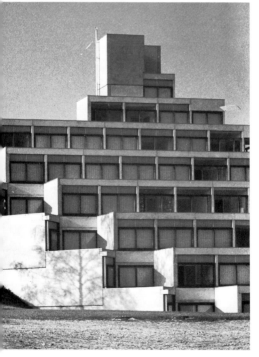

The Commercial Union Insurance Company headquarters (right), in the City of London, was built in 1969. Designed by Gollins, Melvin and Ward, it is one of the few British commercial buildings to match the best American standards. It has glass curtain walls carried on steel hangers suspended from the roof-slab. It shares a paved forecourt, open to Leadenhall Street, with the P & O shipping headquarters by the same architects.

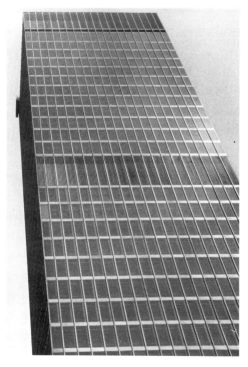

USA, the years of Wright's dominance

UNTIL JUST BEFORE World War II, Frank Lloyd Wright was producing almost the only noteworthy architecture in the United States, a surprising situation considering America's industrial and technological progress and the changes that were already taking place in Europe. There were, however, two exceptions: some clean-lined skyscrapers on the east coast and some distinguished houses on the west coast, where there had been a wholesome tradition of unacademic domestic architecture since Bernard Maybeck and the Greene brothers, in the early years of the 20th century, had built houses in natural materials, somewhat influenced by the Japanese, with a free interpenetration of space resembling that in Frank Lloyd Wright's Prairie houses.

Their principal successor was Richard Neutra, who in 1923 arrived in the United States as an immigrant from Vienna, where he had been influenced by Adolf Loos and Otto Wagner. His loosely planned houses, sympathetically related to the landscape, began with the Lovell House near Los Angeles (1927) and reached a climax with the Kaufmann House at Palm Springs (1947). He and another original house architect, Rudolph Schindler—like Richard Neutra originally Viennese and a disciple of Frank Lloyd Wright—gave the United States its first glimpse of the new European sophistication.

The 1930s witnessed a second climax to Frank Lloyd Wright's own career after his pioneer achievements at the beginning of the century. By now revered, but only as an historic figure, Wright surprised even his admirers by creating in his late fifties and sixties two of his most dynamic and original works—the Pennsylvania house Fallingwater (1936) and the Wisconsin office building for the Johnson

The Johnson Wax Building at Racine, Wisconsin, was the most important work designed by Frank Lloyd Wright before World War II. The main administration building, built between 1936 and 1939, extends horizontally in Wright's favourite dimension, and is a fine example of the use of brick. More offices and the research tower, added between 1944 and 1950, used the same materials. The tower, 15 storeys high, has floors cantilevered from it. Square floors alternate with circular mezzanine floors. The external wall is made of bands of brick and glass tubing.

Twenty-one miles of glass tubing provide the light source for the offices and corridors of the Johnson Wax Building.

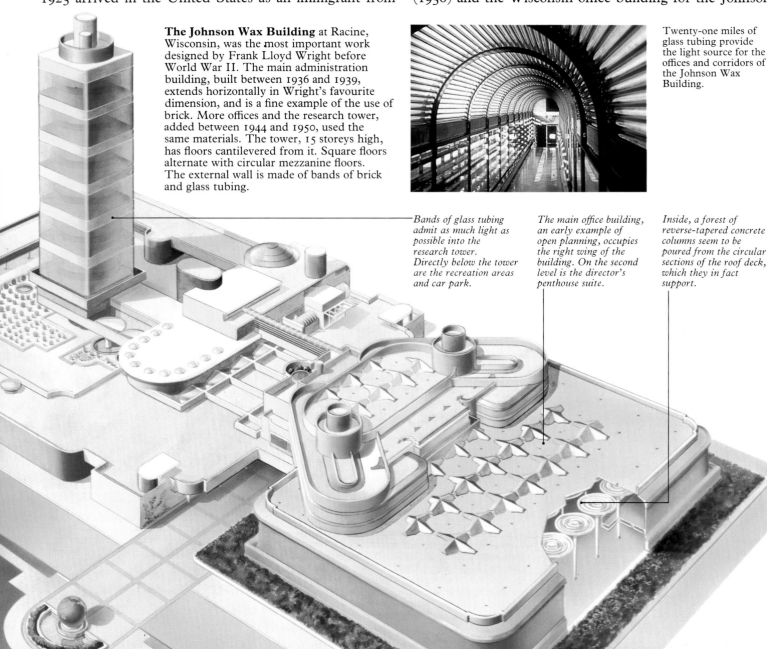

Bands of glass tubing admit as much light as possible into the research tower. Directly below the tower are the recreation areas and car park.

The main office building, an early example of open planning, occupies the right wing of the building. On the second level is the director's penthouse suite.

Inside, a forest of reverse-tapered concrete columns seem to be poured from the circular sections of the roof deck, which they in fact support.

Wax Company (1936–50). Both were remarkable for their range of spatial invention and for an unprecedented assurance in the use of concrete. Also dating from this period is Frank Lloyd Wright's own highly romantic winter home, Taliesin West, which he built in 1938 in the Arizona desert.

The end of the 1930s saw another unexpected development: the arrival, as political refugees, of several powerful and experienced German architects who, both as teachers and as practitioners, transformed the whole American scene within a few years. Of these Mies van der Rohe, appointed professor at the Illinois Institute of Technology in 1938, had the most widespread and lasting influence. The firm of Skidmore, Owings and Merrill, founded in 1936, skilfully adapted Mies's steel and glass idiom to the needs of American business buildings.

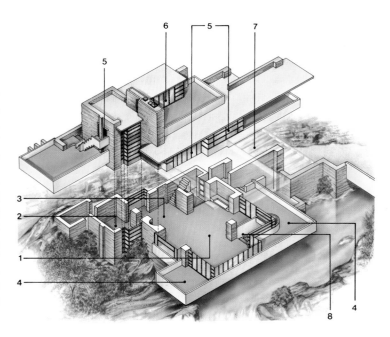

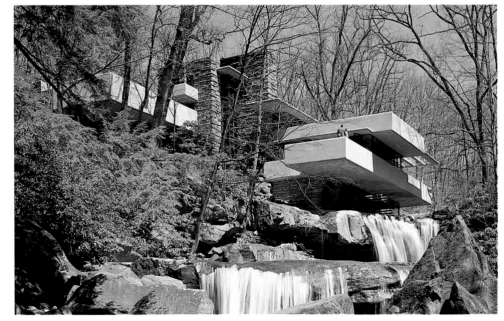

Fallingwater (left), at Bear Run, Pennsylvania, was built in 1936 by Frank Lloyd Wright and is an exercise in the integration of house and landscape, inner and outer space. Poised on a steeply wooded site, its solid core is rooted in the upper part of the slope to counterbalance the terraces cantilevered out over the waterfall below. The plan (above) of the two storeys of the house reveals a pattern of interpenetrating surfaces co-ordinated around the high vertical core of the building. Both storeys are glass-walled to give views of the countryside. The ground floor is raised on piers and contains the main living area (1), with a kitchen (2), dining area (3) and terraces (4). On the second level, bedrooms (5) open on to terraces. A picture gallery (6) creates a smaller upper storey. A glass and concrete skylight (7) stretches over part of the living area below. A suspended staircase (8) leads to the water.

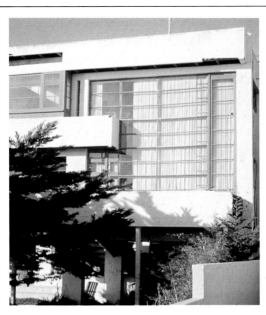

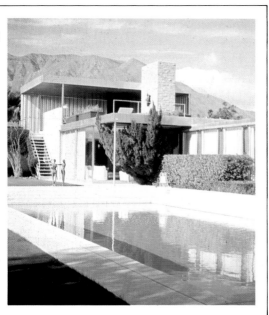

INFLUENCES AND INTERPRETATIONS
Frank Lloyd Wright made a profound impact on younger architects. Rudolph Schindler, a Viennese who settled in America, worked for a time with Wright, and the Lovell Beach House at Newport Beach, California (left), built in 1926, is a blend of Wright's teaching and the influence of European avant-garde architecture. A construction of white-painted concrete, glass and wood, the house is raised on stilts and surrounded with cantilevered terraces in a deliberate opposition of vertical and horizontal elements. Richard Neutra, a compatriot of Schindler's, was much influenced by Wright's conception of the house in harmonious integration with its surroundings. The Kaufmann Desert House (right), built in 1947 at Palm Springs, is a large house with a spreading roof and glass walls which open on to paved courtyard areas.

USA, building high

THE SKYSCRAPER, which was such a prominent feature of American architecture from the 1920s onwards, was the precocious, and occasionally delinquent, child of four grandparents: steel-framed construction, the invention of the electric elevator, high city land values and competitive advertising. The last must be included because some of the most ambitious skyscrapers have hardly been economic as buildings, but have become so because of the commercial value of a company headquarters that visibly outreaches its neighbours.

The first skyscrapers, most of them in Chicago, were relatively simple in form, deriving directly from their frame construction, but when the fashion for skyscraper-building moved to New York, architects expressed their confidence in, and their excitement over, this novel type of city building by modelling them sculpturally and embellishing their exteriors with period or fanciful ornament. The Woolworth Building (1913) by Cass Gilbert, in a kind of Gothic style, and the Chrysler Building (1930) by William van Alen, embellished in a style now known as Art Deco, are prominent examples of this treatment.

Only in the early 1930s did a new generation of skyscrapers emerge which continued the tradition of the 1890s and showed some realization that such buildings could achieve more grace and dignity if they relied on the drama of their upward lines and the repetition of identical windows, rather than on any adventitious shaping of the silhouette or application of ornament. The first skyscrapers to follow this principle were the Daily News Building, New York (1930), by R. Hood, and the Philadelphia Savings Fund Society Building (1932), by Howe and Lescaze.

The pattern was somewhat changed, although not the aesthetic aim, with the invention of metal and glass curtain walling. The first notable glass-walled skyscraper was Lever House, New York (1952), by Skidmore, Owings and Merrill, which also recognized the town-planning principle that one object of building high should be to free space on the ground. It included on its site a two-storey horizontal building containing a large open court and a twenty-one-storey tower. Twenty-one storeys are of course nothing now; one hundred storeys were reached in 1969 in the Hancock Center, Chicago.

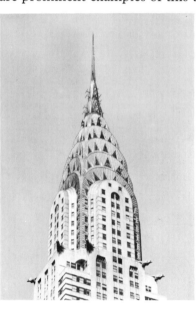

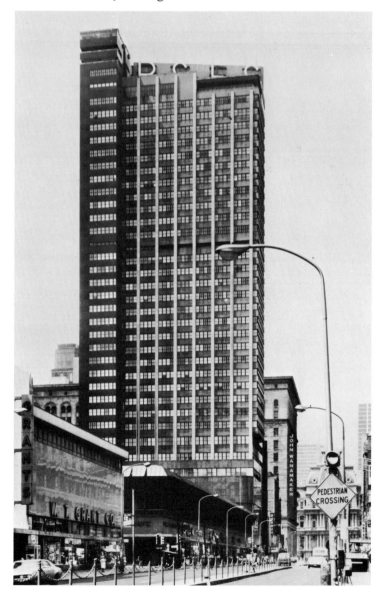

The Philadelphia Savings Fund Society Building (right), erected in 1932, was one of the first architecturally pure skyscrapers. Rejecting the "shaped-tower" designs then prevalent, the architects— Howe and Lescaze—followed the slab style initiated by Louis Sullivan in Chicago, and produced a building of style and distinction.

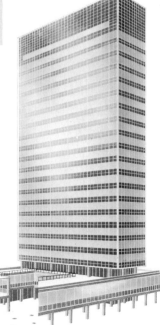

The Chrysler Building is one of the tall New York buildings which feature shaped towers. It was built in 1930 to the design of architect William van Alen, and the fanciful silver sunbursts derive from the Art Deco style.

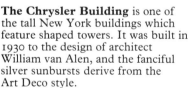

Lever House in New York was built in 1952 by Skidmore, Owings and Merrill. This trend-setting design of a glass-clad tower raised on a low podium was planned to free space on the ground, and was much copied.

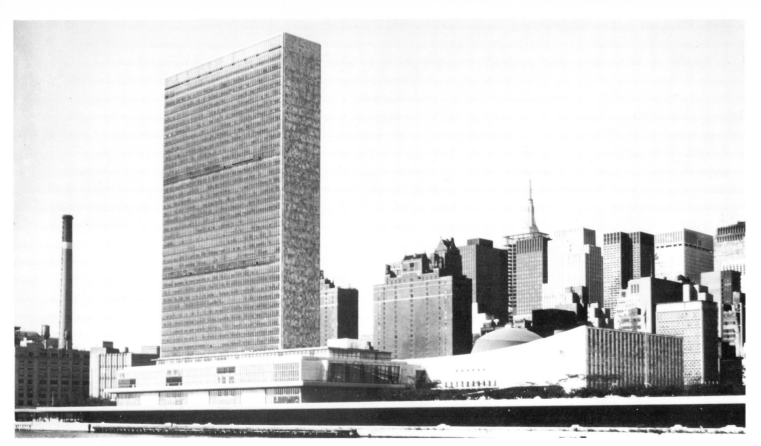

The United Nations Headquarters, on the banks of the East River in New York (above), was the conception of an international committee in which the dominant personality was Le Corbusier. Finished in 1953, the complex comprises the 39-storey glass tower of the secretariat, a conference area, a library and the Assembly—originally meant to be one of a pair. The Assembly and library were designed by Wallace K. Harrison.

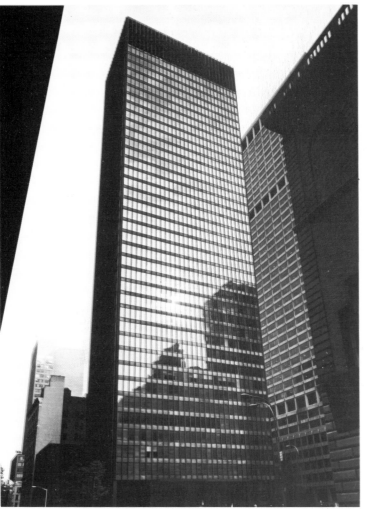

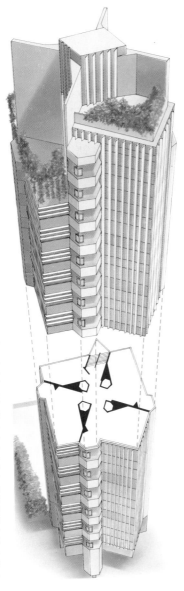

The Seagram Building in New York (left) is an aristocrat among the skyscrapers of the 1950s and 1960s, the ultimate sophistication of the glass box. Designed jointly by Mies van der Rohe and Philip Johnson and erected between 1954 and 1958, it is set back in a spacious plaza, rising with severe elegance to 39 storeys. The steel framework is wrapped in a curtain wall of bronze and bronze-tinted glass.

The Price Tower at Bartlesville in Oklahoma, by Frank Lloyd Wright, is a modification of his design for an apartment tower for the vestry of St Mark's-in-the-Bouverie, New York, which was never executed because of the Depression. The cantilevered 16-storey tower (right), which emerged 25 years later, in 1956, was intended as a structural analogue to a tree, with the floors cantilevered from four hollow cores containing lifts and service ducts. Office suites and apartments are differentiated by the use of external vertical louvres for the residential areas, and horizontal ones for the offices. Each apartment fits into the same height as two office floors.

USA, the outstanding years

BY THE 1950S AMERICAN architecture was the most exciting in the world, befitting a continent of so much economic abundance. Stimulating it was the fact that many of the leading architects were also professors in the architectural schools—something almost unknown in Britain and rare in other countries. Men who were at the same time theorists and practitioners, like Gropius, Louis Kahn, Mies van der Rohe and Paul Rudolph, had immediate influence as well as prestige.

Socially oriented types of building, in which Britain and some other European countries had made so much progress, were however weakest in the United States, especially public authority housing. Among the few exceptions were some schemes in the eastern states by I. M. Pei. Civic buildings showed little conviction or sense of direction—witness the relative failure architecturally of the ambitious Lincoln Center for the Performing Arts, New York, which was begun in 1959; nor was there much advance in the siting of new buildings or control of the environment generally.

The most interesting buildings were those designed for business and industry, following the pioneer work of Albert Kahn in the 1930s. Eero Saarinen's technical center for General Motors at Warren, Michigan, begun as early as 1946, was outstanding. Commercial companies in America appreciated the prestige value of good architecture and therefore became discriminating patrons at a time when the choice of architects elsewhere was too often based on their financial know-how and experience of site development.

University buildings developed interestingly. Some of these led a move away from the predominant steel frame and curtain wall, in spite of the continued success of large firms like Skidmore, Owings and Merrill who had helped to popularize them, and of the fact that Philip Johnson's "glass box" house at New Canaan, Connecticut (1949), remained an object of pilgrimage for young architects. This move was concerned with form rather than space; the building's functional elements were clearly differentiated. It was much influenced by Louis Kahn, who designed the Medical Research Building, Philadelphia (1960), and the Salk Institute, California (1965). Other examples are the buildings of Kevin Roche and John Dinkeloo and Boston City Hall by Kallmann, McKinnell and Knowles, a rare instance of a distinguished civic building.

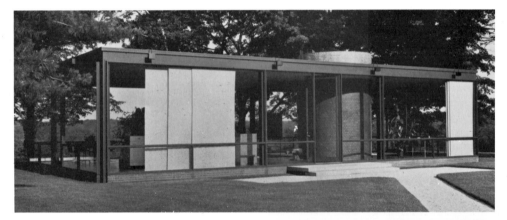

Philip Johnson's Glass House (left), in New Canaan, Connecticut, designed for his own occupation, received more attention than almost any American building of the immediate post-war period. It was built in 1949. Johnson was a disciple of Mies van der Rohe, and the house expresses the master's philosophy while retaining an originality which is Johnson's own. It is a glass box hung on a slender steel skeleton. An off-centre, short brick tower contains the bathroom and fireplaces.

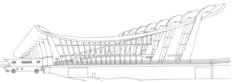

Dulles International Airport (above), near Washington DC, designed in 1958 by Eero Saarinen, is a rhythmic, uncluttered structure of concrete and curving glass walls. Mobile lounges, the architect's invention, made long communicating corridors unnecessary.

The Ford Foundation (far right), built in 1967 by Kevin Roche, John Dinkeloo and Associates, departs radically from the accepted idea of office buildings in New York. Only 12 storeys high, it appears from the street to be a single unit; within, however, is a vertical "garden" (right), open to the public, a courtyard bounded on two sides by office blocks and enclosed by ten-storey glass curtain walls. Air conditioned, and protected by a folding glass roof, the courtyard is visible from each office.

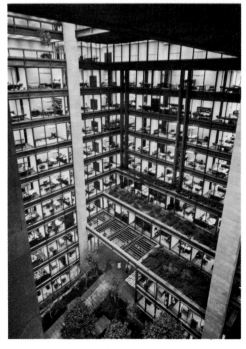

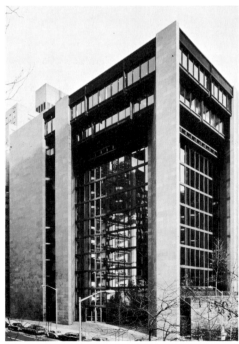

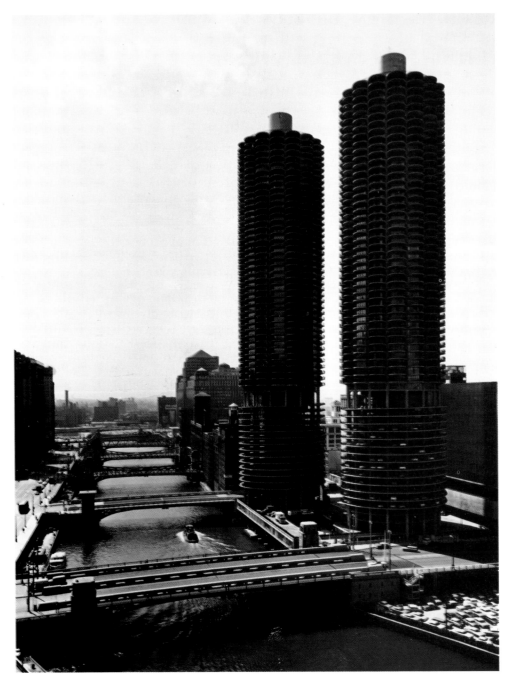

Marina City (left), a compact precinct of offices, apartments, garages, restaurants and, of course, a marina, stands on the river in Chicago. It was built in 1964 by Bertrand Goldberg Associates in an endeavour to solve the problem of crippling land prices by using the minimal ground area. The twin concrete cylinders rise from helical car parks, which spiral up to the 18th floor. Above them, wedge-shaped apartments fan out from a central core containing elevators and services, and end in rings of semicircular balconies whose repeated, rippling pattern enlivens the simple cylindrical shape.

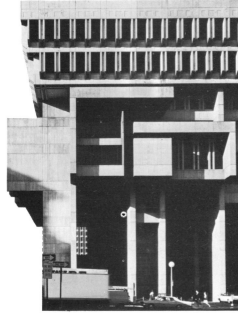

Boston City Hall (above), built in 1967 by Kallmann, McKinnell and Knowles, is the centre of an urban renewal complex. The hall overlooks a courtyard of brick, and above, projecting from the structure, are the mayoral chambers. In conscious contrast, tapering storeys of glass and concrete, containing rooms for functions, are suspended from the flat rectangular roof.

The General Motors Technical Center at Warren in Michigan was, at project stage, an architect's dream: unlimited funds and an undeveloped 900-acre site. Eero Saarinen, who inherited the commission from his father in 1948, responded with a predominantly horizontal design. A spectacular 22-acre lake is the focal point for groups of long, low rectangular buildings—a service area (1), process development section (2), engineering building (3), design office (4) and research department (5). The design complex includes a domed auditorium (6) clad in aluminium. The only vertical element is the stainless steel water-tower (7), which stands in the lake. Brightly coloured brick end-walls enliven the whole composition.

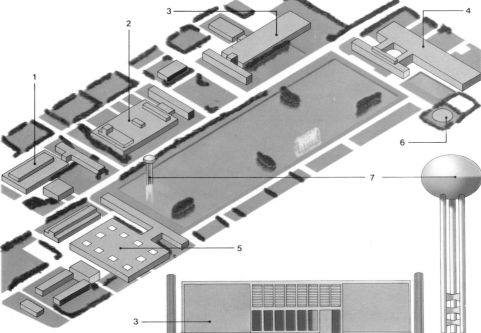

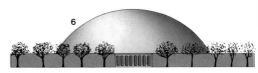

Latin America's distinctive style

THE MOST ARCHITECTURALLY advanced countries in Latin America in the 20th century have been Mexico and Brazil and to a less extent, and almost wholly owing to the dynamic efforts of Carlos Raúl Villanueva, Venezuela.

Mexico was the first to break away from pseudo-historical tradition under the leadership in the 1920s of José Villagrán García, and subsequently produced an increasing number of interesting buildings. They include the vast university city, where the library, designed by Juan O'Gorman in 1953, has a massive rectangular stack-room wholly covered outside with pictorial mosaics. Also in Mexico City is one of the best-designed museums in the world: the Anthropological Museum in Chapultepec Park (1964) by Vázquez and Mijares. The adventurousness of Mexican architecture was enhanced by the arrival in 1939 of the architect–engineer Felix Candela as a refugee from Fascist Spain. He was a pioneer of shell-concrete structures and built increasingly daring wide-span halls, factories and churches. Mexico is also notable for its prefabricated rural schools.

The dramatic emergence in Brazil of a tropical version of the so-called International Style got its initial impulse in 1936 when, as the result of a conflict between the traditionalists and the modernists, a group of young architects, led by Lucio Costa, was appointed to design a Ministry of Education headquarters at Rio. They asked Le Corbusier to be consultant, and although he came to Brazil for only three weeks, the outcome showed how well suited his personal style was to South American conditions and climate; in particular his practice of raising a building on columns to give shady spaces beneath and of covering its façade with a projecting grille to protect the interior from direct sun. This device—the *brise-soleil*—had been invented by Le Corbusier in Algeria a few years before.

Among the architects responsible for the Ministry of Education building was Oscar Niemeyer, who went on with others, including Affonso Reidy, to create a characteristically Brazilian modern architecture. It was lyrical and even Baroque, adapting its forms to the strong sunlight, but also incorporating such traditional elements as the *azulejos*, or Portuguese decorative wall-tiles.

Unprecedented architectural opportunities arose in Brazil in 1956 when it was decided to build a new capital in the almost uninhabited central highlands. The formal, symmetrical lay-out of the city of Brasilia was designed by Lucio Costa. The main public buildings, including the government centre, a spectacular exercise in pure geometry, were by Niemeyer.

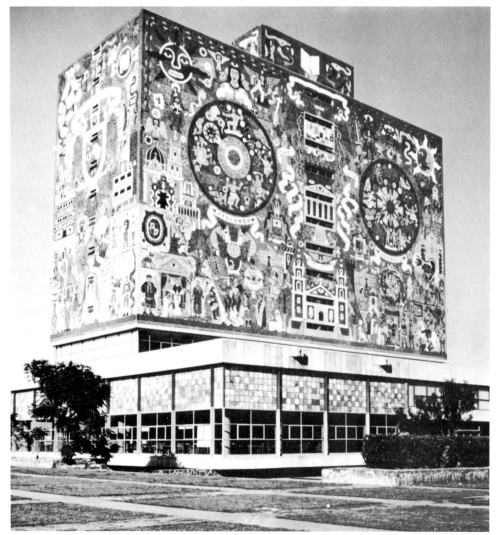

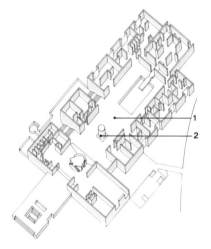

The National Museum of Anthropology (above), set in Chapultepec Park in Mexico City, was built by Pedro Ramirez Vázquez and Rafael Mijares in 1964. It is a two-storeyed structure with display galleries surrounding a long rectangular patio (1), which is partially protected by a large aluminium canopy supported by a single column (2). The walls are faced with rough-hewn granite.

The Central Library (left), built in 1953, is part of the purpose-built "university city" of Mexico City. A reinforced concrete structure, it was designed by Juan O'Gorman with Gustav Saavedra and Juan Martinez de Velasco. The dominant feature is the tall stackroom tower, which is covered all over with coloured mosaics designed by O'Gorman and incorporating symbolic and decorative motifs taken from pre-Hispanic civilizations.

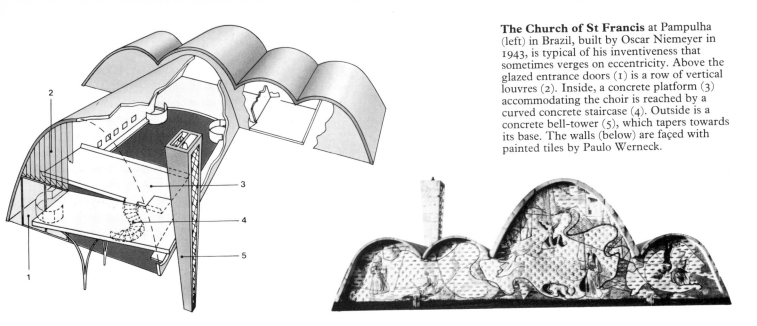

The Church of St Francis at Pampulha (left) in Brazil, built by Oscar Niemeyer in 1943, is typical of his inventiveness that sometimes verges on eccentricity. Above the glazed entrance doors (1) is a row of vertical louvres (2). Inside, a concrete platform (3) accommodating the choir is reached by a curved concrete staircase (4). Outside is a concrete bell-tower (5), which tapers towards its base. The walls (below) are faced with painted tiles by Paulo Werneck.

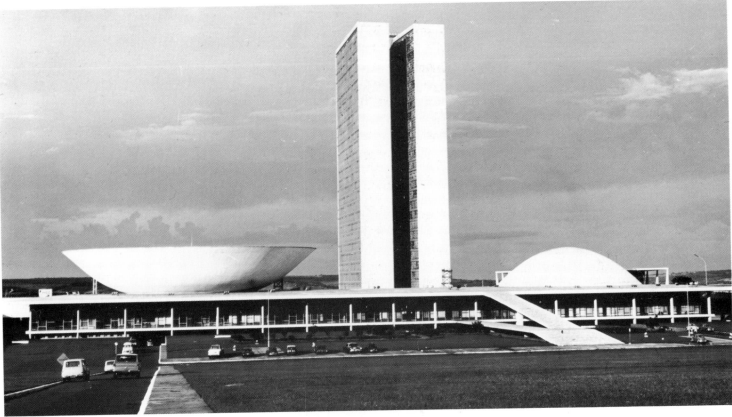

The Palace of the National Congress at Brasilia (above) was designed by Oscar Niemeyer and completed in 1960. It stands between embankments built to provide access at roof level, via the two shorter sides of the building. The double tower is the Secretariat and the convex and concave structures, rising above the long base block, are the Senate Chamber and Hall of the Deputies.

The Alvorada Palace (right), the official residence of the President of Brazil, was the first permanent building to be erected in Brasilia, although it is not part of the administrative complex. Placed on a large artificial plain, facing a man-made lake, it was built in 1958 to Oscar Niemeyer's design. The roof extends beyond the glass walls, protecting them from the sun, and is supported by marble-faced curved columns.

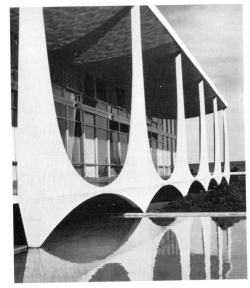

1 Cabinet-room
2 President's office
3 Library
4 Waiting-room
5 Banqueting-hall
6 Entrance hall

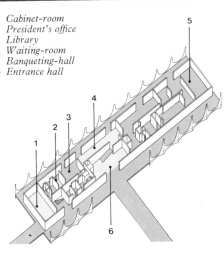

Japan's dynamic new school of architects

JAPANESE ARCHITECTURE, other than orthodox domestic buildings, was dominated by commonplace imitations of traditional Western styles, sometimes with a superimposed Eastern flavour, until a revolutionary change occurred in the 1950s. This was due to two men. The first, who prepared the ground, was the Czech architect Antonin Raymond, who had emigrated to the United States, worked for Frank Lloyd Wright and come to Japan as his assistant in 1919 when Wright was invited to design the Imperial Hotel in Tokyo. Raymond stayed on and became a successful architect in Tokyo, gradually introducing modern Western ideas and techniques as well as revealing to the younger Japanese architects the relationship of their own vernacular tradition to modern concepts of spatial planning.

The other man was Le Corbusier, who had already employed several young Japanese architects, including Kunio Maekawa, in his office in the 1920s. He visited Tokyo in 1955 to design the Museum of Western Art in Ueno Park. Maekawa, Junzo Sakakura and Takamasa Yoshizaka, who worked with him on this project, and others influenced by him, subsequently formed a compact professional group independent of the majority of Japanese architects who were employees of the big contracting firms. They evolved a characteristic Japanese version of the International Style, a peculiarity of which was to give their favourite material, reinforced concrete, an appearance of deriving from timber construction.

The first notable building in this style was the Peace Centre at Hiroshima, designed in 1950 by Kenzo Tange, the most dynamic of the group and the first modern Japanese architect to gain a world-wide reputation. Unlike most revolutionary groups who at first only built privately, Tange and his contemporaries had early opportunities of building on a civic scale because the post-war reorganization of local government required new administrative buildings in all the prefectural capitals. Examples of the new architecture were thus distributed throughout the country. This brilliant school of Japanese architects had other opportunities to display its virtuosity at the 1964 Olympic Games at Tokyo, for which Tange designed a spectacular sports hall, and at Expo '70 at Osaka, for which he designed a vast central arena covered by a space-frame roof (engineered by Yoshikatsu Tsuboi) that showed the Japanese as much at home with steel as with concrete.

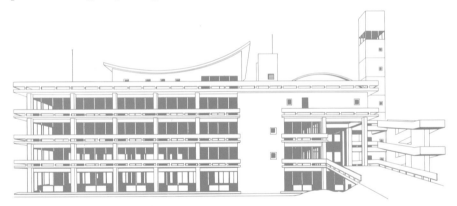

Hajima City Hall (left) was built as a result of the nation-wide plan to reorganize the administration of local government after World War II. It was completed in 1959. The architect, Junzo Sakakura, was, with Maekawa and Tange, the pioneer of Japanese modern architecture. His work is close to that of Le Corbusier, in whose office he worked for eight years. Other buildings of his include the art gallery at Kamakura, one of the significant early works of modern Japan, and the handsome Silk Centre which stands on the waterfront of Yokahama.

The Municipal Festival Hall in Tokyo was built between 1958 and 1961 by Kunio Maekawa for the quincentenary celebrations of the city. It is situated in Ueno Park, close to the Museum of Western Art designed by Le Corbusier, in whose office Maekawa had worked. The building serves many activities; there is an auditorium which can be adapted for concerts, plays, opera and ballet performances, a music library, offices, studios, exhibition rooms and a restaurant. The tops of these various structures can be seen protruding through the flat roof. The building is of reinforced concrete. Maekawa designed a similar building at Kyōto which was completed in 1961.

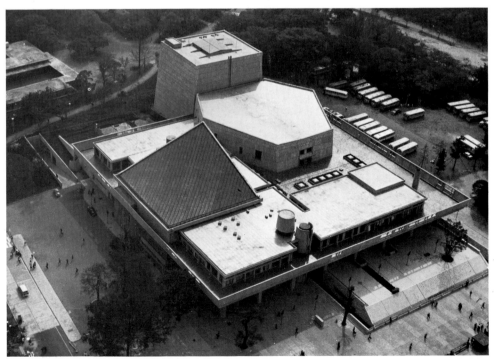

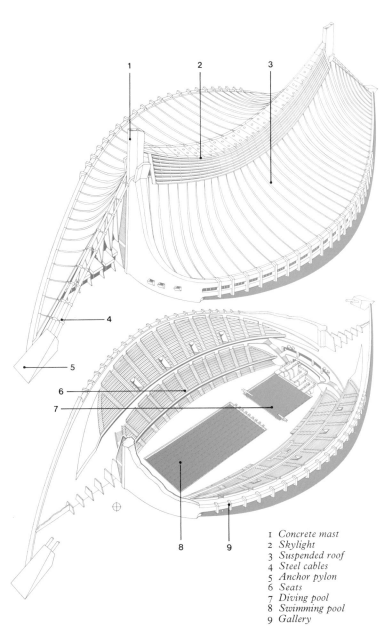

1 Concrete mast
2 Skylight
3 Suspended roof
4 Steel cables
5 Anchor pylon
6 Seats
7 Diving pool
8 Swimming pool
9 Gallery

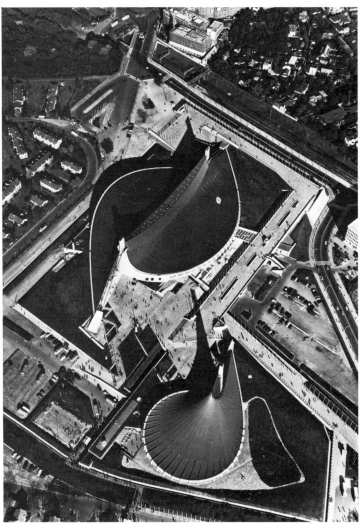

The Sports Halls (above) were designed by Kenzo Tange (the engineer was Yoshikatsu Tsuboi) for the 1964 Tokyo Olympics. Their roofs, suspended from steel cables, show the virtuosity of the Japanese in other materials besides their favourite concrete. The larger hall (left), a swimming arena, had the largest suspended roof in the world—a welded steel net slung from two reinforced concrete masts and two 13-inch-thick steel cables.

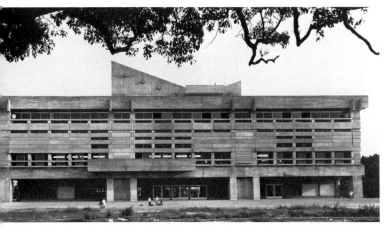

The City Hall at Kurashiki, built by Kenzo Tange in 1960, is a flat-roofed, compact rectangular building. It exemplifies the timber-like articulation of concrete elements typical of many modern Japanese buildings.

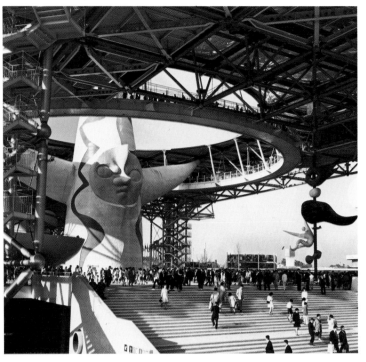

Expo '70, held in Osaka, was planned by a team of architects led by Kenzo Tange. A steel space-frame roof (right), engineered by Yoshikatsu Tsuboi, covered the central plaza, surrounding the "Tower of the Sun" sculpture.

Canada, Australia and India

CANADA HAS INEVITABLY been dominated by her more populous neighbour, and several of the leading United States architects have built in her cities. But since the 1950s Canadian-designed buildings have begun to earn international attention. Outstanding is the redevelopment of central Montreal as one multilevel shopping and business area with interconnecting underground streets, based on a plan by the American I. M. Pei. It includes the robust and original Place Bonaventure (completed in 1968) by Affleck, Desbarats, Dimakopoulos, Lebensold and Sise. The same firm designed the Arts Center at Ottawa (1970). Erickson and Massey designed the beautifully articulated Simon Fraser University in British Columbia (begun 1963) and John Andrews designed Scarborough College, Ontario (1966). The Montreal international exhibition of 1967 gave a helpful impetus to modern Canadian architecture.

Australia is also America-oriented and has some technically sophisticated city buildings, of which perhaps the best is Australia Square, Sydney (1968), by Harry Seidler. The relatively new capital, Canberra, is more notable for its lay-out and planning than for its architecture. Housing progress throughout Australia is inhibited by a preference for sprawling bungalow suburbs. By far the most spectacular building is the Sydney Opera House, designed in 1956 by the Danish architect Jørn Utzon, winner of the competition, who, however, resigned while the building was still unfinished. It was completed in 1973 by Hall, Todd and Littlemore. It is criticized by purists because its sail-like roofs are quite unfunctional and by users because there is nowhere to park cars. But as astonishing in form as it was difficult to construct, it adds an enchanting sculptural ornament to Sydney's waterfront.

As in the case of Brazil and Japan, it was Le Corbusier who brought modern architecture to India, when, in 1951, he laid out the new Punjab capital, Chandigarh (modifying an earlier master-plan by the American architect Albert Mayer), and furnished it with a dramatic hilltop group of public buildings. They exemplify his most monumental and highly sculptural handling of concrete. Under his influence there has grown a lively school of Indian architects, led by B. V. Doshi in Ahmadabad, Achyut Kanwinde and Shivnath Prasad in Delhi and C. M. Correa in Bombay.

A cross-section of the Opera House shows the entrance foyer (1) above the scenery dock (2), the opera stage (3), auditorium (4), north foyer (5) and restaurant (6).

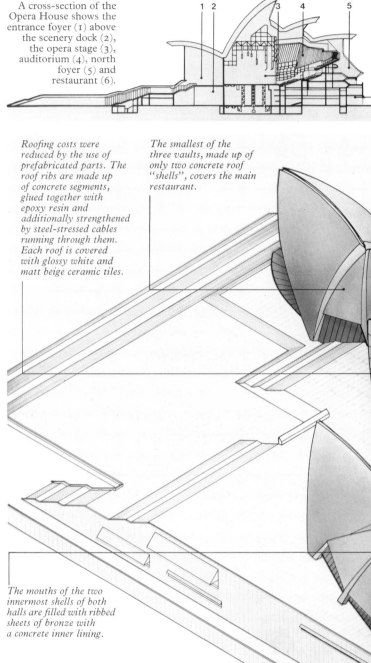

Roofing costs were reduced by the use of prefabricated parts. The roof ribs are made up of concrete segments, glued together with epoxy resin and additionally strengthened by steel-stressed cables running through them. Each roof is covered with glossy white and matt beige ceramic tiles.

The smallest of the three vaults, made up of only two concrete roof "shells", covers the main restaurant.

The mouths of the two innermost shells of both halls are filled with ribbed sheets of bronze with a concrete inner lining.

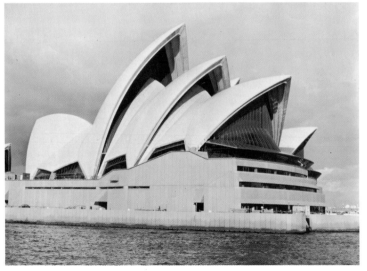

The Sydney Opera House was designed by the Danish architect Jørn Utzon and constructed by Ove Arup and Partners, the engineers, between 1959 and 1973. Set on a spectacular site spread over four and a half acres of Bennelong Point in Sydney Harbour, it is skirted on three sides by water and approached on the landward, the south, side by a gigantic flight of steps. The tallest of the curved concrete roof vaults rises to 221 ft above sea-level and covers the main concert hall; the opera house lies under the second; and the main restaurant under the third and smallest vault. The whole complex stands on a massive podium, which rests partly on the sandstone bedrock at water level and partly on some 550 piers, sunk to 40 ft below sea-level in some places.

The opera hall seats 1,530 and is a smaller version of the concert hall, with a four-vault roof covering entrance foyer, auditorium and north foyer. Beneath its entrance foyer is a scenery dock; dressing and rehearsal rooms are housed beneath the revolving stage.

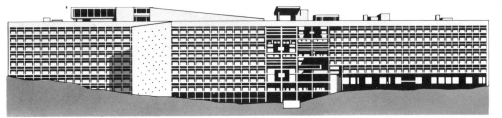

The Secretariat at Chandigarh in India (left) is part of a complex of public buildings, including an Assembly and Law Courts, designed by Le Corbusier for the new capital he laid out for the State of Punjab between 1951 and 1958. The 800-ft-long raw concrete slab of the Secretariat is patterned by its grid of *brises-soleil*, or sun-breaks, one of Le Corbusier's favourite architectural devices.

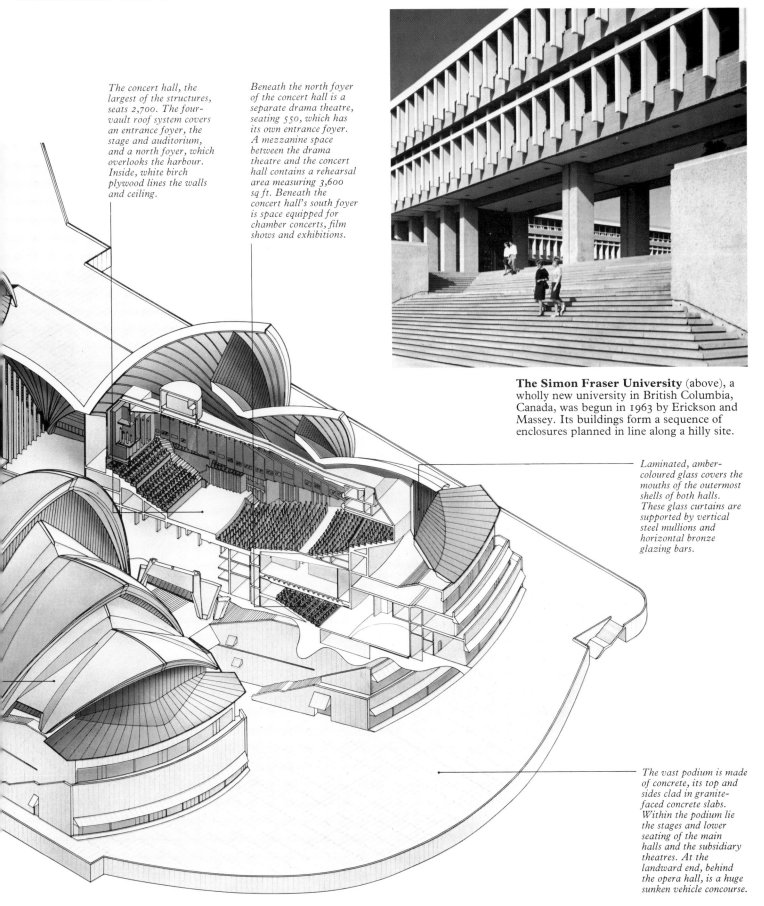

The concert hall, the largest of the structures, seats 2,700. The four-vault roof system covers an entrance foyer, the stage and auditorium, and a north foyer, which overlooks the harbour. Inside, white birch plywood lines the walls and ceiling.

Beneath the north foyer of the concert hall is a separate drama theatre, seating 550, which has its own entrance foyer. A mezzanine space between the drama theatre and the concert hall contains a rehearsal area measuring 3,600 sq ft. Beneath the concert hall's south foyer is space equipped for chamber concerts, film shows and exhibitions.

The Simon Fraser University (above), a wholly new university in British Columbia, Canada, was begun in 1963 by Erickson and Massey. Its buildings form a sequence of enclosures planned in line along a hilly site.

Laminated, amber-coloured glass covers the mouths of the outermost shells of both halls. These glass curtains are supported by vertical steel mullions and horizontal bronze glazing bars.

The vast podium is made of concrete, its top and sides clad in granite-faced concrete slabs. Within the podium lie the stages and lower seating of the main halls and the subsidiary theatres. At the landward end, behind the opera hall, is a huge sunken vehicle concourse.

The Orient 1: The Far East

Beginning with the architectural heritage of the Far East and ending with the greatest buildings of the Americas, more than 1,000 buildings are identified and briefly described in the following sixteen-page gazetteer. The world is divided into eight sections, each indicated by a square on the key map below. Every building and town described can easily be located by its number on the adjacent map; capitals are marked by squares. The gazetteer is designed to extend the geographical scope of the book for those inspired not only to read about but also to discover for themselves the world's great architectural treasures.

JAPAN

Himeji Castle (6), built in the late 16th century, is the antithesis of the grim western fort. Above a sloping stone base rises a white-walled, many-storeyed keep surmounted by upturned pyramidal roofs.
Hiroshima (7). In the Peace Memorial Park, now the city centre, Kenzo Tange's MEMORIAL HALL, 1953, a grey reinforced concrete exhibition gallery, stands beside its grim, ruined predecessor. On Itsuku-Shima, a lovely offshore island, is the ancient MIYAJIMA SHINTŌ SHRINE, its solitary red gateway rising majestically from the sea.
Ise (2). The GREAT SHRINES have been razed and rebuilt, in accordance with Shintō custom, every 20 years since 478. These cypress huts on piles, with wide thatched roofs, were Japan's first architecture.
Izumo (8). The SHINTŌ SHRINE, based upon traditional forms, was designed by Kiyonori Kikutake and built in 1964. Influenced by Wright's Japanese architecture, it is one of the country's most important religious buildings.
Kyōto (3), imperial capital for 1,200 years, encircles NIJŌ CASTLE, a sumptuous if formidable 17th-century palace. Its interior is a masterpiece of the informal domestic style of the period epitomized in the KATSURA PALACE. Among Kyōto's earlier buildings, the 13th-century SANJUSANGENDO, 390 ft long, is the world's longest wooden hall. The 14th-century KINKAKU, the famous GOLDEN PAVILION, was once a palace, and its contemporary, the RYŌANJI, is a typical Zen Buddhist temple. In **Kyōto Matsugasaki**, Sachio Ohtani's 1960s INTERNATIONAL CONFERENCE CENTRE echoes the traditional Japanese wooden building. At **Uji** the BYŌDŌIN is a refined Buddhist temple whose graceful PHOENIX HALL is an exquisite tribute to the 11th-century Fujiwara style.
Nara (4), first imperial capital, is a city of ancient and beautiful temples. The GREAT BUDDHA HALL of the TŌDAIJI, begun in 738, is the world's largest wooden building, and the incomparable KONDŌ of the 7th-century HŌRYŪJI is the oldest monumental building in wood. South of Nara, the 8th-century YAKUSHIJI PAGODA is one of

Japan's oldest buildings in true national style.
Ōsaka (5). Seven miles round, the restored GOLDEN CASTLE stands squarely upon a plinth built to resist both siege and earthquake. Pioneer modern buildings, like the 1930s SOGO BUILDING by Togo Murano, mingle oddly here with the ageless elegance of the 6th-century SHITENNŌJI.
Tokyo (1) was the 16th-century stronghold of the Tokugawa Shoguns, whose MORTUARY TEMPLE is one of Japan's famous monuments and EDO CASTLE, part of the Imperial Palace, their first building. Kenzo Tange's CITY HALL, 1952–7, is an indigenous modern building. The country's first post-war building, the READER'S DIGEST OFFICE, was designed by Antonin Raymond, Wright's pupil, in 1949, and the MUSEUM OF WESTERN ART, 1959, was by Le Corbusier. Kunio Maekawa designed both the FESTIVAL HALL and the GAKUSHIN UNIVERSITY in the 1960s; the futuristic SPORTS HALLS are the work of the versatile Kenzo Tange who also designed the tent-shaped sheet-steel ST MARY'S CATHOLIC CATHEDRAL, completed in 1965. Near Tokyo is the HŌMMŌNJI Buddhist temple.

SOUTH KOREA

Kyŏngju (2), royal city of the Silla Kingdom, has preserved in the curved roofs and elaborate carvings of the 6th-century PULKUK TEMPLE the ancient Chinese timber technique.

Seoul (1). Imperial flights of marble stairs and multiroofed pavilions and pagodas provide an historic breathing space in modern Seoul. The 14th-century KYONGBOK GUNG PALACE is guarded by the immense KWANGHWAMUN GATE.

CHINA

Ch'ang-an, Sian (6). The brick-built BIG GOOSE PAGODA, built in 704, is the one building remaining from the great T'ang capital.
Chi-hsien, Hopeh (3). In the TU LO TEMPLE, the KUAN YIN HALL, built in 984, houses a 50-ft-high Buddhist statue. China's second oldest wooden building, it is a tribute to the simplicity of Sung dynasty timber architecture.
Chiu-hsien, Hopeh (4). The AN-CHI "SAFE CROSSING" BRIDGE, China's oldest extant, was in continuous use from the early 7th century until 1954.
Mount Sung, Shanghai (5). The SUNG YUEH PAGODA, 90 ft high and erected in 523, is the oldest pagoda and the oldest brick building in China.
Mount Wu T'ai, Shansi (2). The FO KUANG TEMPLE HALL, 857, is China's oldest wooden building, built by the T'ang.
Peking (1) is like a Chinese box —cities within a city. At its heart the **Forbidden City**, the IMPERIAL PALACE, begun in 1403, is guarded by the gigantic MERIDIAN GATE. Within its red towered walls lies a labyrinth of ornately roofed palaces, temples and libraries. The **Imperial City**, with the now wall-less GATE OF GREAT PEACE, surrounds the palace; the 15th-century TAI MIAO, a Confucian Temple, is now the Palace of the Workers' Culture. The **Inner City** marks the site of medieval Khan-balik; the ROUND TOWER was the centre of Kublai Khan's exotic palace. In the **Outer City** is the ALTAR OF HEAVEN, three huge, concentric, circular terraces of marble, built in 1420. The triple-roofed, round TEMPLE OF HEAVEN was built in 1889. Northwest of the city is the

SUMMER PALACE, and southwest lies the medieval 12-arched marble BRIDGE OF MARCO POLO, 750 ft long. The MING TOMBS are 30 miles to the north. Among the temples of the **Western Hills** is the 8th-century TEMPLE OF THE RECLINING BUDDHA, famous for its monumental gateways. Not far from the city runs the GREAT WALL, dating from the 2nd century BC.

JAVA

Borobudur (2), built in the 9th century, is the world's largest Buddhist shrine. Its seven vivaciously carved terraces rise majestically to the main stupa, a stark obelisk; inside surrounding bell-shaped lattice stupas sit stone statues.
Chandi Sari (1) is a Buddhist shrine built in the early 9th century and famous for the sculptured panels on the outer walls. It is rectangular in shape and consists of three interconnecting halls.
Prambanan (3). Within the single precinct of the LARA JONGGRANG are assembled 232 Hindu temples, each dedicated to a different deity. The pyramidal, heavily sculpted form of the central shrine is echoed by four serried rows of smaller temples standing guard before the encircling wall.

LAOS

Vientiane (1) was formerly the royal city of a powerful kingdom in old Laos. In the ROYAL PALACE grounds is the WAT PHRA KEO, built in 1563, a typically Laotian pagoda of carved wood raised upon pillars, with a steep, stepped-out roof.

KHMER REPUBLIC

Angkor (1), mysterious and majestic Khmer capital, is scattered over more than 200 square miles of jungle. The great city of ANGKOR THOM, within ten miles of stone wall, is famed for the 200 colossal stone heads, which smile inscrutably across the treetops. ANGKOR WAT is the best known of Angkor's 100 or more 12th-century temples.

THAILAND

Ayutthaya (1) is Siam's old capital. The towered, stupa-like WAT BHUDDAI SVARYA is its oldest temple, built in the 13th century. The columned hall before the main shrine set the theme for Siamese temple architecture.
Bangkok (2), criss-crossed with meandering canals, is dominated by the 242-ft spire of the WAT ARUN, Temple of the Dawn, a stupa-like pagoda incrusted with coloured faience. The frescoed walls of the GRAND PALACE enfold temples sheathed in gold leaf and glass mosaic. The WAT SAKET was built in the early 20th century of Carrara marble, and the WAT PO has a 160-ft-long statue of the Reclining Buddha. The WAT BENCHAMABOPITR typifies Bangkok's ornate style of high gables, stepped-out roofs and elaborate finials.

BURMA

Pagan (1), a 13th-century royal city, is now a haunting ruin on the Irrawaddy plain. Among the 2,000 remaining shrines, the 12th-century ANANDA PAGODA is a cruciform vaulted temple, seven storeys high with a 183-ft gilded spire. The sinuous SCHWEZIGAN, and the classical MINGALAZEDI are among the most beautiful of Burma's pagodas.
Rangoon (2) is everywhere overshadowed by the magical TEMPLE OF SHWE DAGON, its beautiful, tapering 325-ft spire rising above a cluster of 64 lesser shrines, each with its own small spire. The shrine is swathed from foot to *hti*, the ornamental umbrella at the summit, in a coating of sun-reflecting gold leaf, its pinnacles making a fantastic pattern against the sky.

NEPAL

Katmandu Valley (1), where the Buddhist monasteries of Patan and Katmandu were built as early as the 5th century, has always been Nepal's cultural centre. In **Patan**, the GREAT BUDDHA MONASTERY, with its high tapering roof, is built of stone. Four Buddhist stupas surround the city. The ROYAL

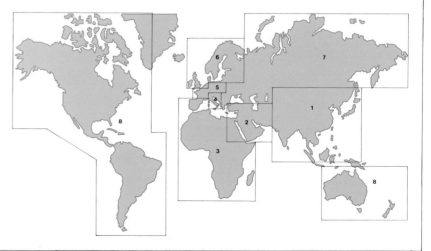

PALACE of **Katmandu** is a maze of courtyards and pavilions, and the GREAT STUPA OF SHIMBU is said to be the valley's oldest shrine. A 6th-century Hindu city, **Bhadgaon's** PALACE OF 55 WINDOWS has a façade of lattice-work and overlooks the central square, where a stone-carved temple confronts a spectacular terracotta temple. The FIVE-TIERED TEMPLE of Bhadgaon is well known, but the oldest tiered-roof temple is in 12th-century **Kirtipur**. In the valley's centre is the ancient STUPA OF BAUDDHA, above whose concrete dome peer the all-seeing eyes of Buddhahood.

INDIA

Agra (6). The crescent-shaped FORT was Akbar the Great's 16th-century stronghold, embracing lavish palaces, mosques and halls. JAHANGIR'S PALACE is in early Mogul style, a blend of Hindu and Muslim elements; the PEARL MOSQUE is a gem of Mogul maturity. In Agra is the incomparable TAJ MAHAL, and the TOMB OF AKBAR, sculpted in white marble, lies six miles to the north.

Ahmadabad (20), founded in 1411, was the birthplace of the true Indo-Saracenic style. Ahmad Shah's JAMI MASJID incorporated fragments of Jain and Hindu buildings but the 16th-century MOSQUE AND TOMB OF RANEE SIPRI achieved a refined synthesis. The MILL OWNERS' ASSOCIATION BUILDING and the MAISON SHODHAN were designed by Le Corbusier in the 1950s. The INSTITUTE OF INDOLOGY is a modern building by B.V. Doshi, an Indian architect.

Ajanta (18). A spectacular series of Buddhist *chaityas*, sanctuaries, and *viharas*, preaching caves, dating from the 2nd century BC, form a gigantic monastery cut into a cliff face, their walls aglow with ancient frescoes. At **Ellora**, 65 miles away, 34 caves were sculpted out of bare rock along one and a quarter miles of sloping hillside. The KAILASA TEMPLE, incrusted with relief sculpture, was carved from the top downwards from a 107-ft-high mountain of rock.

Amber (4), sheltering beneath its great FORT, is now almost deserted. The PALACE OF MAN SINGH I, begun in 1600, is a terraced wilderness of gardens and pavilions resplendent with mosaics, latticed marble and spangled Jaipur decoration.

Amritsar (1), holy city of the Sikhs, was founded in 1577 around a sacred artificial lake. Rising from a platform in the lake's centre and joined to the shore by a long marble ramp, the 18th-century GOLDEN TEMPLE glitters with gilded copper-plated walls and wrought-silver doorways.

Bhubaneswar (10) was the focal point of Orissa's Golden Age of temple-building. The 10th-century MUKTESWAR TEMPLE is the region's typical cactus-shaped shrine; the 127-ft tower of the ornate LINGARAJA TEMPLE is 1,000 years old. The 9th-century BRAHMESWARA TEMPLE is decorated inside and out with relief carvings.

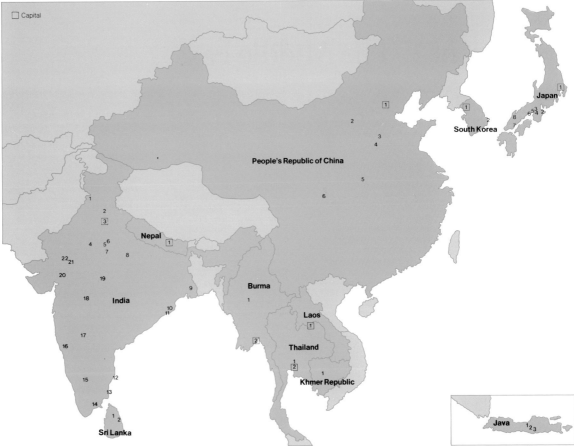

Bijapur (17) is a walled Muslim city built in a predominantly Turkish style. The 17th-century GOL GUMBAZ, an austere mausoleum, has the world's second largest dome, 124 ft in diameter.

Calcutta (9), founded as Fort William in 1690 by an agent of the East India Company, has palatial Neo-Classical houses and public buildings which recall the era of the Raj. Near Clive's octagonal FORT, completed in 1781, is GOVERNMENT HOUSE, begun in 1799. Designed by Captain Wyatt of the Bengal Engineers, it is an imitation of Kedleston Hall in Derbyshire. ST JOHN'S CHURCH, 1787, is a replica of Wren's St Stephen's, Walbrook. The HIGH COURT, 1872, by Walter Grenville, resembles the Cloth Hall at Ypres. The TOWN HALL is in Grecian style with a Doric portico. There is an Italianate National Museum and a domed GENERAL POST OFFICE with Corinthian columns. The OCHTERLONY MONUMENT, 1828, has an Egyptian base, a Syrian column and a Turkish cupola. The vast VICTORIA MEMORIAL, 1906, by Sir William Emerson, is a mixture of Renaissance and Mogul styles.

Chandigarh (2), designed by Le Corbusier, is the Punjab capital, one of the 20th century's few planned towns. It was conceived as an anthropomorphic unit, the CAPITOL, the civic centre, its "head" and the various quarters its "limbs". The HIGH COURT, with double roof, is well adapted to the region's extreme climate.

Delhi (3) was first built seven miles south of the present city, where the QUTB MINAR, the world's tallest free-standing tower, was built 234 ft high in 1199, and the QUWWAT-UL-ISLAM is India's oldest mosque. An early Muslim city, **Tughluq-abad**, was planned in the 14th century. Nearer to Delhi are the 15th-century TOMBS OF THE LODI KINGS, an Afghan dynasty, and the 14th-century SHRINE OF NIZAM-UD-DIN. The PURANA QILA is an early Mogul fort. In **Old Delhi**, the Mogul JAMI MASJID is India's largest mosque; the RED FORT contains Aurangzeb's superb PEARL MOSQUE and Shahjahan's superlative DIWAN-I-AM and DIWAN-I-KHAS. In **New Delhi**, a spacious early 20th-century garden city planned by Sir Edwin Lutyens, are the colonial-style PARLIAMENT HOUSE, PRESIDENTIAL PALACE and SECRETARIAT.

Fatehpur Sikri (5), Akbar's pleasure-dome, was the Mogul capital during its brief heyday. Above its imaginative palaces of white marble and red sandstone soars the glorious portal of the JAMI MASJID, inlaid with geometric designs in marble. This exquisite city, seven miles in circumference, was built in precisely nine years and abandoned after seventeen.

Goa (16). Among the Baroque churches of this former Portuguese colony the CONVENT AND CHURCH OF ST FRANCIS OF ASSISI, with its Manueline portal and richly decorated interior, is one of the finest.

Gwalior (7). The FORT has towered 300 ft above the town since, it is believed, the 6th century. In the 14th century the Tomar ruler, Man Singh I, built the PAINTED PALACE; its 300-ft-long walls, adorned with bright enamelled tiles, form the fort's eastern side.

Khajuraho (8) is the site of more than 25 unique 10th- and 11th-century temples famous for their erotic carvings. The CHAONSUT JOGU, a Jain temple with 64 spire-capped cells, is thought to be the oldest of its kind; the KANDARYA MAHADEV is the largest.

Konarak (11). The TEMPLE OF THE SUN is a colossal stone representation of the Sun God's chariot. Around the base are 24 carved wheels and seven giant stone horses paw the ground in front. Although only the 13th-century ceremonial hall was completed, this temple, with its highly erotic sculpture, is one of India's most beautiful.

Madurai (14), a 17th-century temple city, is dominated by the GREAT TEMPLE, its enclosures lined with superhuman *gopurams*, pyramid-shaped gateway-towers, decreasing in size towards the central court. Here the MINAKSHI TEMPLE is famous for its HALL OF 1,000 PILLARS.

Mahabalipuram (12), a religious centre founded in the 7th century by a Pallava king, is famous for the great rock relief, the Penance of Arjuna, and for the five *rathas*, monolithic stone-carved TEMPLES, the remains of the original "Seven Pagodas" after which the town is named.

Mount Abu (22). Among the DILWARA TEMPLES on the site of the 11th-century Jain capital, the VIMALA TEMPLE, its façade carved with a lacy intricacy, is the oldest and best preserved. The 13th-century TEYAPALA TEMPLE is a masterpiece of Indian sculpture.

Mysore State (15). The TEMPLE at **Somnathpur** is considered the most perfect of the flat-topped, star-shaped temples of the 11th-century Hoysala kings. At **Belur**, the CHENNAKESARA TEMPLE is banded with relief-carved friezes. The HOYLESWARA TEMPLE at **Halebid** is the largest of the three.

Sanchi (19). Although the Buddha never visited this holy spot, the immense GREAT STUPA, the largest of four, enshrines the remains of one of his disciples. Begun in the 3rd century BC, it was enlarged in the 2nd as Buddhism gained in popularity. The 5th-century AD GUPTA TEMPLE on the site is India's earliest extant stone temple.

Thanjavur (13), formerly Tanjore, was capital of the medieval Tamil Chola state. Among its 74 temples, the BRIHADEESWARA, with a 190-ft-high pyramidal tower, is typical of early Tamil architecture.

Udaipur (21), within its bastioned walls, is a fairy-tale town of palaces and gardens around a man-made lake, where the white marble palaces of JAG MANDIR and JAG NIVAS float, each upon its separate island. On a ridge above, the PALACE OF THE MAHARANA UDAI SINGH, the largest in Rajasthan, was built in the 16th century.

SRI LANKA

Anuradhapura (1) is a wonderland of *dagobas*, bell-shaped stupas of Ceylon, which date from the last centuries BC. ABHAYAGIRIYA, 326 ft round and 249 ft high, is the largest. The BRAZEN PALACE, seven storeys high, bristles with 1,600 piers.

Polonnaruwa (2) preserves the traces of an ancient and abandoned Sinhalese capital. Built in the 12th century, the RANKAT DAGOBA still has a near-perfect spire and the LITERARY DAGOBA once housed the sacred scriptures.

The Orient 2: The Middle East

PAKISTAN

Lahore (1), sacked by the Mongols in 1241, was rebuilt by the Moguls. The FORT, famous for its Kashi tile mosaics, was Akbar's first fortress-palace. Within its splendid enclosure is the MOTI MASJID, 1645, the first Pearl Mosque, and the SHISH MAHAL, the Palace of Glass. The city is resplendent with glazed and gilded mosques, including Aurangzeb's IMPERIAL MOSQUE and the TOMB OF JAHANGIR.

Mohenjo Daro (2). Here an ancient city has been unearthed, planned around a central citadel. The anonymous streets of this city are the only clue to a forgotten people, who, 3,000 years ago, evolved the first known Indian civilization.

AFGHANISTAN

Herat (1). Dazzling sunsets irradiate the blue-tiled domes and minarets of this former Timurid capital. The still lovely ruins of the 15th-century MUSALLA AND MEDRESA are a reminder of lost splendours, as is the refined, fluted dome of the TOMB OF GAWHAR SHAD.

IRAN

Choga Zanbil (12), sacred centre of a Mesopotamian city 3,000 years ago, is a six-stage ziggurat. From its well-preserved state, archaeologists have been able to deduce what the top of a ziggurat looked like.

Damghan (6) boasts Persia's oldest Islamic building, the TARIK KHANA MOSQUE, built in the early 8th century. Its style marks the transition from that of the now decayed 6th-century SASSANIAN PALACE to the later Arabian courtyard plan. Highly decorative brickwork distinguishes the 11th-century TOMB-TOWER OF PIR-E-ALAMDER.

Firozabad (16). Ardashir's Glory, the 3rd-century PALACE of the first Sassanian king, is a complex of *iwans*, chambers and courts, all surrounding a large central court. Its mighty 180-ft-wide façade is worthy of a palace built to mark a new era.

Gonbad-i-Qabus (7), visible for miles around, is the oldest Persian tomb-tower, completed in 1007, a cone-capped brick cylinder enhanced only by its ten soaring buttresses and encircling inscriptions.

Isfahan (11), high above the Iranian plateau, was a Safavid city built during the 17th and 18th centuries around the ROYAL SQUARE. On the east side is the MOSQUE OF LUFTULLAH, with a fine floral-tiled dome; on the west is the PAVILION OF FORTY COLUMNS, with delicate frescoes. The ROYAL MOSQUE is set at an angle to its own gateway, and tiled with the turquoise faience, which seems to colour the whole city. The FRIDAY MOSQUE, its great courtyard flanked by two domes, was founded in 760, and the dome of the MEDRESA OF THE SHAH'S MOTHER is adorned with arabesques and white inscriptions. Of Isfahan's five bridges, the KHWAJU BRIDGE is a tribute to Safavid engineering.

Maragheh (2). Persia's earliest mosaic faience decoration can be seen on the brick façade of the GONBAD-I-SIRKH, an early 12th-century tomb-tower. The 12th-century GONBAD-I-QABUS is sheathed in a faience coat.

Mashhad (8) was the centre of Safavid porcelain production. The MOSQUE OF GAWHAR SHAD and the SHRINE OF IMAM REZA display some of Persia's best tilework.

Nayin (10). A little mosque in the desert, the MASJID-I-JAMI is the oldest Persian mosque still in use. Built in the early 10th century, its oblong court is surrounded by "Persian" arches.

Pasargadae (13). Scattered ruins mark the site of the first Achaemenid capital and the PALACE OF CYRUS THE GREAT. Near by, the TOMB OF CYRUS, *c.* 529 BC, is a simple cube.

Persepolis (14). On a promontory above a high plateau, 2,400-year-old relief-inscribed grey limestone monoliths and jutting columns mark the site of Darius I's royal citadel. Part of the PALACE, the terraced APADANA was an audience-hall. The HALL OF ONE HUNDRED COLUMNS contained the throne.

Qum (5). The 16th-century Safavid SHRINE OF FATIMA THE IMMACULATE was a centre of Shi'ite pilgrimage. The main dome is embellished with gilded copper tiles, the iwan with gold stalactites and the portal with brilliant mirror-work. The 15 brick TOMB-TOWERS which surround the city have tiled and domed interiors.

Shiraz (15), with its legendary gardens, was beautified by the 18th-century Vakil of Persia, whose MASJID-I-VAKIL is decorated with native Shirazi *haft rangi* tiles.

Sultaniyeh (3). The MAUSOLEUM OF ULJAITU KHUDABANDA, built in 1320, is one of the most perfect examples of Mongol architecture remaining in a once richly endowed imperial capital.

Tabriz (1). The early 14th-century MASJID-I-JAMI must be one of the world's largest brick buildings. Though ruined, the interior is still beautifully decorated. The BLUE MOSQUE, built in 1465, is one of Persia's few roofed mosques.

Varamin (4) was an important architectural centre in the 14th century. The MASJID-AS-SHARIF is variedly decorated with inscriptions in high relief, blue faience tiling and carved brick.

Yazd (9). Sections of the 12th- to 14th-century mud-brick walls, ornamented in places and fortified in others, have survived in this desert stronghold of Zoroastrianism. The Buvayhid SHRINE OF THE DUVAZDAH IMAM, built in 1036, has a dome set upon a square, and the later Timurid SHRINE OF SHAMS AD-DIN is adorned with fine, painted stucco-work. The MASJID-I-JAMI has a magnificent portal crowned by Persia's highest minarets.

IRAQ

Babylon (3), rebuilt by Nebuchadnezzar in the 6th century BC, was a fortified planned city, entered through the ceremonial ISHTAR GATE. The city is now an extensive ruin, an archaeological site near the town of al-Hillah.

Ctesiphon (2). Just 20 miles from Babylon are the remains of a gigantic vaulted brick hall, the TAQ-E KISRA. Its origins are obscure, but its name, "Arch of Chosroes", suggests that it was once part of the palace of that illustrious 6th-century Sassanian king. The structure marks the site of Ctesiphon, a city which grew from a Greek army camp into a rival of **Seleucia**, the Parthian capital, built on the opposite bank of the Tigris.

Samarra (1). The venerable 1,000-year-old MALIWA, the spiral brick minaret of the GREAT MOSQUE, is one of Islam's most original monuments. Only the formidable towered walls remain of the once-glorious mosque, and even less remains of the city it served, for this sometime capital of the Abbasid Caliphate, built to rival Baghdad, was abandoned after only 56 years.

Ur-of-the-Chaldees (5), built 21 centuries BC, was one of the first great cities. Two temples, a ziggurat and a palace were contained within the sacred precinct, elevated upon a high platform.

Warka (4). The WHITE TEMPLE stood upon a flat-topped, 40-ft-high platform, the earliest form of ziggurat. A courtyard temple, it was once white-washed and decorated with cone-shaped mosaics; built *c.* 3000 BC, it is one of the world's first monumental structures.

TURKEY

Aksaray (11), in an arid desert, was once an important Seljuk city. The ALAY HAN, built 1220–5, was Anatolia's first Royal Han, and the SULTAN HAN the largest.

Ani (15). In the 10th century, when Armenia was a buffer state between Persia and Byzantium, King Ashot III made Ani his splendid capital. Ruling from the great FORTRESS, he ordered the building of the CATHEDRAL and a multitude of CHURCHES, which preserve the Armenian style.

Aphrodisias (8), "the most illustrious city of Aphrodite", whose IONIC TEMPLE was turned into a Byzantine basilica, is still under excavation. A white marble ODEON has been recovered, complete with dressing-rooms.

Aspendos (9). Converted into a palace by a Seljuk sultan, the ROMAN THEATRE, the most complete in Asia Minor, has survived almost intact, its acoustics unchanged for 18 centuries. The theatre at **Side**, near by, is nearly twice the size.

Bergama (4), ancient Pergamum, was formerly the province of Aesculapius, god of medicine. In the lower town the ASKLEPIEION, his temple, had a medical library and a theatre. Upon the 1,000-ft-high ACROPOLIS stands an UPPER CITY, a compound of AGORA, GYMNASIUM and a huge THEATRE.

Boghazköy (13), the 13th-century BC Hittite city, Hattusas, has huge fortified walls pierced by vaulted gateways and still flanked by great towers.

Bursa (3) witnessed the evolution of Ottoman architecture. Although the ULU JAMI, the Great Mosque, is essentially Seljuk in style, the ORHAN JAMI, built in 1417, is one of the first Ottoman mosques. Below the city are the Iznik-tiled TÜRBES of the Ottoman sultans.

Diyarbekir (18), on the Tigris, has seen a succession of rulers. Her walls, a crenellated bastion stretching across the plain, were built in 349 by the Romans, and Roman columns were built into the 12th-century ULU JAMI.

Edirne (1). The SELIMIYE JAMI was Sinan's most mature creation, in which he achieved the Ottoman ideal: a dome larger than that of the Christian Santa Sophia, and one which appeared to float in mid-air. The KULLIYE OF BEYAZIT II, a mosque enclosed by a number of charitable and educational institutions, was built in the 15th century.

Ephesus (6), described as Asia's first and greatest metropolis, is the site of Asia Minor's most impressive classical ruins. The façade of the TEMPLE OF HADRIAN is well preserved, and the 2nd-century LIBRARY OF CELSUS, the best preserved of all Roman libraries. In Ephesus, now called Seljuk, ST JOHN'S BASILICA was built with stones from the TEMPLE OF ARTEMIS, and Greek masonry forms part of the superlative MOSQUE OF ISA BEY, built in 1375.

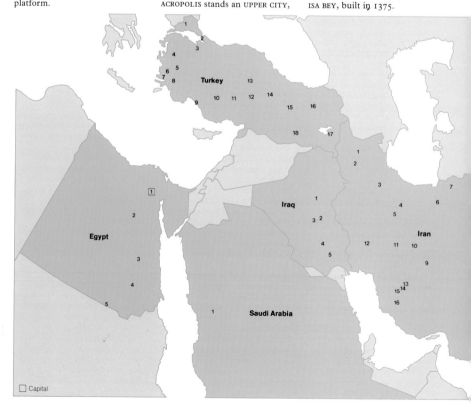

Capital

Erzurum (16), in the far north-east, is high and bleak; the grey, blank walls of the 12th-century Seljuk ULU JAMI look more like a castle than the nearby CITADEL, with its brightly tiled mosque and minaret. The 12th-century ÇIFTE MINARE MEDRESA was a Seljuk Koranic college.

Istanbul (2) is an oriental medley of domes and minarets riding upon a switch-back of hills, the result of 27 centuries of building. In 368, Constantine's great AQUEDUCT was built to supply water to a city which, in less than a century, outgrew its walls. The new FORTIFICATIONS number among the world's greatest defensive systems. The GOLDEN GATE was a majestic entrance to a city of churches, where the ruins of the 5th-century MONASTERY OF ST JOHN OF STUDIUM still exhibits a Byzantine delicacy. The SANTA IRENE was transitional in plan between the early basilica and the dome-centred church, of which Justinian's unforgettable SANTA SOPHIA was the supreme example, and the LITTLE SANTA SOPHIA its prototype. Justinian's architectural adventures extended underground, where 336 pillars support the roof of the beautiful CISTERN OF YEREBATA SAYAR, the city reservoir. The KARIYE MOSQUE was once the Church of Our Saviour in Chora, resplendent with 14th-century Byzantine mosaics, and from the Islamic era dates the hilltop TOPKAPI PALACE, the palace of the Ottoman sultans, and the SULEIMANIYE, Sinan's crowning achievement.

Kaysari (12) boasts the AHMET PASHA MOSQUE, built by Sinan. The most distinctive of the geometrical decoration at which the city's craftsmen once excelled is to be found on the SHAABIYE MEDRESA. To the northwest is the SULTAN HAN, a magnificent Seljuk caravanserai.

Konya (10). Fortress-like, the ALAEDDIN JAMI, built in 1220, has one of the most beautiful interiors of the city's outstanding collection of Seljuk buildings. The INCE MINARE is a famous mid-13th-century dome-chamber mosque. The SIRCALI MEDRESA, 1242, is important, for although ruined, it is lined with the tile and mosaic decoration which evolved in Konya and became synonymous with Seljuk architecture. Meylana's MOSQUE AND MAUSOLEUM is the 13th-century resting place of the founder of the Whirling Dervishes.

Miletus (7), birthplace of Hippodamus, the first town-planner, is now a wonderland of scattered ruins, where the great 2nd-century ROMAN THEATRE and the remains of a gymnasium rub shoulders with a Seljuk caravanserai and the 15th-century MOSQUE OF ILYAS BEY. At **Didyma**, the ruined TEMPLE OF APOLLO was never quite finished; at **Priene**, another of the cities of the ancient Ionian Union, the TEMPLE OF ATHENA POLIOS is outstanding among Greek temples in Asia Minor.

Sardis (5). The TEMPLE OF ARTEMIS, dating from c. 334 BC, is now, like the ancient city, a ruin under excavation.

Sivas (14), in Seljuk country, is a spacious modern city in whose old quarter stand some of the most beautifully decorated Seljuk buildings. The ÇIFTE MINARE, built in 1271, is now reduced to a portal and two minarets, but these exemplify the splendid brick and tilework of the era. The BLUE MONASTERY is named after its enamelled brickwork, and the MUZAFFER BÜRUCIRCI MEDRESA has delicate stone carving. The ŞIFAIYE, with a faience portal and mosaic-tiled interior, was once a hospital.

Van (17), a wild and untamed province, is scattered with small churches and monasteries, each one a tribute to the region's Armenian heritage. One of the finest, the MONASTERY OF AGHT'AMAR, on a small island in Lake Van, was built c. 928.

SYRIA

Aleppo (2), a busy trading city full of fine houses, Turkish baths and graceful KHANS, frames the vast 13th-century CITADEL, the most ingenious and splendid Saracenic castle.

Damascus (5) was an ancient caravan terminus, where the GREAT MOSQUE, the earliest surviving stone mosque, was built c. 706 by the Ummayad caliphs in the centre of a vast colonnaded precinct, the site of the Roman temple of Jupiter Damascenus. From the Ottoman period dates the AZEM PALACE, striped in marble, now a museum of folklore, and the DERVISH MOSQUE, built in 1516. Suleiman the Magnificent's TEKKIYEH, with slim minarets, epitomizes the restraint of Turkish architecture.

Kalat Siman (1). In AD 423, to escape the publicity which his self-inflicted austerities were attracting, St Simeon Stylites retired to the top of a 60-ft-high pillar, where, for 30 years, he preached twice daily to the crowds that thronged its base. On this site a BAPTISTRY was built, four chapels arranged in the form of a cross, with an open octagon over the pillar.

Krak des Chevaliers (3), the greatest Crusader castle, is formidable and immense, strategically placed and ingeniously defended with devious gateways, drum towers and machicolations.

Palmyra (4), centre of the Roman caravan routes, nurtures the remains of the great 1st-century AD TEMPLE OF BEL, a colossal structure set in a walled precinct on the desert's edge. The great TEMPLE OF THE SUN was built upon a platform in the centre of a colonnaded court at the end of a Sacred Way.

JORDAN

Jerash (1), one of the ten cities of the Decapolis along the ancient Nile/Euphrates trade route, is among the best preserved of provincial Roman towns. High on a hill is the great TEMPLE OF ARTEMIS, a courtyard of tall Corinthian columns.

Petra (2) was the first capital of the nomadic Nabataeans in the 2nd century BC, a pink sandstone city of 750 or more rock-hewn tombs. The EL DEIR TEMPLE is the most complete, and the 33 tiers of the 1st-century AD ROMAN THEATRE rise to the countless open tombs in the canyon walls above.

SAUDI ARABIA

Medina (1), an oasis town upon a plateau nearly 3,000 ft above the desert, contains Muhammed's COURTYARD HOUSE and the tombs of the prophet and his family.

LEBANON

Baalbek (2). Above the line of trees which screens the Ancient Roman acropolis, appear the tops of five 60-ft-high Corinthian columns of the TEMPLE OF JUPITER, the highest of antiquity. The TEMPLE OF BACCHUS, beside it, was built in the 2nd century.

Jubail (1), ancient Byblos, was the commercial and religious centre of the Syrian coast from 4000 BC. The OBELISK TEMPLE, built in a stone precinct, is one of its earliest monuments, and the CRUSADER CASTLE, the first in the Levant, is built of stones from antique ruins.

ISRAEL

Bat Yam (1). The TOWN HALL AND COMMUNITY CENTRE, 1959–63 by Neumann, Hecker and Sharon is an extraordinary medley of geometric patterns, a three-storeyed inverted ziggurat.

Jerusalem (2), rosy-walled, is dominated by the golden DOME OF THE ROCK, Islam's oldest monument, its rotunda bright with Turkish tiles. The CHURCH OF THE HOLY SEPULCHRE, a pre-Muslim building dating from the 6th century, is built on the site of Christ's tomb. Even older, the CHURCH OF THE RESURRECTION, 327–35, with an inner circle of columns surrounded by an octagon, influenced Romanesque church plans. The WAILING WALL is part of the city's FORTIFICATIONS, which date back 1,000 years. In this multidenominational city,

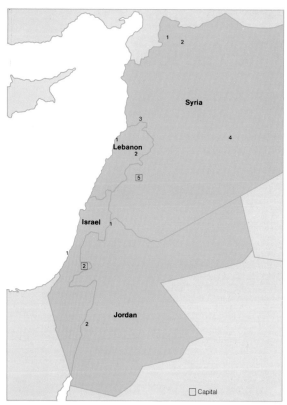

the EL-AQSA MOSQUE is over 1,000 years old. Kiesler's SHRINE OF THE BOOK, 1965, is an underground vault surmounted by a symbolic dome and wall. At **Bethlehem** the fortress-like CHURCH OF THE NATIVITY, erected by Justinian, was restored by the Crusaders.

EGYPT

Abu Simbel (5). The GREAT TEMPLE, six famous statues dominating its great 105-ft-high façade, was recently moved in its entirety to escape flooding.

Beni Hassan (2). The TOMBS, dating from the 3rd to 2nd centuries BC, comprise 39 rock-cut frescoed chambers behind a porticoed façade. At **Tell-el-Amarna** are the remains of Pharaoh Akhnaten's PALACE and new town, which endured from c. 1366 to 1351 BC.

Cairo (1). The great MOSQUE OF IBN TULUN, begun in 876, is Cairo's oldest mosque, clearly influenced by Abbasid building in Iraq. Begun in 979, the AL-AZHAR MOSQUE proclaimed the Fatimid line, whose MOSQUE OF AL-HAKIM, 990–1013, blended Egypt's various styles into a new unity. The later MOSQUE OF AL-AKMAR shows the Fatimid style at its most developed. Saladin was responsible for the great 12th-century CITADEL. The Ayyubids introduced the cruciform mosque plan into Egypt, exemplified in the MOSQUE AND MAUSOLEUM OF SULTAN HASSAN, 1356–63. The MOSQUE AND MAUSOLEUM OF SULTAN BARKUK, outside the city, is typical of many roofed, private mosques. Southwest of Cairo, at **Sakkara**, stands the first major example of Ancient Egyptian architectural planning. The STEP PYRAMID OF ZOSER, begun c. 2778 BC by Imhotep, is the world's first large-scale monument in stone. The MASTABAS OF THI AND AHA are 3rd-century BC rectangular funerary mounds. At **Dahshur**, the NORTH PYRAMID was the first true pyramid. At **Abusir** is the PYRAMID OF SAHURA, its relief sculptures a tribute to the artistic achievements of the 5th Dynasty. The CHEPHREN FUNERARY TEMPLE GROUP, containing the SPHINX, is the most famous group of pyramids at **Giza**; the GREAT PYRAMID OF CHEOPS is the largest of the three on the site.

Luxor (3), with its unfinished TEMPLE, lies near the ancient remains of the city of THEBES, capital of the New Kingdom from the 16th century BC. The TOMBS OF THE KINGS, an arid necropolis, is built into the mountain-side, the sarcophagus a frescoed, columned hall. The RAMESSEUM is a mortuary temple built c. 1301 BC, terminating in a vast hypostyle hall. At **Karnak**, the building of the GREAT TEMPLE OF AMON, the greatest Egyptian temple, spanned 12 centuries. Surrounded by a wall and approached from the TEMPLE AT LUXOR by an avenue of sphinxes, it is sited inside an enclosure of temples with a sacred lake. The unique rock-cut TEMPLE OF HATSHEPSUT at **Deir el-Bahri** is built on terraces. The TEMPLE OF SETI I at **Abydos** has the finest relief carvings remaining from Ancient Egypt. At **Edfu**, the TEMPLE OF HORUS, 237–57 BC, has a fine outer hypostyle hall and enormous, 100-ft-high pylons; and the TEMPLE OF HATHOR at **Dendera** is very similar, with strange capitals inscribed with the goddess's animal head.

Philae (4), in the Upper Nile, was a sacred island where the remains of a vast TEMPLE complex date back to the 4th century BC. When the Nile is high the island is completely submerged and only the great blocks of the 1st-century TEMPLE OF ISIS, and the KIOSK remain visible.

The African Continent and the Iberian Peninsula

MOROCCO

Agadir (1), severely damaged by an earthquake in 1960, has been since replanned. The buildings in the town centre, now a pedestrian precinct, have been designed by a native architect, Elie Azagury. His sunshaded LAW COURTS, 1967–8, is one of Morocco's outstanding modern buildings.

Fez (4). The seven-acre KAIROUAN MOSQUE, the oldest in the country, was founded c. 850 and enlarged in the 12th century.

Meknès (3). More than 25 miles of walls, a triple enclosure, surround the PALACE of Sultan Moulay Ismail built in the 17th century. The walls are pierced by remarkable towered gateways. Near by at **Volubilis**, a 1st-century AD Roman municipium, the ARCH OF CARACALLA, AD 217, was built as a monumental reminder of Roman strength.

Rabat (2). The ornate 12th-century TOWER OF HASSAN, a magnificent Almohad minaret, soars above the ruins of the MOSQUE OF AL-MANSUR. It was intended to be the tallest in the world, but was never completed. To the north, the KASBAH DES OUDAYA is an old fortress with a splendid 12th-century Almohad gateway.

ALGERIA

'Annaba (6) was the site of a Phoenician trading town in the 11th century BC and of the Ancient Roman city of Hippone, which until 1949 was completely hidden under the present town. Excavations have unearthed a remarkable FORUM, its paving still intact, the CISTERNS of Hadrian and the BATHS built in the time of Septimius Severus.

Cherchel (2), the Roman city of Caesarea, has the second-largest AQUEDUCT in Roman Africa.

Constantine (4), on a high plateau surrounded by a ravine crossed by the 420-ft-long, 20th-century El Kantara bridge, is a walled city, its fortifications, including the massive KASBAH, built with Roman materials.

Djémila (3). The remains of the Ancient Roman town of Cuicul were built upon an artificial podium. The TEMPLE OF SEPTIMIUS SEVERUS and the ARCH OF CARACALLA are the best-preserved structures within this splendid columned site, but the BAPTISTRY, built in the 5th century BC, is its most important building.

Timgad (5), was one of the most important cities of the Augustan age, founded by Trajan c. 100 AD. Its lay-out is its most interesting feature, the square plan enclosed 12 insulae in each direction, the forum and civic buildings occupying those south of the centre.

Tlemcen (1), focal point of the old North African trade routes, was Algeria's religious and cultural capital. The GREAT MOSQUE in the town centre was built by the Almoravids in the 12th century. The MECHOUAR was the fortified palace of the Muslim rulers, now a military barracks and hospital. The city is still enclosed by the remains of the ALMOHAD RAMPARTS. The MOSQUE OF SIDI BOU MEDINE was built by the Merinids. In nearby **Mansourah** the ruined MOSQUE was one of their finest buildings.

TUNISIA

Carthage (3), founded in the 8th century BC as a colony by the Phoenicians of Tyre, is now a ruin on the outskirts of Tunis. From the Phoenician period date the PUNIC TOMBS on the site of the citadel of Byrsa. From the Roman city, Colonia Julio Carthago, founded 122 BC, dates the AQUEDUCT, the greatest in North Africa.

Dougga (1), an old Numidian town, has a rare example of a 2nd-century BC LIBYCO-PUNIC MAUSOLEUM. Among Dougga's Roman remains are the ARCH OF SEPTIMIUS SEVERUS, AD 235, is outstanding, and near the 2nd-century CAPITOL is a FORUM surrounded by 6th-century Byzantine walls.

El Djem (6), founded in 45 BC as a colony for veteran Roman legionaries, has the most complete surviving COLOSSEUM in the Roman Empire, the third largest in the world.

Kairouan (5). The GREAT MOSQUE, founded c. 670 and enlarged and restored on many occasions, is the oldest mosque in Africa.

Sfax (7). The medina is surrounded by the original AGHLABITE RAMPARTS, built in the 9th century, and guarded by the 10th-century KASBAH or citadel. One of its oldest buildings is the GREAT MOSQUE, built in 849.

Sousse (4). The GREAT MOSQUE, with arcade-encircled courtyard was begun in 850; the sanctuary is its oldest part, but the building incorporates Ancient Roman columns. The RIBAT is the most important of the monastery–fortresses built by the Aghlabites in the 9th century.

Thuburbo Maius (2), founded in 27 BC by Augustus, is a remarkable ruined city. The CAPITOL is approached by a monumental staircase from the 160 ft sq FORUM, built in the 2nd century AD, which still has a paved market-place. In the THERMAE, the WINTER BATHS consist of 20 rooms, including a FRIGIDARIUM, with its original mosaic floor, and a CALDARIUM complete with heating ducts.

LIBYA

Cyrene (3) was founded at the beginning of the 7th century BC. This Greek colony was surrounded by a defensive wall and laid out according to a grid system in Ptolemaic times. The centre of the town is marked by the TEMPLE OF ZEUS, a gigantic 6th-century BC Doric temple.

Leptis Magna (2), the largest of the three cities of Tripolitania, contains North Africa's most extensive ruins. It was the birthplace of Septimius Severus and covers an area of 250 acres. Its FORUM, SEVERAN BASILICA and MARKET-PLACE, as well as an AMPHITHEATRE and HIPPODROME, have been uncovered. The magnificent PUBLIC BATHS were built during the rule of Hadrian.

Sabratha (1), the most westerly of the three cities of Tripolitania, flourished under Roman rule during the 1st and 2nd centuries AD. The most imposing monument is the THEATRE, built of sandstone.

SUDAN

Meroe (1), capital of the kingdom of Kush from the 6th century BC to the 3rd century AD, lies beside the Nile. Excavations on the site which began in 1902 have unearthed a large city of stone houses, granite pyramids and temples.

ETHIOPIA

Aksum (1). The present CHURCH OF ST MARY OF ZION replaced the earliest church in Ethiopia in the 10th century.

Gondar (2), formerly Ethiopia's capital, is famous for a group of 17th-century CASTLES built by King Fasilidas.

Lalibela (3) is named after its most devout and distinguished monarch, who, legend has it, built the 11 monolithic churches hewn out of solid rock for which the site is famous. They date from the late 12th century.

SOMALI REPUBLIC

Mogadishu (1). The GREAT MOSQUE is a simple stone building whose fat, cylindrical minaret is adorned only with horizontal stone courses. Built in AD 1269, it is one of the city's oldest Muslim buildings.

KENYA

Mombasa (2). The Portuguese began their great castle, called FORT JESUS, in 1592, on the site of a smaller fort begun in 1569. Built on a promontory, it is the finest example of 16th-century military architecture in Africa.

Nairobi (1). H. Richard Hughes, a British architect, designed the TELEVISION CENTRE, and, utilizing contrasting materials, the FEDERATION OF LABOUR HEADQUARTERS, 1960.

TANZANIA

Kilwa Kisiwani (1) was a medieval city-state founded by the Muslims in the late 10th century. The island has many mosques. The GREAT MOSQUE was built in the 13th century and enlarged in the 15th. The great HUSUNI PALACE dates from the 13th and 14th centuries. In the 16th century, Kilwa, an important commercial centre, was held by the Portuguese who built the GEREZA, or fortress, which was reconstructed by the Arabs early in the 19th century.

MOZAMBIQUE

Lourenço Marques (1). The PYRAMIDAL KINDERGARTEN was begun in 1964 by Amancio d'Alpoim Guedes. His YES HOUSE, built in the 1960s, is the administration building of an oil-processing factory.

RHODESIA

Bulawayo (1). A projecting roof shades the AUTO-REPAIR SHOP OF MODERN MOTORS LTD by Berlowitz, Furmanovsky and Kagan. Their RHODESIA PACKING FACTORY building was one of the first factories on the continent.

Great Zimbabwe (2), capital of a lost African culture, was a royal city built during the 16th century.

SOUTH AFRICA

Cape Town (3). The finest buildings date from the era of Dutch colonial influence. Built in 1755, the BURGHER WATCH HOUSE is one of South Africa's finest examples of Dutch colonial architecture, a classical-style building decorated with scrolls and surmounted by a bell-tower. GOVERNMENT HOUSE, begun 1682, but considerably altered, has a fine interior. The town's oldest building is the CASTLE, a bastioned fort shaped like a five-pointed star. It replaced the original wooden fort and was begun in 1666 and completed in 1677. It is built of bricks imported from the Netherlands and stone from Table Mountain. Three miles from the city is GROOT SCHUUR, rebuilt by Sir Herbert Baker for Cecil Rhodes in Dutch colonial style after a fire in 1898.

Johannesburg (2), dominated by a minaret-like television transmission tower, is a city of skyscrapers. The ART GALLERY is its outstanding building, in academic classical style, by Sir Edwin Lutyens.

Pretoria (1). GOVERNMENT HOUSE and the UNION BUILDINGS were major works of Sir Herbert Baker, built between 1905 and 1913.

DAHOMEY

Cotonou (1). The FRENCH EMBASSY by Henri Chomette is Dahomey's finest building. In **Abomey** the ROYAL PALACE, now a museum, and the TOMBS OF THE KINGS are monuments of the 17th-century Fon Empire.

NIGERIA

Ibadan (2). UNIVERSITY COLLEGE by E. Maxwell Fry and Jane Drew utilizes the traditional Yoruba system of cross-ventilation. Tropical sunshades are used decoratively in the CO-OPERATIVE BANK OF WESTERN NIGERIA.

Lagos (1). Nigeria's British tradition is best expressed in Godwin and Hopwood's HANBURY HOUSE where indigenous movable sunshades regulate the interior temperature. A Nigerian, A. Ifeanyi Ekwueme, designed the LABORATORY BUILDING in ST GREGORY'S COLLEGE. Oluwole Olumuyiwa's CRUSADER HOUSE, a radio station, uses movable window panels for shading.

NIGER

Tahoua (1) preserves the striking domed mud buildings typical of this desert region and similar to the Sudanese style.

GHANA

Accra (3). Articulated by sunshades, Fry and Drew's CO-OPERATIVE BANK OFFICES is a six-storey glass tower. The NATIONAL MUSEUM by Drake and Lasdun has a vaulted dome.

Cape Coast (2), one of West Africa's oldest towns, grew up around CAPE COAST CASTLE. Built by the Swedes in 1652, it was reconstructed by the British after 1664. Designed by COMTEC, an Italian firm, UNIVERSITY COLLEGE, 1966, shows the influence of Le Corbusier.

Elmina (1), on the Gulf of Guinea, was the earliest European settlement on the Gold Coast, founded by the Portuguese in 1471. ST GEORGE'S CASTLE was built in 1482.

MALI

Djenne (2). The simple GREAT MOSQUE at Djenne dates from the 14th century and is built of timber plastered with pisé, a puddled clay mixture.

Timbuktu (1). The oldest surviving mosque in West Africa, the DYINGUERÉ BER, dates from the early 14th century. The MOSQUE OF SIDI-YAHIA, in the town centre, was begun in 1400 and took 40 years to build, and the SANKORÉ MOSQUE dates from the mid-15th century.

PORTUGAL

Alcobaça (4). The MONASTERY CHURCH OF SANTA MARIA, 1178, is a simple hall church built of white stone. Despite its Baroque façade, the building retains an air of Cistercian simplicity.

Batalha (3). The MONASTERY, founded in the 14th century in thanksgiving for victory over Castile, was mainly built in the 15th century. The church is simple, cruciform with tall clustered piers and lancet windows, and the façade is a riot of Manueline decoration.

Braga (1). BOM JESUS DO MONTE is one of Portugal's most famous Baroque churches.

Coimbra (2) was Portugal's first capital. Built on a hillside, it is dominated by the high tower, built in the 18th century, of the old UNIVERSITY. The fortified CATHEDRAL was built between 1140 and 1175.

Lisbon (6). The 16th-century JERONIMITE MONASTERY at Belem survived the earthquake of 1755, as did the Manueline TOWER OF BELEM, opposite. By the mid-18th century, the Baroque style was fully developed in Portugal. The CONVENT CHURCH OF MADRE DE DEUS, 1711, is the work of João Frederico Ludovice. Lisbon was gradually rebuilt after the 1755 earthquake, and its boulevards and squares give the city an 18th-century aspect. Outside the SUMMER PALACE OF QUELUZ, built by Mateus Vicente and Robillon, has white and pink Rococo decoration adorning the façade. North of Lisbon, at **Tomar**, is the CONVENT OF CHRIST, begun in the 12th century. The monastery is famous for its Manueline carving.

Mafra (5). The MONASTERY–PALACE has an immense 800-ft-long façade in the centre of which is the church façade. Erected by King João V in the 18th century, after the birth of a son, the monastery is a well-balanced example of Portuguese Baroque.

SPAIN

Avila (7) was surrounded with its towered WALL after a victory over the Moors in 1090. The Romanesque CATHEDRAL, 1160–1211, with its slit windows, ramparts and an apse with small chapels, forms part of the city fortifications.

Barcelona (14). Catalonia developed an early eclectic yet indigenous style of architecture, best seen in BARCELONA CATHEDRAL, the most outstanding example of Catalan Gothic. The PALACIO DE LA AUDENCIA, with a stone staircase in an outer court, is a Gothic town palace, and the CASA DEL AYUNTAMIENTO, the Gothic Town Hall. A Catalan, Gaudi, anticipated the Art Nouveau in his earliest buildings. Few architectural precedents can be recognized in the determined asymmetry of the PALACIO GUELL, 1885–9, with its parabolic grill-covered doorway, and the fairy-tale PARQUE GUELL. CASA MILÁ and the CASA BATTLÓ are eccentric town houses. The SAGRADA FAMILIA, begun in 1882 and not yet finished, is Gaudi's version of Neo-Gothic. Luis Domènech's PALACE OF CATALONIAN MUSIC was begun in 1905–8. From Barcelona, boats make regular crossings to the Balearic Islands, less than 100 miles away. The finest Gothic building in **Palma**, the capital of **Majorca**, is the 13th-century CATHEDRAL, built to celebrate the Reconquest of Spain from the Moors. Its castle-like façade is arrayed with vertical buttresses, and its only decoration consists of a magnificent west portal and a crown of spires.

Burgos (4). Hans of Cologne's twin traceried spires are the most famous feature of the irregularly planned CATHEDRAL, which was begun in the 13th and completed in the 15th century.

Córdoba (10). The GREAT MOSQUE, now the CATHEDRAL, was begun in 785. Mosaics and geometric designs adorn the interior, where arcades of marble columns support banded red and white horseshoe arches rising in tiers to the stellar-vaulted roof.

Gerona (16). The CATHEDRAL, 1312–1598, is a towering hall church. The vault which spans its single, aisleless nave is the widest in Europe.

Granada (12). The palace and fortress of the ALHAMBRA is the only Islamic palace to have survived in Spain. The PALACE OF CHARLES V was built on to it in severely classical style in 1527–68. Beneath the Alhambra the huge CATHEDRAL is a mixture of Gothic and Renaissance design, while the west front, by Cano, is Baroque. The SACRISTY OF THE CARTUJA is a prime example of Churrigueresque decoration, the work of Francisco Hurtado Izquierdo.

León Cathedral (3), built to a French Gothic model, has, unlike any other Spanish cathedral, enormous windows filled with magnificent 13th-century stained glass.

Madrid (8). At the geographical centre of Spain, Philip II ordained the building of the MONASTERY OF EL ESCORIAL in 1559. Begun by Juan Bautista de Toledo, it was completed in 1584 by Juan de Herrera. The same architects designed the ROYAL PALACE OF ARANJUÉZ on the River Tagus 30 miles south of the city. Juan Gómez de Mora, Spain's leading 17th-century architect, was responsible for the lay-out of the PLAZA MAYOR. He designed the CHURCH OF THE ENCARNACIÓN. Pedro de Ribera's HOSPICIO SAN FERNANDO best displays his

Churrigueresque extravagance. The city's 19th-century buildings include the immense CATHEDRAL OF NUESTRA SEÑORA DE LA ALMUDENA, begun in 1880 by Marqués Francisco de Cubas and still unfinished. Modern Madrid's ZARZUELA HIPPODROME was designed by Eduardo Torroja, a concrete engineer, and completed in 1935. Ranging rows of concrete shell vaults surround the stadium. In **Alcalá de Henares**, the UNIVERSITY has a façade built by Mora. The BERNARDAS CHURCH, 1617–26, presaged the Baroque with its oval nave.

Poblet (15). The ABBEY CHURCH, 1151–96, with its beautiful cloisters, was one of the great Cistercian foundations in Catalonia. Not far away is the MONASTERY OF SANTAS CREUS. These are the most important of Spain's 12th-century ecclesiastical remains.

Ripoll (17). The ABBEY CHURCH, 1020, considerably restored, is one of the finest examples of Catalan Romanesque, and has remarkable traceried cloisters.

Salamanca (5). The OLD CATHEDRAL, 1120–78, forms a group with the late Gothic NEW CATHEDRAL. The city's finest example of Plateresque decoration is the façade of the medieval UNIVERSITY, a masterpiece of the art.

Santa Maria de Naranco (2) is a strikingly simple example of Asturian pre-Romanesque architecture, embodying both Visigothic and Carolingian features.

Santiago de Compostela (1). The CATHEDRAL, begun 1078, was influenced by ideas imported from France. It has an 18th-century Baroque façade by Fernando Casas y Nóvoa.

Segovia (6). The perfectly preserved ROMAN AQUEDUCT dates from 80 BC. It still carries water in its half-mile-long channel, which is supported by 118 two-tiered granite arches

of which the tallest is 90 ft high. The fairy-tale ALCÁZAR, with turrets and towers, is a fortified palace on a high rock, dating from 1455. SEGOVIA CATHEDRAL is a late Spanish Gothic building.

Seville Cathedral (11), begun in 1402 on the site of a mosque, is the largest Gothic cathedral in Europe and one of Spain's earliest Gothic churches. The ornate GIRALDA TOWER was the original 12th-century minaret. Its name derives from a revolving bronze figure within it. The 14th-century ALCÁZAR is an example of *Mudéjar* work, a synthesis of Islamic and Christian characteristics.

Tarragona (13). The ROMAN AQUEDUCT, Las Perreras, stands just outside the city. TARRAGONA CATHEDRAL, begun in 1171, is chiefly Romanesque, but its pointed arches heralded the Gothic style in Spain.

Toledo (9). The CATHEDRAL, although built in the 13th century to the French plan, is a fine example of Spanish Gothic. SANTA MARIA LA BLANCA was a synagogue from the 12th to the 13th century and became a Christian church in the 15th century after the expulsion of the Jews. SAN CRISTO DE LA LUZ, a former mosque built in 960, was taken over by Christians in the 12th century. The PUERTA DEL SOL is a 13th-century arched and arcaded gateway whose decoration is an early example of *Mudéjar* decoration. The PUENTE DEL ALCÁNTARA, which spans the River Tagus, was built by the Romans, rebuilt by the Arabs in the 10th century and further fortified in 1258. The academic perfection of the 16th-century AFUERA HOSPITAL is the result of its Italian High Renaissance origins: Bartolomé Bustamente, its architect, had studied in Italy. Enrique de Egas, master of the Renaissance Plateresque style, designed the HOSPITAL OF SANTA CRUZ DE MENDOZA, begun in 1504.

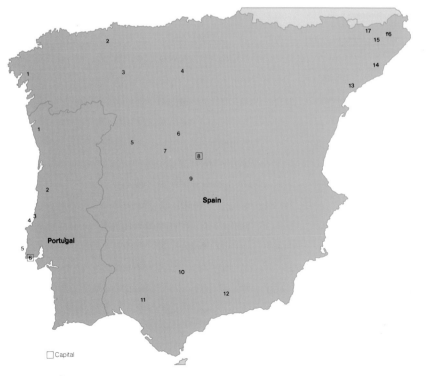

□ Capital

Portugal

Spain

Europe 1: Italy and Switzerland

SICILY

Agrigento (7). The TEMPLE OF CONCORD, *c.* 430 BC, in the famous **Valley of the Temples**, is the best-preserved Greek temple. The TEMPLE OF ZEUS OLYMPIUS, *c.* 510–409 BC, is of unusual design, 173 by 361 ft, and apparently never completed.
Catania (4), replanned by Vaccarini in the 17th century is a Baroque city in which the CATHEDRAL, the PALAZZO MUNICIPALE and the SANT'AGATA, SAN PLACIDO and SANTA CHIARA churches are the central buildings. URSINO CASTLE was built in the 13th century, a bastion against seaborne raiders.
Cefalù (2). The CATHEDRAL is a Romanesque basilica decorated with Byzantine mosaics. Built 1131–1240, it has the austere stone façade and tiny windows of its Apulian prototypes.
Palermo (1). The Norman Romanesque CATHEDRAL has been so altered since it was begun in 1185 that it has lost much of its original character. The CHURCH OF LA MARTORANA has a Byzantine dome and drum with mosaic decoration on a gold background and a detached campanile. The triple-domed CHURCH OF SAN CATALDO, 1161, is decorated simply, like the CHURCH OF SAN GIOVANNI DEGLI EREMITI, 1132–48. The 12th-century PALATINE CHAPEL, once part of Palermo's royal palace, is lined with mosaics. Five miles away, at **Monreale**, the CATHEDRAL has an oriental air. Built of limestone inlaid with black lava and interspersed with coloured marbles, its remarkable Sicilian Romanesque interior is decorated with mosaics. The 13th-century BENEDICTINE CLOISTERS are gorgeously decorated.
Ragusa (6). The 18th-century CHURCH OF SAN GIORGIO by Gagliardi is one of Sicily's few Baroque churches.
Syracuse (5). The GREEK THEATRE, begun in the 3rd century BC, is the finest, and the TEMPLE OF APOLLO, *c.* 565 BC, is the oldest of the remains of this once-important Greek provincial city. Of less remote antiquity is the elliptical parapet-ringed ROMAN AMPHITHEATRE.
Taormina (3). The 3rd-century BC GREEK THEATRE is the second largest in Sicily and complete enough to be used each year for summer festivals.

ITALY

Assisi (16). The CHURCH OF SAN FRANCESCO, 1226, comprises a rock-carved lower church, its walls covered with early 14th-century frescoes, and a Gothic upper church painted by Giotto. The Romanesque CATHEDRAL OF SAN RUFINO was begun in 1144.
Bari (18). City ramparts, archways and piazzas and the massive bastioned CASTLE sustain Bari's medieval mood. The Romanesque CHURCH OF SAN NICOLA is one of southern Italy's oldest buildings, dating from the late 11th century.
Caprarola (25). The PALAZZO FARNESE, a masterpiece of Mannerist architecture, rises above immaculately terraced gardens, an important part of the composition. Vignola's stern façade frames an outer pentagon by Peruzzi, which in turn surrounds a circular court.
Castel del Monte (17) was built in the 13th century under the Emperor Frederick II. Eight mighty towers corner the octagonal keep. Here, Roman symmetry was incorporated into a concentric defensive system.
Cremona (5). Romanesque arches on small marble columns lighten the solidity of the Romanesque CATHEDRAL and the TORAZZO, Italy's tallest campanile. Galleries rim the crown of the octagonal BAPTISTRY, which, with the 13th-century TOWN HALL, completes an impressive complex.
Florence (32). Giotto's 269-ft-high CAMPANILE, embellished with multicoloured marble and bas-reliefs, complements the adjoining, predominantly Gothic, CATHEDRAL, whose magnificent dome was added by Brunelleschi in 1420. Its 270-ft-long nave is one of the longest of any cathedral in the world. The green and white marble 11th-century BAPTISTRY, third building in this famous group, is a domed octagon with marvellously worked bronze doors. Near by is the severe, crenellated PALAZZO VECCHIO, the Gothic Town Hall, dominated by its soaring bell-tower. The venerable, arched PONTE VECCHIO has been a shopping centre since the Middle Ages. SANTA CROCE, begun in 1294 by Arnolfo di Cambio, is one of the largest Gothic churches. Brunelleschi's FOUNDLING HOSPITAL, begun in 1421, was the first Renaissance building by the first Renaissance architect, and the PALAZZO RUCELLAI was one of the first palaces to display the classical Orders. Among Brunelleschi's churches, SANTA MARIA DEGLI ANGELI was one of the earliest centrally planned Renaissance churches. SAN LORENZO, like SANTO SPIRITO, was styled like a basilica, but the NEW SACRISTY was added by Michelangelo in High Renaissance style. His Mannerist leanings become apparent in the LAURENTIAN LIBRARY. The PALAZZO MEDICI, built in 1444 by Michelozzo, was the first Florentine Renaissance palace, and the PALAZZO PITTI, begun *c.* 1458, the most famous. The most representative Early Renaissance town palace is Benedetto da Maiano's PALAZZO STROZZI, built from 1489 to 1539. The PALAZZO UFFIZI was Vasari's 16th-century Mannerist masterpiece. The CHURCH OF SANTA MARIA NOVELLA, 1278–1350, was the first Gothic building to be given a superimposed Renaissance façade, the work of Alberti in the 15th century. To Florence's collection of great churches Michelucci added, in 1962, the CHURCH OF SAN GIOVANNI, simple and striking, built of coarse rubble with a copper roof. Nervi designed the STADIUM in 1930, with a cantilevered roof and ingenious flying spiral staircase. Conspicuous on its high hill is the CHURCH OF SAN MINIATO AL MONTE, Romanesque with antique Roman columns. The coloured patterns of its marbles and mosaics are a tribute to the influence of Byzantium upon this glorious city.
Genoa (35). Among her 400 churches, the Romanesque CATHEDRAL OF SAN LORENZO has a 16th-century tower, cupola and ceiling, and the 13th-century CHURCH OF SAN MATTEO, with a black and white marble façade, was built in 1278.
Ivrea (2). The OLIVETTI ADMINISTRATIVE AND INDUSTRIAL CENTRE was built in four phases between the 1930s and 1950s by Figini and Pollini. The buildings of the Welfare Centre and the Factory are arranged around a piazza in a landscaped setting.
Mantua (7). The immense CASTEL DI SAN GIORGIO, like the PALAZZO DUCALE, was decorated with paintings by the great masters. Begun in 1472, the CHURCH OF SANT'ANDREA, with its triumphal arch façade, and SAN SEBASTIANO, begun a decade earlier, were the only two buildings which Alberti designed in their entirety. Outside the city, the low wings of Giulio Romano's Mannerist PALAZZO DEL TÈ, 1526–34, built around a huge courtyard, form an architectural unity with the well-planned garden.
Maser (11). Set in magnificent grounds, Palladio's excellent VILLA BARBARO is decorated with Veronese frescoes.
Milan (4). The CATHEDRAL is a vast and intricate white marble Gothic edifice adorned with 135 spires and 2,245 statues. Like the sombre CHURCH OF SANT'AMBROGIO it is more northern European than Italian in style. Bramante's CHURCH OF SANTA MARIA PRESSO SAN SATIRO, 1482–94, has a non-existent chancel, cleverly faked in high relief, a delightful demonstration of linear perspective. The polygonal drum he added, together with dome, choir and transepts to the CHURCH OF SANTA MARIA DELLE GRAZIE was imitated widely. Eclecticism governed the design of the 19th-century OPERA HOUSE, and English advice was used in the building of the iron and glass GALLERIA VITTORIO EMANUELE II. In the same pioneering spirit, Ponti's PIRELLI SKYSCRAPER, 1955–8, towers 415 ft above the city, and the strange TORRE VELASCA is a crenellated office block. The OLIVETTI OFFICES, 1955, have a heliport on the roof.
Montepulciano (28). Sangallo the Elder's masterpiece, MADONNA DI SAN BIAGIO, was built on the town's outskirts in 1518–29 on a Greek cross plan. Its two storeys are spanned by two Orders of pilasters, perfectly related.
Naples (21). The imposing 14th-century fortress, CASTELLO NUOVO, with grandiose triumphal arch and battlemented towers, is an austere contrast to the statue-laden 17th-century ROYAL PALACE and to the southern Baroque CERTOSA DI SAN MARTINO, designed by Cosimo Fanzago in the 17th century. Luigi Vanvitelli is best known for the Royal Palace at **Caserta**, the 18th-century summer residence of the Bourbon rulers with long Versailles-inspired gardens. 19th-century architectural themes are represented by Nicolini's OPERA HOUSE, by the monumental CHURCH OF SAN FRANCESCO DI PAOLA and by Quaglia's UNIVERSITY. Designed to seat 60,000, the STADIUM, 1955–7, is a clear case of beauty through function.
Ostia (22). On the outskirts of the modern town are the ruins of the recently excavated OSTIA ANTICA, a Roman city complete with forum, capitol, barracks and insulae.
Padua (10). Built in 1305, the PALAZZO DELLA RAGIONE, the long Town Hall, displays, in embryo form, the Renaissance loggia, a row of depressed arches supported upon columns. Completed just two years later, in 1307, the BASILICA SAN ANTONIO, a pilgrimage church, is Byzantine in inspiration.
Paestum (19). The Classical buildings in the Ancient Greek city of Poseidonia rival the ancient remains of Greece itself. The TEMPLE OF POSEIDON, dating from *c.* 460 BC, approaches the more perfected type of Doric temple. It has 35 fluted columns and a well-preserved entablature. The TEMPLE OF DEMETER, *c.* 510 BC, and the BASILICA, another temple, show an early Ionic influence.
Parma (6). The threefold group of CATHEDRAL, BAPTISTRY and CAMPANILE, built between the 12th and 13th centuries, rounded and octagonal in form and bright with coloured marbles, is one of the finest groups of Romanesque ecclesiastical buildings.
Pavia (3). The CATHEDRAL, begun in 1488 by Bramante, has a superb Early Renaissance interior, and its dome was designed by Leonardo da Vinci. The CHURCH OF SAN MICHELE, built in the 12th century, has a Byzantine-like central cupola and a typically Italian façade. The CERTOSA, outside the town, is a pure example of Lombardian Renaissance style. Begun in 1396 by Visconti, its sculptured façade was designed in the 15th century by Amadeo.
Pienza (27). In the mid-15th century Pope Pius II employed Bernardo Rossellino to convert Pienza, then a village, into a township. His Renaissance CATHEDRAL, simply and classically beautiful, flanked by the PALAZZO PUBBLICO and the PALAZZO PICCOLOMINI, all surrounding a central square, are a fine example of Early Renaissance town-planning.
Pisa (34). Designed by Buscheto, a Greek architect, the CATHEDRAL was begun in 1063. The five-aisled BASILICA has a Saracen-inspired pointed dome and triumphal arch. Dioti Salvi's circular BAPTISTRY is surrounded by a lower storey of half-columns connected by semicircular arches, and the cylindrical CAMPANILE, the Leaning Tower, slants 14 ft from the perpendicular because of a 12th-century construction miscalculation.
Poggio a Caiano (31). One of the earliest Renaissance palaces, the VILLA MEDICI has a loggia by Sangallo.
Pompeii (20). The excavated buildings of this Roman town, buried by volcanic eruption in AD 79, give the most complete picture available of Roman life.
Prato (33). The 11th-century CATHEDRAL was transformed by Pisano in 14th-century Gothic style. Sangallo's SANTA MARIA DELLE CARCERI, completed in 1506, is outstanding among the city's churches.
Ravenna (13) was capital of the western Roman Empire in the 5th century when the MAUSOLEUM OF GALLA PLACIDIA, the earliest cruciform building, was erected. The ORTHODOX and the ARIAN BAPTISTRIES, *c.* 500, exhibit some of the beautiful interior mosaics which characterize Ravenna's Early Christian churches, and the TOMB OF THEODORIC, *c.* 530, houses the ashes of the great King of the Ostrogoths. SAN VITALE, built 526–47, is the West's most interesting Byzantine church, and SANT'APOLLINARE NUOVO, 493–525, has incomparable mosaics. SANT'APOLLINARE IN CLASSE, 534–50, is a three-aisled basilica with a timber roof and an early campanile.
Rimini (14). Alberti's TEMPIO MALATESTIANO, begun in 1450 and sadly never completed, displays the first attempt to adapt a triumphal arch façade to a Gothic building.
Rome (23). The architectural heritage of the Eternal City is an array of ages, styles and moods. Perfectly proportioned and excellently preserved, the late Roman PANTHEON is crowned with a majestic hemispherical dome. Tiers of arcades surround the 1st-century COLOSSEUM, large enough to seat 50,000. The FORUM ROMANUM was the largest public square of the ancient city, and the BASILICA OF MAXENTIUS, begun AD 308, is the most famous Roman basilica, a proof

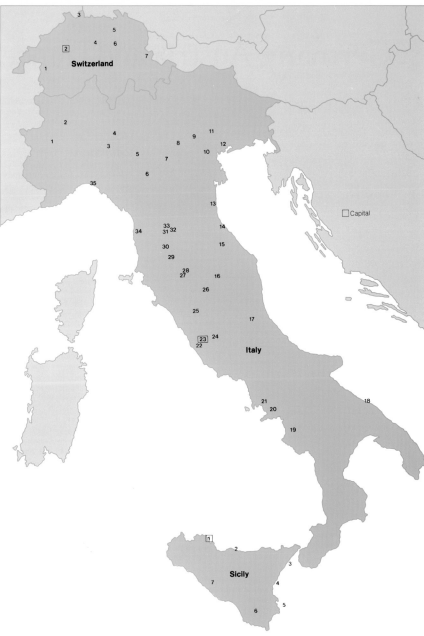

Italy

Switzerland

Sicily

□ Capital

---

the nearby TEMPLE OF VESTA, c. 27 BC, and the 1st-century AD TEMPLE OF THE SYBILS.

Todi (26). One of the finest centrally planned Early Renaissance churches outside Florence, SANTA MARIA DELLA CONSOLAZIONE was designed in 1508 by Caprarola and Peruzzi.

Turin (1). Guarino Guarini, a Theatine monk, designed in the mid-17th century the CHURCH OF SAN LORENZO, with a strange, 36-arched cupola, and the complex Baroque PALAZZO CARIGNANO. Filippo Juvarra, equally gifted, led Turin into the 18th century with the façade of the CHURCH OF SANTA CRISTINA, the rich PALAZZO MADAMA, with a superb staircase, and the immense Baroque STUPINIGI PALACE. His BASILICA DI SUPERGA, a mausoleum, marks the apogee of Italian Baroque. Turin is a fine example of 19th-century town-planning, the work of Frizzi and Promis. The fine PORTA NUOVA RAILWAY STATION is an iron and glass construction and, reflecting contemporary impulses, the PALACE OF LABOUR, built for an exhibition in 1961 by Nervi, has steel columns supported upon palm leaf capitals and is capped by several mushroomed roofs. On the city's fringe are the futuristic FIAT WORKS, 1919–23, by Giacomo Matte-Trucco.

Urbino (15). The twin towers of the castle-like 5th-century DUCAL PALACE flank a slender unpretentious façade. One of the finest of Italy's Renaissance palaces, it has a splendid cloistered courtyard.

Venice (12). Considered by many to be one of the wonders of the world, ST MARK'S CATHEDRAL, begun 1042, extracts the richest aspects of various styles. Its five hemispherical domes are of Byzantine influence, while its stately ornamental superstructure is Romanesque and Gothic. It overlooks ST MARK'S SQUARE, which opens on the Grand Canal and is adjoined by the Gothic Renaissance flamboyance of the pink and white marble DOGE'S PALACE. Among Venice's other architectural masterpieces are the great domed CHURCH OF SANTA MARIA DELLA SALUTE, built to commemorate the passing of a plague in 1630, the gallery-lined, graceful RIALTO BRIDGE and the magesterial CA D'ORO, a medieval palace haughtily poised on a canal edge. Gracing the waterfront is Palladio's CHURCH OF SAN GIORGIO MAGGIORE, 1566. The earliest of Palladio's two Venetian Mannerist churches, the REDENTORE, was begun in 1577. The CATHEDRAL OF SS. MARIA AND DONATO on the **Island of Murano**, built in the 12th century, is Venetian Romanesque.

Verona (8). The famous ARENA is one of the best-preserved Roman amphitheatres. SAN ZENO MAGGIORE, rebuilt from 1138, has one of the earliest naves in Italy, and the CATHEDRAL is both Gothic and Romanesque.

Vicenza (9). The great Gothic Town Hall, the BASILICA, was given its façade by Palladio in the 16th century. His masterpiece was the VILLA ROTONDA, built on a hilltop.

SWITZERLAND

Basel (3). Although it still has a Romanesque east end, the hilltop MINSTER is representative of Swiss Gothic. The restored TOWN HALL was built in the 16th century in classical style. Karl Moser, leading 20th-century Swiss architect, designed the CHURCH OF ST ANTHONY in 1927. in concrete with glass panelling, reminiscent of Perret's designs, but more imposing.

Berne (2). Arcaded streets with 15th-century pillars, carved fountains and stern 13th-century towers crowd Berne's centre. The CATHEDRAL and the TOWN HALL, Switzerland's finest secular Gothic building, were built in the 15th century. The HALEN ESTATE at **Kirchindach**, 1960, is an important example of private enterprise housing.

Chillon Castle (1). Reflected in the still waters of Lake Geneva, the spiky turrets of the 13th-century castle look romantic and picturesque. Built with the help of English Plantagenet military engineers, it is none the less severely functional.

Einsedeln (6). On the shores of Lake Geneva, this PILGRIMAGE CHURCH is one of Switzerland's outstanding Baroque achievements. Built in the early 18th century by Caspar Moonsbrugger, its fantastic interior is the work of the Asam brothers. To the northeast is the ABBEY CHURCH OF ST GALLEN. Its outer appearance is sedate, classical Baroque in the Vorarlberg tradition, but its LIBRARY is an outstanding example of Rococo decoration. The SWISS GRADUATE SCHOOL OF ECONOMICS AND ADMINISTRATION, 1960–3, is by Förderer, one of Switzerland's outstanding modern architects.

Lucerne (4) is famous for its charming medieval quarter with two unique 14th- and 15th-century covered wooden BRIDGES. The 17th-century ALTES RATHAUS is curiously medieval in appearance. The JESUIT CHURCH, 1666–73, was built in a restrained Baroque style. Pupils of Moser built the 20th-century CHURCH OF ST CHARLES and the CHURCH OF ST JOSEPH, the latter with a detached campanile.

Salginatobel Bridge (7), built in 1930 by Robert Maillart, is typical of his low-cost, functional structures which blend aesthetically into the countryside.

Zurich (5), where in 1963 Switzerland's greatest architect designed his own LE CORBUSIER CENTRE, seems to have become a centre for modern architecture. In 1930–2 the NEUBÜHL SCHEME was an advanced method of town-planning using standardized units created by Paul Artaria and Hans Schmidt. Philip Roth's "REIDHOF" SCHOOL, 1963, belongs to the modern movement. The FREUDENBERG SCHOOL, 1958–61, by Jacques Schader, on its hilltop, is one of the finest of Switzerland's modern schools. At **Alstetten**, on the outskirts, Karl Moser designed the CHURCH OF ST JOSEPH, 1938–41, the façade perforated and surmounted by a clock and belfry.

---

of Roman vaulting skills. Built in the 5th century, when Rome had become a centre of Early Christian building, SANTA MARIA MAGGIORE retains much of its original interior and SANT'AGNESE FUORI LE MURA is a faithful replica of the original basilica. Old St Peter's was demolished to build ST PETER'S CATHEDRAL, 1506–1626, the work of many architects beginning with Bramante. The dome, built by Michelangelo, looks down on the wide expanse of ST PETER'S SQUARE, laid out by Bernini and flanked by the VATICAN, for which Bramante designed the main courtyards. A tunnel connects the Vatican with the fortress-like, circular CASTEL SANT'ANGELO, once Hadrian's mausoleum and later a refuge for besieged popes. The austere Tuscan Doric façade of Bramante's TEMPIETTO SAN PIETRO IN MONTORIO signalled the beginning of the early 16th-century High Renaissance in Rome. Sangallo followed in similar style with SANTA MARIA DI LORETO, 1507, and Raphael with the VILLA MADAMA and the PALAZZO VIDONI CAFFARELLI, but

Peruzzi, like Michelangelo irreverent of ancient principles, designed the PALAZZO MASSIMI ALLE COLONNE along unmistakably Mannerist lines. Vignola's IL GESÙ, designed in 1568, with its curved façade, was the first Baroque building. Among the glitter of later Baroque splendour the CHURCH OF SANTA MARIA MAGGIORE and the PALAZZO BARBERINI, its façade by Bernini and its decoration by Borromini, were outstanding. Borromini's SAN CARLO ALLE QUATTRO FONTANE, 1638–40, based on triangular units, was an immediate sensation, and Bernini's SANT'ANDREA AL QUIRINALE, 1668, which was centralized and oval in plan, was copied all over Europe. The outstanding building of 19th-century Rome was the MONUMENT OF VICTOR EMMANUEL II, symbol of the unification of Italy. A fitting beginning to Italy's post-war architecture, Montuori and Associates' RAILWAY TERMINUS, with an immense sweeping, curving roof, was finally completed in 1951. Resourceful and inventive, Nervi built his

magnificent PALAZZO and PALAZZETTO DELLO SPORT in the 1950s and 1960s. Near by, in **Caprarola**, the PALAZZO FARNESE, 1517–34, is the most monumental of Renaissance palaces.

San Gimignano (30). Ringed by ramparts, the town, with its stone palaces and narrow streets, retains its medieval appearance and flavour. Thirteen square towers, remnants of wars fought between rival families, overlook the surrounding countryside.

Siena (29) is a quaint medieval city, where the soaring, slender TORRE DEL MANGIA, with crenellated crown, rises from a wing of the gracious Gothic PALAZZO PUBBLICO, built 1288–1310. The CATHEDRAL is one of Italy's finest Gothic buildings, with a richly sculpted white marble façade, the work of Giovanni Pisano during the late 13th century.

Tivoli (24). The gardens of VILLA D'ESTE, 1550, a former Benedictine monastery, descend in a series of terraces adorned with magnificent fountains. Stucco-coated columns emphasize the purity of line of

273

Europe 2: East and West Germany, Austria and France

EAST GERMANY

Bernau (2). Hannes Meyer, a Swiss architect who succeeded Gropius as director of the Bauhaus, designed the GERMAN TRADE UNIONS SCHOOL in 1930.

Dessau (4). Though the Bauhaus buildings have almost all been destroyed since the 1920s, GROPIUS'S OWN HOUSE survives.

Dresden (5). Only parts of Poppelmann's curious ZWINGER, 1711–22, an enclosure for court pageants, festivals and tournaments, survived the Allied bombing.

Potsdam (3). Germany's leading architect, Von Knobelsdorf, replanned the city from 1744 and built the SANSSOUCI PALACE with vivid Rococo decoration. The OLD TOWN HALL and the NEUES PALAST were by Boumann, a Dutch architect. Schinkel, a native painter, based his NIKOLAIKIRCHE, 1844, on the Roman Pantheon, and Mendelsohn, a Prussian-American, designed the EINSTEIN TOWER in 1919–21.

BERLIN

Berlin (1), devastated and partitioned in 1945, is still capital of East and West Germany. Von Knobelsdorf's SCHLOSS CHARLOTTENBURG has been restored, as has Schüter's ARSENAL. The 19th-century NEUE WACHE, the city gate, and Schinkel's ALTES MUSEUM have survived, as have the vivid red-brick Romantic Classical TOWN HALL and Rachsdorf's weighty Neo-Baroque CATHEDRAL. As architect to AEG, Peter Behrens designed the TURBINE FACTORY in 1909. Poelzig's GROSSES SCHAUSPIELHAUS, 1919, is a dramatic example of late Art Nouveau and Gropius's SIEMENSTADT is a prototype modern housing estate. An interesting post-war building is Egon Eiermann's KAISER WILHELM GEDACHTNIS KIRCHE in West Berlin, with honeycomb-patterned windows. The PHILHARMONIC HALL, 1960–3, is by Hans Scharoun.

WEST GERMANY

Aachen (21). The polygonal domed ROYAL CHAPEL, built 796–804, the centre of the predominantly Gothic CATHEDRAL, was built as Charlemagne's mausoleum and became an important prototype for later German churches.

Alfeld-an-der-Leine (2). The FAGUS FACTORY, 1911, the prototype of the post-war glass curtain-walled buildings, is a rare German example of Gropius's work.

Augsburg (9). The FUGGER CHAPEL, a mausoleum, in the CHURCH OF ST ANNA, was in 1509 one of the first German buildings with Renaissance features. Elias Holl's early 17th-century TOWN HALL and

ARSENAL exhibit a purer Renaissance style.

Bamberg (5). The CATHEDRAL, although built in the early 13th century, is still essentially Romanesque in style. Bamberg was one of the centres of 17th-century Baroque architecture when Georg Dientzenhofer designed the façade of ST MARTIN'S CHURCH and Leonhard Dientzenhofer built the ABBEY OF ST MICHAEL.

Cologne (20). The soaring façade of northern Europe's largest Gothic CATHEDRAL is a breathtaking contrast with the 20th-century precinct before it. Begun in 1248, the cathedral was only completed in 1824–80. The CHURCH OF THE APOSTLES was begun in 1035. The STEEL CHURCH, built in 1928 by Otto Bartning, has steel and glass walls. The CHURCH OF ST ENGELBERT at **Cologne-Riehl** is circular in plan with circular windows, an Expressionist church of 1931–3 by Dominikus Böhm. In the 1914 Werkbund Exhibition the MODEL THEATRE was Van de Velde's last pre-war building, while the ADMINISTRATION BUILDING was one of Gropius's earliest. His FREE-STANDING HOUSES were almost completely prefabricated and he designed the MODEL FACTORY with Franz Hoffmann. The HOUSE OF OSWALD UNGERS, built in the late 1950s, is a significant modern dwelling.

Frankfurt am Main (17). Ernst May, City Architect between 1925 and 1930, planned a number of SUBURBAN ESTATES.

Heidelberg Castle (14), although partly ruined, is still an impressive example of the many castles built in Germany during the 16th and 17th centuries.

Limburg Cathedral (18), beside the River Lahn, was built in 1213–42 and is late Romanesque in style.

The Monastery Church of Maria Laach (19), 1093–1156, a Romanesque church which evolved towards Gothic in the later stages of building, still displays a stylistic unity.

Munich (8). Leo von Klenze's LUDWIGSTRASSE, his Neo-Grecian KONIGSPLATZ, and Karl von Fischer's KAROLINENPLATZ, were laid out in the 19th century. The CATHEDRAL, a faithful post-war restoration, was begun in 1470. A sumptuous palace, the MUNICH RESIDENZ, c. 1560, in Early Renaissance style, is one of the largest in the country. To the north SCHLEISSHEIM, enlarged by Zuccali, is typical of Germany's imported Roman Baroque of the 17th century. Zuccali and Viscardi enlarged the SCHLOSS NYMPHENBURG in 1702. ST MICHAEL's CHURCH is Germany's outstanding Renaissance church. Baroque without and a Rococo fantasy within, the CHURCH OF ST JOHN NEPOMUK was the Asam brothers' most mature work, built in 1733–46. Zimmer-

mann designed the High Baroque pilgrimage church, DIE WIES, near **Steingaden** to the south, after 1745, with a superb ornate oval nave. The RESIDENZ THEATER in Munich, 1751–3, is a Rococo building by a French architect, De la Guêpière. An imposing Neo-Gothic structure, the TOWN HALL was built in the 19th century. For the 1972 Olympic Games, Frei Otto built the OLYMPIC GAMES TENT.

Nuremberg (6). The city's Gothic buildings miraculously escaped destruction during World War II. The façade of the FRAUENKIRCHE has been carefully restored. A hall-church, it was begun in 1354. The CUSTOM HOUSE was built in 1498.

Ottobeuren (10). The ABBEY CHURCH is the finest of J. M. Fischer's Baroque churches in Bavaria.

Regensburg (7). The oldest church in this Bavarian town, the SCHOTTENKIRCHE, is Romanesque, with a rich sculptured portal. The 13th-century CATHEDRAL is noted for its fine stone and glasswork. The Gothic TOWN HALL was built in the days when Regensburg was a semi-independent city-state.

Speyer Cathedral (15) stands, unusually, in the centre of a park. The large, groin-vaulted crypt was begun c. 1030.

Stuttgart (13). Solid, plain ashlar blocks predict post-war modernism in Bonatz's RAILWAY STATION of 1912–26. In 1926, Mendelsohn's SCHOCKEN STORE, marked by horizontal bands of windows, was one of a number he designed in the 1920s. Mies van der Rohe

designed an APARTMENT BUILDING for the Werkbund Exhibition in 1927.

Trier (22). The CATHEDRAL, begun in 1019, has a former Roman basilica as part of its structure. Solidly Romanesque with four stately towers, it forms a group with the Transitional LIEBFRAUENKIRCHE, built in the 13th century and exhibiting both round and pointed arches. Built in 300, the PORTA NIGRA is a defensive Roman gateway.

Ulm (12). The MINSTER, built 1377–1492, its single 529-ft-high openwork spire added in the 19th century to the original design, is noted for its fine carving and masonry. West of Ulm, the ABBEY CHURCH OF OBER MARCHTAL was built 1686–1701 by Thumb and Beer.

Vierzehnheiligen (4). The PILGRIMAGE CHURCH was Neumann's supreme success. Built 1743–72 on the summit of a hill, it is a basilican church with a curving centre-piece between two towers, and its stuccoed and sculptured interior is a masterpiece of Baroque decoration.

Weingarten (11). The ABBEY CHURCH, begun in 1715, was built by a number of Germany's most famous Baroque architects.

Worms Cathedral (16). Supreme example of the German Romanesque, this dignified Rhineland church, built c. 1110–81, retains much of its original plan.

Würzburg (3). Balthasar Neumann carried out his earliest architectural work in this central German city, which he

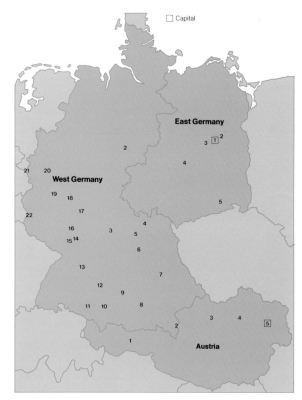

☐ Capital

East Germany

West Germany

Austria

helped to plan. The RESIDENZ, on which he worked with Von Hildebrandt, was his last and major work, begun in 1719.

AUSTRIA

Innsbruck (1). Christoph Gumpp's MARIAHILFKIRCHE, 1647, and Georg Gumpp's later and more complex LANDHAUS represent the birth of Austrian Baroque. ST JOSEPH'S CHURCH, 1717, was built by Herkommer, a Bavarian, and decorated by the Asam brothers.

Melk (4). High above the Danube, Jacob Prandtauer's Baroque MONASTERY CHURCH was built in the 18th century.

Salzburg (2). High above the city the 12th-century CASTLE has fine medieval concentric walling. One of Austria's first Renaissance buildings, the CATHEDRAL was begun in 1614 by an Italian, Santino Solari. The DREIFALTIGKEITSKIRCHE, 1694, and the KOLLEGIENKIRCHE, 1696–1707, are by Fischer von Erlach.

Sankt Florian (3). The ABBEY CHURCH, begun by Carlo Carlone and completed by Prandtauer, is the largest in Upper Austria and an example of pure Baroque.

Vienna (5). A typical German hall-church, ST STEPHEN'S CATHEDRAL, with its lovely 448-ft-high spire, was begun in the 14th century, a medieval building in a Baroque city. As architect to the court, Fischer von Erlach enlarged the old HOFBURG PALACE, adding its gleaming white RIDING SCHOOL and an IMPERIAL LIBRARY, restrained and verging on the Neo-Classical. In 1696, he began the SCHONBRUNN PALACE on the city's outskirts. His finest building was the KARLSKIRCHE, 1716, with two columns in front reminiscent of minarets. Von Hildebrandt's first Viennese building was the PIARISTENKIRCHE, built in 1698. Its two-towered façade curves convexly and its interior, like that of ST PETER'S CHURCH, is oval shaped with a painted saucer dome. He is best known for his palaces, the BELVEDERE, 1714–21, his masterpiece, the DAUN-KINSKY PALACE and the SCHWARZENBERG, 1697–1723, which he designed with Fischer von Erlach. These Austrian architects also designed the best of Vienna's public buildings. Ferstel's VOTIVKIRCHE, 1856–79, and the PARLIAMENT HOUSE were built as part of the Emperor Franz Josef's 19th-century city replanning scheme. In the dying years of a 600-year-old empire, Vienna embraced the Art Nouveau with Olbrich's SEZESSION HOUSE, 1898–9, a symbolic exhibition building, and the delicately ornate MAJOLICA HOUSE, 1898–9, by Wagner, who also designed the eclectic POST OFFICE SAVINGS BANK in 1903. Adolf Loos's STEINER HOUSE, 1910, was the first modern domestic house.

FRANCE

Albi Cathedral (37) towers above the rugged River Tarn, a monument to the war-torn years of its birth. This late 13th-century brick building is a fortress as much as a church.

Amiens (6), France's second-highest cathedral, is regarded as the epitome of French Gothic and is famous for its wood carvings.

Ancy-le-Franc (16). The CHATEAU, the first French step towards the Renaissance style, was designed by an Italian, Sebastian Serlio.

Anet (23). The CHATEAU, designed in 1548 by Philibert de l'Orme, was copied throughout Europe. The entrance, the only remaining part, and the chapel, were the first French buildings in Renaissance style.

Angers (30). The 17 huge mural towers of the 13th-century CASTLE dominate the town. Its curtain walls are 130 ft high. The CATHEDRAL, begun in the 11th century, is a domical cruciform church in the Romanesque style of Anjou.

Angoulême (33), perched like an eagle's eyrie on a high rock outcrop, has a Romanesque CATHEDRAL with bell-tower and sculpted façade in Aquitaine regional style, and four Byzantine-inspired domes.

Arles (43), once a fine port, is the site of a Roman AMPHITHEATRE built before 55 BC. The Romanesque Provençal CHURCH OF SAINT TROPHIME has a classical façade. Ancient Roman influence upon early Provençal churches is apparent at SAINT GILLES DU GARD, near by.

Autun (14) is still guarded by two ROMAN GATEWAYS, dating back to the time of Augustus. Begun in 1120, the CATHEDRAL, with pointed nave vaults and arches and embryo flying buttresses, marks the transition from Romanesque to Gothic. It is celebrated for the original beauty of its stone carvings by Gislebertus.

Avignon (42). The PONT DE SAINT-BENEZET is one of France's rare Romanesque secular works. The PALACE OF THE POPES, 1316–70, was the 14th-century papal residence.

Azay-le-Rideau (29). In this CHATEAU, begun in 1519, grim medieval functionalism gave way to Renaissance elegance.

Beauvais Cathedral (5) is the loftiest Gothic building. Its present choir vault, 157 ft high, replaced an earlier one, just 2 in higher, which collapsed in 1284.

Blois (27). The CHATEAU was built between the 13th and the 16th centuries in three different styles. There is a remarkable octagonal spiral staircase in the Early Renaissance François I wing.

Bourges (26). The CATHEDRAL, begun in the fervour of the 12th-century religious revival, was completed on a less ambitious scale. With the five portals of its Flamboyant west front and fine 13th-century glass, it is one of Europe's most remarkable cathedrals.

Caen (3) was the birthplace of Norman architecture. Here, in 1062, William the Conqueror founded the ABBAYE AUX HOMMES

and, in 1066, his wife, Queen Mathilde, founded the ABBAYE AUX DAMES. Dating from the 14th century, SAINT-PIERRE is in the mature Norman style.

Carcassonne (39), a fortified hill town, rises dramatically from a flat plain. The walls date from Roman to medieval times.

Chambord (25). The CHATEAU, begun in 1519, like many of the early Loire châteaux which ushered the Renaissance style into France, is traditional in style with Italianate decoration.

Chartres Cathedral (24), the outstanding example of French High Gothic architecture, is the finest church in France. It is famous for the figure sculpture on the portals and fine 12th- and 13th-century stained glass.

Chenonceaux (28), begun in 1515 on the medieval square keep plan, was extended by Philibert de l'Orme to form a bridge over the River Cher. Jean Bullant's gallery was a Late Renaissance addition.

Cluny (13), as completed in 1130, was the largest church in Romanesque Europe. Today its ruins still have the earliest French pointed arch.

Conques (36). The CHURCH OF SAINTE FOY, the smallest of the pilgrimage churches, has a famous sculptured tympanum over the West Portal.

Coutances Cathedral (2), 1218–91, is France's purest example of Norman Gothic, a style characterized by twin towers surrounded by turrets and capped by high spires.

Eveux-sur-l'Arbresle (12). The MONASTERY OF LA TOURETTE, 1957–60, by Le Corbusier, is a forceful structure in concrete; the U-shaped monastery and its rectangular chapel surround a central court.

Fontainebleau (18) was the mid-16th-century creation of two Italians: Primaticcio and Rosso. The decoration of the Long Gallery—the earliest in northern Europe—for which they devised strap-work, was copied outside France.

Fontenay (32). The ABBEY, founded in the 12th century, is the oldest surviving collection of Cistercian monastic buildings.

Laon (7) was France's first complete Gothic cathedral, built 1160–1225.

Le Raincy (20). The simple single-aisle plan, the use of glass with reinforced concrete and the 140-ft-high bell-tower made Auguste Perret's CHAPEL OF NOTRE DAME a pioneer building of the 1920s.

Marseille (44). Planned as the first stage in a township environment by Le Corbusier in the 1940s, the UNITE D'HABITA-TION is a bold high concrete building of interlocking rectangular apartments.

Mont-Saint-Michel (1). The ABBEY stands on a solitary rock, savage tides between it and the coast. The Romanesque church is the oldest building, with a Flamboyant Gothic choir.

Nîmes (40) preserves the MAISON CARRÉE, the best-preserved early Roman temple, and the PONT DU GARD, built c. AD 14, was once part of a 25-mile aqueduct. The AMPHITHEATRE is used today.

Orange (41), rich in Roman remains, has an AMPHITHEATRE dating from AD 50 and one of France's finest triumphal arches, the ARC DE TRIOMPHE OF TIBERIUS, dating from 49 BC.

Paris (21). The ABBEY CHURCH OF SAINT DENIS, the first major Gothic building, was begun just outside Paris in 1135. The CATHEDRAL OF NOTRE DAME was begun 30 years later. With the SAINTE CHAPELLE, 1244–8, and the 15th-century HOTEL DE CLUNY, Parisian architecture spans the whole Gothic era. Pierre Lescot designed the Renaissance PALAIS DU LOUVRE. De Brosse, the leading architect of 17th-century Paris, built the PALAIS DE LUXEMBOURG and the CHURCH OF SAINT GERVAIS in classical style, and was succeeded by Jacques Lemercier with the CHURCH OF THE SORBONNE. The CHURCH OF THE VAL-DE-GRACE was built to the design of Mansart, whose masterpiece was the CHATEAU DE MAISONS-LAFITTE, begun 1642. He built the CHURCH OF THE INVALIDES and laid out the PLACE VENDOME. VERSAILLES, still one of the world's largest buildings, was built for Louis XIV outside Paris by Le Vau and Hardouin-Mansart. The INSTITUT DE FRANCE, begun 1661, was Le Vau's purest Baroque building. Soufflot's dome of the PANTHEON, 1787, was a landmark in French Neo-Classicism. From this the Empire Styles were born of which the ARC DE TRIOMPHE is the best-known example and Vignon's MAGDALEN, 1808, is the most famous church. The EIFFEL TOWER is one of the 19th-century's most celebrated iron structures. Guimard's METRO entrances are among the

few surviving structures of the Art Nouveau in France. The APARTMENT BLOCK ON THE AVENUE WAGRAM was one of Auguste Perret's early buildings, and the reinforced concrete BLOCK ON THE RUE FRANKLIN established his reputation. He also modified Van de Velde's THEATRE OF THE CHAMPS ELYSEES in 1910–11. The Y-shaped 1950s UNESCO BUILDING was designed by Breuer, Zehrfuss and Nervi.

Périgueux (34). The Greek cross shape and five domes of the Romanesque CATHEDRAL OF SAINT FRONT betray a Byzantine inspiration.

Poissy (22). White, cubist and raised on pilotis, the VILLA SAVOIE, 1929–31, is typical of Le Corbusier's early work.

Poitiers (31). The triple apses, small conical towers and profuse sculpture of the Poitou Romanesque style are exemplified by NOTRE DAME LA GRANDE, 1130, and SAINTE HILAIRE, rebuilt 1165. The SAINT JEAN BAPTISTRY is France's oldest church.

Rheims Cathedral (8), built within 100 years, is nevertheless homogeneous in style. The sculpture both inside and out is unique and the windows display the first example of bar tracery.

Ronchamp (11). In the irrationalist style of the 1930s, the CHAPEL OF NOTRE DAME is one of Le Corbusier's most imaginative buildings.

Rouen Cathedral (4) was begun in the 12th century, but the central spire, the final addition, was not built until the 19th century. In this cathedral the Flamboyant style first made its appearance. Rouen's PALAIS DE JUSTICE, a reconstruction of

the 15th-century Town Hall is one of France's finest Gothic secular buildings.

Sens Cathedral (17) is transitional in style. Begun in 1144, it displays both round and pointed arches.

Souillac (35). Once a pilgrimage church on the route to Compostela, the ABBEY CHURCH of SAINTE MARIE dates from 1130. Its excellent sculpture belongs to the same school as that of the ABBEY OF SAINT PIERRE at **Moissac**, founded in the 6th century and demolished, but for the gateway and cloister, during the Revolution.

Strasbourg Cathedral (10), begun late in the 12th century, experienced in 1225 a sudden change to the Gothic style. The west front is its finest feature.

Toulouse (38). The largest remaining pilgrimage church, the Romanesque BASILICA OF SAINT SERNIN, 1080–90, has the five-aisled plan of Cluny and a Gothic tower and spire. The PLACE CAPITOLE, by Guillaume Camnas, is a fine example of 18th-century town-planning.

Vaux-le-Vicomte (19). France's leading Baroque architect, Le Vau, designed this magnificent château for Fouquet. It was decorated by Lebrun and its park laid out by Le Nôtre.

Vézelay (15). One of the largest and most famous of France's many Romanesque churches, the pointed cross vault of SAINTE MADELEINE's interior narthex, 1130, is thought to be the earliest in the country.

Vignory (9). The Romanesque church, rebuilt in 1050, was originally a gift from Charlemagne to local monks. The nave is unvaulted in the Carolingian tradition.

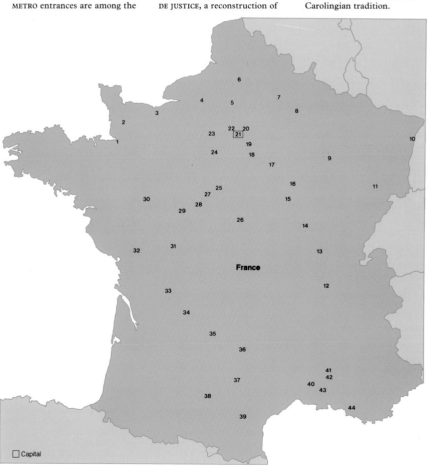

France

☐ Capital

Europe 3: The Low Countries, Britain and Scandinavia

THE NETHERLANDS

Amsterdam (2). The oldest building, the OUDE KERK, 1300, did not receive its steeple until the 16th century. The fine Dutch Palladian ROYAL PALACE by Jacob van Campen was once the Town Hall. The 19th-century RIJKSMUSEUM, like the CENTRAL STATION, emulates the 16th-century Transitional Gothic style. The STOCK EXCHANGE, 1897–1909, by H. P. Berlage, in plain red brick, presaged modern architecture. The fantastic appearance of the EIGENHAARD ESTATE, 1913–21, and the DE DEGERAAD HOUSING DEVELOPMENT, 1917, by Piet Kramer, exemplifies the expressionistic use of Art Nouveau. The newly built ORPHANAGE by Aldo van Eyck utilizes modular units.

Haarlem (1). In the hands of the Dutch master of Mannerism, Lieven de Key, the rectangular MEAT HALL became, in 1602, a building of character.

Hague, The (7). Traditionally the seat of the counts of Holland, the KNIGHT'S HALL in the BINNENHOF dates from 1250. The MAURITSHUIS, c. 1633, first gave a definitive shape to Dutch classicism.

's Hertogenbosch (5). The CATHEDRAL, profusely decorated, is a rare instance of pure Dutch Brabantine.

Hilversum (3). Willem Dudok's VONDEL SCHOOL, built in 1926, is characterized by fine brickwork and long banded windows. Beautifully proportioned, his TOWN HALL, 1928, has been imitated throughout Holland.

Rotterdam (6). The LIJNBAAN PEDESTRIAN PRECINCT, 1953, was the prototype of a now-common city feature. The purposeful and clean-lined two-storey dwellings of the KIEFHOEK HOUSING ESTATE, built in the 1920s, were innovatory for their time. The VAN NELLE FACTORY, 1927–30, was a pre-war experiment.

Utrecht (4). The CATHEDRAL, a major example of French Gothic in Holland, is lined with frescoes. The SCHRÖDER-SCHRÄDER HOUSE, 1924, by Rietveld, is a supreme realization of the two-dimensional De Stijl aesthetic.

BELGIUM

Antwerp (3). The late Gothic CATHEDRAL, 1352–1411, is Belgium's finest and widest. Floris's TOWN HALL, 1561–5, remains the chief monument to Flemish Mannerism.

Bruges (1). A picturesque Hanseatic splendour is still apparent in the ornate and pinnacled TOWN HALL, and in the monumental HALLES and BELFRY. The PALAIS DE JUSTICE is typical of early 16th-century Belgian architecture.

Brussels (4). The CATHEDRAL choir, 1226, is Belgium's oldest Gothic building. The GUILD HOUSES of the GRANDE PLACE display a unity of treatment running through different period styles. The strictly Neo-Classical PLACE ROYALE, part of an 18th-century town-planning scheme, looks down upon the domed PALAIS DE JUSTICE, 1866–73, by Poelaert. The EXCHANGE, 1868–83, is evidence of the 19th-century boom in civic building. The GALERIE DE LA REINE, 1847, an early shopping arcade, is roofed with a semicircular vault of glass in iron frames. Towards the end of the century, Brussels saw the birth of Art Nouveau. Its first manifestation was in VICTOR HORTA'S HOUSE, 1892–3. Horta designed the HOTEL SOLVAY, the MAISON DU PEUPLE, 1896–8, with tendril-like linear decoration, and the HOTEL VAN EETVELDE, 1898–1900. The STOCLET PALACE, 1904–11, by Josef Hoffmann, is an asymmetrical mansion with a tall tower. In severe contrast is the 20th-century CITE MODERNE, 1922–5, by Victor Bourgeois.

Ghent (2). A Romanesque barbican guards the entrance to GRAVENSTEEN CASTLE. The BELFRY, 1300, surmounted by an elegant spire, was a remarkable expression of the city's medieval importance and the half-Gothic, half-Renaissance TOWN HALL of its 16th-century wealth.

Tournai (6). The magnificent black-marbled CATHEDRAL has a Romanesque nave and a Gothic choir.

Uccle (5). The influence of contemporary scientific theories on the aesthetic of Art Nouveau can be seen in the organic unity of BLOEMENWERF, 1895–6, the home of Henri van de Velde.

Ypres (7). Simple and yet richly decorative, the low unbroken façade of the CLOTH HALL, 1200–1304, extends to over 400 ft.

BRITAIN

Anglesey (43). BEAUMARIS CASTLE, 1283–1323, with rings of high curtain walls and mural towers, is illustrative of the active defensive system introduced by Edward I.

Bath (31). The original conduits still bring water to the ROMAN THERMAE, the best preserved in the world. BATH ABBEY, 1501–39, is a Tudor Gothic church with a fan vaulted nave. The Woods's splendid schemes of Georgian terraced houses: QUEEN SQUARE, ROYAL CRESCENT, and the famous CIRCUS, dating from the early 18th century, give the town its supreme elegance. In the city of **Bristol**, only a few miles away, the CATHEDRAL, 11th-19th centuries, is a rare English Gothic hall church. The CLIFTON SUSPENSION BRIDGE was built by Brunel, and the SEVERN SUSPENSION BRIDGE, opened in 1966, has a span of over 3,000 ft.

Bodiam Castle (24), built in the 14th century for coastal defence, has a central courtyard plan.

Boothby Pagnell (10) is one of the earliest-surviving Norman manor-houses in England.

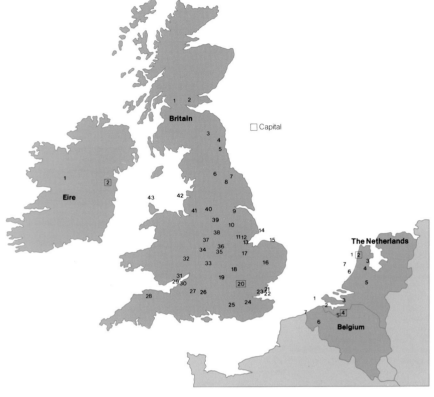

Britain

□ Capital

Eire

The Netherlands

Belgium

Brighton (25). The ROYAL PAVILION was begun in 1786 as a sedate, centrally planned house with a domed rotunda. In 1815 John Nash converted it into a fantasy palace.

Cambridge (17). The UNIVERSITY was founded in 1209 by a group of Oxford students. PEMBROKE, 1663–5, was Wren's first building. KING'S COLLEGE CHAPEL, 1446–1515, has a superb Perpendicular fan vault.

Canterbury (23). The CATHEDRAL was an 11th-century foundation, but the central tower and the nave and transepts are the best examples of English Perpendicular.

Castle Howard (7), built 1699–1712, by Sir John Vanbrugh and Nicholas Hawksmoor, is a large and stately Georgian residence.

Cliveden (19), 1849–51, a great house of the early Victorian period, was designed by Sir Charles Barry.

Compton Wynyates (34), 1520 is a typical Tudor mansion built of red brick, stone and half-timber work.

Coventry (37). The CATHEDRAL, Basil Spence's new building in a warm brick, is a basilica, completed in 1962.

Deal (22). The CASTLE, 1540, consists of two concentric baileys of six circular platforms from which the cannon fired.

Durham (5). The CATHEDRAL dominating a river gorge, is one of Europe's foremost examples of Romanesque architecture.

Earls Barton (36). The CHURCH is noted for its chevroned tower. Once part of a castle it is a rare example of Saxon architecture, dating from the late 10th or early 11th century.

Edinburgh (2). Among the city's 18th- and 19th-century public buildings, the REGISTER HOUSE and UNIVERSITY are fine examples of Georgian architecture. A similar inspiration can be seen in the monumental Ionic columns of Playfair's NATIONAL GALLERY OF SCOTLAND. Classical influence is evident in the Graeco-Roman façade of the ROYAL COLLEGE OF PHYSICIANS, 1850–5, by Thomas Hamilton.

Ely Cathedral (13) was begun on a rock in marshy Fen country c. 1090 and completed in the 14th century.

Exeter Cathedral (28) still has two large transept towers, which were built in 1030, but the present building dates from c. 1275 and, by its completion in the mid-14th century, had emerged as England's finest Decorated cathedral.

Fountains Abbey (6), the earliest Gothic building in England, is now a roofless ruin in a romantic landscape. Dating mainly from the 12th century, it is one of the country's most complete monastic complexes.

Glasgow (1). The SCHOOL OF ART was begun in 1897 by Charles Rennie Mackintosh, who designed HILL HOUSE, 1903, and the WILLOW TEA ROOMS. HOUS'HILL, **Nitshill**, c. 1906, has an extraordinary Music Room.

Gloucester Cathedral (32) was once a great abbey church whose crypt, choir and nave, 1089–1160, are noble Romanesque monuments. The choir has England's largest Perpendicular windows and the cloisters are roofed with Perpendicular fan vaulting.

Haddon Hall (40), its earliest part dating from Norman times, is a stately semi-fortified manor-house of the Perpendicular period.

Hadrian's Wall (3), completed in AD 136, ran 73 miles across bleak hill ridges, a permanent Roman frontier.

Hatfield House (18), an early 17th-century Jacobean mansion of noble aspect, was built to an E-shaped plan.

Holkham Hall (14), a central villa framed by four symmetrically ranged service wings, is a typical late 18th-century Palladian house.

Kedleston Hall (39), designed by James Paine, is a Georgian mansion. It was completed in 1770 by Robert Adam.

Leicester (38). The UNIVERSITY DEPARTMENT OF ENGINEERING, built in 1963 by Stirling and Gowan, reveals a modern attempt to express honestly, the purpose of a building whose form is determined by efficiency.

Lincoln (9). The CATHEDRAL, begun in 1093 and largely rebuilt between 1192 and 1300, possesses in its choir and lesser transepts some of the earliest-known examples of Early English architecture.

Little Moreton Hall (41), a gaily patterned half-timbered Tudor country-house, was built in the mid-16th century.

Little Wenham Hall (16), built in the late 13th century, is the best-preserved manor-house of the period and an early domestic brick building.

Liverpool (42). The METROPOLITAN CATHEDRAL OF CHRIST THE KING was completed in 1967, the work of Sir Frederick Gibberd. The 18th-century ALBERT DOCK was designed by Jesse Hartley.

London (20). The square hall keep of the TOWER OF LONDON was begun by William the Conqueror in 1080. WINDSOR CASTLE, begun outside London just over 100 years later, has a circular shell-keep flanked by two elongated baileys. In the castle grounds ST GEORGE'S CHAPEL is a fine example of the 15th-century style of English ecclesiastical architecture, as is the chapel at ETON COLLEGE near by, England's second oldest public school, founded in 1440. WESTMINSTER ABBEY, a Benedictine foundation of 960, was rebuilt from 1055 onwards so that every phase of English Gothic architecture is included in its walls. Begun c. 1520 for Cardinal Wolsey, HAMPTON COURT PALACE, on the Thames, is an outstanding Tudor brick palace. Inigo Jones built the QUEEN'S HOUSE, at Greenwich, and the BANQUETING HALL, in Whitehall, London's first Italian Renaissance buildings. COVENT GARDEN PIAZZA with ST PAUL'S CHURCH, also by Jones, was an early civic scheme. The present London skyline is still pinnacled by the spires of some of Wren's 53 churches and by the dome of ST PAUL'S CATHEDRAL. He also incorporated John Webb's KING CHARLES'S BLOCK into Greenwich Hospital, now the ROYAL NAVAL COLLEGE. The Baroque ST JOHN'S CHURCH, in West-minster, was designed by Thomas Archer in 1721–8, and ST MARY WOOLNOTH, by Hawksmoor, is in the City. Lord Burlington's Palladian CHISWICK HOUSE was once a country mansion. London's first Classical Revival building was SOMERSET HOUSE, by Sir William Chambers. Robert Adam built SYON HOUSE from 1762. FITZROY SQUARE was one of his town-planning schemes, but John Nash's excellent 19th-century schemes for REGENT STREET and REGENT'S PARK are more famous. Sir John Soane's buildings, the BANK OF ENGLAND and DULWICH ART GALLERY, are less strictly classical. Sir Robert Smirke built the NATIONAL GALLERY and the BRITISH MUSEUM. The PALACE OF WESTMINSTER, by Sir Charles Barry and A. W. N. Pugin, is the most restrained example of the Neo-Gothic style; Walpole's STRAWBERRY HILL at Twickenham is its most fantastic example. In the 19th century England had led the movement in iron and glass architecture with the BURLING-TON ARCADE, 1815, and Brunel and Wyatt's RAILWAY STATIONS, but the only monuments of Art Nouveau were Townsend's WHITECHAPEL ART GALLERY and BISHOPSGATE INSTITUTE. Sir Edwin Lutyens was the foremost architect of the 20th century. A traditionalist, he designed HAMPSTEAD GARDEN SUBURB and the REUTER BUILDING in Fleet Street. The POST OFFICE TOWER was completed in 1966.

Longleat House (30), 1553–80, was the earliest country-house in unmistakably Elizabethan style.
March (12). The CHURCH OF ST WENDREDA, built in 1500, has a famous hammer-beam roof.
Newcastle upon Tyne (4). The ROYAL ARCADE, designed by Grainger and Dobson, was part of a homogeneous planning scheme of the 1820s. The CATHEDRAL architecture belongs to the Late Decorated phase.
Norwich (15). The CATHEDRAL, built c. 1096–1145, has a long, narrow Norman nave and, unusual in England, a triapsidal east end. Beyond the city, the clustered buildings of the UNIVERSITY OF EAST ANGLIA were begun in 1965.
Oxford (33), England's oldest university, was founded c. 1167 by English scholars from the University of Paris. UNIVERSITY COLLEGE was founded in 1249. CHRIST CHURCH was built in 1546 with OXFORD CATHEDRAL as its fine late Gothic chapel. The SHELDONIAN THEATRE, 1664–9, was designed by Wren; the RADCLIFFE CAMERA, 1737–49, was Gibbs's major work, and QUEEN'S COLLEGE, 1709–38, was by Hawksmoor. Not far from Oxford, BLENHEIM PALACE, the most monumental of England's stately houses, was Vanbrugh's major work.
Peterborough Cathedral (11) was one of the great Benedictine abbey churches. It dates from the late 12th century.
Ramsgate (21). The planned asymmetry and steep gables make the HOUSE OF AUGUSTUS PUGIN a personal interpretation of the spirit of medievalism.
Salisbury Cathedral (27), outstanding example of the Early English style, was the only one of England's cathedrals to be planned as an entity.
Stoke Bruerne Park (35), 1629–35, by Inigo Jones, was the first English country-house with a Palladian central block and colonnaded side wings.
Wells Cathedral (29). The wide sculptured screen of its west front is this cathedral's finest feature. A gem of Early English architecture, built from c. 1180 to c. 1425, its exquisite interior has distinctive scissor-like arches supporting the tower.
Winchester (26). The CATHEDRAL, over 560 ft from west front to east end, is the longest of any medieval cathedral in Europe.
York (8). The medieval CATHEDRAL, built mainly in the 13th century, is the largest Gothic church in the country.

EIRE

Clonfert Cathedral (1) is a 13th-century church built on to a 12th-century façade whose portal with sloping jambs is a rare example of Irish Romanesque.
Dublin (2), built on a river delta at the head of Dublin Bay, was at its cultural height in the 18th century when Sir Edward Lovet Pearce laid out a new city in Palladian and Georgian style, and in 1728 designed the OLD PARLIAMENT HOUSE. Two of the most imposing buildings are the CUSTOMS HOUSE and the FOUR COURTS. TRINITY COLLEGE, 1752–98, was given a classical façade by Chambers in 1745. At **Glendalough**, outside Dublin, one of Ireland's famous monastic sites, ST KEVIN'S CHURCH dates from the 10th century.

DENMARK

Århus (1). The TOWN HALL, designed by Arne Jacobsen, was built in 1937.
Copenhagen (3). An unusual spire made up of entwined dragons' tails surmounts the Renaissance EXCHANGE's tower. CHARLOTTENBURG PALACE is typical of the Dutch Palladian style of the 17th century. The early 18th-century FREDERIKBERG, Frederik IV's palace, has lost much of its original simplicity by the addition of flanking wings. Denmark's most gracious 18th-century civic scheme, the FREDERIKSTADEN, centres on the PLACE ROYAL. Its chief boulevard, FREDERIKSGADE, is terminated by the Baroque marble dome of FREDERIK'S CHURCH, designed by Nicolas Jardin and completed in 1894. Christian Hansen's VOR FRUE KIRKE was built around the shell of the Cathedral. Hansen's RAAD-OG DOMHUS, 1803–15, is a combined Town Hall and Court House. A synthesis of Gothic and modern styles distinguishes the early 20th-century GRUNDTVIG CHURCH, by Jensen Klint. The 1920s stark but beautiful POLICE HEADQUARTERS, by Hack Kampmann, illustrates a return to Neo-Classicism.
Gentofte (2). The versatile MUNKEGAARDS SCHOOL, by Arne Jacobsen, provides classrooms with additional teaching space.

NORWAY

Borgund (1). Its highest roofs terminating in carved dragons' heads, ST ANDREW'S CHURCH is one of the finest wooden stave churches to have survived unaltered since the 12th century.
Oslo (2). Of the many fine vistas within this spacious 19th-century city, the combina-tion of the simple, well-proportioned classical ROYAL PALACE and the EXCHANGE, by C. H. Grosch, is perhaps the finest. The central block of Grosch's UNIVERSITY BUILDINGS, 1840, on which he collaborated with Schinkel, contains a hall with murals by Edvard Munch. The FROGNERSETEREN RESTAURANT, 1,000 ft above the fjord, is a well-preserved instance of the *fin de siècle* "Dragon Style" movement, which developed from medieval stave church design. Among the fountains and gardens of the waterfront, the immense CITY HALL is one of Scandinavia's most imposing civic complexes, expressing, among many influences, that of the Bauhaus.

SWEDEN

Hälsingborg (2). The CONCERT HALL, 1932, is the best-known work of Sven Markelius.
Stockholm (1). The medieval character of the RIDDARHOLM CHURCH, a 13th-century Franciscan abbey, has survived 15th- and 16th-century additions. The RIDDARMUSET, the Nobles' Assembly Hall, 1641, is a Dutch Palladian building designed by Simon de la Vallée and Joost Vingboons. Nicodemus Tessin's last and most famous building was the picturesquely sited SUMMER PALACE OF DROTTINGHAM, on **Lake Malaren**, completed at the end of the 17th century. The ROYAL PALACE was begun by his son, who also built the centrally planned CHURCH OF ST KATERINA in 1656. The CITY HALL, by Ragnar Ostberg, is Stockholm's most famous landmark and last important building in the early 20th-century National Romantic style. Erik Gunnar Asplund's CITY LIBRARY, 1924–7, has a circular lending hall rising above the three-storey rectilinear library. He built gay PAVILIONS for the 1930 Exhibition.

FINLAND

Helsinki (3) was largely the creation of Carl Engel, a German, in the early 19th century. At the centre, his SENATE SQUARE covers an area of almost 200,000 sq ft and is dominated by the Lutheran CATHEDRAL OF ST NICHOLAS on an immense podium above a long flight of steps. Near by, in more medieval style, is the HOUSE OF THE NOBLES by George Chiewitz, dating from 1861. The first significant contribution of the 20th century came, appropriately, from Eliel Saarinen. The stark and dramatic granite RAILWAY STATION marked the culmination of Finland's Romantic National phase. Within the clean-lined concrete and glass exterior of the PALACE HOTEL, an important prototype, are offices and car parks. The HOUSE OF CULTURE, also by Aalto, comprises a rectangular five-storey office block connected to a large auditorium, whose curve was produced by the use of specially designed wedge-shaped bricks.
Imatra (2). The CHURCH AT VUOKSENNISKA by Alvar Aalto is a versatile structure serving both religious and other functions.
Otaniemi (4). The POLY-TECHNICAL INSTITUTE, on a rolling wooded site, was part of a larger projected programme designed by Aalto in 1949.
Paimio (5). The TUBERCULOSIS SANATORIUM, 1929–33, by Alvar Aalto, was one of the earliest modern hospitals.
Säynätsalo (1). An interesting red brick, wood and copper construction by Aalto in a parochial situation, the CIVIC CENTRE was built in the 1950s.

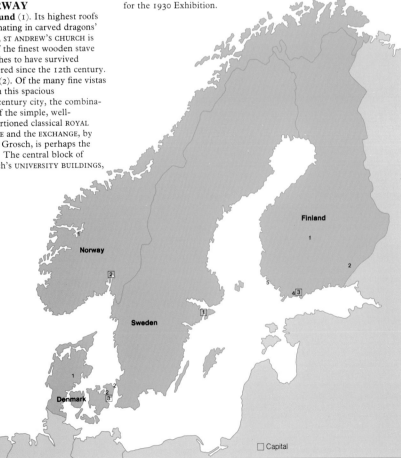

Europe 4: The Soviet Bloc, Greece and Cyprus

U.S.S.R.

Kiev (6) was Russia's first Christian centre. The domed CATHEDRAL OF ST SOPHIA, begun 1037, was the country's first great Byzantine church. ST MICHAEL also dates from the 11th century. Built in the 18th century by Russia's leading Baroque architect, Bartolommeo Francesco Rastrelli, ST ANDREW'S CHURCH, on a hilltop, is similar in plan to the 12th-century CHURCH OF ST PARASKEVA.

Leningrad (1) was called St Petersburg until the Revolution. It was founded in 1703 by Peter the Great, who chose for his new capital an inclement site—the island-scattered mouth of the River Neva, where it flows into the Gulf of Finland. Domenico Tressini from Switzerland designed the first building, the PETER AND PAUL FORTRESS, a pentagonal island castle enclosing the CATHEDRAL OF SS. PETER AND PAUL. The Empress Elizabeth patronized Rastrelli, an Italian, who designed in Baroque style the VORONTSOV and STROGANOV palaces and the SMOLNY CONVENT, and, in the Byzantine tradition, the CATHEDRAL OF THE RESURRECTION. He built the elegant WINTER PALACE for Elizabeth, and the great coastal PALACE OF TSARKOE SELO, and enlarged the PETERHOF, in the **Gulf of Finland**. Under Catherine the Great, Antonio Rinaldi built the MARBLE PALACE and began the CATHEDRAL OF ST ISAAC. The Palladian ACADEMY OF SCIENCES was designed by Quarenghi, who also built the HERMITAGE THEATRE. A Russian serf, Voronikhin, built the CATHEDRAL OF THE VIRGIN OF KAZAN, based on St Peter's in Rome, and the INSTITUTE OF MINES on the plan of Paestum's Temple of Poseidon. Thomas de Thomom's EXCHANGE was based on the same source. The last buildings to be constructed before the Napoleonic invasions were the ADMIRALTY BUILDINGS. To the north of Leningrad, on **Kizhi Island**, the CHURCH OF THE TRANSFIGURATION is a remarkable example of northern Russian wooden architecture. Built in 1714, it has 22 domes. Now within Soviet boundaries, Vyborg was part of the area ceded after war between Russia and Finland. The KARELIA MUNICIPAL LIBRARY, 1927–35, was the first major public building of Alvar Aalto.

Moscow (3). On Kremlin Hill in the CATHEDRAL OF THE ASSUMPTION, 1475, an Italian, Fioravanti, combined in a five-domed cube the traditional Russian Byzantine style with Italian Renaissance decoration and construction methods. The CATHEDRAL OF THE ANNUNCIATION, a Russian Byzantine church, was begun in 1482 by architects from Pskov. The CATHEDRAL OF THE ARCHANGEL MICHAEL was designed in 1505 by Alevisio Novi, another Italian. Also within the massive towered KREMLIN WALLS, which date from the 15th century, are the FACETED PALACE, its façades incrusted with diamond studding, built c. 1490 by two Italians, and the Renaissance GRAND PALACE. The PALACE OF CONGRESSES, 1960–1, by M. V. Posokhin, is a well-constructed Functionalist building in rich materials. The CATHEDRAL OF ST BASIL THE BLESSED, in Red Square, is as fantastic in form as in decoration. It represents the culmination of the Russian Byzantine style. The GUM STORE, 1889–93 by Pomerantsev, has a 1,000-ft-long façade and a galleried iron and glass interior with a domed roof. After 1917 Constructivism prevailed in Russia, governing the design of Konstantin Melnikov's CLUB RUSAKOV, 1925–6. Le Corbusier built the CENTROSOYUS, 1928–36, a steel and glass curtain-wall structure raised on pilotis. In the 1930s the era of Stalinist grandeur began, expressed in immense skyscrapers of which the LOMONOSOV STATE UNIVERSITY, on the city edge, is the most monumental. But an admirable achievement was made in the MOSCOW UNDERGROUND RAILWAY, begun before 1939 and still being extended.

Novgorod (2). The 11th-century CATHEDRAL OF ST SOPHIA, traced in stone the style of its wooden predecessor. The 12th-century CHURCH OF THE NATIVITY, ST GEORGE, in the YURIEV MONASTERY, and ST NICHOLAS have bulbous domes, a stylistic departure from Byzantine traditions and partly the result of adaptation to a cold climate. The 13th-century CHURCH OF ST THEODORE STRATILATES and the CHURCH OF THE TRANSFIGURATION are more simple, with fewer apses and a single dome.

Samarkand (5). Timur's GUR-I-MIR, the 14th-century mausoleum of the conqueror, is covered with turquoise Persian tiles. The mortuary chapel, a square within an octagon, is surmounted by a great glazed dome and drum, a symbol of Timurid architecture. Near by, in the domed buildings of the SHAH-I-ZINDAH, the bodies of Timur's family are buried. In the centre of the ancient town, the REGHISTAN, a Persian-style medresa, is undergoing complete restoration. The MOSQUE OF ULUGH BEG, c. 1430, is a later Persian building.

Vladimir (4). The ornate USPENSKY CATHEDRAL, rebuilt in 1183, is based upon St Sophia in Kiev. The CATHEDRAL OF ST DIMITRI is nearer to the Novgorod style, simple in plan with a single dome supported upon four piers. The CHURCH at **Pokrov**, on the River Nerl is one of the earliest and best preserved, with some of the earliest extant Russian sculpture.

POLAND

Cracow (2). The 10th-century circular stone CHAPEL OF SS. FELIX AND ADAUCTUS is now part of a later palace. The large brick DOMINICAN CHURCH has a medieval Baltic façade and decorated gable. The CATHEDRAL, on the crown of Wawel Hill, has a 14th-century façade with some Renaissance and Baroque features. The 13th-century WALLS, a barbican and ST FLORIAN'S GATE still guard the city, and the 14th-century TOWN HALL stands in the market-place. Parts of the 14th-century UNIVERSITY have been restored. Some of the first Renaissance works outside Italy are in Cracow. The ROYAL CASTLE, on Wawel Hill, was begun, c. 1500, by Franciscus Italus, an Italian. The SIGISMUND CHAPEL, 1519, was the prototype Renaissance chapel in Poland. The CLOTH HALL, 1559, was a Renaissance civic building. Built by the Jesuits, the CHURCH OF SS. PETER AND PAUL was one of their first Baroque churches, modelled on Il Gesù in Rome. The three-storeyed CHURCH OF ST ANNE is decorated with sculpture by Baldassare Fontana. The MUNICIPAL THEATRE, 1891–3, by Zawiejski, is one of Poland's few remaining 19th-century buildings based on the Paris Opera House.

Wroclaw (1). Badly damaged during World War II, the CATHEDRAL has now been reconstructed. It is a brick-built Gothic church to which, in 1716, Fischer von Erlach added his Baroque ELECTORAL CHAPEL to the east end. One of the early reinforced concrete office blocks was Hans Poelzig's COMMERCIAL BUILDING, 1911. Max Berg designed the CENTENNIAL HALL, in 1911 and Eric Mendelsohn the PETERSDORFF STORE, 1927.

CZECKOSLOVAKIA

Brno (2). ST JAKOB'S CHURCH is one of Czeckoslovakia's finest late Gothic churches. The AVION HOTEL, designed by Bohuslav Fuchs, was built in 1927. In 1930, Mies van der Rohe built the TUGENDHAT HOUSE, an early example of open planning. VRANOV CASTLE, rebuilt in 1678–95, stands upon a mountain-side above a rocky gorge. A Baroque castle, its oval saloon, with oval and rectangular windows and painted elliptical cupola, is the work of Fischer von Erlach.

Prague (1). On Castle Hill, on the northwest bank of the river, the CATHEDRAL OF ST VITUS, begun in the 14th century, is Czeckoslovakia's outstanding Gothic building. It is partly the work of Peter Parler, who also built the CHARLES BRIDGE, 1376–8, with a 2,000-ft span and decorated with sculptured figures. PRAGUE CASTLE, near the cathedral, has interesting rooms with unusual decorated ceilings. The POWDER TOWER and the OLD and NEW TOWN HALLS are late Gothic secular buildings and the TÝN CHURCH, built by Peter Parler and Matthias Rejsek, has two strange towers with picturesque finialled turrets. A Renaissance square, TÝN COURT, lies behind it. The BELVEDERE is an early 16th-century Renaissance Palace built by Italians. The ARCHBISHOP'S PALACE was built in 1561 and later given Rococo decoration. The VALDŠTEJN PALACE, by Andrea Spezza, is in a more Mannerist style, but the façade and courtyard are Roman Baroque. The ČERNIN PALACE, designed by Francesco Caratti, has a 465-ft-long façade decorated with columns. The elliptical ABBEY CHURCH OF ST JOSEF was the work of Jean Baptiste Mathey in 1675–94. In 1701 Fischer von Erlach designed the CLAM-GALLAS PALACE, which has sculptured figures by Braun in the splendid doorways. Christof Dientzenhofer made Prague his home and built the CHURCH OF ST NICHOLAS; its remarkable interior has a painted cupola and curved balconies. His son, Kilian, designed the ABBEY CHURCH OF ST NICHOLAS in the Old Town Hall Square, and the CHURCH OF ST JOHN OF THE ROCK. Eclectic and interesting, the 19th-century buildings in Prague are monumental and cheerfully decorated. The NATIONAL MUSEUM, 1885–90, by Joseph Schulz, and the NATIONAL THEATRE, 1881–3, by Josef Zitek, exhibit the designs of many indigenous artists. The PRAGUE SAMPLE FAIRS PALACE, 1924–8, by Tyl and Fuchs, is an early glass curtain-wall building. Karel Prager emerged in the post-war years as Czeckoslovakia's leading architect. His 1964 INSTITUTE OF MACROMOLECULAR CHEMISTRY is a glass curtain-walled building, and the PARLIAMENT HOUSE is built of stone, metal and glass.

HUNGARY

Budapest (2). On the New Hill of Pest, a fine medieval CASTLE was completed in the 14th century. In recent years it has been faithfully reconstructed to the last recorded detail. On Castle Hill the great 13th-century CORONATION CHURCH OF ST MATTHIAS, a Romanesque building which gradually evolved into Gothic, has also been rebuilt. After the Turkish occupation, **Buda** was extensively rebuilt, and the TOWN HALL, 1692, survives. **Pest**, across the river, was expanded, and the UNIVERSITY CHURCH, 1730–42, was built in Austrian Baroque style by Andreas Mayerhoffer. In the 19th century the Emperor Franz Josef rebuilt the second capital of his Austro-Hungarian Empire. Mihály Pollack designed the Romantic Classical NATIONAL MUSEUM, and the PARLIAMENT BUILDING, 1883–1902, by Steindl, is a huge Neo-Gothic edifice with a central dome. Schikedanz completed a vast scheme in the northeast of the city. The NATIONAL THEATRE was built in the 1960s, with abstract designs on the façade.

Fertöd (1). The ESZTERHÁZY PALACE, now an agricultural research centre, is the largest and finest palace in Hungary. Built by Erhard Martinelli in 1720, it was later extended by Miklos Jacoby.

ROMANIA

Voronet (1). The 16th-century MONASTERY CHURCH is perhaps the most original of Moldavia's painted churches. Inside and out its entire surface is covered with frescoes.

BULGARIA

Rila Monastery (1), high in the mountains, was founded in the 10th century. The monks' cells were built in arcaded galleries which overlook the polygonal courtyard. The church, which was rebuilt in the 18th century, is a Byzantine-style basilica with five domes and an arcaded narthex, and is decorated inside with splendidly executed frescoes.

YUGOSLAVIA

Gračanica (3). The MONASTERY CHURCH, 1321, is perhaps the most remarkable example of medieval Serbian architecture, a blend of Roman and Byzantine influences.
Split (2). DIOCLETIAN'S PALACE, begun in the late 3rd century, was a vast, rectangular building, heavily fortified, covering an area of eight acres. From the 7th century, a medieval town grew up within and around its walls. Near the eastern Silver Gate, Diocletian's ornate mausoleum was converted into a CATHEDRAL. Few changes were made to the Roman building, which is an octagon surrounded by a low peristyle of Corinthian columns. Internally it is circular with a hemispherical brick dome, the forerunner of the Byzantine dome. A graceful CAMPANILE was added in the late 14th century; five storeys high, it tapers to a 16th-century octagonal crown. The nearby Temple of Jupiter became the BAPTISTRY, and the monumental peristyle between the two buildings became the town's MAIN SQUARE. The transitional style of the palace foreshadowed the development of Byzantine architecture.

Zadar (1). With an inner row of columns supporting a circular wall, the CHURCH OF ST DONATO, c. 812–876, is an outstanding example of a pre-Romanesque stone-built church. The CATHEDRAL and the CHURCH OF ST GRISOGONO are fine examples of Italian-style stone-built Romanesque churches of which many examples survive along the Adriatic coast.

GREECE

Aegina (11). The TEMPLE OF APHAIA, graceful and archaic, built in 490 BC on a raised terrace on a rocky hill, has fluted grey limestone columns rising to simple Doric capitals.
Athens (12). Above the city, the glory of Classical Greece, the PARTHENON, 447–432 BC, crowns the ACROPOLIS. Near by, the tiny temple of ATHENA NIKE, c. 427 BC, epitomizes Ionic elegance, and the ERECHTHEION, 421–405 BC, culmination of the Ionic Order, has an exquisite caryatid PORCH OF MAIDENS. On the side of the Acropolis is the THEATRE OF DIONYSUS. Hewn into the rock, it was originally Greek, c. 330 BC, but was much modified by the Romans, while the ODEON OF HERODES ATTICUS, a theatre-like concert hall, is Roman. Among other treasures in the city below are the colonnaded STOA OF ATTALUS, reconstructed to its original form, and the best-preserved temple in the world, the THESEION, 449–444 BC, in the Doric style. Built to accommodate 50,000, the STADIUM, begun in 331 BC, has been restored in modern times for Olympic Games. Among the Byzantine churches which have survived is the CHURCH OF THE VIRGIN GORGEOPEKOS, a diminutive building in white pentelic marble, a strange mixture of Greek Classical and early Byzantine styles and sculptures. Built c. 875 and enlarged in the 13th century, the CHURCH OF THE KAPNIKAREA is similar, but has three polygonal apses at the east end and a small dome decorated inside with gold mosaics. ST THEODORE, c. 1065, of stone and brick, is shaped like a Greek cross with a polygonal dome. Two of Greece's most important modern buildings are the UNITED STATES EMBASSY, by Walter Agropus, and the HILTON HOTEL. Outside Athens, on **Mount Hymettus**, the MONASTERY OF KAISERIANI, beautifully frescoed, has recently been restored to its former Byzantine brilliance. Amid harbour-town factories 14 miles east of Athens, the once-paramount religious centre of **Eleusis** lies in ruins. Walls, monumental gates, triumphal arches and temples surround the important 5th-century BC TELESTERION.
Bassae (17). Most perplexing temple of Ancient Greek architecture, the 5th-century BC TEMPLE OF APOLLO is unusual in that it faces north and south, is curiously elongated and mixes Doric, Ionic and Corinthian features.
Daphni (13). On the ancient sacred way from Athens to

Eleusis the 11th-century MONASTERY OF DAPHNI guards a mountain pass, and records, in its exquisite mosaics, the apogee of Byzantine art.
Delos (9) had five AGORAS, or market-places, because for centuries it was the populous centre of Aegean trade. Now the small granite island is one of the finest sites for Greek, Hellenistic and Graeco-Roman remains. Three TEMPLES TO APOLLO, adjacent to one another, are studies in the styles of the 6th, 5th and 4th centuries BC.
Delphi (19), oldest and most sacred of the sanctuaries, is the loveliest ancient site in Greece. Here the oracle was consulted.

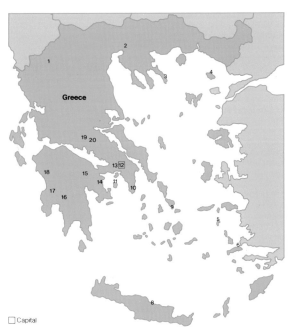

Greece

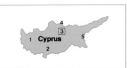

Cyprus

☐ Capital

A rare THOLOS, or rotunda, of pentelic marble, a well-preserved raised THEATRE, and a unique WALL of polygonal masonry surround the important TEMPLE OF APOLLO, c. 510 BC.
Epidaurus (14). Set deep in the hillside, the ancient THEATRE, a splendid 55-tiered geometrical design, is perhaps the finest and most complete in Greece. Above the theatre is the SANCTUARY OF ASCLEPIUS, where from all over the Ancient World the sick came to be healed.
Hosios Loukas (20), one of Greece's outstanding Byzantine monasteries, stands on a hilltop, the site of a shrine founded in the 10th century by Luke the Stiriote, a prophet and orthodox ascetic. The larger of the monastery's two churches is famed for its beautiful mosaics.
Knossos (8). An elaborate complex of frescoed courts, halls of state, royal suites and service and craftsmen's quarters, the PALACE OF KING MINOS, begun c. 2000 BC, covers four acres. It typifies the ancient Minoans' sophistication and splendour. Many buildings have two or three storeys, and in the queen's

rooms was the first ever water closet. At **Phaistos** there is another remarkable palace of the ancient Cretans.
Kos (6). On the windswept terraces, two and a half miles from the city, are the remaining baths, fountains and temples of the imposing ASKLEPION, a medical centre founded after 357 BC.
Meteora (1). Remotely and inaccessibly located upon pinnacles of rock, five or six small churches remain of 30 built in the 14th century. ST BARLAAM and ST STEPHEN are the best preserved, Byzantine in style with painted frescoes.
Mistra (16). This long-dead city preserves exquisite 14th- and

15th-century Byzantine architecture. Most beautiful of the reconstructed churches is the PANTANASSA, now belonging to nuns, which was built in 1365 and combines slender architecture and fine frescoes.
Mount Athos (3). A male stronghold from which all women are banned, the peninsula is devoted to 20 Greek Orthodox monasteries, treasuries of medieval art, which date from AD 963. Athonite churches have unusual transepts and narthex.
Mycenae (15). On a rocky ridge between Corinth and Agros, massive ramparts and tombs, built in cyclopean blocks of stone and still largely intact, recall the might of the prehistoric Mycenaean civilization whose kings fought the Trojan War. The four monoliths of the 13th-century BC LION GATE are surmounted by a majestic early monumental sculpture. Still complete, the magnificent TREASURY OF ATREUS, c. 1325 BC, has a 44-ft-high unsupported vault, unparalleled until the building of the Roman Pantheon.
Olympia (18). One of the grandest temples in mainland Greece, the Doric TEMPLE OF ZEUS, c. 470 BC, dominated the vast sacred precinct, where every four years for a millennium the Greeks gathered for the Olympic Games.

Patmos (5). Resembling no other monastery in Greece, the 11th-century MONASTERY OF ST JOHN has immense sharp-sided walls, towers and battlements like a medieval fortress.
Rhodes (7). A succession of wide walls, towers, bastions, lunettes, ravelins and barbicans, the fortifications of the old city, built by the Knights of St John from 1310 to 1522, were restored by the Italians between 1912 and 1943.
Salonica (2). Reflecting centuries of Byzantine and Ottoman Turkish rule, the city's magnificent architecture includes the 5th-century domed CHURCHES OF ST GEORGE and ST SOPHIA, both with fine mosaics, and the five-aisled BASILICA OF ST DEMETRIUS, AD 500–50.
Samothrace (4). A rich sacred centre in Hellenistic times, the ruins of the awesome SANCTUARY OF THE GREAT GODS boast the largest circular building in Greek architecture. From here came the famous Winged Victory of Thrace, now in the Louvre.
Sounion (10). Prominent on the headland with the sea on three sides stand 16 white marble columns, remains of the Doric TEMPLE OF POSEIDON, one of the modest temples built by Pericles in 444–440 BC.

CYPRUS

Famagusta (5). Here, the CATHEDRAL OF ST NICHOLAS is also a model of early 14th-century French Gothic architecture. At **Salamis**, the TOMBS OF THE KINGS date from the 8th century BC. The city WALLS are a tribute to Venetian engineering skills. The Venetians in 1489 began the remodelling of the Lusignan fortifications, and made Famagusta one of the most impregnable fortified cities of the Middle East.
Kyrenia (4). The PALACE OF VOUNI, to the west, has been reconstructed. It dates from the 5th century BC, the period of Persian influence in Cyprus. KYRENIA CASTLE dates from the period of Venetian rule, the late 15th century. It was founded by the Byzantines and Lusignans. Not far from Kyrenia is the CASTLE OF ST HILARION, part of the Byzantine system of coastal defences. The ABBEY OF BELLAPAIS, three miles east of Kyrenia, is one of the finest Gothic monuments in Cyprus. The church dates from the 13th century. The ruined cloisters are among the abbey's most beautiful features.
Limassol (2). The great KOLOSSI CASTLE, 7 miles west of Limassol, was the Grand Commandery of the Order of the Knights of St John. **Curium**, near by, was an Ancient Greek city kingdom, where the THEATRE dates from the 2nd century AD.
Nicosia (3). The CATHEDRAL OF ST SOPHIA, now the Selimiye Mosque, was founded in 1209. Its French Gothic character contrasts oddly with the two Turkish minarets on the west façade. It was built by French craftsmen following the Crusade.
Troodos Mountains (1). The island's principal monastery is KYKKO, founded in the 12th century.

Two Continents: The Americas and Australia

CANADA

Montreal, Quebec (2). A 19th-century Gothic revival produced the twin-towered Neo-Gothic CHURCH OF NOTRE DAME, 1824–43, by James O'Donnell. Less grandiose is the CATHEDRAL OF ST JAMES, 1875–85, a smaller version of St Peter's in Rome, by Joseph Michaud and Victor Bourgeau. The CHURCH OF THE ASSUMPTION, built in 1863–5 by Bourgeau, and the CHURCH OF NOTRE-DAME-DE-GRACE, which was completed in 1851 by John Ostell, exemplify the mid-19th-century Baroque revival. Built for EXPO '67, the UNITED STATES PAVILION, designed by Buckminster Fuller, was a geodesic dome 200 ft high. The WEST GERMAN PAVILION by Frei Otto and Rolf Gutbrod is a stressed skin construction, and Safdie's HABITAT '67 is a mass housing complex.

Toronto, Ontario (1). A Neo-Romanesque style was adopted for the UNIVERSITY COLLEGE, 1856–8, by W. C. Cumberland, and also for the CITY HALL, built in 1890 by E. J. Lennox. In contrast, Viljo Revell's monumental CITY HALL of 1958–65, together with John Andrews's SCARBOROUGH COLLEGE, 1964–6, have placed Canada at the forefront of architectural innovation.

UNITED STATES

Ácoma, New Mexico (20). The CHURCH AND CONVENT OF SAN ESTEVAN, a mid-17th-century Spanish mission centre, was built by the Ácoma Indians.

Bear Run, Pennsylvania (12). FALLINGWATER, 1936, is Frank Lloyd Wright's most famous building.

Boston, Massachusetts (4). Belonging to the Colonial phase of American architectural history, the PAUL REVERE HOUSE, c. 1676, is of timber-frame construction. Among the churches of the period, CHRIST CHURCH, 1723, is a simple, Wren-like brick building with a square tower and timber steeple. KING'S CHAPEL, built 1749–54, is a stone church with an Ionic portico. The STATE HOUSE crowns Boston's Beacon Hill. Built 1795–1808 it is a dignified monument to American Neo-Classicism. H. H. Richardson's TRINITY CHURCH, built 1872–7, established his reputation. The PUBLIC LIBRARY, 1887–93, based on St Geneviève in Paris, was built by McKim, Mead and White. The CITY HALL, built in 1967, is Boston's finest modern building, by Kallmann, McKinnell and Knowles.

Buffalo, New York (13). The GUARANTY BUILDING, built by Adler and Sullivan in 1894–5, was an early skyscraper.

Cambridge, Massachusetts (3). HARVARD, the United States' oldest university, was founded in 1636. MASSACHUSETTS HALL, the oldest college, dates from 1718.

HARVARD HALL is an example of mid-18th-century American collegiate architecture. The GRADUATE CENTER, 1949–50, was designed by Walter Gropius. Le Corbusier built the CARPENTER CENTER FOR THE VISUAL ARTS in 1961–3. STOUGHTON HOUSE, 1883, was built by H. H. Richardson. The MASSACHUSETTS INSTITUTE OF TECHNOLOGY has provided scope for some of America's most innovatory architecture. In 1947, Alvar Aalto's BAKER HOUSE was built. Eero Saarinen designed the AUDITORIUM BUILDING in 1952–5.

Capen House, Topsfield, Massachusetts (2), is one of the finest 17th-century colonial houses in the United States.

Charlottesville, Virginia (11). The UNIVERSITY OF VIRGINIA was designed in 1817–26 by Thomas Jefferson and became the prototype for later American campus universities.

Chicago, Illinois (17), was the birthplace of the skyscraper and home of the Chicago School. The last building in Chicago to have load-bearing walls was built in 1891, the 16-storey MONADNOCK BUILDING by Burnham and Root. Their RELIANCE BUILDING, of 1890–4, carried a light coating of terra-cotta and had a metal frame. In 1903–4, the CARSON, PIRIE, SCOTT STORE, 21 storeys in height, was Louis Sullivan's great achievement. Influenced by the Chicago School, in 1904 Frank Lloyd Wright designed the UNITY CHURCH in Oak Park, based on a square module and built of concrete, a new material. ROBIE HOUSE, built of fine brick with low-pitched, hipped roofs, has the horizontal emphasis of Wright's style. Mies van der Rohe was the architect of the PROMONTORY APARTMENTS, 1949, two severe 22-storey blocks. At the Architecture Department of the ILLINOIS INSTITUTE OF TECHNOLOGY, Mies was commissioned in 1938 to design the new university campus. More recent towers in Chicago have included Mies van der Rohe's LAKE SHORE DRIVE APARTMENTS, built in 1951, MARINA CITY, two circular towers each housing 4,000 people, designed by Bertrand Goldberg in 1964 and completed in 1967, and the curved LAKE POINT TOWER, built by Schipporeit-Heinrich Associates in 1968. The JOHN HANCOCK BUILDING, 1,105 ft high, was designed by Skidmore, Owings and Merrill.

Dallas, Texas (19). Completed after Frank Lloyd Wright's death, the KALITSA HUMPHREYS THEATRE was his last work.

Dearborn, Michigan (14). The GEODESIC DOME, built by Buckminster Fuller in 1953 for the Ford Rotunda, is the first example of the use of this structure in industry.

Farnsworth House, Plano, Illinois (18), is a steel-and-glass box, a private dwelling, designed by Mies van der Rohe.

Lincoln, Massachusetts (1). A compact and functional building, GROPIUS'S HOUSE, which he designed in 1938 with Marcel Breur, is a long, low structure of timber-box construction.

Los Angeles, California (22). A rambling concrete slab structure, its balconies supported by steel cables from above, the LOVELL HOUSE, 1927–9, by Richard Neutra, represented a breakthrough in the new skeleton frame technique. The LOVELL BEACH HOUSE at **Newport Beach, California** was designed by R. M. Schindler.

New Canaan, Connecticut (7). A deceptively simple glass box, the GLASS HOUSE, 1949, by Philip Johnson, and the BREUER HOUSE I, built on a hillside in 1947, is rectangular in plan.

Newport, Rhode Island (5), was the adopted home of Peter Harrison, a trader who became America's leading architect of the immediate pre-Revolutionary period. His first building, the REDWOOD LIBRARY, 1749–58, is a Palladian style timber building. The SYNAGOGUE, completed in 1763, shows the influence of Gibbs, and the WILLIAM WATTS HOUSE of 1874, though considerably enlarged, is unmistakably in the style of Norman Shaw. In the BRICK MARKET, begun in 1761, Harrison returned to English Palladianism for his inspiration.

New York (8) is a city of extravagant dimensions, incongruously blended with aspirations of architectural tidiness. The DYCKMAN HOUSE c. 1783 is its oldest building. ST PAUL'S CHAPEL, 1764–6, is a colonial church. On Fifth Avenue the VANDERBILT MANSION, 1879–81, was designed by R. M. Hunt. TRINITY CHURCH, by Richard Upjohn, was built 1839–46, a Gothic Revival building which is now dwarfed by office buildings. James Bogardus designed the LAING STORES, built 1848–9, and the HARPER BROS. PRINTING WORKS, 1854. The Gothic-style WOOLWORTH BUILDING was an important landmark in the development of the skyscraper. Built by Cass Gilbert it is 792 ft high with 52 storeys. The EMPIRE STATE BUILDING, built in 1932 by Shreve, Lamb and Harmon, was the highest office building in the world, with 82 storeys, until 1975, when the WORLD TRADE CENTER, two 1,350-ft-high 110-storey towers, was completed to the designs of Minoru Yamasaki and Associates and Emery Roth and Sons. The ROCKEFELLER CENTER is a campus of high-rise buildings begun in 1931 and finished in 1939. The CHRYSLER BUILDING, 1930, by William van Alen, was the first

skyscraper to top 1,000 ft. The helical, concrete GUGGENHEIM MUSEUM was completed in 1956, the year of Wright's death. LEVER HOUSE is a modern office building built in 1952 by Skidmore, Owings and Merrill. The glazed SEAGRAM BUILDING, was by Mies van der Rohe and Philip Johnson. Le Corbusier, Oscar Niemeyer and Sir Howard Robertson collaborated in the design of the UNITED NATIONS BUILDING, 1947–52, the famous glass curtain-wall SECRETARIAT HEADQUARTERS dominating the complex. The LINCOLN CENTER FOR THE PERFORMING ARTS was completed in 1957, a Formalist building designed by Wallace K. Harrison, Philip Johnson and Eero Saarinen. The FORD FOUNDATION was a departure in 1967 from what had become the traditional form of office building in New York; it is an L-shaped 12-storey block.

Philadelphia (9). Built of stuccoed rubble, MOUNT PLEASANT is a colonial house in Georgian style and dates from the mid-18th century. CHRIST CHURCH, built in 1727–54, is a colonial church. The Declaration of Independence was signed in INDEPENDENCE HALL, 1791. The CARPENTERS HALL, 1770–1, was built for the master carpenters of Philadelphia, a simple Georgian building. Walter's FOUNDERS HALL in GIRARD COLLEGE is a notable example of Greek revivalism, like the MERCHANTS' EXCHANGE, 1832–4, by William Strickland. The CITY HALL, 1874–1901, by John McArthur, is in French Second Empire style. The PENN MUTUAL LIFE INSURANCE BUILDING, begun in 1850, is an interesting example of an early building with a cast-iron façade, the work of G. P. Cummings. Louis Kahn designed the RICHARDS MEDICAL RESEARCH BUILDING in the UNIVERSITY OF PENNSYLVANIA, completed in 1960, a dramatic building and an example of Brutalism. ROBERT VENTURI'S HOUSE was built in 1962–4.

Racine, Wisconsin (16). The HELIO RESEARCH LABORATORY AND TOWER was Frank Lloyd Wright's 1950s scheme for the Johnson's Wax Company.

Taliesin West, Arizona (21). Built of canvas, glass and timber in an arid desert, Frank Lloyd Wright's house was completed in 1938.

Warren, Michigan (15). A linked series of low cubes flanking a lake, the GENERAL MOTORS TECHNICAL CENTER was designed by Eero Saarinen in 1948.

Washington, D.C. (10) was planned by Pierre Charles L'Enfant, a French architect and engineer, in the last quarter of the 18th century. The WHITE HOUSE was designed by James Hoban in the English Palladian style and was built between 1792 and 1829. The CAPITOL, 1792–1867, was designed by

Dr William Thornton. His Palladian building was rebuilt by B. H. Latrobe after being damaged. The great cast-iron dome over the central rotunda was the work of Thomas Ustick Walter. In nearby **Chantilly,** the DULLES INTERNATIONAL AIRPORT was Eero Saarinen's last project in 1958.

Yale University, New Haven, Connecticut (6), is one of the country's older universities. CONNECTICUT HALL, founded 1750, is a colonial building. FARNHAM HALL, built in 1869–70 by Russell Sturgis, expresses the historicism of 1870s college architecture. The ART GALLERY, 1952–4, was Louis Kahn's first major building. Eero Saarinen's HOCKEY STADIUM, completed in 1958, has the first of his suspended roofs. The Wright-inspired ART AND ARCHITECTURE BUILDING was built in 1961–3, designed by Paul Rudolph, the Dean. Philip Johnson and Richard Foster designed the KLINE BIOLOGY TOWER, 1965–6.

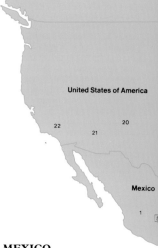

MEXICO

Chichén-Itzá (13), the great Maya–Toltec capital, was founded c. 530, and after the 7th century became the centre of a Renaissance of Maya culture. The HOUSE OF THE VIRGINS dates from this period. The CASTILLO, the main temple, is fully restored. A late Toltec building, it is nine-tiered. The central plaza of this ancient city contains temples and pyramids, the BALL COURT and the ASTRONOMICAL OBSERVATORY.

Cuilcuilco (6). The ARCHAIC STEPPED PYRAMID, built c. 500–300 BC, must be Mesoamerica's oldest ceremonial building.

El Tajín (3). A steep staircase climbs to the summit of the GREAT TEMPLE, the most important remaining monument of the Totomac people.

Labná (12). The GREAT GATE is one of the few monumental gateways found in Maya cities. Labná's most important building is the GREAT TEMPLE.

Mexico City (5). The extraordinary architectural contrasts of the Mexican capital are best displayed in the PLAZA OF THE THREE CULTURES, the site of **Tenochtitlán**, where the remains of an Aztec wall squat in the shadows of the 16th-century Spanish colonial CHURCH OF SANTIAGO, which in turn is overlooked by the FOREIGN MINISTRY, a post-World War II skyscraper. The hub of the city is the PLAZA DE LA CONSTITUCIÓN, where the 17th-century PALACIO NACIONAL, once the residence of Cortés and built on the foundations of Montezuma's Palace, stands near the ultra-Baroque METROPOLITAN CATHEDRAL, begun in 1570 and completed c. 1810. The CATHEDRAL, built in 1718–37 by Jerónimo Balbás, is the largest in the Americas. The MERCEDARIAN CLOISTER, begun in 1634, and the VIZCAÍNAS, a school for poor girls, built 1734–53 by Pedro Bueno, are important vestiges of Spanish America. The vast external mosaics of the LIBRARY, in UNIVERSITY CITY, on the outskirts, are a tribute to Mexican heritage and reflect the country's historical pride. A gaily coloured box, the building was designed by Juan O'Gorman and built in 1953. Felix Candela, an outstanding concrete engineer born in Spain, designed the COSMIC RAY PAVILION in 1951. Felix Candela's first commission as architect and engineer was the CHURCH OF THE MIRACULOUS VIRGIN, 1954. CELESTINO'S WAREHOUSE, built in 1956, has a folded plate roof and is an example of umbrella concrete construction. LOS MANANTIALES, built at **Xochimilco** in 1958, is an octagonal concrete restaurant. The SPORTS PALACE, 1966–8, is perhaps Candela's greatest building. On the city's outskirts is the great TEMPLE OF TENAYUCA, dating from 1200.

Mitlá (9). The Zapotecs, who in the mid-14th century abandoned Monte Albán, moved to Mitlá, six miles to the southeast. "GOVERNMENT HOUSE" is the most complete building.

Monte Albán (8), the first Zapotec temple-city, is spread across a group of hills above the Valley of Oaxaca. The city dates from the 1st century AD to c. 950.

Ocotlán (1). The SANCTUARY, begun c. 1745, replaced an earlier structure built after successive appearances of the Virgin to an Indian. Its exuberant façade is an example of colonial Churrigueresque. Near by at **Tlaxcala** is the CHURCH OF SAN FRANCISCO, the oldest Christian building in the continent, founded in 1521 by Cortés. Its beams are made of cedarwood from nearby forests.

Palenque (10). The buildings of this Maya city are famous for their rich stucco and stone ornament.

Teotihuacán (4). The PYRAMID OF THE SUN, with a 750-ft-sq base and a height of 216 ft, is part of a great ceremonial complex of buildings in one of Mexico's most splendid ancient cities, built in the 2nd century AD by an unknown people.

Tula (2). The TEMPLE OF QUETZALCOATL is Tula's best-preserved Toltec building.

Uxmal (11). The HOUSE OF THE MAGICIAN is a later example of Maya architecture dating from the 12th to the early 13th century AD. The NUNNERY, covered with rain god masks, consists of four groups of buildings around an inner court. The GOVERNOR'S PALACE is one of the most beautiful Maya buildings.

Xochicalco (7). The remains of a FORTRESS look out over the largest RITUAL BALL COURT in Mesoamerica, 75 yds long.

GUATEMALA

Tikal (1). In this most recently rediscovered and possibly the largest and oldest of the Maya cities, the unbroken stairway rises imperiously to the entrance of the GREAT JAGUAR TEMPLE, 230 ft high, the most important architectural monument in a city of temple pyramids.

HONDURAS

Copán (1). The jungle has engulfed most of the temples, pyramids and palaces of this mysteriously abandoned Maya city, but the RITUAL BALL COURT has survived.

VENEZUELA

Caracas (1), centre of a rapid mid-20th-century population explosion, was replanned by Maurice Rotival. The CERRO PILOTO housing development scheme of 1955, designed by Guido Bermudez, is one of the largest to have been planned and is notable for its superb site, facing a high mountain. The EDIFICIO POLAR by M. Vegas Pacheco, a pupil of Mies van der Rohe, was the best-designed skyscraper of the 1950s in Latin America. Rising high above the Plaza Venezuela. The UNIVERSITY TOWN was planned by Carlos Raúl Villanueva, Venezuela's pioneer architect of the 20th century who designed the DOS DE DICIEMBRE HOUSING ESTATE in Caracas for over 12,000 people, and the EL PARAÍSO, a smaller estate.

COLUMBIA

Popayán (1), 15,063 ft above sea level and founded in 1536, was a city of major religious and cultural importance in the colonial era. Among the fine examples of Spanish colonial architecture in this city the UNIVERSITY was founded in 1640 and the CATHEDRAL dates from the 17th century.

ECUADOR

Quito (1). Spanish and Italian styles were blended in the CHURCH OF SAN FRANCISCO, one of Latin America's most important colonial monuments of the 16th century.

PERU

Cuzco (3). From here, a small settlement in the 15th century AD, the Inca culture evolved. One of the city's oldest monuments, the WALLS, of coursed, black andesite masonry were built by the skilful Incas. The ACCLAI HUASI, the House of the Chosen Women, has notably fine mortarless stonework. SACSAHUAMAN is an enormous fortress above the Inca capital. The Jesuit CHURCH OF THE COMPAÑÍA, begun in 1651, is an important building of the early colonial period.

Lima (1). The CATHEDRAL, a mixture of Neo-Classical and Baroque features, was begun in 1543 and completed c. 1750 after 200 years of rebuilding in a constant battle against earthquakes. The TORRE TAGLE PALACE, built in the 18th century, shows the influence of Moorish Spain. The QUINTA DE PRESA, its adobe walls coloured pink, recalls the Austrian Rococo style. It was built in 1766 and until 1820 was the seat of the Court of the Inquisition.

Machu Picchu (2), the only unsacked INCA CITY, was only rediscovered in 1911 high up on the mountain from which it takes its name.

Sillustani (4). Among the few pre-Inca ruins is a CHULLPA, a circular burial tower.

BOLIVIA

Sucre (2). Here, the SAN FRANCISCO UNIVERSITY, one of the oldest in South America, was founded c. 1624. The 17th-century BASILICA METROPOLITANA is one of the finest of the surviving colonial churches in this city.

Tiahuanaco (1). The pre-Incan ruins near Lake Titicaca date from c. AD 500–1000 and were built by a people whose history is very obscure. The GATEWAY OF THE SUN is a monolithic structure.

BRAZIL

Brasilia (2). Oscar Niemeyer designed most of the strange, futuristic structures of Brazil's administrative capital during the 1950s.

Ouro Preto (4). The steeples of 11 graceful old churches mark the skyline of this hillside town. The CHURCH OF SÃO FRANCISCO was built between 1766 and 1794 by Francisco Lisboa, a native. Niemeyer's HOTEL, built in 1940, blends sympathetically with its colonial setting.

Pampulha (3). Niemeyer's CHURCH OF ST FRANCIS OF ASSISI, built in 1943 of reinforced concrete, is a series of parabolic arches. Niemeyer and Costa together designed the CASINO PAMPULHA and the YACHT CLUB in 1942.

Rio de Janeiro (5) boasts one of Brazil's earliest colonial Baroque churches, SANTO BENTO, built in 1652. A. J. V. Grandjean de Montigny designed the CUSTOMS HOUSE in 1826 with a distinct French Empire flavour. His pupil, J. M. J. Rebelo, built the ITAMARATÍ PALACE in 1851–4. In 1937, Oscar Niemeyer's first building, the DAY NURSERY, was built in Rio, based on the ideas of Le Corbusier, who also influenced the design of the MINISTRY OF EDUCATION AND HEALTH, 1937. NIEMEYER'S HOUSE was built in 1942. An open-plan building on three levels, it pioneered the use of an interior ramp. Le Corbusier planned the UNIVERSITY in 1936. The PEDREGULHO ESTATE, 1953 by Affonso Eduardo Reidy, is one of the longest housing units in the world. SANTOS DUMONT AIRPORT was begun in 1938.

Salvador (1). Richly carved, the most important church in this coastal town, one of Brazil's oldest cities and now called Bahía, is SÃO FRANCISCO, 1701.

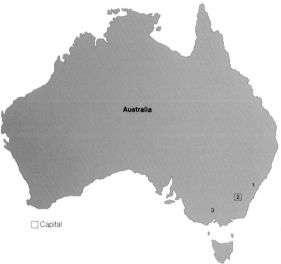

Australia

□ Capital

AUSTRALIA

Canberra (2), spacious, planned and 20th century, was based on designs by Walter Burley Griffin, a Chicago architect.

Melbourne (3). Built in the 19th century, the HOUSES OF PARLIAMENT, with a dignified dome, verge on the monumental. The TREASURY is classical, the CATHOLIC CATHEDRAL Neo-Gothic and the ANGLICAN CATHEDRAL was designed by William Butterfield, temporarily imported from England. The PUBLIC LIBRARY, a later building in reinforced concrete has, unusually, a great dome, and the NATIONAL ARTS CENTRE is entirely indigenous modern and magnificent.

Sydney (1). Convicted of forgery and transported in 1814, Francis Greenaway, a pupil of Nash, became the country's first Government Architect. The 19th-century Sydney he planned has succumbed to the ravages of progress and expansion, but his stately HYDE PARK BARRACKS still carry a hint of Palladian inspiration, and the GOVERNMENT HOUSE STABLES are pure crenellated Regency. ST JAMES CHURCH, his finest monument, has a copper spire. In the same pioneering spirit the HARBOUR BRIDGE became in 1933 the world's largest arch bridge. Futuristic and controversial, the OPERA HOUSE, designed by Jørn Utzon, was completed after much delay in 1973.

Glossary

Abacus The flat slab between the top of a capital and the architrave.
Abutment Solid masonry placed to resist the lateral thrust of an arch or vault; also the place of junction.
Acanthus A plant whose leaf forms are used as a decorative motif on Corinthian and Composite capitals.
Acropolis The citadel of a Greek city where the chief temples and monuments were built, as at Athens.
Acroteria Plinths for statues and ornaments at the apex and ends of a pediment; also the figures themselves.
Agora The Ancient Greek equivalent of the Roman forum, that is an open space for assemblies and markets.
Aisle In a church, one of the lateral divisions parallel with the nave, chancel or choir.
Ambulatory A continuous aisle around a circular building; the aisle around the east end of a Christian church.
Amphitheatre A circular or elliptical building with tiered seating and an open central arena, as used by the Romans.
Antefixes Ornamental blocks fixed vertically along the edge of a tiled roof to conceal the ends of the tiles.
Apse A semicircular or polygonal termination, usually to a church sanctuary.
Aqueduct An artificial channel, often an elevated masonry structure, conveying water from its source to its destination; it was invented by the Romans.
Arcade A range of arches supported on piers or columns, either free-standing or BLIND, that is, attached to a wall.
Arch A curved structure of wedge-shaped blocks designed to span an opening and supported only at the sides. CORBELLED ARCH: a "false arch" consisting of blocks of masonry, each laid to overlap the one beneath until the gap is bridged by a single slab; DIAPHRAGM ARCH: a stone arch spanning the nave of a church with no roof vault; HALF-ARCH: an arch from the springing line to the apex only; HORSESHOE ARCH: often found in Islamic buildings, it can be either a pointed or a round horseshoe; LANCET ARCH: a narrow pointed arch, its span shorter than its radii; OGEE ARCH: an arch of double curvature, the lower convex, the upper concave; PARABOLIC ARCH: its curve is a parabola, a conic section (the intersection of a cone and a plane parallel to its side); POINTED ARCH: an arch with its two curves meeting at an acute angle; also called an EQUILATERAL ARCH; RELIEVING ARCH: an arch built into the wall above a true arch, to relieve it of some of the load and thrust; ROUND or SEMICIRCULAR ARCH: the simplest of arch forms, made up of a semicircle of voussoirs; SEGMENTAL ARCH: an arch consisting of a segment of a half-circle; SQUINCH, SQUINCH ARCH: an arch built diagonally across the corners of a rectangular space, a series of squinches converting the rectangle into a circle or octagon; STILTED ARCH: an arch springing from a point above its imposts, so that the sides seem vertical at the bottom; TREFOIL or TRILOBE ARCH: two cusps divide the arch into three lobes.
Architrave The beam or lowest part of an entablature; also the moulded frame around a door or window.
Ashlar Squared hewn stone laid in regular courses with fine joints.
Atrium In Roman domestic architecture, an inner court covered along the sides; also the forecourt, sometimes cloistered, of Early Christian and Byzantine churches.
Axial planning The placing of several buildings or parts of a building along a single line.

Bailey The open area or court of a castle; also called a ward.
Baldacchino A canopy over an altar, throne or tomb. It may rise from columns or hang from the ceiling.
Baptistry A building, often separate from the church, containing a font for the baptismal rite.
Barbican A fortified outwork defending the entrance to a castle.
Basilica In Roman architecture, a public hall used for the administration of justice. In Early Christian and later architecture, a building consisting of nave and aisles, with windows above the level of the aisle roofs (a clerestory).
Bastion A projection on the curtain wall of a castle, placed to allow surveillance and defence.
Batter A slight inward sloping given to walls (battered = sloping).
Battlement A defensive parapet with alternating openings (embrasures) and solid portions (merlons).
Bay A compartment of a building: in churches, the space between one column or pier and the next, including the vault or ceiling covering it; also any unit of a wall surface divided by large vertical features or, on exteriors, by windows. The term is also used for projecting windows.
Bema In Ancient Greece, a speaker's platform. In Early Christian churches, a raised stage for the clergy. It constitutes the germ of the transept when expanded laterally in later architecture.
Bent entrance A defended entrance involving one or more sharp changes in direction.
Boss An ornamental projection covering the intersection of the ribs of a vault, or sometimes of beams in open wooden ceilings.
Bracket A member projecting from a vertical surface to form a horizontal support. A CONSOLE is an ornate type of bracket.
Breastwork In military architecture, a fortification thrown up breast-high for defence.
Brise-soleil A screen used as a sun-break; now, frequently a permanent arrangement of horizontal or vertical louvres used to shade window openings.
Buttress A mass of masonry built up against a wall to add support or to resist the pressure of an arch or vault. ANGLE BUTTRESS: two buttresses meeting at the corner of a building; CLASPING BUTTRESS: formed when a solid pier of masonry encases a corner; DIAGONAL BUTTRESS: one placed at the corner of a building and equidistant from both walls; FLYING BUTTRESS: an arch or half-arch springing from a detached pier and abutting against a wall to take the thrust of a vault; SETBACK BUTTRESS: two buttresses set back from a corner.

Caldarium The hot-water room in a Roman public baths.
Campanile The Italian term for a bell-tower, usually free-standing.
Cantilever A structural member, such as a beam, girder, step or balcony, which projects beyond the line of support.
Capital The head or crowning feature of a column or pilaster.
Caravanserai A rest house for caravans on the main trade routes in Anatolia and Persia; also called a han.
Cartouche A shaped tablet enclosed in an ornamental frame or scroll. It often has an inscription or heraldic device.
Caryatid A carved female figure used in Greek and later buildings as a column or support.
Casemate A vaulted chamber with embrasures built into the thickness of ramparts or other fortifications and used as a barracks, a battery, or both.
Cast-iron An iron-carbon alloy distinguished from steel by containing quantities of cementite or graphite, which make it unsuitable for working.
Cella The main body of a Classical temple.
Central planning Planning symmetrically, or nearly so, in four directions.
Chancel The portion of a church reserved for the clergy and containing the altar and choir.
Chapterhouse A building attached to a cathedral, collegiate or conventional church and used for the assembly of clergy or chapter.
Château The royal or seigniorial residence and stronghold of medieval France; the early fortified château reached its culmination in the late 15th century. The 16th-century château, with gardens and outbuildings, was only lightly fortified. By extension, any grand country-house.
Chevet The French term for the combination of an apse, its surrounding ambulatory and radiating chapels.
Choir The part of a church where services are sung, normally in the west part of the chancel but sometimes extending into the nave, although in large medieval churches the choir often sat beneath, or west of, the crossing. The term is sometimes applied to the whole chancel.
Circus In Roman architecture, a long enclosure with rounded ends and with tiered seating around a central open space; in the 18th century, a circular range of houses; in modern terms, a circular road or street junction.
Clerestory The upper window-level of a large building rising above adjacent roofs; in particular, the top range of windows in the nave of a basilican church above the arcade and triforium.
Cloisters A covered arcade around a quadrangle connecting the monastic church to the domestic parts of the monastery.
Coffering Sunken ornamental panels in ceilings, vaults and domes.
Colonnade A row of columns supporting an entablature or arches.
Column A vertical cylindrical support, usually consisting of base, shaft and capital. In Classical architecture, it is part of an Order.
Composite A Roman addition to the Classical Orders. Its capital combines the volutes of the Ionic capital with the acanthus leaves of the Corinthian.
Concourse An open space.
Concrete Cement mixed with coarse and fine aggregate (such as pebbles, crushed stone, brick), sand and water. In some form, it has been used since the time of the Ancient Romans. PRE-CAST CONCRETE: components of concrete cast in a factory or on site before being placed in position; PRE-STRESSED CONCRETE: a development of reinforced concrete. Reinforcing steel is replaced by wire cables in ducts, so positioned that compression is induced in the tension area of the concrete before it is loaded. This is done by stretching the cables before or after the concrete is cast; REINFORCED CONCRETE: since concrete is strong in compression and weak in tension, reinforcing steel rods are inserted to take the tensile stresses which, in a simple beam, occur in the lower part.
Corbel A bracket or block projecting from a wall to support a roof beam, vault or other feature.
Corinthian The third of the Classical Orders. Characteristics: a high base, sometimes a pedestal; slim, fluted column shaft with fillets; bell-shaped capital with acanthus-leaf ornament.
Cornice The projecting upper section of an entablature; also the moulded projection completing a wall, door, etc.
Counterscarp In fortifications, the outer wall or slope of a defensive ditch.
Crenellate To indent or embattle.
Crossing The space at the intersection of the nave, chancel and transepts in a cruciform church.
Cupola A dome, especially a miniature dome with a lantern-top.
Curtain wall In castles, the surrounding fortified wall. In modern architecture, an outer non-load-bearing wall.
Cusp A projecting point on the inner side of an arch, window or roundel.
Cyclopean In pre-Classical Greek architecture, masonry consisting of large irregular stones; also any polygonal masonry on a large scale.

Dome A concave roof, usually hemispherical or elliptical, on a circular or polygonal base. A section through a dome may be pointed, semicircular or segmental. SAUCER DOME: a dome with a segmental section and no drum; GEODESIC DOMES, invented this century by R. Buckminster Fuller, are structures of metal, plastic or even cardboard based on tetrahedrons or octahedrons; ONION or BULB DOMES are external shapes only.
Donjon A castle keep.
Doric The first and simplest of the Classical Orders. Characteristics: no base; relatively short columns, their surface fluting meeting in a sharp arris, or edge; a plain echinus and square abacus. ROMAN DORIC was similar, but had a base.
Dormer window A small, gabled window projecting from a sloping roof.
Drum The circular or polygonal wall supporting a dome; also a section of a circular column.

Eaves The lower edge of an overhanging roof.
Echinus The convex moulding beneath the abacus of a Doric capital; the corresponding part of an Ionic capital, with egg and dart decoration.
Embrasure An opening in a castle wall or parapet; also an obliquely recessed door or window.
Enceinte An enclosure, especially in fortifications.
Engaged column A column attached to a wall or pier.
Entablature The upper part of a Classical Order, between columns and pediment, consisting of architrave, frieze and cornice.
Entasis The slight swelling given to a column shaft to counteract the optical illusion that it is thinner in the middle.

Façade The exterior of a building on one of its principal sides, usually containing an entrance.
Faience A general term for glazed earthenware used for pottery or to decorate buildings; named after Faenza, in Italy, where much ceramic ware was made from *c.* 1300.
Fenestration The arrangement of windows in a building.
Fillet A narrow band between mouldings, or separating the flutes in columns.
Finial An ornament crowning a pinnacle or other architectural feature.
Fluting Vertical grooves on columns and pilasters.
Forum In Roman architecture, a central open space usually surrounded by public buildings and colonnades. It corresponds to the Greek agora.
Frieze The middle section of an entablature; also the continuous band of relief around the top of a room or building.
Frigidarium The cold-water room in a Roman public baths.

Gallery An upper floor, open on one side to the main interior of a building (for example, the galleries above the aisles of a church), or to the exterior. In medieval and Renaissance houses, a long, narrow room.
Gazebo A look-out tower or elevated summer-house which commands a view; often incorporated in a garden wall.
Giant Order An Order of columns or pilasters extending through two or more storeys of a building.
Greek Cross A cross with arms of equal length.

Hall-church A church with nave and aisles of the same height.

Hammer-beam roof A late Gothic roof form in which massive beams project horizontally from the top of the wall but do not meet their corresponding members on the opposite side.

Hypostyle A hall in which the roof (usually flat) is supported by columns throughout the building.

Impost The projecting member on which an arch rests.

Infilling Material used to fill up or level.

Insula The Roman multistorey apartment house or tenement block.

Ionic The second of the Classical Orders. Characteristics: a moulded base; tall, slim column shafts with columns separated by fillets; capitals decorated with volutes.

Iwan A vaulted hall with an imposing arched opening; a feature of Sassanian and Islamic architecture.

Joggle A masons' term for joining two stones by means of a notch in one and a corresponding projection in the other.

Keep The inner stronghold of a castle, equipped to serve as the chief living quarters permanently or during siege.

Lady Chapel A chapel dedicated to the Virgin Mary; it normally lies east of the church chancel and projects from the main building.

Lancet A tall, slim, pointed window, characteristic of Early English work.

Lantern A small windowed tower or turret crowning a cupola or dome.

Latin Cross A cross with one arm longer than the other three.

Light The glazed area between the uprights of a window.

Loggia A gallery, open on one or more sides, sometimes columned; it may also be a separate structure, usually in a garden.

Lunette A semicircular window or solid panel in a dome, arch, vault, etc.

Machicolation A projecting parapet on a castle wall or tower with floor holes through which missiles could be dropped on the enemy.

Martyrium A building erected at a site of martyrdom or containing the relics or grave of a martyr.

Medresa The Islamic theological school, in form closely resembling a mosque.

Megaron The principal hall of a Mycenaean palace.

Metope The space between two triglyphs on the frieze of a Doric entablature.

Mezzanine A low storey between two tall ones; usually between the ground and first floors.

Mihrab A prayer niche in a mosque in the wall facing Mecca.

Minaret The tall tower of a mosque from which the call to prayer is made.

Miniature or Dwarf Order A miniature Order of columns or pilasters.

Mosaic Surface decoration made up of small cubes of glass or stone (tesserae) set in cement.

Mosque The Muslim place of worship.

Moulding Projecting or recessed bands used to ornament walls, doors, etc. They may be plain or decorated.

Mullion The upright dividing a window into two or more lights.

Naos The sanctuary of a Greek temple, where the cult statue was housed.

Narthex The arcaded porch or vestibule of Early Christian and some later basilican churches.

Nave The whole of the church west of the crossing; more specifically, the central space bounded by the aisles.

Obelisk A square, tapering pillar ending in a pyramid.

Oculus A round window or opening.

Orders Designs of columns and their

entablatures, especially of the five CLASSICAL ORDERS as used in Ancient Greece and Rome. The Greeks developed the Doric, Ionic and Corinthian Orders, to which the Romans added the Tuscan and the Composite. Renaissance designers adapted Roman models, creating many variations, but in the later Classical Revival there was strict adherence to Greek and Roman originals.

Oriel A bay window supported on corbels.

Pagoda As known in China and Japan, this is a multistoreyed wood or stone tower, part of a Buddhist temple complex.

Pavilion An ornamental building, often a summer-house; also a projecting subdivision of a building, forming a central feature of the main façade.

Pediment A triangular gable above an entablature in Classical architecture; a similar feature over any window or door.

Pendentives Inverted triangular concave segments, one of the means by which a circular dome is supported above a square or polygonal compartment; used in Byzantine, Romanesque, Renaissance and later work.

Piano Nobile The raised main floor of an Italian Renaissance palazzo.

Piazza An open public place surrounded by buildings.

Pier A heavy, masonry support, often composite in section and thicker than a column, but fulfilling the same function.

Pilaster A rectangular column projecting from a wall merely as a decoration but conforming to the Orders.

Pillar A detached upright support which deviates in shape and proportion from the Orders.

Pilotis Pillars or stilts supporting a raised building.

Pinnacle The crowning feature on a buttress or parapet; it resembles a small conical or pyramidal turret.

Podium The stone base on which a temple or other structure is built.

Portcullis The vertically opening iron gate at the entrance to a fortress.

Portico A colonnaded entrance to a building.

Postern A small secondary entrance, sometimes concealed and usually at the rear of a castle, town or monastery.

Propylaeum The monumental entrance to a Greek sacred enclosure.

Purlin A horizontal roof beam resting on the principal rafters and supporting the subsidiary ones.

Putti Painted or carved representations of small naked boys.

Pylon A tower-like Ancient Egyptian gateway with central opening and sloping sides.

Pyramid In Ancient Egyptian architecture, a vast monumental stone tomb with a square base and with sloping sides that meet in an apex.

Qibla The direction of Mecca; by extension, the wall in a mosque that faces Mecca.

Quadrangle A rectangular courtyard surrounded by buildings.

Rib A projecting band, either structural or decorative, separating the cells of a groined vault.

Rondel or roundel A circular panel, disc or medallion; also a similarly shaped panel in a stained glass window.

Rood screen In many medieval churches, the chancel screen carrying the rood, or cross.

Roof A covering over a building. It can be flat, pitched or shaped. Types include a HELM ROOF, which has four inclined faces joined at the top, with a gable at the foot of each; a HIPPED ROOF, with sloping, instead of vertical, ends; a LEAN-TO ROOF, with only one slope, built against a higher wall; a MANSARD ROOF, which has a double slope,

the lower being longer and steeper than the upper; a SADDLEBACK ROOF, a normal pitched roof; a HYPERPARABOLOID ROOF, a special form of double-curved shell, its shape a continuous plane developing from a parabolic arch in one direction to a similar inverted parabola in the other.

Rose A circular window with mullions radiating like the spokes of a wheel.

Rustication A method of building masonry: the blocks or courses of stone are emphasized by deeply recessed joints and often by a roughened surface.

Sacristy A repository for sacred vessels in a church.

Sahn The inner court of a mosque.

Sanctuary The most sacred part of a church or temple. In Christian churches, the area containing the main altar; also known as the presbytery.

Screens passage The passage at the service end of a medieval hall between the screen and the buttery, kitchen and pantry.

Shell structures Support features formed from a single or double curved surface and composed of materials (such as concrete) that are resistant to bending. The shell's thickness is slight in ratio to its surface area.

Shoin A style used in Japanese noble residences. It evolved from the 12th century onwards and reached its most perfect form in the Katsura rikyū. Special features in the rooms are alcoves for displaying paintings, large sliding panels as doors, and a vestibule where shoes are left. These features became traditional in urban domestic architecture.

Skyscraper A tall multistorey building of steel-frame construction.

Solarium A sun terrace or loggia.

Spandrel The triangular surface or space between two arches or between an arch and a wall.

Springer or **springing line** The point at which an arch rises from its support.

Stalactite Islamic ceiling ornament made up of squinch arches to resemble natural stalactites.

Steel-frame construction The technique of hanging the outer walls of buildings on load-bearing metal frames.

Stoa A detached colonnade or portico.

Strap-work Interlaced bands of relief ornament on ceilings or walls.

Stucco Plaster or cement used as low-relief decoration on ceilings or walls; also plaster applied to entire façades to simulate stone.

Stupa In Buddhist architecture, originally a burial mound; later a Buddhist or Hindu monument for relics surrounded by an ambulatory.

Stylobate In Classical architecture, the top step of the platform on which a colonnade is placed. The three steps of a Doric temple collectively form the CREPIDOMA.

Sukiya A simple and austere Japanese style in which little buildings were added on to each other, sometimes surrounding an open courtyard.

Tatami Rice straw mats used to cover floors in Japanese houses. Multiples of the basic tatami unit (roughly 6 ft x 3 ft) have for centuries been employed to determine the size and proportion of rooms.

Temenos A sacred precinct in which stood a temple or other sanctuary.

Tepidarium The warm-water room in a Roman public baths.

Terracotta Baked unglazed clay used for construction and decoration.

Trabeate Built of horizontal beams and vertical posts.

Tracery The ornamental stone framework holding the glass in a Gothic window. PLATE TRACERY, the earliest and simplest type, is solid stone in which openings have been cut for the glass. BAR TRACERY (tracery proper) uses stone ribs in complicated patterns. Variations include CURVILINEAR TRACERY, made up of sinuous lines and circles; and FLAMBOYANT TRACERY, literally "flame-shaped" and characterized by an upward tendency and profuse ornament.

Transept The projecting arms, usually between nave and chancel, in a cruciform church. The north and south arms are always called the "north transept" and the "south transept". Occasionally there is an additional transept east of the crossing.

Tribune In a church, an upper gallery above the aisles; also a projecting platform or balcony in a church or theatre.

Triforium The raised arcaded corridor between the aisle arcading and clerestory in the nave of a church.

Triglyph The fluted block between two metopes in a Doric frieze.

Tuscan A Roman addition to the Classical Orders, it resembles Doric, but has a base and unfluted columns.

Tympanum The triangular space enclosed by a Classical pediment; also the area between the lintel of a doorway and the arch above it.

Undercroft A vaulted underground room.

Vault An arched ceiling or roof of stone or brick. BARREL VAULT: a continuous vault of semicircular or pointed section, also called a WAGON or TUNNEL VAULT; CORBEL VAULT: a vault built on the same principle as the corbelled arch; CROSS or GROIN VAULT: a vault formed by the intersection at right angles of two barrel vaults, the compartments thus formed meeting at a groin; DOMICAL or CLOISTER VAULT: a dome rising direct on a square or polygonal base, and with surfaces separated by groins; FAN VAULT: a form of rib vault in which the bay divisions and vaulting compartments are ignored and the ribs radiate from the wall-shafts in a fan-like pattern; LIERNE VAULT: a ribbed vault in which liernes (tertiary ribs), which do not spring from the wall supports, are added to link the main ribs and tiercerons (secondary ribs); RIB or RIBBED VAULT: a development of the groin vault, in which groins are replaced by arched ribs built across the sides and diagonals of the vaulted bay to form a support for the infilling. The vault can be QUADRIPARTITE, SEXPARTITE or have any number of compartments. SEGMENTAL VAULT: a vault whose section is a segmental arch; STELLAR VAULT: a vault with ribs, secondary ribs (tiercerons) and tertiary ribs (liernes) arranged to form a star pattern.

Viaduct A long series of arches carrying a road or railway.

Villa In Roman architecture, the landowner's residence or farmstead on his country estate; in Renaissance architecture, a large country-house; in 19th-century England, a grand detached house, usually on the outskirts of a town; in modern terms, a small detached house.

Volute A spiral scroll, especially on an Ionic capital.

Voussoirs The wedge-shaped stone blocks forming an arch.

Wainscot Timber panelling on walls.

West front The main façade, lying west of the nave in most large churches.

Westwork A tower-like element, with an entrance and vestibule and a chapel above, found in Carolingian and Romanesque churches.

Wrought-iron Malleable iron with only small amounts of other elements, but containing elongated particles of slag, more rust-resistant than steel and more easily welded.

Ziggurat In Mesopotamia and pre-Hispanic America, a stepped pyramid supporting a temple or an altar.

Ziyada The outer court of a mosque.

Index

A reference which is in a caption only and is not the subject of the adjoining illustration has the suffix c (e.g. 164c). Page numbers in italics refer to illustrations.
The various forms of 'Saint' (e.g. San, Santo, St) are given in each case as S.

Index

About the Authors

Anthony Blunt was Professor of History of Art at London University and Director of the Courtauld Institute of Art until his retirement in 1974. He was also Surveyor of the Queen's Pictures. His numerous books on architecture and art include *Artistic Theory in Italy, François Mansart, The Nation's Pictures, Art and Architecture in France, 1500–1700, Philibert de l'Orme, Nicolas Poussin* and *Sicilian Baroque*.
(AUTHOR OF PP. 156–67, 172–87, 196–200).

Sir Hugh Casson, Professor of Environmental Design at the Royal College of Art from 1953 to 1975, was Director of Architecture at the Festival of Britain from 1948 to 1951. He was a member of the Royal Fine Arts Commission and, as a practising architect, lectured extensively in Europe and the United States. His published works include *Victorian Architecture* and *Inscape: The Design of Interiors*.
(AUTHOR OF PP. 210–17)

Nirad C. Chaudhuri's books include *The Autobiography of an Unknown Indian, A Passage to England, The Continent of Circe*, for which he received the Duff Cooper Memorial Prize for 1966, and biographies of Friedrich Max Müller and Clive of India.
(AUTHOR OF PP. 24–31)

Alec Clifton-Taylor, an author and journalist, lectured on art at London University from 1934 to 1939 and from 1946 to 1957, and extensively all over the world. His books are *The Pattern of English Building, The Cathedrals of England* and *English Parish Churches as Works of Art*.
(AUTHOR OF PP. 80–3, 94–107, 114–29)

Robin Fedden was Deputy Director-General of the National Trust. His many books include *The Land of Egypt, Syria, Crusader Castles* (with J. Thomson) and *The Continuing Purpose: A History of the National Trust*.
(AUTHOR OF PP. 46–51, 130–40)

Peter Kidson was Reader in History of Art at the Courtauld Institute of Art, London University. He is the author of *Sculpture at Chartres, A History of English Architecture* (with P. Murray and P. Thompson) and *The Medieval World*.
(AUTHOR OF PP. 52–76)

James Lees-Milne is the author of many books on Renaissance and Baroque architecture. Formerly Historic Buildings Adviser to the National Trust, his books include *The Age of Inigo Jones, Earls of Creation, St Peter's* and *English Country Houses: Baroque*.
(AUTHOR OF PP. 168–71, 188–95)

Seton Lloyd, Emeritus Professor of Western Asiatic Archaeology at London University, is the author of many archaeological and architectural works, including *Foundations in the Dust*, a history of the exploration and excavation of Mesopotamia, *Early Anatolia* and *Art of the Ancient Near East*.
(AUTHOR OF PP. 38–45)

Peter Murray is Professor of History of Art at Birkbeck College, London University, and is a former President of the Society of Architectural Historians of Great Britain. In collaboration with his wife, Professor Murray wrote *The Dictionary of Art and Artists* and *The Art of the Renaissance*. His other publications include *A History of English Architecture* (with P. Kidson and P. Thompson) and *The Architecture of the Italian Renaissance*.
(AUTHOR OF PP. 142–55)

John Julius Norwich, 2nd Viscount Norwich, is Chairman of the Venice in Peril Fund and a member of the Executive and Properties Committee of the National Trust. He has made some 30 television documentaries. He is the author of two books on the Norman kingdom of Sicily, *A History of Venice*, and *The Architecture of Southern England*. He is now working on a history of the Byzantine empire.
(AUTHOR OF PP. 32–6, 78–9, 84–93)

Dennis Sharp was General Editor to the Architectural Association, London, and Senior Lecturer in Architecture at the Architectural Association School. He is also Consultant on Architecture and Design to the Open University. A practising architect, he has written a number of books on architecture, including: *Modern Architecture and Expressionism, The Picture Palace, A Visual History of Twentieth-Century Architecture* and (with T. and C. Benton) *Form and Function*.
(AUTHOR OF PP. 222–5, 228–31, 234–9)

Sir James Richards was Editor of the *Architectural Review* from 1937 to 1971. A leading architectural historian, critic and broadcaster, he is the author of many books on modern and historical architecture. Among these are *Introduction to Modern Architecture, Castles on the Ground, The Functional Tradition in Early Industrial Buildings* and *The Professions: Architecture*.
(AUTHOR OF PP. 202–9, 218–21, 226–7, 232–3, 240–65)

John Thomson is, with R. Fedden, the author of *Crusader Castles*. As an undergraduate at Cambridge University, he did field work on medieval architecture in Italy and Turkey. Since then he has pursued his interest in castles both in Europe and the Middle East. He is a member of the British Diplomatic Service.
(AUTHOR OF PP. 108–13)

William Watson was Professor of Chinese Art and Archaeology in London University, at the School of Oriental and African Studies. His published works include *The Sculpture of Japan, Archaeology in China, China before the Han Dynasty* and *Cultural Frontiers in Ancient East Asia*.
(AUTHOR OF PP. 12–23)

ACKNOWLEDGEMENTS

Photographers

Photographs on each page are listed from left to right in descending order. Abbreviations used are: CMD/P: C. M. Dixon/Photoresources; RHA: Robert Harding Associates; AFK: A. F. Kersting; HL: Holford Library; P: Pictor; CLI: Colour Library International; SCL: Spectrum Colour Library; FLH: F. L. Harris; AA: Courtesy of Architectural Association.

12 Paolo Koch 15 William Macquitty, Magnum/Bruno Barbey, CMD/P 16 Orion Press, Japan Information Centre, London 17 Werner Forman Archive, Orion Press 18 RHA 19 RHA, Magnum/Bruno Barbey, Magnum/Rene Burri, William Watson 20 Douglas Dickins, Orion Press 21 Douglas Dickins, Tony Stone Associates 22 Orion Press, Photoresearchers/George Holton 23 Photoresearchers/Dana Levy 24 Werner Forman Archive 26 Douglas Dickins, Douglas Dickins, Tony Stone Associates 27 RHA, AFK 28 Werner Forman Archive 29 Luc Ionesco, John Massey Stewart 30 Both pictures: AFK 31 Nirad Chaudhuri, AFK, AFK 32 Ferdinand Anton 34 HL/Chapman, HL/Chapman, CLI 35 HL/Chapman 36 All pictures: Loren McIntyre 38 Vorderasiatisches Museum 40 Roman Ghirshman; from "Tchoga Zanbil" (Vol. 1, 1966, Planche VI) 41 Jane Taylor 43 Roger Wood, HL 44 P, SCL, Oriental Institute Chicago 45 Aerofilms 46 Hirmer Fotoarchiv 48 Both pictures: SCL 49 HL, HL, HL, AFK 50 Both pictures: HL 51 Jane Taylor, Werner Forman Archive 52 Scala 54 CMD/P, Ronald Sheridan, CMD/P 55 SCL, Susan Griggs Agency/Reflejo 56 James Austin 58 Sonia Halliday 59 Scala 60 Jean Roubier, Hirmer Fotoarchiv 61 Susan Griggs/Reflejo 62 CMD/P, Scala 63 CMD/P 64 Sonia Halliday/Birch, others: American School of Classical Studies at Athens 66 Magnum/Erich Lessing 68 Mansell Collection/Alinari, Bidarchiv Foto Marburg 69 AFK, Mansell Collection/Alinari, Werner Forman Archive 70 Scala 71 RHA, Ronald Sheridan, CMD/P 72 Scala 73 CMD/P, Jean Roubier, AFK, AFK 74 Scala 75 Both pictures: Mansell Collection/Alinari 76 Jean Roubier, Fototeca Unione 78 Sonia Halliday 80 FLH, Jean Roubier 81 P, P, Scala 82 P, Scala,

CMD/P 83 Scala 84 Magnum/Erich Lessing, Jane Taylor 85 Magnum/Erich Lessing, Bernard Cox 86 Scala 87 Magnum/Erich Lessing, Magnum/Erich Lessing, Reresby Sitwell, P 88 First four Jane Taylor; John Julius Norwich, Jane Taylor 89 Magnum/Erich Lessing 90 Scala 91 CLI, P 92 Scala, P 93 Angelo Hornak 94 Agence Top/Michael Nahmias 96 FLH, Scala 97 Jean Roubier, Jean Roubier 98 FLH 99 Ronald Sheridan, HL, Woodmansterne: Nicholas Servian F.I.I.P. Ltd. 100 Angelo Hornak, AFK 101 Scala 102 FLH, CMD/P 103 Scala, FLH, Scala 104 Jean Roubier, FLH 105 Hamlyn Photo Library, Scala 106 CMD/P, Sonia Halliday 107 John Bethell/R.J. Mainstone 108 AFK 110 Sonia Halliday, AFK, P 111 Crown Copyright, reproduced with the permission of the Controller of Her Majesty's Stationery Office 112 John Thomson, British Tourist Authority 113 Spanish Tourist Office, AFK, Aerofilms 114 Agence Top/Michael Nahmias 116 CMD/P, Jean Roubier 117 Tony Stone Associates, others: Jean Roubier 118 Both pictures: Sonia Halliday 119 CMD/P, Sonia Halliday, HL 120 Michael Kaufman, FLH, FLH 122 Michael Kaufman, FLH, FLH 123 HL, Picturepoint, Michael Kaufman 124 P, Jean Roubier 125 Jean Roubier, AFK 126 Both pictures: Scala 127 All pictures: Scala 128 Popperfoto 129 Mansell Collection, Country Life 130 HL/Photo Clyde 133 Ronald Sheridan, Popperfoto, HL 134 John Hanley 135 Jane Taylor, RHA 136 John Julius Norwich, Jane Taylor 137 All pictures: Jane Taylor 138 P, Scala, Tony Stone Associates 139 Scala 140 SCL, Sonia Halliday, John Bethell/R. J. Mainstone 142 Scala 144 Scala 145 Scala, Angelo Hornak 146 Scala 147 All pictures: Scala 148 Scala 149 Scala, FLH, Jean Roubier 150 Both pictures: FLH 151 Electa Editrice, Scala 152 Jean Roubier, Mansell Collection 153 Scala 154 Electa Editrice, Scala 155 Angelo Hornak 156 Jean Roubier 158 Jean Roubier, Scala 159 Douglas Dickins, CMD/P, Jeremy Whitaker 160 Jeremy Whitaker, HL, Jean Roubier, Courtauld Institute 162 FLH, Scala 163 Bernard Cox, Douglas Dickins, Portuguese Tourist Office 164 Both pictures: Jean Roubier 165 Jean Roubier 166 Both

pictures: AFK, 167 Both pictures: AFK 168 John Bethell, Jeremy Whitaker, AFK 169 Angelo Hornak, AFK 170 AFK 171 AFK, AFK, FLH, AFK 172 Mansell Collection 174 Scala, FLH, FLH 175 Scala, FLH 176 AFK, Scala 177 FLH, Private collection, FLH 178 Giraudon, Bulloz 179 Agence Top/D. Bouquignaud, AFK 180 Lucien Hervé, Jean Roubier 181 Bulloz 182 AFK, Picturepoint, Bernard Cox 183 Rapho/Everts, Scala 184 AFK, Private collection 185 FLH, AFK, HL 186 Giraudon, Scala 187 Scala, Douglas Dickins, Barnaby's Picture Library 188 Michael Photo Library 189 Bernard Cox, John Bethell, AFK 190 AFK 191 Angelo Hornak, John Bethell, Angelo Hornak/courtesy National Trust, Jeremy Whitaker 192 Both pictures: AFK 193 John Bethell, Victoria Art Gallery, Bath 194 John Bethell, AFK 195 Jeremy Whitaker/courtesy Duke of Northumberland, AFK, Mansell Collection (T. Hisham) 196 Christian Baugey 198 Brazilian Embassy, Hamlyn Photo Library 199 P, Christian Baugey, Carlos Etchenique, P 200 Douglas Dickins, Mansell Collection 202 Ronan Picture Library 204 AFK, SCL, British Rail Photo Unit 205 Cooper-Bridgeman/Gordon Roberts 206 Roger Viollet 207 P 208 AFK, Bulloz, Popperfoto 209 Wayne Andrews 210 Royal Academy of Arts/Hardwicke, Angelo Hornak, Michael Kaufman 211 Bettman Archive 212 AFK, Angelo Hornak 213 Popperfoto, Michael Kaufman, Angelo Hornak 214 Rapho/Ciccione 215 Bernard Cox 216 AFK 217 Popperfoto, Novosti Press Agency, Scala 218 Angelo Hornak 220 AFK 221 Michael Kaufman, J. M. Richards, Wayne Andrews 222 John Jacobus, Van Phillips 223 Dennis Sharp 224 Both pictures: Bildarchiv Foto Marburg 225 Hamlyn Photo Library/Keith Gibson, Architectural Press Manfredi Nicolletti, Alistair Service, Architectural Press/ Foto Mas 226 Hedrich Blessing 227 Hedrich Blessing, P 228 Dennis Sharp 229 Archives de l'Architecture Moderne, AA, Bildarchiv Foto Marburg 230 Dennis Sharp, Burkhard Verlag 231 Burkhard Verlag, Archives de l'Architecture Moderne 232 Architectural Press 234 John Jacobus, Burkhard Verlag 235 John Jacobus, Hubert Jan Henket, Hubert Jan Henket, Archives de

l'Architecture Moderne 236 Both pictures: Dennis Sharp 237 Bildarchiv Foto Marburg, Bildarchiv Foto Marburg, Popperfoto 239 Bildagentur Mauritius, P, P 241 AA, Bildagentur Mauritius 242 Pirelli, Milan 243 Bildagentur Mauritius, P. Marzari 244 Cement and Concrete Association 245 Both pictures: Cement and Concrete Association 246 Lennart Norstrom, Ralph Erskine, Hälsingborgs Konserthus 247 G. E. Kidder Smith, Danish Tourist Board 248 CMD/P, Museum of Finnish Architecture, J. M. Richards 249 J. M. Richards, P, J. M. Richards 250 AFK 251 AFK, HL, SCL 252 Brecht Einzig, Denys Lasdun/Brecht Einzig 253 SCL, Architectural Press/de Burgh Galwey, Architectural Press/Peter Baistow 254 AA 255 Ezra Stoller, AA, AA 256 Angelo Hornak, Wayne Andrews 257 P, Angelo Hornak 258 All pictures: Ezra Stoller 259 Ezra Stoller, Hedrich Blessing 260 Christian Baugey 261 P, RHA, Picturepoint 262 Architectural Press/Kiyoshi Otsuji 263 Orion Press, Architectural Press/Toshio Taira, J. M. Richards 264 Bildarchiv Mauritius 265 British Columbia Government

Artists

Terry Allen, Malcolm Lee Andrews, Arka Graphics, Arthur Barbosa, Bateson and Stott Ltd., Marilyn Bruce, Harry Clow, David Cox Studios, Terence Dalley, Dateline Graphics, Enzo de Grazia, Dan Escott, Peter Fitzjohn, Eugene Fleury, Chris Forsey, Garden Studios, Gilchrist Studios, Vana Haggerty, Jackson/Day Designs, Sarah Janson, Launcelot Jones, Don Kidman, Harold King, Ivan Lapper, Peter Levasseur, Linden Artists, Kevin Maddison, Jim Marks, Dennis Mills, Mitchell Beazley Studio, Olive Moroney, Peter Morter, Bill Ody, Product Support (Graphics) Ltd. Profile Art Services, Mike Saunders, Saxon Artists, Chris Simmonds, Ronald Steiner, Stobart/Sutterby, Alan Suttie, Wolfe Stoerl, Technical Graphics Ltd., Eric Thomas, Venner Artists, Dick Ward, David Watson, Alan Whiteman, Roy Wiltshire, Anne Winterbotham, Harold Wright